Irwin Allen Televi
Productions, 1964-

ALSO BY JON ABBOTT

Stephen J. Cannell Television Productions:
A History of All Series and Pilots (McFarland 2009)

Irwin Allen Television Productions, 1964–1970

A Critical History of
Voyage to the Bottom of the Sea,
Lost in Space, *The Time Tunnel*
and *Land of the Giants*

JON ABBOTT

McFarland & Company, Inc., Publishers
Jefferson, North Carolina, and London

To the memory of Irwin Allen, Richard Basehart, Paul Carr, Kevin Hagen, Jonathan Harris, Kurt Kasznar, Howard Lydecker, Guy Williams, Paul Zastupnevich, and all the other craftsmen and performers no longer here with us to read these words about their significant and valued contribution to our enjoyment of these wonderful shows.

The present work is a reprint of the illustrated case bound edition of Irwin Allen Television Productions, 1964–1970: A Critical History of *Voyage to the Bottom of the Sea, Lost in Space, The Time Tunnel* and *Land of the Giants, first published in 2006 by McFarland.*

LIBRARY OF CONGRESS CATALOGUING-IN-PUBLICATION DATA

Abbott, Jon, 1956–
Irwin Allen television productions, 1964–1970 : a critical history of *Voyage to the Bottom of the Sea, Lost in Space, The Time Tunnel* and *Land of the Giants* / Jon Abbott.
p.   cm.
Includes bibliographical references and index.

ISBN 978-0-7864-4491-5
softcover : 50# alkaline paper ∞

1. Allen, Irwin, 1916–1991.
2. Irwin Allen Productions—History.
PN1992.92.I79A23 2009   791.4502'32092—dc22   2006019840

British Library cataloguing data are available

On the cover: Irwin Allen on the set of *The Time Tunnel* (ABC/Photofest)

Manufactured in the United States of America

McFarland & Company, Inc., Publishers
Box 611, Jefferson, North Carolina 28640
www.mcfarlandpub.com

Contents

"When we are in a hot corner it is stories we want, not the high poetic function which represents the world. We want incident, interest, action, and to the devil with your philosophy."

—Robert Louis Stevenson

"Most TV shows are what I call Donna Reed's living room. Donna goes to the door, opens the door, and there's John the milkman. But John's got a problem, so they go into the living room, sit on the couch and talk for seven pages. 'Oh John, you found out your wife is giving you a surprise birthday party and you don't want her to know that you know.' They shoot the seven pages and they go home for the day. Me, if I can't blow up the world in the first ten seconds, then the show's a flop."

—Irwin Allen

Preface

If you were watching a color science-fiction television series during the 1960s, the chances were pretty good you were watching an Irwin Allen presentation. There were, after all, only 79 episodes of *Star Trek*, and only 43 of *The Invaders*, whereas Irwin Allen produced 274 episodes of his four different series, over 200 in color. Irwin Allen's TV career began with the submarine adventure series *Voyage to the Bottom of the Sea*, based on his own feature film of the same name, and continued with *Lost in Space*, *The Time Tunnel* and *Land of the Giants*.

Some people love the Irwin Allen shows; others consider them the perfect example of how *not* to do SF TV. Personally, I think the latter opinion is unfair and unjustified. There are many ways to define SF TV. When Georges Méliès was making *A Trip to the Moon (Le Voyage dans la Lune)* in 1902, widely regarded to be the first science-fiction film, he was not thinking about scientific accuracy or presenting the true future, whatever that might be. He was thinking about just two things: showmanship and special effects. Sixty years later, Irwin Allen was thinking about the same things—and not without good cause. Serious science fiction films traditionally died a death at the box office, and the failure of such films as the speculative future musical *Just Imagine* and the portentous *Things to Come* in comparison with hits like the *Flash Gordon*, *Superman*, and *Buck Rogers* serials had shown Hollywood the path to take. Allen's efforts were one third Jules Verne

and Sir Arthur Conan Doyle, one third the Republic, Universal, and Columbia serials, and one third the bug-eyed atomic monster movies of the '50s. They were also undoubtedly one hundred percent Irwin Allen! Allen had a 'house style'—similar in many ways to the pulp magazines of the '40s and '50s—that permeated all four of his series; stock players, the same writers and directors, crossover props, sets, and locations, familiar plots, gimmicks, and obsessions all gave his shows a specific look. Allen's tricks and techniques, some of which he adapted from earlier examples, and some of which he devised and popularized by himself or perpetuated by the re-use of '50s props and musical scores, would continue to influence other producers from *Star Trek* onwards (Gene Roddenberry loved flashing lights and lurch scenes as much as Allen). The British producer of an adaptation of a fairytale story involving miniature people for the BBC once grudgingly but admirably admitted that he screened episodes of *Land of the Giants* to learn "what not to do" and ultimately ended up using every one of the series' tricks.

Irwin Allen may well have demonstrated how not to do serious, precognitive, or scientifically accurate SF for sniffy purists, but it was never his intention to do so. Irwin Allen's TV shows were made as commercial entertainments, not to comment on the human condition, deliver dire warnings, or speculate about the future (although on rare occasions they did all three). Not only are

1

his four 1960s SF shows a model demonstration of how to make exciting, successful, entertaining action adventure in the fantasy genre, not only are they still phenomenally popular around the world all these years later, but they have been used consistently as blueprints for contemporary TV series—although sadly by people who still haven't managed to take on board most of the television truths Allen discovered those long decades ago. If they had, then *Fantastic Journey*, *Voyagers*, *Otherworld*, *seaQuest*, *Earth 2*, and *Sliders*, to name but half a dozen owing a nod to Irwin Allen, would all have enjoyed much longer runs.

As a fervent fan of the Allen series, I have promoted, praised, defined and defended them in many articles in my twenty-year career writing for TV and sci-fi media magazines (see bibliography). Research for those articles provided a wealth of information and inspiration that led to this book.

In these pages, you will find writer, director, and guest cast for all 274 episodes of these four Irwin Allen series, plus trivia, comment and criticism, background, interview quotes, and as much information on the guest players' other work in the TV and film fantasy genre as space permits. Irwin Allen used the same writers and directors on all his series, and many of the same guest actors, a few of whom appeared six or seven times in different episodes of different series. With so many episodes to cover, and so many names making more than one appearance in Allen's four series, repetition was not a luxury afforded to me, so for the maximum information on the writers, directors, and particularly actors' credits, I strongly advise the use of the index. Most of the guest players are mentioned in detail somewhere in the text.

With all due respect to those who have gone before me, there has been very little intelligent writing about the Irwin Allen shows, and I have done my best to redress the balance over the years. Something snaps in the minds of even some of our most intelligent critics when the name of Irwin Allen is mentioned, and knee-jerk name-calling and ludicrous generalizations replace the more objective commentaries afforded to the shortcomings of, say, Roger Corman, *Star Trek*, or *Doctor Who*. What fair-minded critic, in the face of all television's history of short-run disasters, instant cancellations, and acknowledged failures, could seriously call *Lost in Space* "the worst sci-fi show ever"?—and yet this has happened twice. It was beloved by mainstream audiences around the world (a clue there, perhaps), rated well for three seasons, had many fine moments (as we shall see), is still in reruns today, and retains a devoted army of fans. Yet the slurs persist. Fortunately in recent years we have been blessed with the fascinating research and revealing, objective interviews of U.S. writers such as Mike Clark, Bill Cotter, Kyle Counts, Joel Eisner, Richard Messman, Paul Monroe, Mark Phillips, Ian Spelling and Tom Weaver in the pages of *Starlog* and others, and the exemplary efforts of a U.S. TV executive named Kevin Burns to get out the magnificent soundtracks of the Allen shows and his superb documentary, all of them going out under the banner of *The Fantasy Worlds of Irwin Allen*.

And we owe special thanks to the casts and supporting casts, all the wonderful guest players, Irwin Allen, Paul Zastupnevich, the writers and directors, the set decorators, designers, film editors and music editors who made these four shows the most extraordinary, creative, exciting and entertaining adventure series ever to air on 20th century television.

Jon Abbott, 2006

Irwin Allen: An Introduction

There's a place for message SF. Rod Serling burnt himself out hammering out literate and moving paeans to the human condition in his enduring classic *The Twilight Zone*, using the SF medium to get across messages that the more direct, reality-based programming of the heavily censored '50s and '60s TV industry did not allow. Leslie Stevens and Joe Stefano were meticulous visionaries, enthused with the potential of film and fantasy to grab the audience by the throat and expose their fears and imaginations to *The Outer Limits*. Gene Roddenberry used *Star Trek* to confront philosophical and human issues in a television environment filled to capacity with genies and witches, talking horses, hillbilly millionaires, and secret agents talking into their clothing (wonderful, funny shows all, but variety is the spice of life).

Unlike those other icons of '60s SF TV—Rod Serling, Stevens and Stefano, Gene Roddenberry—Irwin Allen had no messages to impart and no philosophies to expound. Any politics to be found in his series were usually the result of adhering to Hollywood formula and tradition rather than political convictions. Allen was a showman, pure and simple. If it was eloquence, scientific accuracy, or profound commentary on the meaning of life you were looking for, then it was best not to look in Irwin Allen productions—but for superb special effects of the day, excellent sets, superior guest performances, action and adventure, hardnosed heroes, horrible monsters, sinister villains, and all-out fast-paced escapism that has yet to be matched, then Irwin was your man. His series were adventure shows, with the emphasis on visual spectacle and action. As one light-hearted commentator once pointed out, "If you criticize Irwin Allen's shows for being implausible, you're missing the point.... Radiation, pollution, overpopulation, starvation, the new ice age—all are very real problems. But there's nothing like watching grown men roaming around the cosmos with no income worries or mortgage problems when we need cheering up."

Critics may point to the Irwin Allen series and say "that could never happen." And for some reason, the same people who justifiably applaud AIP, Universal's monsters, Alland and Arnold, Serling and Stefano, *Star Trek*, *Doctor Who*, DC Comics, Marvel Comics, and Hammer films have said just that. The fairytale scenarios in *Lost in Space*, the monster mayhem of *Voyage to the Bottom of the Sea*, the time-traveling in *The Time Tunnel*, the tiny people of *Land of the Giants* not crushed by the forces of gravity—no, that could not happen. But that is exactly the point of making these shows, watching them, enjoying them. *They could not happen*. Therein lies the pleasure of them, the joy in surrendering to them for 49 minutes an episode. They could not happen. Only in our dreams and in our imagination could they happen. Do we dare point out that the same applies to *The X-Files* and *Buffy the Vampire Slayer*?

The writer and comic actor John

Irwin Allen (far left) on the set of *The Lost World*. Seated opposite are various cast members including Michael Rennie (heavy coat), Claude Rains (glasses), and David Hedison (captain's hat). Hedison would wear the hat again—every time Allen used stock footage of him from this film in *Voyage to the Bottom of the Sea!*

Cleese once said that he could never understand the appeal of science-fiction, as the real world is so much more interesting. When science-fiction takes itself so seriously, as so many contemporary series of the 1990s did, I sympathize with his point of view. What storyline in *Star Trek: Deep Space Nine* or *Babylon 5* could compare with the intrigues of ancient Rome, Greece, or Byzantium? What fictional conspiracy yarn could beat what we know about the Kennedy assassination or Watergate? What is the point of seeing modern-day politics played out in a cartoon cavalcade of guttural sounds and

silly names by actors in prosthetic foreheads with scales and glaring eyes? But when we need to escape from the misery of the news broadcasts, or the tyranny of historical or scientific fact, that is when the door to the wacky worlds of Irwin Allen and his colleagues in sheer, unadulterated fantasy seems so inviting.

The opening scene of "Deadly Blackmail," the first of just three episodes of Irwin Allen's aborted late-'70s *Return of Captain Nemo* project (later edited down to the feature-length *The Amazing Captain Nemo*), shows the huge hi-tech innards of a sophisticated super-submarine. Standing incongruously in the aisle between two lengthy banks of mammoth winking, blinking computer banks manned by glistening golden cyborgs is an eccentric little old man dressed in baggy trousers and a cardigan who looks as though he should be sitting by the fireside with a cat, or maintaining a musty old library. A metallic door slides open, and in stomps a towering metallic giant hidden behind a ferocious face mask. He stops at the side of the impish old man to make his report ... Only a liar or a dullard could fail to be hooked by an opening ten seconds like that! The Allen series have no higher pretensions either to elevate them, or sink them.

Irwin Allen was born in New York in 1916. He studied journalism and advertising in college, and moved to Hollywood in 1938 to become a magazine editor. A year later, he was writing and directing a Hollywood celebrity radio show, and the influences that would form his attitude to film and TV began to show themselves.

Allen was always impressed with the Big Names of Hollywood, and the whole star system environment. He ran a literary agency, becoming an agent for screenwriters, and wrote a syndicated Hollywood gossip column. Clearly, he knew stars better than he knew scripts, which were often the weak link in his productions ("Never let your business manager choose your scripts!" fumed Joan Fontaine, when asked about her role in the *Voyage to the Bottom of the Sea* feature film), and his fascination for spectacle first manifested itself in documentary form.

His earliest films were fascinating and factual in theme, the Academy Award winning *The Sea Around Us* in 1950, and the 1956 feature *The Animal World*, in which he first mixed fact and special effects with dinosaur sequences by the famous stop-motion specialists Willis O'Brien (*King Kong*) and Ray Harryhausen. But he swiftly found that facts got in the way—or, at least, they worked better purely as a springboard

into more fantastic realms. This lead to his ambitious but laughable star-studded 1957 feature *The Story of Mankind*, which related famous historical events Hollywood-style within a fantasy framework—that of a heavenly courtroom with the Devil and the "Spirit of Mankind" introducing vignettes illustrating both sides of the coin. *Halliwell's Film Guide* called it "a hilarious charade, one of the worst films ever made, but full of surprises, bad performances, and a wide range of stock shots" (it sounds as if he enjoyed it). Thus was born Allen's tendency to utilize stock footage, which manifested itself in all his '60s sci-fi shows, particularly *Voyage to the Bottom of the Sea* and *The Time Tunnel*. Why not? Without it, certain stories could not be told. With it, the possibilities were endless. A number of Irwin Allen regulars put in appearances for *The Story of Mankind*, including Vincent Price, Peter Lorre, and the Marx Brothers. Allen had previously produced the Groucho Marx feature *Double Dynamite* in 1951, and Groucho Marx was one of Allen's best friends. Dee Hartford, Groucho's niece, would make a number of appearances in Allen's TV series, most notably as the android Verda in *Lost in Space*.

Appropriately enough for a showman like Allen, his next film was *The Big Circus* in 1959, which again featured Price and Lorre in the cast, and was described by the same Leslie Halliwell as a "fast-paced melodrama that makes little sense but generally provides the expected thrills." Again, he might have been talking about Allen's fantasy series.

In 1960, Allen returned to his beloved dinosaurs with his updated adaptation of Sir Arthur Conan Doyle's *The Lost World*, which starred Claude Rains (star of the original *The Invisible Man* in 1933) and newcomer David Hedison (who had appeared in the '50s Fox sci-fi horror *The Fly* and a submarine adventure, *The Enemy Below*). This time, Allen chose to forsake textbook accuracy and create his dinosaurs by dressing up real lizards and superimposing them with the action on miniature sets. This footage was quite effective and subsequently turned up in one form or another, sometimes more than once, in every single TV series Allen produced in the 1960s!

In 1961, Allen turned even further toward fantasy with his feature film *Voyage to the Bottom of the Sea*, which starred Walter Pidgeon of the classic 1956 feature *Forbidden Planet* as Admiral Nelson, the role later essayed by Richard Basehart in Allen's subsequent TV series of the same name. Co-starring were Peter Lorre, Joan Fontaine, and Allen regular Michael Ansara with his then-wife Barbara Eden (of *I Dream of Jeannie*), with Robert Sterling as Captain Crane; David Hedison was coerced into accepting the role of Crane in the TV series.

Next came Allen's 1963 adventure, *Five Weeks in a Balloon*, again with Lorre, Sir Cedric Hardwicke from *The Story of Mankind*, Red Buttons from *The Big Circus*, and Richard Haydn of *The Lost World*. All these feature film yarns were written by Charles Bennett, a Hollywood veteran who had written scripts for Hitchcock and DeMille, and who went on to contribute occasional scripts for Allen's various TV series before retiring. Next, Allen moved into TV with his four successful 1960s sci-fi series, the first of them making Fox's reputation as a TV supplier. These series were, of course, *Voyage to the Bottom of the Sea*, which began in 1964 and closed in 1968, *Lost in Space* (1965–1968), *The Time Tunnel* (1966–1967) and *Land of the Giants* (1968–1970).

Allen used many of the same technical craftsmen on his films, and took many of them to television with him, including composer Paul Sawtell, who composed the *Voyage to the Bottom of the Sea* theme (Allen's other themes were provided by John Williams of *Star Wars* and *Superman* fame), award-winning special effects wizard Lyle B. Abbott (who won further awards for his team's work on *Voyage* and *Time Tunnel*), and costume designer, occasional bit player and all-purpose right-hand man Paul Zastupnevich, the man who made the monsters and clothed the aliens and astronauts alike.

Allen was a contradictory man, a time-is-money tyrant when he came down on to the set, but generous with his praise and often handing out lavish and impromptu gifts. He was loyal to the people who worked for him, using the same craftsmen, lieutenants, writers and performers on all his shows, from the highest producer or award-winning technicians to the lowliest bit-players. He was dictatorial, unpredictable, blunt and arbitrary, but despite this, he was admired and respected, and his loyalty was returned. He retained the services of the same people on his productions over decades, including the writers, who were on the receiving end of most of his mercurial tirades and consequently have been the most venomous and revealing about the man in return. Allen was hard on his writers, and sometimes unfair and unreasonable. But although often critical of their scripts, performers such as Richard Basehart, Robert Colbert, Don Matheson and Whit Bissell were always ready and willing to participate in his productions. Said *The Time Tunnel's* Robert Colbert, "Irwin Allen had three shows on at once. That's what I call a guy with moxie!"

Stories about Allen are legion. Here was a man who used stock footage until it fell apart, yet forbade writers to refer to stock in their scripts and spent a fortune initially establishing a series; the *Time Tunnel* set was massive, and *Land of the Giants* the most expensive series on television while it was in production. Here was a man who, when told the cost of a spaceship for a *Lost in Space* alien snapped "Let him walk!" ... and then let the show be canceled rather than take a cut in the budget. Here was a man who once walked onto the set of *The Time Tunnel* and announced in front of the entire cast how he'd love to do a show that didn't require any actors ... and yet who idolized the big-name Hollywood greats.

The extensive use of stock footage—or even the building of a completely new story around action sequences from another source or a previous episode—was not a new phenomenon, nor was it unique to the Irwin Allen productions. The old Universal, Monogram, Republic and Columbia movie serials of the '40s and '50s, to which the early episodes of *Lost in Space* and the heroics of all four Allen series owed an enormous debt, and the B-movies from the same studios and others, often employed material from other sources and earlier films to save on the budget, and as late as the 1970s Universal (who started the trend with their *Flash Gordon* serials) were still employing footage from films such as *Duel* and *Earthquake* in series such as *The Incredible Hulk*. Like Allen, acclaimed productions from such cost-conscious British producers as ITC and Hammer frequently reused footage, performers, sets, and locations.

Allen's series were the natural successors of the movie serials (as were the TV westerns of the '50s and '60s and the Stephen J. Cannell series of the early '80s), and even found further jobs of work for many of the performers in those adventures, including actor turned casting agent Larry Stewart and such serial and SF B-movie veterans as Whit Bissell, John Zaremba, John Crawford, Harry Lauter, Ross Elliott, Billy Benedict, Lyle Bettger, Peter Brocco, Richard Carlson, Eduardo Cianelli, Tris Coffin, Charles Drake, Paul Fix, Byron Foulger, Michael Fox, Arthur Franz, Bill Hudson, Victor Jory, Jock Mahoney, Hugh Marlowe, Gerald Mohr, and Lyle Talbot.

Forty years on, Irwin Allen's series are still popular and successful enough in the marketplace for 20th Century Fox to license stylish merchandise, including DVDs, soundtrack CDs, collectors' models, and trading cards, often under the Fantasy Worlds of Irwin Allen logo, the title of a superb 1990s documentary celebrating his work.

Irwin Allen was a master craftsman, supervising all four of his fantasy series with the consummate skill, care and attention of a champion showman. He was first and foremost an entertainer, and his responsibility was not to the science fiction purists or point-scoring Trekkers who have reviled his work in comments ranging from knee-jerk habit to an almost perverse obsession, but to the studio, the TV stations, and ultimately the mass audience, which he consistently pleased. Allen was no storyteller, like the other aforementioned giants of fantasy TV—he was into spectacle, and to that extent, he delivered the goods.

Allen was, above all else, an ideas man. His inventive and creative use of the budget, ably assisted by costume designer Paul Zastupnevich and story editor William Welch, among others, splashing out on pilots, props, sets, and special effects, but cutting corners elsewhere by the judicious recycling of costumes, equipment, and stock footage, resulted in some of the finest escapist fantasy ever produced. Many of Allen's '60s special effects were simple fireworks, model work, colored lights, electronic sounds, and making people appear and disappear by simply stopping the camera while the cast remained motionless and the actor stepped offscreen. Others were Emmy award-winning and state-of-the-art, superior to anything past or then-current.

It's true that some Irwin Allen episodes had a few rough edges in terms of sets and effects (who could forget the beach-ball minefield from Lost in Space's "The Golden Man?")—but mostly, they were superb. The planet set from Lost in Space and the Time Tunnel itself were magnificent optical illusions. The Tunnel complex was possibly the most striking single set ever produced for SF TV (the vortex effect won an Emmy); Robert Kinoshita's Lost in Space Robot puts other film and TV tin men of the period to shame (other than Forbidden Planet's Robby, which Kinoshita also realized); and the modelwork for the Jupiter Two, the Seaview and the Flying Sub (by Howard and Theodore Lydecker, who made Captain Marvel and Rocketman fly decades earlier and brought Atlantis to life in Republic's extraordinary Undersea Kingdom) makes the spaceships and satellites of Star Trek and The Outer Limits look sick in comparison. Furthermore, not only were the Allen series state-of-the-art in their day, they are still visually impressive now. With the exception of their hilariously casual use of nuclear power, an occasional outdated attitude toward women, and the odd hippie or odder hairstyle, the fantasy environment of the four series, coupled with their reluctance to follow fads, has conspired to make them, like Gerry Anderson's puppet shows and Hanna-Barbera's cartoons, both fashionably, appealingly retro and yet timeless.

Allen was obsessed with spectacle and special effects, and a little less concerned with logic and characterization. Much has been made in print of his "no quibbling" dictates when faced with a plot hole, and his description of The Time Tunnel as "a running and jumping show," a quote that turns up everywhere (including my text—twice). But he got lucky—what characterization there was in his series came due to the efforts of the talented story editor Tony Wilson, and performers such as Richard Basehart, Jonathan Harris, Kurt Kasznar, John Crawford, and Kevin Hagen, who brought color and integrity to their varied, energetic and challenging performances. Anyone can ride a horse into a wild west town or sit in a suit behind a desk and dole out orders to TV cops, but it takes serious talent and ability to make pulp SF work. And in Guy Williams, Mark Goddard, David Hedison, Del Monroe, Robert Colbert, James Darren, Gary Conway, Don Marshall, and Don Matheson, Allen had some of the best small-screen tough guys and heroes an adventure show could ask for. Where are the heroes of contemporary TV who could hold a candle to John Robinson, Doug Phillips and Tony Newman, or Mark Wilson? Where are the

TV villains to compare with Dr. Smith, Alexander Fitzhugh, or Inspector Kobick? They just don't make 'em like that any more.

Allen left series TV to return to his farcical film career (*The Poseidon Adventure* and *The Towering Inferno* were followed by such legendary turkeys as *The Swarm* and *When Time Ran Out*), and later produced a string of TV movie disaster films and a lame star-studded adaptation of *Alice in Wonderland* (a *Pinocchio* project was aborted, for which we may be truly thankful). The early termination of Allen's delightfully nutty and naive *Return of Captain Nemo* project for Warners in the late '70s—wallowing in all the traditional Allen trademarks—after only three episodes would seem to have indicated the end of the line for Allen's particular brand of innocent fantasy. However, in recent years the Allen series have been rediscovered, and since *Star Wars* and its progeny have reminded audiences that they are allowed to find science-fiction funny and exciting as well as thought-provoking, there's fresh interest—and, with hindsight, a fresh perspective—for the weird and wonderful films and series of the '50s and '60s of which Allen was one of the most prolific practitioners.

1 *Voyage to the Bottom of the Sea*

September 1964–March 1968

Voyage to the Bottom of the Sea was Irwin Allen's first television series and ran from 1964 until 1968 (the pilot was filmed in 1963). Based on his mediocre but successful 20th Century Fox feature film of the same name, it was the first of a small number of television series that turned out to be superior to the films that spawned them (20th Century Fox's *Peyton Place*, M*A*S*H, *Alien Nation*, and *Buffy the Vampire Slayer* among them). It was also the series that established 20th Century Fox as a major force in TV production and producer Irwin Allen as one of the most powerful and successful TV providers of the 1960s. However, the series only came to exist in the first place because Allen and Fox had the foresight to keep the $40,000 worth of submarine sets to use in the future. The series, concerning the exploits of an atomic research submarine, independent of, but working for, the U.S. government, was therefore viable financially because Allen had kept all the standing sets—the *Seaview* itself cost more than most pilot films of the day.

The 600 foot long submarine *Seaview*, represented in the series by several different models of varying length and sophistication to perform different functions, is mostly distinguished by its glass viewscreen at the nose of the vessel and the fins on the back. Working under Fox's special effects wizard Lyle B. Abbott, who won several Emmys for his work for Allen over the years, the *Seaview*,

and its splendid manta-like Flying Sub introduced in the second season, were guided on wires by special effects man Howard Lydecker, who had worked on the old Captain Marvel and Rocketman adventures of the '40s for Republic using the same technique to make the heroes fly. Some of his earliest work, with brother Theodore Lydecker, included the highly regarded *Undersea Kingdom* serial. As with Allen's other series, the show benefitted from some of the finest movie-standard technicians Fox had to offer, including legendary cinematographer Winton Hoch (who photographed the visually stunning western classic *She Wore a Yellow Ribbon*).

Contrary to popular myth, *Voyage to the Bottom of the Sea* featured monsters, aliens, and science-fictional concepts from the earliest episodes. However, it is true to say that initially there were fewer of them. The stories started out in a fairly sober and straightforward fashion during the first monochrome season, and then settled into the more familiar and popular monster-of-the-week format of the second, third and fourth color seasons that most folk remember, returning to many of the same themes and storylines portrayed in the first season, but in a more fantastical manner. The series benefitted vastly from the arrival of color, at which time the entire submarine was given a facelift and redesign, and in style and execution it looks today as if there were five years rather than six months between the filming of the first and second seasons. The first season had a spartan look and a try-everything-once approach to scripts that ranged from espionage capers to '50s-style sci-fi, while the second season looked sharp, glossy, and lavish. The third and fourth seasons suffered from budget cuts and a dearth of fresh ideas, but thanks to the standing sets and expertise employed, still managed to look good and provide the requisite thrills and spills.

Memorable first season episodes included the first flying saucer episode, "The Sky Is Falling" (featuring extensive footage from the opening scenes of *The Day the Earth Stood Still*), a remake of Allen's 1960 film *The Lost World* as "Turn Back the Clock," Robert Duvall as an alien recovered from the seabed in "The Invaders," J.D. Cannon as a murderous and cowardly gloryhound in "The Condemned," a rampaging '50s-style robot in "The Indestructible Man," and the first two blobby monster yarns, "The Price of Doom" and "Cradle of the Deep."

As the first season was filmed in black and white, and broadcasters have the easy option of taking three color seasons, the earliest episodes are not seen nearly as often as the color ones, and this is unfortunate as they feature some intriguing ideas and interesting players; Ed Asner appears far removed from his amiable, *Lou Grant* persona in "The Exile," as a brutish dictator marooned at sea with Admiral Nelson, Leslie Nielsen appears as an incompetent submarine commander in "The Creature," and George Sanders is a double agent in "The Traitor." Other guest stars included Carroll O'Connor, June Lockhart, James Doohan, Henry Silva, Nancy Kovack and Richard Carlson.

With the start of the second season, *Voyage* drifted into a brief flirtation with entertaining Bond-ish spy stories provoked by the release of the underwater-based *Thunderball* and the pervasive secret agent mania of the period, turning out such high quality yarns as "The Cyborg," "Escape from Venice," "Time Bomb," "The Left Handed Man," "The X Factor," "The Peacemaker," "The Deadliest Game," and "The Machines Strike Back." As good as they were, ratings fell—audiences were suffering a surfeit of *Bond/UNCLE* adventures everywhere, and it quickly became apparent from the ratings surge every time the series featured sea-creatures and aliens that the viewers wanted to see the submarine, and more of the monsters they had been teased with earlier.

There then followed the series' best period of imaginative, underwater-based sci-fi with a variety of unusual and original story ideas. Highlights included "Leviathan," with a spectacular undersea confrontation between giant mutated scientist Liam Sullivan and the *Seaview*, the legendary "Monster from Outer Space" (a bodysnatching balloon blob!), "Deadly Creature Below," with a recurring red-eyed seaweed monster, the self-explanatory "Terror on Dinosaur Island," Kevin Hagen as an obsessed scientist pursuing a giant whale in "The Shape of Doom," the giant spider and "The Monster's Web," James Darren as "The Mechanical Man," and mad scientist John Dehner and "The Menfish." The third season opened with the famous living brain, aka the "Monster from the Inferno," while other brains of varying intelligence conjured up the self-explanatory "Werewolf," SF veteran Hugh Marlowe's "Thing from Inner Space," "The Plant Man," Lyle Bettger's seaweed "Creature," plus "The Heat Monster" (a living flame), "The Fossil Men" (living rocks!), "Shadow Man," "The Wax Men," and "The Mummy." In the fourth season, time travelers, immortals, Venusians, "Deadly Amphibians," a killer gorilla, "The Abominable Snowman," and "The Return of Blackbeard" would follow. Almost all of these were enormous fun, but scattered among them were lackluster and creature-less espionage thrillers and interminable heroes-turn-bad/impostor yarns set tediously throughout the *Seaview*'s corridors.

Shortly after the start of the third season location shooting had ground to a halt, the writing started to get lazy, stock footage and other short cuts were rampant, and the actors were getting tired and frustrated. Although the fourth and final season started well (lots of money and effort clearly went into the first four stories aired), the scripts were getting more and more ludicrous, and budget cuts were taking their toll. By now, the *Seaview* had encountered silver-suited space aliens, a variety of over-sized underwater creatures, ghosts, a mermaid, bogus pirates, and even killer dolls and leprechauns. By the end of the second season, Allen's dictatorial approach had alienated the better writers, and lame scripts, with a cheap and threadbare look about their execution showed that the series had run its course; even when the ideas were good ("Return of Blackbeard," "Flaming Ice," the infamous and magnificently ambitious "Lobster Man"),

Armed and angry, Richard Basehart (left) and David Hedison hunt down the show's scriptwriters? Despite the absurdity of some of the stories, Allen—quite wisely—would allow no humor or sarcasm to creep into the series. *Voyage to the Bottom of the Sea* was grim, earnest, action packed and relentlessly suspenseful.

there were no stories to back them up, and when the ideas weren't there, nothing would have been on the screen at all had it not been for the superb casting, sets, photography, and special effects miniatures (one could always count on some pyrotechnics or a scene or two with the Flying Sub to liven up the duds). Happily, after a handful of some of the worst episodes ever, the series ended on a high note with "No Way Back," a time travel yarn of second season quality. However, even during its weaker

seasons, the series was outrating all direct competition by far and still turning out the occasional gem.

Voyage to the Bottom of the Sea succeeded firstly because Irwin Allen knew exactly how to make a colorful and suspenseful adventure series, and secondly because of the commanding and credibility-enhancing presence of actor Richard Basehart in the lead, an inspired choice for the role of Admiral Nelson—portrayed in the film by *Forbidden*

Planet's Walter Pidgeon. Pidgeon's Nelson came across as a pompous dictatorial bore, but Basehart's Nelson was warmer and more human, while retaining the aloofness and authority of command. Although wonderful in the role, Basehart made no secret of the fact that he did *Voyage* purely for the money (he was coping with an expensive divorce from his first wife), and was openly contemptuous of the series' fantasy elements. He particularly hated the monsters, although supporting players have confirmed his negative attitude was entrenched from the earliest episodes. For Basehart, who possessed a reasonably impressive and prestigious list of film credits, it was a voyage to the bottom of his career, and while many guest stars interviewed over the years have pronounced Basehart to have been distant, unfriendly, and even pompous, others—including the regular cast—have had nothing but good words for him. Clearly, he was a man you had to get to know. It is common knowledge he got through many of the later episodes with a few stiff drinks (so did many of the audience by that point!), but one thing everybody is unanimously agreed on is the integrity of his performance and the authority that he brought to his role and the series. Whatever Basehart ultimately thought of his time on *Voyage*, it certainly didn't prevent him from working for Allen again, nor did it diminish the respect his supporting cast held for him. He later appeared in two Allen pilots, *City Beneath the Sea* and *The Time Travelers*, and Allen's TV movie *Flood*. He appeared in over sixty films and TV movies, with TV guest shots in *Rawhide, The Naked City, Twilight Zone, Ben Casey, Alfred Hitchcock, Gunsmoke, Ironside, Hawaii Five-O, Columbo, Little House on the Prairie,* and *Streets of San Francisco.* One of Basehart's last jobs was providing opening narration for the *Knight Rider* series and a guest appearance in the pilot; he died in 1984 shortly after providing voiceover work for the 1984 Olympics TV coverage, ironi-

cally the same month as Walter Pidgeon, the first Admiral Nelson. Basehart did not live to see the revival of the series on cable and satellite, and so, due to his professionalism, his dissatisfaction with the series has only become known through interviews with his fellow actors. Whether his attitude toward the series would have mellowed over the years, or whether the show's continued prominence and popularity would have annoyed and embarrassed him is something we shall never know. It is fair to assume that, like many other actors of his era, he would have found the show preferable to much contemporary fare in terms of content and technical quality, but no doubt frustrated that while *La Strada* and *The Brothers Karamazov* are forgotten by all but film buffs, he is remembered by his public today for *Voyage to the Bottom of the Sea.*

The role of Captain Crane, played in the film by Robert Sterling, went to David Hedison after much persistent badgering on the part of Allen, who phoned him relentlessly until he agreed to the role. It was colleague Roger Moore, then playing *The Saint,* who advised a prevaricating Hedison during a trip to London to jump at the chance of a long-running series, which, he pointed out, would provide the financial security to do any role he wanted afterwards. Hedison, dissatisfied with his film career, took the plunge—literally! Hedison later enjoyed the opportunity to do much theater work, and reluctantly turned down a role in *Twin Peaks* because he was committed to a theater engagement. Like many 1960s TV heroes, David Hedison moved into smooth villainous roles after *Voyage,* guest-starring on innumerable TV series as hapless hero or deceitful rogue, including *Cannon, Wonder Woman, Charlie's Angels, Love Boat, Fantasy Island, Hart to Hart, The Fall Guy, Hotel, Matt Houston, Knight Rider, Dynasty, The Colbys,* and *The A-Team.*

The rest of the crew were faceless (and in many cases nameless) to all but the most devoted of viewers. The first chief, Curley Jones, had almost nothing to do, and was played by the tough-looking Henry Kulky, who sadly died during production of the first season; a former wrestler known as Bomber Kulkavich, he had enjoyed an extensive career in early TV and film (appearing alongside Richard Basehart in Sam Fuller's *Fixed Bayonets* in 1951). The fish-eyed Terry Becker was brought in for season two as Chief Francis Sharkey, and quickly ran with the role, turning what was essentially a bit part into comic relief, fast becoming the third most prominent member of the cast and a major asset to the show. With his constantly distraught and puzzled expressions of dismay, and short-tempered desperation, poor old Sharkey never quite knew what was going on, only that he didn't like it! Although Becker played dimwitted comic relief on *Voyage*, he was actually a very educated man, and later directed TV episodes of series such as *Mission: Impossible* and *M*A*S*H*, becoming a producer on high-school drama *Room 222*. The luckless Robert Dowdell, cast as Crane's right-hand man Lt. Cmdr. Chip Morton, was undoubtedly given all the most hilariously silly lines, and was quickly relegated to repeating Crane's commands and asking obvious questions for the benefit of plot exposition. While Basehart got through the more fantastic moments of the plots by having Nelson in a form of constant denial (no matter what silliness had befallen the sub in previous weeks, Nelson steadfastly remained in a state of disbelief), and Hedison's Crane got through the proceedings by clenching his fists, his teeth, or any other available part of his anatomy, poor Chip Morton had to spell everything out in straightforward lines of dialogue. Del Monroe, mutinous crewman Kowski in the feature film, grabbed a couple of extra letters in his name to become the more loyal Kowalski in the series, while Paul Trinka became crewman Patterson. In the third season, each had a story built around

them. Allan Hunt was briefly added as Riley, a surfer type, in a misguided and hamfisted attempt to pull in the teenage audience during the second season, and Arch Whiting was the radio man inevitably named Sparks. Many other familiar faces flitted through the exploits of the *Seaview* each week, but few were credited, although SF veteran Paul Carr made a handful of appearances in the first season as crewman Clark before getting killed off in the second season under the name of Benson. The ship also managed to get through three ship's doctors (Richard Bull, Wright King, and Wayne Heffley), which wasn't surprising, given the bizarre nature of some of the crew's ailments, which could turn them into beast-men, yeti, or crazed psychotics at the drop of a plot point! Cuts, bruises and burns were more often outnumbered by outbreaks of violent psychosis, lycanthropy (three times!), or transformations into fossil men or alien bodysnatchers ... quite often, the crew were literally not themselves!

It's intriguing to note that the *Seaview* was a military vessel masquerading as a craft devoted to purely scientific research, whereas by the time Steven Spielberg was reworking Allen's series in the 1990s into the hapless *Earth 2* and the hopeless *seaQuest DSV*, times had changed to the extent that the submarine was now a military vessel commandeered and converted for scientific studies. Although the scientific missions the *Seaview* took on were genuine, Nelson had little time for any scientific data once the ship was endangered, and was quick to destroy anything that got out of hand. Needless to say, there was some repetition of plot developments within the limited surroundings of a submarine. The tunnel-visioned obsessive scientist was a favorite springboard into catastrophe, and during the third season in particular, there were numerous episodes in which the regular cast became the bad guys, either through transformation or impersonation. At one point in the series, the writers suddenly hit on the idea of having the crew elude their various adversaries by climbing through the ship's ventilation system, and a number of episodes employed this ruse.

The series was memorable for several recurring characteristics—a tendency to have various crew members taken over by alien forces; the famous lurching scenes whenever the submarine was attacked or disabled (Allen or the director would bang a bucket to tell the actors when to change direction while the camera rocked); the showers of sparks from the control panels whenever something malfunctioned; a lot of wandering around corridors looking for threats real or imagined (and interminably long and boring when you're just a kid watching in black and white); giant sea creatures outside the ship, and growling monsters loose inside it; Admiral Nelson's complete inability to believe in anything the slightest bit strange during 110 episodes featuring things that were very strange indeed; Captain Crane's complete inability to lock up proven nutcases or keep a close watch on obvious screwballs instead of letting them wander round the sub unattended causing trouble; major trouble makers guarded by one lone crewman instead of a good dozen; and the series' innocently naive attitude toward nuclear power and radiation (early escapades in the nuclear reactor room were initially accompanied by radiation suits, but this minor detail encumbered the actors and was soon dispensed with—by then the entire crew were probably so irradiated it hardly mattered!). And, like a number of series with a strong female following, the cast was all-male, resulting in a commendable lack of the sort of gooey romantic sub-plots that slowed down so many episodes of *Star Trek* and others.

Allen's notorious and skilful use and re-use of library footage also livened up the show beyond normal budgetary possibilities. Hedison was a contract player for Fox, and had appeared in a number of films including *The Enemy Below*, *The Fly*, and Allen's *The Lost World*. Both *The Enemy Below* and *The Lost World* were plundered extensively for stock footage in *Voyage to the Bottom of the Sea*, which deserves some sort of award for most creative re-use of library footage (no film from *The Fly* was ever used, but Allen did filch some of the set decoration for the *Seaview*). Every single set piece from the *Voyage* feature film was used at some point in the series, often more than once, as was a large chunk of the series' pilot in "The X-Factor." A lengthy piece of underwater footage with a bomb from "The Peacemaker" turns up in "The Mermaid," as does the death of a crewman (Roy Jenson) first filmed for "The Menfish," while a sequence in an undersea cavern from the second season's "The Mechanical Man" turns up in the fourth season's "The Terrible Leprechaun." The third season episode "No Escape from Death" offered no escape from stock footage, using tinted scenes from four different previous episodes. It was asking for trouble to sit down to a meal on board the *Seaview*, as the sub was invariably attacked just as the dinner bell sounded. Allen had filmed a mess in the mess hall sequence for the feature, and had no intention of letting it go to waste, using it repeatedly in the early episodes. Still, all this chicanery was preferable to those clip shows everyone else used to do to cut corners which simply had the cast sitting around reminiscing ...

Following the demise of the series, bumped to make way for the premiere of Allen's *Land of the Giants* after all concerned (except Allen) agreed that the undersea series had run its course, the *Seaview* later turned up in an episode of *Wonder Woman*, while the Flying Sub, including the interior,

Opposite: **Western Publishing's Gold Key imprint published some wonderfully lurid comic books during the series' run which captured the spirit of the show perfectly.**

GOLD | VOYAGE TO THE BOTTOM OF THE SEA   12c

KEY

10133-705
MAY

VOYAGE TO THE BOTTOM OF THE SEA

RICHARD BASEHART

1967, CAMBRIDGE PRODUCTIONS, INC. AND TWENTIETH CENTURY-FOX TELEVISION, INC.

From the frozen wastes of time, a million-year-old beast comes to life aboard the Seaview!

was used in Allen's pilot film *City Beneath the Sea* (no matter how many times the Flying Sub was destroyed, and even though there was only ever one in operation, the craft was always described as FS1!). While the series was in production many *Voyage* creatures turned up in Allen's companion series *Lost in Space*, notably in "The Raft," "A Change of Space," "The Prisoners of Space," "Hunter's Moon," "The Time Merchant" and "Anti-Matter Man," as did assorted props. The bridge set of *Voyage* is used as an underground base for an invasion force in the *Lost in Space* episode "The Lost Civilization," and redressed sections of the *Seaview* were used to represent other submarines in 1965's *Our Man Flint* and the 1966 *Batman* feature. Portions of the *Seaview* also turn up in *The Time Tunnel* ("Raiders from Outer Space") and *Land of the Giants* ("Graveyard of Fools").

Although filmed in the 1960s, *Voyage to the Bottom of the Sea* was set in the late '70s/early '80s. What was then the future is now the past, but the series' military setting avoided problems with dated styles and fashions, and of course the vast majority of episodes took place undersea. This has proven advantageous to the series for syndication purposes. The first year looks and feels as old as it is, but the second, third and fourth seasons still look great.

Voyage did not have any of the thoughtful philosophy or moral dilemmas of the heavier SF material of the preceding years, such as *The Twilight Zone* or *The Outer Limits*, but it was not intended to. More often than not, its politics, if that's not too strong a word for a series that never intended any, were of the particularly naive but reassuring nature that permeated 1950s and 1960s SF TV series. Early episodes reflected the Cold War atmosphere of the period, particularly prevalent in the first season, when many of the *Seaview*'s earliest adversaries were working for a "foreign power" ("The Mists of Silence," "The Price of Doom," "The Magnus

Beam," "No Way Out," "Long Live the King," "Hail to the Chief," "The Exile"). A cautious alliance was formed between the super powers when the entire world was threatened, such as in the episodes "Hot Line" or "Time Bomb," reflecting the conservative/liberal mix of the Kennedy era, and although obviously partisan, *Voyage* was essentially a fair and honest show, never portraying an entire nation's people as bad, only their military or government. The nature of the series and its setting made the political notion of America as policeman of the world inevitable, but many other episodes featured alternative adversaries to hostile governments, such as extra-terrestrials, undersea races, mad scientists, and other lone gunmen and dangerous obsessives. These were invariably left unguarded to roam the sub, even when their potential threat was known! Such illogical behavior was not unusual on *Voyage*; discovering that one of their number is an impostor and a murderer sent to kill off everyone else in "The Death Ship," everyone immediately and obligingly splits up to wander the corridors of the *Seaview* alone...!

Hedison confronted all these menaces with grim resolve and poker-faced determination, but it was Basehart's cautious disbelief and careful delivery of otherwise lifeless and absurd dialogue that gave the more outrageous episodes whatever credibility they possessed. His sense of authority and bemusement gave the show a dignity and gravity it would otherwise never have enjoyed. A few episodes were achingly boring, others stupid beyond belief, but when the show was good it was great ... and it was usually good. Most episodes of *Voyage* are hugely entertaining and eminently watchable, and the series is certainly one of a kind, the longest-running science-fiction series on American TV until *Star Trek: The Next Generation*. Allen's series were state-of-the-art in their day, but today's huge advances in special effects technology have rendered the look and style of '50s creature features and 1960s SF TV extinct, but for reruns. Films and TV of the sort made by Roger Corman, George Pal, William Alland and Jack Arnold, and Irwin Allen, to name but a handful, will never be made this way again, and many of the craftsmen and performers are gone. That's one of the best reasons to hunt them down and enjoy them for what they are.

The Cast

REGULAR CAST: Richard Basehart (Admiral Harriman Nelson), David Hedison (Captain Lee Crane), Robert Dowdell (Lt. Commander Chip Morton).

RECURRING CAST: Del Monroe (Kowalski), Terry Becker (Chief Francis E. Sharkey), Henry Kulky (Chief 'Curly' Jones), Paul Trinka (Patterson), Allan Hunt (Riley), Arch Whiting ('Sparks'), Paul Carr (Clark), Richard Bull, Wayne Heffley (ship's doctors).

BACKGROUND CREW: Ray Didsbury, Pat Culliton, Robert Doyle, Mark Slade, Nigel McKeand, Gordon Gilbert, Derrick Lewis, Joe E. Tata, Jerry Catron, Robert Pane, Robert Lipton, William Stevens, Bill Burnside, Buddy Garrett, Scott McFadden, Paul Stader, Jim Stader, many others.

VOICE ARTISTS: Dick Tufeld, Ray Didsbury, Paul Zastupnevich.

The Episodes

FIRST SEASON (1964–1965)

Eleven Days to Zero

wr. and dir. Irwin Allen

The Seaview sets sail for the Antarctic to detonate a bomb that will prevent earthquakes devastating the world with tidal waves, but enemy agents want the disaster to occur to undermine world security.

GUEST CAST: Eddie Albert (Dr. Fred Wilson), Bill Hudson (Captain John Phillips), John Zaremba (Dr. Claude Selby), Theo Marcuse/Werner Klemperer (Dr. Gamma), Booth Colman (Chairman), Hal Torey, Barney Biro (committee members), Christopher Connelly (crewman).

"Eleven Days to Zero" was a busy affair, with plenty of action to sell the series. Originally filmed in color in 1963, it was then slightly tinkered with and aired, as was the entire first season filmed, in black and white in 1964. Both a monochrome and a color version of the revised pilot exist, the monochrome version altered to feature the first season credits sequence. The pilot was inevitably made up of any action sequences Allen could legitimately lift from his feature film, bearing in mind that it had been made with a completely different cast. Scenes with a shark and the squid's tentacles came from the movie, as did numerous shots of the kitchens and corridors being rocked as the vessel is attacked. Also lifted was a scene involving depth charges necessitating a diving team repair job on the sonar. Not being able to re-use the scenes of the sky on fire from the cinema version clearly rankled Allen, and so the feature film's plot—and said footage—were consequently rehashed for the second season episode "The Sky's on Fire," the title of which at least telegraphed such chicanery to those who recalled the feature! Furthermore, those color scenes filmed for the pilot that *were* new would later be re-used themselves in the color episodes of the series (most significantly "The X Factor").

Between the original color pilot, and the eventual broadcast version in black and white, all the scenes with the bad guys were refilmed or tinkered with. Bizarrely, the Bondian villain (named in the credits but never referred to in the dialogue as Dr. Gamma) was portrayed by two actors, both typecast as shifty villainous types. Scenes shot for the original pilot feature Theo Marcuse, best known as the wizard Korob in *Star Trek's* Hallowe'en episode "Catspaw," although he also took minor roles in two classic *Twilight Zones* ("The Trade-Ins" and "To Serve Man") and was superb in "The Leeches" for *The Invaders*. Other roles included *The Outer Limits* ("Fun and Games"), *The Time Tunnel* ("Devil's Island"), and *Batman* ("Death in Slow Motion"/"The Riddler's False Notion"). He was well-served by the '60s spy fad, and appeared in three episodes of *The Man from UNCLE* ("The Recollectors Affair," "The Minus X Affair," and "The Pieces of Fate Affair"), episodes of *Get Smart, I Spy,* and *The Wild Wild West,* and the comedy spy features *The Last of the Secret Agents* and *The Glass Bottom Boat.* Reshot scenes and new voiceovers are Werner Klemperer, a villain in episodes of *The Man from UNCLE* ("The Project Strigas Affair"), *Lost in Space* ("All That Glitters"), and a later *Voyage* ("The Blizzard Makers"), but soon to become irreversibly associated with the slapstick role of Colonel Klink, a wonderful creation and personal triumph in the otherwise problematic '60s sit-com *Hogan's Heroes.* He has appeared in cameos as Klink in episodes of both *Batman* and *The Simpsons.* Oddly, Marcuse gets sole credit in both versions, and yet it is Klemperer we see in the single, shadowy shot of Gamma's face! Equally bizarre is that both actors' voices are used in different scenes. Marcuse, a fine actor, is reduced to little more than a glorified stand-in. When the sub pursues the *Seaview* in the original pilot, and the captain protests that he can't take his vessel any deeper (more feature film footage), the shadowed villain silently gives the thumbs down; in the series' episode, we cut to Gamma giving spoken commands. Gamma was intended to be a regular nemesis for Nelson and his crew, but the network apparently disliked the idea and vetoed it, and the series was almost certainly better for it.

This episode introduces Captain Crane to the *Seaview* when the previous commander is killed by agents of the villain in the opening scene. The crew's hostility toward their new commander in the pilot was justified by the shooting of fresh scenes in which Crane tests security by sneaking aboard the sub in drydock and punches out Kowalski. New scenes were added in which Crane makes amends with Kowalski and in which Nelson and Crane discuss said test. These are the scenes which occur between Nelson's meeting with the government brass and Nelson and Crane in Nelson's cabin debating the security of their Top Secret mission, and they did indeed improve, enhance and clarify the story. The added dialogue between Nelson and Crane concerning the nature of the *Seaview* and her crew is particularly strong and insightful into the characters and series premise, and very well written and played. This scene, and those showing tension between the crew and the new commander suggest forthcoming character development that was not acted upon. A gloom-and-doom scene with Crane on the radio to Nelson was added to the air attack scene to heighten suspense, and the scene with Nelson and the government brass (one of whose number was John Zaremba of *The Time Tunnel*) was slightly re-edited. All the changes seem to have improved the finished product. The most interesting difference between the color pilot and the first episode of the series was that the theme music had been changed; the color pilot has a Gershwin-style piano score at the close credited to Paul Sawtell and Sidney Cutner which is strongly reminiscent of the theme for *The Naked City* TV series of all things.

The script for "Eleven Days to Zero" is credited to Allen, and there seems little reason to dispute it. So much of the pilot consists of footage and plot structure from the feature film credited to Allen and the sour Charles Bennett (see the section on "Secret of the Loch" for further discussion of this) that it was more a case of what to take out rather than adding anything new. It is of course a truncated version of the feature film, with all those elements not re-used here being rehashed in the series' version of the feature film scenario, "The Sky's on Fire." The opening credits roll over newsreel scenes of devastation that have since become cliché, and bear all the hallmarks of Allen's obsession with disaster and catastrophe. Particularly amusing is Eddie Albert's speech to the Washington committee, which is full of hilariously sensationalistic adjectives as Wilson luridly details the horrors that the tidal waves will inflict on large portions of the globe with all the demented glee of a tabloid newspaper!

Playing crewmen in the pilot were Mark Slade, who left the show after the first few episodes to re-surface in the seafaring sit-com *The Wackiest Ship in the Army* the following season, another film-to-series, but would eventually be best known for his role in the western series *The High Chaparral*, and—uncredited—Christopher Connelly, who was to leave the claustrophobic confines of the *Seaview* and cross the lot to Fox's long-running 1960s prime-time soap *Peyton Place*, which made a minor star of him. Connelly, who some years later appeared in the late '70s mini-series of *The Martian Chronicles*, his only other TV SF credit, appears in a number of early publicity stills for the series and is often mistakenly billed in these as Arch Whiting (Sparks). Another oft-repeated error is that the series later featured two exploratory vessels named the *Flying Fish* and the *Sea Crab*; these articles and reference books are working from outdated press releases and sales material. Ultimately, both these concepts were merged into what became the Flying Sub.

Both Slade (whose initial character was killed off in the feature film, and re-named in the series, from Smith to Malone) and Del Monroe (Kowalski) were the only players to transfer from the film to the series;

while Slade went to serve on what was surely only the second wackiest ship in '60s TV after the first few *Voyage* episodes had been filmed, Monroe appeared in virtually every episode of the series until the end of its run.

Bill Hudson had appeared in Bert Gordon's *The Amazing Colossal Man* and *Attack of the Fifty Foot Woman* in the '50s and was now playing bit parts at Fox, including a *Batman* ("Instant Freeze/Rats Like Cheese"). A recurring character in the 1954 series *Rocky Jones, Space Ranger*, his other films included *The She Creature*, *The Man Who Turned to Stone*, and *Moon Pilot*. Booth Colman appears again in "The Mist of Silence," presumably as the same official, and appears in Irwin Allen's unsold pilot *The Time Travelers*. Other credits include episodes of *Boris Karloff's Thriller*, *The Outer Limits*, *The Wild Wild West*, *The Invaders*, *Galactica '80*, and *Star Trek: Voyager*. He also played Doctor Zaius in the 1974 *Planet of the Apes* TV series.

Hal Torey appears in the films *War of the Colossal Beast*, *Earth vs. the Spider*, *The Cosmic Man*, and *Invisible Invaders*. He has minor roles, again as a military man, in the pilot for Allen's next series, *Lost in Space*, and the second season *Voyage* episode "The Monster from Outer Space." John Zaremba would return in the second season as Vice Admiral Johnson in "Time Bomb" before taking up his regular role in *The Time Tunnel* as Doctor Swain the following season.

Shortly after this episode aired, guest star Eddie Albert—later to be irrevocably identified with the long-running '60s hickcom *Green Acres*—appeared in the excellent and underrated "Cry of Silence" for *The Outer Limits*. Ironically, *The Outer Limits*, a wonderful series, was cancelled partly because *Voyage* had bumped it from its safe slot on Monday evenings. *Voyage* would in turn be bumped—advantageously—to Sundays, replacing *Wagon Train*, where it would remain for the rest of its run. Production no: 6008. Note: 7202 is the first episode of the series to be filmed; there was no 7201.

The City Beneath the Sea

wr. Richard Landau, dir. John Brahm

A treasure hunt turns sour when Captain Crane encounters an undersea city whose inhabitants have designs on the surface world.

With Hurd Hatfield (Leopold Zeraff), Linda Cristal (Melina), John Alderson (the innkeeper), Al Ruscio (Dmitri), Peter Brocco (Xanthos), Peter Mamokas (Nicolas), Joey Walsh (Atlas).

David Hedison trots jauntily around a backlot Greek island in this acceptable if routine first episode aired, leaving Richard Basehart to hold the fort in the *Seaview*. Although it would have benefitted greatly from color, the rather straightforward and underdeveloped story is a passable time-waster.

This episode, like many of the first season, was originally to feature Theo Marcuse's Doctor Gamma as the villain, but the network had already forced this character's excision from the pilot (see "Eleven Days to Zero"). "Irwin loved the idea of this guy" writer Richard Landau told *Starlog*, "but the network didn't, and they got rid of him fast. They felt that kind of villain was old hat—and he was!" The story idea was already there when Landau was recruited to write for the show. Landau had written "Wolf 359" for *The Outer Limits*, the infamous miniature civilization story memorably parodied in both *The Simpsons* and *South Park*, and later contributed the enjoyable "The Indestructible Man" to *Voyage*, his only other story for the series after a falling out with Allen during the writing of it. He also scripted the 1951 feature *The Lost Continent*, co-wrote the 1955 adaptation of *The Quatermass Experiment* (aka *The Creeping Unknown*), and wrote for *The Green Hornet* and *The Wild Wild West*. In the 1970s, he wrote for *Space: 1999* and produced the final season of *The Six Million Dollar Man*.

John Brahm later directed "Hot Line" for *Voyage*, and the memorable "Zzzzz" and "The Bellero Shield" for *The Outer Limits*. Films include *The Undying Monster* and *The Mad Magician*. He did not stay long with *Voy-*

age, and his two episodes were sandwiched between a large number of assignments for *The Twilight Zone*, *Boris Karloff's Thriller*, and the *UNCLE* franchise. Linda Cristal would later join short-term crewman Mark Slade and "Mist of Silence's" Henry Darrow as a regular on *The High Chaparral*. Hurd Hatfield was on the way down when he made this guest appearance; his underwritten, nothing-to-do role was down to being the rewritten and unwanted Doctor Gamma. His best known credit is probably 1945's *The Picture of Dorian Gray*.

As with many of the early episodes, there is a huge cast, and many of the supporting actors only had one or two scenes in the entire episode. Production no: 7204.

The Fear Makers

wr. Anthony Wilson, dir. Leonard Horn

An experimental nerve gas that induces growing panic in its victims is employed by an enemy agent to sabotage the Seaview, but he is unaware as to just how experimental the unstable substance is.

With Lloyd Bochner (Dr. Martin Davis), Edgar Bergen (Dr. Arthur Kenner), Robert Doyle (Prior), William Sargent (Anders), Walter Brooke (Dan Case), Ed Prentiss (Philip James), Martin Kosleck (Davis' superior).

Although his most famous SF TV role was as the terrified translator of alien dialects in the legendary *Twilight Zone* episode "To Serve Man," Lloyd Bochner's career throughout the '60s and '70s consisted mostly of smarmy, deceitful villainy, and this episode sees him in fine form, slipping and sliding around the *Seaview* as a traitorous psychologist employing not so subtle mind games to unhinge the sub's crew with the aid of a sinister "fear gas" hidden in the ventilation system. Unknown to even him, the gas is unstable, making him as vulnerable to its ultimate effects as anyone else, and the scenes of him panicking when this comes to his attention are not only reminiscent of "To Serve Man," but the most fun in the episode. He would be back as a paranoid warmongering general in "The Deadliest

Game," a second season episode, where his credits are listed in detail. Somewhat less typical casting was Edgar Bergen, father of actress Candice Bergen, and best known for his bizarre career as a ventriloquist—bizarre as he was best known on the radio. He gives a perfectly competent performance here as Bochner's innocent colleague. The network was clearly impressed—they moved the episode forward to the series' all-important third week on the air.

A number of familiar bit players round out the cast. Martin Kosleck, always a bad guy, was cast to type in a single scene as the instigator of the enemy plot (possibly another Doctor Gamma replacement). Other roles include *Boris Karloff's Thriller*, *The Outer Limits*, *Get Smart*, and numerous episodes of the *UNCLE* series. Walter Brooke later played the role of D.A. Scanlon in *The Green Hornet*. William Sargent, here the ill-fated submarine captain in the teaser, would also come to grief in "The Conscience of the King" in *Star Trek*, and two fine episodes of *The Invaders*, "Genesis" and "Dark Outpost." Ed Prentiss also appeared in *The Wild Wild West* and *The Invaders*.

Anthony Wilson was story editor on Allen's *Lost in Space* and *Land of the Giants*, where he made invaluable contributions to both. He also wrote "Beach Head," the excellent pilot for *The Invaders* and "Come Wander With Me," a poor *Twilight Zone*. "The Fear Makers" falls somewhere in between, competently written but a little slow; it's what one might call an actors' episode, as it gives the cast a chance to chew the scenery, a challenge accepted head on by Richard Basehart, who relished any chance to show some genuine emotion. Between them, Bochner and Basehart just about keep the episode interesting.

Leonard Horn would direct a number of first season episodes of *Voyage*, including "The Mist of Silence" (his first), "The Sky is Falling," "Submarine Sunk Here," "The Magnus Beam" and "The Condemned." He

also directed "Invaders from the Fifth Dimension" for *Lost in Space*, and three classic episodes of *The Outer Limits*, "The Man Who was Never Born," "The Zanti Misfits," and "The Children of Spider County." Given the imagination shown in his episodes of *Lost in Space* and *The Outer Limits*, his work on *Voyage* is quite routine. For the second season of *Voyage* he directed "The X Factor" and "Terror on Dinosaur Island," and in 1975, the impressive WWII-based pilot for the *Wonder Woman* series. Production no: 7207.

The Mist of Silence

wr. John McGreevey, dir. Leonard Horn

Captain Crane and members of his crew are abducted and threatened with execution during a Latin American uprising.

With Mike Kellin (General D'Alvarez), Alejandro Rey (Ricardo Galdez), Rita Gam (Detta Casone), Henry Delgado/Darrow (Captain Serra), Edward Colmans (President Fuente), Booth Colman (Chairman), Weaver Levy (Oriental Colonel), Armand Alzamora (Spanish Major), Doug Lambert (Williams), Joe E. Tata (Farrell).

John McGreevey, a former writer of pulp SF, was best known on TV for his work on comedy shows, and yet here turns in the darkest, grimmest episode of the entire series. McGreevey later wrote for *The Flying Nun*, a particularly lame '60s sit-com on which Alejandro Rey was a regular, at which time Rey complimented him, saying that "The Mist of Silence" had given him "the rare opportunity to play a character that had some substance!"

"The Mist of Silence" in the title is in fact a mysterious fog that envelops a small boat carrying Crane and some of his crew (the story apparently grew from a germ of an idea inspired by the legend of the Mary Celeste, although the filmed result recalls *The Incredible Shrinking Man*). The men wake up in a cell in one of those many unidentified Latin American banana republics of old Hollywood and it's up to Nelson and a group of freedom fighters supporting the former President, now a drugged puppet in the hands of the local tyrant, to save the day. The *Seaview* is hardly seen at all, except for one token bit of business involving an aerial attack and some depth charges, all footage from the *Voyage* pilot.

As with many of the early episodes, there is quite a large cast in comparison with later seasons. Mike Kellin, here playing the leering despot D'Alvarez, appeared as a similarly smirking alien in "The Deadly Games of Gamma Six" for *Lost in Space* and as a haunted submarine crewman in "The Thirty Fathom Grave" for *The Twilight Zone*. Doomed by Hollywood stereotyping to always play the bad guy, Kellin clearly decided to go with the flow and make a meal of it. Alejandro Rey's other fantasy credits include *Boris Karloff's Thriller, I Spy, The Girl from UNCLE, Night Gallery, The Bionic Woman, The Amazing Spider-Man,* and *Knight Rider*. Edward Colmans and Henry Delgado both appeared in "Tourist Attraction" for *The Outer Limits*. Often cast as a Spanish or Mexican supporting player, Colmans' other credits include the feature *War of the Worlds* and episodes of *My Favorite Martian, Get Smart, I Spy, The Time Tunnel,* and *The Wild Wild West*. Henry Delgado later anglicized his name to Darrow, presumably to avoid constant stereotyping in south-of-the-border roles, but achieved his greatest success playing Manolito in the western series *The High Chaparral*. Under the name of Darrow he would appear in *The Wild Wild West*, the 1975 pilot for *The Invisible Man, The Gemini Man, The Incredible Hulk, Airwolf, Knight Rider, Star Trek: The Next Generation,* the 1992 pilot for *Time Trax, Star Trek: Voyager,* and *Babylon 5*. Booth Colman is presumably playing the same official he played in the pilot.

Joe E. Tata had worked for Horn before, on two of his episodes of *The Outer Limits*, and was a regular bit-player in Fox productions. Although he plays Farrell, the unfortunate crewman who gets shot, he

would turn up alive and well as various unnamed crewmen in further episodes as well as several episodes of *Batman, The Time Tunnel,* and *Lost in Space*. This was director Leonard Horn's first *Voyage* assignment, although "The Fear Makers" aired first. Production no: 7203.

The Price of Doom

wr. Harlan Ellison, dir. James Goldstone
> *An unidentified enemy agent aboard the Seaview sabotages a scientific expedition.*

With David Opatoshu (Dr. Karl Reisner), Jill Ireland (Julie Lyle), John Milford (Philip Wesley), Steve Ihnat (Dr. Pennell), Pat Priest (Karen Pennell), Dan Seymour (General), Ivan Treisault (enemy operative).

Harlan Ellison, author of the notorious *cause celebre* for *Star Trek*, "The City on the Edge of Forever," was the first writer to introduce a monster to *Voyage to the Bottom of the Sea*, later the series' staple diet and saving grace after all the tiresome Red Menace villains of the early episodes. A prolific writer of 1960s TV, Ellison's other SF work included "Demon with a Glass Hand" and "Soldier" for *The Outer Limits*, "The Pieces of Fate Affair" and the superb "Sort of Do-it-Yourself Dreadful Affair" for *The Man from UNCLE*, as well as the more routine "Shatterday," "Paladin of the Lost Hour," and "Gramma" for the 1980's *Twilight Zone*, and story editor and consultancy posts on the '80s *Twilight Zone* and *Babylon Five*. His working relationship with Allen was abrupt and short-lived—a story conference for the series apparently ended with Ellison sliding down the boardroom table to punch the lights out of network executive Adrian Samish. According to a published fanzine interview with Ellison, a model of the *Seaview* fell onto Samish, hospitalizing him, and Ellison found himself blacklisted from all further ABC writing assignments—Samish vetoed every hiring thereafter, including a much coveted *Batman*. However, it is highly unlikely that any relationship between Allen, notoriously controlling and intimidating toward writers, and Ellison, famously volatile and independent, would have ever developed. In this instance, Ellison claimed that the argument began when Allen and his executives started adding blatant absurdities and clichés to his story. He ultimately exercised his right to replace his credit with a pseudonym and chose Cordwainer Bird, the most derogatory and foolish pen name he could think of.

As ungracious and extreme as Ellison's behavior was, he was either seriously off-form for this episode, or the rewriting was destructively vindictive. It is hard to believe that much of Ellison's original script remains. Clichés and cornball concepts abound (such as a bit of business with a cigarette lighter, and Reisner's six months to live), and the dialogue, which is usually his strength and positively sings in an Ellison script, is particularly poor. Dialogue was never *Voyage's* strong point, but some of the exchanges in this episode are exceptionally dire, and way below the high standards to be found in his work for *Burke's Law* and *The Man from UNCLE*. Ellison has always refused to discuss, or even identify, his uncredited TV work, so we can only speculate, but "The Price of Doom" (a meaningless title, changed from Ellison's own very un-Allen-like "Mealtime") shows every indication of having been not so much tampered with as completely torn up and stamped on. The villains, in particular, are the usual high-living Reds (Ivan Treisault as another substitute for the abandoned Dr. Gamma no doubt, and hefty Dan Seymour, the poor man's Victor Buono) surrounded by fine wines and art, a Hollywood tradition and *Voyage* cliché that serves two functions—firstly to distinguish them from the unpretentious, uncomplicated blue-collar TV audience and make them suspiciously over-intellectual, and secondly as visual shorthand to portray total corruption in countries otherwise known to be poor. The poverty of Communist nations naturally never reached the higher echelons, of course; Allen's *Voyage* Reds, like everyone else's at the time, are always swilling wine or brandy, surrounded by antiques and oil paintings that the proles will never see. The monstrous creature itself, which looks good when bubbling and gushing forth from the science lab beakers in a mass of tentacles and ooze, but then becomes a rather obvious spiky inflatable balloon, is destroyed in the traditional B-movie manner of finding a convenient delete-where-applicable Achilles heel (this time it's cold), and the manner of the discovery of this fatal flaw is hopelessly lame.

Familiarity with Ellison's style, prejudices, and love of the macabre and subversive suggest that the opening scene in the icy laboratory where the scientist and his sexy wife meet their demise began on Ellison's typewriter, along with such notions as a reformed guilt-ridden Nazi scientist and the cowardly and arrogant representative of big business, but again we can only guess. As the badly written capitalist bully, John Milford is adequate. David Opatoshu shines as the repentant scientific researcher, and comes off the best, along with the ever-reliable Richard Basehart. Both performers have a history of destabilizing bad dialogue and making it work. Steve Ihnat, who appeared in the two-parter "The Inheritors" for *The Outer Limits* and as Garth in the *Star Trek* episode "Whom Gods Destroy," is solid as the doomed professor, and Pat Priest (bland Marilyn in *The Munsters*) is delightful as his bubbly wife, while Jill Ireland is as reliably and consistently bad as ever, giving yet another dismal performance in a TV career saved only by her swingin' London stripper in "The Five Daughters Affair" (aka *The Karate Killers*) for *The Man from UNCLE* and an adequate showing in *Star Trek's* famous "This Side of Paradise." Several other roles in *UNCLE*, mostly facilitated by her marriage at the time to series star David McCallum, were on a par with her unconvincing turn here.

David Opatoshu turned up in many fantasy TV series of the '60s. A frail-looking yet authoritative type, usually bearded, he is often a diplomat, professor, or scientist. He was particularly good as a treacherous academic in "The Alexander the Greater Affair" for *The Man from UNCLE* (released as the feature *One Spy too Many*), and the weak, insanely pragmatic Anan Seven in "A Taste of Armageddon" for *Star Trek*. Other roles include *The Twilight Zone, The Outer Limits, The Time Tunnel, The Invisible Man, The Bionic Woman, The Six Million Dollar Man, Cliffhangers,* and *Buck Rogers in the 25th Century*. He was still working in the late 1980s, turning up in an episode of *Alien Nation*. John Milford appeared in "The Children of Spider County" for *The Outer Limits* and episodes of *Get Smart, The Invaders, Land of the Giants, Ghost Story, Planet of the Apes, The Six Million Dollar Man, The Gemini Man, The Bionic Woman, The Amazing Spider-Man, Wonder Woman,* and *Knight Rider*.

James Goldstone directed "The Sixth Finger" and "The Inheritors," two highly regarded episodes of *The Outer Limits*, and "Where No Man has Gone Before" and "What Are Little Girls Made Of?" for *Star Trek*. Goldstone loved his *Outer Limits* assignments, but had ambitions that went beyond weekly television series, and was less impressed with the sci-fi environs of *Star Trek* and *Voyage to the Bottom of the Sea*. Indeed, his second *Star Trek* was done, he says, purely as a favor, and he worked alongside Allen when, as so often befell directors in the '60s, the series he had initially been offered was canceled. When this happened, directors would be given a take-it-or-leave-it substitute, and Goldstone found himself pressganged to serve on the *Seaview*. Although he was no more fond of Allen than Ellison, and refused to work when Irwin came on the set to supervise, he returned to *Voyage* to direct "Doomsday," "The Human Computer," and "The Exile." However, like so many of those who worked both in front of, and behind

the cameras on classic TV shows, when invited to re-watch his *Voyage* episodes for a 1994 interview with Mark Phillips, author of McFarland's *Science-Fiction Television Series 1959–1989*, he willingly came to the conclusion that they were not as bad as he had recalled. "I was really amazed at how good the plankton looked. On the set (it) looked terribly fake ... made out of big balloons, and the air pumps that made them move were so noisy we had to loop all of the actors' lines. The secret was not to stay on it too long, and instead play the people's reaction to the danger ... not that the plankton is terrifying, but that the people are terrified. That (opening) scene worked based on one criterion, and that's whether you cared about the human beings." Other credits include *The Man from UNCLE* ("The Brain Killer Affair") and several episodes of *Amos Burke—Secret Agent*. Despite his animosity towards Allen, the offer to direct Irwin's 1980 feature *When Time Ran Out* was too lucrative to pass over. But, said Goldstone, "Irwin and I got along no better on that twenty million dollar picture than we did on those five day *Voyages*." Production no: 7210.

The Sky Is Falling

wr. Don Brinkley, dir. Leonard Horn
The Seaview is attacked by an energy-draining spaces.

With Charles McGraw (Rear Admiral Tobin), Adam Williams (Chief), Frank Ferguson (Air Force General), Joseph di Reda (alien).

The series' first foray into close encounters was a relatively serious one compared with the army of invading extra-terrestrials to appear in the third and fourth seasons. The storyline, if not its execution, has echoes of Alland, Arnold, and Bradbury's 1953 feature film *It Came from Outer Space*, with essentially benevolent and detached aliens attracting attention by mistake and taking recognizable human form to make a swift departure. The dialogue makes its point but is not terribly profound, with Nelson failing to make the obvious defense that a second, rescue saucer is being encouraged by the alien to make the same rush to judgment he is so angry with Earth for making; there seems to be as much lack of understanding and communication on the aliens' part as on Earth's, a flaw often overlooked in discussions of *It Came from Outer Space,* in which the so-called peaceful aliens steal identities, terrify the locals, and fire ray guns! Despite being obviously intelligent, the alien here willfully misinterprets the behavior of the armed forces as Nelson fights his corner with words. Perhaps because of his distaste for science fiction, Basehart misses a chance to play the alien in an unusual manner, playing his lines as the extraterrestrial in the same way he does for Nelson. Compare this with Robert Duvall's attempts to sound awkward and unusual in "The Invaders" a few episodes later.

The alien saucer is a customized model of Klaatu's ship from the famous and vastly superior *The Day the Earth Stood Still,* with some silly colored lights added, and the opening scenes employ the familiar opening footage from that film. Although Allen frequently employed Bernard Herrman's distinctive score from that film in his series (often in *Lost in Space* and *Time Tunnel,* and extensively in the *Voyage* episodes "The Indestructible Man" and "The Mummy," to name but two of many), he wisely doesn't jog audience memories here, although the familiar ominous hum of that film's saucer is used at one point, alongside more clichéd bleeps and bloops. Apparently new footage, or perhaps discarded footage from the film, shows the saucer over the sea. The episode's author, Don Brinkley, wrote some of his best work around the less friendly extraterrestrials of the same network's *The Invaders,* including such superior episodes as "Vikor," "Quantity: Unknown," "The Ivy Curtain," "Wall of Crystal," and "The Pursued." He wrote one other episode for *Voyage,* "Hail to

the Chief." Regular first season director Leonard Horn was also no stranger to extraterrestrial encounters, having previously directed three classic episodes of *The Outer Limits;* he would later direct the stylish first season episode of *Lost in Space,* "Invaders from the Fifth Dimension."

Although poor Henry Kulky had not yet passed away (the actor died shortly before the end of the first season), there is a different, unnamed Chief in this episode, suggesting the actor's unavailability. Taking the role was Adam Williams. Character actor Frank Ferguson (credits include "The Marionettes" for *Land of the Giants*) is a typical warhorse general, while Charles McGraw makes the most of his handful of opportunities to raise the character of "Trigger-Happy" Tobin above his stereotypical purpose of hawkish antagonist, particularly when Nelson enters the spacecraft. Otherwise, his character is there to perform the same irritating disagreeable tension as later cardboard authoritarians would on *Star Trek,* but with more depth.

Joseph Di Reda, glimpsed briefly as the alien, also appeared in the somewhat less classy "Invasion from Outer Space" for *The Green Hornet.* As the script tells us that this alien visage is too horrible for humans to see (an old sci-fi chestnut also swiped from *It Came from Outer Space*), showing a mortal face with goo on it was an unnecessary embellishment; this fellow seems far less disconcerting than being faced with a duplicate of yourself. Production no: 7209.

Turn Back the Clock

wr. Sheldon Stark, dir. Alan Crosland Jnr

The Seaview searches for a missing scientist with the expedition's sole and apparently amnesiac survivor, and discovers a prehistoric world beneath the sea.

With Nick Adams (Jason Kemp), Yvonne Craig (Carol Denning), Vitina Marcus (native girl), Les Tremayne (Dr. Denning), Robert Cornthwaite (Dr. Zeigler), Robert Patten (Kemp's Doctor).

From the moment *Variety* reviewed the *Voyage* pilot, Allen was being castigated in print for re-using earlier footage to cut costs, but little did his critics know—they hadn't seen anything yet. No television series before or since has recycled earlier material quite so brazenly or so frequently as *Voyage to the Bottom of the Sea*. With the exception of the feature film material, this episode was Allen's first and most shameless re-use of film footage, employing almost all the action sequences from his 1960 feature *The Lost World*, and although it did not go unnoticed by the viewers of the time (several letters of complaint appeared on the *TV Guide* letters page), Allen continued the practice throughout his TV career, and in particular on *Voyage to the Bottom of the Sea* and *The Time Tunnel*. However, whereas the stock film footage of *The Time Tunnel* was used only to set the scene for the adventures to follow and represent expensive battles and set pieces during the story, *Voyage to the Bottom of the Sea* frequently used its own set pieces, and those from other films, to construct new stories or take cheap short cuts. Fortunately, Allen's stock footage was always expertly integrated with the freshly-filmed material, although this didn't impress the *TV Guide* complainants, and ultimately put paid to any hope Allen had of building a weekly series around *The Lost World*.

Replying to three sarcastic letters following the October 1964 airdate (including one pointing out that *The Lost World* had aired twice on TV in the last year), Allan Balter replied: "Fact is, there was a minimum of stock footage from *The Lost World*, no more than you ordinarily find in any (TV series) of this sort like *Twelve o'Clock High* or *Combat*. We did use one very spectacular cut in which two monsters fought and fell over a cliff. It would have cost a fortune to re-do this." Fact is, Balter's reply was disingenuous at best and a downright lie at worst, but in those days there was no home video to contradict readers' memories and ABC tellingly left "Turn Back the Clock" out of the summer reruns. Although there is no stock footage from the movie in the first two of the four acts (just in the pre-credits teaser), three lengthy sequences are plundered in acts three and four, including the one Balter admits to, and the entire climax of the adventure is lifted from the movie and identical to it. "Turn Back the Clock" virtually becomes *The Lost World* in its second half. Certainly, stock footage was a valid cost-cutting ploy, and Allen used it frequently and justifiably, and to excellent effect, as did many other producers. However, as enjoyable as "Turn Back the Clock" is as an individual episode, this was an instance in which Allen had gone a clip too far; it was one thing to use existing footage to represent a new situation in a fresh story, but this episode was little more than a scene by scene recreation of Allen's 1960 feature utilizing not just the ever-familiar dinosaur fight (which unrepentantly returns two years later in *Time Tunnel's* "Chase Through Time" for another outing) but many other set pieces as well through the devious recasting of Hedison and Marcus in both. Consequently, for those who have seen the original film in color, this episode is interesting only as a monochrome curiosity. For those who have not seen *The Lost World*, a peculiar sense of *deja-vu* will be forthcoming when they do, and as professional and as entertaining as this piece of work is, it serves only to devalue both Allen's feature film and the *Voyage to the Bottom of the Sea* series.

As the network never exercised its repeat option on the episode, it wasn't seen again until syndication. This is a shame, as the new framing sequence and guest cast is quite good. Scriptwriter Sheldon Stark, a former comic-book writer, goes to some trouble to explain away the more fantastic elements of the story in some very well-written scenes, but contributes little in the way of new ideas other than a ludicrous secret agent-style blow-gun that Nelson just happens to carry in his shoe; no doubt there'll be a call coming through from Maxwell Smart at any minute! This episode was Stark's only contribution to *Voyage to the Bottom of the Sea*, but he did go on to write for *The Man from UNCLE, Batman, The Green Hornet, Mission: Impossible,* and "On a Clear Night You Can See the Earth" for *Land of the Giants.*

Alan Crosland directed "The Mice" and "The Mutant" for *The Outer Limits*; for whatever reason, although he was very prolific in TV SF, this was his only work on any of the four Irwin Allen series. The son of silent film director Alan Crosland Snr., his other TV credits include numerous episodes of *The Twilight Zone, The Wild Wild West, The Six Million Dollar Man, The Bionic Woman,* and *Wonder Woman.* There is nothing remarkable or outstanding in any of them, and some of the *Wonder Woman* episodes make the jaw drop. Otherwise, most of the episode's interest comes from some welcome and familiar supporting players, lead by the beautiful Yvonne Craig, who was great fun in spy films such as *One Spy too Many, One of Our Spies is Missing,* and *In Like Flint,* wonderful as the green-skinned seductress in *Star Trek's* "Whom Gods Destroy," and fondly remembered as Batgirl in the third season of the *Batman* TV series. She is also the only plus in the classic turkey *Mars Needs Women.* Her only other work for Allen was the awful "Wild Journey" for *Land of the Giants.* Craig spends most of her time here screaming, but she does it well—her reaction when she first goes nose-to-nose with a giant lizard is very good.

The equally striking Vitina Marcus first appeared as the native girl in Allen's 1960 feature film adaptation of *The Lost World,* and recreated her role here for the benefit of reusing the footage. Such amiable cooperation made her an Allen favorite, and her loyalty (and ability) secured her a considerable amount of further work with Allen, including another *Voyage,* "The Return of the Phantom." The ill-fated Nick Adams,

star of two short-lived TV series, *The Rebel* and *Saints and Sinners,* also starred in the "Fun and Games" episode of *The Outer Limits.* He was best known for attaching himself first to James Dean, and then Elvis Presley, although he never appeared in an Elvis film (Yvonne Craig did two). Adams is excellent in his role here as Kemp. Les Tremayne (whose credits include *The Monolith Monsters* and *The Angry Red Planet*) plays the small role of Carol's father well, and Robert Cornthwaite (who later appears in the second season as a General in "The Deadliest Game") has just one scene—one of the best in the film—as a paleontologist angered when he believes Nelson has tried to deceive him with a fake dinosaur bone. His mood shift is very well played. Although Mark Slade is credited for appearing as crewman Malone, and Del Monroe as Kowalski, they are both barely seen, but another crewman with a couple of lines gets no credit at all! Patterson is seen briefly in a background shot. Production no: 7205.

The Village of Guilt

wr. Berne Giler, dir. Irwin Allen
Nelson and his crew investigate rumors of a giant sea monster off the coast of Norway.

With Richard Carlson (Lars Mattson), Anna-Lisa (Sigrid), Steven Geray (Oscar Dalgren), Frank Richards (Otto Hassler), G. Stanley Jones (Anderson), Erik Holland (Gartern), Torben Mayer (the innkeeper), Greger Vigen (young boy), Kort Falkenberg (father).

Despite being directed by Allen himself and guest-starring SF veteran Richard Carlson, this episode was held over until the show was up and running. Although the first episode of the series filmed, it was the eighth episode to air. As network policy is traditionally to hold a weak episode until the first few have hooked the audience, this would seem to indicate they considered it a weak one. Alternatively, it's possible they were struck by a sense of *deja-vu.* Directing an episode of *Voyage* for the second and last time, Allen has the gall to use stock footage from the pilot already, in the sequence where Crane dives and orders full speed ahead. A clumsy cut closes the scene with a reference to Norway as their destination. Fortunately for Allen, the network's decision to hold this one back helped hide the repetition. The episode itself is built around the octopus attack footage from the *Voyage* feature film, the creature being the village's guilty secret. The network's random shuffling of the episodes prepared for broadcast also obscures the fact that the first few episodes made are noticeably landbound.

Although he helmed his four 1960s pilots, this was the only series episode of his shows that Allen ever directed personally. Writer Berne Giler, who also wrote "Hot Line" for *Voyage*, later moved on to the *UNCLE* franchise, where he wrote several enjoyable adventures for both *The Man from UNCLE* and *The Girl from UNCLE*. He was the father of David Giler, who co-wrote Fox's 1979 hit *Alien*.

Richard Carlson was a veteran of several somewhat earlier sci-fi classics, including *The Magnetic Monster*, *It Came from Outer Space*, *Riders to the Stars* (which he also directed), and *The Creature from the Black Lagoon*. He is underused and forgettable here. His main claim to fame on TV was the 1950s Red Menace series *I Led Three Lives*, which co-starred John Zaremba of the *Voyage* pilot and *The Time Tunnel*. Shortly after this episode of *Voyage* he starred in the war series *McKenzie's Raiders*. Erik Holland's numerous credits include *The Man from UNCLE*, *The Invaders*, *Star Trek*, *The Six Million Dollar Man*, *The Bionic Woman*, *Galactica '80*, *The Incredible Hulk*, and the 1994 *Stargate* feature film. Frank Richards appeared in several episodes of *The Adventures of Superman*. Torben Meyer had a small role in David Hedison's 1958 feature *The Fly*. Child actor Greger Vigen appears in *Bewitched* ("Little Pitchers Have Big Fears") that same year. Production no: 7202.

Hot Line

wr. Berne Giler, dir. John Brahm

Two Russian scientists aid the Seaview in averting a political catastrophe when a Soviet satellite malfunctions and threatens to fall on America—but one of them is a phoney.

With Michael Ansara (Gregory Malinoff), Everett Sloane (Gronski), Ford Rainey (U.S. President), James Doohan (aide), John Banner (Russian Chairman), Robert Carson (SAC General).

By a twist of fate, writer Berne Giler's only other contribution to *Voyage* aired directly after his first, "The Village of Guilt"; John Brahm previously directed the second episode aired, "The City Beneath the Sea."

"Hot Line" is a standard acceptable suspense thriller marred by one fatal flaw—the inclusion of an elaborate and unnecessary location shot sequence which reveals to the audience the identity of the impostor scientist. There is little suspense left in wondering whether the world will blow up or not in a continuing weekly series.

Michael Ansara had appeared in a different role in the *Voyage to the Bottom of the Sea* feature film, and would appear again in season two as the commander of a hostile submarine in "Killers of the Deep." Here, he looks and speaks much as he did in the feature, but without the religious fervor. Everett Sloane is excellent as the fake Gronski, and the scene in which Nelson tricks him into revealing himself is the highlight of an otherwise routine episode. Ford Rainey returned as the President in "Doomsday," and played a somewhat more famous American President when he appeared as Abraham Lincoln in "The Death Trap" for *The Time Tunnel*.

Adding interest are two bit parts played by soon-to-be-familiar faces. This was the second of two minor roles in *Voyage* for James Doohan, later to be cast as Scotty on *Star Trek*. He had appeared in the same capacity in "Hail to the Chief," in which he was given the name of Larry Tobin, although that episode had yet to air. He would also at some point be considered as a new Chief for *Voyage,* presumably during contract negotiations with Terry Becker for the third season as he has said that he had to choose between that offer and the role of Scott. He also appears prior to *Star Trek* in "Valley of the Shadow" for *The Twilight Zone,* "The Shark Affair" and "The Bridge of Lions Affair" (aka *One of Our Spies is Missing*) for *The Man from UNCLE,* "A Strange Little Visitor" for *Bewitched,* and "The Expanding Human" for *The Outer Limits.* Later, dogged by the role of Scott, he took a recurring role in the Saturday morning series *Jason of Star Command,* appeared in the *Star Trek* feature films, and an episode of *Star Trek: The Next Generation* ("Relics"). John Banner would later be instantly recognizable as Sgt. Schultz from the popular sit-com *Hogan's Heroes.* This same year he also guested in *The Man from UNCLE* in "The Neptune Affair." The rocket capsule used in this episode would become a familiar prop in Allen's series, later turning up in "The Indestructible Man," and then utilized in *Lost in Space* the following year in "Welcome Stranger." Production no: 7208.

Submarine Sunk Here

wr. William Tunberg, dir. Leonard Horn

The Seaview *drifts into an undersea minefield, and several explosions send the sub to the bottom seriously damaged.*

With Carl Reindel (Evans), Eddie Ryder (Harker), Robert Doyle (Blake), Paul Comi (Bishop), George Lindsey (Collins), Wright King (ship's doctor).

If you are going to make 110 episodes of a series about a submarine, then sooner or later you are going to do the old trapped-on-the-seabed-with-the-air-running-out chestnut, so you might as well get it out of the way early. The honor fell to writer William Tunberg, and it was his only work for Allen, or indeed for any 1960s sci-fi show, although he shares an SF TV writing credit with Fred Freiberger on *The Wild Wild West* ("The

Night of the Dancing Death"). Although the *Seaview* crunching onto the bottom of the sea became a regular occurrence in later seasons, it would only be as a plot development rather than the entire storyline. This is the paint-by-numbers version, a steadily suspenseful episode, but it's not made clear once rescue arrives exactly how the *Seaview* and its crew are going to be raised through the minefield. And was Morton's the only diving bell available?

The underwater minefield footage came from the *Voyage to the Bottom of the Sea* feature film, and great chunks of this episode are used as set pieces in a third season episode titled "No Escape from Death" with a similar storyline. Richard Basehart has an obvious stand-in for the flooded compartment sequence which is recycled constantly throughout the series. Yes, all your favorite submarine clichés are here. The death by deep pressure scene is surprisingly flat, even though the horror of Collins' demise is left to the imagination, with the camera scanning the faces of the crew as they hear his plaintive cries for help.

Bizarrely, Paul Comi, who plays Bishop, is not credited, even though he has a larger role than some of those who are. He would return to the series in the second season, as an escaped convict in "Deadly Creature Below," and also appears in the *Time Tunnel* episode "Massacre." Wright King makes his one and only appearance as the *Seaview* doctor in this episode. Ten years earlier, he had been partner to a puppet in the 1954 editions of the *Johnny Jupiter* kids' show. During the '60s King chalked up appearances in *The Twilight Zone, The Invaders,* and in the '70s *Logan's Run.*

Generally, actors who played recurring roles as crewmen were either anonymous throughout the series, or acquired character names, but unusually, Robert Doyle appears in three different episodes under three different names—he was Prior in "The Fear Makers," is called Blake here, and is reincarnated as Werden in the second season episode "And Five of Us Are Left." He was also the loutish villager in "The Sixth Finger," an episode of *The Outer Limits*, and returned in that series' second season for "The Expanding Human." Other credits include *My Favorite Martian*, *The Man from UNCLE*, *The Girl from UNCLE*, and *The Invaders*.

The reason, of course, for the presence of Ryder, Reindell, Lindsey and Doyle as one-off crewmen for this episode was quite simply because actors were needed, rather than the more familiar faces of recurring extras and stunt men, many of whom were often the cast's stand-ins earning extra pay for doing double duty as crewmen. Production no: 7212.

The Magnus Beam

wr. Alan Caillou, dir. Leonard Horn
A foreign despot has a powerful magnetic beam to bring down aircraft that the Seaview must render inoperable.

With Malachi Throne (General Gamal), Monique Lemaire (Luana Rossi), Jacques Aubuchon (Abdul Azziz), Mario Alcalde (Major Amadi), Joseph Ruskin (Inspector Falazir).

Rather amusingly, this episode was pulled from its place in the running order and shown a few weeks later during an early 1990s rerun in Britain when its plot—Middle East tin-pot tyrant shoots down Western planes—uncannily echoed real world events during the Gulf War. Bizarrely, Malachi Throne does look alarmingly like a comic-book version of a certain Middle East despot in this episode! In fact, it's simply a routine but enjoyable espionage caper, with the Fox backlot European street doubling for the side streets of Jakarta and, rather more obviously, the dock of the Nelson Institute utilized as General Gamal's hideaway for his magnetic beam. Despite a couple of phoney-looking rocks standing around, the set is all too familiar.

Writer and sometime actor Alan Caillou claimed a colorful past as a wartime spy

himself, and went on to frequently appear in, and write for *The Man from UNCLE*. He also wrote, and appeared in, various episodes of *Boris Karloff's Thriller* and wrote B-movies *Village of the Giants* and *Kingdom of the Spiders*. As an actor he also appeared in the TV movies *Sole Survivor* (with Richard Basehart) and *The Questor Tapes* (an unsold Gene Roddenberry pilot), and the short-lived sit-com *Quark* (as a recurring character who was a disembodied head).

Malachi Throne appeared three times in *Voyage to the Bottom of the Sea*, again in the first season in "The Enemies," and as Blackbeard the Pirate in the fourth season. Similarly robust roles included "The Thief of Outer Space" for *Lost in Space*, and Singh in "The Night of the Long Knives" and Machiavelli in "The Death Merchant," both for *The Time Tunnel*. Joseph Ruskin, a familiar TV bad guy, would later appear for Allen in *The Time Tunnel* ("Revenge of the Gods") and *Land of the Giants* ("Terror-go-Round" and "The Secret City of Limbo," the latter alongside Malachi Throne). Character actor Jacques Aubuchon appeared in *The Twilight Zone*, *The Man from UNCLE*, *The Green Hornet*, *Land of the Giants*, and *Project UFO*. Mario Alcalde has credits for *The Wild Wild West*, *The Man from UNCLE*, and *The Immortal*. Monique Lemaire has minor roles in *Batman* ("The Thirteenth Hat/Batman Stands Pat") and *The Time Tunnel* ("Reign of Terror," as Marie Antoinette). Production no: 7213.

No Way Out

wr. Robert Hamner, Robert Leslie Bellem, dir. Felix Feist
A defector rescued by the Seaview from behind the Iron Curtain refuses to disclose valuable enemy information until Nelson and Crane return to free his lover ... but no-one is aware that an expert assassin is on board the Seaview to make sure their prize never talks.

With Jan Merlin (Victor Vail), Danielle De Metz (Anna Ravec), Thann Wyenn (Anton Koslow), Oscar Beregi (Colonel Lascoe), Don Wilbanks (Wilson), Richard Webb (Parker).

A perfectly competent and typical spy caper of the period ultimately falls victim to the same recurring flaw in so many of these sorts of stories once the identity of the assassin is revealed. Nelson and Crane *know* that his mission is to kill the defector, and yet there is still only one guard outside the sick bay, and not a soul inside. Also, Crane has no qualms about delivering Anna to the same mismanaged danger zone, where she is also at risk. Obviously the assassin will make straight for his target, so why is there no small army waiting for him? All this illogical silliness in the last ten minutes doesn't ruin the episode, but it does mar it a little.

This was writer Robert Hamner's first contribution to *Voyage*, and his only collaboration. Possibly Bellem provided the story idea—this was his only effort for *Voyage*, while Hamner went on to write "The Ghost of Moby Dick," "The Last Battle," "The Human Computer," and "Cradle of the Deep" for the first season, and "The Abominable Snowman" for the fourth. He joined the *Lost in Space* writers with the third season of that show, where he produced a string of excellent light-hearted Smith-and-Robot yarns. Hamner wrote one episode of *The Time Tunnel*, "Attack of the Barbarians," and "A Taste of Armageddon" for *Star Trek*. A prolific writer in all dramatic genres, he created the late–'70s cop show *SWAT* and was later the story editor on the *Wonder Woman* TV series. Robert Bellem had been a writer on the *Adventures of Superman* series in the '50s.

Danielle De Metz was television's resident French beauty in the '60s, although she often portrayed other nationalities convincingly, including a fiery Italian in *The Girl from UNCLE* ("The Catacombs and Dogma Affair"). Here, she's an unconvincing East European in an unconvincing script. She was at her best playing the girlish European innocent. Her films include *Return of the Fly* and *Valley of the Dragons*, and her many TV roles include episodes of *Boris Karloff's*

Thriller, I Spy, I Dream of Jeannie, and a fair number of *The Man from UNCLE*. The young crew-cut Jan Merlin was innocent teenage astronaut Roger Manning in the early '50s TV series *Tom Corbett, Space Cadet*, but ten years later was almost exclusively playing sneering Aryan-style bad guys. He appeared three times in *Voyage to the Bottom of the Sea*, as an assassin in this first season story, a wicked assistant in the second season's "The X-Factor," and a Nazi officer in the third season's "Death from the Past," and did a fine turn as a menacing, emotionless silver alien in *Time Tunnel's* "Visitors from Beyond the Stars."

Thann Wyenn was also busy throughout the '60s, but as one of those faceless character actors adept at any minor supporting role. His films include the underrated 1957 creature feature *The Beginning of the End*, and his TV work includes several episodes of *The Man from UNCLE* and *The Twilight Zone, Boris Karloff's Thriller, Honey West, The Invaders, The Girl from UNCLE, Get Smart, The Six Million Dollar Man*, and *Knight Rider*. Oscar Beregi, a familiar villainous character in '60s TV, was the commandant of "Devil's Island" in *The Time Tunnel*.

This was Richard Bull's first appearance as the *Seaview* Doctor, a role he played periodically throughout the entire series. After "No Way Out," he appeared in "Mutiny," "Doomsday," "The Invaders," "The Saboteur," "The Amphibians," "The Traitor," "The Return of the Phantom," "Monster from the Inferno," "The Brand of the Beast," "The Creature," "Death from the Past," and "The Fossil Men." Other roles included *I Spy, The Man from UNCLE*, and *Amazing Stories*. The episode also marks bit-player Pat Culliton's first credit. During the course of the series he would appear as crewmen or aliens in numerous episodes, with credited appearances including "No Way Out," "Doomsday," "The Creature," "The Enemies," "Jonah and the Whale," "The Mummy," "Terror," "Deadly Amphibians,"

"The Terrible Leprechaun," "Time Lock," and "Savage Jungle." He also worked on *The Time Tunnel* ("The Day the Sky Fell In," "Revenge of the Gods," "Visitors from Beyond the Stars," "Idol of Death," and "Billy the Kid") and *Land of the Giants* ("Genius at Work" and "Panic"), and appeared in a recurring role on the *Starman* series of the mid-'80s. The ill-fated Parker is played by Richard Webb, who, ten years earlier, had been TV super-hero *Captain Midnight*. Later TV credits included *I Dream of Jeannie*, *Get Smart*, *Star Trek*, *I Spy*, and *The Six Million Dollar Man*. Allen used him again for a bit part in his unsold pilot *The Time Travelers*. Production no: 7214.

The Blizzard Makers

wr. Joe Madison, William Welch, dir. Joseph Leytes

It's snowing in Florida ... and the machinations of a mad scientist are to blame.

With Werner Klemperer (Frederick Cregar), Milton Seltzer (Dr. Charles Melton), Sheila Mathews (Melton's wife), William Boyett (Air Force Lt.), Kenneth McDonald (surgeon), Biff Elliot (telephone man).

A curiously plodding and uninvolving affair, although it picks up at the end when the action shifts to bad guy Frederick Cregar's island lair, an over-familiar outdoor cavern seen repeatedly not only in *Voyage*, but in *Time Tunnel* ("Kill Two by Two" and "Idol of Death") and first season *Lost in Space*. However, Basehart is at his best and Winton Hoch sure does photograph snow beautifully. Some unintentional humor is provided by an arch scene in Cregar's cells when Crane spots a bugging device and he, Kowalski, and Curley have a very forced, knowing conversation about how they really, *really* hate BUGS.

Werner Klemperer, the son of famous orchestral conductor Otto Klemperer, had played the unwanted Doctor Gamma in the *Voyage* pilot, and was here promoted to visible villainy as the callous Cregar, although

like so many of William Welch's adversaries, he is disposed of in a perfunctory manner at episode's end. Welch went on to become one of Allen's most valued right-hand men, and worked on all his series, but most extensively for *Voyage*, to which he contributed 34 of the 110 episodes. He was fast rather than good, but his episodes weren't bad either. All three of his first season episodes were collaborations, a result of his function as story editor for that year, but his solo outings during the second season, when he was associate producer, were among the series' best. Had he had the luxury of time, he might have achieved much more (his "Night of the Long Knives," for *The Time Tunnel*, is excellent), but unfortunately he quickly showed himself to be adept at writing yarns around Irwin's plentiful supplies of stock footage, and once Allen realized where his talents lay, it swiftly became his job to pinch-hit across all of Allen's series, constructing stories built not just around existing footage, but specific props and sets as well. Many of Welch's later scripts for Allen's shows are consequently notable primarily for requiring no new sets or props at all, and his work began to exhibit signs of laziness and cynicism (he openly joked to another writer of having written a *Voyage* episode in which absolutely nothing happens—probably one of the fourth season runarounds).

Milton Selzer was a busy character actor of the period often cast as a weak everyman carrying a huge burden. He appeared in *The Twilight Zone* ("Hocus, Pocus, and Frisby" and "The Masks"), and episodes of *The Man from UNCLE*, *Get Smart*, *The Invaders*, *Mission: Impossible*, *The Six Million Dollar Man*, and *Wonder Woman*. Sheila Mathews married Irwin Allen. Other appearances in his series include "Return from Outer Space," "The Space Vikings," and "Princess of Space" for *Lost in Space*, and "Deadly Lodestone" and "Wild Journey" for *Land of the Giants*. She can be seen complaining about her robot dressmaker in Allen's pilot film

City Beneath the Sea. Bit player William Boyett's acting career spans over three decades of TV SF, frequently cast as a pilot or a cop (he later co-starred in the glossy cop show *Adam 12*). His credits include *Forbidden Planet* and episodes of *The Outer Limits, I Spy, Batman, The Invaders, The Man from UNCLE, Circle of Fear, The Six Million Dollar Man, The Gemini Man, The Incredible Hulk, Amazing Stories,* and *Star Trek: The Next Generation.* Kenneth McDonald had met an underwater menace of his own—he had a minor role in *The She Creature.* Biff Elliot confronted "The Devil in the Dark" in *Star Trek* and appeared in two episodes of *Planet of the Apes.*

Neither Madison nor Leytes worked again for Allen, or have any further fantasy series credits. Production no: 7215.

The Ghost of Moby Dick

wr. Robert Hamner, dir. Sobey Martin

A distraught wife tries to prevent her vengeful husband from pursuing a giant whale that crippled him and killed their son.

With Ed Binns (Dr. Walter Bryce), June Lockhart (Dr. Ellen Bryce), Bob Beekman (Jimmy Bryce).

Voyage was Allen's first series, and in this first year of TV production, during which *Voyage* was his only on-air project, he is starting to accumulate his regular stable of malleable writers and directors (it was Irwin's way, or the highway, and free spirits did not last long). This was writer Robert Hamner's first solo contribution to *Voyage* (he had previously co-written "No Way Out" with Robert Bellem, where his credits are detailed). It was also Sobey Martin's first work for Irwin Allen.

A prolific director for Allen, he was a former MGM film editor in the '30s who became a documentary maker after WWII but quickly gravitated to the populist end of the market when television began, taking on adventure formats such as westerns and cop shows before working exclusively for Irwin

Allen until his retirement in 1970. He has been described by one reference work as a sort of TV midwife, and that is certainly true of his time with Allen, where he was relied on to churn out episodes one after another while the actors were left to their own devices. If you were a good performer, this was a blessing; if you were getting it all hopelessly wrong, there was no hope of being told so when Martin was in charge. One actor on the Allen series recalled him lining all the performers up in a row for their close-ups, another remembers him nodding off in his chair until the set-ups were ready! However the fact remains that all his work for Allen is not merely adequate, but imaginative and exciting. During the first season of *Voyage to the Bottom of the Sea* (1964–'65), Martin directed more episodes than anyone, dividing his time the following season (1965–'66) between the second year of *Voyage* and the first of *Lost in Space.* Martin left both series during the 1966–'67 season to devote his full attention, such as it was, to *The Time Tunnel,* and directed almost half the episodes. Following the demise of *Time Tunnel,* he returned to *Lost in Space* for the third and last season (1967–'68). The following year, Allen put him to work on *Land of the Giants,* where once again he directed almost half the first season (1968–'69) and many of the second (1969–'70). Of Allen's 274 SF TV episodes, Martin directed about one sixth.

June Lockhart, daughter of actors Gene Lockhart and Kathleen Lockhart and mother of Anne Lockhart, was best known for her role in children's adventure series *Lassie* during the '50s. As a result of this appearance in *Voyage,* she was the first cast member signed for Allen's next series, *Lost in Space,* in which she portrayed Maureen Robinson.

Ed Binns' other credits include the B-movie *Curse of the Undead* and two *Twilight Zones.* He was to go to another watery grave ten years later in the movie *Night Moves.* Richard Basehart was among the cast of the

1956 movie adaptation of *Moby Dick*. Stock footage from this episode was later used in the second season episode "The Shape of Doom," another giant whale yarn with Ahab overtones. Production no: 7216.

Long Live the King

wr. Raphael Hayes, dir. Laslo Benedek

A young prince is under the protection of the Seaview so that he can ascend to power before unfriendly forces can take over.

With Carroll O'Connor (Old John), Michael Petit (Prince Ang), Michael Pate (Colonel Meger), Sara Shane (the Countess), Jan Arvan (Georges), Peter Adams (Johnson).

It's a Christmas episode, and it originally aired December 21st, 1964. So—was he an angel? God? Or possibly Santa Claus? Either way, Carroll O'Connor, as a mysterious shipwrecked do-gooder who befriends the frightened young prince, turned in an impressively restrained performance where many others would have laid on the sentiment with a trowel. Michael Pate plays another of his shifty stooges, Sara Shane is suitably sophisticated as the Countess, and Michael Petit, who plays an almost identical role as a young prince in "The Four Steps Affair" for *The Man from UNCLE*, is well cast as poor orphaned Ang, another role easy to get wrong but done right here. Young Michael Petit also appeared in *The Outer Limits*, and *The Munsters*. One of the better child actors of the '60s, he was particularly good in an episode of *The Beverly Hillbillies*. The casting saves a routine episode and makes it a fairly good one.

Carroll O'Connor and Michael Pate worked together again in "The Last Patrol," a superior episode of *The Time Tunnel*. Pate later returns in the first season episode "The Traitor," playing the same kind of role, although the fourth season *Voyage* episode "Flaming Ice" offers a change of pace as a near-unrecognizable Pate plays a quality alien, a frost man. Always the bad guy, he also appeared in *Boris Karloff's Thriller, Get Smart, The Man from UNCLE, Honey West, Amos Burke–Secret Agent, Batman, The Wild Wild West*, and *Mission: Impossible*.

Hungarian-born Laslo Benedek will forever be known as the director of the 1954 feature *The Wild One*, and later directed "The Buccaneer" for *Voyage*, an early template for the *Die Hard/Under Siege* school of scriptwriting. Sara Shane also co-starred in Benedek's *Wolf 359*. This was writer Raphael Hayes' only contribution to the Allen canon ... or indeed, any other SF TV series of record. Production no: 7211.

Hail to the Chief

wr. Don Brinkley, dir. Gerd Oswald

When the President of the United States is injured in an accidental fall, enemy agents seize the opportunity to attempt an assassination on board the Seaview.

With Viveca Lindfors (Dr. Laura Rettig), Malcolm Atterbury (Commander Jamieson), David Lewis (Dr. Kranz), Tom Palmer (Dr. Taylor), John Hoyt (General George Beeker), Edward Platt (Morgan), Nancy Kovack (Monique), Susan Flannery (secretary), Laurence Kerr (Oberhansley), James Doohan (Larry Tobin), Berry Kroeger (Chairman), Paul Sorensen (enemy agent).

For some reason, ABC clearly didn't think much of this episode as they buried it in Christmas week, a sure sign of a weak episode being hidden, and yet it is actually quite good (once you get past the foolishness of performing delicate surgery on a rockin' and rollin' submarine). Don Brinkley had written "The Sky is Falling," and some of the best episodes of *The Invaders*. He also wrote "The Survival School Affair" for *The Man from UNCLE* and spent the 1970s working on medical soaps. His daughter is Christie Brinkley, a famous model.

The German-born son of actress Kate Waldeck and director Robert Oswald, director Gerd Oswald came to Hollywood in 1938. Working his way up through the ranks, he secured his first directing assignment in 1956 with the grim murder mystery

A Kiss Before Dying, but turned to television in the 1960s, where he did his best work for *The Outer Limits*. Episodes of the original *Star Trek* and the '80s version of *The Twilight Zone* were so disappointing they seemed to come from a different director. With the single exception of "Specimen: Unknown," acknowledged by everyone to be a disaster, all his other *Outer Limits* episodes ("OBIT," "Corpus Earthling," "It Crawled Out of the Woodwork," "The Invisibles," "Don't Open Till Doomsday," "Fun and Games," "The Chameleon," "The Form of Things Unknown," "Soldier," "The Expanding Human," "The Duplicate Man," "The Premonition") are excellent, with his collaborations with writer/producer Joseph Stefano masterpieces of the medium. No less than seven of his thirteen episodes are acknowledged classics. His experiences on *Star Trek* were less rewarding. "The Conscience of the King" is thoroughly mediocre and undistinguished, while "The Alternative Factor" is widely regarded as one of that series' major misfires. Despite presiding over two of the biggest turkeys in otherwise excellent SF series, in both cases the episodes concerned ("Specimen: Unknown" and "The Alternative Factor") were infamously troubled productions, and neither was the fault of Oswald, who bravely boarded sinking ships in both cases. Despite the enormous artistry evidenced in his *Outer Limits* work, and obvious enthusiasm for directing, there appears to have been no ambitious gameplan in Oswald's overall TV career (traditional tosh like *Perry Mason* and *Bonanza* brush with the more ambitious *Rawhide* and *The Fugitive*), and his films are a disparate lot, suggesting that his attitude was that of a working man grateful for employment. How else to explain his taking on of TV episodes in trouble or the likes of *Gentle Ben* and *Daniel Boone* in his resume? Although Oswald was responsible for many of the finest episodes of *The Outer Limits*, his efforts on *Voyage*, like fellow *Outer Limits* directors John Brahm and Leonard Horn, are

less distinguished; only the scenes with Susan Flannery's treacherous eyelash-batting secretary and Kowalski's interception show any of the usual Oswald flair, although Viveca Lindfors, looking scarily similar to Natasha in the *Rocky and Bullwinkle* cartoons, comes off well.

Again there is a large supporting cast of familiar faces. John Hoyt appeared in almost all the major science-fiction series of the '60s, often more than once. He did two *Twilight Zones*, three superb *Outer Limits*, the *Star Trek* pilot and two excellent *Time Tunnels*. Malcolm Atterbury appeared in the films *I Was a Teenage Werewolf*, *Blood of Dracula*, and *How to Make a Monster*. He also turns up in *The Twilight Zone* and *The Invaders*. David Lewis was the hapless Warden Crichton on several episodes of *Batman*. Edward Platt was the exasperated Chief on *Get Smart*, and came to a sticky end as the stuffy principal in "The Man with the Power" on *The Outer Limits*. He appeared twice more in that series, in "Keeper of the Purple Twilight," and "The Special One." Usually blonde, Nancy Kovack managed to appear in virtually every cult fantasy show of the '60s before retiring to marry conductor Zubin Mehta of Three Tenors fame; in "Hail to the Chief" and *Star Trek's* "A Private Little War" she is equally bewitching dark-haired. She appeared in the pilot of *Bewitched* and several other episodes, as well as *The Man from UNCLE*, *I Dream of Jeannie*, *Honey West*, *Batman*, *I Spy*, *The Invaders*, *Get Smart*, and *The Invisible Man*. Susan Flannery would return in "The Traitor" and the second season episode "Time Bomb." Viveca Lindfors did not do much sci-fi, but she did appear in the 1994 feature *Stargate*. Production no: 7206.

The Last Battle

wr. Robert Hamner, dir. Felix Feist
Nelson is abducted by die-hard Nazis forcing scientists of varying specialized fields to work for them.

With John Van Dreelen (Schroeder), Joe De Santis (Miklos), Rudy Solari (Tomas), Dayton

Lummis (Reinhardt), Ben Wright (Brewster), Eric Feldary (Deiner), Sandra Williams (stewardess).

Writer Robert Hamner was specifically instructed to write a story around a standing set on the Fox lot that had been built for the film *Von Ryan's Express* ... and when Allen's *Voyage* episode headed for the small screen before the movie opened on the big screen, there were ructions at 20th Century Fox when the film producers found out about it! A few phone calls apparently smoothed things over. Once again, as with "No Way Out," Hamner's script was handed to Hollywood veteran Felix Feist, whose career went back to the silents.

Felix Feist had been working in Hollywood since the 1920's, but hadn't made a film since 1955. Like many other old timers, he was trying to build a career in television when he died in 1965, shortly after becoming one of a number of producers on Fox's groundbreaking primetime soap *Peyton Place*. Among his last pieces of work as a director were the final episode of *The Outer Limits*, "The Probe," and "No Way Out," "The Last Battle," "The Indestructible Man," "The Saboteur," "The Amphibians," and "The Enemies" for *Voyage to the Bottom of the Sea*. For the cinema he directed the 1953 feature *Donovan's Brain*, one of the earliest living brain movies—although Curt Siodmak's book had already inspired *The Lady and the Monster* (1944); Feist also directed the 1933 film *Deluge*, one of the earliest disaster movies and which provided footage of tidal wave destruction for a number of 1930s and '40s serials.

John Van Dreelen was television's special guest Nazi for three decades. He was back for more villainy in the third season's "Death from the Past," this time as a Nazi officer revived from suspended animation. His films include *Beyond the Time Barrier* and *The Leech Woman*, and his TV credits *The Twilight Zone*, *The Man from UNCLE*, *I Spy*, *The Wild Wild West*, *Mission: Impossible*, *Get Smart*, *The Six Million Dollar Man*, *Wonder Woman*, *Knight Rider*, and *Airwolf*. Rudy Solari was Casino in the '60s series *Garrison's Gorillas*, and also appears in episodes of *The Outer Limits*, *Star Trek*, *The Bionic Woman*, and *The Incredible Hulk*. Dayton Lummis appears in "The Night of the Long Knives" for *The Time Tunnel*. His brief expositionary role there as Gladstone is a small gem, and he made a good fairytale king in *Jack the Giant Killer*. Ben Wright, a busy British-born bit player, appears in the same *Time Tunnel* scene. His brief appearances in 1960s SF TV are numerous. Production no: 7220.

Mutiny

wr. William Read Woodfield, dir. Sobey Martin

Admiral Nelson suffers from paranoia after encountering a giant jellyfish while lost at sea.

With Harold J. Stone (Admiral Starke), Jay Lanin (Captain of the Neptune), Lew Brown (Lt. Commander Jackson), Steve Harris (Fowler).

This was the third script for the series by William Read Woodfield, although it was the first aired. His first effort, "Doomsday," ran the following week. It is mainly notable for starting the series' infatuation with giant sea creatures, in this case an enormous jellyfish. The creature effects are not flawless, but the finished result is quite good. As for the human guest stars, the blustering Starke is a buffoonish straw man played without much subtlety—or choice in the matter—by Harold J. Stone, perpetually typecast as comedy gangsters or over-the-top military commanders, although Basehart gets the chance to act. It's a trivial point, but the submarine destroyed by the sea creature is Jefferson in the credits, but (clumsily) changed to Neptune in the show. Production no: 7219.

Doomsday

wr. William Read Woodfield, dir. James Goldstone

When Russia neglects to inform the rest of the world that it is launching a series of communications satellites, the Seaview is put on war alert.

With Donald Harron (Corbett), Sy Prescott (Corporal), Paul Genge (General Ashton), Ford Rainey (U.S. President).

This was the first script for the series by William Read Woodfield, brought aboard by associate producer and later writing partner Allan Balter. Woodfield wasn't keen, but Balter was a friend and desperate for scripts, and Woodfield was attracted by the money.

Woodfield, who had written for the series *Sea Hunt*, had a very low opinion of the series and claims to have dashed this episode—his version of *Doctor Strangelove*, or *Fail Safe*—off in two days. He also claimed, in a *Starlog* interview, that Basehart and Hedison both considered this to be their finest script so far, and perhaps it did have more resonance during the era of Duck and Cover and the Bay of Pigs. Director Goldstone has said that he, Basehart, and Harron were provoked into many concerned discussions on the topic during filming. Today, however, it simply looks dated, melodramatic and corny, particularly the interruption of the bizarre frat-house-style party to add gravitas to the situation, and the unintentionally hilarious scenes in sick bay of the doctor trying to perform delicate eye surgery on Kowalski while depth charges explode all around them, a laughable over-egging of the plot (particularly as the script forgets to tell us Kowalski came out of it just fine). Apparently, the end of life on earth wasn't jeopardy enough.

Having said that, Donald Harron and Richard Basehart give exceptional performances, Harron being one of those invaluable and extraordinary players capable of delivering a fresh and unique performance each time. Some actors are cast for type, and specialize in always reliably and competently playing the same sort of role to perfection in every case. Deserving of even greater accolades, but rarely getting them, are the actors who give numerous completely different characterizations each time. Harron was

Robin Hood for *The Time Tunnel* ("Revenge of Robin Hood") and a bombastic Australian UNCLE agent in "The Four Steps Affair" and the *UNCLE* feature *To Trap a Spy*, but you'd never know it until you matched the credits. Ford Rainey, also the U.S. President in "Hot Line," is very good in his sober, solitary scenes with Basehart.

Despite the grim tone of "Doomsday," several outtakes in the *Fantasy Worlds of Irwin Allen* documentary appear to have come from this episode, including one of David Hedison unable to insert the fail-safe key. It's amusing to note that in his scenes in the episode, Crane always has his key already in place! Familiar library music later frequently used in *The Time Tunnel* can be heard in several scenes. Production no: 7217.

The Invaders

wr. William Read Woodfield, dir. Sobey Martin

An alien being of advanced intelligence but from the dawn of time is found on the seabed in suspended animation.

With Robert Duvall (Zar/alien).

This was the fourth of seven solo scripts for the first season by William Read Woodfield. It also marks the fourth and final appearance of Allen's full dive sequence in the first season, here interspersed with footage of Duvall's bald, earless alien creeping around the *Seaview* (*Voyage* never filmed anything if it had already been filmed before—previously, this footage had been used in the pilot, "The Village of Guilt," and "The Price of Doom"). It's a strangely flat script, enriched by Duvall's comic-bookish wickedness. His other early TV work included "The Chameleon" and "The Inheritors" for *The Outer Limits*, and the memorable "Chase Through Time" for *The Time Tunnel*, where his work is discussed in more depth. The episode's main claim to fame is that it is the first Irwin Allen show to use the electronic popping sound effects that would become so prevalent in all his series, particularly *Lost in Space*. Production no: 7221.

The Indestructible Man

wr. Richard Landau, dir. Felix Feist

A data-collecting robot returning from a space mission is retrieved from the sea by the Seaview, *but becomes a rampaging menace.*

With Michael Constantine (Dr. Brand).

The Russian capsule from "Hot Line" has had USA painted on the side and been given a door. Inside is a wonderful Saturday morning serial-style robot that, incredibly, is never seen again in any other Irwin Allen episode. The capsule, however, would go on to be seen time and time again. Go figure.

It's a wonderfully silly and enjoyable episode, with plenty of cheap thrills as the poor uncredited fellow inside the costume gingerly makes his way around the *Seaview*, hoisting himself through the submarine's doorways to the strains of Bernard Herrman's theme for Gort from *The Day the Earth Stood Still* (unlike, say, *Them*, *It Came from Outer Space*, or *The Beast from 20,000 Fathoms*, much of the influence this film and *Forbidden Planet* has had on the psyche of the general public as to what constitutes pulp SF must surely come from the constant re-use of those film's props, costumes, or music!). The storyline is a *Voyage* cliché, the misguided but well-meaning scientist, who in his desperation to keep his experiment active, is blind to the harm his pet project is causing around him. This is its fifth appearance out of nine in the first season alone, and the task of making the scientist three-dimensional this time falls to Michael Constantine, an anonymous but familiar face in American TV who has looked much the same for forty years. Fantasy/SF TV credits include episodes of *The Twilight Zone*, *The Outer Limits*, *I Spy*, *The Invaders*, *Night Gallery*, *Airwolf*, and *Friday the 13th*, but he was best known for his co-starring role in the highly regarded schoolroom drama *Room 222*, co-produced by *Voyage's* Terry Becker.

Amusingly, at one point, Nelson and Crane debate the cause of a crewman's death, completely oblivious to the giveaway clue that the door has been ripped off its hinges! This is one of those classic moments when the staging lets down the scriptwriter's vision—what ends up on the screen is not what the writer had in mind.

This was Richard Landau's second and last script for *Voyage* (he previously wrote "The City Beneath the Sea"). Allen unfortunately had a reputation for bullying and intimidating writers, and Landau was one of the few who wouldn't stand for it, and did not contribute again. Production no: 7222.

The Buccaneer

wr. William Welch, Al Gail, dir. Laslo Benedek

A notorious thief takes over the Seaview *in an attempt to use it to attack a ship carrying the Mona Lisa.*

With Barry Atwater (Logan), George Keymas (Igor), Emile Genest (French Captain), Gene Dynarski (guard).

Basehart and Hedison do *Die Hard!* A by-now-familiar plot from 1990s action thrillers is given an early and suspenseful test run in this episode, in which a gloating, over-confident and arrogant cultured plotter and his highly-trained, highly prepared and super-efficient gang of thugs take over a plane, boat, building or in this case, the *Seaview* for an ulterior motive involving an even greater crime that the hostages must prevent. Here, it's the theft of the Mona Lisa, *en route* to a loan-out by yacht. The author makes no claims of provenance, but this may well be the birth of this old chestnut; if not, it's certainly one of the concept's earliest examples, and both are 20th Century Fox productions.

Al Gail was Irwin Allen's cousin, and co-wrote both this episode and "The Traitor" with William Welch for the first season. He performed an emergency rewrite on the second season episode "The Monster's Web," and as writers willing to work with Allen became increasingly difficult to find, Gail began to turn in competent but unspectacular solo scripts for the fourth season, such as "The

Return of Blackbeard" and the infamous "The Lobster Man."

Barry Atwater (here billed as G.B. Atwater, as he was in many early stage, film, and TV performances) will forever be remembered by fantasy fans as vampire Janos Skorzeny in the TV movie *The Night Stalker*. He's excellent in the *Man from UNCLE* episode "The Sort of Do-it-Yourself Dreadful Affair," and appeared in four episodes of *Mission: Impossible* during the series' lengthy run. He also gets to play a rather disgusting looking zombie on "Corpus Earthling," an excellent episode of *The Outer Limits*, and played Surak in the *Star Trek* episode "The Savage Curtain." Other credits include *The Twilight Zone, Bewitched, The Invaders, The Wild Wild West*, and *Night Gallery*. He returns to *Voyage* to play no less a personage than Benedict Arnold, in the very last episode, "No Way Back." Hard-faced heavy and stunt man George Keymas returns in "The Lost Bomb" and also has credits in *The Twilight Zone, The Wild Wild West, Mission: Impossible, The Man from UNCLE, The Invaders, Night Gallery*, and *The Six Million Dollar Man*. Gene Dynarski, a busy bit-player, appears as an alien in the fourth season episode "Journey into Fear." A little more recognizably, he appears in two *Star Trek* episodes, "Mudd's Women" as a miner and "The Mark of Gideon" as an official.

Ray Didsbury was Richard Basehart's stand-in during the making of *The Satan Bug*, a stodgy thriller wasting a good idea and great cast that was filmed between the *Voyage* pilot and the start of the series. He followed Basehart to *Voyage*, and frequently appeared as a crewman during the series' run, often acting as voice coach and voiceover artist as well. Didsbury had been whacked and zapped in previous episodes ("No Way Out" and "The Invaders" to name but two), and here he is shot down during an escape attempt. If a crewman wants to stay alive on a TV show he should always make sure he at least has a name ... but the anonymous

Mr. Didsbury manages to get bopped, chopped and dropped in several episodes!

Mr. Logan doesn't get his painting, but Fox's Mona Lisa ends up *Lost in Space* the following year when it turns up in the grasping possession of Doctor Smith in the first season's "Wish Upon a Star"! The footage of the military police being dumped in the water when the *Seaview* submerges comes from the feature film. Interestingly, Crane and the others make a huge fuss about the callousness of the act, when in the film it is Nelson who submerges, and everyone assumes they'll be fine! Production no: 7223.

The Human Computer

wr. Robert Hamner, dir. James Goldstone

Crane sets sail in the Seaview *as the sole operator of the super-sub to test a new computer system that has dispensed with human beings.*

With Simon Scott (Dr. Reston), Ted De Corsia (foreign General), Harry Millard (enemy agent), Herbert Lytton, Walter Sande (military officials).

Without a doubt, the dullest, slowest Irwin Allen episode of any of his series ever made. The entire story consists of David Hedison wandering apprehensively around the deserted set of the *Seaview*. Perhaps he was looking for a script.... It was, of course, what's called a bottle show (a quick and easy episode, made on standing sets either to cut costs or make up time), something Hamner had already provided with "The Last Battle" and would try to achieve with monster mash "Cradle of the Deep," his next script. The lengthy cast is deceptive—the rest of the *Seaview* crew leave quickly, and most of the other players appear briefly in just one scene as the military prepare the experiment.

David Hedison, perhaps unsurprisingly, actually enjoyed the episode, and what there actually is onscreen is largely due to his and director James Goldstone's efforts. "The zoom lens wasn't used much back then, and I would dolly in while zooming out" explained Goldstone to interviewer Mark Phillips.

"David Hedison and I also decided to play speechless suspense, and we did that by using his body language, the way he moved down a corridor and so on." And then there is the opportunity to study the set (nothing else is happening). "I loved the main set" said Goldstone. "The control room was marvelous. The art director, Bill Creber, was brilliant. They had no budget, but somehow he came up with these marvelous things." One major computer bank of pointlessly random flashing lights had previously been in David Hedison's lab in his Fox feature film *The Fly*. Hedison later entered into an ill-fated production company venture with this episode's co-star Harry Millard that resulted in one very bad unreleased film before Millard passed away. However, there was one happy result—while searching for locations in Italy, Hedison met his future wife. Production no: 7224.

The Saboteur

wr. William Read Woodfield, Allan Balter, dir. Felix Feist

Crane is brainwashed to sabotage an important mission.

With Warren Stevens (Forester), Bert Freed (Dr. Ullman), Russell Horton (Parker), James Brolin (Spencer).

In an early example of the series' contrived synchronicity, this episode was made back-to-back with "The Traitor," a yarn in which Nelson must play the deceiver. Here, it's Crane's turn to be the bad guy. This doubling up of ideas would become commonplace as the series went on and every crew member got the chance to turn bad in one form or another and save money on guest stars, but at this point in the first season, it's more a shortage of inspiration than cash. Both "The Traitor" and "The Saboteur" were produced next to each other, although the network wisely split the two by a few weeks for transmission. This was the fifth of seven solo scripts for the first season by William Read Woodfield, and as might be expected with Woodfield it's a cleverer script than baddie Basehart's adventure, although the twist is telegraphed, so to speak, to more alert audiences by the casting. As the two chief suspects (one of them is believed to be the brainwashed Captain Crane's traitorous on-board contact), guest stars Warren Stevens and Bert Freed both play their cards close to their chests. Not so David Hedison, who—instead of playing his role confused and disconcerted by the brainwashing—goes into smirking villain mode, and transforms into a grinning fool as he goes about his treacherous business. After a dull, slow start during which a mysterious offscreen voice (almost certainly Werner Klemperer, offscreen villain of "Eleven Days to Zero" and onscreen villain of "The Blizzard Makers") laboriously gives the transformed Crane his instructions, the episode picks up once the *Seaview* sets sail and becomes genuinely intriguing. However, Crane is turned into a murderous traitor far too easily, and what should have been a spectacular climax to the story, when the *Seaview*'s glass nose is shattered, is sadly muted and brief. A couple of times during a fight scene the sturdy walls of the *Seaview* are even seen to wobble ...

This was the first of three appearances in *Voyage to the Bottom of the Sea* by Warren Stevens, who played different roles in "Deadly Invasion" and "Cave of the Dead." He worked extensively for Irwin Allen, appearing in "One Way to the Moon" for *The Time Tunnel*, "Brainwash" and "A Place Called Earth" for *Land of the Giants*, and as a would-be regular in Allen's short lived *Return of Captain Nemo* project.

Bert Freed was the police chief in the classic *Invaders from Mars*. He returns in the second season's "The Silent Saboteurs" and also appeared in episodes of *The Outer Limits*, *The Munsters*, *The Green Hornet*, *Kolchak: the Night Stalker*, and *Knight Rider*. James Brolin, later to star in the long-running series *Marcus Welby MD* and *Hotel*, was a bit-player at Fox in the '60s, and can also be found in a couple of episodes of *Batman* in minor roles. Bizarrely, the crewman Parker is referred to comically as 'Fred' in the credits—Woodfield having a bit of fun—before someone presumably realized that as a serving crewman, he had to be referred to by a surname. Production no: 7226.

Cradle of the Deep

wr. Robert Hamner, dir. Sobey Martin
Unnatural experiments on board the Seaview *with the speed of evolution create a monstrous life form from a microscopic particle.*
With John Anderson (Dr. Janus), Howard Wendell (Dr. Benton).

One of the earliest monster episodes is hindered by bad dialogue accompanied by bad performances, a fatal combination. The actors struggle valiantly with their lines, but Hedison, Carr and Anderson are uncharacteristically bad, with only Basehart providing a solid performance—ironic, given that Anderson has told in an interview how he took Basehart aside at lunch to complain about his attitude. "Dick spent the entire morning snickering over every line and poking fun at the story" said Anderson. "I was shocked. Dick wasn't just my friend, he was one of the finest actors I had ever known.... I couldn't believe that he could act in such a childish, destructive, and insensitive manner...." Anderson confronted Basehart about his concerns, pointing out that the bad script was a challenge and that he needed all the skills of both of them to make the part work. Basehart apologized, realized Anderson was right, and the gentlemanly disagreement was resolved, with Basehart once again taking the art of acting seriously, if not Irwin Allen and the sci-fi series he was stuck with. Actually, it's Hedison who's made to look stupid by the script, in the idiotically played scene when the lack of oxygen affects the crew. Hedison rages at the insubordination of it all when it's clear that the crew have been overcome in some way, and are not in their right minds. In contrast, Basehart gets all the good scenes!

As monster episodes go, this one—like most of the first season creature features—is relatively tame compared with the shenanigans of the color episodes, with the blob just getting bigger offscreen. "It was just sitting there on the floor, obviously made of plastic and red ink" groaned Anderson. "Sometimes, what you are asked to believe is so either banal or bizarre that you have trouble with it" echoed Paul Carr. "We had to believe that a pulsating piece of plastic was a sea monster of some kind. It was awful!" However, it's hard to see how any props department of the day could have done any better with a "blob brief"! This episode apparently had some trouble getting on the air because of network fears about offending religious fundamentalists with its origins of life theme, although oddly the two scenes in which Basehart confronts the religious implications are the only moments the non-monster scenes come to life.

John Anderson was the sinister Ebonite in "Nightmare" for *The Outer Limits*, and appeared in four different *Twilight Zone* stories—"A Passage for Trumpet," "The Odyssey of Flight 33," "Of Late I Think of Cliffordville," and "The Old Man in the Cave." Later in his career he appeared in episodes of *The Incredible Hulk*, *Project UFO*, *Greatest American Hero*, *Voyagers*, *Starman*, *Star Trek: The Next Generation*, and *Quantum Leap*. He also appeared with Basehart in the disappointing pre-*Voyage* feature film *The Satan Bug*.

Poor jittery crewman Clark disappears after this episode, his last of four (perhaps not surprisingly, as he is arrested), but Paul Carr would return in the second season to meet a grisly end as the similarly scared crewman Benson in "Terror on Dinosaur Island." For some reason, most likely the unavailability of regular *Seaview* doctor Richard Bull, another familiar crewman, Richard Basehart's stand-in Ray Didsbury, usually the helmsman in the first season, is wearing the stethoscope in sick bay. However, the episode's biggest credibility problem is not Doctor Didsbury or the plastic blob, but a recurring flaw, particularly in that first year. Once again in this series, two obvious stunt doubles damage suspension of disbelief in the scenes where Clark fights Janus in the lab. Of all the 1960s fantasy series, only *The Avengers* could match *Voyage* for ill-matched fight doubles. Production no: 7227.

The Amphibians

wr. Rik Vollaerts, dir. Felix Feist

Two over-enthusiastic scientists get carried away in their zeal for experimentation and turn themselves into amphibians.

With Skip Homeier (Dr. Jenkins), Curt Conway (Dr. Winslow), Zale Parry (Angie), Frank Graham (Danny).

Rik Vollaerts wrote the *Star Trek* episode "For the World is Hollow, and I Have Touched the Sky" and "The Bookworm Turns/While Gotham Burns" for *Batman*. His first of a number of scripts for *Voyage* treads familiar ground for the series, with two over-ambitious and subsequently deranged single agenda scientists turning themselves, and then kidnapped divers, into water-breathers, although these were somewhat tame compared to the army of Gill-Men that stomped aggressively through the color seasons. Events just about hold the interest, as does the lovely Zale Parry as the female amphibian, but the episode is slow, repetitive, and talky, enlivened mostly by the diving sequences.

Richard Basehart is mostly absent from this episode, presumably due to a production overlap with his exhaustive screen time in "The Exile." Given Hedison's small role there, and Allen's similar catch-up strategy filming *Lost in Space* the following year (in which cast members were split between two adventures), it is likely that "The Exile" and "The Amphibians," sharing consecutive production numbers, were filmed simultane-

ously.

Veteran B-western player Skip Homeier appeared three times in *Voyage*, returning as an evil Senator in the third season episode "The Day the World Ended" and an alien from outer space in the fourth season episode "Attack." He had worked once before with both Richard Basehart and Henry Kulky on the 1951 war film *Fixed Bayonets*. Other TV SF roles included "The Expanding Human" for *The Outer Limits* and two appearances on *Star Trek*, once in the infamous Nazi episode "Patterns of Force," and again as the cauliflower-eared guru Doctor Sevrin in the dire "The Way to Eden," as well as episodes of *The Addams Family*, *Ghost Story*, *The Six Million Dollar Man*, *The Bionic Woman*, *The Incredible Hulk*, and the 1979 TV movie *The Wild Wild West Revisited*.

Curt Conway also appeared in *The Outer Limits*, in "Moonstone" and "Keeper of the Purple Twilight," and in "He's Alive" for *The Twilight Zone*. Production no: 7229.

The Exile

wr. William Read Woodfield, dir. James Goldstone

Nelson is trapped at sea on a life-raft with a brutal dictator seeking asylum in the U.S. in exchange for military secrets.

With Ed Asner (Premier Alexei Brynov), David Sheiner (Josip), Harry Davis (Konstantine), James Frawley (Semenev), Jason Wingreen (Mikhil), Michael Pataki (officer).

This was the sixth of seven solo scripts for the first season by William Read Woodfield, and once again, James Goldstone was assigned to direct. As in "Mutiny," Nelson is adrift in the open sea again, this time with a brutish dictator of reddish hue. A typical 1960s-style teaser worthy of *UNCLE* or *The Avengers* has the tyrant Brynov's firing squad being gunned down while he lives to escape. Basehart carries this episode quite well, and has several scenes with some meat on, and although apparently there was much derisive jocularity on the set regarding the script (the production number is close enough to "Cradle of the Deep" to hope that the filming took place before Anderson gave Basehart his talking-to), this is actually one of the more dramatic and thoughtful scripts in the series by a writer Basehart usually respected. From the point of view of an actor, it's difficult to imagine what any performer worth his salt could have found to complain about other than being dumped in the Fox water tank for the second time that season, although Asner is well-known for his left-wing politics, while writer Woodfield was equally unabashed in his anti-communist fervor.

For the cast, Goldstone had assembled a small stock company of reliable old friends— which was probably wise. "We shot on a water tank, with these six guys on a rubber raft, and they were very uncomfortable. We had fog blowing past and wind machines on them ... the rehearsals were improvised and crazy." As ever with a Woodfield script, there is much flimsily disguised Red-bashing, with little doubt as to the true nature of the tyrant's home country, and it is here that Woodfield succumbs. "That script was written almost overnight" said Goldstone, thirty years later. "It was based on (Hitchcock's) *Lifeboat* and (then Russian premier) Kruschev. Some of the lines are wonderfully funny—'Today you kill me! Tomorrow I kill you!' is hysterical. It belongs on (1950s comedy revue) *Your Show of Shows!*"

However, the script has its moments, particularly when Basehart and Asner are left alone on the raft, each trying to outlive the other, political philosophies meaningless as they struggle simply to survive another hour. After the earlier mayhem and melodramatics, there is an opportunity for two consummate actors to act, and with Basehart and a strong cast of above-average guest players dominating the action, a reasonable straight drama results, with not a blob in sight. Sheiner does his usual slimy stooge act (see also "The Ivy Curtain" for

The Invaders and "The Alexander the Greater Affair" aka *One Spy too Many* for *The Man from UNCLE*), Davis is as ever the frail collaborator (see "The Bridge of Lions Affair," aka *One of Our Spies is Missing* for *The Man from UNCLE*), and Asner offered a neat line in slobbish, bullying villainy before becoming cuddly conservative Lou Grant in the late '70s overtly liberal and groundbreaking *Mary Tyler Moore Show* and *Lou Grant* series.

Asner was another who had previously worked with Basehart between his filming of the *Voyage* pilot and the start of the series when they made *The Satan Bug*, the tedious suspense thriller with a great cast but somnambulistic direction and editing. Although he'll always be known to TV viewers as the brashly philistine but unrelentingly fair news editor Lou Grant, Asner had a prolific if less rewarding career during the '60s as a burly, crop-haired, heavy-lidded thug with leery, swiveling eyes that, should they swivel in your direction, would quickly necessitate a change of pants. He was an unlucky cop obliterated by a radioactive dustball in *The Outer Limits* ("It Crawled Out of the Woodwork"), an evil THRUSH agent in the guise of a used car salesman in *The Girl from UNCLE* ("The Double-o-Nothing Affair"), and leader of an alien plot, and later venal bartender, in *The Invaders* ("Wall of Crystal" and "The Miracle"). In the 1970s, Asner appeared in two fantasy-oriented TV movies, the stylish supernatural horror *The Haunts of the Very Rich*, and the speculative *The Last Child*, and, much later, in an episode of *The X-Files*, "How the Ghosts Stole Christmas."

David Sheiner's dour, humorless countenance stared blandly out at viewers in numerous 1960s series, particularly *The Man from UNCLE*, in which he appeared in four different episodes. He also appeared in episodes of *The Twilight Zone*, *I Spy* (twice), *The Invaders*, *Mission: Impossible* (four again), *Planet of the Apes*, *The Six Million Dollar Man* (twice), *The Amazing Spider-Man*, *Manimal*, and *Automan*. Harry Davis' credits also include *Mission: Impossible* (the pilot, plus two others) and *The Man from UNCLE* (twice). Both Sheiner and Davis appear in the second season *Voyage* episode "The Death Ship."

James Frawley, who later turned to directing, appears again in "Killers of the Deep" during the second season. He also appeared in the pilot for *The Outer Limits*, "The Galaxy Being," and in that series' only two-part episode, "The Inheritors," also directed by James Goldstone. Other credits include *The Man from UNCLE*, *My Favorite Martian*, and *I Spy*. Michael Pataki had a recurring role in the short-lived *Amazing Spider-Man* series as a police captain. His other SF TV credits include *The Twilight Zone* ("A Quality of Mercy"), *Star Trek* ("The Trouble with Tribbles") and episodes of *Batman*, *The Invisible Man*, *Star Trek: The Next Generation*, and *The Highwayman*. Bit player Jason Wingreen has literally dozens of credits in fantasy series, all of them minor roles. Production no: 7228.

The Creature

wr. Rik Vollaerts, dir. Sobey Martin
> *An incompetent commander puts the* Seaview *at risk as he tries to cover up his own fatally bad judgment.*

With Leslie Nielsen (Captain Adams).

This was the second *Voyage* script by Vollaerts to be produced, and the dialogue is much better than "The Amphibians." The plot, however, is already quite familiar, with another vain stressed-out zealot trying to convince himself and everyone else that he has not been to blame for his disasters. The creature is a giant devil fish, or Manta Ray, the menace created by the straightforward process of putting a regular sized Manta into the tank with the *Seaview* model. Simple, and quite effective.

Leslie Nielsen starred in the 1956 classic science-fiction film *Forbidden Planet*, but he was in television by the early 1960s, where he would stay for the next twenty five years playing dramatic roles exceptionally well, until, perversely, he—and we—discovered his comedic talents in the popular movie spoof *Airplane!* and subsequent TV series *Police Squad!*, which in turn resulted in constant work in further send-ups and parodies. Previously, he had appeared primarily in cop shows and TV movies, although he turned up in *The Wild Wild West* ("The Night of the Double Edged Knife") and the final *Man from UNCLE*, a two-parter titled "The Seven Wonders of the World Affair" and released as the feature *How to Steal the World*, in which a memorable demise was spoiled by the decision to speed up the film. This performance, and a couple of turns in *Night Gallery*, hinted at the clown behind the straight face.

A surviving blooper, however, on view in the 1995 documentary *The Fantasy Worlds of Irwin Allen*, hints that Basehart and Hedison had their moments of hilarity too. A dramatic scene where Hedison reaches for a communications device, only to pull the wiring from the wall, ends with both breaking up into laughter. It also demonstrates Allen's wisdom in destroying most of the outtakes from his series as we now can't help but notice that the scene has subsequently been completed with the wire still loose onscreen. Production no: 7230.

The Enemies

wr. William Read Woodfield, dir. Felix Feist
> *A drug that induces uncontrollable hate is utilized by callous scientists to set Nelson and Crane against each other.*

With Henry Silva (General Tau), Malachi Throne (Dr. Shinera), Robert Sampson (Captain Williams), Tom Skerritt (Richardson).

We had seen the "fear gas"—now, here was the "hate drug" and yet another episode opening with yet another doomed sub suffering a fate the *Seaview* must both investigate and avoid. This was the last of seven solo scripts for the first season by William

Read Woodfield, who was fascinated by magic acts, sleight of hand, and optical illusions, and built this episode around an opportunity to show off a room that used optical trickery to make people look bigger or smaller than they were without the use of trick photography. Although the effect allowed actors to cross the screen back and forth, whereas the conventional split screen effects of the 1960s did not, unless rear projection was used, such subtleties were probably lost on the mainstream TV audience of the time, who were used to such size-play, especially in the Irwin Allen series. Otherwise, it's a fairly nondescript episode, with Henry Silva cast in a typical role as a Red Chinese sadist, and the island lagoon Nelson and Crane are trapped on by now beginning to look remarkably familiar and more than a little over-employed. The cave entrance had been used in "The Blizzard Makers."

Henry Silva appeared in two excellent episodes of *The Outer Limits*, "Tourist Attraction" and "The Mice," but understandably sleepwalks through his role here. Other roles include *Boris Karloff's Thriller, I Spy, Mission: Impossible*, and *Night Gallery*. He also portrayed Killer Kane in the pilot film for *Buck Rogers in the 25th Century*. Malachi Throne had already appeared in *Voyage*, as General Gamal in "The Magnus Beam," and would appear again in the fourth season in "The Return of Blackbeard." He did a vast amount of work for Irwin Allen, and the clichéd callous Oriental scientist he portrays here is hardly his finest moment, although he carries it off as well as might be hoped. Ordinarily, *Voyage* employed performers of the race portrayed, and this was an unusual lapse that dates the episode.

Robert Sampson, a familiar TV face, also comes to a sorry end in "The Mutant," an enjoyable episode of *The Outer Limits* in which he gives his best TV SF performance; he looks desperately uncomfortable in his *Star Trek*, "A Taste of Armageddon." This is a brief, pre-opening credits appearance.

Other, sometimes more substantial roles for Sampson include episodes of *The Twilight Zone, I Spy, Wonder Woman*, and *Knight Rider*. Tom Skerritt, also seen here only briefly, was the Captain of the *Nostromo* in the 1979 creature feature *Alien*. He had a more substantial role in "The Death Trap," an episode of *The Time Tunnel*, and "The Devil's Platform" for *Kolchak: the Night Stalker*. *Voyage* regulars Pat Culliton and Robert Lipton both appeared as crewmen in the previous episode, "The Creature," suggesting that the submarine sequences were filmed at the same time. Production no: 7231.

Secret of the Loch

wr. Charles Bennett, dir. Sobey Martin

Investigating the deaths of scientists supposedly killed by the legendary Loch Ness Monster, Nelson and Crane discover murderous spies and an enemy submarine.

With Torin Thatcher (Professor MacDougall), Hedley Mattingley (Inspector Lester), George Mitchell (Angus), John McLiam (assassin), Joe Higgins (magistrate), Tudor Owen (crofter).

Back in 1934, writer Charles Bennett had written a minor British feature titled *Secret of the Loch* based on the tourist trap myth of a prehistoric creature that supposedly lived at the bottom of the impenetrable Loch Ness in Scotland. It was a natural for him to rework it, title and all, for the *Voyage to the Bottom of the Sea* series. Basehart and Hedison stand around as if trapped in a vintage Ealing film themselves as the supporting cast compete to see who can provide the most stereotypical Scots accent (Basehart briefly performs a splendid one), and in their skepticism (although well-founded under the circumstances of the story) Nelson and Crane seem to have forgotten their own recent encounters with prehistoric monsters and sea creatures. Bringing the episode alive as the treacherous and phoney MacDougall is Torin Thatcher, later "The Space Trader" in *Lost in Space*. Other TV includes *Boris Karloff's Thriller, The Time Tunnel, Star Trek, Land of the Giants*, and *Night*

Gallery. He is best remembered for his performances as evil wizards in *Seventh Voyage of Sinbad* and *Jack the Giant Killer.*

Hedley Mattingley, a regular in the 1960s series *Daktari*, was usually cast as stuffy British types and also appeared in *The Man from UNCLE, My Favorite Martian, I Spy,* and *Get Smart.* Prolific bit player John McLiam worked for over five decades in films and TV. He appeared four times in *The Twilight Zone,* and in episodes of *The Outer Limits, Honey West, The Invaders,* and *Ghost Story,* Woody Allen's superb 1973 sci-fi satire *Sleeper,* the 1974 pilot for *Planet of the Apes,* the 1975 pilot for *The Invisible Man, Voyagers, V, Beauty and the Beast,* and *Star Trek: The Next Generation.* George Mitchell appeared in episodes of *The Time Tunnel* and *Land of the Giants.* Tudor Owen was the captain of the Lusitania in the interesting *Twilight Zone* episode "No Time Like the Past."

Writer Charles Bennett had scripted Allen's feature films *The Story of Mankind, The Big Circus, The Lost World, Five Weeks in a Balloon,* and the feature version of *Voyage to the Bottom of the Sea.* His disdain for Allen (no doubt assisted by the fact that his career was hurtling downhill after previous work with prestigious names like De Mille and Hitchcock), the *Voyage* series, and TV in general is on record, and by the 1960s apparently extended to his audience. This script, and his second season effort "Escape from Venice," are cynical tosh, but not too bad, and "The Heat Monster" is enjoyable nonsense, but "The Deadly Dolls" and "The Terrible Leprechaun" are absolutely dire. He also wrote "The Night of the Eccentrics" for *The Wild Wild West* and "Terror-go-Round" for *Land of the Giants.* He claimed to have written for *Time Tunnel,* but if he did, it was neither credited nor produced. If Bennett "loathed TV," as he told *Starlog* magazine, then he went out of his way to create a self-fulfilling prophecy as to its awfulness. Production no: 7232.

The Condemned

wr. William Read Woodfield, dir. Leonard Horn

An over-zealous grandstanding Admiral soaking up the praise and publicity for another man's work endangers the integrity of valuable and groundbreaking depth pressure experiments and the safety of the Seaview itself to steal the glory ... and commits murder to conceal his mistakes.

With J.D. Cannon (Admiral Bentley Falk), Arthur Franz (Professor Archer), Alvy Moore (Hoff), John Goddard (Tracy).

This was the second of seven solo scripts for the first season by William Read Woodfield, who later teamed up to write eight more scripts for the second season with former associate producer Allan Balter. It's a mystery why the network held this episode back so long until the end of the season, as it is a strong example of first season *Voyage* at its best. One of Paul Zastupnevich's most wonderful monsters gets its first showing here, a swirling mass of seaweed with two bulbous red eyes (we know they're red because the creature shows up again in the color episodes of both *Voyage* and *Lost in Space*), but it's J. D. Cannon, best known as Chief Clifford in the '70s cop show *McCloud,* who steals the show, giving a marvelous performance as the callous, self-serving scientist Bentley Falk. It takes some doing to outshine the monster in an Irwin Allen show, but with the help of Woodfield's script, fine supporting players (particularly John Goddard as the poor schmuck Tracy), and some superb direction by Leonard Horn (the scenes in the diving bell are magnificently evil and claustrophobic), the always welcome Cannon gives one of the best performances of his career. A larger-than-life brutal buffoon like Falk is always going to be a borderline parodic portrayal, but Cannon makes him real. He's the star of the show.

Cannon's other notable SF TV appearance was in "Beach Head," the pilot for *The Invaders,* in which he's excellent as a skeptical cop. Unfortunately, "The Organization," his other *Invaders,* near the end of the series, with its cartoon-show mobsters, is one of the worst in the series. He also appeared in *The Wild Wild West, Mission: Impossible,* and *The Highwayman* ("Send in the Clones"), a short-lived Glen Larson show of the late '80s in which he joined *Battlestar Galactica's* Terry Carter in a thinly-veiled send-up of their roles in Larson's *McCloud.*

Arthur Franz, as the true brains behind Falk's experiments, featured in numerous sci-fi B-movies of the 1950s, including *Flight to Mars, Back from the Dead, The Flame Barrier, Monster on the Campus,* and *The Atomic Submarine* (a forerunner of *Voyage*), but most notably as the stereotypical pipe-sucking scientist in the classic science-fiction film *Invaders from Mars.* TV roles followed in the 1960s, including *The Invaders, Land of the Giants,* and, later, *The Six Million Dollar Man.* Production no: 7218.

The Traitor

wr. William Welch, Al Gail, dir. Sobey Martin
A double agent threatens the safety of Nelson's sister in an attempt to barter for missile secrets.

With George Sanders (Major Gen. Fenton), Michael Pate (Hamid), Susan Flannery (Katie).

A very ordinary spy melodrama, as once again an enemy agent gets on board the *Seaview,* although this time there is more to it. The suave, urbane villainy of George Sanders graced a number of TV productions as the former star's career waned, most notably as THRUSH agent Emory Partridge in two editions of *The Man from UNCLE* ("The Gazebo in the Maze Affair" and "The Yukon Affair") and as the first of three different incarnations of Mr. Freeze in the *Batman* TV series. His films included *Things to Come, The Ghost and Mrs. Muir, From the Earth to the Moon,* and the cult favorite *Village of the Damned.* "The Traitor" is a tolerable time waster that manages to hold the attention, although only the scene where Sanders turns up on the *Seaview* has any kind of *frisson.* In one scene, lights are turned out to obscure the use of a stunt double, but once

again Basehart's fall guy is obviously too tall. Production no: 7225.

SECOND SEASON (1965–1966)

Jonah and the Whale

wr. Shimon Wincelberg, dir. Sobey Martin
Nelson and a Russian scientist are examining the remains of a ruined underwater experimental base when their diving bell is swallowed whole by a giant whale.

With Gia Scala (Dr. Katya Markhova).

Shimon Wincelberg had scripted the pilot film for *Lost in Space* earlier that year which had sold the series to CBS and then been carved up to form the basis of that series' first four episodes. Allen now requested that Wincelberg come up with a high concept storyline to open the second season of *Voyage,* and he more than delivered, suggesting a storyline in which the series' stars were seen inside a giant living whale. (There's nobody called Jonah in the episode; the title refers only to the Biblical story.) It has to be said that the colored lights and inflatable bags that make up the innards of the whale look like exactly what they are, but the episode is imaginative and intriguing, nonetheless, and apparently partially shot on sets built for Fox's big screen feature *Fantastic Voyage* that year (a curiously stodgy film, slow to get started and plodding thereafter, *Fantastic Voyage* was a marvelous idea about a group of miniaturized scientists traveling through a human body in a submarine-type craft that could have benefitted greatly from some Irwin Allen-style pizzazz). The sets also show up in "The Derelict," the second episode of *Lost in Space,* filming at around the same time.

This episode also introduces Terry Becker as Chief Francis E. Sharkey (Henry Kulky, the previous Chief, had passed away near the end of the first season) and Allan Hunt as crewman Stu Riley, who—like Chekov in *Star Trek*—was introduced to

New cast members Allan Hunt and Terry Becker join their colleagues for a second season photocall. Left to right: Richard Basehart, David Hedison, Allan Hunt, Terry Becker, and Robert Dowdell.

attract teen audiences. With his painful period surfer slang he dates the series badly, but fortunately he quickly blended into the rest of the crew, and was gone altogether by the end of the second season. All together, Hunt appeared in only sixteen episodes as Riley, but in the later episodes, with the character toned down and given less prominence, he became an asset to the show, rather than the embarrassment he is in this episode.

Gia Scala (real name, Giovanna Scoglio), playing a Russian scientist here, was in fact an Italian actress who had very limited success during her stay in Hollywood. This is her only TV SF credit. Wincelberg later wrote the first draft of the

pilot for *The Time Tunnel,* and the *Star Trek* episodes "Dagger of the Mind" and "The Galileo Seven" (co-written with Oliver Crawford). Production no: 8201.

Time Bomb

wr. William Read Woodfield and Allan Balter, dir. Sobey Martin

Foreign agents inject Nelson with a deadly liquid that will turn him into a human bomb when he comes into contact with radiation.

With Ina Balin (Litchka), Susan Flannery (Katie), John Zaremba (Vice-Admiral Johnson), Richard Loo (Li Tung), Richard Gilden (Tal), Harold Dyrenforth (doctor), Lee Millar (soldier), Jon Kowal (police officer), Frank Delfino (enemy agent).

As the 1965–'66 season began, America

and Europe were in the grip of the kitsch secret agent fad and hi-tech spy-mania enveloped films and TV. Unless you were around at the time to experience it firsthand, it's difficult to effectively convey just how pervasive and all-encompassing this trend was in the media of the day. The early 20th century passion for westerns spread itself more evenly across five decades; the 1950s sci-fi craze restricted itself mainly to the B-movie/drive-in circuit; the 1970s obsession with police dramas and the 1990s *X-Files* fad only applied to television ... but the public's secret agent obsession in the mid–'60s crossed all media, from novels, movies and TV to cartoons, comedy, comics and commercials. It lasted from about 1964 to 1969, but permeated virtually everything throughout 1965 and 1966.

The spy-mania of the 1960s was far removed from the Cold War paranoia of the 1950s, even though the adversaries were often the same vaguely Russian, vaguely Red-Chinese sorts. These wild and improbable adventures were more rooted in swinging '60s escapism and the jet-set affluence and glamour of the rapidly shrinking world of the Kennedy era, than 1950s Cold War paranoia and the dirtier global policing beginning in Vietnam as the Kennedy dream died. Indeed, whereas earlier spy yarns had involved themselves with very real threats from Germany, Japan, and Russia, and consequently were grim and grey, conservative and conformist, and thick with repression, the spy shows of the mid–'60s were bright, colorful, relentlessly upbeat for all the casual death and mayhem displayed, and surprisingly progressive in '60s terms; although women were invariably portrayed as treacherous Mata Hari types (dark hair) or scatty sex toys (blonde hair), *The Man from UNCLE* featured an American and a Russian working together for a worldwide organization against a global threat, *The Avengers* and *Honey West* offered up TV's first tough, resilient and resourceful female stars, and *I*

Spy made television history by making the inter-racial heroes, one white hipster, one black scholar, equal partners. While these series broke convention, equally entertaining fantasies served merely to confirm or reinforce political prejudices, the most popular and prominent of these being *Mission: Impossible*, a pro–CIA fantasy that finally went off the air as the true dramas of Vietnam and Watergate unfolded. Before becoming story editors, and later producers on that series, William Read Woodfield and Allan Balter had been turning out thinly-veiled Reds-under-the-bed yarns for a variety of shows; Woodfield's included first season *Voyage to the Bottom of the Sea* (notably "Doomsday," "The Saboteur," "The Exile," and "The Enemies"), while Balter had penned the extraordinary "One Hundred Days of the Dragon" for *The Outer Limits*, a glorious and gripping exercise in fear that uncomfortably predicted a Presidential assassination, although from without rather than within. The passing of the years did not change their tune; as late as the early 1980s, Woodfield and Balter were story editors on Glen Larson's laughable sub-*Mission: Impossible* travesty *Masquerade*.

Not every episode of *Voyage* that Woodfield and Balter penned was rooted in Cold War hostilities (they first became a writing team on *Voyage*), but their work together on the color episodes frequently featured sinister Orientals and other thinly-disguised foreign powers of the sort *Mission: Impossible* specialized in (by the 1980s, they were able to come out of the closet completely and name the villains implicitly on *Masquerade*). Please note that the author is not suggesting that the Communist countries of this era were not a threat (they certainly were, particularly to their unfortunate neighbors), although certainly the McCarthyite fear of Communism created far more fear, insecurity and social upheaval within America than any Communist cabal of infiltrators could have hoped to achieve; I am simply noting these attitudes as prevalent in the pop culture of the time, as films, novels, comics and TV moved away first from Nazi spies, and then Red Menace antagonists, to more colorful and fantastic science-fictional ones (*THRUSH, SMERSH*, etc.) as the free world, now recovered from the effects of post-war austerity, became happier and more frivolous.

Visually and thematically, there could have been five years between the first and second seasons of *Voyage* rather than a few months, and Woodfield and Balter's "Time Bomb" inaugurated a slew of Bondian fantasies in the weeks to follow that occasionally even forgot to include the submarine! This episode's nod to the James Bond/ UNCLE fad has John Zaremba (from *The Time Tunnel* and the *Voyage* pilot) doling out a variety of Q-type gadgets to Nelson, which the episode spends more time describing than using, and a quintessentially typical spy show scene worthy of *Get Smart* in which a young boy playfully firing a ray-gun is in fact an evil midget (Allen regular Frank Delfino) shooting deadly drugs! There's also lots of that sly, wry, pseudo-sophisticated banter that the Bond/UNCLE genre specialized in—everybody is trying to be sparklingly witty (with the emphasis on trying) and no sentence is complete without a smirk or a raised eyebrow. Most significantly though, while we see little of the *Seaview*, this episode introduces the Flying Sub on its wobbly but invisible wires for the first time (more about this vessel under "The Left-Handed Man"). As for the episode itself, there's rarely a dull moment, with Ina Balin excellent as the traditional femme fatale and Susan Flannery as the good girl agent Katie, a lovely, likeable character introduced in "The Traitor" as Nelson's ersatz sister, but after this episode never seen again; in an interview with *Starlog*, Woodfield revealed that the intention was to introduce a Bondian girlfriend for Crane named Tiffany Loveland—close call! Later, Flannery—who had

also previously appeared in the episode "Hail to the Chief" as a treacherous secretary—appeared in the memorable Pearl Harbor episode of *The Time Tunnel*, "The Day the Sky Fell In," and in *The Green Hornet* episode "Trouble for Prince Charming." Production no: 8203.

And Five of Us Are Left

wr. Robert Vincent Wright, dir. Harry Harris

The Seaview sets out to rescue some long-lost survivors of a WWII submarine sinking who were marooned on a Pacific island and have been there ever since, presumed lost at sea and unaware of the outcome of the war. The situation is complicated by the presence on the Seaview of the embittered son of one of the officers, a volcanic reaction on the island, and a similar occurrence within the Japanese officer in the group, who is unable to come to terms with the thought that Japan surrendered.

With Robert Doyle (Werden), Philip Pine (Ryan), Teru Shimada (Nakamura), James Anderson (Wilson), Ed McCready (Hill), Kent Taylor (Johnson), Francoise Ruggieri (Brenda).

This "...was one of the few episodes that dealt with people, and a semblance of reality, as opposed to giant clams and aliens!" announced author Wright to *Starlog* magazine. However, so many things are going on in this episode that none of them seem to get covered properly, with all situations being resolved far too simplistically.

Philip Pine was the vice president in the superb Cold War episode of *The Outer Limits*, "One Hundred Days of the Dragon," and the evil Colonel Green in "The Savage Curtain" for *Star Trek*. He was most memorable though as the terrified cop who stops a car and finds an alien monstrosity that sends him into shock in "*Genesis*," a superb early *Invaders*. Other credits include *Adventures of Superman, The Twilight Zone, The Wild, Wild West, Get Smart, Circle of Fear*, and *The Six Million Dollar Man*. His films include *The Lost Missile* and *Phantom from Ten Thousand Leagues*, a super-cheap B-movie with a *Voyage*-style monster which also starred his co-star here, Kent Taylor. Taylor's film credits include the even cheaper *The Day Mars Invaded Earth*, and *The Crawling Hand*. He worked again for Irwin Allen in *Land of the Giants* ("The Deadly Dart").

Bit player Teru Shimada, usually cast in minor roles as foreign dignitaries (*Batman*, *The Man from UNCLE*, etc.) gets one of his best and biggest opportunities in this episode, and excels. James Anderson would portray a pirate in the memorable *Time Tunnel* episode "Pirates of Dead Man's Island." Ed McCready frequently played bits on *Star Trek*. Production no: 8202.

The Cyborg

wr. William Read Woodfield, Allan Balter, dir. Leo Penn

Invited to inspect the work of Dr. Tabor Ulrich in the study of cybernetics, Nelson finds he has been lured into a trap to drain his knowledge and place it within a cyborg duplicate of himself to take his place on board the Seaview.

With Victor Buono (Dr. Tabor Ulrich), Brooke Bundy (Gundi), Nancy Hsuer (Tish Sweetly), Fred Crane (cyborg), Tom Curtis (technician), Nick Colasanto (reporter), Stanley Schneider (crewman).

A talky first half is redeemed by some excellent visual effects and fine performances from Basehart and campy screen villain Victor Buono as mad scientist Ulrich, a typically Bondian gloater of the period— all he needs is a cat on his lap! The second half is faster paced end-of-the-world stuff, with a tense nuclear countdown; Woodfield regarded it as one of his best scripts for the series, and he's right. It has a genuinely clever *denouement* as the Cyborg is exposed. Of the visuals, the cyborg-making process is particularly good, certainly superior to the jokey creation of similar beings in the later *Lost in Space* episode "The Space Destructors," which has many parallels here, in particular the appearance of the cyborgs. The episode also has a few things in common with the pulpy *Star Trek* episode "What Are Little Girls Made Of?," which appeared the following year. There are also some striking,

if unlikely visuals as Nelson's mind is plundered for his knowledge. A thoroughly nonsensical prop of a cut-out human figure filled with lights looks good, but seems to serve no practical purpose—except perhaps to the props department, which used the thing repeatedly on all Allen's series at one point or another, most prominently for "The Dream Monster," an episode of *Lost in Space* in which an alien scientist is also creating cyborg-types, "The Condemned of Space," the third season opener for *Lost in Space*, and in "Raiders from Outer Space" for *The Time Tunnel*, in which it was used as a torturous brain-draining device.

A bulky, hammy, and often hilarious character actor, Victor Buono enlivened numerous TV series episodes of the '60s and '70s as various assorted villains, all of them larger than life, all very, very different and very, very camp, notably King Tut in five *Batman* stories and Professor Schubert in six episodes of the dismal *Man from Atlantis*. He is the under-used villain in the *Matt Helm* film *The Silencers*, and leader of the mutants in *Beneath the Planet of the Apes*. Credits include three appearances in *The Wild Wild West*, and wonderful work in *Boris Karloff's Thriller*, *The Man from UNCLE*, *I Spy*, *The Girl from UNCLE*, *Get Smart*, *Night Gallery*, and the TV movie *More Wild Wild West*.

Brooke Bundy appeared in "The Deadly Games Affair" for *The Man from UNCLE* and over twenty years later was Chief Engineer in the *Star Trek: The Next Generation* episode "The Naked Now." Nancy Hsueh's exotic appearance kept her busy in the spy shows of the period, including *The Man from UNCLE*, *I Spy*, and *The Wild Wild West*. Stunt player Fred Crane would return for the forthcoming episode "The Left-Handed Man." Nick Colasanto, in one of a number of 1960s bit parts before playing mobsters in the '70s, later became Coach in *Cheers*. Production no: 8205.

Escape from Venice

wr. Charles Bennett, dir. Alex March

Accused of murder, Captain Crane is pursued through the labyrinthine streets of Venice by the real killers, an important code to a secret weapon locked in his head.

With Renzo Cesana (Count Staglione), Vincent Gardenia (Bellini), Delphi Lawrence (Julietta), Rachel Romen (Alicia), Margot Stevenson (Betty), Danica D'Hondt (Lola Hale), Tommy Nello (Antonio), Ken Tilles (gondolier), Freddie Roberts (croupier).

A lively, entertaining and typically '60s caper that further indulges the spy mania of the period. Venice is the only city in the world that can be cut off entirely from the outside world, as the script tells us twice. The James Bond/UNCLE influence is well to the fore in this episode, with the secret code in the form of a melody (a daffy idea which appropriately also reared its head in the spy spoof comedy Get Smart, in "Hubert's Unfinished Symphony"), a little old lady holidaying from her teaching job becoming implicated in the spying shenanigans (the UNCLE trademark), and a casino boss with an exotic foreign name as the bad guy! Nelson's secretary even refers to Crane by his first name before correcting herself to give the implication that Crane is a bit of a girl-magnet, in the grand tradition of The Man from UNCLE. As in all secret agent thrillers of the period, life is cheap, and nobody is who they appear to be—a gondolier produces a deadly knife and murders Crane's contact, a waiter is not merely a waiter at all, but a stooge for the villain, and a store owner (familiar character actor Vincent Gardenia) is a grasping foil for the highest bidder! There's a laughable scene in which the schoolteacher, the innocent abroad drawn into the caper at her country's bidding in the grand tradition of The Man from UNCLE, must deviously let Nelson know that Crane has contacted her—and so produces a cheap souvenir of a *crane* (hint, hint) to alert Nelson to her newfound

role ... thus immediately ensuring that everybody in the vicinity would have immediately noticed this bizarre sight! Happy days.... To further date the episode, the music is scored by *Batman* composer Nelson Riddle.

Amusingly, the *al fresco* cafe where Nelson meets the Count, and then the schoolteacher, is the Nelson Institute dock gussied up with a few tables, parasols and plants; it also doubled for a fort in the Sudan in *Time Tunnel's* "Raiders from Outer Space." Other street sets are also familiar, some of them used again in "The Deadliest Game" a couple of weeks later, others familiar from other European exploits in *Voyage* and *Time Tunnel*; the famous rubber lamp post from *Time Tunnel's* "Reign of Terror" also puts in a Hitchcockian appearance. Venice, of course, is represented by library footage, pleasingly and cleverly integrated. The submarine doesn't actually feature at all in this episode, except in a couple of brief scenes (interestingly and unusually shot by director March), and the only underwater action is Crane's fight in the canal, although we do get to see the Flying Sub in action. Kowalski and Patterson are also absent, although Sharkey and Riley get substantial roles. Danica D'Hondt's Lola Hale—confusingly similar in appearance to Lawrence's Julietta—is another one-shot stab at giving the series a steady female liaison at the Institute. No substitute for Katie or Tish, she's not seen again—but then, neither were they. Although named Lola in the credits, the dialogue twice sounds like Lily, or Lilith. The sets, lighting and photography are excellent and the colors rich, and for all the clichés and thudding then-contemporary slang used by Riley and Sharkey, this is an hour well spent. Production no: 8204.

The Left-Handed Man

wr. William Welch, dir. Jerry Hopper

Despised industrialist Noah Grafton seeks to influence government by placing his own puppet Secretary of Defense in power, the much-loved and respected Admiral Penfield, a benevolent, likeable fellow of flawless character whose carefully cultivated image is to be Grafton's mask of respectability ... but Penfield's daughter becomes aware that Penfield is in Grafton's pocket, and turns to Admiral Nelson to expose the scheme, unleashing a deadly escapade into espionage and political duplicity.

With Barbara Bouchet (Tippy Penfield), Cyril Delevanti (Noah Grafton), Regis Toomey (George Penfield), Charles Dierkop (the assassin), Michael Barrier (Cabrillo), Judy Lang (Angie), Fred Crane (Lasher).

More spy capers, and one of the more substantial and thoughtful story ideas from the Allen stable. The only clue that it's a Welch script, rather than a Woodfield/Balter, is that everything is resolved with an explosion, a Welch trademark. Again, the *Seaview* is hardly to be seen, although there is a splendid, lengthy scene showing off the Flying Sub, as Crane takes Admiral Penfield on a spectacular fairground ride to end 'em all as he demonstrates the *Seaview*'s latest toy. One wonders if this sequence was originally intended to premiere the Flying Sub for the viewers too.

As this is the episode that features most, if not all, of the series' Flying Sub footage, it is here that we should pause to salute the masters of early 20th century special effects, the brothers Lydecker.

The Flying Sub, like the *Seaview*, the *Jupiter Two* from *Lost in Space*, and all the miniatures seen in the Irwin Allen series up until 1966, were produced by Howard Lydecker. Howard and Theodore Lydecker began their special effects careers shortly after the advent of sound, their earliest credits gracing the legendary Gene Autry serial *The Phantom Empire* made by Mascot Studios in 1935 and Republic's *Darkest Africa* in 1936, for which they created the flying batmen of Joba, their first occasion to put human figures into flight, and the creatures' jungle city. For the next twenty years, from 1936 to 1956, they worked exclusively for Republic, the classiest of the low-budget serials operations, where they built miniature cities, full-size futuristic vehicles, and made

models of both men and machinery fly. Among their finest achievements was their showcase production, the glorious *Undersea Kingdom*, which demonstrates all their skills and techniques, plus the Flying Wing (an early Flying Sub prototype) for 1937's *Dick Tracy*, similar craft in *Spy Smasher* (1942) and *Flying Disc Man from Mars* (1951), and the flying effects for *Adventures of Captain Marvel* (at a time when Columbia's *Superman* was being made to fly through animated inserts) and the various incarnations of Republic's Rocketman, which were hugely effective for the time and done simply with dummies attached to wires. By filming outdoors in natural daylight, rather than a false studio environment, and giving some thought as to where to place the camera for maximum credibility, the authenticity of the effect was enhanced considerably. Titles graced with their work during this period included *Fighting Devil Dogs*, *The Mysterious Doctor Satan*, *The Adventures of Captain Marvel*, *Spy Smasher*, *Captain America*, *The Purple Monster Strikes*, *King of the Rocket Men*, *Flying Disc Man from Mars*, *Radar Men from the Moon*, and *Zombies of the Stratosphere*. They also designed the famous disembodied Martian leader effect for 1953's *Invaders from Mars* and worked on the films *Tobor the Great*, *The Underwater City*, *Our Man Flint*, and *Way ... Way Out*. Library footage of miniature buildings being destroyed was utilized in *Earth vs. the Flying Saucers*. Howard Lydecker passed away during the series' run, while working on his most ambitious project to date, the attack on Pearl Harbor for the suspenseful *Tora! Tora! Tora!* (although he got no screen credit for it). It is no doubt partly due to his untimely death that *Voyage to the Bottom of the Sea* chose to make do with the existing footage of the Flying Sub for its final two seasons.

This episode also features the first Sharkey/Kowalski bit of business, as the double-act that would provide the series' heavy-handed and mercifully brief comic relief is inaugurated. Cyril Delevanti makes a fine evil, aged, silver-haired villain, and Barbara Bouchet is a rare treat for the guys in this invariably male dominated show. Delevanti appears in four episodes of *The Twilight Zone*, as well as episodes of *Adventures of Superman*, *Boris Karloff's Thriller*, *My Favorite Martian*, *Mission: Impossible*, and *I Spy*. Bouchet also appeared in an excellent *Man from UNCLE*, "The Project Deephole Affair," and the *Star Trek* episode "By Any Other Name."

Charles Dierkop, the hippie cop from *Police Woman*, was a regular bit-player on *Voyage*, and also the villain's stooge in Allen's pilot film *City Beneath the Sea*; here, he's the Bondian assassin of the title, with a deadly gun in place of his right arm. Regis Toomey, a more conventional cop in the popular *Burke's Law*, was well cast as the ambivalent Penfield offered up as the puppet of evil industrialist Grafton, and later portrayed the retiring doctor in "Pirates of Dead Man's Island" for *The Time Tunnel*. Truth is stranger than fiction dept: he was a good friend of Ronald Reagan! Truth is stranger than fiction part two: William Welch was a former political speech writer. Production no: 8207.

The Deadliest Game

wr. Rik Vollaerts, dir. Sobey Martin

With the President trapped in an undersea nuclear fortress, a paranoid five-star general attempts to launch a missile attack on Cold War countries.

With Lloyd Bochner (General Hobson), Robert F. Simon (U.S. President), Audrey Dalton (Lydia Parrish), Robert Cornthwaite (General Michaels).

As complex and intriguing as the second season's high quality spy stories were by '60s standards, these quasi-adult espionage capers held little appeal for the 7.30. Sunday night audience *Voyage* was catering for, and ratings plummeted. In the months to come, the ratings would reliably rise every time there was a monster to hand, dependably

dip every time there wasn't. This episode at least takes the series back underwater again for some *Seven Days in May/Twilight's Last Gleaming*-style political chicanery as the *Seaview* races against time to prevent a military coup not in the usual un-named banana republic, but the U.S.A. itself, as nuclear Armageddon looms yet again. Irwin Allen liked the nuclear reactor room set in the undersea base so much he later incorporated it into the *Seaview*, where it played a major role in numerous third and fourth season episodes.

Lloyd Bochner, a veteran of screen villainy, had already been up to mischief on the *Seaview*, in the first season's "The Fear Makers," and is an obvious villain here, giving one of his best SF TV performances. He will, however, forever be primarily known as the poor chump who misread "To Serve Man" in the classic *Twilight Zone* episode of the same name. He menaced *UNCLE* on numerous occasions, smarmed his way through episodes of *Honey West*, *The Wild Wild West*, *The Green Hornet*, *Mission: Impossible*, *Bewitched*, *The Six Million Dollar Man*, *The Bionic Woman*, *The Amazing Spider-Man*, *Battlestar Galactica*, *Manimal*, and *The Highwayman*, and was superb as a Dracula-like vampire in *Superboy* during which he inadvertently sinks his teeth into a lead pipe...

Robert F. Simon, a military man for over three decades in U.S. TV (most memorably in "The Zanti Misfits" for *The Outer Limits*), is here promoted to President. He often played Darrin's father in *Bewitched* and was J. Jonah Jameson in the 1970s *Amazing Spider-Man* series. Audrey Dalton faced a *Voyage*-like sea creature in the excellent 1957 monster movie *The Monster That Challenged the World*. She appeared several times in *Boris Karloff's Thriller* and episodes of *The Wild Wild West* and *The Girl from UNCLE*. Robert Cornthwaite was Zeigler in the first season's "Turn Back the Clock" and appeared in the SF classics *The Thing* and *War of the Worlds*. Production no: 8206.

Leviathan

wr. William Welch, dir. Harry Harris

En route to assist a scientist exploring undersea fissures with an apparent breakthrough discovery, Nelson and his crew are subjected to constant hallucinations of oversized sea-creatures that have been planted in their minds to make them doubt their senses when they confront the horror that awaits them.

With Karen Steele (Cara Sterling), Liam Sullivan (Dr. Anthony Sterling).

Looking decidedly out of place among the international espionage capers of 1965, this story is more typical of later entries and at least offered a welcome diversion from the secret agent yarns. The ratings improved dramatically. For a start, the *Seaview* is back to playing a major role in the proceedings, with non-stop underwater action involving a variety of giant-sized sea-creatures including a mutated human being. We are back to the deranged obsessive scientists of the first season again, as an underwater-based researcher becomes giant-sized, along with most of the sea-life in the area. The scenes with the oversized scientist wrestling with the sub are obvious in their simplicity, but quite gripping nonetheless, and most unpleasant for trouper Liam Sullivan, more accustomed to far less strenuous roles. Sullivan spent a whole day weighted down in twelve feet of filthy, dirty water, submerged in a full set of clothes, and wrestling with the eight-foot model of *Seaview* while holding his breath. A week later, Allen, dissatisfied with the footage, sent him down again, but—much to Irwin's annoyance—after literally almost drowning the first time, Sullivan insisted on the tank being half-drained, so that he could get air. It's fair to say that no working actor would today undergo such trials for a weekly TV show—a barrage of union rules and health and safety demands would ensure the use of a stunt-man. There has been some controversy over the years over Sullivan's developing freshly-sprouted fangs for the final attack, but this author casts his minority vote of approval.

Footage of the undersea lab and the Flying Sub arriving and departing from it would be re-used extensively throughout the series. As with the later *Star Trek* episode "The Man Trap," salt was the key to the secret, providing the *Seaview* crew with some ridiculously explicit hallucinations to order; watch in the tag, as David Hedison ad-libs a gag with the salt and then scatters it over his dinner—for a split-second, there's apprehension written all over Robert Dowdell's face, as he realizes the salt is still supposedly contaminated ... but the scene stayed.

Liam Sullivan was Nexus in the *Lost in Space* episode "His Majesty Smith" and Parmen in the *Star Trek* episode "Plato's Stepchildren." He also appears in *The Twilight Zone* as the headmaster in "The Changing of the Guard." Other roles include "The Silence" for *The Twilight Zone*, "The Brain Killer Affair" for *The Man from UNCLE*, "Crypt" for *Logan's Run*, and "Gun on Ice Planet Zero" for *Battlestar Galactica*.

Karen Steele was married to Hollywood movie director Budd Boetticher. Her other two claims to fame in the pulp sci-fi arena besides "Leviathan" were as one of "Mudd's Women" in *Star Trek* and the co-starring role in the film *Cyborg 2087*, a likely source of inspiration for the *Terminator* movies. Production no: 8211.

The Peacemaker

wr. William Read Woodfield, Allan Balter, dir. Sobey Martin

An idealistic and naive scientist turns a powerful super-bomb over to a hostile nation in the mistaken belief that they will use it to secure world peace, and narrowly escapes death when he discovers that he's been duped. Contacting Seaview with an assurance to disarm the undersea bomb he has presented them with, he is rescued by Crane and a female agent and smuggled back to freedom in a junk, where he is held in contempt as a traitor ... but instead of disarming the bomb, he ensures that only he can control it, intending to blackmail the world into peace.

With John Cassavetes (Dr. Everett Lang), Irene Tsu (Su Yin), Whit Bissell (General Connors), Dale Ishimoto (Premier), Lloyd Kino (police officer), Lee Kolima (junk captain), George Zaima (scientist), Walter Woolf King (Hansen), George Young (Lang's accomplice).

An entertaining espionage thriller, with much of the action taking place away from the *Seaview* (the nation concerned is "behind the Bamboo Curtain"!). The most frighteningly credible scene however takes place between crewman Riley and the gung-ho Chief Sharkey, the former of whom is guarding the room where the by now quite demented scientist has stationed himself, threatening to detonate the bomb himself if his demands for peace aren't met. Sharkey has just cajoled Riley into joining him in a clumsy grab for the detonator when Commander Morton arrives just in time to cancel the order as Riley is letting Sharkey in! Underwater bomb disposal footage from this episode was later used in the third season episode "The Mermaid," with new dialogue dubbed in.

Film actor, film director, and star of '60s series *Johnny Staccato* John Cassavetes probably never did live down the day he tried to blow up the world in a vain attempt to hold it together! He only ever did TV work to finance his more personal film projects, and was often very rude and contemptuous toward his fellow actors toiling in the arena of popular entertainment making the sort of films people actually wanted to watch. In fact, "The Peacemaker" is an entirely acceptable episode, with well-integrated stock footage of China and the European street dressed up to the nines for the land scenes. Irene Tsu has a string of cultish credits including Elvis movie *Paradise, Hawaiian Style*, schlock sci-fi *Women of the Prehistoric Planet*, and the silly John Wayne Vietnam movie, *The Green Berets*. She was mostly used for decoration in beach movies and spy films in the '60s, but roles improved later, especially thanks to a run on the offbeat quality medical drama *St. Elsewhere*. Credits include episodes of *My Favorite Martian*, *The Man from UNCLE*, *I Spy*,

The Wild Wild West, *Future Cop*, *Wonder Woman*, *Airwolf*, and *Star Trek: Voyager*. In an interview for *Filmfax* magazine, Tsu told how Cassavetes childishly tore buttons off his wardrobe and caused other irritations during the production. Playing a military man is Whit Bissell, who later portrayed much the same role as General Kirk in *The Time Tunnel*. Production no: 8212.

The Silent Saboteurs

wr. Max Ehrlich, Sidney Marshall, dir. Sobey Martin

Crane and Sharkey are hindered on a mission to put a deadly force-beam out of action that is destroying returning spacecraft from Venus when two secret agents turn up, both claiming to be the contact they are supposed to meet with.

With Pilar Seurat (Mona), George Takei (Cheng), Bert Freed (Halden), Alex D'Arcy (Lago), Phil Posner (Stevens), Robert Chadwick, Ted Jordan (astronauts).

Richard Basehart is absent from this episode, represented only by pre-filmed inserts as Crane reports to him. Max Ehrlich also wrote the story for the *Star Trek* episode "The Apple," rewritten by Gene Coon; here, his story was passed on to story editor Sidney Marshall for revision, possibly due to Basehart's absence. Robert Dowdell takes up the slack, asking fewer silly questions than usual!

Guest star George Takei was only months away from being cast as Mr. Sulu in *Star Trek*, by which time he had also guested on *The Twilight Zone*, *I Spy*, and *Mission: Impossible*. Later, while maintaining his ties to the *Star Trek* franchise, he would appear in episodes of *The Six Million Dollar Man*, *Beyond Westworld*, and *Space Cases*. Like Hsueh and Tsu, Pilar Seurat was another Oriental actress who benefitted from 1960s stereotyping, and got her turn on *I Spy*, *The Wild Wild West*, *The Man from UNCLE*, and *Star Trek*. Bert Freed had previously appeared in the first season episode "The Saboteur" (now he was surrounded by more saboteurs, but they were silent ones!).

The first season's episodes had been set a few years into the future, in 1973. For reasons never made clear, second season stories were occasionally pre-fixed with random dates ranging from 1976 (like this one) to 1978 and back again. In the third and fourth seasons, the arbitrary dating would range from 1976 to 1982. This was particularly odd, as there was never any obvious reason why any of the episodes should have been pinned down to a specific time. In fact, because of the science, politics, and fictional U.S. Presidents, *Voyage to the Bottom of the Sea* becomes more credible when the time period is kept deliberately vague. 'Futuristic' dates now set far in the past needlessly date the show. Production no: 8209.

The X Factor
wr. William Welch, dir. Leonard Horn

A bizarre kidnapping plot unfolds when Nelson follows up intelligence reports from a colleague that a toy manufacturer is using his factory as a front to smuggle scientists abroad as mannequins.

With John McGiver (Alexander Kaber), Jan Merlin (Henderson), Bill Hudson (Captain Shire), George Tyne (Dr. Liscombe), Anthony Brand (technician).

The story concerns a toy factory, and so lo and behold, sure enough, the first sight we see is professional mime Larry Dean being wheeled on in his familiar toy soldier suit. Dean appeared in several TV episodes at around this time, always portraying a mechanical man, and made numerous appearances on such diverse productions as *Bewitched*, *Lost in Space*, and *Land of the Giants*. He also appeared twice on *The Lucy Show* (once in the legendary shop window scene as a mechanical butler). A limited specialty act to be sure, but the wackiness of '60s TV kept him gainfully employed. The most notable aspect of this episode though is Allen's brazen re-use of the first season's pilot teaser (filmed in color but released in black-and-white) as part of the action in this story; it had been aired only just over a year earlier as the introduction to "Eleven Days to

Zero." Welch and Allen even went so far as to recast Bill Hudson in the new role of Captain Shire (he previously played Captain Crane's predecessor as commander of the *Seaview* so that he could die again in the attack footage!

That said, it is a marvelous sequence, ingenious and spectacular, and there is a shot—presumably filmed for the pilot—of Nelson being found by a bad guy and looking down the barrel of a gun as he staggers to safety that had not been used originally. Nevertheless, it was one of Allen's most audacious cheats, and actually didn't fit the new story all that well. When wicked Alexander Kaber is threatened by an inspection of his premises by Nelson and Shire and ominously suggests that "anything could happen on such a dangerous drive," he surely didn't mean for his assassins to attract obvious attention by blowing the car off the road in a helicopter machine-gun attack—it does rather throw undue suspicion on him! The rest of the episode though, making considerable and conspicuous use of the Fox studio lot (also seen in "Time Bomb"), is great fun, with a memorably appropriate end for the evil Kaber (John McGiver). Kaber is listed in the credits as 'Alexander Corby,' but for whatever reason his name was changed between script and production; interestingly, there is another Alexander Corby in the *Star Trek* episode "What Are Little Girls Made Of?," although this wouldn't appear for another year. However, the name may have been registered and the script in production.

This is the last in *Voyage's* string of Bondish, *UNCLE*-like spy yarns (Kaber is the usual smug gloater, referring both to "my country" and a "European division" *ala UNCLE's* THRUSH), and director Leonard Horn even films the action scenes in the in-your-face hand-held *Man from UNCLE* style, which is presumably deliberate as it wasn't his usual approach. Leonard Horn had directed a number of first season episodes of

Voyage, but directed only this episode and "Terror on Dinosaur Island" before moving on. Known for taking his time (it's surprising how many Allen assignments he secured, given Allen's time-is-money philosophy of direction), Horn photographs the action sequences from every available angle, making this a very atypical *Voyage*.

A familiar face in film and TV of the 1960s as a stuffy authority figure mostly employed in comedy series and films, John McGiver was the boss of the inept Mr. *Terrific* in the deservedly little-seen '60s super-hero spoof. He always played exactly the same sort of role, and as Kaber, he is perfectly and typically cast. He is pompous and difficult again in "Sounds and Silences" for *The Twilight Zone* and a splendid villain in the excellent *Man from UNCLE* episode "The Birds and the Bees Affair." Jan Merlin, busy B-movie player and co-star in the 1950's series *Tom Corbett, Space Cadet*, made several appearances in Allen series, most of them for *Voyage*. Previously he had played a bad guy in the first season's "No Way Out," and would be back for more in the third season's "Death from the Past." Most memorably though, he was one of the silver-skinned aliens who made an Arizona community in 1888 a ghost town in "Visitors from Beyond the Stars" on *The Time Tunnel*. Tony Brand has a bit part as a Trojan warrior in "Revenge of the Gods" for *The Time Tunnel*. Although Brand is credited, the crewman who makes up the fourth member of Crane's shore party and has far more to do, is not, despite being a familiar face from many episodes. In fact, he's Ray Didsbury, Richard Basehart's stand-in, about whom more can be found under the first season episode "The Buccaneer."

Although many of the *Seaview* crewmen became familiar from appearing in numerous, often consecutive episodes, these extras often stood in whenever background people were needed in other scenes. For example, one of the men in the control center de-stroyed in the first season's "The Creature" is a short, stocky, bushy-haired fellow seen in many episodes as a *Seaview* crewman, and in this episode, a tall, broad, dark-haired extra who wheels in Larry Dean's soldier at the start and is later seen reporting to Kaber's right-hand man that the factory is under attack, is another frequently seen crewman. As Crane and his men attack, he and the other men working for Kaber are joined by reinforcements including ... the short, stocky guy! Allen clearly assumed no-one would notice, and no doubt most viewers didn't, but many of these bit-players were used with great regularity, and when episodes are *viewed* with great regularity (particularly stripped daily) they become very recognizable. Production no: 8214.

The Machines Strike Back

wr. John and Ward Hawkins, dir. Nathan Juran

When an automatic undersea U.S. defense system starts firing missiles at American cities, Nelson allies himself with Admiral Halder, the co-creator of the weapons, unaware that Halder himself is orchestrating the chaos in an insane bid to seize power in his own country.

With Roger C. Carmel (Admiral Halder), Francoise Ruggieri (Captain Trober), Bert Remsen (Senator Kimberly), John Gallaudet (Admiral Johnson), Al Shelly (Murphy/diver).

This is the first contribution from western series stalwarts and former pulp SF mag writers John and Ward Hawkins, who worked extensively on shows such as *Bonanza* and *The High Chaparral*. Admiral Nelson always was a bit of a hawk; here, he defends a computerized undersea defense system that goes awry, launching missile strikes against U.S. cities. It's all part of a plot by an evil counterpart and former colleague Admiral Halder (Roger C. Carmel), from one of those deliberately ambiguous foreign lands of indeterminate, apparently Iron Curtain origin. Halder, who helped build the devices, is now controlling them for his own ulterior purposes. The episode ends with Nelson assuring the military and a liberal senator (played by Bert Remsen as a shrill, near-hysterical irritant and obstacle) that it couldn't possibly happen again!

It's interesting to note how the political climate has changed over the years; today, someone taking Nelson's stance would be the bad guy, endangering world peace with needless and dangerous weaponry. After such episodes as "Doomsday," "The Human Computer," "The Deadliest Game" and "The Peacemaker," to name but four of many, Nelson might have figured out by now that their nukes were as dangerous to themselves as their enemies! The corruption of the system by one of its creators would be deemed proof that the concept of the drone missiles was a bad one! However, rather than the episode being a warning against such deadly deterrents, the missile system stays in place at episode's end. Regardless of the dramatic device of things going wrong for the sake of the adventure, most pre–'70s stories of this type were intended to make the viewer feel secure that disaster had been averted rather than alarmed that such events might happen in the first place.

Roger C. Carmel is of course best known as Harry Mudd from *Star Trek*; he was also Colonel Gumm in the *Batman/ Green Hornet* team-up and Roger Buell in the first season of the mid–'60s sit-com *Mothers-in-Law.* Carmel milked his girth, twinkling eyes and bushy handlebar moustache for all they were worth in a period of TV and cinema that treasured and exploited character actors to their fullest, and he was frequently seen giving a broad, almost vaudevillian performance as a scoundrel in 1960s TV. He turns up in two episodes of *The Man from UNCLE*, "The Quadripartite Affair" and "The Ultimate Computer Affair," and three episodes of *I Spy*, "Affair in T'Sien Cha" (the pilot), "Red Sash of Courage," and "The Barter," which shows Carmel doing what he did best, as his shabby Mudd-like stooge is set up to take a fall. Another classic Carmel performance can be found in the light com-

edy *Breezy*, in which he plays the jealously salivating best friend of a middle-aged man who has attracted the charms of a free spirit hippie girl.

Francoise Ruggieri was briefly seen as Crane's date in "And Five of Us Are Left." She also appears in the *Lost in Space* episode "The Sky is Falling" (no connection with the *Voyage* episode of the same title). Bert Remsen, a familiar TV face in supporting roles, also appears in "One Hundred Days of the Dragon" for *The Outer Limits*. The undersea headquarters of the bad guys is the miniature first used in "Leviathan"; the interior, with the tell-tale fishtanks in the background, is often used as Admiral Nelson's lab, here redressed with a new false wall. There are numerous original shots of the *Seaview* with the drone sub, which interestingly is painted in the same style as the Flying Sub, yellow with a light blue streak, leading to speculation that it might originally have been built either as a prototype Flying Sub or as another piece of *Seaview* hardware. It looks fine in some shots, but like a fast food toy in others. The missiles are particularly poor. Production no: 8215.

The Monster from Outer Space

wr. William Read Woodfield, Allan Balter, dir. James Clark

A returning space probe crashes into the sea with an amoeba-like alien life form attached to the outside that seizes control of the Seaview *crew.*

With Hal Torey (Naval Commander), Preston Hanson (Mission Control), Lee Delano (technician).

"It's some sort of alien life form alright ... but it's like nothing we've ever seen before!" In fact, it's a giant inflatable hairy plastic bag with tentacles and a skin problem, and it's like *everything* we've seen before. The opening scene, in which a rather cut-rate control room tracks the return of the space probe is the first of many unintentionally hilarious sequences, littered with space-age pseudo-scientific gobbledygook; the first words out of the flight director's mouth upon being informed that the probe is carrying a living extraterrestrial hitch-hiker are "We must kill it!"—probably the only sadly realistic line of dialogue in the whole episode. Fortunately for him and us, this rather rash assumption that the creature is hostile is rapidly proven correct by events.

Picked up by the *Seaview*, the alien life form is gradually taking over the crew of the submarine *Invaders from Mars*-style, who immediately start behaving like shifty Grade-Z movie villains as soon as they've been absorbed into the amoeba-creature's being—for this is Woodfield and Balter's Red Menace in extraterrestrial form, taking over mortal minds, "each (one) a segment under some sort of central control." "Don't fight us, Admiral" begs the possessed Captain Crane, "We're all one. Eventually everyone in the world will be part of one great organism." Okay, thanks guys, we've got it. Similarly thinly-veiled stories were a dime-a-dozen in 1950s and 1960s SF—a well-known example is "This Side of Paradise," for *Star Trek*. So much so, that often, lazy and/or knee-jerk critics would assume a Red Menace sub-text even when there wasn't one! The dialogue is appallingly bad; one page of particularly excruciating exposition between Nelson and Sharkey aboard the Flying Sub—just in case nobody had ever seen a 1950s monster movie before—is wisely played for laughs by Basehart and Becker, who turn the wooden conversation into light banter. At another point in the episode, also on board the Flying Sub (during a scene which introduces us—for no particular reason—to a fog-cutting device in the vehicle), Basehart catches Becker out with an ad-lib.

As any creature-feature afficionado knows, alien life forms are always susceptible to an ordinary common-or-garden element which destroys them—air, fire, water, salt-water, electricity, and so on; just delete where applicable. This episode is, of course, no exception. Interviewed by Mike Clark for *Starlog* magazine, Woodfield tried to deny all knowledge of the episode, and attempted to palm the blame off on Robert Hamner! (Possibly he was recalling "Cradle of the Deep").

Trivia buffs will note that in Nelson's lab, which in the previous episode "The Machines Strike Back" doubled as the bad guys' headquarters, the door that led to the airlock in Halder's control room now leads to a handy cupboard. The blobby monster in this episode reappears in the third season as a hallucination in "The Day the World Ended." At a sci-fi convention, David Hedison revealed that the poor man working the suit had to be led around everywhere, blind as a bat—bizarrely, he was actually inside it. Most of one would-be exciting scene ended up on the cutting room floor when a weakened door prepared for a one-time-only shot showing the monster and its human stooges smashing into Nelson and Sharkey's last stand laboratory proved remarkably resilient to the weight of the actors. When they finally broke through, tumbling on top of the creature they had just forced through, everybody collapsed in laughter; this scene had to be replaced by a side-on shot of Nelson and Sharkey being confronted by Crane and Morton, although a few seconds of the creature forcing its way through the set can still be seen. Unfortunately, all this occurred on one of the days Irwin Allen was proudly showing guests around his playpen.

For all its corniness though, the episode keeps moving, and is quite entertaining. There is obviously some padding, such as the Flying Sub fog-cutting sequence and the lengthy underwater attack on the creature with torches, but these add to the episode's enjoyment rather than subtract, and once the chase is on for Nelson and Sharkey, the action improves considerably. The episode also features the famous climbing-through-the-air-vents ploy that became a regular fixture on this series—as did Wayne Heffley, who makes his debut as one of the two recurring ship's doctors; he would appear in three further episodes, "The Menfish," "The Monster's Web," and "Deadly Creature Below." This was James Clark's only *Voyage to the Bottom of the Sea*; Fox kept him gainfully employed on *Batman*, which was *Batman's* gain and *Voyage's* loss— he does quite a good job here with some very silly material, and although it is impossible to forget that we are looking at what is plainly a balloon inflating and deflating, the scenes showing the monster appearing and reappearing are as effective as might be hoped. Rather than being banished for this debacle, Clark, a former film editor turned director of sentimental animal movies and family films, should have been considered an asset to the series who might have vastly improved some of the third and fourth season improbabilities. Production no: 8213.

Terror on Dinosaur Island

wr. William Welch, dir. Leonard Horn

Crane mounts a rescue mission to save Nelson and Sharkey, marooned on a mysterious prehistoric island after the Flying Sub has crashed, unaware that one of his search party is a vengeful deranged crew member who wants him dead.

With Paul Carr (Benson).

It's stock footage time again, as Captain Crane pays his second trip to *The Lost World*—or his third, if you count David Hedison's starring role in the film this is ripped off from. Allen uses all the footage he couldn't fit in last time, plus a couple of shots from other dinosaur movies, but unlike the first season episode "Turn Back the Clock," which took sequences from the film in large chunks to exploit the fact that Hedison appeared in both, and was essentially just a brazen remake, this episode uses the dinosaur footage to supplement an original story, *ala The Time Tunnel*. In fact, this time it's Nelson and Sharkey who spend most of their time on the island, and Crane, Kowalski, Patterson and Allen regular Paul Carr as the deranged Benson who come to rescue them. The footage is flawlessly and skillfully

integrated with the new action, and a far more creative job has been done than with "Turn Back the Clock," with a shot of Sharkey trying to free the Admiral from a rockslide superimposed in the foreground of the dinosaur battle, although absurdly, a woman's scream carelessly remains on the soundtrack in one part of this sequence. Allen certainly had some gall using the dinosaur fight again after the previous season's *TV Guide* debacle.

The island set is well made, but we are obviously in the studio. Scenes of a volcano exploding and the fatal flooding that sparks the adventure are also stock (the flooding from "Submarine Sunk Here" is seen yet again in "The Shape of Doom," "No Escape from Death," and many others), but despite all this, it's an entertaining and enjoyable episode with some nice scenes between Nelson and Sharkey, including a rare attempt at intentional humor as Nelson makes a fire out of Sharkey's little black book of phone numbers. As if this isn't amusing enough, as Nelson tears out the pages he ad-libs "Hey, I used to know (her)...!"

The scenes in which the *Seaview* is attacked by one of the prehistoric creatures undersea are splendid, despite the over-familiar flooding scenes, and the story moves along at a cracking pace with Horn making the most of the opportunities afforded by the large island set. The crew don't know if Nelson and Sharkey are alive or dead, it's a race against time before the island sinks into the sea, and there's good footage of the Flying Sub out of control. It all becomes quite exciting at the end.

Paul Carr was a regular face on '60s scifi shows, and particularly *Voyage to the Bottom of the Sea*, having appeared as crewman Clark several times in the first season. He would be back, as Clark, in stock footage employed in "No Escape from Death." Production no: 8217

Killers of the Deep

wr. William Read Woodfield, Allan Balter, dir. Harry Harris

In pursuit of a submarine stealing nuclear missiles, the Flying Sub is shot down, and while Nelson is picked up by an American destroyer, Crane is found by the enemy sub.

With Michael Ansara (Captain Tomas Ruiz), Patrick Wayne (Fraser), James Frawley (Manolo), Bruce Mars (Bosun's Mate), John Newton (Commander Lawrence), Dallas Mitchell (Destroyer Sonar Operator), Gus Trikonis (Submarine Sonar).

This is the second Flying Sub to be destroyed in as many episodes, and also another episode plundering a previous feature film. It's quite an exciting entry, bearing in mind that much of the episode was stock footage, and that it's a straightforward sea battle adventure, with no bizarre creatures or alien invaders. It's rather like a war film—indeed, much of it *is* a war film!—but the tension never flags, and for once Woodfield and Balter keep the episode surprisingly Red-free and void of dated jingoism. In fact, the whole episode is joyously free of clichés, with none of Woodfield's sneering foreign Generals or nervy crewmen cracking up.

Like Star Trek's "Balance of Terror," produced that same year, this is an episode that shows the aching futility and waste of war in a non-preachy way. The men in both vessels are strapping young lads far too young and brave to die, but each group is devoted to destroying their opposite numbers in a battle that will ultimately mean nothing. The inclination toward showing the American destroyer running on clean-cut apple pie power and the enemy sub full of leering psychopaths is admirably resisted to create an authentic sense of despair and loss at the idea that anyone should perish in this senseless confrontation. Even Michael Ansara, who always *looks* like a villain, is not portrayed as the usual vicious, self-interested bungler but a bold officer as devoted to his country as Nelson and Crane are to theirs;

contrast this performance with his deliberately evil and callous military man in the superb "Secret Weapon" for *The Time Tunnel*, both episodes filmed within months, maybe weeks of each other at a time when Ansara had his head shaved for a stage role in *The King and I*.

The idea of having Nelson on board the U.S. ship that is hunting the sub, and Crane on board the sub which is attacking and being attacked is an inspired one that keeps an edge-of-the-seat atmosphere throughout the episode. Particularly well-handled by Basehart and Hedison is the obvious regret they feel as each assumes the other lost at sea, subdued while they both try to deal with the immediate issue of the enemy. Their necessarily repressed anger and dismay at the sequence of events that have suddenly unfolded as they get on with the job at hand—Nelson taking command of the destroyer and hunting the sub, Crane's constant acts of self-sacrificing sabotage—are pitched at exactly the right level, with no casual dismissive matter-of-fact response to the presumed death of a long-time friend and colleague, but no *Star Trek* histrionics or emotionalism until the immediate danger is dealt with. A very real sense comes across that they will be mourning later.

Due to the extensive use of (spectacular and well-integrated) stock footage, the *Seaview* plays a minimal role in this story. Interestingly, Hedison also featured in the 1957 war film much of the footage is taken from, *The Enemy Below*. Some of the stock music is recognizable from *The Time Tunnel*.

Michael Ansara had appeared in a different role in the *Voyage to the Bottom of the Sea* feature film, and in the first season episode "Hot Line." James Frawley, today a director, previously appeared in "The Exile." Today, bit player Gus Trikonis is also a busy director, his work having included episodes of quality series *Wiseguy* and *The Flash*. Patrick Wayne is the son of John Wayne. Production no: 8216.

Deadly Creature Below

wr. William Read Woodfield, Allan Balter, dir. Sobey Martin

A huge near-indestructible sea creature and two escaped convicts picked up at sea endanger some undersea missile tests and a valuable guidance system.

With Nehemiah Persoff (Dobbs), Paul Comi (Hawkins).

A good, strong, solid adventure episode that opens with the escape of the convicts and throws in a gigantic roaring sea monster to liven things up. Highlights include the theft of the Flying Sub by the convicts, who drive it straight to the bottom and into the waiting clutches of the undersea life-form.

The creature, one of Paul Zastupnevich's best, was first seen in the first season's "The Condemned," used again as a tree creature in the *Lost in Space* episode "The Raft," a specimen of "The Keeper," and as one of the alien jurors in "The Prisoners of Space," and returns for a third time in *Voyage* in "Secrets of the Deep." The stock music in this episode can be heard in *Batman, Lost in Space* and *The Time Tunnel*. This episode became the subject of a 3-D View-Master reel.

Nehemiah Persoff also appeared in "Secret Weapon," an episode of *The Time Tunnel* made at around the same time as this story, and later, "Land of the Lost" for *Land of the Giants*. Paul Comi was the unpleasant Bishop in the first season's "Submarine Sunk Here." Production no: 8218.

The Phantom Strikes

wr. William Welch, dir. Sutton Roley

The Seaview encounters the ghostly wreck of a sunken German U-boat, but only Nelson knows the true identity of the supernatural survivor the Seaview picks up shortly afterwards—the cold, embittered spirit of the captain whose career was cut short in life, and now wants to resume it in Crane's body.

With Alfred Ryder (Captain Krueger).

A silly, dreary episode which even top-notch director Sutton Roley can't enliven, although it seems to be one of the series' best

remembered, and spawned a sequel a few weeks later. Even the adventurous Roley's camera looks lost as it bobs and weaves around the set looking for interesting shots. However, Nelson has an interesting globe of the world in his cabin that illuminates and doubles as a light, and there is some nice model work of the *Seaview* and the ghostly U-boat to look at. Roley manages two nice shots, one when Krueger first comes aboard the *Seaview*, his red-hued face peering down to the control room from outside the sub, and another superb visual when he finally leaves, walking into oblivion. Only three scenes in the whole tedious hour bring the show to life; Morton's rescue from the Flying Sub fire, Kowalski rather uncharacteristically cracking up under the strain of Krueger's presence, and the aforementioned finale. Nelson's reticence to let the crew—or at least Crane—in on his knowledge about Krueger is irritatingly stupid, and Nelson's constant withholding of pertinent, often life-threatening information for no obviously apparent reason was a constant character flaw in a number of Welch's scripts. Why doesn't this man trust his captain and crew with valuable information that their success depends on?

Alfred Ryder, the sole guest star in this episode, was to return as Krueger in the appropriately titled "Return of the Phantom" from the same writer and director at the end of the season. In the third season, Ryder made another appearance, this time in a different role as an obsessed scientist in "The Heat Monster."

Sutton Roley, whose career spanned *Wagon Train* and *Gunsmoke, Lost in Space* and *Voyage to the Bottom of the Sea, Starsky and Hutch* and *Hawaii Five-O* and *Mission: Impossible* to *Airwolf* is one of the few TV directors whose work is often instantly recognizable, distinguished by an almost pathological desire to employ unusual camera angles for no obvious reason. As ingenious as his tricks were, the viewer was always made aware that he or she was watching a highly stylized film, and it is said that the mark of a truly good director is to make the audience forget that. Nevertheless, there is something to be said for flair. On *Starsky and Hutch*, he'd shoot through bead curtains; on *Hawaii Five-O*, he'd have the cameraman crouch down behind a car door. Although this breaks the number one rule of the good director, by making the viewer instantly aware that they are watching a fiction through a camera, the creativity is fascinating and welcome in a medium dominated by fast and rudimentary direction, and his approach suited the already unreal environment of SF TV, if not the cop shows and westerns. His *Man from UNCLE* efforts are extraordinarily weird, his *Invaders* dreamlike and disconcerting; for "The Phantom Strikes," he insisted on removing one entire side of the *Seaview* so he could shoot from behind the control panels in one long tracking shot. He did not drop by the Irwin Allen factory too often (he did four *Lost in Space* and three *Voyage*), but whenever he did, the results were always memorable. When Roley could prove to Allen that his antics would not cost money, as he did for the *Seaview* one take tracking shot sequence (which particularly excited the often bored Richard Basehart, although some of the traditionalists on the set got excited in a more negative way), Allen was always receptive and willing to give him a chance. Interested parties should particularly seek out "The Oasis" and "Anti-Matter Man" for *Lost in Space*, "The Innocent" for *The Invaders*, and "The Seven Wonders of the World Affair," aka the feature *How to Steal the World*, for *The Man from UNCLE*. He would be back on board the *Seaview* for "Dead Men's Doubloons" and "Return of the Phantom." Production no: 8219.

The Sky's on Fire

wr. William Welch, from Charles Bennett and Irwin Allen, dir. Gerald Mayer

With the Van Allen radiation belt surrounding the Earth on fire, and the world in chaos, the Seaview speeds to a missile launch site with a solution, while awaiting an on-board team of experts to agree the plan.

With David J. Stewart (Professor Weber), Robert H. Harris (Professor Carleton), Frank Marth (Admiral McHenry), Dick Tufeld (newsreader's voice).

This episode is basically a rewrite of the feature film, with a few significant changes by Allen's fix-it man William Welch. Many people, recognizing Allen's predilection for re-using an abundance of stock footage, assume this story to be a rather obvious attempt to absorb the bulk of the feature film into the series, but for the amount of film actually re-used here, it hardly seems to have been worth the effort; paradoxically, many other episodes used far more stock from the feature, notably the series pilot "Eleven Days to Zero" and "The X Factor."

Clearly, a straightforward rewrite of the feature was not only unnecessary, but pointless, as the decision to focus on the feature film plot point of the validity of Nelson's theory turns the movie's foregone conclusion into an absolute inevitability on the series. We *know* on a continuing series that the world must be saved, and that scientist Weber, poor schmuck, is wrong in his genuine belief that Nelson's solution will have the reverse effect, because he's made the mistake of arguing with the star of the show; Nelson's coming back next week, and he isn't. In the feature film, the dissenting scientist is left blustering at the U.N., and the attempt to prevent the missile launch is left (mostly) in the hands of religious zealot Alvarez, a demented defeatist. Here, it's the scientist himself trying to prevent Nelson from carrying out a democratically arrived-at decision, and with his own life not at stake (he's safe on the *Seaview*), and no religious mania evident, his motivation in murdering his opponents lacks logic. If he believes himself to be right, why not wait to be vindicated by Nelson's blunder? Weber is clearly not motivated by any altruistic desire to save lives as he spends the entire episode threatening them!

Had the opposing view to Weber's been held by a non-regular, with Nelson in the middle, there might at least have been some doubt as to who had got their calculations right ... but Weber's not merely mistaken, he's a bona-fide loony too, further loading the dice. There's little logic to his panicky bumping off the others—their votes are already known, and killing poor McHenry doesn't change the odds anyway. Also, given that Weber is not a devious enemy agent, but simply fanatically misguided, and bearing in mind that he had no reason to believe that the vote would go against him, there's the little matter of the spiked ring he wears to drug the crew—why on earth would he have such a thing? Interestingly, in the film, Nelson is a brave maverick, defying known U.N. instructions; now, as a series regular, he must be seen to be backing the authorities, and Weber is the dissenter. Similarly, in the film, Kowalski—called Kowski—is a genuine mutineer who deserts the ship. Here, the ludicrous plot device of a drug must be employed to avoid blotting the copy books of series regulars.

On the plus side, the shots of the sky on fire—which of course are from the film—are just as impressive the second time around as window-dressing as they were the first, and the Flying Sub sequence offers a measure of excitement, as ever. Stewart and Harris are well-cast (one can certainly sympathize with poor old Carleton's literally world-shattering indecision more than Nelson did), and Weber's final exposure as a bad guy finally provides the episode with some much-needed tension as he holds the crew at gunpoint past the deadline. Ultimately, though, the episode is brought down by a total lack of logic, and for the sake of a hastily written filler, Allen undermines and diminishes the value of his feature film original.

Of the performers, David J. Stewart appeared in *The Man from UNCLE*, in "The Monks of St. Thomas Affair" at around this time, while Robert H. Harris was a B-movie veteran, with credits including *How to Make a Monster* and *The Invisible Boy*. He returns to Allen for the *Land of the Giants* episode "Collector's Item." Frank Marth is one of those familiar faces who has never been off the screen since the earliest days of TV—appearances span *Bilko* to *Airwolf*, and he looks exactly the same throughout the thirty years between the two. A veteran of innumerable TV cop shows and action adventure series, his TV SF roles have been limited, but he was seen more than once as one of *The Invaders*, most memorably in "The Innocent."

Behind the scenes, Irwin Allen was wrestling with a decision of his own; contract negotiations with Terry Becker had broken down, and the hunt was on to find another actor to replace him as the Chief. Sharkey's ludicrous survival after falling on top of a live grenade in this episode was actually a part of this. The character had initially been killed off until Allen, unable to find a satisfactory replacement, caved in. Consequently, Sharkey makes a remarkable recovery! With the exception of two very brief appearances in "The Shape of Doom" and "The Death Ship" (presumably inserts filmed at another time), this was Chief Sharkey's last appearance during the second season; he missed five of the last seven episodes completely, and did not play a substantial part in the series again until the third season.

The voice of Dick Tufeld, narrator for *Lost in Space* and *The Time Tunnel* and voice of the *Lost in Space* Robot, can be heard relating tales of worldwide catastrophe as the *Seaview* taps into a news broadcast ... just as he did in the feature film. Later Tufeld voices the "Monster from the Inferno" in the third season opener. Production no: 8220.

Graveyard of Fear

wr. Robert Vincent Wright, dir. Justus Addiss
   A scientist desperate to use the Seaview *to re-*

trieve papers and formulae lost at sea to sustain a fountain of youth potion for his lover neglects to inform Nelson and Crane that their vessel—and many before it—was sunk by a monstrous, mutated giant Portuguese Man O'War ... which, along with the desperate scientist, then endangers the Seaview and all aboard.

With Robert Loggia (Dr. Ames), Marian Moses (Karyl Simmons).

As with his previous script for *Voyage*, "And Five of Us Are Left," writer Robert Vincent Wright has too much going on in this action-packed episode to truly do justice to the immortality theme, which is brushed aside for the exciting scenes with the mutant Man O'War. Wright's scripts really needed a 90 minute slot to flesh out all his ideas, but at least his episodes never dragged (the episode has probably the shortest teaser and most abrupt ending in the series!).

While the business with the creature is exciting stuff, and the character of the scientist Ames is drawn well, the character of the 230 year old Karyl Simmons is never really clearly defined. At one point, Ames refers to the work of the many scientists before him, with whom Karyl may have either been colleague, guinea-pig, or both, but later at the close of the story makes an odd speech about how he "created" her. If so, how could she be 230 years old? In addition to this, the role could have benefitted from better casting; with all due respect to the actress, who creates a three-dimensional portrait of fear with very little screen time, the part of Karyl, being as small and undemanding as it is, could have certainly been enhanced by casting a knock-out beauty in the role. After all, Ames and those before him have risked everything to sustain this woman's life. And while there may have been little point in retrieving Ames' work for Karyl's benefit, it's never quite made clear why the *Seaview*, the mutant menace now dealt with, doesn't make some effort to retrieve his notes; possibly, a "there were some things man was not meant to know" speech got crowded out of the running time.

Once again, this episode suffers from the annoying contrivance of letting an obviously addled troublemaker run around the ship unguarded and unhindered, a tradition of the series from the beginning to the end, but this carelessness is a minor irritant quickly overshadowed by the action scenes, which are taut and suspenseful, and there are several good shots of both monster and the *Seaview*, with the Flying Sub added to the action later and a nice touch of horror at the end. All said and done, an enjoyable episode.

Robert Loggia starred in a '60s spy series titled *T.H.E. Cat*, and in the 1980s was *Mancuso, FBI*. He was as often a gangster as a cop, and has some good scenes in the brutal *Scarface*. Among many more substantial roles in later years, he portrays a military man in the fun alien invasion film *Independence Day* and was megalomaniac Senator Tony Kreutzer in the superb and underrated *Wild Palms* mini-series. Marian Moses can be found looking much healthier in *The Man from UNCLE* in an episode titled "The Girls from Nazarone Affair." Production no: 8221.

The Shape of Doom
wr. William Welch, dir. Nathan Juran

A whaler is lost in restricted waters with all hands, except for the man who caused the disaster—Dr. Alex Holden, an obsessive scientist who has injected the whale that rammed his ship with a growth serum. With Holden's notes lost at sea, the whale has not only become his only chance of securing valuable tissue samples, but swallowed an undersea nuclear bomb.

With Kevin Hagen (Dr. Alex Holden).

This was *Voyage's* third giant whale story after "The Ghost of Moby Dick" and "Jonah and the Whale," and needless to say, uses footage from the first season's "Ghost of Moby Dick" just as "Jonah and the Whale" did. In fact, the opening pre-credits teaser is from that episode. Once again, Nelson's the villain by today's standards, as in "The Machines Strike Back," which also concerns itself with TV's stunning naiveté in the 1960s where nuclear power was concerned, here supporting a farcical plan to blow a canal through the bottom of the sea with a series of nuclear explosions (which the President himself, and a boatload of other dignitaries are going to watch, yet!), while Holden's experiments (which Nelson really ought to be intrigued by) depend solely on the whale that has swallowed one of the charges and is now swimming around like a giant doomsday bomb ("Yes, we'll lose your whale, and a few fish besides..." shrugs Nelson as he proposes an explosive demise for the hapless mammal). In the years to follow, such a storyline would sentimentally concern itself with saving the whale, and the guys nuking the ocean would be the bad guys! In fact, Nelson's quite mean and stupid in this one, showing no sympathy at all for Holden's work or dilemma, even if Holden is supposed to be even crazier (Hagen, being a wonderful actor, doesn't play Holden as a clichéd loon, but as earnest and passionate about his work, and so becomes sympathetic). Nelson takes an almost sadistic pleasure in refusing Holden's request; ironically, in the "Ghost of Moby Dick" episode, it's Nelson who takes Holden's position in this episode, briefly becoming almost as irrational. In fact, Nelson is never particularly consistent in his support or condemnation of his fellow scientists—sometimes he is understandably unsympathetic, as in the first season's "The Creature" or the later "Thing from Inner Space," sometimes remarkably tolerant, as in "The Condemned," where he grudgingly works with Bentley Falk for the good of the research, or in "The Indestructible Man," in which several of his crewmen have been brutally dispatched, other times oddly detached from the aims of his colleagues, as here, and in the previous episode.

The notion of a growth serum is reminiscent of the natural phenomena discovered by yet another deranged scientist, Dr. Sterling in "Leviathan" (it's so typical of Irwin Allen that it has to be a *giant* whale!), and during the course of the series the *Seaview* would be constantly plagued by a variety of giant-size phenomena such as this creature (although why anyone would want to enlarge a whale is never fully rationalized!), the Manta in "The Creature," the spider in "The Monster's Web," and the previous story's Man O'War, while the obsessive whale-hunter had already been done in the aforementioned "Ghost of Moby Dick." Despite the absurdities of the nuclear aspect, this episode is rather more enjoyable than that one, thanks largely to another superb performance from the underrated Kevin Hagen, whose numerous appearances in Irwin Allen productions (as well as other films and series) were always above average, and who excels as the desperate Holden, particularly strong when he first comes aboard the *Seaview*, dominating the screen completely; he can also be seen to advantage in "The Death Merchant" for *The Time Tunnel* and "The Yo-Ho-Ho and a Bottle of Rum Affair" for *The Man from UNCLE*. As the demented Holden, he has a central role, and makes the most of his screentime, stealing the show in every scene; the other performers are practically knocked off the screen every time he's on the set—and he does his own stunts in the fight scenes.

Another idiotic (and typically *Voyage*) plot point has a single Master At Arms escorting the crazed Holden to his cabin, when it's clear he's about to go off the deep end—and he does, easily overpowering the solitary crewman and beating up Riley and Kowalski in his desperation. As a result, yet another wacko scientist is loose on the *Seaview* with a vested interest in screwing up Nelson and Crane's careful plans. All in all, it's absolute nonsense made eminently watchable by the powerful performances of Basehart and Hagen. Hedison has nothing to do, and Dowdell and Becker have only a couple of lines; the Flying Sub's out of commission, so we get to see the return of the mini-sub instead, which the tall and broad Hagen looks ridiculously uncomfortable inside. Despite such indignities as this and his *Time Tunnel* cabbage-headed alien, his roles for Irwin Allen were actually meatier than those he received from Rod Serling on his *Twilight Zones*, and his substantial credits are listed under "His Majesty Smith" for *Lost in Space*. Production no: 8222.

Dead Men's Doubloons

wr. Sidney Marshall, dir. Sutton Roley

The demented descendant of a 16th century pirate is convinced that he is his ancestor reincarnated, and acts out an elaborate charade to sabotage an underwater communications system.

With Albert Salmi (Captain Brent), Allen Jaffe (Sebastian), Bob Swimmer (pirate), Stan Kamber (sailor), Robert Brubaker (Admiral Howard).

A thoroughly amusing and positively absurd yarn, which suggests from the teaser that we are seeing another reincarnated sea captain in the manner of Roley's previous "Phantom" assignment of a few episodes earlier. In fact, Brent (played with great enthusiasm by Albert Salmi, who was also Tucker the phoney space pirate in two episodes of *Lost in Space*—"The Sky Pirate" and "Treasure of the Lost Planet") is ultimately revealed to be a simple raving lunatic, a foreign agent with orders to sabotage the elaborate undersea defense system the *Seaview* is checking out. Why he has gone to such elaborate lengths to pretend that it's a pirate galleon shooting at the *Seaview* and the Flying Sub for what is supposed to be a covert sabotage operation is never explained, and would make a great sequel for a more inspired writer. Where did he get two dozen demented crewmen and the approval of his masters to mount such an extraordinary charade? His pirate masquerade is purely an attention-attracting conceit that is not only quite unnecessary but also detrimental to the assignment. It also makes complete nonsense of the opening teaser, which shows

him all at sea and shouting curses into the sky several centuries earlier, an event that is ultimately revealed as a complete fantasy on the part of the madman Brent. In this story though, any attempt at rationalization would just make the premise less credible, not more so ... and then we'd cheat ourselves out of seeing the *Seaview*, and then the Flying Sub, shot at by a 16th century galleon! All might have been explained by some supernatural conclusion linked to the teaser, but it is never forthcoming.

Nevertheless, such minor details should not be allowed to stand in the way of a cracking good yarn, and what a boring episode this would have been without the period dressing. As it is, we get lots of footage of the galleon and the Flying Sub, and an exciting action-filled climax. The sets and costumes are wonderful—as usual—and Sutton Roley's direction is as imaginative as ever. One particularly good scene has Nelson and Crane entering the unhinged spy's cabin aboard the *Seaview*, completely oblivious to the huge Jolly Roger flag that unfurls behind them as they close the door! The pirate footage used for the sequences in 1524 and when the Flying Sub is being attacked is later employed in the pirate episode of *The Time Tunnel*, "Pirates of Dead Man's Island," as is the small set representing the deck of the pirate ship. Salmi makes a commendable effort to play Brent differently from Tucker, affecting a bizarre accent, but although usually a wise strategy against stereotyping, on this occasion may have been a mistake. Given the absurdity of the episode anyway, he perhaps should have taken the ball and run with it, as over-the-top as he was in *Lost in Space*.

As well as portraying the wily Tucker in *Lost in Space*, Salmi made notable *Twilight Zone* appearances in the episodes "Execution" and "Of Late I Think of Cliffordville." Production no: 8223.

The Death Ship

wr. William Read Woodfield, Allan Balter, dir. Abner Biberman

Scientists on board the Seaview *during the testing of a new computer system that will eliminate the need for a crew are systematically done away with by an unidentified saboteur who intends to use the Seaview's missiles to destroy a seabound peace conference.*

With Lew Gallo (Vice Admiral Stroller), June Vincent (Ava Winters), Elizabeth Perry (Tracy Stewart), David Sheiner (Arthur Chandler), Herb Voland (Glenn Carter), Harry Davis (Dr. Frank Templeton), Ivan Triesault (Klaus), Ed Connelly (Rourke), Ross Elliott, Alan Baxter (enemy agents).

This is essentially the old dark house gimmick, transferred to the *Seaview's* submarine setting, but despite it's obvious familiarity, the writers pull it off well. Although many sources, including 20th Century Fox, credit regular *Voyage* writers William Read Woodfield and Allan Balter with the script, the episode itself credits the names of Michael Lynn and George Reed. In fact, these names were pseudonyms—this episode marked the end of Woodfield and Balter's relationship with *Voyage* and Allen when they refused to rewrite the story's ending (to blame the murders on an invisible alien!) when filming ran late.

Although a meticulously crafted suspensor, this was a shameless rip-off from another source, in this case a direct steal from the Agatha Christie novel *Ten Little Indians*, complete with twist ending intact. Consequently, although an efficient and polished yarn, the plot is such a brazen swipe that anybody with the slightest knowledge of Christie's cheat will spot the catch immediately. It's an odd departure for the series to attempt a murder mystery, so it's fortunate that the result was well written. If the episode has a single minor flaw, it is that no-one ever assumes that either Nelson or Crane might be the murderous betrayer; after all, although *we* know that the stars of the show are in the clear, nobody else is supposed to know that Nelson and Crane have

to come back next week! The other regulars are absenteed early in the tale, and half the guest cast wiped out by the end of the second act.

This episode turned out to be a bit of a disaster for Irwin Allen, and Abner Biberman was another director who did not return to the Allen stable after having had the misfortune to be associated with a troubled production (Biberman's direction was awful anyway ... poor Lew Gallo looks ridiculous wedged in the bridge/nose doors!). The episode lost Allen two of his most prolific and successful writers and he ended up filming the original ending anyway!

Lew Gallo appeared twice in *The Time Tunnel* (a minor role in "The Day the Sky Fell In," and as the alien Vokar in "Chase Through Time") and as Sgt. Smith in the *Lost in Space* yarn "Flight into the Future." He would return to *Voyage* in the third season episode "Deadly Waters." Both David Sheiner and Harry Davis appeared in the first season episode "The Exile," where more detail may be found. Herb Voland was more readily associated with sit-com material ranging from *Bewitched* to M*A*S*H, as was June Vincent (*Bewitched* and *The Ghost and Mrs. Muir*). Ivan Treisault had a minor role in the first season's "The Price of Doom," where his other relevant credits are listed. Elizabeth Perry appeared in the *Outer Limits* episode "The Brain of Colonel Barham," Alan Baxter in "OBIT."

The enemy agent who initiates the plan is uncredited, but is plainly Ross Elliott, who also appeared in two episodes of *The Time Tunnel*, "One Way to the Moon" (again as a saboteur for an unidentified foreign power) and "Visitors from Beyond the Stars." The rest of the story but for this scene takes place entirely on board the *Seaview*, and all else is stock footage; the drone sub sequence comes from the *Voyage* feature film, and had already been used in the series pilot. The story idea of an all-purpose, all-powerful computer replacing the crew later resurfaced in

Star Trek, in "The Ultimate Computer." Production no: 8210.

The Monster's Web

wr. Peter Packer, Al Gail, dir. Justus Addiss

While testing his new super-fuel, Captain Gantt's submarine is destroyed by what he claims is a giant underwater spider. When the fuel is discovered to be dangerously volatile at a certain depth, the Seaview has two deadly threats to contend with—the explosive fuel still in the wreck of the sub and the spider the arrogant and unlikable Gantt insists is still lurking down there.

With Mark Richman (Captain Gantt), Barry Coe (Bill Balter), Sean Morgan (Nuclear Sub Sonar).

This episode bears a strong resemblance to "The Shape of Doom" a few weeks earlier, and a number of other episodes in which an obsessed scientist is so devoted to his work that he ignores the inherent dangers to life and limb. There's never a dull moment, the spider monster looks quite good, and the scenes with Gantt's sub hitting the spider's web and the Flying Sub wrapped up like a fly are strong images. Footage of the spider's web is used to represent an alien saucer's threat to pad out the climax of the third season episode "Day of Evil."

Despite the similarities of the episode to standard *Voyage* fare, in particular the first season's "The Creature," Peter Packer was a writer more regularly employed on *Lost in Space,* where he wrote nearly half the series. This was his only contribution to *Voyage;* he later also made a single contribution to *Land of the Giants* ("The Flight Plan"). Al Gail's name on the credits is down to a rewrite necessitated by a sudden illness suffered by Richard Basehart midway through filming; he had only completed a couple of scenes aboard the Flying Sub before he became unable to continue. His sudden unavailability is obvious if you're looking for it; a number of scenes employ a double (a scene of Nelson entering the Flying Sub is shot with the stand-in literally hiding under his hat), other

scenes use existing footage and voiceovers, and he's clearly missing from the climax. That said, the show has made the best of a bad job. In the following episode, "The Menfish," Nelson's lines are taken by guest actor Gary Merrill as Admiral Parks (Merrill was briefly considered as a permanent replacement for Basehart), and he's also absent from the next, "The Mechanical Man," which seems to have required less extensive rewrites (as David Hedison has cynically but honestly observed, lines were interchangeable, and if one player was absent, everyone would be moved up a notch in the script). The character of Bill Balter appears to be a rare in-joke in an Irwin Allen show, as Allan Balter, formerly with *The Outer Limits,* is one half of the William (Bill?) Woodfield/Allan Balter writing team. Given the circumstances of their departure one wonders who put the gag in, and whether Irwin noticed it. Allen had a quite sensible and justified aversion to onscreen private jokes, which always remind the viewer that he or she is watching a fictional film or TV show, so destroying the tenuous illusion of reality. With the sort of fanciful material Allen produced, this was a hazard to suspension of disbelief he could not afford.

Mark Richman, sometimes billed as Peter Mark Richman, later returned to the series for "Secrets of the Deep." A frequent player in SF TV, Richman appeared twice in *The Outer Limits* ("The Borderland," "The Probe"), twice in *The Invaders* ("The Leeches" and "The Inquisition"), and in episodes of *The Man from UNCLE* ("The Seven Wonders of the World Affair," aka the feature *How to Steal the World*), *Land of the Giants* ("Panic") and *Star Trek: The Next Generation* ("The Neutral Zone"). Production no: 8224.

The Menfish

wr. William Read Woodfield, Allan Balter, dir. Tom Gries

A scientist working on board the Seaview starts abducting crewmen to turn them into amphibious menfish.

With Gary Merrill (Admiral Park), John Dehner (Dr. Borgman), Victor Lundin (Hansjurg), Lawrence Mann (diver), George Sims (Bailey), Roy Jenson (Johnson).

Question: What do you get when you cross a man with a fish? Answer: Standard man-into-monster B-movie material, complete with hypodermic needles and lab coats, unwilling participants, rampaging rubber-suit monsters, deformed stooge, and a mad criminal doctor who wants to take over "ze verld!" As Admiral Parks, Gary Merrill (Senator Clark in the pilot film for *The Time Tunnel* at around this time, where his credits are discussed) was standing in for hospitalized series star Richard Basehart. The transition is made smoothly, other than one brief scene in which the *Seaview* doctor mentions the results of an autopsy; when Crane orders that the results go no further, the doctor points out that he usually informs the Admiral ... but as this Admiral is not Nelson, there seems little good reason for making this point. The episode is paradoxically made more credible by Nelson's absence, as Parks succumbs far too easily to Borgman's implanted device that makes him do his bidding; Nelson was surely tougher than Parks is portrayed here.

Dehner's Borgman is a good villain, cut from the same slice of ham as his demented mad scientist in the *Man from UNCLE* two-parter "The Prince of Darkness Affair," released theatrically as *The Helicopter Spies.* Victor Lundin, here playing Borgman's stooge, would return as a creature himself in the fourth season as "The Lobster Man," and also appeared in Allen's *Time Tunnel* as Karnosu the native in "The Crack of Doom." He was quite disappointed to find his emotional climactic scene at the end of this episode trimmed down to the bare basics by Allen, who apparently snapped at director Gries that "we're not doing *Playhouse 90!*"

These three characters dominate the action along with Hedison as Captain Crane and Dowdell's Chip Morton. This was Wayne Heffley's final appearance as the *Seaview* doctor, after which Richard Bull returned to the role, and of the other regulars, only Kowalski puts in a blink-and-you-miss-him appearance in the exciting climax. Trivia collectors may notice that two regular background crew members are given names in this episode—Collins and Forrester. As tempting as it might be to assign these names to them permanently, the truth is that it could have been any extras in those scenes. The Menfish themselves look suspiciously like hobby-kit models of the Creature from the Black Lagoon until they become cute little fishy-sized monsters. Once the stunt-men climb into the suits, they actually look quite impressive for what they are, particularly when they're in the water. The underwater scenes when the first creature grows to man-size are well-handled, although Borgman takes his own sweet time using the control device, primarily, it seems, so that the audience can enjoy a lengthy underwater struggle between the Manfish and three divers. Less effective are the scenes in which Borgman has the upper hand over Crane and Parks. Numerous chances to fight back are offered by the clumsy direction, most noticeably when Crane walks right past Borgman, whose gun is practically falling out of his pocket! A minor but glaring continuity error has Crane unbuttoning his shirt to put on diving gear, but then having it buttoned up again when the camera returns seconds later.

While the episode takes a while to get moving, it holds the interest, but the fun really starts when the Menfish finally appear. The scene in which stunt-man Roy Jenson decides to sneak a look at the creature and it breaks free is well played, particularly when the creature crashes through the wall to attack Crane, as is the colorful chaotic climax in which—provoking memories of "Leviathan"—the Manfish grows to gigantic size, thus offering the opportunity for the man in the monster suit to wrestle with the

Seaview model. Tom Gries, who later went on to direct feature films and TV movies, did not return to *Voyage to the Bottom of the Sea,* but did direct an above-average *Batman* adventure the following year featuring the Riddler. The Manfish costume did reappear however, constantly; the sequence with Roy Jenson is used again in "The Mermaid," which features the creature-suit again, as does "The Thing from Inner Space" and "Night of Terror." Jenson, incidentally, is that rare gift, a stunt man who can act. He's a white-haired cult member in Dehner's aforementioned *Man from UNCLE* episode, and was one of the ill-fated THRUSH agents invading UNCLE headquarters in the very first *Man from UNCLE* pilot "The Vulcan Affair," aka *To Trap a Spy.* He's excellent as a hood in *The Outfit* and a biker in *The Gauntlet,* two 1970s crime thrillers. Gries featured him prominently in his *Batman* episode, "A Riddle a Day Keeps the Riddler Away"/"When the Rat's Away, the Mice Will Play," a series highlight.

The monster suit—which was the *raison d'etre* for this episode—also turns up in the *Lost in Space* episode "A Change of Space," filmed at around the same time. The chronology of this episode is interesting; Allen apparently walked in to Woodfield and Balter's office with the costume and asked them to write a story around it, and yet the hot-tempered duo had departed the show during the hasty filming of "The Death Ship," which has a much earlier production number, indicating that both these episodes had lengthy production problems. Production no: 8225.

The Mechanical Man

wr. John and Ward Hawkins, dir. Sobey Martin
    An unfeeling human-like android with telepathic powers develops ambitions to rule the world, and to continuously boost his powers must drill into the heart of a volcano, causing destruction around the world.

With James Darren (Dr. Peter Omir), Arthur O'Connell (Dr. Paul Ward), Cec Linder (Van Druten), Robert Riordan (Ralph Vendon), Seymour Cassel (Jensen).

Flawless comic-book SF, with James Darren of *The Time Tunnel* guesting as the deadly android Mr. Omir; it was his appearance here that lead him to be cast immediately afterwards in *Time Tunnel* the following season, reunited on several occasions with busy Allen director Sobey Martin. Needless to say, further details on Darren can be found there.

Although the title of this episode suggests a traditionally robotic menace of the sort found in the first season's "The Indestructible Man," this is another of the series' occasionally inappropriate titles. Darren's android has a light show under his jacket and wears a cool pair of shades to hide his power, but otherwise takes human form. The effects and sets are as excellent as ever, and the opening teaser showing Darren's bared back a mass of flickering lights and wires is notably memorable; equally so, a later scene in which he stands perfectly still and unperturbed on the bridge as the *Seaview* crew are hurled around in one of the series' popular lurch scenes, and his arrival in the air-lock bone-dry in a suit and tie! As the android Omir, Darren is perfectly cast, his deliberately monotone delivery colluding perfectly with his blandly perfect good looks and flawless smooth skin to create a human-like android who—for once—doesn't move as comfortably as a human or show flickering eyelids, stubble, etc. So many films and series episodes simply assume that by announcing that someone is an android automatically makes them one.

The absence of any regulars with character (Basehart is still away, and the contract-haggling Terry Becker glimpsed only briefly in stock footage) puts the cardboard Crane and the slow-witted Chip Morton center stage, creating an episode that is pure Marvel Comics from start to finish, with Arthur O'Connell especially cartoonish as the android's stereotypical feeble inventor. Both he and Darren keep admirably straight-faced while mouthing the most outrageous B-movie dialogue; although story editors on *Bonanza* and *The High Chaparral*, the Hawkins brothers' origins as pulp SF writers shine through plainly here. "What have I created?" pleads O'Connell to the heavens; "I possess power your infantile minds could never even dream of!" announces Darren! Great stuff, and amazingly a step up for both Darren and O'Connell, who previously appeared together in the trend-setting teen torment movie *Gidget*, which begat an army of sequels and imitators. The sequence in the caverns with Morton, Kowalski and Jensen is later re-used shamelessly in the fourth season's "The Terrible Leprechaun." Production no: 8226.

The Return of the Phantom

wr. William Welch, dir. Sutton Roley

Shortly after the body of the supernatural Gerhardt Krueger is committed to the ocean, Nelson is visited by the ghost of a native girl who warns him that Krueger's ghost will return.

With Alfred Ryder (Captain Krueger), Vitina Marcus (Lani/Maria).

This final second season episode saw Richard Basehart return to the series after his two and a half episode absence. Marginally more interesting than its precursor from the same writer and director, "The Phantom Strikes," this is more "The Phantom, Part Two" than a sequel, continuing as it does directly on from the original—complete with references to Kowalski's state of health (he broke down in "The Phantom Strikes") and the damage inflicted on the Flying Sub. Sadly, such detailed attention to minutia does not extend to the main body of the plot, which sports a huge discrepancy—despite at least a dozen witnesses to Krueger's departing speech and ghostly departure at the close of "The Phantom Strikes," this story commences with only Nelson being aware of Krueger's true nature. Crane and Morton are once again skeptics, even

though they and numerous crewmen saw Krueger dissolve through the nose of the sub after a revealing discourse on the nature of the modern world. The episode opens with a recap showing Krueger being riddled with bullets by the crew and buried at sea, but then completely overlooks the closing scene in which all was revealed. A lengthy sequence in which Nelson tries urgently to convince Morton that Krueger is of supernatural origin is consequently quite ridiculous. Either Welch forgot how his own story ended, or brazenly ignored it and dismissed that final scene. Amusingly, published interviews with others on Allen's staff reveal that writer Welch actually believed in all this hokum about ghosts and reincarnation, which accounts for the prolific number of ghost stories on the series which—alongside the "Phantom" stories—included "The Haunted Submarine," "Cave of the Dead," and "The Return of Blackbeard."

No doubt both Basehart and Hedison enjoyed this rare opportunity to stretch their acting abilities (Hedison declared it his favorite episode), with a straitjacketed Basehart getting to go crazy when the ghostly Lani appears, and Hedison playing a man possessed, complete with Krueger's corny accent. Director Sutton Roley creates some imaginative ghostly illusions with Krueger and Lani, notably when Lani appears in sick bay, and when she is in Nelson's cabin for the second time, and particularly when Krueger enters Crane's body in sick bay in classic tried-and-true "look behind you!" fashion. The scenes in the island cemetery lack Roley's usual flair, although Hedison and Marcus are good, but there's another good shot when Krueger leaves Crane's body; Crane, in close-up, slumps to the ground, revealing a red-hued Krueger behind him. The only let-down is a clumsy shot of Krueger disappearing in the Flying Sub—instead of fading away, he blinks out in traditional Irwin Allen fashion with an electronic pop, and the cut is clumsy. Otherwise, it's a model lesson of how to do an effective ghost story with limited television resources, and a good end to a thoroughly enjoyable and diverse second season. Although there were still many excellent episodes to come, neither the series—or the scripts—would be this good again, and overall, *Voyage to the Bottom of the Sea* is seen to its best advantage during the second season; the third and fourth would bring budget cuts and script problems, but there was still much more fun to come. Production no: 8227.

THIRD SEASON (1966–1967)

Monster from the Inferno

wr. Rik Vollaerts, dir. Harry Harris

A powerful, disembodied living brain attempts to take the Seaview as a 'body,' and makes Crane its zombie slave.

With Arthur Hill (Lindsay), Dick Tufeld (brain voice).

The fourth of six episodes by Rik Vollaerts, this is a curious choice as a new season opener, more like an end-of-season throwaway than an incitement to watch some of the splendid episodes to follow. The monster of the title is the blustering brain itself, which does nothing but sit in a tank glowing and spouting Marvel Comic supervillain dialogue. There's no inferno. In fact, we're offered no explanation as to where the brain might have come from and why, although Nelson speculates that it's from outer space, a conclusion the brain verifies in one of many empty threat diatribes near the close of the episode. Embracing many recurring clichés of *Voyage*, including the lurching sub, atomic threat, troublesome visiting scientist, and bodysnatched crew, it's all very reminiscent of the second season's "Monster from Outer Space," which was marginally more entertaining in its sheer awfulness, although this one has vastly superior visuals.

Still—who could hate a disembodied

brain movie? Disembodied brains have been a staple of the movies since Baron Frankenstein first planted a used one in his monster, and among the more notorious have been *Donovan's Brain*, *The Brain from Planet Arous*, and *The Space Children*. Arthur Hill, whose career during the '70s seemed to consist of being cast as the surprise bad guy in numerous films and TV productions (each surprise thus being less surprising), has a nothing role as guest scientist Lindsay, but center stage is taken by the brain, a static adversary voiced by Dick Tufeld, very recognizable here as the voice of the *Lost in Space* Robot, who probably has more dialogue than anybody else in this episode but doesn't rate a credit. The presence of Tufeld, and a back-handed compliment in the form of a jokey nostalgic reference during a scene in a 1989 episode of *Baywatch* (talk about throwing stones in glass houses!), are this episode's only claims to notoriety. Production no: 9201.

Werewolf

wr. Donn Mullalley, dir. Justus Addiss

While exploring a radioactive volcanic island, a scientist is bitten by a wolf that has been exposed to radiation and contracts a contagious virus that transforms him periodically into a werewolf.

With Charles Aidman (Dr. Hollis), Douglas Banks (Witt).

The first of three episodes by Mullalley, and also the first of three werewolf yarns (the others are by story editor William Welch). "Werewolf" is an entertaining monster mash with a very basic plot, but plenty going on to keep things humming. Some carefully credulous dialogue ("If I'm going to turn into a tortured creature like Hollis I want to know why" says Nelson; "I'm sorry, Admiral" says the doctor, "but I don't know how to cure a werewolf! Incantations and witches' broths were never my strong subject!") help to surmount the presence of the Teenage Werewolf-style creature bounding around the *Seaview*, and creates just the right balance between B-movie cynicism and poker-faced wolf-hunting. As the unfortunate scientist whose carelessness initially exposes him to the virus, Charles Aidman, who narrated the 1980s *Twilight Zone,* and also appeared in the original *Twilight Zone* series in the legendary but overrated "Little Girl Lost," brings integrity to a difficult and thankless role. He also appears in "The Pit," an episode of *The Invaders* which has a great opening scene as Aidman's college professor hallucinates saucers on campus. Bit player Douglas Banks is offed in the teaser; he lasts a little longer in two *Land of the Giants* episodes, "The Golden Cage" and "Sabotage."

Highlights include Aidman silently undergoing the transformation into werewolf as his cell door is opened, with Nelson and the doctor so engrossed in their discussion that they haven't noticed, and the teaser, with fellow boffin Banks frozen in fear with an expression of panic and resignation combined at the sight of the wolf poised to strike. The only low points in this episode are two rather forced bits of business between Sharkey and Patterson, hopelessly unfunny banter which appear to be padding. Curiously, Kowalski does not appear in this episode. Trivia freaks will recognize two of the series' most frequently seen un-named crewmen bit players in the background of the corridor scene when the werewolf is first discovered.

Of the other two werewolf stories in *Voyage,* the second, "The Brand of the Beast," is a sequel to this story, with Nelson's previously allayed fears of infection proving correct after all. In the unrelated "Man-Beast," it's Crane who becomes the creature. Mullalley's other *Voyage* episodes were "The Plant Men" and "Destroy *Seaview*"; one of his earliest writing credits was the highly regarded 1933 feature *Mystery of the Wax Museum,* a co-written adaptation of a stage play. He also wrote for *Kolchak: the Night Stalker.*

This was Justus Addiss' third *Voyage* assignment; he had previously directed two second season stories, "Graveyard of Fear" and "The Monster's Web," and would become a regular *Voyage* director for the third and fourth seasons. Addiss was not a very good director, frequently throwing away opportunities for the moment, and it is tempting, if perhaps a little unfair, to assume that the more impressive moments in this episode are down to the talents of the performers rather than anything Addiss brought to the table. Production no: 9202.

The Day the World Ended

wr. William Welch, dir. Jerry Hopper

As all the lights showing the locations of the world's nuclear submarines blink out, the Seaview personnel come to the uncomfortable conclusion that they may be the last people on Earth ... a supposition backed up when the sub surfaces and they wander the deserted streets of New York.

With Skip Homeier (Senator Dennis).

In fact, the VIP politician being given the grand tour is a master hypnotist with the entire crew under his spell, an intriguing absurdity given credence by the man's success at getting himself elected a Senator. This is an entertaining episode, reminiscent of the first season's nuclear Armageddon yarns "Hot Line" and "Doomsday," giving equal time to all the regulars and offering a good long look at the outside of 20th Century Fox's Century City Plaza doubling as the deserted New York. This courtyard was often used in 20th Century Fox productions, particularly the *Batman* series, and most prominently during the 1966 *Batman* feature film the same year this episode was filmed, in the sequence near the end when Batman and Robin land the Batcopter on a pile of mattresses. We then see Nelson and Sharkey turn the corner where they enter what appears to be a movie theater. The outside of this building was also frequently used in the *Batman* series, notably the opening scenes of "The Penguin Goes Straight," when the fowl fellow runs for office, and in the second half of the Archer tale. The blob creature footage employed when Kowalski and Crane hallucinate has been lifted from "The Monster from Outer Space."

Skip Homeier previously appeared in "The Amphibians" during the first season. He would return to play an alien in the fourth season episode "Attack." Production no: 9205.

Night of Terror

wr. Robert Bloomfield, dir. Justus Addiss
Nelson, Sharkey, and a geologist are swept away to a volcanic island, where a strange mist gives them hallucinatory visions.
With Henry Jones (Dr. Sprague), Jerry Catron (pirate).

Plot elements from the two previous episodes come together in this story, with another volcanic island, and more hallucinations. Here, a strange mist causes the cast to undergo nightmarish visions, including the inevitable giant lizards, a popular Irwin Allen potboiler plot that also turns up in *Lost in Space* ("Flight into the Future") and *Land of the Giants* ("Nightmare" and "Graveyard of Fools"). We also see spore-spraying plants *ala The Outer Limits* ("Specimen: Unknown") and *Star Trek* ("This Side of Paradise") which will also show up in the later *Voyage* "Savage Jungle." The notion of seeing things that may or may not be real also echoes the theme of the second season episode "Leviathan." Finally, the old quicksand pit is a favorite jeopardy element of the Irwin Allen series, and turns up in all his series on numerous occasions.

Despite all these standard Irwin Allen elements, this was apparently writer Bloomfield's only contribution to the series (and indeed the entire Allen canon). So dependent on stock footage, existing props and costumes, and standing sets is this episode that it's a surprise that it wasn't written by Welch, or that the writer didn't do more work for Welch. This is paint-by-numbers

Irwin Allen. The island, jungle and quicksand pit sets were regularly seen on the Allen series (the lizard, jungle, *and* quicksand all show up in "Chase Through Time" in *The Time Tunnel*, and "Graveyard of Fools" for *Land of the Giants*), and the spiky tree-colored creature was a dressed up monster suit that appeared several times in *Lost in Space* with various trimmings (including "The Prisoners of Space" and "Hunter's Moon") and *Voyage* (including "The Menfish" and "The Thing from Inner Space"). The laser rifle is a prop from *Lost in Space*. However, one novel difference here is that most, if not all of the lizard footage is not swiped from *The Lost World*, as was the usual practice, but filmed especially for this episode—the script initially specified a giant alligator, scrubbed for safety reasons (probably a good idea, as an episode of British SF puppet show *Thunderbirds* involving giant alligators did indeed run into difficulties!).

The episode works quite well, except for a ludicrous finale, when Nelson decides for no immediately apparent reason that the lizard has to be destroyed. The *Seaview* fires a Polaris missile that's big enough to have taken out the entire island and swamped Crane's tiny little rescue dinghy, and Nelson survives staying on the island simply by doing the human equivalent of scurrying down a rabbit hole! To top it off, the tidal wave takes out the island anyway!

Henry Jones later appeared in two further episodes in the fourth season, as a new character, the time traveling Mr. Pem. He also appeared in *Lost in Space* as Smith's Cousin Jeremiah in "The Curse of Cousin Smith" and in the "Werewolf" episode of *Kolchak: the Night Stalker*, and was a series regular on the MTM sit-com *Phyllis*. Jerry Catron became a victim of "The Fossil Men" during the third season and the slimy rubber bodysnatching bats of *Star Trek's* homage to *It Conquered the World*, "Operation: Annihilate."

The first season of *Voyage to the Bottom*

of the Sea was set in the year 1973, then nine years into the future, a statement made several times during the season. By the third season, writers were randomly, and pointlessly, attaching future dates ranging between 1978 (this one) and 1982. This episode, production number 9204, is introduced as 1978, then twelve years into the future, while "The Day the World Ended," no. 9205, but shown previously, is introduced as 1980. Although dates were neither necessary or desirable, this peculiar occasional affectation continues for the rest of the third and fourth seasons, even though most episodes aren't given a time period at all! Production no: 9204.

The Terrible Toys

wr. Robert Vincent Wright, dir. Justus Addiss

The Seaview is attacked by a flying saucer after retrieving a mysterious man from the sea. In the old man's possession are six innocent-looking toys, quickly revealed to be devices operated by the aliens.

With Paul Fix (Sam Burke), Francis X. Bushman (elderly alien spokesman).

Robert Vincent Wright boarded the *Seaview* at the start of the second season; this was his third of four contributions. Despite the rather silly premise (sinister, dangerous toys were a recurring cliché in 1960s fantasy series), this is not such a terrible episode, even though it sounds absurd ... and is. Paul Fix, a veteran bit player, mostly in westerns, appeared in *The Time Tunnel* ("The End of the World") at around this time.

Fans will recognize certain strains of background music from both *Lost in Space* and *The Time Tunnel*, while *Voyage* followers will easily spot the blatant use of underwater footage from "The Monster's Web," possibly inserted to bring the episode up to time (rather ironic, as two of Wright's previous episodes, "And Five of Us Are Left" and "Graveyard of Fear," are too packed with material for justice to be done to all the ideas). As the elderly occupant of the saucer, former silent movie actor Francis X. Bushman looks like he brought his wardrobe from *The Story of Mankind* with him. A suitably weird ambience is evoked by his presence, but it would have been nice if this peculiar imagery had been imaginatively explained; the old man is clearly in the thrall of the aliens—was he another abductee?

Obviously pleased to be working, at around the same time as this episode, Bushman had also played minor roles in the AIP quickie *The Ghost in the Invisible Bikini* and a *Batman* ("Death in Slow Motion/The Riddler's False Notion"). Bizarrely, Irwin Allen has cited this routine, nondescript and somewhat ludicrous episode—alongside "Jonah and the Whale"—as being his favorite *Voyage* ... but he was enamored with old movie stars, and Bushman died shortly after filming this episode, so it seems highly likely that sentimentality accounts for this ridiculous choice. The toys were storebought and customized, and difficult enough to be filmed in a threatening manner without the added handicap of being assigned to unimaginative Justus Addiss. Production no: 9206.

Day of Evil

wr. William Welch, dir. Jerry Hopper

Aliens send a duplicate of Admiral Nelson on board the Seaview to launch a nuclear missile attack that will trigger a holocaust to destroy the Earth.

Another hostile flying saucer, with a storyline recalling the first season's "The Sky Is Falling." The door was left open for a follow-up that never materialized; note how that ol' budget-cruncher Welch saved on guest stars by having the regulars do doubletime as the bad guys. This ploy would become over-used to the point of absurdity during the last two seasons, despite the fact that the network were clearly unimpressed, and held the episode back a few weeks. Watch Nelson's escape from Sharkey on the way to the brig, and you'll see a stunt-man substitute for Sharkey when Crane uses a judo flip. Production no: 9203.

Deadly Waters

wr. Robert Vincent Wright, dir. Gerald Mayer

While investigating a sunken atomic sub, the Seaview *is stranded at the bottom of the ocean as disaster piles upon disaster.*

With Don Gordon (Stan Kowalski), Lew Gallo (Kruger), Harry Lauter (Commander Finch).

Don Gordon, often seen on TV as a stressed out misfit or hood, appeared in "The Four of Us are Dying" and "The Self-Improvement of Salavatore Ross" for *The Twilight Zone,* tour-de-force "The Invisibles" for *The Outer Limits,* and "The Trial" for *The Invaders;* fans of *Voyage* have always been slightly bemused that while Kowalski's brother has a first name in this episode, the Kowalski who appeared throughout the series' four year run was never given one! Robert Vincent Wright's fourth and final script for the series—his others were "And Five of Us Are Left," "Graveyard of Fear" and "The Terrible Toys"—appears to have solved the problems of the first two, providing the requisite action scenes while retaining the human conflict he liked to include. While the theme of the cowardly crewman who everyone dislikes is a somewhat old-fashioned storyline (and already familiar to *Voyage* from "Submarine Sunk Here," "Doomsday," "Terror on Dinosaur Island," and others), the plot keeps moving and there is only one script point that keeps nagging—knowing that Stan Kowalski was unstable, and having made the dangerous trip across to the disabled Flying Sub, why didn't Crane simply stay there and help Nelson repair the vehicle instead of risking the journey back? The simplistic design of the suit also lets down Wright's script and introduces a laughable flaw to the finished film, which is built around the exclusivity of the diving suit's operation—in the grand tradition of Republic's Commando Cody, there are only three different colored buttons on the suit controls; how difficult could it have been to explain their function before it was used by Crane or Nelson? Production no: 9207.

The Thing from Inner Space

wr. William Welch, dir. Alex March

A phoney, status-seeking adventurer leaves his film crew to die when a savage sea-creature storms ashore on the island where they're filming. While Nelson is none too impressed by the would-be hunter's desire to return to the island for further glory-seeking, crewman Patterson's father was on the doomed first expedition and he wants revenge.

With Hugh Marlowe (Bainbridge Wells), Dawson Palmer (Creature).

Veteran creature feature leading man Hugh Marlowe (*The Day the Earth Stood Still, Earth vs. the Flying Saucers, World Without End,* etc.) appears as the wretched explorer and self-publicist Bainbridge Wells, who leaves his film crew to die at the hands of a *Black Lagoon*-style creature (*Lost in Space* monster man Dawson Palmer in a customized monster suit from "The Menfish" and "Night of Terror"). It's a pleasure to see Marlowe again, and he gives a fine performance of stiff terror and treachery recalling his weak and unsavory character in *The Day the Earth Stood Still.* Certain plot points recall "And Five of Us Are Left" and "Terror on Dinosaur Island," in that we again have a bitter crew member determined to join the second expedition for an ulterior motive ... This time, it's Patterson, meaning that both Kowalski and Patterson as series regulars have been given a little backstory and center stage action back to back. A hugely enjoyable episode. Production no: 9208.

The Death Watch

wr. William Welch, dir. Leonard Horn

Nelson and Crane find themselves aboard a deserted Seaview, *where they are to be participants in a bizarre experiment whereby they are given subliminal commands to try and kill each other.*

Terry Becker gives one of his best performances in the series in what was otherwise one of the most tedious and dreary episodes made. Similar to the equally monotorious first season episode "The Human Computer," which had Crane stalked on board a deserted *Seaview* by a mystery man, this episode features only Nelson, Crane and Sharkey with a disembodied control voice (which sounds very much like Sue England, who voiced the evil robot in "Deadliest of the Species" for *Lost in Space*). Written by Welch, and using only standing sets and no guest stars or supporting players, this must have been simplicity itself to direct and has all the hallmarks of a making-up-time job; it could have easily been completed in just two or three days, but curiously Leonard Horn was not a director known for his haste. There's an excellently filmed and staged fight sequence at the climax and a nice tag, but otherwise this is a major snoozerama from start to finish. Production no: 9210.

Deadly Invasion

wr. John and Ward Hawkins, dir. Nathan Juran
Tiny capsules taken on board the Seaview *are discovered to be miniature spaceships, containing alien beings who can plunder minds and take the form of the familiar images they discover.*

With Warren Stevens (alien leader), Brent Davis (crewman).

More hostile alien invaders, as another shape-shifting, form-changing alien being this time takes on the appearance of one of Nelson's old colleagues. This was the second of three *Voyage* appearances for Richard Basehart's former roomie Warren Stevens; the others were "The Saboteur" in the first season and "Cave of the Dead" in the fourth season. A veteran of SF TV, other roles in the '60s included *The Twilight Zone*, *The Outer Limits*, *The Time Tunnel*, *The Man from UNCLE*, *Star Trek*, and *Land of the Giants*. In 1978, he appeared as a supporting player in Allen's short-lived *Return of Captain Nemo* project, guest-starred in *Wonder Woman*, and in the 1980s was one of a number of old-timers who appeared in a salute-to-the-'60s *Twilight Zone*, "A Day in Beaumont."

Also working under the names Jerry Juran and Nathan Hertz, director Nathan Juran started out as an art director on such films as *Doctor Renault's Secret* (1942), and rapidly became a master of most adventure genres, including historical, fantasy, and sci-fi for film and TV, working for William Alland and Irwin Allen, and with Ray Harryhausen, but he never escaped the B's. Juran couldn't fix a script if his life depended on it, and some of the greatest lapses in logic, even for an Irwin Allen show, had his name on the front, but he could stage the action masterfully. He also couldn't control or guide his actors (Jonathan Harris gave some of his very best and very worst performances in Juran's *Lost in Space* episodes), but his casting choices were immaculate, and some of television's very best character actors turn up in Juran's work. Consequently, he didn't have to coax a performance out of them, just stand aside and let them get on with it. Juran worked on all Allen's shows, overseeing two dozen episodes altogether, at least half of which are among the most memorable, as well as three or four total turkeys. None of the gems or the stiffs were *Voyage* episodes, although this is his least impressive of the three he handled. When the scriptwriters had done their job properly (it was not his responsibility, after all, to story-edit) and the actors were on the money, Juran could make gold ... but he couldn't make gold out of tin. Production no.: 9209.

The Haunted Submarine

wr. William Welch, dir. Harry Harris
When the Seaview *encounters a centuries-old square-rigger sailing on the surface, strange events start to occur as ghostly moaning and laughter is heard in the corridors and Nelson finds his crew frozen in time.*

A dual role for star Richard Basehart as he plays the ghost of Admiral Nelson's wicked slave-trading ancestor, who is doomed to a Flying Dutchman type of existence for his crimes. This is essentially a rehash of the tiresome Phantom episodes "The Phantom Strikes" and "Return of the

Phantom," even to the extent of being written by that ol' ghost-buster himself, William Welch. Basehart gives a fine performance as both characters, and the crew are uniformly excellent when frozen in time—not a blink among them, although Terry Becker wobbles a bit in the corridor scene ... as well he might! Once again, as in "The Phantom Strikes," for no immediately apparent reason, Nelson keeps the presence of the ghost a secret from the rest of the crew—even though their experiences with the Phantom (not to mention the numerous reports of moaning and laughter in the corridors from the crew) would have been quite enough to prevent them from disbelieving him. At one point early in the episode, Crane suggests these reports of inexplicable superstitious activity might simply be the result of the crew requiring some long overdue shore leave—Nelson certainly seems to need it, given his behavior in this one, giggling like a silly child when faced with a foam-covered Sharkey (assaulted in poltergeist fashion by a fire extinguisher), and refusing to confide in Crane even after the Captain has realized all is not right. The usual massive holes in logic are in Welch's script—the ghostly Nelson immediately departs when discovered, even though seconds earlier he claimed to be able to destroy the sub, and despite all the weird occurrences and attacks, Nelson still goes all coy when Crane not unnaturally asks for an explanation. The episode's illogical plotting is quite irritating, with only Richard Basehart's performance to keep it interesting. Poor David Hedison struggles with an impossibly idiotic role, and gives his best performance while frozen.

Basehart apparently relished doing this episode as it gave him something different to do, but actors' favorite episodes are invariably selected not by overall quality but by how central the performer was to proceedings and how much the personal benefit from the script. This is certainly true for "The Haunted Submarine," and given Base-

hart's known dissatisfaction with his lot on the show, it is surprising other treats were not served up to keep him sweet. He was certainly capable of delivering. Production no.: 9215.

The Plant Man
wr. Donn Mullalley, dir. Harry Harris
   A scientist is controlled telepathically by his evil twin, who has plans to create an army of plant monsters.
   With William Smithers (Ben Wilson/John Wilson).

Another dual role, this time for guest star William Smithers, who plays both twin brothers. Smithers was also the renegade starship captain who created a new Nazi Germany on an impressionable planet in the *Star Trek* episode "Patterns of Force," and the cowering, treacherous witness to the actions of *The Invaders* in the memorable "The Innocent." In the 1970s, he showed up in *The Six Million Dollar Man* and *The Amazing Spider-Man*. Once again though, it is Richard Basehart's three-dimensional performance that provides this episode with its momentum, particularly in the Flying Sub sequences ... although the giant version of the plant monster gives the Flying Sub such a whack that Nelson and Wilson couldn't possibly have really survived! The other cast members have little to do in this episode except throw themselves back and forth as the submarine lurches, although Voice of Doom Chip Morton gets to deliver another of his timeless lines as he describes the situation on board the sub to Nelson. As in "Leviathan" and "The Menfish," a large-size version of the enemy menaces the sub from the outside, while the regular-size create mayhem on the inside. The smaller versions of the plant creatures that run amok on board the sub are never terribly convincing as a menace, not least because we don't see enough of the duplicating process that makes them a threat, although the scenes in which they emerge from the reactor room from within the foliage are quite striking in a '50s/'60s special effects kind of way. The plant creatures would later show up in the third season *Lost in Space* episode "The Flaming Planet," but it's kind of doubtful whether Ben Wilson intended his army of plant men to be decked out in tin hats and battle kit...!

Mullalley's other *Voyage* episodes were the okay "Werewolf" and the dismal "Destroy Seaview." Production no.: 9212.

The Lost Bomb

wr. Oliver Crawford, dir. Gerald Mayer

Nelson's efforts to defuse a super-bomb are hindered by an enemy submarine and a double agent.

With John Lupton (Dr. Bradley), Gerald Mohr (Mr. Vadim), George Keymas (Commander Zane).

A moderately entertaining time-killer, but certainly nothing special; the villain is revealed very early in the story, and there's little suspense to be had from a bomb which will destroy the *Seaview* and "half the world" since we know it won't. Once again, we get a glimpse of the series' cavalier use of nuclear weaponry despite constant near-catastrophe, and Nelson's hawkish favoring of the atomic deterrent. It is, of course, quite absurd that this super-bomb should have been undersea in the first place, as when the *Vulcan* submarine blows up the cargo plane originally carrying the bomb, the explosion would have detonated the device anyway—otherwise, why all the fuss about firing on the *Seaview?*

Gerald Mohr, here quite obviously reading his lines off cue cards, was Morbus in the *Lost in Space* episode "A Visit to Hades" and the voice of Reed Richards in the 1960s *Fantastic Four* cartoons from Hanna-Barbera. John Lupton gave a superior performance in "The Alamo" for *The Time Tunnel*; his SF/fantasy credits also include *Jesse James Meets Frankenstein's Daughter.* George Keymas had previously appeared in the first season episode "The Buccaneer."

Oliver Crawford wrote "The Galileo Seven" for *Star Trek* and "The Clones" for *Land of the Giants,* two memorable editions of those series, but this decidedly unmemorable episode was his only contribution to *Voyage to the Bottom of the Sea.* Gerald Mayer had previously directed "Deadly Waters" and "The Sky's on Fire" and would return for "The Heat Monster." "Task Force" for *The Invaders* is his only other SF TV credit. The Cessium bomb is a familiar prop later redressed as the device aliens use to intimidate the staff of *The Time Tunnel* in "Raiders from Outer Space" this same season and used as a deadly laser gun when placed on its side and made mobile inside the Robot in *Lost in Space's* "Trip Through the Robot." The *Vulcan* sub, and much of this episode's premise, would later reappear in the episode "Rescue." Production no.: 9211.

The Brand of the Beast

wr. William Welch, dir. Justus Addiss

The werewolf virus Nelson contracted in the earlier episode is triggered by exposure to radiation during a crucial attempt to stop Seaview's power source exploding the sub. Now Nelson prowls the Seaview ... and there's still no cure for the affliction.

This sequel to Donn Mullalley's "Werewolf" is a much more simple and less impressive affair than its predecessor, with all the careless illogicality that we have come to expect from William Welch's contributions to the series. Suspension of disbelief requires the protagonists to behave as they might be expected to. In this story, there is absolutely no reason for Nelson to endanger the ship and crew by keeping his affliction a secret—his excuse at the end of the episode that Crane had enough to worry about is absurd as the creature's behavior has been endangering a rescue mission at every turn. He lies to the doctor, lies to Crane, puts Sharkey in an impossible position, wrecks the Flying Sub, steals the diving bell and rampages through the circuitry room! If the werewolf had been a guest star crewman, they might have got away with that rationale, but from the Admiral it's just plain daft, and a replay of exactly the same flaws to be found in Welch's "The Phantom Strikes" and "The Haunted Submarine." Why won't Nelson take his trusted colleagues into his confidence? Like many of Welch's scripts for *Voyage* and *Land of the Giants*, this is simply a forty-nine minute runaround for existing sets, quickly and conveniently wrapped up when the close of the fourth act approaches (even the ship in peril is forgotten), and the first of a style of creature features in the latter half of the series which simply involved the crew chasing a growling bogey-man around the sub's corridors ("The Mummy," "Fatal Cargo," "The Abominable Snowman," "Man-Beast," etc.). The novelty here is that the creature is Admiral Nelson, with Basehart giving a far better performance than the episode deserves, although it's certainly not Basehart under the monster mask.

This episode is one of director Addiss' better efforts, with one stand-out moment when Crane pursues the werewolf saboteur from the Flying Sub and grabs his leg on the stairs, looking up to be greeted by a snarling wolfman's countenance. Elsewhere it's paint-by-numbers, with all the usual trademark scenes and stock footage. Nitpickers may ask why Crane takes a radio message from Sparks in the control room when his little alcove is right there.... Production no.: 9213.

The Creature

wr. John and Ward Hawkins, dir. Justus Addiss
  The Flying Sub is utilized to destroy a giant sea creature which is gradually taking over the crew of the Seaview.
  With Lyle Bettger (Dr. King).

This was the second of two episodes with this title, the first being from the B&W season, and although it's another giant plant monster, it bears a closer resemblance to Woodfield and Balter's corny "Monster from Outer Space" and Rik Vollaerts' third season opener "Monster from the Inferno,"

as members of the crew—beginning with Crane—gradually become as one with the creature. Apart from the monster, which is wonderful (and returns in "The Astral Traveler" for *Lost in Space* a few months later), the episode has little about it that's special, although we see some good effects work with the creature and the Flying Sub, and one nice shot when the crew under the control of the creature are in the brig and attempt *en masse* to hypnotize Kowalski as the camera intimidatingly pans along the bars on their faces. There's no reds-under-the-bed subtext this time, as there was with Woodfield and Balter's effort; "The Creature" is simply a perfect example of the potboilers that *Voyage* turned out each week during the third season—bubbling along just enough to keep you watching, but evaporating into nothing at the end! Lyle Bettger also appears in "Invasion" for *The Time Tunnel*. Production no.: 9214.

Death from the Past

wr. Sidney Marshall, dir. Justus Addiss
  Two Nazi officers are woken from suspended animation and promptly resume WWII.
  With John Van Dreelen (Von Neuberg), Jan Merlin (Froelich).

This was a second *Voyage* appearance for John Van Dreelen and a third for Jan Merlin. Leith Stevens' style of background music from *Land of the Giants* is recognizable in some scenes, and it's rather offputting here to be watching *Voyage* but hearing *Giants!* Like Marshall's previous solo script for *Voyage*, "Dead Men's Doubloons," this yarn begins with an incident in the past and then moves into the series' present day. Despite being the show's story editor for three seasons, Marshall didn't exactly wear out his own typewriter keys, and contributed only two more (awful) scripts to the series, "Nightmare" and "The Death Clock," his lack of inspiration a small mercy, given the abysmal quality of his efforts. Fans of the absurd will be heartened by the wobbling cardboard Nazi rockets, which wouldn't have been out of place in an amateur dramatics production. It's just as well they fizzle out like cheap fireworks ... Production no.: 9216.

The Heat Monster

wr. Charles Bennett, dir. Gerald Mayer

A research scientist wants to help a fiery alien that has turned up at his Arctic research station, but the alien, a mobile sentient jet of flame, is an evil menace.

With Alfred Ryder (Dr. Bergstrom), Don Knight (Sven).

This episode is essentially a rewrite of the 1951 feature *The Thing from Another World* with elements of the *Outer Limits* stories "The Bellero Shield" (the heat monster arrives via exploratory spaceward laser beam), "The Galaxy Being" (scientist attempts benevolent contact with extraterrestrial) and "Behold Eck" (Bergstrom suggests that the alien destroyed the base by accident and meant no harm). It is improbable that Bennett was drawing from these episodes; rather, he was more likely just following pulp sci-fi convention. Some background music is familiar from *The Time Tunnel* and *The Day the Earth Stood Still* and the arctic footage is lifted from the *Voyage to the Bottom of the Sea* feature film, which writer Charles Bennett also scripted. The only thing sillier than guest star Alfred Ryder's Nordic accent is Britisher Don Knight's Nordic accent and a monster that is simply a jet of flame dollied around the set. Oddly enough, most hostile alien creatures on U.S. TV tend to speak with the voices of TV news anchormen, and this one's no exception. Ryder's scientist, sole survivor of an Arctic outpost contacted by the alien force, insists that Nelson and Crane should not attempt to destroy the creature, but as usual the hawkish Nelson rather hastily disagrees, and is naturally backed up by developments in the script. As the alien is quickly revealed to be as hostile as assumed (casually setting Nelson alight is a clue), the message appears to be a rather paranoid one completely at odds with sci-fi like *The Outer Limits*, which usually shows the aliens as innocents and the scientists who protect them as heroes. Here, Bergstrom is portrayed as a naive cowardly crazy man, with destroyers Nelson and Crane the common-sense heroes. There is always the possibility that Bennett intends to portray the *Seaview* regulars as intellectually unprepared for the arrival of alien visitors (Bergstrom's defense is quite rational), but frankly it doesn't seem likely; *Voyage* wasn't known for complex and ambiguous concepts, and Bennett was a bored and careless writer. More likely, the story just follows popular Hollywood tradition. Fortunately, the episode is good fun, and a fast pace keeps the tension mounting as the crew are cooked by the evil alien.

Ryder was previously the phantom sea-captain in the two earlier episodes "The Phantom Strikes" and "Return of the Phantom." His other numerous SF TV credits include a phoney psychic in "The Borderland" for *The Outer Limits*, another deranged scientist in "The Man Trap" for *Star Trek*, one of *The Invaders* in "Vikor" and "The Ransom," and the bitter master of the orphanage in "The Night of Thrombeldinbar" in *Land of the Giants*, fine episodes all. Don Knight also appears in the pilot episodes of *The Time Tunnel*, *Fantastic Journey*, and *Manimal*, and enjoyed a regular co-starring role as a villain in the short-lived early '70s series *The Immortal*. Other credits include *Bewitched*, *Night Gallery* and *Circle of Fear*, and an episode of time-travel show *Voyagers*. Production no.: 9217.

The Fossil Men

wr. James Whiton, dir. Justus Addiss

Former mariners who became transformed by strange properties into rock-like creatures in an undersea grotto add to their number by throwing luckless visitors into a fiery pit, and now intend to increase their number with the Seaview crew.

With Brendan Dillon (Captain Jacob Wren), Jerry Catron (Richards).

One of the most memorable episodes, "The Fossil Men" has a *Seaview* shore party ambushed by tragic rock-men that lumber out of the cliff-face (not out of a cave—out of the cliff-face!) on another of those mysterious islands so beloved of this series. One stand-out sequence has Sharkey discover and fire an ancient flintlock, thus hitting the cliff-face and bringing out the Fossil Men, with the apologetic words "I didn't know it was loaded!" Says Nelson wearily, "That is the saddest phrase...!" Another highlight is the revealing of crewman Richards' transformation, and the creatures rampaging through the *Seaview* with little use for doors. Having seen one of the creatures rip through the wall into the corridor as if it were, er, cardboard, it seems a little optimistic—and a waste of a good door—to lock a captured Fossil Man in one of the storerooms! The major flaw of the episode though is the newsanchor-style voice of Jacob Wren, the creatures' leader; Brendan Dillon gave a superb performance as Colonel Fettrech in "The Night of the Long Knives" for *The Time Tunnel*, and with his voice now dubbed, nothing of his performance remains, obscured as he was by the monster suit. This change may have been made in desperation by Allen, who was enraged to find Basehart and Becker mocking the script by allegedly changing the dialogue, and even more enraged when it was pointed out to him that they had read the dialogue as written. The background music in the grotto scene is from *The Day the Earth Stood Still*, and much used by Allen. The grotto itself is the island set, the molten lava familiar stock. All shots of the *Seaview* in this episode were taken from previous stories; the Fossil Men were later seen in the *Lost in Space* episodes "Cave of the Wizards," made that same year, and "Flight into the Future" the following year. Jerry Catron was the grinning pirate in "Night of Terror."

Sadly, on the strength of this episode at least, which is in fact a rather good yarn

undermined by the last minute interference, this was James Whiton's only contribution to *Voyage to the Bottom of the Sea*. Events during filming undoubtedly made sure of that. He did, however, contribute "The Napoleon's Tomb Affair" to *The Man from UNCLE*, the only other fantasy TV credit found for him. Production no.: 9218.

The Mermaid

wr. William Welch, dir. Jerry Hopper

The crew suspect Crane of being overdue for some extended shore leave when he claims to have seen a mermaid swimming around.

With Diane Webber (the mermaid), Roy Jenson (crewman).

Like Doctor Smith's space-siren in the *Lost in Space* episode "Wild Adventure," Crane's mermaid disappears every time he calls a witness. Happily, unlike "Wild Adventure," not much time is wasted on the old you-must-believe-me routine, and the episode splits up into two equally enjoyable halves (or quarters, by the time you've accounted for the length of footage lifted from elsewhere), as Crane, having finally found and captured his mermaid, attempts to persuade her to help locate a deadly bomb primed to go off, and her hostile amphibian protector is running amok on the sub.... Unfortunately, the menfolk of her race are somewhat less attractive, being scaly, savage, and decidedly jealous. Fans of *The Time Tunnel* will recognize some familiar background music during these scenes.

The bomb disposal sequence in this story has been lifted wholesale from the second season episode "The Peacemaker," with new dialogue dubbed over the footage, while the scaly creature is *Voyage's* regulation monster suit ("The Menfish," "Night of Terror," "The Thing from Inner Space," and *Lost in Space* episode "A Change of Space"), with some footage lifted from "The Menfish"; particularly familiar is the scene in which the creature escapes from the sub by attacking a curious crewman played by stunt-man

Roy Jenson. The mermaid footage is lifted as well, which is why Crane declines to wear his usual wetsuit in this episode; he had to match up with the source material. *Playboy* model Diane Webber had played a mermaid before, in an obscure 1962 feature, *The Mermaids of Tiburon*, which had been directed by John Lamb, now working as the *Voyage* series' underwater photographer, and which—believe it or leave it—was later re-released with additional footage as the soft-porn film *Aquasex!* Production no.: 9219.

The Mummy
wr. William Welch, dir. Harry Harris

A 3,000 year old mummy sabotages all attempts to take it back to its place of origin, taking control of Crane and sending the Seaview *to the bottom as it runs amok around the sub.*

Good fun. Ever since Karloff first presided over the rebirth of Egyptian dead in the 1933 *The Mummy* and provoked four direct sequels and a horde of imitators, these bandaged reanimated corpses have been a staple of pulp fantasy. Here, this classic movie monster shambles around the *Seaview* corridors displaying dubious mystical powers to the strains of library music from *The Day the Earth Stood Still* and various pieces used frequently in *The Time Tunnel*. A shot of Chief Sharkey looking horrified as the mummy advances towards him is used again, printed in reverse, when the mummy is destroyed. Production no.: 9220.

The Shadowman
wr. Rik Vollaerts, dir. Justus Addiss

A shadowy alien being takes possession of Commander Morton to prevent the Seaview *assisting in the launch of a space probe.*

David Hedison proves the existence of "The Mermaid" (Diane Webber).

One of those episodes everybody remembers (including the makers of the 1980s *Twilight Zone* series, who swiped the concept almost identically for their own episode titled "The Shadow Man"). Here, the shadowman is an alien life-form, flitting around the *Seaview* in an attempt to sabotage the space race. The result is a cheaply created but superbly menacing adversary, part actual shadow, part bit player clad in black. Very effective, and very cost-effective. Production no.: 9221.

No Escape from Death
wr. William Welch, dir. Harry Harris

While investigating the appearance of an unidentified Sealab, the Seaview *is rammed by an enemy submarine and sent to the bottom.*

If anything can be said in defense of the inordinate amount of shamelessly rehashed stock footage used in this episode for all the major set pieces, it is that Irwin Allen was at least imaginative in his execution of cheater clip shows. Most series would simply have created an excuse for the cast to sit around and reminisce about past exploits while the producers cashed in on a budget-crunching time-saver, but at least with Allen's blatant recycling there's fun to be had in admiring the way previous footage is integrated into the new. Essentially a remake of the first season textbook suspenser "Submarine Sunk Here," but with a third season creature slant, "No Escape from Death" uses cleverly tinted footage from the monochrome first season episodes, employing the much-used flooding sequence alongside Nelson's near-drowning from "Submarine Sunk Here" (Nelson has an obvious stand-in for the flood scene), crewman Clark's crawl through the air ducts from "Hail to the Chief," the giant Portuguese Man O'War from "Graveyard of Fear," and the inside-the-whale footage from the first color story "Jonah and the Whale." Paul Carr appeared in several first season episodes as Clark, and is resurrected here, after earlier being renamed Benson for the episode "Terror on Dinosaur Island" and killed off! Production no.: 9222.

Doomsday Island

wr. Peter Germano, dir. Jerry Hopper

When a gigantic egg is brought on board the Seaview, it breaks open to reveal a monstrous amphibious creature—the first of an alien army that will invade the Earth.

With Jock Gaynor (Scorpian leader).

This was without a doubt one of the most farcical episodes of the series, even by third season standards, but it is enormous fun. The monster suits were particularly below par, and although they are later reused for two classic third season *Lost in Space* episodes the following year, "The Time Mer-

chant" and "Anti-Matter Man," they were used only for alien stooges and kept in the background. The costume was not really strong enough to carry a story; although the creature faces are okay, and the eyes particularly good, the body suits are obviously sparsely decorated and spray-painted wetsuits, and the bright red color of them doesn't help credibility much. The whole thing then falls apart completely when the creature opens its mouth to speak—or rather, doesn't open its mouth to speak—and out comes this booming, sonorous news-anchor voice, just as in "Monster from the Inferno," "The Heat Monster," and "The Fossil Men." To add insult to injury, everyone is carrying around ridiculous brightly-colored plastic toytown guns that would become regular fixtures for the remainder of the season! At least the opticals are good; there are some good shots of the Flying Sub whizzing around, and if the set-pieces are familiar—the creature throwing crewmen about, the *Seaview* in a race against time to a) get off the bottom and b) fire their missiles, people appearing and disappearing and being paralyzed in time—they are at least fast-paced and well-executed. The episode doesn't have a single boring minute, but that doesn't stop the deficiencies of the story from piling up, such as how the Scorpian (their spelling—it's *not* a scorpion) thinks he's going to get his red rubber gloves on the *Seaview*'s atomic reactor if he blows the sub up first. On the other hand, any creature that can lift the inside of the Flying Sub out of its shell and embed it in a cave wall probably has a few more tricks up his sleeve. It's also not made very clear that Crane and Kowalski are apparently watching the events aboard the *Seaview* on the Scorpian scanner.

Other typical Allen trademarks beside the booming alien voices, the aliens' power to freeze our heroes, and ability to travel instantaneously include the usual cavernous hideaway, and the dangerous island; the opening scene of this episode with Nelson and Sharkey in the Flying Sub searching for the errant rock, and the notion of an island appearing and disappearing are reminiscent of "Terror on Dinosaur Island," while the alien lair resembles that of the invaders in *The Time Tunnel's* classic "Raiders from Outer Space" the same year—although in that particular episode, the aliens' equipment also included the familiar tubes and pipes of the *Seaview* missile room! Familiar library music includes a splendid piece familiar to *The Time Tunnel* as the amphibian first prowls the ship, and the inevitable strains from *The Day the Earth Stood Still* as the amphibian approaches two unsuspecting guards (although one of them is looking straight down at the advancing creature's shadow!). Peter Germano co-wrote the infamous Halley's Comet episode of *The Time Tunnel*, "The End of the World," and although this episode of *Voyage* is entirely typical of the Allen series, these were Germano's only two contributions to the Allen shows. While his *Time Tunnel* is an intelligent and literate adventure, this is a good ol' monster mash with some of the daftest dialogue ever uttered by an alien invader. David Hedison grits his teeth and glares, while Basehart adds the usual gravitas. Jock Gaynor later turns up in human form in the fourth season's "Man of Many Faces." Production no.: 9223.

The Wax Men

wr. William Welch, dir. Harmon Jones

An evil circus clown emerges from crates of wax exhibits on their way to Washington and starts substituting wax duplicates for the crewmen.

With Michael Dunn (the clown).

A legendary episode, and quite silly even by Irwin Allen standards. Michael Dunn, an actor of restricted height, was recurring villain Dr. Loveless on western spy-fantasy series *The Wild Wild West*, and the wicked Mr. Big in the *Get Smart* premiere, and was also seen in "Plato's Stepchildren"

for *Star Trek*. Here, his presence and bizarre costume livens up an otherwise standard takeover story. Making up for the typically inane William Welch dialogue is Harmon Jones' inventive direction; he's no Sutton Roley, but he keeps what could be a dull plod around the standing sets interesting and lively. Unfortunately, this was to be his only episode of *Voyage*, although he did return to direct on *Land of the Giants*. All the action takes place inside the *Seaview*, but the wax make-up is good—particularly on the bogus Nelson—and the final scenes showing the melted wax men, puddled in the crew's clothing, is effective. With a plot as absurd as this one, it seems futile to point out the holes in logic, such as how the clown replaced over a hundred crewmen, or how he knew what they looked like beforehand. As for the true cargo, the alleged Atlantean statues seem lost forever, as the clown is no condition to explain what he did with them—or indeed, how he went from clown to would-be world conqueror ... Very '60s. Production no.: 9224.

The Deadly Cloud

wr. Rik Vollaerts, dir. Jerry Hopper

As a wave of freak-of-nature disasters sweep the Earth, Crane takes the Flying Sub to investigate a mysterious cloud that has appeared over the ocean, and is absorbed by a metallic alien being, whose extraordinary powers he inherits when he returns to the Seaview as an inhuman slave.

With Robert Carson (Jurgenson), Bill Baldwin (aide).

A rather shabby episode very similar to "Day of Evil" and a dozen others, with little to commend it other than a striking alien. The last two episodes of the third season are both further variations of the crew-are-not-themselves yarns, in which various regulars are being possessed or brainwashed. There's a distinct impression that the show was stuck for scripts as the season came to an end, with Crane playing bad guy one week and Nelson the next; certainly, neither

"Deadly Cloud" or "Destroy *Seaview*" bring a single new idea to the series between them. In fact, of 26 episodes in the third season, all but ten of them involved crew members being taken over or replaced by doubles!

"Deadly Cloud" is very much a tired, end-of-the-season episode. There's no logic to events, and a noticeable absence of effects shots showing any of the key incidents; we never once see the cloud itself, for example. What we do get is lots of badly integrated shots of swaying palm trees, volcanic lava, and crumbling buildings. The dialogue is dreary and carelessly written, and uncharacteristically for an Allen show, the stock disaster footage is very clumsily glued together. The episode is further encumbered by a series of not very successful tension-is-mounting cutaways to a Washington base that rather obviously consists of two uncharismatic actors, a desk, a map, and a curtain. One scene that does work is the one just before the opening credits, when we glimpse a brief blink-and-you-miss-it shot of the alien materializing in the Flying Sub.

Otherwise, oh dear. The submarine setting has absolutely no relevance to the story whatsoever, and all the set pieces have been seen in previous episodes. The *Seaview* crewmen are still carrying around silly bright plastic ray-guns that look like they came out of a cereal packet, and there's a noticeable lack of background music in some scenes, almost as if there wasn't time to score the whole thing. David Hedison, however, gives one of his better performances and none of the other regulars let the side down either. No-one, however, expected to be coming back for a fourth season at this point. Robert Carson previously appeared in the first season episode "Hot Line," and also played a military man in a *Lucy Show* set in a submarine at around this time, titled—fairly enough—"Lucy and the Submarine." Production no.: 9225.

Destroy Seaview

wr. Donn Mullalley, dir. Justus Addiss

A mysterious disembodied voice controls a brainwashed Admiral Nelson as the Seaview goes in search of a powerful element that will create a super-weapon for the nation that possesses it.

With Arthur Space (Dr. Land), Jerry Catron (enemy diver).

A rather slapdash end to the third season, marred—like "Deadly Cloud" before it—by some mind-numbing dialogue and a poorly structured plot with a rushed, once-through-the-typewriter feel offering nothing new to the regular viewers and much that was familiar. At many points in the episode it seems that the only thing keeping certain characters alive is the fact that they have contracts to come back in the next episode, although *Voyage* was very lucky to get a fourth season after this. Sharkey is hardly fazed by a gunshot wound that looks very serious, a number of people are blithely zapped with laser beams that look fatal, and although he has orders to blow up the *Seaview*, Nelson uses only knock-out gas on Kowalski and the rest of the crew. Yet again, characters are seen running around with those little yellow cereal packet ray guns; other characters, such as the enemy divers, have *Lost in Space* laser rifles. The character of Dr. Land is a meaningless one, and the absence of any kind of visual evidence of an adversary makes the threat seem as contrived and as empty as it is. The entire episode looks like the afterthought it almost certainly was. Mullalley's other *Voyage* episodes were "Werewolf" and "The Plant Man," both far superior to this.

The anonymous Arthur Space was a veteran of '50s B-movies and matinee serials, having appeared in the serials *Canadian Mounties vs. Atomic Invaders* and *Panther Girl of the Congo*, and the features *Target Earth* and *Twenty Million Miles to Earth*. TV work included *Adventures of Superman*, *The Wild Wild West*, and 1970s superman *The Six Million Dollar Man*. Production no.: 9226.

FOURTH SEASON (1967–1968)

Fires of Death

wr. Arthur Weiss, dir. Jerry Hopper

An expert in volcanic activity supposed to be assisting the Seaview in dampening an active volcano is actually an aged alchemist determined to live forever ... even if he has to blow up the Southern Hemisphere to do it.

With Victor Jory (Dr. Turner).

Victor Jory (memorably a rampaging pirate in *The Time Tunnel's* "Pirates of Dead Man's Island") guests as an aged alchemist determined to live forever ... even if he has to blow up half the world to do it. For what became the fourth season opener (although actually the fourth episode to be put into production that season), Allen appears to have pulled out all the stops, creating an excellent cavernous volcano set and filming new special effects footage, some of which was—amazingly—not used again, and building an exterior of a portion of the Flying Sub, showing a door from which the characters emerge at the back of the craft. This construction was rarely seen, but appears again in the equally elaborate "Journey with Fear" and again in "The Death Clock." The story is non-stop action and makes for an exhausting forty-nine minutes (there are only two scenes of plain dialogue, and one of those is the tag!), although it's unclear why David Hedison is written out midway through the story. Perhaps he was unwell, filming another story, or just didn't fancy being painted gold! Whatever the reason, the honor falls to golden boy Chip Morton, in the first of just two stories (the other is "Journey with Fear" a few episodes later) in which his character has anything substantial to do!

Victor Jory, a film actor nearing the end of his career, and star of the infamous *Cat-Women of the Moon*, was actively busy in television at this time, and plays Turner energetically. Annoyingly, and unfairly, many actors are uncredited in this episode, including the performer who plays Brent, whose role is larger than Patterson's in this story! Production no: 1304.

The Deadly Dolls

wr. Charles Bennett, dir. Harry Harris

An evil puppet master intends to replace the Seaview crew with duplicates.

With Vincent Price (Professor Multiple).

Despite the presence of the wonderful Vincent Price, this episode is absolute drivel from beginning to end. Little of the plot makes sense, with one bizarre event after another taking place without explanation on the grounds that—as alien beings—Multiple and his doll-men can do anything. As a result, the finished story lacks structure, credibility, and suspense, and is little more than a disjointed and disorganized collection of strange occurrences. What the episode does boast is some superb new special effects sequences, including the scenes where the energy creature attacks the Flying Sub with force blasts, and the shots of the *Seaview* glowing with nuclear energy. However, the puppets are absolutely ridiculous, and Vincent Price, Allen's old pal from *The Story of Mankind*, and busy in both film and TV at this time, is completely wasted as Multiple as all the best lines go to Nelson's idiotic puppet.

Price was a prolific actor who had made a name for himself in the horror genre (primarily in the early 1960s with drive-in movie king Roger Corman), and had appeared alongside David Hedison (then Al Hedison) in the 1950s creature feature *The Fly*. He also made several appearances in the *Batman* series at around this time, as the villainous Egghead, and in the late '70s starred in the very quickly canceled SF vehicle *Time Express*. A *Man from UNCLE* episode from this period, "The Fox and Hounds Affair," showed just how good Price could be as a villain with the right material, and just how wasted he was in *Voyage* (although Price was hardly being choosy at this time—one of his

TV guest appearances was in an episode of lowbrow sit-com *F Troop*, in a story titled "V is for Vampire"!).

Writer Charles Bennett was retired when Allen cajoled him into doing the occasional script for his TV series, but he must have needed the money because his attitude toward Allen bordered on hatred and his 1992 emergence from retirement, in his nineties, omitted his work with Allen. This is not surprising, as Bennett wrote some very poor material for the series, all his scripts having a once-through-the-typewriter feel as if he was making them up as he went along rather than starting with any kind of story ideas beyond the central premise. Furthermore, the concept of dolls replacing the crew had already been done before on the series in the third season, in the comparatively less stupid but equally wacky "The Wax Men," to which this episode bears a strong resemblance. Production no: 1303.

Cave of the Dead

wr. William Welch, dir. Harry Harris
The Seaview *becomes a victim of the curse of the Flying Dutchman, a square-rigger of ghostly folklore.*
With Warren Stevens (Van Wyck).

Yet another of William Welch's life-after-death ghost stories in the spirit, so to speak, of "The Phantom Strikes," "Return of the Phantom," and "The Haunted Submarine." Welch really did believe all this stuff with a passion, and claimed he'd recorded ghostly wails in his own house. This one may be the best of the four, and features a bizarre scene in which everybody on the submarine is replaced by a literal skeleton crew. There are however, a few loose ends, as might be expected from a Welch script. We never learn where Van Wyck first came from in relation to his pose as a Navy official (the episode starts with him aboard the Flying Sub with Nelson), and he seems to be all but forgotten during the mid-section of the story. Also, it's not quite clear how Nelson managed to knock a ghost unconscious

when they were in the diving bell. There are also more new effects shots as in the previous two episodes, and more to follow in the next episode, "Journey with Fear." This was SF TV veteran Warren Stevens' third and final *Voyage*, after "The Saboteur" and "Deadly Invasion." Production no: 1305.

Journey with Fear

wr. Arthur Weiss, dir. Harry Harris
Crane and Morton are abducted by aliens to the planet Venus in experimental space capsules being launched from the Seaview.
With Eric Matthews (Major Wilson), Gene Dynarski, James Gosa (aliens).

"Journey with Fear" might well have been titled *Cockroach Creatures from Venus* had it been made ten years earlier—they don't make 'em like this any more. Once the viewer gets past the total insanity of a vertical rocket the size of the *Seaview* being launched from *inside* the *Seaview*, without ripping the entire vessel to shreds, this particular episode is enormous fun. Think 20th century *Doctor Who* with a budget. An excellent cavernous set, beautifully lit and photographed, with superb monster suits from the ingenious Paul Zastupnevich (who created all Irwin Allen's fabulous array of monsters and aliens for *Lost in Space*, *Voyage*, and *Time Tunnel*) both go toward creating some wonderful visuals. The alien Centaurs (bearing absolutely no resemblance to anything remotely like a human horse) are cleverly designed, with layered legs similar to those used for Zastupnevich's legendary later Lobster Man and clever head masks with visible mouths and concealed eye holes in the layered face mask topped by two purely decorative bulbous eyes on top. Put in context with the SF material that preceded it, the creatures, sets and miniatures on *Voyage* looked fabulous. It's like an episode of submarine puppet show *Stingray* with real people.

Inside the alien suits are bit players Gene Dynarski and James Gosa. Both kept busy throughout the 1960s, Gosa also finding gainful employment underneath a giant plastic lump of what appears to be sentient doggie poo in "Target Earth" for *Lost in Space*, and in human form for *The Man from UNCLE* ("The Master's Touch Affair") and *Land of the Giants* ("Underground"). Dynarski appeared in two *Star Trek*, "Mudd's Women" and "The Mark of Gideon," as well as the first season *Voyage to the Bottom of the Sea* "The Buccaneer." Other credits include episodes of *Batman*, *Land of the Giants*, *The Invisible Man*, and *Star Trek: The Next Generation*. Eric Matthews, who plays the ill-fated Major Bob, also appears in the *Lost in Space* episode "Two Weeks in Space" as an evil alien.

Of the regulars, Crane and—for a change—Morton dominate, although Nelson, Kowalski and Sharkey also have a fair amount of screen time. A sequence with Sharkey giving Patterson one of his trademark pep talks in the control room appears to have been added to make up time. For Robert Dowdell, this was one of his better episodes with regard to having something to do other than recite the silliest lines of dialogue every week. The scenes in which he is blinded actually gave him the opportunity to act for a change, which he does quite well. The sinister chair in which he is placed also turns up in the *Lost in Space* episode "The Flaming Planet," while the pendant orbs are standard Irwin Allen alien issue and can also be seen on the *Time Tunnel* episode "The Kidnappers" among others.

Two new rooms magically appear aboard the sub for the impossible rocket launch, and are never seen again. The control center occupied by Nelson is clearly the *Seaview* control room partitioned off and filled with Irwin's job lot computer banks. Most of them are immediately familiar—indeed, the Time Tunnel control room personnel are probably mounting a search for most of them even now ... As for the room in which the rocket ship is supposedly

launched from, the launch procedure is particularly amusing, which consists of everyone running out into the corridor (presumably after lighting the blue touch paper). The atmosphere on Venus is also pleasingly suitable for humans too—just a little humid...

There is little point in looking for logic in what is simply an action adventure romp, but one can't help observing that due to a lack of any serious thought in the scriptwriting, the aliens are actually only guilty of jumping to conclusions, and the actions of every Earthman they encounter only serve to fuel their paranoia and doubt. In fact, the Centaurs' assumptions are understandable, and identical to Nelson's in other extraterrestrial episodes. Every verbal threat is met not with an explanation or the hand of friendship, but attack and deceit. On every occasion, the Earth people attack first—they even went into orbit with guns! No-one is asking *Voyage to the Bottom of the Sea* to be something it's not—it's a monster mash, and that's that—but it would have been a simple matter to add a couple of lines to justify the acts of aggression toward the aliens. Instead, their assumed hostility is only implied by the conventions of the genre, a common *Voyage* trademark. There are other minor inconsistencies too, such as why the Centaurs would even set up a base on an unstable planet, and why they cower from the thruster jets on the capsule when they can just materialize inside, or even walk around them! Production no: 1307.

Sealed Orders

wr. William Welch, dir. Jerry Hopper
Dangerous fumes cause Nelson and his crew to experience bizarre hallucinations.

"Sealed Orders" is yet another late entry to the series with a plot that makes no sense at all. Apart from rehashing the tired old all-alone-on-the-sub routine from "The Human Computer" and "The Death Watch," two other monumental bores, the story is riddled with minor and major idiocies.

Minor examples would include how easy it was for ordinary seaman Kowalski and Chief Sharkey to play around with the hangar for a neutron bomb, the fact that the circuitry room (from which weekly devastation and calamity is frequently wrought!) never seems to be manned (except occasionally by one guy looking the wrong direction), and why Kowalski's search party for the missing circuitry room crew are all brandishing guns! (Tough ship!) On a greater scale, where were the hundred-plus crew while their top officers were running around the sub hallucinating that no one was around?

One person who *was* around during filming was Richard Basehart's son Jack from his first marriage. Visiting his father on a rare trip from Italy to the U.S., he appears pointlessly as the in-jokingly named Jackson. A little too pointlessly, in fact—the vanity-casting bone tossed to daddy Basehart leads viewers to wonder why this new young crewman is pointedly introduced, only to never appear again. It might have made more sense for Jackson to have been behind the hallucinations, rather than remain a mystery cameo for the ages.

The episode's real problem, though, lies with the moldering storyline. If William Welch absolutely had to cobble together another cost-free bottle episode (and one can only presume he was instructed to do so after the expenditure on the likes of "Fires of Death" and "Journey with Fear"), we might have asked for two considerations. Firstly, that he not resort to the old empty ship routine yet again, and secondly that he use a few more clips. Two brief shots of creatures from "Night of Terror" and "The Thing from Inner Space" do not make an exciting episode, and the psychedelic sequences, to coin the vernacular of the period, come far too late in the day to make any of this interesting. A major dud. Production no: 1306.

Man of Many Faces

wr. William Welch, dir. Harry Harris

As the Seaview *races to disable an underwater super-magnet causing the Moon to be drawn towards the Earth, the crew are menaced by a master of disguise.*

With Jock Gaynor (Dr. Randolph Mason).

The first of the fourth season episodes to be put into production, this is a slight and clichéd affair, understandably held over until the new season was safely away. There's quite a bit of action away from the sub, recalling the early first and second seasons, and the story is completely absurd—mostly because the master of disguise flitting about the *Seaview* in the guise of virtually every crew member in the episode appears to be mysteriously able to change his height, build, and bone structure too! It's all embarrassingly reminiscent of those lovely old Hanna-Barbera cartoons where the villainous disguise expert could be anyone with a twirl of his cape. Had the man of many faces been a shape-shifting alien, *Voyage* could probably have carried this preposterous plot off (it is, after all, good, silly fun), but we are ultimately asked to believe these remarkable quick changes are the work of a mere mortal—and a thoroughly absurd choice of mortal too, although an obvious one, as he's the only suspect we're ever given. Furthermore, did nobody else—say, a couple of hundred observatories or astronomers—not notice the moon getting closer to the Earth? Aspects of this story resemble the *Voyage* feature film plot—Nelson against the world, the *Seaview* a fugitive sub pursued by the authorities, a fatally misguided scientist whom Nelson opposes, and the usual library film of climate chaos! A sadly predictable way to start the fourth season, and a wise decision from the network to bury it.

Bit players Howard Culver and Bradd Arnold portray the TV interviewer and studio attendant. Production number: 1301.

Fatal Cargo

wr. William Welch, dir. Jerry Hopper

A monstrous white gorilla rampages through the Seaview, murdering people at the will of a jealous scientist.

With Woodrow Parfrey (Leo Brock), Jon Lormer (Dr. Blanchard), Janos Prohaska (the gorilla).

As well as being a perfect textbook example of the archetypal color episode of *Voyage to the Bottom of the Sea*, complete with misguided scientist, slimy treacherous villain and raging pea-brained monster storming around the ship until zapped into oblivion, "Fatal Cargo" also offers the perfect opportunity to give credit where it's due to one of the many unsung heroes of the golden age of SF TV.

Underneath the gorilla suit is the late, great Janos Prohaska (and yes, his name is misspelled in this episode's closing credits—but he had the unusual accolade for a professional monster man of often *getting* an on-screen credit), a creative genius who, if you have seen most of the vintage sci-fi series, you have seen performing at least a dozen times. Indeed, the white gorilla featured in this episode is also—with added horn, spikes and tail—the Mugato that jumped Captain Kirk in the 1968 *Star Trek* episode "A Private Little War."

Killer gorillas date back to the dawn of cinema, and are usually—and wisely, no doubt—portrayed by actors in suits. So common was the comic or deadly gorilla in film that several actors specialized in them by bringing their own gorilla suits to the party, including stunt-man Ray 'Crash' Corrigan, formerly the human lead of the serial *Undersea Kingdom* among others, Steve Calvert, who purchased Corrigan's suit from him and continued in the same vein, and George Barrows, whose work was usually restricted to playing obvious fakes in sit-coms such as *The Lucy Show* and *The Beverly Hillbillies* etc., and is best known in SF circles for being the furry wearer of the diving helmet in the in-famous '50s turkey *Robot Monster*. Prohaska, however, who also did his share of *Lucy Shows*, went one better. A Hungarian-born stuntman, acrobat, and circus performer, he prided himself on creating an element of doubt in the audience, and duplicated as best he could the real mannerisms of simians, so that whereas Barrows and his colleagues would give their gorillas human mannerisms for laughs (such as rolling their eyes or the good old gag of putting a chummy arm around the shoulder of a blissfully unsuspecting comedian preparing for his double-take), Prohaska would prefer to play it straight and go for those is-it-or-isn't-it moments. Compare, for example, the lumbering white gorilla of "Fatal Cargo" with the similar but sweet and cuddly "Abominable Snowman" padding around the *Seaview* a few episodes later—like this one, great fun, but so obviously a guy in a suit in longshot. Like his 1950s predecessor Paul Blaisdell, Prohaska specialized in all types of monsters and creatures for the burgeoning fantasy market of the time, but rather than wait for producers to come to him (although they soon did), Prohaska busily designed and created his own monster suits in his Santa Monica workshop and then turned up at the offices of Daystar, Desilu, or Irwin Allen to tout for work while showing off the suit. In fact, the *Star Trek* episode "The Devil in the Dark" was specifically written around just such a pitch from Prohaska, who—after a Desilu audition in his chimp suit for *The Lucy Show* (presumably for the playful "Mooney the Monkey" episode)—scuttled into the neighboring *Star Trek* offices in a more elaborate version of the oversized microbe outfit he'd created for an *Outer Limits* episode, "The Probe."

One of Prohaska's first jobs in the monster market had been to wear the extraordinary Thetan costume made by Projects Unlimited for the early *Outer Limits* episode "The Architects of Fear," as his acrobatic ability and muscular legs enabled him to endure the painful stilt legs. However, even he was unprepared for his first stint wearing the head; it was freshly and extensively glued, and he reeled around and nearly passed out. As a backhanded compliment, the final scenes were blacked out and censored by many of the U.S. regional broadcasters, who considered the creature way too scary! Next, Prohaska wore his own circus monkey suit as Darwin the intelligent monkey in "The Sixth Finger" (an outfit which later provided more monkey business for the 1964 teen movie *Bikini Beach!*). A couple of *Outer Limits* monsters also turned up in the *Star Trek* pilot "The Cage," as did, apparently, Prohaska, wearing one of them.

Prohaska also provided and wore a giant-beaked blue and orange bird suit for "Forbidden World," a second season *Lost in Space*, a comical and unthreatening outfit which later turned up on two episodes of *Bewitched* (producer William Asher was familiar with Prohaska's work as he was also the man behind the beach movie series). Early '70s TV viewers may recall *The Andy Williams Show*, which ran from 1969 to '71, a mix of singing acts and comedy skits with recurring characters doing variations of the same bit every week; Prohaska portrayed the legendary Cookie Bear, a post-Yogi moocher in a huge tie who would ring Williams' doorbell each week with a fresh scam to unsuccessfully filch cookies. At the same time he was plaguing Williams' surreal suburbia he was wearing his gorilla suit in "Comeback" and "The Marionettes" for *Land of the Giants*, and operating the formidable rock creature in the *Star Trek* episode "The Savage Curtain." Tragically, he was set to work on the 1974 TV version of *Planet of the Apes* when in pre-production he and several others working on the series were killed in a helicopter crash while scouting locations.

One has to wonder where Prohaska would be today, had he lived. Would his creativity have taken him onto greater things during the special effects revolution of the late '70s and 1980s? Or would he, like Ray Harryhausen, have had to retire gracefully, a respected relic of the past? One suspects that today he would at least be a regular on the convention circuit, but he died on the cusp of developments that would have either excited and inspired him, or put him out of business as a dinosaur.

Although dispensed with before the opening titles, elderly bit player Jon Lormer, with no less than three bit parts in *Star Trek* to his name, but usually relegated to playing preachers in such classics as *Twilight Zone*'s "Execution" and *The Invaders*' "Valley of the Shadow," gets one of his more substantial roles here as the ill-fated and naively trusting Doctor Blanchard, done away with by the wicked Woodrow Parfrey, one of TV's great slimeball villains, who spends most of the episode mincing around the corridors of the *Seaview* in the shadows, slithering around the walls like a slug while being eyed suspiciously by a doubting Admiral Nelson, who's got the poor slob's number from the minute they meet on the island! Invariably cast as a malevolent man, often a mad scientist or corruptible professor, Parfrey hit 1960s TV with perfect timing, appearing in no less than five *Man from UNCLE* adventures, most of the supernatural sit-coms (including four *Jeannies*), *Batman*, *Lost in Space*, and many other spy shows (including *Honey West*, *Get Smart*, and *Mission: Impossible*).

"Fatal Cargo" is *Voyage* at its most enjoyable. As with all the monster episodes, whether it is rampaging aboard the ship or floating around outside, there is never a dull moment ... and whether they were Prohaska's work or not, the *Voyage* monsters are some of the best ever devised for TV. Sinister music trumpets every event, and there is plenty of the unintentionally funny dialogue that afficionadoes adore, including the sort of classic doom-laden remarks that precede every development—"I just hope that tranquilizer keeps on working!" and "I don't care how strong he is, he'll never get out of here!"

Ordinarily, the daftest lines seem to go to poor old dopey Chip Morton out of a sort of perverse sense of tradition, but this time the honor goes to Sharkey, who snaps "Don't just stand there with your teeth in your mouth, get going!" Huh?? The trick pen business echoes the well-known "The Cybernauts" episode of *The Avengers* a couple of years earlier, and is a familiar device in fantasy TV. The episode also offers the usual superb production values—great sets, excellent photography, and the best miniature model work in TV SF. Production no: 1309.

Time Lock
wr. William Welch, dir. Jerry Hopper
A wargamer from the future is snatching famous historical figures from the past, and intends to add Admiral Nelson of the Seaview to his collection.
With John Crawford (Alpha).

In "The Kidnappers," a flawed but thoroughly enjoyable episode of *The Time Tunnel*, a ruthless alien scientist has abducted various figures from the history books, ranging from Roman philosopher Cicero to 20th century madman Adolf Hitler, and keeps them in a zombie state on his home world in the far future. This is an inferior but still entertaining rehash of the same idea, in which the oddly attired Alpha (John Crawford in a silver neck brace and shades) collects military memorabilia with a difference—he kidnaps living specimens and transforms them into soulless zombie slaves.

The second episode put into production for the fourth season, this one—like "Man of Many Faces"—was also held over to be buried in a quiet week. Plainly one of Welch's cost-cutting shows to order, employing existing materials, Alpha's two silver-skinned stooges are lazily costumed straight from wardrobe in Allen's standard silver spacesuits and quilted jackets, and so look remarkably similar to the members of the drone society in "Chase Through Time," another episode of *The Time Tunnel*. Alpha's desk is a familiar prop (seen in *Time Tunnel's*

"The Kidnappers" and *Land of the Giants'* "Secret City of Limbo" among others), and he sits before the over-used computer bank from *The Time Tunnel*. The time machine is plainly one of the freezing tubes of the *Jupiter Two* from *Lost in Space*.

Although happy with his other work for producer Irwin Allen on *Lost in Space* and *The Time Tunnel*, Crawford was less than satisfied with his sojourn on the *Seaview*; having played the role with a silky, sadistic attitude, he was instructed by Allen to redub the entire episode in more traditionally menacing tones. This absurd decision makes the obvious dubbing on Crawford look like a character in a bad foreign movie. Allen did not make many bad decisions while producing nearly 300 hours of fantasy TV, but those he made were mostly on *Voyage*; Alpha's dubbed monotone is up there with the redubbed Fossil Man and the talking Snowman still to come. None of the imposing figures Alpha has snatched are identified by name, or credited in the cast, including the Mongol warrior and Roman centurion who do most of his dirty work and the two skull-capped, silver-suited, silver-skinned accomplices on board the *Seaview*.

As in all Welch's rush jobs, the menace is dispatched in an explosion when the episode needs to end. Here, however, the willful destruction of Alpha's base now that he's gone seems a little rash, if not sadistic, as no attempt has been made to restore or return his other captives from past battlefields who have already been shown to be frozen, but still alive! When Nelson sets his bomb and flees, they are all left to face the explosion in frozen fear! The original and official synopsis for this episode indicates that the explosion from Crane's grenade launcher was supposed to blow a hole in the wall to reveal a city of the future, but ultimately this was never shown. An inferior job at portraying this may have been attempted, as the scene cuts rather rapidly. Director Jerry Hopper does his best with the material, producing several nice shots of Alpha's base. The sequence in which the crew are put into a form of paralysis on the *Seaview* bridge is well done, as worried eyes in frozen bodies swivel nervously, and he cuts to the immobile faces of Alpha's victims as often as possible to create an eerie sense of dead eyes watching.

While his role as a villain in *Voyage to the Bottom of the Sea* was spoilt, Crawford is clearly having great fun as Chronos, another malevolent manipulator of time he portrayed later that same season in "The Time Merchant" for *Lost in Space*. A versatile performer when given the chance, he appeared in four very different episodes of *Time Tunnel* in four very different roles.

What might charitably be written off as an example of synchronicity appears to be occurring a year later as the ten-part *Doctor Who* story "The War Games" employs a similar premise to both "The Kidnappers" and "Time Lock." Production no: 1302.

Rescue
wr. William Welch, dir. Justus Addiss
The Seaview *pursues an enemy submarine that has been attacking other vessels, unaware that a traitor on board is working against them.*
With Don Dubbins (Chief Beech).

Conventional underwater antics, with an enemy sub and double agent. As is so often the case with *Voyage*, the enemy agent is easily identified by the viewer as the only new face in the episode, although in this case we are made aware of his treachery early. The submarine is the *Vulcan* from "The Lost Bomb" and others, and the presence of William Welch as writer suggests one of Allen's budget crunchers utilizing stock footage and standing sets. All this aside, a very entertaining episode. The scene where the divers are deliberately sent out with the wrong air tanks by the bad guy is quite chilling, and reminiscent of the callous murders of the two frogmen in "The Machines Strike Back." Production no.: 1310.

Terror
wr. Sidney Ellis, dir. Jerry Hopper
After answering a distress call from botanists on an island, an invading alien intelligence is accidentally taken on board the Seaview *and possesses several crew members and Admiral Nelson.*

This was to be Sidney Ellis' only filmed contribution to the series due to the show's imminent cancellation, and what a dud. Expenditure consists of some plastic orchids and a glowing light effect and the entire exercise is plainly intended to do nothing but fill 49 minutes with scenes of bogus jeopardy. It's tough to care about any of it, although the sequence with the Flying Sub attacking the *Seaview* is reasonable, and the alien light force is thoughtfully animated, looking particularly good when it disappears into or emerges from the *Seaview*'s walls, like the alien intelligence in *Star Trek*'s "Day of the Dove." Full marks to the cast for trying to look interested. In the 1980s, Ellis worked with another pop culture icon and prolific contributor to Americana, Stephen J. Cannell, as story editor on *The A-Team* and *Hunter*.

Jerry Catron and Pat Culliton regularly appeared in *Voyage* as crewmen, or in other minor roles, and turn up here too, alongside Brent Davis, who was a crewman in "Deadly Invasion," a marine in *Time Tunnel*'s "Kill Two by Two," and put a monster suit on for the *Lost in Space* episode "Target Earth." Bit player Damian O'Flynn, who portrays the ill-fated Dr. Thompson, appeared in episodes of the '50s *Adventures of Superman* series, the *Batman* pilot, and the pre-credits teaser of "The King of Diamonds Affair" for *The Man from UNCLE*. He finishes work before the opening credits of this episode too. Production no: 1308.

A Time to Die
wr. William Welch, dir. Robert Sparr
Day turns to night, constellations shift, satellites disappear from the sky, and radio waves go dead when the Seaview *is hurled through time by Mr. Pem, an evil eccentric scientist.*
With Henry Jones (Mr. Pem).

This episode introduces the character of Mr. Pem, a sort of American version of Doctor Who, an eccentric inventor and evil meddler who plunges the *Seaview* submarine through time back to the prehistoric era with a pocket watch that is drawing its power from the *Seaview's* nuclear reactor by amplifying it tenfold. By the time Mr. Pem made his first of what would be two appearances, the series was in its fourth year and on its last legs, and like many of the series' final episodes, "A Time to Die" fails to fulfill its potential. We are never presented with any backstory to Pem himself, and only the efforts of impish character actor Henry Jones flesh him out. Whatever entertainment value Pem possesses is down to Jones, but the character is still just a boring little man. A considerable portion of the show is devoted to laborious running about in circles, and a further chunk is devoted to Pem rerunning scenes of a previous adventure to series star Richard Basehart through his office door—not projected *on* to his office door, *through* his office door! At just two minutes long, it seems more like ten, and downgrades the episode considerably, especially as the view through the door offers a variety of different camera angles. Lazily written, the episode never properly explains Pem's motives, intentions, abilities, or indeed how the *Seaview* has apparently returned to the present day. Most baffling of all is the sequence where Nelson is inexplicably trying to turn the *Seaview* reactor back on. Why? It powers their adversary, who needs to be defeated first.

Henry Jones had previously appeared as Sprague in the third season's "Night of Terror" and as Smith's Cousin Jeremiah in the *Lost in Space* story "The Curse of Cousin Smith." He was a more subdued, but equally mad adversary for *The Man from UNCLE* in "The Neptune Affair," returned again in "The Cap and Gown Affair," portrayed "The Leprechaun" in *Bewitched,* and chalked up a number of other roles in SF TV including recurring mad scientist on *The Six Million Dollar Man* in three episodes, "Day of the Robot," "Run, Steve, Run," and "Return of the Robot Maker." Like many great character actors, Jones enhanced bit parts (he's perfect as a mob doctor in early '70s thriller *The Outfit*), but a little of him went a long way, and Allen's eccentrics frequently overstayed their welcome. Production no: 1317.

Blow Up
wr. William Welch, dir. Justus Addiss
> *Nelson cracks up and the crew plots mutiny.*

Another William Welch runaround on standing sets to fill an hour, like "Sealed Orders" and "Terror" this season. Nelson behaves oddly out of character for the duration of the show after untested breathing apparatus makes him paranoid. And that's it. It had all been done before, most noticeably in the first season episode "Mutiny." Despite the absence of any appealing audience hook, Basehart no doubt enjoyed the opportunity to act a little, and it's his performance as a delusional paranoid that is the episode's sole attraction as he once again demonstrates both his acting ability and his value to the series. Bizarrely, the perpetually pedestrian Justus Addiss chooses this episode to actually direct, rather than sleepwalk through an assignment. Production no: 1313.

Deadly Amphibians
wr. Arthur Weiss, dir. Jerry Hopper
> *The Seaview is attacked by an amphibious underwater race.*
> With Don Matheson (amphibian leader).

"Deadly Amphibians" may not be one of the great episodes of *Voyage,* but it is certainly a typical example of how much fun the series could be at it's most entertaining. The episode starts with a bang—literally—and one of the show's famous lurch scenes, and has a great opening teaser as we first glimpse the aliens joyously celebrating the sinking of the *Seaview.*

The effects sequences—graced with reasonable monster suits and underwater scenes of the amphibians that recall *The Creature from the Black Lagoon*—are peppered with moments of genuine suspense, such as Sharkey and Crane silently recovering from the sonic ray together, the tapping on the airlock that turns out to be Kowalski returning, and the creatures lurking behind rocks to menace the divers. Other memorable shots include Kowalski being dragged off through the water as Crane and Sharkey look on helplessly, and the amphibian emerging from behind a rock. This was *Voyage* working at it's best—the monster suits look twice as good in the water, and such underwater sequences as those here were what made the series special as SF TV—creating monster suits out of wetsuits was an inspired way of producing competent and impressive special effects to 1960s standards on a TV budget. The action never lets up from the moment the episode begins, and Jerry Hopper, one of the series' most skilful directors, keeps the camera moving and the frame busy. And even though Crane first sights the creatures alone, we are spared the endless credulous doubting scenes that slow down so many similar yarns. Kowalski's transformation into one of the amphibians—and subsequent miracle cure—is absurdly hokey, but works in the context of an already silly story ... and although the amphibian leader is named as Proto in the closing credits, at no time during the episode is the leader referred to by this name, a common occurrence in *Voyage*. Exactly how Crane's mere rolling over onto the cables somehow shorted the sonic cannon is not clear...

Guest star Don Matheson—and only in an Allen show could you get guest star credit as the creature-of-the-week?—was a familiar name, if not yet a familiar face, to Irwin Allen's viewers. He had previously appeared twice in two very different episodes of *Lost in Space*, first as an alien being in the lyrical, sensitive "The Sky Is Falling" during the first season, and then later as a super-android sending up a certain Kryptonian super-hero in the comical "Revolt of the Androids," one of the funniest second season stories.

At the time of this episode's production, Matheson was on the payroll awaiting the start of *Land of the Giants*, the fourth and final Irwin Allen SF show that would ultimately take *Voyage's* time-slot the following season. Allen didn't want his newcomer's face exposed to the public until the show's debut, so he put him to work terrorizing the *Seaview* under a monster mask. According to Matheson, Richard Basehart was so astonished to hear actual lines of dialogue emanating from a stunt-monster, he stopped filming and demanded to see the face of the young newcomer in the suit! Watch closely during the scene when the amphibian leader confronts Nelson in his laboratory, and you'll catch a baffled Richard Basehart mouthing Matheson's lines along with him...

Irwin Allen had a knack for finding strong, likeable leading men that male and female viewers could admire for their own reasons—Hedison, Dowdell, Guy Williams, Mark Goddard, Robert Colbert, James Darren—and Matheson's Mark Wilson in *Land of the Giants* was in this grand tradition. He deserved better than to fade from sight after *Land of the Giants*, but by then it was the '70s, and TV was into quirky characters for leading men—*McCloud, Columbo, Kojak, Cannon, Quincy* etc.—and by the time two-fisted, square-jawed types came back into vogue in the '80s, Matheson's moment had passed, and he was reduced to guest roles on shows including *Falcon Crest* (a recurring role as a bad guy), and a *Murder She Wrote/ Magnum* crossover story. Married for a while to *Giants* co-star Deanna Lund, his daughter Melissa was a player on the much-mocked sit-com *Mr. Belvedere* and appears in the SF video comedy cheapie *Virgin Hunters, aka Test Tube Teens from the Year 2000* (without wishing to raise expectations too high, this is unusual of its genre for actually being funny and clever in places). Production no: 1314.

The Return of Blackbeard

wr. Al Gail, dir. Justus Addiss

The ghost of the legendary pirate Blackbeard materializes aboard the Seaview at a politically sensitive moment and causes mayhem with his supernatural powers.

With Malachi Throne (Blackbeard).

Malachi Throne chalks up yet another robust performance in an Allen production, this time as Blackbeard the pirate. Throne had previously appeared twice in *Voyage to the Bottom of the Sea*, during the first season in "The Magnus Beam" and "The Enemies," and made seven appearances in Allen productions all told. Here, he is ill-served. Sadly, this nondescript story typical of fourth season *Voyage* does him no favors; what a great second season story this might have been, when everyone was trying just a little bit harder. Clumsily written and unimaginatively directed, a fine idea is thrown away by lackluster efforts behind the scenes. Why could director Justus Addiss not show some of the imagination he exhibited on the mediocre "Blow Up"?

Writer Albert Gail was Irwin Allen's cousin, and co-wrote "The Buccaneer" with William Welch for the first season. He performed an emergency rewrite on the second season episode "The Monster's Web" when Richard Basehart was taken ill midway through filming, and as writers willing to work with Allen became increasingly difficult to find, began to turn in competent but unspectacular scripts for the fourth season. This was his first solo outing; the second and final was "The Lobster Man," another fun episode that could have benefitted from a stronger script and greater effort from Addiss.

Although the cast are probably having a great time in their pirate costumes, the same cannot be said for the poor viewers. There are numerous groaners featuring illogical behavior from the cast—Kowalski arrives at the scene of the alarm call and assumes the smoldering Jolly Roger symbol to be "a joke," even though everyone's on high security alert and an alarm has been heard ... and when Nelson absurdly asks Sharkey if the puzzled crewman has "seen Blackbeard," the scene is played as a wacky double-take moment. As anyone knows, this sort of material only works if the audience can believe in it as they watch ... and that means that no matter how absurd the events portrayed, the actors must play them straight. There also has to be an internal logic to the behavior of the players, which this episode noticeably fails to provide. To compound the disappointment, scenes that should be dramatic or surprising fall flat because Addiss fails to do anything with them—Blackbeard's arrival on the bridge at the climax of the opening pre-credits teaser is anti-climactic, as having appeared, Blackbeard promptly disappears ... and the confrontation with the first crewman falls flat because no-one can be bothered to film reaction shots.

Writer and story editor Al Gail's ideas were as typical and as creative as anybody's on the series, but his scripts are hopeless—they have nowhere to go, and so go nowhere. Furthermore, we are never sure exactly how this return of Blackbeard has occurred. Is he a ghost, an immortal, or reincarnated? He has the attributes of a ghost, but where does his futuristic technology come from? Where did he get the force field device, or the ability to control men's minds? Hampered by the bored direction of Addiss and the unquestioning, careless script of Gail, this episode has none of the fun of "The Sky Pirate" in *Lost in Space*, none of the energy of the second season's "Dead Men's Doubloons" (the other *Voyage* pirate episode), and none of the thrills and pace of *Time Tunnel's* "Pirates of Dead Man's Island." All in all, the weakest of Allen's pirate sagas, and quite a missed opportunity. Production no: 1316.

The Terrible Leprechaun

wr. Charles Bennett, dir. Jerry Hopper

When the Seaview undertakes a mission off the coast of Ireland, an evil leprechaun sees the perfect opportunity to get his magical hands on some gold buried under the seabed.

With Walter Burke (the leprechauns), Seymour Cassell (Jensen).

Terrible indeed, as we take a voyage to the bottom of the barrel courtesy of the semi-retired Bennett, who returned to work for Fox on an ultimately unrealized film script in the early '90s in *his* early 90s. The leprechaun(s) are played by Walter Burke, "The Toymaker" from *Lost in Space*, and who was seen in two superb episodes of *The Outer Limits*, "The Invisibles" and "The Mutant." Burke was wonderful in *The Outer Limits*, and fun in *Lost in Space*, but—despite appearances in *Bewitched, I Dream of Jeannie* and *The Munsters*—this is certainly his silliest role! Nevertheless, he plays both parts perfectly, and what there is to enjoy here is contributed by Burke and Paul Zastupnevich's wonderful leprechaun suits.

There is one flaw, though. Despite the costume change, the script does not make it immediately clear that we are dealing with two leprechauns (note that the episode title is in the singular). It's typical fourth season cheapness for Allen to use the same actor for both roles, as competent as Walter Burke is. This was doubly confusing to those of us originally watching in black and white! And cowardly crewman Jensen has now died twice—the sequence with Morton, Kowalski and Jensen in the undersea cavern is swiped from the second season episode "The Mechanical Man." Production no: 1321.

The Lobster Man

wr. Al Gail, dir. Justus Addiss

An alien crustacean turns up aboard the Seaview, feigning friendship.

With Victor Lundin (Lobster Man).

A great concept and monster suit, but the story and direction leave much to be desired. Writer Albert Gail was back at the typewriter, and although "The Lobster Man" is not as disappointing as Gail's other fourth season solo outing "The Return of Blackbeard," it's still a let-down. The main failing is a lack of set pieces (we don't even get to see the Lobster Man perform his rescue), while what is there is sunk once again by the leaden and bored direction of Justus Addiss. Fortunately, the striking costume and the question of the alien's motives (although betrayal is pointedly forthcoming) keep the episode interesting and entertaining.

Only Irwin Allen could have or would have dared to present a Lobster Man as a serious proposition, and the concept has been fondly remembered as hilarious ever since (the only straight-faced predecessor was Roger Corman's legendary *Attack of the Crab Monsters* in 1957, although this belonged to the lower end of the oversized menace trend, an offshoot of the big bug or nature-runs-amok genre begun by *Them!* in 1954). In 1989, there was even a spoof sci-fi film titled *Lobster Man from Mars*, and the short-lived super-hero send-up *Once a Hero* featured a clumsy Lobster Man as a joke. At around the same time this *Voyage* episode was produced, *The Beverly Hillbillies* had a running joke about a macho hunky actor—Larry Pennell's Dash Riprock (real name: Homer Noodleman)—being perpetually threatened with the role of 'Crab Man' if he didn't play ball with his bosses, and threats such as "being fitted for his claws" or "driving the Crabmobile" were bandied about! Still, all this aside, guest star Victor Lundin, although under-used in his most substantial SF TV appearance, is superbly menacing and imposing as the Lobster Man. He had previously appeared in *Voyage* in "The Menfish" as well as episodes of *Get Smart, Batman, The Man from UNCLE*, and *Babylon 5*.

The story features a number of illogicalities—Nelson takes absurd fatalistic chances with the sonic gun, and the creature turns hostile and abandons his pretence with ridiculous haste. How does the Lobster Man know of Crane's reference to the Trojan Horse, and if the space capsule is to be transformed into a bomb, where will the alien be when it goes off? Like many fourth season episodes, budget restrictions and careless writing prevent this episode from achieving its potential as a great cult classic. The deadly duo of Gail and Addiss strike again... Production no: 1320.

Nightmare

wr. Sidney Marshall, dir. Charles Rondeau
Crane finds himself alone on the Seaview, the victim of an extraterrestrial plot.
With Paul Mantee (Jim Bentley).

Almost laughably bad. Crane finds himself alone on the *Seaview* ... which by now is becoming a very tired plot device indeed. This is the fourth such story, after "The Human Computer" in the first season, "The Death Watch," and "Sealed Orders" from this same season. To add insult to injury, Crane cracks up almost immediately—not too impressive for the heroic lead, and crewman Patterson, when discovered, follows suit. The one moment of interest comes right at the end, when guest star Mantee transforms into a pulp movie alien—actually one of the alien outfits from *Time Tunnel's* "Raiders from Outer Space," modeled in the style of the Metaluna mutant from *This Island Earth.*

As with Robert Sparr, director Charles Rondeau had boarded the *Seaview* at the end of its voyages, but unlike Sparr, who drew some fun assignments, Rondeau's three scripts were all turkeys. Rondeau had been gainfully and frequently employed during the heyday of the Warner Brothers TV factory in the early '60's, when that studios westerns and detective shows were production line prolific, but with the demise of the Warners TV boom he had flitted from one series to another, trying his hand at everything,

staying nowhere long and apparently taking anything that came along. Although some of his assignments were on prestigious or successful series, he did not settle, working on every type of show and genre from *Gunsmoke* to *Batman.* For the fourth and final season, *Voyage* veered wildly each week between high concept schlock SF episodes ("Fires of Death," "The Deadly Dolls," "Journey with Fear," "The Return of Blackbeard," "Deadly Amphibians," "The Terrible Leprechaun," "The Lobster Man," "The Abominable Snowman," "Flaming Ice") and obvious cheap fillers ("Rescue," "Terror," "Blow Up," "Nightmare," "The Edge of Doom," "The Death Clock"), and Rondeau's were all from the second variety. None of them were well written or particularly creative beyond the initial idea (Marshall's script here is cynical, time-filling, cost-cutting rubbish), but at least the high concept schlock was fun because of the creatures. Case in point, the next episode.... Production no: 1319.

The Abominable Snowman

wr. Robert Hamner, dir. Robert Sparr
A scientist at an arctic research station mutates into a monstrous snow-beast and runs amok aboard the Seaview.
With Dusty Cadis (Rayburn), Bruce Mars (Hawkins), Frank Babich (corpsman).

Schlock heaven. Writer Robert Hamner was a prolific writer in all dramatic genres, and had written many first season episodes of *Voyage.* However, he had by this point moved over to *Lost in Space,* to that series' great advantage. Although *Voyage* was by now scraping the bottom of the barrel for writers, this would be Hamner's only contribution to the show outside the more sober first season. Even though he adapted to the new *Voyage*—now festooned with aliens and monsters—effortlessly, he has maintained in interviews that he doesn't even remember writing this yarn!

One can certainly forgive him for disavowing all knowledge.... As the title betrays, this is easily one of the silliest episodes of the series, free of leprechauns, killer clowns and wax men it's true, but graced with a fearsome monster hindered by the awkward minor detail that ... he's kind of cute. Unlike Janos Prohaska's lumbering white furry gorilla of "Fatal Cargo" a couple of months earlier, which actually looked like it might tear someone's head off, the Abominable Snowman—not in the least bit snowy, other than being white—resembles nothing short of a great big cuddly soft toy that would be hard put to hug someone to death. Also, whereas Prohaska would go out of his way to move around in an animalistic manner, Snowy trips around the *Seaview* corridors a little light in the loafers to be frank, acting and looking for all the world like the guy in a furry white suit he is. He pads here and there around the *Seaview*, and in one hilarious scene, is sitting on top of the ship's torpedoes, looking down on the crewmen as they search the missile room. When he jumps down, he doesn't leap, but swings down with gymnastic flair like the well-trained athlete the stuntman obviously is!

For the first half of the episode, the crew don't know what they're up against, which is fortunate as Crane and the doctor can barely get their lines out in one scene, and the Admiral wisely stays in his cabin for the first half of the episode, emerging only to be seen visibly holding back his laughter when Snowy has him trussed up in the reactor room ... Once the creature opens his mouth to speak perfect American anchorman English the episode totally loses it, as does Basehart, helplessly looking upstage to avoid the camera's gaze!

The revelation half way through the episode that the mutant creature (it's not really a snowman, although it is quite abominable, as it kills about thirty people altogether) can talk is the last straw in a glorious debacle littered throughout with unintentional laughs. It rather reminds one of the old joke about the faithful dog who suddenly chastised his master for buying a different dog food. When the master expresses surprise that after all these years his dog has spoken, and asks why he never has before, the dog replies "Well everything's been all right until now!" In all fairness, director Robert Sparr does his best, but it's not good enough, and he makes some bad choices. What tension the episode possesses comes courtesy of a director who has forged ahead whereas so many others would have thrown up their hands and left the actors to be totally humiliated rather than merely partially embarrassed. Sparr manages a nice aerial shot in the missile room scene as the creature hides above them, and does his best to create tension with ominous shadows on walls and scuffling footsteps; the problem is, even the Snowman's silhouette and feet are adorable. The one scene that does work is the very first shot of the creature—a full-on close-up of his powder-puff visage filling the camera menacingly before the opening credits. But it's all downhill from there. In another scene, shortly after the second death, Kowalski is making his way through the corridors in a time-killing game of hide and seek (carrying one of those silly bright yellow cereal packet-style ray guns prominent toward the end of the series), only to change places after much ominous stalking with another, more expendable crewman at the last minute—who, of course, gets to be victim number three! The scene is doubly bizarre for not allowing the unfortunate extra Kowalski encounters a speaking part. Lines are something the supporting players are spared. As Ray Didsbury revealed in his *Filmfax* interview, the production was keeping costs down by not allowing the crewmen lines, as speaking parts caused higher payments to the actors. Basehart put a stop to it as soon as he realized what was happening, but the practice is plainly apparent in this episode, particularly in this scene where Kowalski nearly fires at his soon to be ill-fated colleague coming round a corner. The poor guy can only exhale and shake his head. It may have been a mercy. While we can excuse Sparr, who also directed *Star Trek's* "Shore Leave" and several episodes of *The Wild Wild West*, there is no denying the episode boasts some dire golden turkey dialogue, even for *Voyage*.

Snowy initially appeared in three *Lost in Space* episodes, locked in a cage in "Space Circus" and "Hunter's Moon," and in a single scene sequence for "Revolt of the Androids" (it's the opening scene, so you can also catch him in the next week trailer at the end of "Treasure of the Lost Planet"), and so it's possible that Allen and his people knew the creature was weak—it was never intended to carry an episode. However, corners were clearly being cut during the fourth season, and our furry friend appears to have been promoted. As Hamner has understandably developed amnesia over this travesty, we can only speculate as to whether he wrote an abominable snowman story and had this suit thrust upon him, or whether he was requested to write a cheap episode around the suit. Possibly the latter, as he can't remember it.

Despite all the above mockery, "The Abominable Snowman" is a hugely enjoyable time-waster, precisely because it is so silly, and it represents exquisitely a certain kind of *Voyage to the Bottom of the Sea* episode synonymous with the last two seasons. The scenes where the creature runs amok in the reactor room and the sub duly tosses back and forth sparks a-flyin' are quintessential *Voyage*, and part of the series' charm. As remarked earlier—they don't make 'em like that any more.... Production no: 1315.

Secrets of the Deep

wr. William Welch, dir. Charles Rondeau
Renegade scientists based in a Sealab surrounded by dangerous undersea creatures hold the sea's shipping lanes to ransom.

With Peter Mark Richman (Hendrix).

More two-faced double-agents inside the sub and malevolent plant creatures outside the sub. This is rather obviously another cheater, cobbled together cheaply to cut corners, usually because of budget overruns on other episodes. William Welch knew every prop and piece of footage in all four of Allen's series; every time an episode was needed on the cheap, Welch would have the job of putting one together using existing materials only. "Secrets of the Deep" has all the hallmarks of one of these episodes. Every incident is built around existing footage and stock shots from other episodes, the seaweed monster having previously appeared in "The Condemned" and "Deadly Creature Below." As a story, "Secrets of the Deep" doesn't stand too much close examination, with the villain Hendrix acting in a particularly illogical manner. Working—as we soon learn he is—for the blackmailers, many of his demands or his actions make little sense. Events occur more to utilize stock footage than they do to advance the story; for example, why does Nelson risk his life in the diving bell when the Flying Sub, launched later, would be so much more efficient? (Answer: to re-use tinted footage from "The Condemned"). Why isn't Hendrix satisfied that the *Seaview* can't search for the sea lab after the initial attack? He doesn't want it found, but not only insists the diving bell is launched, but asks to go down with it! And despite apparently having enough force to cause a tidal wave, an explosion does very little harm to the Flying Sub. Why does Hendrix tell Sparks to send a message of gibberish and say it's authorized by Nelson, when he knows his lie will be so quickly and easily exposed? And why does Hendrix need to plant a signal device in the *Seaview* to assist the second attack when the first was launched without one? And where on earth does that ridiculous enormous aerial come from out of his ring!?! Hendrix also seems to have been abandoned and ignored by his colleagues, although this is never actually stated. The giant fish could destroy him as well as the crew of the *Seaview*, and when he asks for all the mutated sea creatures to be cleared away for his escape, he still falls foul of the giant swordfish.

Mark Richman, sometimes billed as Peter Mark Richman, previously appeared in "The Monster's Web." His Hendrix is an obvious villain from the start, but as a series of set pieces to while away the time, it will do. Production no: 1312.

Man-Beast

wr. William Welch, dir. Jerry Hopper

Agreeing to test a new serum that will allow humans to take diving bells deeper than ever before, Crane is unaware that the experiment he has volunteered for will transform him into a raging beast-man.

With Lawrence Montaigne (Dr. Braddock).

Captain Crane's turn to change into a werewolf-type, courtesy of a crazy scientist. Interestingly, Richard Basehart is completely absent from the first half of the episode, giving the distinct impression that we are taking another *Voyage* without him, but he then turns up in the latter half to save the day.

This was not to be Hedison's last venture into lycanthropy; ten years later he would appear in several episodes of the awful *Fantasy Island* series, giving a truly dreadful performance as a man haunted by lycanthropy in a yarn also titled "Man-Beast." The werewolf make-up and transformation in the *Fantasy Island* farrago is seen only once, and is lamentably bad. There was something about the sheer lameness of *Fantasy Island* that seemed to provoke poor performances; the usually excellent Allen regular Kevin Hagen appears in the companion storyline in that episode, and he gives an uncharacteristically appalling performance too. Here, however, make-up legend Dan Striepke comes up with a typical yet original wolfman make-up for Hedison to work with, and work this dedicated actor does.

"I think that was our undoing" David Hedison complained once. "The rock men, the lobster man, the mummy...." But for all

his dislike of the show's monsters, Hedison, as in *The Fly*, his famous '50s creature feature, insisted on playing the creature himself, and by his own admission, "had a ball." It's a reasonably entertaining episode for us too, and Hedison had no qualms about looking as frazzled as the make-up people could make him during the lead-ups to his transformations. As in "Deadly Amphibians," director Jerry Hopper keeps the plot hopping with creative camera angles, full, busy, sets, and a few genuine moments of suspense, particularly in relation to the transformations. The only flaw comes in the form of some confusion over how much Crane knows about his condition. We are lead to believe throughout that Crane is completely oblivious to his alter-ego and his actions as the creature, but then when Nelson confronts him, he seems to know everything, and recalls and laments the death of a crewman.

Guest star Lawrence Montaigne deserves a special place in the SF TV Hall of Fame for the distinction of having played a Romulan, a Vulcan, an Invader, a THRUSH agent, and an American-Indian who stumbles through the Time Tunnel. Here, as the mad wheelchair-bound scientist Braddock—in all fairness to the Hall Of Clichés, the wheelchair does have a role to play in the story—Montaigne seems almost Spock-like; he was, in fact, the unlucky suitor in *Star Trek's* "Amok Time." Production no: 1323.

Savage Jungle

wr. Arthur Weiss, dir. Robert Sparr

The Seaview becomes a floating greenhouse when another race of plant-men make an appearance.

With Perry Lopez (Keeler), Pat Culliton (first commando).

Another episode produced on the cheap, utilizing stock footage of ordinary things which attain menacing significance because they are where they shouldn't be, and an abundance of rubber plants! The alien is conveniently in human form and

Seaview uniform, and the three commandoes are simply regular Allen bit-players clad in camouflage outfits and inexplicably covered in regulation silver paint. The device Nelson uses to clear away the plants is idiotic both in execution and concept, and much of the episode is able to be padded with drawn-out scenes of everybody stumbling around and collapsing from lack of oxygen, series regulars wandering around through the plants, and Keeler changing his soldiers back and forth from doll-size. There was apparently some sort of personality conflict between Lopez and Culliton, although it doesn't show up onscreen. Lopez also appeared twice in *The Time Tunnel*, in "Massacre" and "Night of the Long Knives." Production no: 1322.

Flaming Ice

wr. Arthur Browne Jr., dir. Robert Sparr

Frost Men from an icy alien world attempt to steal the Seaview's nuclear reactor to repair their downed saucer ... flooding the Earth in the process.

With Michael Pate (Gelid), Frank Babich, George Robotham (Frost Men).

One of the better-looking of the last few *Voyages*, even though the Frost Men's lair has been done on the cheap; the *Time Tunnel* computers can be seen in the background along with several other familiar bits and pieces cobbled together. The concept was probably an easy sell to Allen at this late date because of the potential for using snowbound stock footage from the pilot, but "Flaming Ice" still required a little more effort into putting it together than most of the back end of the final year. The story has the usual rushed, random collection of jeopardy scenes and once-through-the-typewriter dialogue of this point in the series, and the aliens have their usual handy powers of force fields and teleportation as required; one has the distinct feeling that Kowalski was supposed to be hit by something in the early sequence watching the sub with Patterson—instead, it just looks like he's slipped. As for

why the aliens should make such a production out of showing off their fatal weakness to Nelson, that's just plain poor writing. Resembling the sort of beings that used to terrorize the crews of puppet shows *Fireball XL-5* and *Stingray*, the Frost Men exist only to imperil the *Seaview*, however irrationally, and their weapons work to the advantage of the script, sometimes leaving their captives powerless, sometimes allowing the victims to come out of the effects. It's not Michael Pate's shining moment in the Allen series (he had first season *Voyages* "Long Live the King" and "The Traitor" and *Time Tunnel* villainy in "The Last Patrol" and "The Walls of Jericho" to his credit), but he comes through it okay. Fellow Frostie Frank Babich previously appeared in the series as the first onscreen victim of "The Abominable Snowman." Robert Dowdell does not appear in this episode.

The end result is an entertaining and unusual addition to the series that makes a welcome change to the plethora of bodysnatching/empty sub fillers of the final weeks as long as you don't think about the story too much, which is not big in the logic department. This was Arthur Browne's only script for Allen's series; even though he had just written the Elvis Presley film *Clambake*, there are no giant clams! Production no: 1324.

Attack

wr. William Welch, dir. Jerry Hopper

An arrogant but benevolent alien assists the Seaview against an invasion force from his world that intends to destroy every major city on Earth.

With Skip Homeier (Robek), Kevin Hagen (Komal).

This one should have been better than it was, but the budget cuts are now seriously hurting the show. The aliens look decidedly threadbare, the leader decked out in an old *Lost in Space* outfit and his stooges looking like refugees from one of *The Time Tunnel's* historical epics. Allen doesn't even bother to paint them a different color. There is an impressive matte shot of the saucer fleet, but it looks suspiciously as though it has come from somewhere else. Although everything's been put together on the cheap, the spacious alien command center is nicely built, albeit with familiar props. Kevin Hagen, who had a vast array of variable TV SF credits including later playing Inspector Kobick in *Land of the Giants*, previously appeared in the more rewarding role of Doctor Alex Holden in the second season's "The Shape of Doom" and also appeared as malevolent aliens in *Lost in Space* for "His Majesty Smith" and *The Time Tunnel* for "Raiders from Outer Space," each time looking quite different. As for poor Skip Homeier, appearing in his third *Voyage* after "The Amphibians" in the first season and "The Day the World Ended" in the third, he still had *Star Trek's* mind-blowingly bad "The Way to Eden" to film for his resume. At least he's the only alien in this episode not to have to wear a silly costume. This is the second to last episode of the series produced. Production no: 1325.

The Edge of Doom

wr. William Welch, dir. Justus Addiss
Nelson must work out which one of his crew members has been replaced by an impostor.

Another daft impostor yarn similar to "Man of Many Faces," and on the face of it, slightly more credible for having the villain impersonate just one person. This time however, the failings are with the story, which is absurd, as Nelson tries to ferret out the fake (believing Crane to be the phoney) with the aid of the other two possible suspects ... neither of whom are ordered to stay in each other's company. Instead of summoning all three men and simply trying to use medical or scientific methods such as dental or fingerprinting identification—or even just trying to rip a few fake faces off—he sets up a series of demented psychological tests that endanger the ship! The Flying Sub also plays

a similar pivotal role, as in "Man of Many Faces." Despite the colossal stupidity of it all, the build-up to the impostor's revelation is quite suspenseful, and if you suspend all logic, the episode is fun ... but it's no wonder the network held it back to a point when the ratings didn't matter any more. Production no: 1318.

The Death Clock

wr. Sidney Marshall, dir. Charles Rondeau
Crane enters the fourth dimension.
With Christopher Robinson (Mallory).

Like "The Edge of Doom," this episode was held back from the middle of the series until near the end, and it's not difficult to see why. As a villainous adversary, Chris Robinson is bland and nondescript, with little to distinguish him and little for the actor to work with. The Space Time Unit the story revolves around is an all-purpose device used not to explore notions of time and space but simply as an excuse for a variety of set pieces utilizing standing sets and library footage. The one unique special effect—the ghostly Crane rising from his comatose form—is reused from "Return of the Phantom." Nevertheless, while logic plays little part in the proceedings, David Hedison's performance saves the episode from being a complete loss, as it was well known he appreciated any opportunity to extend his performance from Crane's usual stiff persona. The set pieces are at least capable of holding the interest, if not sustaining the episode's tenuous grip on credibility. Production no: 1311.

No Way Back

wr. William Welch, dir. Robert Sparr
Time-traveling madman Mr. Pem transports the Seaview through time again, to the American War of Independence, where he's done a deal with a notorious American traitor.
With Henry Jones (Mr. Pem), Barry Atwater (Major General Benedict Arnold), William Beckley (Major John Andre).

Mad scientist Mr. Pem returns in this

very last episode of *Voyage to the Bottom of the Sea*, and happily in a superior adventure that at least ensured the *Seaview* sailed into syndication with some of its original class intact. This was Henry Jones' third *Voyage*; he previously appeared as Sprague in "Night of Terror" and as Mr. Pem in "A Time to Die." This is much better than Pem's first appearance. William Beckley is very good as the tragic Andre, while Atwater (the modern-day vampire in *The Night Stalker* and "The Buccaneer" from *Voyage's* first season) makes a fine Benedict Arnold, sensibly played not as a seething villain but a military man on an opposing side. There's a twinge of nostalgia as *Time Tunnel* library music is played for the last time during the scenes with Arnold and Andre. Production no: 1326.

Episodes in Order of Production

FIRST SEASON (32 EPISODES)

6008 Eleven Days to Zero
7202 The Village of Guilt
7203 The Mist of Silence
7204 The City Beneath the Sea
7205 Turn Back the Clock
7206 Hail to the Chief
7207 The Fear Makers
7208 Hot Line
7209 The Sky Is Falling
7210 The Price of Doom
7211 Long Live the King
7212 Submarine Sunk Here
7213 The Magnus Beam
7214 No Way Out
7215 The Blizzard Makers
7216 The Ghost of Moby Dick
7217 Doomsday
7218 The Condemned
7219 Mutiny
7220 The Last Battle
7221 The Invaders
7222 The Indestructible Man
7223 The Buccaneer
7224 The Human Computer
7225 The Traitor
7226 The Saboteur
7227 Cradle of the Deep
7228 The Exile
7229 The Amphibians
7230 The Creature
7231 The Enemies
7232 The Secret of the Loch

SECOND SEASON (26 EPISODES)

8201 Jonah and the Whale
8202 And Five of Us Are Left
8203 Time Bomb
8204 Escape from Venice
8205 The Cyborg
8206 The Deadliest Game
8207 The Left-Handed Man
8209 The Silent Saboteurs
8210 The Death Ship
8211 Leviathan
8212 The Peacemaker
8213 The Monster from Outer Space
8214 The X Factor
8215 The Machines Strike Back
8216 Killers of the Deep
8217 Terror on Dinosaur Island
8218 Deadly Creature Below
8219 The Phantom Strikes
8220 The Sky's on Fire
8221 Graveyard of Fear
8222 The Shape of Doom
8223 Dead Men's Doubloons
8224 The Monster's Web
8225 The Menfish
8226 The Mechanical Man
8227 The Return of the Phantom
    (Note: there is no number 8208. Despite the late numbering, it is possible this was the abandoned second season opener concerning spies and surfers, devised to introduce the character of Riley, and abandoned due to prohibitive costs. Whatever the storyline, 8208 was apparently abandoned.)

THIRD SEASON (26 EPISODES)

9201 Monster from the Inferno
9202 Werewolf
9203 Day of Evil
9204 Night of Terror
9205 The Day the World Ended
9206 The Terrible Toys
9207 Deadly Waters
9208 The Thing from Inner Space
9209 Deadly Invasion
9210 The Death Watch

9211 The Lost Bomb
9212 The Plant Man
9213 The Brand of the Beast
9214 The Creature
9215 The Haunted Submarine
9216 Death from the Past
9217 The Heat Monster
9218 The Fossil Men
9219 The Mermaid
9220 The Mummy
9221 The Shadow Man
9222 No Escape from Death
9223 Doomsday Island
9224 The Wax Men
9225 Deadly Cloud
9226 Destroy Seaview

FOURTH SEASON (26 EPISODES)

1301 Man of Many Faces
1302 Time Lock
1303 The Deadly Dolls

1304 Fires of Death
1305 Cave of the Dead
1306 Sealed Orders
1307 Journey with Fear
1308 Terror
1309 Fatal Cargo
1310 Rescue
1311 The Death Clock
1312 Secret of the Deep
1313 Blow Up
1314 Deadly Amphibians
1315 The Abominable Snowman
1316 The Return of Blackbeard
1317 A Time to Die
1318 The Edge of Doom
1319 Nightmare
1320 The Lobster Man
1321 The Terrible Leprechaun
1322 Savage Jungle
1323 Man-Beast
1324 Flaming Ice
1325 Attack
1326 No Way Back

—— Episodes in Order of Broadcast ——

FIRST SEASON (32 EPISODES)

6008 Eleven Days to Zero
7204 The City Beneath the Sea
7207 The Fear Makers
7203 The Mist of Silence
7210 The Price of Doom
7209 The Sky is Falling
7205 Turn Back the Clock
7202 The Village of Guilt
7208 Hot Line
7212 Submarine Sunk Here
7213 The Magnus Beam
7214 No Way Out
7215 The Blizzard Makers
7216 The Ghost of Moby Dick
7211 Long Live the King
7206 Hail to the Chief
7220 The Last Battle
7219 Mutiny
7217 Doomsday
7221 The Invaders
7222 The Indestructible Man
7223 The Buccaneer
7224 The Human Computer
7226 The Saboteur
7227 Cradle of the Deep
7229 The Amphibians
7228 The Exile

7230 The Creature
7231 The Enemies
7232 The Secret of the Loch
7218 The Condemned
7225 The Traitor

SECOND SEASON (26 EPISODES)

8201 Jonah and the Whale
8203 Time Bomb
8202 And Five of Us Are Left
8205 The Cyborg
8204 Escape from Venice
8207 The Left-Handed Man
8206 The Deadliest Game
8211 Leviathan
8212 The Peacemaker
8209 The Silent Saboteurs
8214 The X Factor
8215 The Machines Strike Back
8213 The Monster from Outer Space
8217 Terror on Dinosaur Island
8216 Killers of The Deep
8218 Deadly Creature Below
8219 The Phantom Strikes
8220 The Sky's on Fire
8221 Graveyard of Fear
8222 The Shape of Doom

8223 Dead Men's Doubloons
8210 The Death Ship
8224 The Monster's Web
8225 The Menfish
8226 The Mechanical Man
8227 The Return of the Phantom

THIRD SEASON (26 EPISODES)

9201 Monster from the Inferno
9202 Werewolf
9205 The Day the World Ended
9204 Night of Terror
9206 The Terrible Toys
9203 Day of Evil
9207 Deadly Waters
9208 The Thing from Inner Space
9210 The Death Watch
9209 Deadly Invasion
9215 The Haunted Submarine
9212 The Plant Man
9211 The Lost Bomb
9213 The Brand of the Beast
9214 The Creature
9216 Death from the Past
9217 The Heat Monster
9218 The Fossil Men
9219 The Mermaid
9220 The Mummy
9221 The Shadow Man
9222 No Escape from Death
9223 Doomsday Island

9224 The Wax Men
9225 Deadly Cloud
9226 Destroy Seaview

FOURTH SEASON (26 EPISODES)

1304 Fires of Death
1303 The Deadly Dolls
1305 Cave of the Dead
1307 Journey with Fear
1306 Sealed Orders
1301 Man of Many Faces
1309 Fatal Cargo
1302 Time Lock
1310 Rescue
1308 Terror
1317 A Time to Die
1313 Blow Up
1314 Deadly Amphibians
1316 The Return of Blackbeard
1321 The Terrible Leprechaun
1320 The Lobster Man
1319 Nightmare
1315 The Abominable Snowman
1312 Secret of the Deep
1323 Man-Beast
1322 Savage Jungle
1324 Flaming Ice
1325 Attack
1318 The Edge of Doom
1311 The Death Clock
1326 No Way Back

Production Credits

Created and produced by Irwin Allen. Assistant to producer: Paul Zastupnevich. Story editor: William Welch (first season). Story editor: Sidney Marshall (second, third and fourth seasons). Art direction: William J. Creber, Stan Jolley, Louis Korn, Jim McGuire, Rodger E. Maus. Art direction supervisor: Jack Martin Smith. Set decoration: Walter M. Scott, Bert Allen, Sven Wickman. Also: Robert De Vestel, Stuart Reiss, Norman Rockett. Costume design and wardrobe: Paul Zastupnevich. Director of photography: Robert J. Bronner, Carl Guthrie, Winton Hoch, Sam Leavitt, Paul Vogel. Special effects: Lyle B. Abbott, Howard Lydecker. Music: Paul Sawtell, Lennie Hayton, Harry Geller, Leith Stevens, Hugo Friedhofer. Also: Alexander Courage, Robert Drasnin, Irving Gertz, Jerry Goldsmith, Michael Hennagin, Joseph Mullendore, Nelson Riddle, Herman Stein, Morton Stevens. Music editor: Morrie McNaughton. Also: Harry Eisen, Music supervision: Leonard Engel, Lionel Newman. Theme music: Paul Sawtell. Sound effects editor: Robert Cornett, Don Hall Jr., Ralph Hickey. Also: Don Higgins, Dickie Le Grand. Production supervisor: Jack Sonntag. Production manager: Gaston Glass, Hal Herman, Les Warner. Unit production manager: Hal Herman, Harry Templeton. Unit production coordinator: Jack Stubbs. Assistant directors: William McGarry, Norman August. Also: Les Warner, Jack Stubbs, Gil Mandelik, John Bloss, Gil Kissel, Wilson Shyer, Dink Templeton, Ad Shaumer (pilot only). Underwater photography: John Lamb. Film editors: James Baiotto, Robert Belcher, Roland Gross, Dick Wormell. Also: Frederick Baratta, Jack Gleason, John Holmes, Homer Powell, Dolf Rudeen, George Watters. Make-up: Ben Nye. Hair styling: Margaret Donovan. Post production supervisor: George Swink. Post production co-ordinator: Robert Mintz. Associate producer: Joseph Gantman, Allan Balter (first season), William Welch, Frank La Tourette (second sea-son), Bruce Fowler (third and fourth seasons). In charge of production: William Self. Cambridge Productions for 20th Century Fox.

2 *Lost in Space*

September 1965–March 1968

Like all science fiction, *Lost in Space* is first and foremost of its era. Yes, it was a juvenile show—but it was a family show aimed at kids, and kids liked it. A few adults were caught glancing at the screen too—Allen had a knack for making programs that were difficult to ignore if you were in the room at the same time! Many vintage TV series are a delight to see again in a charming sort of way, and *Lost in Space* is no exception. It still stands up as good entertainment in its own right, and Allen's shows come from an age when science-fiction and fantasy TV shows were watched by everyone, not just an elite clique of enthusiasts.

Irwin Allen was a showman, pure and simple, and *Lost in Space* (and his other hit TV series *The Time Tunnel*, *Land of the Giants*, and *Voyage to the Bottom of the Sea*) were intended as spectacle, adventure, and entertainment. The early *Lost in Space* was the equivalent of a high-budget Saturday morning serial, cliffhanger endings and all, and on that level it worked splendidly. It later became more of a light comedy, and it still worked—it was funny.

With the fear and paranoia of the '50s on the wane, America was now looking forward to the future, and was more afraid of foreign powers misusing atomic energy than of the technology itself. President Kennedy, for overt political reasons, had made his rousing speech about how America was going to go to the stars and space was seen

as an attainable "final frontier." Science-fiction of the period speculated on when, not if, humankind was going to colonize the stars, recklessly putting ambitious dates (now long past) for the first moon landing, first moon base, first permanently manned space stations, first families in space. Outer space was ours. We were going to colonize it, police it, live there, farm there, vacation there. It was an exciting and compelling concept in Kennedy's optimistic space-age America, exploited to the hilt by both *Lost in Space* and *Star Trek*, both of which transposed western pioneer mythology to a space age setting.

Both *Star Trek* and *Lost in Space* were initially conceived as series echoing the brave pioneer spirit of the Old West. That *Star Trek's* U.S.S. *Enterprise* ended up policing the galaxies for politicians and *Lost in Space* also ended up jettisoning the covered wagon parallels is indicative of the change in mood in America following the tragedy of Kennedy's assassination. There is no greater gauge of public mood and opinion than pop culture, and the escalation of the Vietnam conflict and the arrival of a liberal, light-hearted environment in a Europe largely untroubled by and ignorant of events in Southeast Asia resulted in a surge of light-hearted escapism on American television and the almost total disappearance of any serious dramatic content until the early 1970s. Having begun as relatively straight Hollywood pulp

SF, *Lost in Space* gradually transformed, almost un-noticeably at first, into a pantomime spoof with Doctor Zachary Smith as the Grand Dame and Will Robinson the Principal Boy.

Leader of the Robinson expedition was Professor John Robinson, played by Guy Williams, formerly TV's heroic *Zorro* for Disney. A perfect leading man for adventure fantasy, he was excellent in the films *Captain Sindbad* and *Damon And Pythias*. Playing his wife Maureen—very much the typical kindly mother figure but also a scientist and pioneer woman in her own right—was June Lockhart, fresh from a similar motherly role in TV's *Lassie*. From an acting family, she was the daughter of Gene and Kathleen Lockhart, and mother of Anne, who would later play the role of Sheba in the 1970s *Battlestar Galactica*. Approached by Allen after a guest appearance in *Voyage to the Bottom of the Sea*, June Lockhart was the first to be cast. TV guest spots prior to casting included *Bewitched* and *The Man from UNCLE*.

Angela Cartwright (who had just appeared as one of the kids in *The Sound of Music*, and grew up before American audiences on the sit-com *Make Room for Daddy*) was daughter Penny, and busy child actor Billy Mumy (fresh from numerous guest appearances including *Bewitched*, *The Munsters*, *I Dream of Jeannie*, and three memorable episodes of *The Twilight Zone*) was the youngest member of the party, Will Robinson. A chimp from neighboring jungle show *Daktari* was drafted in to play alien pet Debbie the Bloop in a woolly balaclava!

Enjoying, if that's the right word, a very chaste holding-hands romance were John's colleague and pilot Major Don West (played by Mark Goddard) and the oldest Robinson daughter Judy (Marta Kristen). Mark Goddard had three series under his belt already, the western *Johnny Ringo*, the cop show *The Detectives*, and the failed and forgotten sit-com *Many Happy Returns*. Marta Kristen had done some small TV roles, and one of her

earliest films was cult beach movie *Beach Blanket Bingo*, in which she played a mermaid. Kristen's Judy was little more than an attractive decoration to entice older adolescents to the screen, although she was promised more at the outset, as were all the Robinson family players. But everyone was so incredibly warm and wonderful, that one important ingredient was missing—conflict. The fundamental concern was sustaining the theme on a weekly basis. Earthquakes, floods, lost cities and bizarre weather conditions would soon exhaust their appeal, and some human drama was needed.

The problem was solved by a fortuitous and last-minute addition to the cast by story editor Anthony Wilson. The cause of the Robinson's misfortune of becoming lost in space would be the wicked Dr. Zachary Smith, an agent for a foreign power and reluctant stowaway played by Jonathan Harris. The sinister spy plot device had proven an invaluable asset in getting the crew of the *Seaview* in mortal danger in *Voyage to the Bottom of the Sea* every other week, and seemed an obvious ploy in getting the Robinson's vessel, the *Jupiter Two*, into equally sticky situations. It proved ultimately to be the series' salvation, and the series' major bone of contention when the colorful, comical creation of Doctor Zachary Smith inevitably—along with the famous Robot, another last minute fix—stole the show.

The Robot, the other ingenious late addition, was designed by Bob Kinoshita, an art director who was also responsible for building Robby the Robot of *Forbidden Planet*, MGM's 1956 sci-fi feature, and many people confuse this character with the unnamed *Lost in Space* Robot (Harris said he wanted to call him Claude, but was vetoed!). Inside the Robot was dancer and stunt-man Bob May, who spoke the lines and later ad-libbed many impromptu routines with Jonathan Harris' Smith. The Robot's dialogue was later re-dubbed by announcer

Dick Tufeld, a disappointment to May, but a wise decision. Tufeld had known creator/producer Irwin Allen since his radio days, and had coincidentally worked as narrator on Guy Williams' *Zorro* series. He would also contribute narration to *The Time Tunnel*, and voice-overs for almost all Allen's series, including the alien menace in the *Voyage to the Bottom of the Sea* episode "Monster from the Inferno."

The fact that the Robinsons' Environmental Control Robot had no name allowed the spiteful and deliciously petty Smith to assail the poor chap with a variety of alliterative insults which became a trade-mark of the show. The "animated weather-machine" was soon known by many popular put-downs, from addle-pated armor-bearer and computerized clod to cybernetic simpleton, disreputable dunce, tin-plated traitor and lead-lined lump! But the Robot usually had the last laugh when troublemaker Smith came to grief.

Whatever *Lost in Space* might have become later, the last minute addition to the show of Harris and the Robot was undoubtedly a wise move. Smith started out as an all-out, no-holds-barred villain, but once he (and Allen and his writers) realized that he would have to throw in his lot with the squeaky-clean Robinsons to enable them to exist together, he first became little more than a liability to the party, and then ultimately a bumbling, sneaky buffoon. As the series wore on, and the Robinsons and Smith accepted each other, the quite blatantly murderous Smith gradually transformed from evil would-be killer to clownish comic relief, as Harris' flamboyant and theatrical off-set persona gradually crept onstage. Like many of TV's recurring nasties—Frank Burns (*M*A*S*H*), Howard Hunter (*Hill Street Blues*), Dr. Craig (*St. Elsewhere*), J.R. Ewing (*Dallas*)—he rapidly grew in audience affection to become the villain you love to hate.

When he was evil, he was despicably evil, jaw-droppingly selfish, and unbelievably short-sighted. The first scene in the series to show Smith and the Robot in a comedic light—in "The Oasis"—has Smith taking a shower in the Robinsons' precious limited water supply while the tone-deaf Robot joins him in a tuneless chorus from *The Barber of Seville!* When divine retribution came, as it always did, it was a thunderbolt that sent Smith screaming, briefly repentant, to the supposed safety of the spaceship. Smith's transgressions—and his comeuppance—were taken—and treated—seriously. By the second season, Smith's escapades had become antics, far less operatic than the grand scale of the first season's crimes. He was now more confident, and supremely arrogant—but he had become a comic figure, offering no real menace to the Robinsons, and the sense of menace threatened by the formerly hostile environment of space had also dissipated. With weaker alien visitors on display (first season e.t.s all evidenced a sense of unknown danger, even the friendly ones), and no location filming of any description, the second season lacked any sense of threat or hardship—the Robinsons were now a happy band of campers, no longer threatened by adverse and extreme weather conditions, and good-naturedly tinkering with weather devices and look-out post radios rather than fleeing for the safety of the force field, struggling to grow crops, or battling harsh terrain. Travels in the Chariot were day trips, lacking any life-saving urgency, machinery was fixed at leisure. Mrs. Robinson's laundry came out of the washing machine ready-wrapped in polythene; Penny and Judy had time to style their hair; Smith had acquired nightwear and any other accoutrements he might require for his delusional exploits. He was just another kid, good-humoredly tolerated by the head-shaking, hard-working Robinsons.

With more years of theatrical experience behind him than the rest of the cast put together, and two previous series (*The*

Third Man and *The Bill Dana Show*), Harris knew a golden opportunity when he saw it. A natural scene stealer, Marta Kristen jokes in interviews that Harris would always make sure he got the last word in any altercation ... and in scenes where he doesn't have dialogue, the viewer will always catch him handwringing or eye-swiveling, head darting back and forth between speakers like a nervous pigeon, to ensure that any group dialogue scene becomes a scene about Smith's reaction to it. He was a delightfully funny extrovert and hammy performer who reveled in his role as the evil and self-centered Smith, who boards the *Jupiter Two* moments before lift-off with the intention of blowing them all to kingdom come, having just performed his official business of passing the family fit for their five year journey where no family has gone before. Smith's (un-named) superiors have ordered him to destroy the space project, and the malevolent medic reprograms the ship's guardian and protector, the impressive mobile device known only as "the Robot"—to do just that. Inadvertently trapped on board the ship at lift-off (the scene showing Smith screaming in terror, unprotected by the suspended animation shielding the Robinson family, is memorably chilling), Smith is forced to remove the Robot's power pack to prevent him carrying out his new orders ... but Will, unaware of Smith's actions, reactivates the Robot, and the mechanical man promptly goes berserk, throwing the ship way off course in the process, and causing the family to become lost in space. Smith puts the family through a harrowing series of events while calling the shots until the ship crash-lands. The Robot is returned to the family, and they must now find a way to either return to Earth or proceed to Alpha Centauri, their original destination.

The pilot film, filmed in 1964, was eventually pulled to pieces and used as the basis for four of the first five episodes. The storyline, written by Shimon Wincelberg, was divided into impressive set-pieces, and each of the future *Lost in Space* writers assigned to write a story around the events. These included the meteor storm, the crash-landing, the journey across the planet, the deserted city, the sea storm, and the famous giant cyclops monster among others. Many excellent miniatures were built, including one of the Chariot, while the actors' doubles were sent out to the Arizona desert with the full-sized version to film inserts of the Robinsons traveling over the planet's rocky terrain; the sequence of the Chariot crossing the planet's ocean, one of the most exciting in the series, was filmed at the giant water tank Fox had built for *Voyage to the Bottom of the Sea*. Sadly, CBS was one year behind the other networks in going to color, and this is doubly sad because as well as making the first and best season rarer in reruns, photos from that year show that the colors of the sets and costumes were at their best, many of the cast clothed in stylish red and blue rather than the kaleidoscope of Carnaby Street colors that followed.

During the course of their adventures in space and on the surface of a hostile and unpredictable planet, the Robinson party are boiled, roasted, chilled and soaked from one end of the planet to the other; the Robot runs amok; Professor Robinson and his wife are cast adrift in space; they encounter a colossal space-station housing alien fellow-travelers; crash-land; get trapped in the ruins of an ancient civilization during an electrical storm; entombed in an ancient crypt during an earthquake; travel across a frozen sea; and discover that the planet's soil turns plants into monsters and monsters into giants! Marooned on the one planet for the whole of the first season (Allen originally conceived the series as a sci-fi version of Johann Wyss' novel *Swiss Family Robinson*, hence the family's name), the Robinsons set off on an adventurous and genuinely exciting trek across the planet for the first few episodes (without Smith, as this footage

This famous image of the Cyclops monster terrorizing the Chariot appeared everywhere when *Lost in Space* was launched in a blaze of publicity.

came from the original Smith-less pilot film) in the intriguing Chariot, an impressive all-terrain tank-like bus, before returning to the camp-site for a mostly excellent first season of adventures. Although the Chariot would be used again that season for a couple of expeditions, it sadly remained stationary or studio-bound for the rest of the series, but for stock footage inserts.

The greatest gift to the historian, social commentator, or archivist is that of 20/20 hindsight, and with this advantage we can see how, episode by episode, at key moments in the series' development, *Lost in Space* gradually changed from a straight dramatic show with moments of comedy into a light comedy show with moments of drama. It wasn't intentionally planned or decided, but it was no accident either.

Although the first season was filmed in black and white, it is generally agreed that these were by far the best episodes of *Lost in Space*—and they are beautifully photographed and directed. Viewers new to the series, or more familiar with the direction the show took in later years, will be surprised to see how different these first episodes are from the later, lighter-hearted color ones that play the most. These stories are much more dramatic, the planet they are marooned on is more desolate, and the series is graced with the occasional outdoor shoot or crane shot. Billy Mumy, Angela Cartwright and Jonathan Harris are much younger-looking, the Robinson family play a much larger part in the proceedings, and the Robot is a little clumsier and more robotic than the "bubble-headed booby" of later years. Most significantly, arch-villain Doctor Zachary Smith was a much a nastier piece of work, far removed from his later image as a loveable old loon.

In "The Sky Is Falling" for example, there is genuinely dramatic tension when Will disappears after the arrival of an alien family, and Smith gradually ferments an atmosphere of bigotry and paranoia within the camp. The relationships between the characters are much more realistically portrayed, and most episodes offered morality tales to the viewers, while paradoxically being more adult in the storytelling. Professor Robinson's insistence in this story that the alien family should be treated as friendly until proven otherwise is clearly contrasted with Smith's unreasoning fearfulness, while in "His Majesty Smith," the Robinson family insist on retaining the real Smith, with all his faults and flaws over a friendly, helpful, but phony android double that is a more attractive proposition. Intelligent, sensitive stories such as these, "My Friend Mr. Nobody," and the Capra-esque Christmas episode "Return from Outer Space" were exclusive to the B&W first season, and the later episodes with similar opportunities, such as "The Golden Man," "Visit to a Hostile Planet," and "Target Earth" opted for a different, lighter approach to similar themes. The only reason that the more fanciful episodes of later seasons worked as they did were because these early stories had laid the groundwork and set out the parameters of the series.

Yet the first season also had moments of broad humor more typical of the later years. "The Space Croppers," by Peter Packer, is one of the earliest examples of the more loony stories, featuring a family of space-hillbillies in which the son turns into a werewolf at full moon. Smith, unaware of this, intends to marry the mother to secure a passage to Earth, his usual goal. Generally Packer stayed on pure B-movie sci-fi themes for later episodes leaving the sillier concepts to other writers, yet it was he, with his "Welcome Stranger" and "Ghost in Space," who initially opened the door for some of the dafter stories.

The second season opened in September 1966 with "Blast Off into Space." This episode is the first of four which, like the first year, string together to form one complete lengthy adventure. The second season was the first to be filmed in color, and opens with a forced evacuation from the planet where they have spent their first year, and the *Jupiter Two* is briefly in flight again, the Robinsons back in space for the first time since the *Jupiter Two* crash-landed in the first season. During the course of this mini-series of sorts, the planet they spent the first season on is destroyed by Nerim, an elderly prospector, played by film veteran Strother Martin, who has been mining the planet for valuable "Cosmonium," and whose blasting has done irreparable damage to the already volatile make-up of the planet. Once in space again, Professor Robinson is insistent that they head for their original destination of Alpha Centauri to colonize, while Smith tries a number of ploys and threats to get the ship on course for Earth. After some excellent opening episodes, showing the characters and series at their best (and during which they narrowly miss a chance to return to Earth again), the *Jupiter Two* eventually crash-lands on a new unexplored world where they would spend the second season (the Robinsons have to arrange another hasty evacuation in the first episode of season three, which finds them periodically traveling through space and stopping off at a variety of other worlds). Like many second seasons for returning series, the first few episodes resembled the first season. There is another act of sabotage by Smith, another space walk, another crash landing, another inhospitable planet that mysteriously brightens up after the initial exploration.

A series of spoofy, humorous episodes follow, primarily concerning Will, Smith, and the Robot, as the series found the formula to sustain it for the next year and in the memories of the general public. The best of the second season episodes were those that religiously adhered to the winning formula in which stories concerned themselves almost exclusively with the exploits of Will, Smith and the Robot, with John Robinson and Don West charging in at the last mo-ment to bail them out of whatever dilemma Smith had got them into. Some of the episodes featuring zany rather than lethal space visitors, worked quite well—"Mutiny in Space," in which Will, Smith, and the Robot are shanghaied, "The Android Machine," which has some great comedy in it, and the sequels "The Toymaker" and "Revolt of the Androids," all of which work on their own level. Other stories, such as the dreadful "West of Mars," "The Girl from the Green Dimension" (a sequel to "Wild Adventure"), and the silly "The Questing Beast" are hopelessly over the top. *Lost in Space* never misfired more badly than when the show was *trying* to be funny. Some writers tried to deliberately inject comedy sequences into the show, not realizing that the humor was inherent in the performances and came naturally.

Interspersed with the space sultans, viking warriors, pirates, ghosts, and magicians of the second year, all of which were colorful and fun, were a handful of straight SF concepts, which made for quite exciting stories while still including the Smith and Robot double act. In "Trip Through the Robot," the Robot balefully trundles out of the camp to fade away for the good of the Robinson party after Smith has created a power shortage. Wandering into a misty valley declared off-limits by Robinson, he is turned into a giant, and Smith and Will must enter his works to reverse the growing process, only to get trapped inside when the Robot starts to return to normal size. In "Wreck of the Robot" wacky silent aliens with blank, glittery faces and bowler hats (!) take the Robot apart during another whiny act of loyal self-sacrifice (the Robot's constant exposure to Smith has turned him into something of a martyr by now!), and in "The Mechanical Men" he becomes the leader of a race of tiny Robots in his image. In "The Colonists" the menfolk are captured by Amazons and are put to work while the women are treated wonderfully, while in

"The Phantom Family," the Robinsons are gradually replaced by duplicate impostors. Other enjoyable episodes with Smith and the Robot on top form include "The Dream Monster," "Cave of the Wizards," "The Prisoners of Space" (which includes clips from early episodes), and "The Galaxy Gift," which guest stars horror film veteran John Carradine.

Lost in Space became a hit in six weeks, largely through positive word of mouth. Each week, more viewers came on board. One thing all the books and most of the fans are agreed on is that Lost in Space deteriorated in quality over its three years, a view also held by Bill Mumy, Angela Cartwright, and the late Guy Williams. On the face of it, this is true in general terms, but it's worth playing Devil's Advocate for a minute.

Firstly, the ratings were consistent for the show's entire three year run. They never declined, except for the summer repeats (which still held more than half the audience), and the second season started particularly well, even against the second season of pop culture phenomenon Batman. Also, it's not true that the first year was the sensible season and everything got silly when the show went to color. Yes, all the really excellent episodes in dramatic terms were in the first season (the third year's "Anti-Matter Man" being a memorable exception). However, first season episodes such as "Ghost in Space," "The Space Trader," "His Majesty Smith," "The Space Croppers" and "A Change of Space" are all entirely typical of second season fare, almost blueprints for the seasons to come. What creates this illusion of a clearly defined switch in styles between first and second season may be that the first season was filmed in crisp, clear monochrome like such classic shows as The Twilight Zone and The Outer Limits, whereas the second season looks much more garish because it was CBS' first year of color TV. Unfortunately, many of the props and planet backgrounds look much less convincing

when painted in bold primary colors. The second season also looks flatter and more studio bound, as the close of the first year also brought about the end of such luxuries as the debut season's highly effective crane shots and location filming. Top-notch directors such as Leo Penn, Paul Stanley, Leonard Horn and Sutton Roley (but for one episode, not uncoincidentally, "Anti-Matter Man") did not return (although most of the later directors—Harry Harris, Sobey Martin, Don Richardson—are already firmly in place by the end of the first season).

Although the writer of the pilot, Shimon Wincelberg, had long since departed, story editor Wilson had by now gathered together a small cache of regular and reliable writers. Of these, Peter Packer and Barney Slater were the most prolific, while Carey Wilber (who also wrote for The Time Tunnel and Star Trek) and Bob and Wanda Duncan also made regular contributions. The Duncans later wrote for The Time Tunnel and Land of the Giants. These five writers wrote every second season episode of Lost in Space but two (and those two were major turkeys). Although some new contributors were bought in for the third year, including, most advantageously, Robert Hamner from Voyage to the Bottom of the Sea, Packer and Slater between them provided over half the third season episodes filmed. Whereas Packer would usually use Smith to get the Robinsons into trouble, Slater usually turned out yarns in which the bad things happened to Doctor Smith.

For the third and final season, the series enjoyed a higher budget and a complete face-lift, including new theme, opening credits, costumes, and props. The Jupiter Two spent much of its time in space and—to its slight detriment—moved away from the popular Smith/Will/Robot formula to give equal time to other cast members. Smith inevitably remained the catalyst of most adventures, and the main instigator of the family's adventures and misfortunes, but did not always dominate the action. By the end of the first season, and throughout the entire second season, almost every episode had centered around the increasingly bizarre exploits of Smith and his two dupes, the impressionable and loyal Will, and the Robot, much to the chagrin of the three women in the cast and Guy Williams, the series' supposed lead, who found themselves increasingly pushed into the background. Williams understandably complained to Allen and his agent, and this resulted in several episodes in the third season revolving around other cast members, most notably "Hunter's

Moon," specifically commissioned to placate Williams with the central role. While it was always a pleasure to see more of Williams, a stoic television tough guy in the grand tradition of the Hollywood hero (he also shares center stage with Smith, Will and the Robot in "Anti-Matter Man" and "The Time Merchant"), episodes focusing on Judy or Penny ("The Haunted Lighthouse," "A Day at the Zoo," "Princess of Space," and "Space Beauty") were often crushingly dull. Kristen's few moments of glory in the spotlight served only to illustrate her youthful lack of ability and the vapidity of the character she

Suntanned and refreshed, the cast of *Lost in Space* pose to promote the third season. Left to right, Billy Mumy, Mark Goddard, Marta Kristen, Jonathan Harris, June Lockhart, Guy Williams, Angela Cartwright.

had been given to work with, while Angela Cartwright, no longer the wide-eyed child of such first season gems as "My Friend, Mr. Nobody" had quite literally grown out of her role.

The notable thing about the third and final season of *Lost in Space* was that when it was good, it was far superior to the second season, but when it was bad, it was much, much worse. The second season may have been more inclined to go the comedy route, but Smith and the Robot were genuinely funny in those stories, and the quality and formula of the episodes were consistent. With the second season formula abandoned and the show unwilling or unable to return to its straight SF origins, third season episodes were wildly variable in both style and quality, from those almost as good as the first season, to some even worse than the lows of the second year. Episodes such as "Collision of the Planets" starring a young Daniel Travanti in a delinquent biker role he's probably still trying to forget, the heavy handed "Princess of Space" and dated generation gap story "The Promised Planet" were far worse than almost anything in the second season. Superior third season episodes include "The Condemned of Space" (guest starring *Forbidden Planet's* Robby the Robot, his second appearance in the show), "Deadliest of the Species" (the Robot gets a girlfriend!), "Anti-Matter Man" (great effects and ideas), and "The Time Merchant" (Smith's character comes full circle).

Fans of the comedic episodes will appreciate "Two Weeks in Space" and "Castles in Space," while "The Space Primevals" and "Fugitives in Space" (with *Hill Street Blues'* bear-like Michael Conrad hidden underneath excellent John Chambers make-up) have a good time with the relationship between Smith and Major Don West; others, including "Kidnapped in Space," "The Flaming Planet," and the notorious "The Great Vegetable Rebellion" are great fun.

In the poorer third season stories, the absence of Smith from certain scenes left a gaping void, but the best of the third season yarns involved the entire family, such as "Visit to a Hostile Planet," "Target Earth," "Deadliest of the Species," and "The Space Creature." Mark Goddard, who, as Williams' side-kick, found his lines being given to Williams in order to placate him, eventually had more to do when Williams walked off the set a couple of times. Later, for episodes such as "Castles in Space," Williams and June Lockhart would film inserts to explain their absence from the main story. Making their point in a more subtle manner, Angela Cartwright has told how, in one episode, she, Marta Kristen, and June Lockhart, all stood in line with their little fingers extended *Invaders*-style (this other popular SF series was also running at the time) for a sequence in which they noticeably had little else to do!

In later years, in interviews given to various fan publications, all the actors, including Williams, were philosophical about the direction the show eventually took in the heady and chaotic environment of 1960s TV, a period renowned for its wacky television. They maintain that despite their status in the series, and the nature of some of the plots, the cast for the most part, took it in their stride, with Harris apparently treating the entire cast and crew to a continuous supply of lollipops every day. Arguments and disputes have been acknowledged but downplayed, and all of the cast are reliably on record as having said that the show was fun to make, and that they enjoyed themselves (although Mark Goddard has told how he burst into tears when he saw the silver spacesuit he had to wear!). The two things that the entire supporting cast agree on was that no-one but Jonathan Harris, the juvenile audience, and the network liked the direction Smith's character went in (Williams called it "giving the show 'the cutes'"), and that "The Great Vegetable Rebellion" was without a doubt the silliest show they ever made! Jonathan Harris repeatedly argued that the evil Smith could not have been credibly sustained for the run of the series, and he was probably right. However, the long-circulated belief that Smith was to have been killed off after the first few episodes is not true.

Irwin Allen's attempts to keep the peace in the third year by giving more screen time to the other cast members improved some episodes while damaging others, but it got the series out of a rut. However, the family atmosphere deliberately cultivated in the first year, with the fatherly talks and motherly worries, and any developing relationship between Don West and Judy were almost entirely absent in favor of the colorful and bizarre absurdity that had become the overwhelming fashionable factor in most '60s TV. As enthusiasm for the era of absurdist TV personified by *My Favorite Martian, Bewitched, The Monkees, Batman,* and *The Wild Wild West* and later adopted by *The Man from UNCLE, The Avengers, Voyage to the Bottom of the Sea,* and even *Star Trek,* began to wane, the crew and cast inevitably began to sense the axe falling.

The story goes that Irwin Allen was certain of a fourth season, but fell out with CBS over budget cuts, and certainly the cast expected to return. Jonathan Harris was scheduled to dine with one of the CBS executives the very morning he read of the cancellation. "Oh and by the way, I did not call him for lunch!" he snapped to an interviewer! June Lockhart heard about it at a showbiz party. "I think that's for the best at this point" she told the messenger. "The show had run its course and it was enough for all of us" she explained to an interviewer. "It was time to go on to other things." Young Billy Mumy burst into tears. Despite his opinion that the quality of the series had declined, he was inconsolable. "But I lived to tell the tale!" he joked.

However, June Lockhart's assessment that the show had run its course was prob-

ably right. It is doubtful that Guy Williams would have returned for a fourth season, Mark Goddard and Marta Kristen were tired, Angela Cartwright had quite literally outgrown her role from sweet older sister to young woman and spare part, and Jonathan Harris had aged visibly from carrying the lion's share of the workload for three years. It was plainly apparent that the cast and writers were burnt out. Although the third season is remembered favorably by fans, about a third of the episodes are pretty bad and the production values on those and a few more were looking a little threadbare. Also, in terms of ratings, the series had started the season badly and although picking up as the year went on, a fourth season could have seen the series close down ignominiously. The episode titled "The Time Merchant" had taken the premise full circle and Smith had found redemption; of the following final six episodes produced, only the last had any class (a decline masked by the network's jumbling of the production order). If it didn't exactly bow out in style, *Lost in Space* could at least leave the field with an excellent batting average. It was, as Lockhart had said, time to go.

A glance at the U.S. TV schedules of 1965, '66, and '67 will not reveal many contemporary dramas grappling thoughtfully with the social evils of the day. It will show family westerns, rural sit-coms, fantasy, and variety shows. The closest the TV schedules of the period came to serious drama was with medical shows *Doctor Kildare* and *Ben Casey,* spy shows *Mission: Impossible* and *I Spy,* war shows like *Twelve O'Clock High* and *Combat,* the soap *Peyton Place,* and *The Fugitive* and *The FBI*—all great shows, all of them as phoney baloney as the genies and talking horses. These few straight shows were surrounded, dominated and opposed by conventional and conservative variety shows and feel-good Americana ranging from *The Lucy Show, F-Troop* and *The Flintstones,* to *Lassie, Bonanza,* and *Daniel Boone.* In 1965, during its first season, *Lost in Space* shared Wednesday evening with *Gidget, Green Acres, The Beverly Hillbillies, Ozzie and Harriet, The Big Valley,* and *The Virginian.* In this environment, *Lost in Space* was radical, cultish stuff.

Lost in Space was pioneering in creative concept as well as premise. Today, a science fiction film or show is not considered complete without a funny robot (*Silent Running, Star Wars, Battlestar Galactica, Buck Rogers, Space Cases*), or—if aiming for respectability—a humorous android (*Logan's Run, Star Trek: The Next Generation*). Failing that, we will be offered a wacky, loveable alien (Willie in *V*, Albert in *Alien Nation*, Vir in *Babylon 5*, Quark in *Deep Space Nine*, Neelix in *Star Trek: Voyager*), the '80s and '90s equivalent to the wisecracking boy from Brooklyn in the '40s and '50s. All these contemporary sci-fi ingredients were, if not pioneered by *Lost in Space*, popularized by the show and acknowledged as a successful and essential part of the mix. *Lost in Space* also gave us the heroic kid—Billy Mumy's Will Robinson was followed by Barry Lockridge in *Land of the Giants*, Scott Jordan in *Fantastic Journey*, Jeffrey Jones in *Voyagers*, and of course the infamous Wesley Crusher in *Star Trek: The Next Generation*. Furthermore, the premise of *Lost in Space*—the group, or family lost, stranded, wandering somewhere—has been the basis of such subsequent series as *Land of the Giants, Land of the Lost, Fantastic Journey, Logan's Run, Otherworld, Star Trek: Voyager, Earth 2, Sliders, Space Cases,* and many others—with *Land of the Giants, Fantastic Journey* and *Earth 2* adding a wicked troublemaker to the list.

Following the series' cancellation, Guy Williams retired from acting, moving to Argentina, where he possessed real estate and his *Zorro* character was fondly remembered. He died of a heart attack in 1989, aged 65.

June Lockhart continued to act, moving straight from *Lost in Space* to the later years of sit-com *Petticoat Junction*, and has appeared in episodes of fantasy series *Greatest*

American Hero, Amazing Stories, and *Babylon 5*, a dreary 1990s space opera on which Bill Mumy appeared. She played a blink-and-miss-it role in the film *Strange Invaders* (with Mark Goddard, whose daughter Melissa produced the film), spoofed *Lassie* on an episode of *It's Garry Shandling's Show* (on which Dick Tufeld later worked, sometimes onscreen), and sent up TV moms on an episode of *Roseanne* which referred to *Lost in Space*. Other films have included such schlock as *Troll* (alongside daughter Anne, who also appeared with her in a *Magnum* episode), *CHUD II, Out There,* and the dire 1997 *Lost in Space* feature film travesty.

Following *Lost in Space*, Marta Kristen secured guest roles in *Trapper John, Fame, Scarecrow and Mrs. King, Remington Steele,* and *Murphy Brown*, and appeared in legendary exploiter *Terminal Island* and Roger Corman's *Battle Beyond the Stars*. Billy Mumy subsequently appeared in episodes of *Lancer* (story-edited by Anthony Wilson), *Here Come the Brides, The Rockford Files,* and a short-lived series called *Sunshine*, before pursuing a music career. Today, Mumy is still active in both acting and music, and enjoys a high profile in fantasy and sci-fi circles, writing comic book scripts (including a short-lived *Lost in Space* title) and guest-starring in the *Captain America* feature film and an episode of *The Flash*, two very underrated super-hero outings (Mumy is a big comics fan). He's provided voices for *Ren and Stimpy, Batman,* and *Animaniacs*, and appeared regularly in *Babylon 5* as Lennier. He also appeared in three episodes of *Superboy* and made a hilarious guest appearance alongside friend Mark Hamill of *Star Wars* fame in an episode of *Space Cases*, a series he co-created for Nickelodeon with colleague Peter David.

In the '70s Angela Cartwright appeared in Allen's film *Beyond the Poseidon Adventure*, and guested in episodes of *Logan's Run* and *Airwolf* before retiring to be a full-time wife, mother, and business-person. The sister of Veronica Cartwright, the actress who appeared in *Alien* and the *Invasion of the Body Snatchers* remake, she still gets together regularly with the casts of *The Sound of Music* and *Lost in Space*. Mark Goddard became an agent, dabbled in writing, worked in daytime soaps (*One Life to Live* and *General Hospital*, the latter during a brief run of episodes featuring June Lockhart), played on Broadway, and appeared in such cult fantasy films as *Blue Sunshine* and *Strange Invaders*. He played a villain in the non-SF but equally cultish *Roller Boogie*, which despite the ghastly title boasts Linda Blair and Beverly Garland as co-stars. Today, he is a teacher of underprivileged children.

Bob May returned to the stage, but appeared in the Robot suit for promos and guest spots on *Good Morning America*, *Vegas*, and *Studs*, and in person with other *Lost in Space* cast members on *Family Feud*. The Robot has appeared without him (!) on the *Mystery Island* segment of *The Banana Splits*, for which he was seriously and badly altered (although later, happily restored to pristine condition), *The Tonight Show with Jay Leno* and in the background of an episode of *Space Cases*. May appeared once more as the Robot (with Mumy, Lockhart and Harris) in a bit of business for *The Fantasy Worlds of Irwin Allen*, a superb documentary by Fox executive Kevin Burns hosted by June Lockhart and the now adult Bill Mumy and featuring numerous Irwin Allen associates.

Once returned to Earth, Jonathan Harris made two appearances in the sit-com *Bewitched* (one, "Samantha on the Keyboard," alongside recurring *Lost in Space* guest player Fritz Feld, both doing the same shtick). He was also reunited with Don Adams from *The Bill Dana Show* for some undistinguished villainy during the final season of *Get Smart*, and turned up in a bizarre and legendary *Land of the Giants* episode as the Pied Piper of myth, an intergalactic traveler it turns out. Harris is wonderful in the pilot film for *MacMillan and Wife*, titled "Once Upon a Dead Man," in which he appears again with

Kurt Kasznar of *Land of the Giants*. In the '70s he played kindly Professor Gampu in the Saturday morning kids series *Space Academy*, and guested in *Night Gallery* for old friend Rod Serling. One of his final on-screen appearances, before retiring to voiceover work (including that of Lucifer in *Battlestar Galactica*), was in an episode of the feeble *Fantasy Island* in a brief comical scene as the judge of a wine-tasting competition. As a voice artist, he can be heard as one of *The Three Musketeers* on Hanna-Barbera's *The Banana Splits*, as Uncle Martin in the animated version of *My Favorite Martian*, as Doctor Smith in a failed pilot for an animated version of *Lost in Space*, and as a pompous flower in Filmation's *Snow White—Happily Ever After*. Financially secure from *The Third Man*, *The Bill Dana Show*, and *Lost in Space*, he retired from on-screen acting after his comedy cameo in *Fantasy Island*. Subsequently, and apparently by choice, he worked only as a voice artist, contributing to *A Bug's Life* (the dialogue for which includes the line "Oh, the pain!"), and *Toy Story 2* among many, many others. "I love doing what I'm doing now" he said during a publicity tour in Britain for the video release of *Lost in Space*. "You don't have to learn any lines, you just pick up the script and do it. I have no further interest in films. Firstly, I don't like the people who are doing them. Secondly, I don't like what they're doing!" He lived long enough to see the mess made of the show in the 1997 film of *Lost in Space* (he died in 2002), and one can only concur. The producers perversely managed to exactly reverse the characters of the entire cast— John Robinson became an insecure wimp, Maureen an unsupportive and difficult wife, Judy a tease, Penny a brat, and Will a problem-causing troublemaker (not out of a desire to do right, as in the series, but to make mischief). Harris was suitably astute when offered a cameo in the film (an offer the surviving cast all, perhaps understandably, took up, other than Bill Mumy, who was cruelly rebuffed when he tried to contribute), managing to be both politely courteous yet pointedly curmudgeonly all at once.

Today, the Robinsons, Don West, Smith, and the Robot, live on in syndication, reaching new generations of viewers with each screening. While locked away firmly in the 1960s Hollywood definition of science-fiction, they remain, like many '60s shows, pleasantly timeless. Say what you like about *Lost in Space*, (and many have), but it was never dull! It is a series that can be heartily recommended to anyone who hasn't checked their sense of wonderment and humor in at Alpha Control.

The Cast

REGULAR CAST: Guy Williams (Professor John Robinson), June Lockhart (Maureen Robinson), Mark Goddard (Major Don West), Billy Mumy (Will Robinson), Jonathan Harris (Doctor Zachary Smith), Angela Cartwright (Penny Robinson), Marta Kristen (Judy Robinson), Bob May (Robot), Dick Tufeld (Robot voice and narrator).

The Episodes

FIRST SEASON (1965–1968)

The Reluctant Stowaway

wr. Shimon Wincelberg, dir. Tony Leader

October 16, 1997 ... and the world anxiously awaits the lift-off of the Jupiter Two, *as the pioneering Robinson family set off into space to start a colony on Alpha Centauri ... unaware that they have a hostile saboteur with them, who has been trapped on board.*

Critics of Irwin Allen looking to relieve themselves of some of their prejudices should perhaps start here. "The Reluctant Stowaway" is a textbook example of high production values, crystal-clear storytelling, model casting, structure, and suspense. Unlike so many more contemporary pilots, as a scene-setter, it sets the scene; this is perhaps why Allen's series stayed in production and are still popular forty years later, while later confused and misconceived series clearly inspired by Allen's shows floundered around trying to find an audience and a direction as they struggled to stay on air. Whatever one may say about Allen's series once in progress, and whatever purists might say about his approach to SF, or indeed science, the initial concepts were professionally prepared TV shows confidently ready to roll.

With this in mind, perhaps one of the most surprising facts about *Lost in Space* is that in the original pilot for the show, Doctor Smith and the Robot were not present. They were only included as an afterthought by story editor Tony Wilson when it was soon realized that the Robinsons would need a resident trouble-maker—a "Long John Silver" figure in his words—to create conflict (it was not to sell the show; CBS had already bought the series and promoted it).

Although the first episode is credited to "S. Bar-David," this is the pen name of Shimon Wincelberg, who also wrote the original Smith-less and Robot-less pilot from which much of the footage from the first few episodes is taken. Wincelberg later wrote the first draft of the pilot for *The Time Tunnel*, as well as the first color episode of *Voyage to the Bottom of the Sea*, "Jonah and the Whale." It fell to Wincelberg to write stowaway saboteur Smith and the Robot into the series in "The Reluctant Stowaway" (revealing that it was Allen who asked for an ordinary name for the villain; Wincelberg complied in the most literal way possible), but the rest of his pilot footage was incorporated into the next few episodes. Wincelberg also wrote the first season episode "Invaders from the Fifth Dimension," the end of his involvement with *Lost in Space.*

The following year, Wincelberg contributed to two scripts for *Star Trek.* These were "Dagger of the Mind" (which begins with a furtive stowaway emerging from his hiding place, as Smith does here) and—with Oliver Crawford—"The Galileo Seven" (which has the shuttlecraft *Galileo* under siege by savage monsters in a situation not too dissimilar from the one the Robinsons find themselves in from the Cyclops when they're in the Chariot in episode four, another Wincelberg scene from the pilot).

Director Tony Leader was involved in a dispute with Jonathan Harris on the pilot when the actor found himself unable to be enclosed in the hidden compartment in his introductory scene. Ultimately, a double was used ... although a better cause for concern might have been just exactly how the hidden compartment—complete with mechanical chair—got into the *Jupiter Two* in the first place! Exactly what function did this device have? Leader then directed the third episode "Island in the Sky" and ended his association with the series. His other fantasy/SF credits include the classic *Twilight Zone* episode "Long Live Walter Jameson," the less memorable "The Midnight Sun," and the routine "For the World Is Hollow, and I Have Touched the Sky" for the third season of *Star Trek.* The mediocrity of his single *Star Trek* episode, which comes nowhere near the two *Lost in Space* or *Twilight Zone* episodes in visual creativity, is a major disappointment. Leader's heart was apparently with the western genre, where he has done the bulk of his work. He did, however, direct cops and robbers, as well as a number of *I Spy* episodes and the SF film *Children of the Damned.*

The indomitable Doctor Smith dominates the series from the off, with the Robinsons spending most of the first half hour in suspended animation, a portentous metaphor for the months to come. The characters have still not quite become established as the ones we would later know—in some scenes, Professor Robinson is referred to as Doctor Robinson, while Doctor Smith is occasionally addressed as Colonel Smith. Note also that the Robot moves both his legs independently in this episode and the third. This was clumsy in appearance and hard work for Bob May, and this Saturday morning serials approach was later dropped and replaced with tracks and wires. In occasional shots, when this was impractical or time-consuming, May would wear the top half of the costume only and walk without the legs, which was also hard work! Directors filmed May from the waist up with varying degrees of success, but even the youngest viewers could—and would—figure out what was going on beneath the line of the camera!

The President of the USA in 1997 is portrayed by Ford Rainey, who had previously played the role in "Hot Line" and "Doomsday," two episodes of *Voyage to the Bottom of the Sea* (set in the '70s!) and would play Abraham Lincoln in "The Death Trap," an episode of *The Time Tunnel.* He was demoted to a mere General in Allen's short promo film for *The Man from the 25th Century,* an unsold series concept. Other SF roles include two episodes of *The Invaders,* "Panic" and "Summit Meeting," and "I, Robot" for *The Outer Limits.* He was frequently cast as figures of authority, and never failed to transcend the visual cliché and give them depth. Rainey also appeared in "The Bionic Woman" and "The Return of the Bionic Woman," two landmark episodes of *The Six Million Dollar Man,* and then in "The Bionic Dog," an episode of the *Bionic Woman* series. He also had brief roles in episodes of the classy '80s series *Wiseguy* and *China Beach.*

Of the other named players, Hal Torey (the military officer) appeared in the *Voyage to the Bottom of the Sea* episode "The Monster from Outer Space" and the film *Earth vs. the*

Spider. Brett Parker was a technician in the pilot for *The Time Tunnel,* also directed by Allen. Visible as one of the news reporters (lean and bearded) is Paul Zastupnevich, Allen's right-hand man, monster-maker and costume designer. The television newsman is portrayed by Don Forbes. Production no.: 8501.

The Derelict

wr. Shimon Wincelberg, Peter Packer, dir. Alex Singer

The Jupiter Two *is swallowed by a colossal spaceship.*

This second episode of the series is a classy affair, with stylish sets and direction, good performances and script, and constant tension, both in the spacewalk scenes at the beginning, and the adventures aboard the derelict ship, the set for which includes many items built for the feature *Fantastic Voyage* and used in the second season opener for *Voyage to the Bottom of the Sea,* "Jonah and the Whale," filmed at around the same time. Footage of the derelict spaceship exterior is used repeatedly during the series' third season.

This is the only episode from the first two seasons of *Lost in Space* not to end with a cliffhanger; it closes with the Robinsons heading for an "Earth-like planet." There is also no footage from the original pilot. It's also the first episode to feature the writing of Peter Packer, one of the series' most frequent and prolific contributors, and was probably conceived opportunistically to utilize the aforementioned set before it was struck. Packer's trademark—an assumption that all space aliens are inherently menacing—shows itself immediately. Indeed, if "The Derelict" has any fault, it is that the Robinsons seem to show little remorse other than for their own loss when the alien creature is shot by the panicky Smith. However, the chickens come home to roost in the second season episode "The Prisoners of Space"...!

Director Alex Singer did not return to *Lost in Space,* but did direct Allen's unsold pilot *The Time Travelers* many years later in 1976. Indeed, he flitted from series to series throughout his career, his other fantasy/SF work including "Earth, Air, Fire and Water" for *Ghost Story* and "The Collectors" for *Logan's Run.* Some of his final work was on *Star Trek: The Next Generation.* Production no.: 8502.

Island in the Sky

wr. Shimon Wincelberg, Norman Lessing, dir. Tony Leader

Smith causes the ship to crash-land on a nearby planet after Professor Robinson is lost on a space-walk. The Robinsons set out across the temperamental terrain in their all-purpose mobile vehicle the Chariot in search of the Professor.

Smith's at his most evil in this one, but we also see glimpses of the lighter Smith to come in a chess playing sequence with the Robot (vanity, cheating, lying, bluffing) and his remorse when he realizes the consequences of his command to the Robot to eliminate the Robinsons. This is the first sign we get that Smith feels something toward the group, particularly the innocent and trusting Will. Everyone gets a good scene in this story, Don and Judy after the crash landing, where we witness Judy's feelings for Don coming to the fore, and Penny and Maureen in the scene with the space-chimp Debbie (still to be determined a "bloop" at this point) that Penny has acquired. If only such strength and definition had remained in the characterizations as the series continued.

Exactly how much of this is due to writer Norman Lessing is difficult to assess, as for whatever reasons, Lessing did not work on the series—or indeed any other Allen productions—again. However, only the crash landing of the *Jupiter Two* is footage from the original pilot, and as the ship originally crashed with the Robinson party still asleep in their freezing tubes, this is the real reason why Major West must "ride out the crash" in one during the crash landing—he's in shot.

This was director Tony Leader's second and last episode of *Lost in Space*, undoubtedly filmed back to back with the pilot. There are no flaws in this episode at all, although it's not quite clear why the cliff face John Robinson has fallen next to is electrified. The Chariot is a wonderful creation (although exactly how much assembling Don had to do on his own gives one pause for thought), and the cliffhanger ending, with the Robot advancing murderously toward Will at the location of the stranded Chariot, is a doozy! Production no.: 8503.

There Were Giants in the Earth

wr. Shimon Wincelberg, Carey Wilber, dir. Leo Penn

The Robinsons are alarmed to discover that fierce winter conditions are approaching, and they must journey to the other side of the planet.

Writer Carey Wilber became associated with the series with this episode, and later penned some of the more over-the-top comedic episodes. He had previously been a writer on the 1950s *Captain Video* show, and would later write "Space Seed" for *Star Trek* and three episodes of *The Time Tunnel*. However, much of this episode is composed of pilot footage, and the only significant new sequences concern Will and the Robot, Smith avoiding his share of the chores, and the giant plant mutations. In very general terms, most of the first half of this episode is fresh material, and most of the second half comes from the original pilot. As post-pilot additions to the series, Smith and the Robot must stay with the ship when the Robinsons venture forth in the Chariot to accommodate this footage.

The plot device of having Will disobey his parents and then save the day becomes a little over-used in this episode, having been employed three times before the episode is even half way through! Firstly, he disobeys

his father's orders and has to be rescued from the Chariot, but saves himself from the Robot; then he saves Smith and the women from the giant plant's tentacles, then loses the Robot, but saves his father and Major West from the Cyclops, and so on ... However, the episode still manages to be one of the best and most well-remembered in the series, possibly because, as Mark Goddard has suggested, the young audience wanted to see Will Robinson be the hero (its overuse here though, does serve to illustrate how necessary the addition of Smith was to the recipe). But there's much more to "There Were Giants in the Earth" than this happy crowd-pleaser. Background music, performances, script, photography, and equal time for all the cast members all combine to show all the characters off to their well-defined best in a model example of how the show could be at its finest. The action and adventure gives the illusion of being non-stop, but one of the best sequences—a rare pause in the action at a campfire—was simply an attempt to pad out the pilot. This delightful scene delineates and defines the characters beautifully.

Director Leo Penn (actor Sean Penn is his son) worked in all TV drama genres extensively, effortlessly flitting from cops to cowboys to doctors, and did two jobs for Irwin Allen apparently back to back in 1965—this additional footage to go with the pilot and the *Voyage to the Bottom of the Sea* episode "The Cyborg"—but did not return to the Allen fold. The following year he directed "The Enemy Within" for *Star Trek*, and "The Little John Doe Affair" for *The Girl from UNCLE*. Prior to directing, he was an actor, playing in fantasy serials of the sort *Lost in Space* was initially modeled on, such as 1948's *Brick Bradford*, the 1949 *Batman and Robin*, *Mysterious Island*, *The Lost Planet* and others. The music in the scenes set in the ancient underground city is taken from Bernard Herrman's wonderful score for the 1951 film *The Day the Earth Stood Still*, which was used extensively in the original pilot and would be used frequently throughout the rest of the series.

Many sources, including some members of the *Lost in Space* cast, credit former football player Lamar Lundy as being the man in the monster suit portraying the Cyclops, while 20th Century Fox records credit regular *Lost in Space* monster man Dawson Palmer. However, a behind-the-scenes *Lost in Space* trading card picture clearly shows Lundy in costume, and he's credited in the original unaired pilot. It seems, therefore, as though Lundy played the part in the pilot footage, with Palmer appearing in the suit for additional footage. Another incongruity is onscreen, and refers to the Robinsons having domesticated "the planet's strange ostrich-like animals." These creatures can actually be seen in the original pilot (the relevant clip can be seen in the documentary *The Fantasy Worlds of Irwin Allen*), but having no obvious use and being something of a liability and unnecessary expense they were quickly and wisely eliminated from the series; however, this single reference to them was (inadvertently?) left in.

Smith's carelessness and laziness comes to the fore in this episode, particularly during the garden sequences. This is also the first episode in which we see the Robot moving without his leg pieces—that is to say, filmed from the waist up, with Bob May wearing only the top half of the suit for greater mobility. In long shots, he now moves on hidden wires, rather than shuffling along independently. The chimp is referred to as "the Bloop" after the strange blooping noises it makes, and Smith's normal day clothes also debut. The *Lost in Space* we know and love is starting to take form, but in the process, some virtues of the early episodes are being lost forever.... Production no.: 8504.

The Hungry Sea

wr. Shimon Wincelberg, William Welch, dir. Sobey Martin

The planet shifts its orbit again, and the Robinsons must cross a frozen sea to return to their spaceship.

This episode features two of the most exciting sequences in the series, one made for the pilot, the other for this episode—the approach of the searing heat wave, and Smith's attempts to warn them of the impending danger, first by radio, then with the Robot, and the dangerous journey across the storm-tossed sea of the title, and temporary loss of Don. Substantial parts of the original pilot are exploited in this episode, and in no other part of the adaptation is it more apparent that Smith and the Robot were added to the mix later. However, the seams are quite invisible, and one would still have to know that Smith and the Robot were added later to notice it, with Smith defiantly staying with the ship and the Robot to excuse their absence as the Robinsons trek across the planet without them in order to make the most of Irwin Allen's set pieces. All the Robinson family footage of the deserted city and the sea has come from the pilot, with only the heatwave sequence being new. William Welch was an expert at writing stories around existing props and footage Allen already had handy, a trademark of his work, particularly on *Voyage to the Bottom of the Sea* and *Land of the Giants*. As this episode, more than any other, consists of scenes from the pilot, Welch clearly had little to do here but put Jonathan Harris on auto-pilot and piece the scenes together. However, two important character moments also occur in this episode— Smith's unexpected change of attitude toward the Robinsons, albeit for the usual selfish motives, and the eruption of the simmering arguments between John Robinson and Major West following their earlier bickering in "There Were Giants in the Earth." Another Allen veteran, Sobey Martin (about whom, more later) directs. The background music for the opening scenes recapping the adventures in the deserted ancient city in this episode is different from the previous episode—this time, John Williams' score is used. Production no.: 8505.

Welcome Stranger

wr. Peter Packer, dir. Alvin Ganzer

When long-lost astronaut Jimmy Hapgood turns up on the Robinsons' planet in his tiny rustbucket spacecraft, John and Maureen consider taking the opportunity to send Will and Penny back to Earth with him.

With Warren Oates (Jimmy Hapgood)

As well as literalizing *Lost in Space's* western pioneer motif by portraying a long-lost astronaut as a cowboy figure (complete with hat and light-hearted wild west punch-up music from the music library), the first episode of the series proper (in other words, not to have a premise dictated by the pilot footage) introduces the friendly visitor plot that became a recurring trademark of the series throughout all three seasons of its production—colorful eccentric shows up at the Robinson camp (after having been discovered outside it by Will or Penny), charms the family, and then turns out to have a sinister motive. "Welcome Stranger" is a little more subtle in this respect, as things don't turn ugly because Hapgood is a bad one, but because of a genuine conflict of opinions and goals—the Robinsons want their kids to get home, Hapgood doesn't want to take them, and doesn't think they should have been taken into outer space in the first place. Later on in the series, this motivation, and the agonizing the Robinsons go through because of it, wouldn't hold water, as the kids are probably safer with their parents than in a frail Earth-bound space capsule, but this early in the series, when the Robinsons' future seemed to hold menace and peril rather than the fun and adventure that was eventually experienced, it was a whole different ball game. Here, the series' barely-seen dark side shows—the urgent desperation to get the kids home, regardless of what fate awaits the rest of them, the anger when

Hapgood refuses. Lightening that darker-than-usual tone is the decidedly unsubtle cowboy-out-of-time subtext, which is hammered home with a relentlessly heavy hand; the western library music is accompanied by every cowboy movie buzzword in the book, as guest player Warren Oates sprays the regulars with corny wild west verbiage. Ironically, the cowboy-as-anachronism theme was one Oates would be irrevocably associated with throughout his career.

Warren Oates was an actor with an easy-going, world-weary style who was most often cast in westerns. He had been a regular on the short-lived contemporary rodeo show series *Stoney Burke* (the only other TV series produced by Daystar, the *Outer Limits* production house), and acquired minor cult status among film buffs in the 1970s due to his frequent and almost exclusive association with fashionable directors such as Burt Kennedy, Monte Hellman and Sam Peckinpah. Frequently appearing in TV westerns, he was also known to SF TV buffs for "The Seventh Is Made Up of Phantoms," a mediocre *Twilight Zone* in which a group of soldiers find themselves mysteriously spirited back to the Indian Wars and Custer's Last Stand (he also had a bit part in "The Purple Testament" for that series), and the memorable *Outer Limits* yarn "The Mutant," co-written by many hands including *Voyage to the Bottom of the Sea* contributor Allan Balter and later *Lost in Space* and *Time Tunnel* post-production supervisor Robert Mintz, in which he played a deranged and power-crazed astronaut turned telepathic killer and actual bug-eyed monster, orbs literally popping out of his head after exposure to radioactive rain. However, film buffs will more likely remember him in the title role of the early John Milius film *Dillinger*, as the luckless cruel father in Terrence Malick's *Badlands*, and as washed-up thugs in Peckinpah's *The Wild Bunch* and *Bring Me the Head of Alfredo Garcia*. While his *Outer Limits* episode is the best of the four SF TV offerings, the

Lost in Space episode takes an easy second place and is an ironic prophecy of the sort of roles that would make him an academics' icon in the '70s.

Oates dominates the episode, putting everyone else in the shade. "He was a cerebral actor, and had much impact when his villains, losers, and heroes were complex figures" wrote Danny Peary in his book *Cult Movie Stars*. "You usually felt his character's pain, and even if you didn't like who he was or what he did, you felt empathy for him." He died in 1982, ironically the very year the Jimmy Hapgood character supposedly left Earth for Saturn ...

This was Alvin Ganzer's only episode of *Lost in Space* and his only work for Irwin Allen. He had previously directed some very mediocre episodes of *The Twilight Zone* and spent most of the mid–'60s directing episodes of *The Man from UNCLE*, only two of which—"The Girls of Nazarone Affair" and "The Birds and the Bees Affair"—stood out from the rest. The opening sequence of this story, with Will, Smith and the Robot idling away the time with a musical interlude, survives only in the previous episode's trailer. This episode opens with an establishing shot of the storm and the *Jupiter Two* that wasn't in the trailer, and then jumps straight forward to John Robinson's arrival on the upper deck. The capsule was an existing prop which had already appeared in the *Voyage to the Bottom of the Sea* episodes "Hot Line" and "The Indestructible Man."

"Welcome, Stranger" also establishes Smith's later frequent practice of swiping various essential bits and pieces from the ship. And we never do learn how the Robot got by without his purloined parts...! Production no.: 8506.

My Friend Mr. Nobody

wr. Jackson Gillis, dir. Paul Stanley

Young Penny's invisible friend turns out to be not a figment of her childish imagination, but an alien life force.

One of the few episodes built around one of the series' minor characters to work, "My Friend, Mr. Nobody" is a gentle fairy tale worthy of *The Outer Limits* or *The Twilight Zone*. This story also authentically captures the day to day banality of the shipwrecked family's existence ... John and Don laboring at the drill site for fuel, Maureen and Judy passing the time with traditionally perceived women's interests (styling hair and baking pies!), Smith and the Robot idling away their time at chess (an earlier episode, "Island in the Sky," had established Smith's penchant for playing against the Robot, a recurring scenario gradually chipped away at by the later comedy bits) ... and of course, poor Penny, a lonely little girl bored out of her mind until an alien life force alone for centuries until now, gives her the attention and adventure she craves.

When asked to define what made his successful sit-com so different from all those that had come before it, Jerry Seinfeld quipped "No hugs, no learning!" He might also have been describing *Lost in Space*, for in the 1960s, TV censors forbade Don and Judy, and even married parents John and Maureen, from showing what they bizarrely perceived as too much affection for each other ... and certainly no one in the Robinson party ever learned from past experience, as this is the first of many episodes in which warning bells should be ringing loud and long when the kids try to tell their parents something. Although as the first of its kind, this might be argued to be the episode which teaches the Robinson elders *not* to be so quickly dismissive of their youngsters' reports, numerous other episodes (for example, "The Dream Monster," "The Thief of Outer Space" and "Mutiny in Space" among many) would have Will and Penny's escapades regarded as imaginative fantasies when they were enthusiastically related to the scoffing, condescending adults. John and Maureen learn nothing from this story and Penny's strange encounter with an "imaginary" invisible friend!

One person who *does* learn his lesson in this story is Don West, who would never again be so completely taken in and lead astray by Smith's Machiavellian manipulations and his plainly suspicious industriousness and eagerness to be a hero. This landmark episode also features one of Smith's earliest insults to the Robot—"you blundering bucket of bolts!"—although Smith's hypocrisy is typically to the fore when the Robot is required to save the day, and we hear "Go, my metallic hero!"...

Like many first season stories, the episode is crafted with great care and thoughtfulness to offer a credibility within the context of the show's parameters that isn't present later in more hurried entries. Writer Jackson Gillis, more usually scripting episodes of *Perry Mason* in the '60s, or *Adventures of Superman* in the '50s (he wrote the well-regarded "Panic in the Sky" as well as fourteen others), but as likely to be contributing to *Knight Rider*, *Wonder Woman* or *The Equalizer* as *Mission: Impossible*, *Columbo* or the new *Perry Mason* in later years, would be drafted in on later occasions to pen episodes for the Penny character on the strength of "My Friend, Mr. Nobody." However, those third season stories—"The Haunted Lighthouse," "A Day at the Zoo," "Princess of Space," and "Space Beauty" (for Judy)—are all so poor, one can hardly believe they come from the same writer ... especially as Gillis had one more gem up his sleeve, "The Magic Mirror," and the second season's passable but comedic "The Thief of Outer Space." While accepting *Lost in Space* assignments, he also wrote for *The Wild Wild West* ("The Night of the Whirring Death" and "The Night of the Gruesome Games"), *The Man from UNCLE* ("The Galatea Affair"), *The Girl from UNCLE* ("The Phi Beta Killer Affair"), *I Spy* ("Lisa" and "This Guy Smith"), and later the awful "Our Man O'Reilly" for *Land of the Giants*. As "My Friend, Mister Nobody" is a classic of 1960s SF TV, let alone among the finest episodes

of *Lost in Space*, the sheer dreadfulness of his third season abominations for the series is unforgivable; Allen was not known for rewriting scripts, only meddling with storylines or rejecting them, so Gillis' later sci-fi efforts—like his *Land of the Giants* and *Wonder Woman* contributions—must be condemned as pure hackery. The third season stories built around Judy or Penny are among the worst in the series.

One can only rave about "My Friend, Mister Nobody" though. There's a freshness to be found in such considerations as Penny gradually teaching the life force words over a period of days (so many extraterrestrials effortlessly speak Earth language), and the fact that Smith and the Robot haven't quite got their trademark double act down pat yet. Scenes such as that outside the sealed cave entrance would later evolve into the beloved Smith and Robot answering back/removal of power pack routine.

Unusually, this is one of the very few episodes aside of those constructed from pilot footage in which the next week trailer forms a part of the story—a sequence with some diamond jewelry being worn by Penny, Smith now (temporarily) cognizant that diamonds are worthless in outer space, something he will soon forget for the sake of numerous later stories. More often, these trailers were simply the first scene of the next episode. "My Friend, Mister Nobody" also benefits—like "Welcome Stranger"— from some of the more creative camerawork that would be completely absent from the second and third seasons, including crane shots of the huge cyclorama planet set and a few outdoors shots filmed at the same location as the search for Professor Robinson in "Island in the Sky." These short scenes of various cast members *en route* to the studio sets in both "Welcome Stranger" and "My Friend, Mister Nobody" look as though they were filmed at the same time.

Whatever Irwin Allen's failings in the scientific credibility department (and he wisely knew that the mass market audience cared no more for pure scientific accuracy than he did), he knew how to make exciting, thrilling television. The spectacular climax to this episode is fast and furious, and packed quite a punch to a 1960s audience weaned on *Captain Video* and *Tom Corbett* or the quiet gentle profundities of most *Twilight Zones*. If Irwin Allen knew anything it was how to keep the kids glued and the adults peering curiously over the tops of their newspapers or paperbacks.

Providing the voice of the alien lifeforce was bit player William Bramley, who can be seen in person in minor roles in various other TV fantasy productions of the 1960s, including *The Girl from UNCLE, Bewitched, The Invaders, Star Trek, I Dream of Jeannie*, and *Land of the Giants*. He also provided the voice for Robby the Robot's guest appearance as an evil "Robotoid" in "War of the Robots" a few weeks later.

Director Paul Stanley had worked with Jonathan Harris on *The Third Man*, but did not stay with any series long, and this was his only *Lost in Space*. Another first season director with the prestigious *The Outer Limits* on his various credits, he was available for Allen only once more, for *The Time Tunnel* (the excellent "Night of the Long Knives"). His work is discussed in detail there. A charming fairytale story that shows Penny off to her best advantage, "My Friend, Mr. Nobody" starts off as a gentle yarn but then storms toward a cataclysmic finale.... Production no.: 8507.

Invaders from the Fifth Dimension

wr. Shimon Wincelberg, dir. Leonard Horn
Aliens plan to steal Smith's brain, but the devious doctor strikes up a deal to deliver the gullible Will to them instead.

This is a very straightforward basic episode with very little substance in story, but more or less a blueprint for all the future Smith-dupes-Will episodes that were to

come, in which Smith would sell out the Robinsons to save his own skin. Indeed, Jonathan Harris frequently referred to Smith "selling Will to the aliens" as a sort of character description shorthand. Although the thin plot results in a fair amount of padding, that padding is what audiences wanted to see—Smith skulking about being wicked, the Chariot crossing the planet, and the flying jet packs—and what the episode lacks in content it makes up for in strong images; the disembodied alien heads (the simple old illusionist's art of black costume against black background), the long, spindly fingers on the alien control panels, the superbly alien ship, and the cheap but clever effects inside the alien ship (simply a dark stage with large sheets of polythene reflecting the light)—they all look great. All this is enhanced by John Williams' music from the opening episodes; the scores backing the jet pack scenes (although this time it's Don in flight) and the passage of the Chariot across the planet are identical to the ones used in "There Were Giants in the Earth" and "The Hungry Sea" respectively. Angela Cartwright is absent from this episode but for one small scene, presumably due to the amount of screentime she had in "My Friend, Mr. Nobody," which, as a minor, was restricted by legal and educational requirements. Once again, John and Don exchange words (over the jet pack). This episode also establishes that the Robot isn't quite as brave as they programmed him to be (see also "The Toymaker," "Anti-Matter Man," and "The Time Merchant," among others), as he wavers when ordered to attack the aliens!

The Robot had two methods of moving after the pilot was filmed; one was to put the entire Robot body on invisible wires and wheel him along in a straight line, the other—for scenes requiring more complicated moves—was to remove the base and let poor, dedicated Bob May shuffle along, carrying the entire weight of the kit on his shoulders. Even as kids watching the show, it was painfully obvious to my generation—and I'm sure subsequent audiences—when Bob May was being wheeled along and when he was walking under his own power, as the Robot would glide smoothly when on the wheels and lumber along swaying awkwardly when walking! However, this episode is notable for being the only one where the cameraman accidentally shows Bob May's feet coming out of the bottom of the Robot's famous "Bermuda Shorts" get-up—the nickname for the cut-off legs which removed the Robot's feet and let May walk the Robot along. Perversely, it's easier to spot in real time than in freeze-frame, but watch when the Robinsons order the Robot to attack the alien ship and if you've a full picture, you'll see it. It's not immediately obvious unless you're looking for it, but once you know it's there, it's impossible to miss! As kids, we were always trying to catch the cameraman out, but although the more adventurous directors frequently came close to it, this is the only time it happens in the entire series.

This was Leonard Horn's only contribution to *Lost in Space*, but he had previously worked extensively on *Voyage to the Bottom of the Sea*. He was also responsible for three of the very best episodes of *The Outer Limits*, directing "The Man Who Was Never Born," "The Children of Spider County," and "The Zanti Misfits," classics all. In fact, when the aliens are speaking their own language in this episode, they sound just like the Zanti! Horn's final work was on the excellent if oddly named *New Original Wonder Woman* pilot in 1975.

Bit players Ted Lehmann and Joe Ryan portrayed the aliens. Ryan was The Magister in the *Time Tunnel* episode "Chase Through Time" and also appeared in *Land of the Giants* ("Double Cross"). Production no.: 8508.

The Oasis

wr. Peter Packer, dir. Sutton Roley

Ignoring warnings not to eat the strange food of the planet before the Robinsons have tested it, Smith eats a fruit which affects his mind, turning him into a dangerous paranoid even as he grows into a giant, just as the garden seeds and the cyclops before him.

Much has been made of the tolerance the Robinsons showed toward Doctor Smith, despite his best efforts to do them in, sell them out, or generally endanger them with his incompetence and stupidity. This episode deals with the situation in two ways—firstly, by having the Robinsons kick him out of the camp, and Smith petulantly go, courting sympathy all the way (a recurring theme to be found in a number of episodes including "Wish Upon a Star," "Attack of the Monster Plants," "Forbidden World," "The Dream Monster," "The Mechanical Men," "Mutiny in Space," and others), and secondly by exaggerating a condition (through tainted fruits) that Smith has clearly been suffering from since the *Jupiter Two* launched with him trapped aboard a ship of frozen would-be corpses—plain, ordinary insanity. The only way to explain away the erratic behavior of Doctor Smith in any episode of *Lost in Space* is to presume him quite mad. How else to explain bathing in the ship's water supply or expecting a hero's welcome when he returns to Earth when the entire world now realizes he was a saboteur? To abandon him in any way would have been heartless because—just as the Galactic Tribunal correctly assumed in the second season's "The Prisoners of Space"—the delusional Doctor Smith is mentally incompetent, with each episode demonstrating a different facet of mental illness. Of course *Lost in Space* was a popular entertainment, not intended to be analyzed so seriously, and Smith causes trouble because his function in the show requires him to cause trouble, but for those looking for explanations in story terms, there it is.

When Doctor Smith started getting more fan mail than anybody, CBS actually hired psychologists to investigate why the kids loved this villain so much. They promptly reported back what the rest of us can see is self-evident—like the wicked cartoon cats who come to grief when they misbehave, children identified with the petulant and self-absorbed Smith more than the idealized juvenile leads, as likeable—and liked—as they were. This episode more than any demonstrates why; Smith is disobedient and thoughtless, evokes sympathy when the chickens come home to roost, and stomps off in a nobody-loves-me tantrum before everything turns out okay in the end! Like all successful comedic characters, Smith is a big kid.

Here, continuing the theme begun when the Robinsons first crash-landed, the soil is growing everything to extreme proportions but poisoning it in the process. Typically, Smith—like a child—can't wait either for common courtesy or routine scientific tests to be carried out and preemptorily tucks in to the juicy fruits the Robinsons have so laboriously gathered, so growing to enormous size. So far, each episode of the series proper has been defining a Smith characteristic for future employment—"Welcome, Stranger" his self-interest, "My Friend, Mr. Nobody" his lust for material wealth, "Invaders from the Fifth Dimension" his short-term thinking. In "The Oasis" we see the birth of the—literally—overgrown child. However, nitpickers may well want to wonder why the giant Smith can't be seen across the flat desert from miles away!

Harris seems ill at ease in the special effects sequences as the giant, as their requirements clearly restrict his performance, but his sequence with June Lockhart and then the rest of the cast when he realizes he may have eaten poisonous fruit is a tour-de-force, utterly convincing and frightening—his horror is ours. This is Harris actually acting, as opposed to just having fun with Smith as in so many later episodes. However, all was not well on the set—Guy Williams had begun to notice that Jonathan Harris was now dominating the show, and

a sequence in which the Robinsons discussed their plight with Smith placed in the foreground of the picture reacting to their remarks is said to have particularly upset him, as he felt his position as the series' lead was being undermined. In truth, it was—the scene focused entirely on Smith, and to add insult to injury, Harris was a consummate scene stealer. It was Roley's decision to film Williams' scene with Smith in the foreground that apparently provided the extra straw on Guy Williams' back.

Perhaps hampered by the confines of the matte work for the giantism effects scenes, this is one of Sutton Roley's less elaborate directorial adventures, although both in this episode and "All That Glitters" a few weeks later, he would make ample and excellent use of the false perspective planet set. Here, he shows off only once, faking a shot that makes it look as though Maureen Robinson takes the elevator from the lower to upper deck in one continuous take, when in fact the two sets stood separately! By accident or design, when Smith plots in his cabin, a reverse shadow of Smith can be seen on the wall as he thinks his dark thoughts. If intentional, this is quite subtle for Roley. Most impressive though is Roley's use of the huge sound stage, made even larger by clever optical illusion. In the riverbed scenes, and the search party sequences, the planet's surface looks huge—and yet the entire episode, but for one brief shot of the Robinsons just before they find the oasis, is shot in the studio. The giant effects are the standard but effective split screen techniques of the day married with a few clever camera angles.

Roley was not the only legend in his own lunchtime on the set that week. Another contributor who put that little bit extra into his efforts than his fellows was the ingenious and creative monster man Janos Prohaska, portraying the giant bloop—or chimpanzee to you or me—in the monkey suit he wore in *The Outer Limits* for "The Sixth Finger" and various other assignments. Prohaska also provided and wore a giant-beaked blue and orange bird suit for "Forbidden World," in the second season. Production no.: 8509.

The Sky Is Falling

wr. Herman Groves, Barney Slater, dir. Sobey Martin

The Robinsons encounter a language barrier with visiting aliens, and when Will disappears, Smith fosters doubt and mistrust.

With Don Matheson (Rethso—alien father), Francoise Ruggieri (Moela—alien mother), Eddie Rosson (alien boy)

This is *Lost in Space* trying to do a *Twilight Zone*-style morality fable about fear and mistrust. Intelligent and well-mounted, it works quite well, but mostly as a suspenseful yarn about parental concern. Extraterrestrial would-be fellow colonizers arrive on the planet, mother, father, and son, the same, but different. Then Will disappears. Unknown to both sets of nervous parents, the alien boy has fallen ill, and Will has stayed with him. The colonizers are suitably alien and mysterious, and for once don't automatically speak the English language—although it seems aliens only fail to do this in films and TV when the story is about an inability to communicate! A well-considered performance by Jonathan Harris, surprisingly subdued and subtle as a paranoid and malicious fear-monger, and without the usual comical histrionics he usually indulged in, gives a quiet strength to this stylish, straightforward study in the triumph of common sense and trust over suspicion and bigotry. It's a simple, timeless message piece, beautifully realized. The alien family are well cast and played, and this is probably the only Irwin Allen production that presumes—rightly, in this case—that less is more.

However, there are flaws. Curiously, the episode is so busy trying to communicate an anti-prejudice message itself that the story's logic suffers to the extent that Smith, ever mistrustful and suspicious, stirring up fear and uneasiness, has a valid point.

Oddly, when Will goes missing, it doesn't occur to anyone to go to the alien camp and pool information, as any parents would. Although Smith suggests the Robinsons should visit the alien encampment as aggressors, there's no reason the Robinsons couldn't visit the new neighbors in the spirit of friendship, and the aliens are equally at fault. They haven't made any attempt to contact the Robinsons, despite being aware of their presence, and may indeed be hostile. It also doesn't ring true that the Robinsons would sit around the *Jupiter Two* all night when they know that something must have happened to Will, alien involvement or not. Even if they don't go to the alien camp, they would still all be out searching for him (when your son goes missing for twelve hours, his safety overrules all other considerations). In short, there is a large expanse of middle ground between charging in with laser rifles, and sitting around doing nothing. If they had asked the aliens for help, they would have found out the other boy was missing too.

The wrap-up scene is also rather odd, as the Robinsons appear to know all about the aliens now, including that they are "Taurons," although we do not learn how they eventually communicated. And as was the case several times in Irwin Allen shows, the aliens are given names in the closing credits that are never used in the program.

The Christmas episode "Return from Outer Space" a few weeks later is a follow-up episode of sorts, although it provokes a small anomaly. In a rather nice effect, the Tauron's transporter beam slices cleanly through a rock to deposit the aliens on the planet in this episode, yet when Will uses the machine in "Return from Outer Space," it deposits him gently on a rooftop.

Don Matheson would return in a different role, as Ikar the android, in the second season's "Revolt of the Androids," a very different style of episode. While waiting to assume his regular role as passenger and businessman Mark Wilson in Allen's then-forthcoming *Land of the Giants* series, Allen again put him to work, this time in a monster suit for "Deadly Amphibians" in *Voyage to the Bottom of the Sea*. Francoise Ruggieri also made two appearances in *Voyage to the Bottom of the Sea*, first briefly as Captain Crane's girlfriend in "And Five of Us Are Left" at around the same time this episode was filmed, and then later again in "The Machines Strike Back" in a more substantial role as the villain's aide. No further SF TV credits could be found for young Eddie Rosson.

The prolific Herman Groves has declined to recall his single script for Irwin Allen when invited by American researchers, claiming understandably that he has written hundreds of TV scripts, and "The Sky is Falling" would appear to have been given a reworking by Barney Slater. One can read too much into things, but it was his only script for the series, and for Allen. It may be an illustration of the alleged tensions on the set that Guy Williams ensures he gets the last line in both this episode and "The Oasis" by ad-libbing. Marta Kristen once stated that Harris always made sure he got the last line! On a lighter note, Billy Mumy's face when a cake disappears is a picture! Clearly this was a scene the young lad could identify with! This is director Sobey Martin's second *Lost in Space* assignment. Production no.: 8510.

Wish Upon a Star

wr. Barney Slater, dir. Sutton Roley

Exiled once more from the campsite, Smith discovers a magical device that will grant him anything he desires.

With Smith having now stormed out of the camp twice, writer Slater cements one of the series' running storylines, a plot device that would be used several times during the series run (see "The Oasis"). On the subject of "The Oasis," although it would have hindered the progress of the story to have

fussed about it, it is slightly jarring to see both Will and Smith tucking into the magic apples in this story so soon after the recent events of that episode, in which tainted alien fruit caused so much trouble.

Smith caused difficulties in two primary ways in the series, first through his desperation to return to Earth, secondly through his greed. Throughout both types of stories ran his selfish streak of self-preservation, even at the expense of his companions. All three character flaws are to the fore in this episode, an entirely typical one that starts slowly but picks up the pace as it goes along, establishing Smith's greed for treasures and luxuries first displayed in "My Friend, Mr. Nobody" and central to the later, similar "His Majesty Smith" and "All That Glitters." Guy Williams gets to do one of his splendid fatherly scenes with the kids that all but disappeared after the first year (replaced as they were with brief admonishing platitudes), a miniature of the *Jupiter Two* puts in an appearance when Smith overreaches with the thought transference device, and the John Williams music (re-used from the initial score) includes his delightful anti-gravity theme from when Will and Penny were floating in space during "The Reluctant Stowaway" for a surreal scene in which Smith prances around showing off the "magic helmet," an appropriately absurd-looking device. The audience will recognize the western theme from "Welcome Stranger" when Will and Penny are fighting, and the theme from "My Friend, Mr. Nobody," along with more familiar much-loved tracks. Note how Will unquestioningly accompanies his father and Don to the rescue when Smith gets his come-uppance from the "monster," actually a wise benevolent alien with an unfortunate tendency to behave like the Frankenstein monster that leaves his actions open to misinterpretation, particularly by the terrified and guilty Smith. Director Roley doesn't get the chance to indulge his trademark stylistic pretensions much, but slips in one curious shot of the Robinsons gathered around an apple, and creates an exciting studio-bound chase (no mean feat).

The alien for this episode (portrayed by regular monster man Dawson Palmer) bizarrely turned up in a sequence of light-hearted publicity shots for *Voyage to the Bottom of the Sea*, despite never appearing in that series, and it was also one of the very rare occasions, if not the only one, where Richard Basehart conceded to be photographed with one of Irwin Allen's monsters, a notoriously touchy subject with that show's star. Possibly as they were gag shots, and the creature feature episodes of *Voyage* had not yet begun in earnest, he was a little more easy-going about it.

This episode is another of the series' quaint and touching morality tales, of which there were many in the first season ("The Sky Is Falling," "All That Glitters," etc.). Here, Smith's magic wishing machine corrupts the family and makes them selfish and indolent by providing everything without effort or price. Finally, Smith gets too greedy, and loses everything. There was always a lesson to be learned from first season *Lost in Space*. Yes, they are obvious and preachy, but they were aimed at a young audience, and often the best episodes. Although director Sutton Roley stated he found Williams "pompous," he has also said that this was one of his favorite episodes because it said something, and in John Robinson, Guy Williams created a firm but fair father figure to aspire to, a man who could deliver a sermon with class; the way he deals with Penny's deceit—"You lost far more than you gained"—is beautifully written and performed. This whitebread mortal Superman did occasionally come across as self-righteous and maybe even a little pompous, but he was always right. When the series became about laughing at naughty Doctor Smith in the second season, Smith still got punished for his misdeeds (Jonathan Harris made sure of that), but the moral base of

the family unit and the cohesion and contrast that John Robinson brought to it with his "family meetings," was the greatest loss. Today's television offers us supposedly more credible dysfunctional families that we can identify with on such classy, funny shows as *Roseanne*, *The Wonder Years*, *The Simpsons* and *Malcolm in the Middle*, but as was demonstrated by the phenomenally popular *The Cosby Show*, there is room for model families that the audience can aspire to. The problem is that *The Cosby Show* wasn't nearly as funny, and drama would rather present the viewer with a succession of backstabbing family units offering up the psychological violence of soaps. In "Wish Upon a Star," the main theme is getting something for nothing and the old adage that if it seems to good to be true it probably is, but the subtext is Smith's loneliness as he sits with all his wealth and possessions. The most significant scene, beginning with one of the earliest examples of Smith spitefully and pointlessly baiting the Robot, is the one where John Robinson refuses to let Smith take the Robot back to the derelict spaceship with him for company. Like the children, Smith learned after the fact, but he never took the lessons on board—he is still trying to hang on to the thought machine right to the end! Production no.: 8512.

The Raft

wr. Peter Packer, dir. Sobey Martin

Smith botches a chance to return to Earth by launching a life-raft prematurely with Will as his unwilling passenger.

This was Peter Packer's fourth script for the series, and Sobey Martin's third directing assignment on the show. It's a solid story, and an enjoyable entry for the first season, that offers brief poignant character scenes interspersed with obvious plot developments and childishly fun scary monster moments. Although this episode concentrates primarily on developing the relationship between trusting Will and scheming Smith, all the Robinsons get substantial scenes before the life raft's take-off. There are also a couple of famous firsts in this episode—the Robot cracks his first insolent joke toward Smith, although he has still not developed his personality and is still being switched on and off as required. Also, although Smith has never been seen exactly leading the charge, this episode features the first time Harris adopts the soon to be familiar pose of holding Will in front of him as a human shield when a monster approaches.

"The Raft" is not a first season highlight, but by no means is it a write-off to be ashamed of. There are only a few minor quibbles and gaffes, easily dismissed—for example, when Will and Smith are moving through space, Harris sways to denote movement and Billy Mumy doesn't. Someone should have caught that and matched their performances. Once again, Will eats untested fruit—and the story even refers to the oasis.

The reactor unit that becomes the raft—Irwin has borrowed the diving bell, inside and out, from the *Seaview*—is enormous and would have left a huge hole in the *Jupiter Two* when removed. We can also only hope they won't need it again in the future! This would seem to be an appropriate point to mention that the *Jupiter Two* exterior barely looks big enough to hold the two decks inside, let alone the Chariot, the diving bell/reactor unit and goodness knows what else as the series progresses (we shall not, yet, mention the enormous Space Pod that suddenly arrives from nowhere in the third season!). The *Jupiter Two* is science fiction's answer to Felix's magic bag.

One of the standing jokes about the *Lost in Space* series is that Smith and the Robinsons seemed to have endless resources on board that provided whatever was needed for any particular adventure (only once did we ever see anyone actually making anything, and that was Smith's dressing gown being prepared by Maureen during the second season's "Deadly Games of Gamma Six"), and it stretched credibility to breaking point. The castaways possessed, or discovered, whatever the scriptwriters required and the story demanded, and such suspensions of disbelief are a part of all television series, from the silliest to the most sophisticated, so there is little point in going on about it. However, the occasional attempt at explanation, however lame or unconvincing, would have been welcome.

There is another import from *Voyage to the Bottom of the Sea* in this episode—the bug-eyed tree monster is the red-eyed seaweed creature that made several appearances in *Voyage* (in the episodes "The Condemned," "Deadly Creature Below," and "Secrets of the Deep") and returns again to *Lost in Space* as a fearsome jury member in the second season's "The Prisoners of Space," as well as bit-playing in "The Keeper" and "Hunter's Moon." In fact, so much of the episode relies on existing materials—we see the jet pack search footage and the Chariot search footage again—that "The Raft" seems more like a William Welch filler show than an original idea. However, Jonathan Harris is not really on form in this episode, only coming to life in the final confrontation with the monster. It would have been nice to see Smith make more of a meal out of being wrongly accused, but otherwise his role in this story, although entirely typical, has some meat on it—there is a touching scene when the marooned Will, stranded with Smith, asks if Smith will be his substitute father. Smith is still a three-dimensional character at this point, rather than just willfully screwing up to advance the story, and Harris plays the moment with subtlety. This is still a glimpse into the future though—an entirely predictable sequence of events storywise, with the fun coming from the monster of the week, here a stationary tree that will suddenly come to life and go "boo!" Production no.: 8511.

One of Our Dogs Is Missing

wr. William Welch, dir. Sutton Roley

The Robinsons are inclined to blame nightly disturbances on a friendly stray dog from an earlier test flight, but the truth is somewhat more alarming.

The patronizing attitude *Lost in Space* often displayed towards women is very much to the fore in this particular episode, although it should always be remembered that it was a common attitude assumed and accepted as the norm by both sexes at the time the series was originally produced in the mid–'60s. The women do the cleaning and the cooking, the men do the macho stuff. Most significantly in this episode, Will gets to join the work party while his older sisters are left behind at the homestead (he also, despite being the youngest of the three Robinson offspring, accompanied the men when they went out to face the alien in "Wish Upon a Star"). During this episode, Maureen is shown as capable and reliable, but also dependent on her husband and unsure of her ability to protect the spaceship as well as the men might (a worry validated by Judy losing her gun, Penny wandering around unchaperoned, and Maureen's error in letting the force field run dry and her inability to reassemble the weapons). She is nervous and insecure, but anxious not to let John be aware of her concerns—which he detects anyway, and rushes back to his grateful and relieved womenfolk to take command and save the day. There was no malice or prejudice in this—most women did not consider this deference to male strength and protectiveness anything but normal in the 1960s, and in many cases enjoyed and expected the protective attitude of men like John Robinson. Indeed, the majority of 1960s women would have felt abandoned, insulted and neglected to be treated in any other way. As the 20th century proceeded to shift and change, and continues to do so into the 21st century, there is no right or wrong here, only an illustration of changing perceptions within society. Attitudes to perceived male and female roles in the '70s, '80s and '90s are just as outdated today, and there is no point in getting outraged, censorious and politically correct about yesterday's definitions of male/female expectations. However, in today's world of equal opportunity and the in-your-face heroics expected and exhibited by women as well as men today in popular culture, this episode does come over as jarring, condescending, and quaintly old-fashioned.

Social history lecture over, we can return to the show. More significant from the point of view of the *Lost in Space* series in this story is Smith's foolishness dismantling the weapons, which seems willful and difficult to believe. Doctor Smith is exceptionally barmy in this episode, further supporting the thesis ventured in the section on "The Oasis" that one can only justify his behavior by accepting that he's genuinely insane. The episode is almost a parody of the first season formula, with Smith spreading fear and paranoia among the castaways with his one hundred percent record of always being wrong. Here though, his incorrect assumptions about the dog make no sense, even by Smith's flexible standards of stupidity, and neither does his behavior. In stories so far, Smith's actions have been motivated by fear, self-interest and self-preservation, and his opinions, if self-serving and small-minded, have been a valid opposing point of view. For example, in "The Sky Is Falling," although his attitude toward the aliens is negative and unhelpful, he might have been right. In "The Derelict," his fear was understandable, in "The Oasis" he was motivated by hunger, in "The Raft" by his determination to go to Earth rather than Alpha Centauri. Here, he's being an ass because he's the show's comic relief (believing the dog to be a hostile alien) and resident plot-serving trouble-maker (the ruined weapons and the "posse"). In even his most deluded moments Smith knows very well that he can't reassemble the guns, and so his brainless malice in taking them apart is quite simply unbeliev- able. As the first season goes on, his actions become both more predictable (making the Robinsons look stupid and short-sighted) and less credible (making trouble not through his character, but because it is his function in the show).

Apart from the scene where Penny searches for the dog and the monster watches her, Sutton Roley uncharacteristically directs without much flair (the opening footage of the Chariot is slightly different from the pre- vious episode's cliffhanger, using a different take when the Robot gives his warning). As ever, Roley tries to work around the failings of the standard issue furry monster suit, which is one of Paul Zastupnevich's less in- spired outfits, and the creature is mostly used as a tease throughout the story, lurking in the shadows and providing a don't-go- away moment for all three act breaks and the teaser. Eventually though, the show must deliver, and the final unavoidable con- frontation with the monster displays all its deficiencies, while the use of pretty dumb blonde Judy as the stalking horse is entirely typical and clichéd even in 1965. In long- shots the monster's just a guy in a bear suit, and although Roley choreographs an excit- ing finale, it looks phoney, and Marta Kris- ten can quite visibly be seen landing on a mattress when she and Don roll down the rock slope. Nitpickers may also wonder, dur- ing the food raid scene, where the Robin- sons got ham from at this late stage, as they are not breeding pigs! Interestingly, when Judy's gun disappears, taken by the dog, no- one considers the obvious assumption that Smith might have stolen it, and later, Penny seems to forget that the dog took it, even though she saw it go. The famous and often- used promotional still of an armed Maureen Robinson being surprised by the creature while apparently searching for it never actu- ally occurs in the show—in fact, although this is June Lockhart's episode, she is the only cast member not to be seen anywhere

near the monster! Billy Mumy's Will Robin- son is absent from a large part of this episode, presumably to accommodate his domination of "Return from Outer Space."

As for the dog, I am not alone in ask- ing—in fact, everyone who has ever seen the episode has asked—what became of the poor animal? Never seen again, or spoken of again (despite his elevation to *Lassie* status at the climax), we can only assume he wandered off into the night to be blown to bits with the rest of the first season's forgotten char- acters in the second season opener "Blast Off into Space," in which the volatile planet they have spent 29 episodes on finally ex- plodes as the Robinsons flee. It is quite plau- sible, given again the time period the episode was produced in, that the dog was initially supposed to die a heroic death sav- ing the Robinsons from the monster, but that either the network or Irwin Allen de- cided this was too strong, although there is no evidence of this. It remains, alongside the sudden appearance of the infamous third season Space Pod, one of the series' most brazen unexplained continuity issues. Production no.: 8513.

Attack of the Monster Plants

wr. William Read Woodfield, Allan Balter, dir. Justus Addiss
Alien plants create a duplicate of Judy.

This is the third (after "The Oasis" and "Wish Upon a Star") of many stories in which the tolerant Robinsons flip out and send the silly Smith into exile, although this time he certainly does deserve it. Banished from the camp after deserting John and Don at a time of great danger, and then deliber- ately dithering before sending assistance, Smith sidles off sulkily with two valuable fuel canisters. The fuel turns out to be food to the indigenous vegetation of the planet, and the plant life promptly grows to enor- mous size with the power to replicate objects and people. Then Judy, missing for a while, turns up at camp strangely different ...

In this story, the volatile alien world is once again spawning malevolent giant-sized life-forms, this time wittering, twittering, giggling plants with the ability to create flawed imitations of first fuel canisters and then Judy Robinson (there is a missed opportunity when Smith discovers the plant, as this happens off-camera). Despite the schlocky almost self-parodic episode title, this is an atmospheric, surprisingly grim and darkly sinister entry this far into the series, with new-to-the-show writers Woodfield and Balter returning to the evil capable-of-anything Smith of the first few episodes, and Woodfield, Balter and Addiss bypass Harris' comedy bits to capture Smith's madness quite skillfully...

Clearly drawn from the 1956 pulp sci-fi classic *Invasion of the Body Snatchers*, it was to be the last appearance of the purely evil Smith. Banished from the camp, Smith skulks about petulantly exploiting the plants' flawed abilities and the gullibility and naive niceness of the younger Robinsons (who, although they have mislaid the last episode's new dog, appear to have rediscovered their "bloop" chimp). Marta Kristen is unusually good as the evil duplicate, the fate of whom is conveniently glossed over when the story abruptly finishes.

Director Justus Addiss was new to the series, and did most of his work for Allen on *Voyage to the Bottom of the Sea*. Here, his direction is stagey but interesting, and vastly superior to his work on *Voyage*, which was a catalogue of disappointments and missed opportunities. His few assignments for *Lost in Space* are unusual only for his habit of filming the Robot's speaking scenes in extreme close-up. As well as being the dullest director on *Voyage to the Bottom of the Sea*, he also directed a few undistinguished episodes of *The Twilight Zone*. Although he never worked on that series, he was the long-term partner of *I Dream of Jeannie* co-star Hayden Rorke.

Writers Woodfield and Balter wrote extensively for the *Voyage to the Bottom of the Sea* series, but made only two contributions to *Lost in Space* (the other was the second season's poor "Wild Adventure"), which is a shame because although the plot is straightforward derivative pulp sci-fi, they have a nice handle on Smith, whose immoral spitefulness to the crew member most sympathetic toward him for once generates appropriate anger from the family and Major West that is a long way from the "dear old Doctor Smith" routines of other episodes. Interestingly, the Robinson party bring much of their trouble upon themselves for baiting the wicked old man in the first place, exploiting Smith's own gullibility with obviously fraudulent threats to leave him on the planet. Smith, being truly capable of such spite, assumes they mean it. Production no.: 8514.

Return from Outer Space

wr. Peter Packer, dir. Nathan Juran

An abandoned alien device sends Will back to Earth, in small-town America at Christmastime, where nobody will believe that he's the young astronaut who set off for Alpha Centauri a few months earlier.

With Donald Losby (Davey Sims), Reta Shaw (Aunt Clara), Walter Sande (Sheriff Baxendale), Sheila Mathews (Ruth Templeton), Harry Harvey Jr. (Mr. Grover), Robert Easton (Mr. Lacy), Keith Taylor, Johnny Tuohy (bullies)

This Christmas story, in the grand tradition of Hollywood smalltown schmaltz—America as we would nostalgically wish it—has Will returning to Earth for the holiday season in snow-covered Vermont, but unable to convince anybody as to his true identity. It's Billy Mumy's favorite episode. Most actors, when asked about their favorite episodes, will name the ones in which they got to stretch, or do the most, and this has certainly been the case with the actors from *Lost in Space* when giving interviews. But while this is very much Billy Mumy's episode, so were many other first season adventures, and this really is one of the best, a cozy and bittersweet confection for Christmas week

1965 that is sadly poignant but warm and fuzzy as well.

Billy Mumy, like fellow child actor Ron Howard, was American boyhood personified, Hollywood style. He had the big eyes, the freckles and the tousled hair of a Huckleberry Finn, and that, alongside a mother who had connections, a lengthy stay in hospital with only the television for fun, and a photographic memory for remembering lines, kept him gainfully employed as a professional child actor. James Stewart called him "the only child actor worth a damn!" Whereas Ron Howard got the good boy roles as the ideal child, Billy Mumy's trademark was mischief. Polite to your face, you got the feeling this was a scamp who would be in trouble the minute you turned your back on him—not theft, vandalism and drugs trouble, but stuck-up-a-tree, head-through-the-railings, broken-a-window trouble.

Many early *Lost in Space* stories were about the frustrations of youngsters not being believed. You would think, after the events of "My Friend, Mr. Nobody," not to mention all the other escapades in the intervening episodes, that the Robinson parents would have learned to at least listen to their children's tales by now, but in a pattern that continued throughout the series, no credence is ever given to Will's wide-eyed discoveries of visiting aliens and extraterrestrial devices. In this episode, it clearly costs them all a trip home—a revelation that they are surprisingly sanguine about. Of course, the writers were aiming squarely at seducing young audiences, who were expected to identify and sympathize with Will's predicament—oh, why won't grown-ups just listen? They knew that the stories would click with youngsters exasperated by not being able to persuade their parents to do exactly what they wanted all the time! As Mark Goddard has perceptively pointed out, the kids wanted to see Will save the day and rescue everybody, and that was exactly what he did

in many first season stories before Smith and the Robot took over the show completely in the second season, necessitating that Professor Robinson and Major West come in with ray guns blazing for want of a role in the format. By the second season the original formula would have been difficult to sustain anyway, because Billy Mumy was inevitably growing up and becoming a more responsible lad. By the third season, the kids were really too old to be convincingly duped by the ever-suspect Smith. However, they were also getting too old not to be believed once in a while!

As warm and cozy as this episode is, there is a subtle sense of sadness hanging over the proceedings that goes far beyond Will's tragic failure to get a message to Alpha Control or bring his family home. Although the point is unspoken, the Vermont boy Davey has clearly lost his parents and lives with his Aunt (his room is in her house), and he's the lucky one. The other boys in the story—sad, surly little bullies—are on a bus headed for the children's home. Will is home, back on Earth, but alone—and still no-one is listening to him. All the men are gruff authority figures short on words and low on patience. All the women are kind, but condescending and not listening. All the boys but Davey are unhappy and unfriendly. The only parents to be found in the episode are Will's, thousands of miles away in space, and there is a lovely long-distance shot of Smith angrily chasing the Robot, arms flailing, Smith collapsing exhausted on a rock after taking the usual few steps, that the audience immediately finds funny and familiar, and gives the impression that when Will returns to the barren planet and the marooned *Jupiter Two*, he has *now*, in fact, really come home. This is no contrived Christmas schmaltz with all the trimmings (you have to pay attention to see that it's Christmas at all), it's actually quite a melancholy piece.

The episode required an unusually

large cast. Reta Shaw was born to play Aunties, Grannys, and housekeepers (she had a regular role as such in the '60s fantasy sitcom *The Ghost and Mrs. Muir*, appeared in a fair number of episodes of *Bewitched*, and can be seen in Disney's *Mary Poppins*), but she also had numerous opportunities to stretch a bit. She had a memorable role in an episode of *I Spy* ("Lisa") as a tough old bird who gets bumped off by a hit and run assassin, making such an impact in the few moments she's on screen that it makes her murder all the worse, while in one of two *I Dream of Jeannie* episodes she appeared in ("Jeannie and the Wild Pipchicks") she had a ball playing a tough military officer who gets magicked into a coquettish vamp! She also had a bizarre role—but then, who didn't?—in *The Man from UNCLE* ("The Suburbia Affair") as a schoolteacher in the employ of bad guys THRUSH, meeting her end while pounding away on a piano! In *The Girl from UNCLE*, in "The Fountain of Youth Affair," she's an elderly dowager pleading for a rejuvenation treatment. Here though, she's in full cuddly Auntie mode, gushing honey and concern as only she could.

The other cast members are equally interesting. Donald Losby, who plays young Davey, had previously played an antennaed alien in a *Twilight Zone* episode, "Mr. Dingle the Strong," some years earlier. Young Keith Taylor, who had recently appeared in an episode of sci-fi sit-com *My Favorite Martian*, appeared again in *Lost in Space*, in the third season's "The Promised Planet," and in *Land of the Giants* ("Sabotage").

Robert Easton, who plays the town's newspaper reporter had recently provided the voice of Lee 'Phones' Sheridan for Gerry Anderson's superior puppet series *Stingray*. Usually cast as dim-witted hicks, his on-screen credits include *Adventures of Superman*, *The Munsters*, *Get Smart*, *Kolchak: the Night Stalker*, and *The Bionic Woman*. Films include *Voyage to the Bottom of the Sea* and the Man

from UNCLE feature *One of Our Spies is Missing*.

Sheila Mathews, later to become Mrs. Irwin Allen, also appears in the second season's "The Space Vikings" and the third season's "Princess of Space," as well as *Voyage to the Bottom of the Sea* ("The Blizzard Makers") and two episodes of *Land of the Giants* ("Deadly Lodestone" and "Wild Journey"), the Allen pilot *City Beneath the Sea*, and Allen's 1985 fiasco *Alice in Wonderland*. You can also see her milling around in *The Towering Inferno*. Bit player Walter Sande has a minor role in the *Voyage to the Bottom of the Sea* episode "The Human Computer" and appeared in the sci-fi features *Red Planet Mars*, *Invaders from Mars*, *War of the Worlds*, and *The Navy vs. the Night Monsters*, the last of which interrupted a clear run of Martian invasion movies! Ann Dore (the town councilor) is the lab assistant in "The Crash," the pilot for *Land of the Giants*.

In a rare attack of continuity for *Lost in Space*, the device that sends Will home is revealed to belong to the Taurons, the alien race the Robinsons encountered a few episodes earlier in "The Sky is Falling." Of course, exactly how the Robinsons knew the alien visitors were called Taurons at the close of that episode, when the entire story had been built around the fact that they couldn't communicate, is another matter! The Hatfield scenes have a musical score in the tradition of 1940s Hollywood schmaltz, and make an interesting contrast with the outer space scenes scored with the usual Johnny Williams background themes from the *Lost in Space* music library, and of course these are by now so familiar that it only serves to increase the familiarity the castaways' planet—outer space is Will Robinson's home now. And whereas the previous episode, "Attack of the Monster Plants," had been the darkest episode since the earliest offerings, "Return from Outer Space" features some of the earliest—and funniest—comedic scenes between Smith and the

Robot, a foretaste of the lunacy and bickering to come. Smith's sad relationship with the mechanical man hasn't been so clearly signposted since they were alone in the *Jupiter Two* in "The Hungry Sea," but this time it's played for laughs (Smith is also seen removing the Robot's power pack, later an over-used ploy). While the Robot is still very much a traditional mechanical man given specific commands and answering specific questions, Bob May is starting to have some fun with the costume, and change is in the air.... Production no.: 8515.

The Keeper

(part one of two)
wr. Barney Slater, dir. Sobey Martin
    An alien collector of life-forms from various planets decides to add Will and Penny to his collection.
    With Michael Rennie (the Keeper)

The series' only two-parter was a slow, spooky tale with some nice scenes when the kids are under the Keeper's spell. While *The Simpsons* wickedly joked—in their sci-fi convention scenes in the episode "Mayored to the Mob"—that it was Smith who, in these more cynical times, should not be left alone with the children, "The Keeper" is actually a model lesson to kids in not going off with strangers—the scenes in which the smooth-talking alien gently coerces the kids into his spaceship with promises of magic and furry animals are quite creepy. In reality, Billy Mumy and particularly Angela Cartwright, are clearly having a whale of a time pretending to be mesmerized by the Keeper's staff! It was also a happy two-parter for Doctor Smith himself; Michael Rennie had previously worked with Jonathan Harris on the syndicated series *The Third Man*, and they had become the best of friends—"The Keeper" was an enjoyable reunion for both of them.

Most of all though, "The Keeper" is a treat for the audience. Widely regarded, along with the third season's "Anti-Matter Man," as an example of the series at its best,

there are several delights—another fabulous spaceship design, following on from the ship in "Invaders from the Fifth Dimension" (the interior's bank of light controls makes a reappearance), with simple but effective false perspective corridors and a superb—if familiar—selection of Paul Zastupnevich's menagerie of monsters. Smith's release of the creatures is an amusing parade of every monster suit Irwin had available (including a regular-sized Cyclops) going round and round in circles. Emerging from the Keeper's ship at the end of the episode (and the beginning of the next) we see the Cyclops monster, the furry beast from the opening sequence (later to return in "The Magic Mirror" and "The Prisoners of Space" with amendments), the alien from "Wish Upon a Star," and the bug-eyed seaweed creature from "The Raft" and several editions of *Voyage to the Bottom of the Sea*. Cynics will say they see Allen and Zastupnevich raiding the costume closet for every available bear suit, while apologists and continuity freaks may point out that there is no reason the Keeper shouldn't have captured examples of the alien races already seen in the *Lost in Space* universe! One suit is new—the hideous bat creature dispatched by the Robot.

Michael Rennie's great claim to fame will always be his role as Klaatu, the alien visitor in the classic sci-fi film *The Day the Earth Stood Still* (indeed, Allen often employed that film's distinctive score in his series, and does so here). He had worked for Allen before, playing Lord Roxton in Allen's 1960 version of *The Lost World*, and would soon portray the Captain of the *Titanic* in the pilot for *The Time Tunnel*. Other fantasy/SF TV roles for Rennie have included the Sandman in *Batman*, two excellent episodes of *The Invaders*, and a THRUSH agent in "The THRUSH Roulette Affair" for *The Man from UNCLE*. His films include the time-travel fantasy *Cyborg 2087*, and George Pal's *The Power*. Production no.: 8516.

The Keeper

(part two of two)
wr. Barney Slater, dir. Harry Harris

Smith inadvertently releases the Keeper's alien captives while trying to steal his spacecraft to return to Earth.

With Michael Rennie (the Keeper)

Smith's double-act with the Robot began in earnest with this excellent two-parter. Bob May has his first large speaking part in this episode, so this is where Dick Tufeld, who dubbed the Robot's lines, really starts earning his money! May too—he spends a lot of this story in the famous 'Bermuda Shorts' kit designed to allow the Robot to walk freely. Unfortunately, but delightfully, the Robot walks a little *too* freely when photographed from the waist up. However, it is Smith who utters the immortal words "Oh, the pain, the pain" in this episode, for the first time since "Invaders from the Fifth Dimension." It will be his catch-phrase for the rest of the season, turning up in "The Sky Pirate," "The Magic Mirror," "The Challenge," "The Space Trader," "The Space Croppers," and frequently thereafter.

An exciting sequence has the Chariot under siege by a giant spider, while the Keeper's mysterious controlling device—in this case, an electronically humming staff—was a handy gimmick that would reappear in various forms throughout all Allen's series. If one of Paul Zastupnevich's monsters appeared on *Lost in Space*, it was pretty much a sure thing that it would eventually turn up on *Voyage to the Bottom of the Sea* later, or vice versa. A few weeks after this episode, the giant spider turned up in a splendid *Voyage to the Bottom of the Sea* episode titled "The Monster's Web." Later, with cartoonish buggy red eyes added, the spider would turn up dog-sized, rather than house-sized, in the second season episodes "Forbidden World" and "The Prisoners of Space." The Alien Leader is portrayed by Wilbur Evans.

Over on the ABC network, at exactly the same time as parts one and two of "The Keeper" aired, part one of the first two *Batman* episodes were also broadcast (although, as twice-weekly half-hours on separate days, they only overlapped half of *Lost in Space*). The effects of this pop culture phenomenon on *Lost in Space* and 1960s television in general were powerful and immediate—astonishingly sudden in fact. So successful was the camp formula of *Batman*, that other series—with the coercion of the networks—were seduced along the same path. Not only was *Lost in Space* encouraged to become as wacky and off-the-wall as possible, but a similar fate befell numerous other series, including *The Man from UNCLE*, which soon shared many of the same scriptwriters and background score as *Batman*. Straight-faced shows were encouraged to let their hair down, while those series which were already fantastical were required to become moreso. *Batman* was filmed literally next door to *Lost in Space* and *Voyage to the Bottom of the Sea*, and perversely, the first half of each week's *Batman* episode was scheduled directly against the first half hour of *Lost in Space*, the two half-hours of *Batman* almost symbolically replacing rock and roll show *Shindig* and the thirteen year old sit-com *Ozzie and Harriet*. Production no.: 8517.

The Sky Pirate

wr. Carey Wilber, dir. Sobey Martin

Will is captivated by Alonzo P. Tucker, a 19th century "pirate," actually a storytelling wastrel, snatched from Earth by aliens and who created a colorful new identity for himself upon his escape.

With Albert Salmi (Alonzo P. Tucker)

A touching story about a Smith-like slacker who, like the would-be saboteur Smith, has improvised a fantasy life after being cast into space against his wishes, and enchants Will with his elaborate adventures as a space buccaneer.

In 1952, film director Raoul Walsh made his buccaneering action film *Blackbeard the Pirate* for RKO, and Robert Newton's hilariously outrageous performance defined the Hollywood pantomime pirate for the next fifty years. To create Alonzo P. Tucker for *Lost in Space*, the "town nuisance" abducted by aliens for suspended animation and occasional study in 1876, Albert Salmi chewed the scenery so enthusiastically that he made Newton look like a skinny nibbler, and—usually cast as dull thugs and blue-collar nobodies—is clearly having the time of his life with one of his most substantial and memorable roles. This episode, understandably one of Bill Mumy's favorites, is an entertaining mix of second season silliness and first season innocence, a sentimental morality tale mixed with a comedy Smith, a wonderful guest performance by Salmi, and a blobby monster finale. Carey Wilber's first original script for the series (previously he wrote extra scenes for "There Were Giants in the Earth" to accommodate pilot footage) wrings every last ounce of sentiment out of Will's boyish fantasy adventure with the rascally fantasist and thief Tucker, the would-be pirate who "ain't got a shred o' harm in him"!

As the story progresses, Will idolizes the genial visitor, until he's exposed as a sham after Tucker's indiscretions catch up with him in one of the classy and well-staged monster attacks that made the first season so much more thrilling than subsequent years. Of course, Tucker is yet another two-faced, truth-twisting second-rate rogue just like Smith—he even has an antagonistic robot companion to irk him—and dear, sweet, innocent gullible Will is being conned yet again. The scenes where Will realizes he's been had, and Tucker realizes that Will would have liked and accepted him without the embellishments are poignant. Just as Tucker realizes he finally has respect from Will, he loses it on exposure, and the adjustments to reality that both have to make in the final scenes are quite moving. Salmi played many similar roles in his career, often playing an inadequate scoundrel, but he was

never better than he was here, and the only comparable script he ever had in quality was *Twilight Zone*'s superb "Execution."

Salmi makes his entrance as Tucker in much the same way Warren Oates made his as the space cowboy in "Welcome Stranger"—roaring at Smith from the top of a large rock. For his part, Harris is still smothered in eye mascara to look sinister, but playing Smith much lighter, with lots of comedy shtick—the fainting, the running on the spot, the brazen lies to the Robinsons ... we even see the first of many versions of the old look-behind-you! bits of business, where the audience, but not Smith, knows the menace is approaching, while Harris milks Smith's ignorance to the hilt. It's this episode that has June Lockhart's memorable line "Don't you 'dear madame' me, Doctor Smith!," and Doctor Smith does his "Oh the pain, the pain" routine. Without lines at all in this episode, but for a couple of ad-libbed goodbyes to Tucker, are Penny and Judy. One minor oversight has Tucker refer to "young Bill" rather than Will (although the character's name is William, so it could conceivably be shortened to Bill—it's the only time Tucker refers to "the nipper" by name).

The role served both Salmi and Wilber well. Salmi, at his best playing twinkle-eyed rogues, would return as Tucker the space pirate in "Treasure of the Lost Planet," a talky but fun second season sequel also by Wilber ... and a few months after this episode aired, was back as a would-be pirate of sorts in the *Voyage to the Bottom of the Sea* episode "Dead Men's Doubloons," giving much the same performance without the sentiment. Although he wisely affects a different accent for the *Voyage* episode, it is odd, and one wishes he had replayed Tucker. He also appeared in an episode of *Gentle Ben* portraying exactly the same sort of character in a near-identical storyline at around the same time as this. In television, if you buy something once, they'll sell it to you again. He worked again for Irwin Allen in a nondescript dual role as two brothers in the *Land of the Giants* episode "Graveyard of Fools," and had a minor role in the feature film *Escape from the Planet of the Apes*, but his best work in the SF arena was for *The Twilight Zone*, where he had two meaty, well-written starring parts, appearing in the aforementioned "Execution" and the enjoyable "Of Late I Think of Cliffordville." Production no.: 8518.

Ghost in Space

wr. Peter Packer, dir. Sobey Martin

Doctor Smith is convinced that he's being haunted by the ghost of a long-dead relative. In fact, he's inadvertently released an invisible gaseous creature from a nearby swamp.

This is essentially the *Lost in Space* version of *Forbidden Planet*, except that the invisible creature with the heavy footprints (the same technique used for that film) is not a creature from the id (that premise would be employed later, in the third season story "The Space Creature"), but a creation of a mixture of elements brought about by Smith's usual contrary behavior. It was Packer, with his story "The Oasis," who first portrayed Smith as basically deranged, and while his subsequent paranoid behavior was put down to contaminated fruit, this episode pretty much established him as a touch demented (a point also picked up on by William Welch in "One of Our Dogs is Missing" and Woodfield and Balter with Smith's astonishing behavior in "Attack of the Monster Plants")! It might be argued, by those seeking a logical explanation for the character's transformation, that his experiences so far had unhinged him since his early murderous villainy, and that he had never quite recovered from his experiences as an isolated stowaway in space or on the planet, where he'd been faced several times by the prospect of death. His cowardice and selfish scheming in earlier episodes had been deplorable but understandable, but there

was no rational reason at all for him to assume, as he does in this story, that he's been haunted, least of all by a relative!

We are now well into the sillier episodes of the series now, with Smith playing the fool and everyone almost symbolically changing into what would be their second season outfits during this episode. Smith's disdain for his new outfit was no act—Jonathan Harris (quite rightly) didn't like the yellow jersey he'd been presented with, and soon returned to his familiar darker garb, disposing of the yellow one in a surprising moment of continuity in the later episode "All That Glitters" by giving it to a visiting alien. Harris wore the light jersey in only three episodes—this one, and "War of the Robots" and "The Magic Mirror," which appear to have been made back-to-back. The other cast members would now wear their new outfits for the rest of the first and the whole of the second season. While there's nothing wrong with them, most followers of the series, including myself, tend to prefer the earlier costumes—as did cast member Billy Mumy, who as a comic-book obsessed youngster, frequently presented a bemused Paul Zastupnevich with his own costume designs ... none of which were ever used, of course!

Although this episode is good fun, and the action scenes with the invisible monster quite well realized with obvious but adequate and effective special effects, Smith's ravings about his Uncle Thaddeus do get quite tiresome after a while, and instead of plots and goals we get antics and comedy relief. We also witness the beginnings of the series' later cavalier disregard for logic. Twice the creature vanishes suddenly, popping out of the picture for no apparent reason other than as a convenience to the plot, and we never get an explanation as to why the creature later becomes visible, why Will became invisible, or why he returned to normal. In fact, Allen could have saved his money on the monster suit—the creature is much more fearsome as an invisible force, and the rubber feet look particularly silly, especially as they are supposed to be heavy enough to make the menacing footprints in the ground, yet bounce around like clown shoes.

Although it is not mentioned, the cage is the one the Keeper left behind. This is probably due not so much to continuity as happy coincidence and prop department convenience. It is almost pointless to ask where Smith got all the equipment and robes for the exorcism.

The 1956 feature film *Forbidden Planet* quite plainly provided inspiration to both *Star Trek* and *Lost in Space*, the two major space adventure series of the '60s, and *Lost in Space* even employed the same production designer during the first season, the talented Robert Kinoshita, who realized both Robby the Robot for *Forbidden Planet* and the Robot for *Lost in Space*, and whose props designs ensured that *Forbidden Planet* offered some provenance to the look of *Lost in Space*. This episode not only lifts the invisible monster storyline from that film, but uses the same special effects techniques of a collapsing portion of flooring to create the illusion of footprints appearing in the sand, and concealed wires to hurl about the scenery. The ghostly séance music mixed in with the traditional *Lost in Space* tracks comes from another science fiction feature, 1951's *The Day the Earth Stood Still*, frequently plundered by Allen for background music—it is used heavily in "The Keeper" for *Lost in Space*, "The Mummy" for *Voyage to the Bottom of the Sea*, and "The Ghost of Nero" for *The Time Tunnel*, to name but three of many. Director Sobey Martin makes excellent use of the sets. Production no.: 8519.

The War of the Robots

wr. Barney Slater, dir. Sobey Martin

Will finds and reactivates a dangerous "Robotoid," and the Robinson Robot must defend the family that has ignored him for the new intruder.

In "The Keeper," the Robot had more lines and screen time than usual. In this episode, the "mechanical misfit" very noticeably moves up from prop to cast member, and has developed significant beginnings of a personality. We witness his timidity, his devotion, and his jealousy; one of his more entertaining traits was his self-pity! Only the Robot suspects the viper in the nest, but his warnings are interpreted as self-interest ... Smith also starts his name-calling in earnest, unleashing a barrage of insults and typically small-minded spitefulness toward one of his few real friends! It is ironic that the story concerns a robot that is supposedly more powerful than the Robinson's robot because it possesses free choice, as this is the first episode to show the Robot as a companion in adventure with Will and Smith capable of independent thought and even feelings, as opposed to a mechanical information machine that needs to be activated and asked questions or given orders. The Robot now speaks without first being spoken to; previously, he would only be seen doing this when issuing his famous "warnings!" While "The Raft" and "The Sky Pirate" had seen Smith mellow a little toward Will and the other family members, the previous episode, "Ghost in Space," cemented the friendship between Will and Smith, and we see the Smith/Will/Robot triumvirate firmly established as the episode opens, the three of them "gone fishin'." Although Smith still bosses him around, everybody now asks and receives information from the Robot.

The scene where Will discovers the Robotoid covered in weeds and foliage is suitably chilling and carries an air of menace. For once, it isn't Smith who's the cause of the trouble, but Will, who reactivates the Robotoid against repeated warnings from the Robot. It was also the episode in which the cast of the series finally realized that Bob May actually enjoyed being inside the tin man and playing his role as the Robot—and how seriously he took it! He famously watched Robby beat up his empty spare

Robot suit from offstage like a distraught parent!

Robby the Robot was designed by the same man who created the *Lost in Space* Robot, Bob Kinoshita, and first appeared in the 1956 feature *Forbidden Planet*, proving popular enough to have the juvenile feature *The Invisible Boy* written around him in 1957. His design was a major turning point in the appearance of robots up to that point. Art director on both *Forbidden Planet* and *Lost in Space*, Kinoshita's designs added enormously to the visual strength and quality of both. Robby returned in a second episode of *Lost in Space*, as the robot guard of a space penitentiary in "The Condemned of Space," the third season opener. Naturally, nobody remarks on the similarities between that robot and the Robotoid from "War of the Robots"! Inside Robby on both occasions is stunt player Eldon Hanson.

Seriously under-used since, Robby has nevertheless made a number of other television appearances, including "Lurch's Little Helper" for *The Addams Family*, the *Columbo* episode "Mind Over Mayhem," and the *Wonder Woman* episode "Spaced Out." His most bizarre appearance though must surely have been an episode of *The Man from UNCLE* known as "The Bridge of Lions Affair" (aka the feature *One of Our Spies is Missing*), in which his headpiece had been removed and used as a part of a sinister rejuvenation machine. Robby also appears in *The Twilight Zone*, as the punchline of two episodes, "Uncle Simon" and "The Brain Center at Whipple's." As ever, the episode liberally raids the score of *The Day the Earth Stood Still*, this time for the scenes with the Robotoid.

Robots in the 1960s were still objects of total fantasy. The scene where the Robotoid magically mends Maureen's ruined watch echoes the often absurd abilities of Robby in *Forbidden Planet*, and the regular *Lost in Space* Robot would often possess supernatural powers at the whim of a scriptwriter that had absolutely nothing to do with what a mechanical man might feasibly be capable of. Both robots were seen by their writers as all-purpose, all-powerful wonders of science, their limitations decided by the dictates of the story rather than plausibility.

Angela Cartwright is completely absent from this episode, but for her appearance in the trailer for the following episode, "The Magic Mirror," which centers around her. Similarly, Will doesn't feature in "The Magic Mirror." No attempt is made to explain either the absence of Penny in this episode or the absence of Will in the next! It is highly likely that these two episodes were made simultaneously; the absence also of the Robot in the following episode strongly suggests that Allen may have been making up production time. Allen would split his cast again, toward the end of the series, right down the middle for "All That Glitters" and "The Lost Civilization," but with an explanation. Production no.: 8521.

The Magic Mirror

wr. Jackson Gillis, dir. Nathan Juran

Penny encounters a strange alien boy who lives in an ethereal dimension on the reverse side of mirrors.

With Michael J. Pollard (mirror boy)

It wasn't all foolishness after "The Keeper." "Haven't you ever wondered what's behind mirrors? Well, this is!" says guest star Michael J. Pollard to Penny in this charming fairytale in which Will and the Robot are virtually absent. This episode, by the author of the first season gem "My Friend, Mr. Nobody," promised a brief return to the fairy tale qualities of wonderment, imagination and horror that had blessed the better episodes of 1965. The mirror dimension is beautifully realized, particularly the way mirrors are used as windows, even if the leftover props from 1962's big budget *Cleopatra* would later become a little overfamiliar from repeated use in *Batman* and later episodes of *Lost in Space*, including "The Ghost Planet" and "The Prisoners of Space." Still, nice to know Fox was getting some of their money back (*Cleopatra* nearly bankrupted the studio; it was saved by *The Sound of Music*). The episode's monster, on the other hand, is one of the most ridiculous yet, a big furry fellow with a patently false eye on a stalk! He would be back in the second season's "Prisoners of Space." Another moment of madness between script and execution comes when Smith warns Penny of an impending cosmic storm, as wind and thunder and lightning assail them. "Is there?" asks Penny innocently, as the full might of a typical Irwin Allen maelstrom surrounds them ...

No doubt on the strength of the superb "My Friend, Mr. Nobody," writer Jackson Gillis was called in to write another story focused almost entirely on Penny. Gillis was clearly required to repeat his triumph here, and throughout the series was established as Penny's writer. While his third season efforts are appalling, his first season work is exemplary. Here he's conceived a nice storybook concept with excellent direction, and the mirror dimension is well realized, including the windows in the boy's world in which the other sides are mirrors. It doesn't work as well as it might have done due to the casting of the quirky Michael J. Pollard rather than a more conventional Prince Charming type, which would have added poignancy rather than pathos to this story of loneliness and unrequited love. Cartwright grew out of her role in subsequent seasons and became a bit of a spare wheel, but in the first season she was perfectly cast as an intelligent, growing adolescent—far less trouble than Will, but still needing guidance and attention. By contrast, Pollard was condemned by his appearance to play overgrown kids and weirdoes in perpetuity.

Although in his mid-twenties when he filmed this episode, Michael J. Pollard had a podgy, imp-like face that made him look younger than he was, and was always cast as oddballs. In "The Magic Mirror" he is supposed to be sympathetic rather than sinister,

but he still comes across as rather discomfiting in his scenes, all of which are with Angela Cartwright but for a brief encounter with Smith. For poignancy, the role called for a wide-eyed waif; when Pollard's needy mirror-boy hungers after Penny's company one recoils more than one sympathizes. Pollard did much TV in this vein during the '60s, appearing in *Honey West*, *I Spy*, *Star Trek*, and *The Girl from UNCLE*, and was much better when being menacing; his supposedly pitiable *Star Trek* delinquent is equally unsympathetic. His main claim to fame was stealing every scene he appeared in during the glossy gangster flick *Bonnie and Clyde* in 1967. Since then, it's been mostly B-movies and straight-to-video fare. In the late '80s he was perfect casting as interdimensional elf Mr. Mxyzptlk (Mix-yez-pitel-ik) in the *Superboy* series ("Meet Mr. Mxyzptlk" and "Mr. and Mrs. Superboy").

Bill Mumy misses this episode completely, almost certainly due to his large amount of screen time in the episodes either side of it, "War of the Robots" and "The Challenge." Also absent is the Robot, prominently featured in "War of the Robots" of course. Bereft of his mechanical Aunt Sally, Smith spends the episode hurling his alliterative insults at the Bloop— "Simian simpleton, blithering Bloop, hirsute horror!"... It turns out to be the highlight of the episode! Production no.: 8520.

The Challenge

wr. Barney Slater, dir. Don Richardson
Will is challenged to a duel by a hostile alien youngster ... but if he wins, his family loses.
With Michael Ansara (father), Kurt Russell (son)

An enjoyable yarn unfolding predictably with plenty of action. The ending, like Slater's following episode, "The Space Trader," just seems to fizzle out rather than conclude. And yes, it is the Kurt Russell of *Escape from New York* and *The Thing* fame. A child actor of the '60s, he also appeared in a fair number of Disney films, the Elvis movie *It Happened at the World's Fair,* and *The Man from UNCLE,* in "The Finny Foot Affair." This and *UNCLE* were his only appearances in fantasy TV before his Disney films in the 1970s and action adventure roles as an adult in the 1980s. Michael Ansara appeared in all the Irwin Allen series, often more than once (asked about them, he could only say that the entire Irwin Allen experience blended together in his memory), and during a lengthy acting career in all dramatic genres, his extensive fantasy series credits spanned four decades, from the colorful '60s to the dark and grim sci-fi soaps of the '90s (five decades if you count one of his earliest appearances in *Abbott and Costello Meet the Mummy!*). Often typecast in militaristic roles, he was also the brainwashed Quarlo in "Soldier" for *The Outer Limits,* appeared three times in *Voyage to the Bottom of the Sea* (the film and the episodes "Hot Line" and "Killers of the Deep"), and as a Klingon in "Day of the Dove" for *Star Trek.* Frequently cast as warriors or other similarly aggressive individuals, he portrayed an Arab chieftain in *The Man from UNCLE,* a murderous Eastern vizier in *The Girl from UNCLE,* a medieval warlord in *Bewitched,* and the Blue Djinn in *I Dream of Jeannie.* Then married to that series' star Barbara Eden, he inevitably made several other appearances on *Jeannie.* He appeared twice in *The Time Tunnel,* as a Cold War Commisar and a silver-skinned alien, and as a callous giant scientist in *Land of the Giants.* In the early '80s, he played a recurring role as Killer Kane in the *Buck Rogers in the 25th Century* series, in "Escape from Wedded Bliss," "Ardala Returns," and "Flight of the War Witch." Most recently he was Elric, leader of the Technomages in "The Geometry of Shadows" for *Babylon 5,* reprised his Klingon role of Kang in *Deep Space Nine's* "Blood Oath" and "The Muse," and appeared in "Flashback" for *Star Trek: Voyager.*

This is the second time (the first was "The Raft") that Smith adopts his soon to be familiar pose of shielding himself from horrors with poor Will! Smith also coins the legendary epithet "bubble-headed booby" in this episode during a blatant comedy bit with the Robot, and the episode continues the extraordinary tradition of having Smith effortlessly appropriate any equipment he desires from nowhere, in this case a trainer's outfit as he coaches Will. In the trailer for the next episode we find Smith decked out with beret, smock, easel, canvas, and paints...! Also in the trailer, and the opening scenes of the following episode is a clumsy cut masking the oft-told tale of how the Robot tipped over, with Bob May inside it, while going up the ramp of the *Jupiter Two.* The outfits worn by Quano and his father in this episode would turn up several times again, including on John Robinson in the season finale "Follow the Leader" and the main adversary in the similar second season episode "The Deadly Games of Gamma Six." For those upset by the 1960s role of women discussed in episodes like "One of Our Dogs Is Missing," there's a rousing defense of sexual equality in this story when the Robinsons confront the unpleasant machismo of Quano and his father. The episode's monster is a shambling plant-like thing with insect-like bug eyes, but—almost as if the episode had overrun—the story ends abruptly without the obligatory fight; the Robinsons simply walk away to leave father and son to their challenge (when Russell returns to the cave, you can catch a quick unintentional glimpse of the monster hiding behind a rock before he actually emerges). Curiously, the name of Kurt Russell's character is Quano, remarkably similar to Ansara's Quarlo in the "Soldier" episode of *The Outer Limits,* which features Ansara in a very similar role as here—ruthless, unemotional warrior. Production no.: 8522.

The Space Trader

wr. Barney Slater, dir. Nathan Juran

Smith is ostracized for selling the Robot to an alien trader, but then digs a deeper hole when he exchanges the Robot for himself.

With Torin Thatcher (the Trader)

This is *Lost in Space's* version of *Faust*, of course, and a rather routine episode at that, although it holds the attention. American television was not taking itself terribly seriously at this point, thanks to the overnight success of *Batman*, and CBS had decided to fight ABC's fire with fire, raising the profile of Smith, Will and the Robot at the expense of the others. The series' already tenuous grip on logic was thrown to the winds, and following the absurd prop acquisitions on display in "Ghost in Space," this episode sees no problem with providing Smith first with a complete Bohemian artist's get-up, and later a pile of World War One sandbags and tin hat—this latter provision particularly pointless and unnecessary (even the Robinsons have found a massive water tank somewhere). Harris is no longer remotely wicked as Smith, just foolish and selfish, and although according to interview materials he was apparently married with a son, he now confidently plays Smith as gay as a summer fair (Harris always wore a massive ring on his wedding finger as if to fend off career destroying bigots). The storyline of "The Space Trader"—Smith selling his soul for lavish meals during a food rationing period—gives Harris the leeway to literally make a meal of the script, and he munches away mercilessly to keep up with Torin Thatcher's usual fruity, theatrical performance, as the two overpowering hams vie to dominate the screen. Several publicity pictures featuring Jonathan Harris messing about with the Robot were released at around this time, and several exist showing Smith with his mysteriously acquired artist's equipment, he and the Robot at the easel, beret and paint palette to the fore. Visually, and factually, we are still in season one, but

in every other respect we are in season two territory—the over-reliance on silliness, the dominance of Smith and the Robot, the relegation of the Robinsons to the background, the excessive re-use of props, would all be trademarks of the second and third seasons. The Trader's spaceship, for example, is the same one first seen in *Voyage to the Bottom of the Sea's* "Hot Line" and "The Indestructible Man," and later redressed for Tucker in "The Sky Pirate." We would see it, and its base, again.

By his own admission, director Nathan Juran frequently hired Torin Thatcher (all but one of his Allen appearances were directed by him), and he appeared with superb results as evil wizards in Juran's feature films *Seventh Voyage of Sinbad* and *Jack the Giant Killer*. A blustering, intimidating type who bullied all supporting players off the screen with his broad performances, Thatcher was the callous MacDougall in "Secret of the Loch" in *Voyage to the Bottom of the Sea*, a stubborn scientist in "The Crack of Doom" for *The Time Tunnel*, and a humiliated time-server in "Nightmare" for *Land of the Giants*. In a reversal of his usual screen persona, he was a cowardly official in the *Star Trek* episode "Return of the Archons." He easily dominates every scene he's in, even overshadowing Smith at times, and Harris resorts to his usual tactics in such situations of becoming even more extreme and hysterical in response. As the Trader, Thatcher is well-cast, but the episode is talky, and we see far too much of Smith and the Trader bantering back and forth, a pantomime pair as camp as a row of tents. The only times *Lost in Space* ever bordered on the tedious was when the guest character was a pain in the ass ("Curse of Cousin Smith," "Mutiny in Space," "The Questing Beast"), and the Trader is thoroughly obnoxious and unpleasant to be around. Smith uses his "Oh, the pain" catchphrase, and for the third time of what would be many, clasps Will in front of him as a shield when terrified—this time by the

Trader's dogs, in an episode without the usual bug-eyed monster. Pay attention and you can quite plainly see Harris and Mumy switching places with their stunt doubles behind a rock as they enter the Trader's camp for the first time and are greeted by the dogs.

One of Bob May's most often-told anecdotes is how he was knocked cold while inside the Robot suit during a scene in which he was required to ascend the ramp of the *Jupiter Two* with several other cast members, one of whom inadvertently stepped on the wires that were pulling him inside the ship, so causing him to keel over backwards when the wire was released. The scene in question is right at the beginning of this episode, a long-shot showing John, Don, the Robot, and Will rushing into the spaceship when the cosmic storm starts, and a clumsy cut shows when the incident occurred. While May presumably recuperates offscreen, the Robot stands stationary at the door of the ship, bubble askew, when John rushes back down the ramp to get Smith. May's first words on coming to—"Is the Robot all right?" "I hadn't signed a contract at the time," May explains, unconvincingly. On a 1980s TV reunion on the short-lived *America* show, the story was wheeled out yet again. "What you forget and I remember is that when he went over he was in three different parts, that's what I couldn't understand!" quipped Mark Goddard. Production no.: 8523.

His Majesty Smith

wr. Carey Wilber, dir. Harry Harris

Smith is chosen by an alien race to be their new leader, and smugly contemplates a new life of ease ... unaware that he has been selected as a useless and expendable sacrifice!

With Liam Sullivan (Nexus), Kevin Hagen (alien)

The second story in a row in which Smith carelessly enters into a contract with aliens due to his short-sighted greed. A brutish alien being uses android humans to trick Smith into becoming a sacrificial vic-

tim, and replaces the real Smith with a kindly, hard-working duplicate. There are similarities to "Wish Upon a Star" and the story unfolds predictably, but it's always fun watching Smith unravel as he gets his comeuppance. Once again, Jonathan Harris camps it up in another yarn built completely around the lighter side of Doctor Smith, with plenty of opportunity to dominate the action—and unlike "The Space Trader," he has center stage all to himself; guest players Liam Sullivan as an emotionless android and Kevin Hagen as a surly, Slavic, beast-like alien are mere straight men. Sullivan was the ill-fated scientist who turned into a giant sea creature for the classic *Voyage to the Bottom of the Sea* episode "Leviathan" a few months earlier. He has a somewhat more comfortable and less strenuous assignment here. Other TV SF roles include "The Brain Killer Affair" for *The Man from UNCLE*, more regal chicanery as Parmen in the *Star Trek* episode "Plato's Stepchildren," and the headmaster in "The Changing of the Guards" for *The Twilight Zone*. He had previously appeared alongside Jonathan Harris in "The Silence," another episode of *The Twilight Zone*. Kevin Hagen, always a class act in any role he played (and he played many for Allen) appeared as extraterrestrials in *Time Tunnel* and *Voyage to the Bottom of the Sea*, as well as taking more conventional mortal roles in those series too. In *Land of the Giants* he held a recurring role as occasional nemesis Inspector Kobick, chalking up fourteen appearances before becoming a semi-regular as the town doctor in the long-running 1970s series *Little House on the Prairie*. He made no less than four appearances in *The Time Tunnel*, as a Greek warrior in "Revenge of the Gods," a government agent in "Secret Weapon," a Confederate soldier in "The Death Merchant," and an alien invader in "Raiders from Outer Space." He appeared twice in *Voyage to the Bottom of the Sea*, as an obsessed scientist in "The Shape of Doom," one of his best roles, and as an extra-terrestrial in

"Attack." He also appeared in several superior episodes of *The Man from UNCLE* ("The Hong Kong Shilling Affair," "The Yo-Ho-Ho and a Bottle of Rum Affair," and "The J for Judas Affair") and for *The Twilight Zone* as an ill-fated astronaut in "Elegy" and a more routine, earthbound part in "You Drive" as a concerned work colleague. Even when playing his three aliens for Allen he tried to give each a different flavor, and here adopts a curious Russian/Balkan accent, no doubt inspired by the hefty, hairy make-up that disguises him. The alien spaceship is the same one, interior and exterior, used in the two-parter "The Keeper," although the outside has been dressed with a rock surrounding to disguise it. Android muscleman Ronald Weber, along with much of the costuming, turns up in the second season episode "The Deadly Games of Gamma Six." This is an entirely typical edition of the series, complete with Smith's familiar "let's not tell your parents" routine when the crown is first discovered, the best moment perhaps being the medley of familiar *Lost in Space* menace melodies that accompany Smith's sudden realization that all is not what it seems when the androids are deactivated.

In the original synopsis, the crown was supposed to make Smith "do a little jig" and then float off his head when Will touched it. All this was simplified in filming. Also excised, or never filmed, was a dinner table scene with Smith passing up his meal to prepare his dossier for Nexus (not very likely!), which he was supposed to offer in the pre-credits sequence. The spaceship is referred to as a cave. Also missing is the Robot's instruction to stop disrupting the Andronican signal home when they think they have Smith back. Production no.: 8524.

The Space Croppers
wr. Peter Packer, dir. Sobey Martin

Smith tries to court the mother of a family of space hillbillies in order to get passage back to Earth, but he is unaware that the son is a werewolf and the daughter is a witch growing carnivorous plants!

With Mercedes McCambridge (Sybilla), Sherry Jackson (Effra), Dawson Palmer (Keel)

Watching Jonathan Harris dominate episodes like "The Space Trader," "His Majesty Smith," and "The Space Croppers," one can see how some of the show's audience and cast members began to get a little frustrated as Smith became a pantomime dame who would not leave the stage. The series was no longer about survival on an alien world, and the Robinson family had not even had a couple of token scenes to themselves since "The Challenge." The show is no longer about jeopardy, but comedy. It probably didn't help that guest actress Mercedes McCambridge told *TV Guide* that "Jonathan certainly ruled the roost" when she was on the show. Although Smith's attempts to flatter the hillbilly woman into taking him back to Earth in their ship are quite funny, these scenes go on much too long, and this is a tiresome and disappointing episode that fizzles out rapidly after a great opening. It's quite dispiriting when—after a tense and exciting beginning—these buffoonish Hollywood hicks make their appearance. It's also an uncharacteristic contribution from Peter Packer, who usually avoided the eccentric oddball aliens of the series' later episodes in favor of hostile, pulp-mag bug-eyed monster types. While these characters have a definite Packer dark streak, this comedic episode (one of the first to be deliberately conceived as such) is a big letdown. It seems likely that the storyline was inspired by the popularity of the then top-rated sit-com *The Beverly Hillbillies*, on which Mark Goddard had guest-starred a couple of times prior to the start of *Lost in Space*. Oddly, while Packer then stayed clear of Earth-culture-influenced aliens, he had set a precedent which other writers—notably Carey Wilber and Bob and Wanda Duncan—would follow continuously the following season.

Of the guest cast, Mercedes McCambridge was a well-known character actress who here turns in a strong performance strongly reminiscent of Bea Benaderet's Cousin Pearl on *The Beverly Hillbillies*. She played numerous tough old birds in various productions over the years, but none tougher than her other encounter with the supernatural, providing the voice for the possessed girl in the nasty 1970s horror film *The Exorcist*. Sherry Jackson flirts once more with the supernatural in the 1972 film *Curse of the Moonchild*, and also appeared as the android lover of Doctor Corby in the *Star Trek* episode "What Are Little Girls Made Of?" She had previously co-starred with Angela Cartwright in the sit-com *Make Room for Daddy*. Dawson Palmer was the series' regular monster man, and this is one of two episodes (the other is "Revolt of the Androids") in which he appears in human form. In the original story synopsis, we find that the werewolf was called off by a whistling sound in the pre-credits encounter. Curiously, he leaves shoe-prints rather than footprints when he changes back from wolf to mortal! The episode opens with a crane shot showing Smith disdainfully throwing Will's earlier costume into the time capsule, an establishing shot not seen in the previous week's trailer. Presumably, the remark by Effra that they "once visited Earth" was a half-hearted attempt to explain away the existence of stereotypical Southern folk in alien form. The scenes with the Robinsons destroying the overgrown plants are strongly reminiscent of the climax to "Attack of the Monster Plants." In the first draft of the script, Will falls into one of the plants and is rescued by the werewolf, rather than being forced into its clutches, and Effra's attentions toward Don are to spite her mother for falling for Smith's well-hidden charms. It's rather sweet that Don would turn away the obvious charms of Effra considering the state of his love life while lost in space, but then she does come across as a bit of a bunny boiler and it would be a shame to ruin his chances with Judy...! Production no.: 8525.

All That Glitters

wr. Barney Slater, dir. Harry Harris

Smith acquires the Midas Touch when he steals an alien treasure from a fugitive from the law.

With Larry Ward (Ohan), Werner Klemperer (Bolix)

Possibly to get ahead on the production schedule, or perhaps to make up for time already lost, the cast split into two groups for the next two episodes, with surprisingly satisfying results. Smith and the women headline this adventure, and the guys and the Robot dominate the following story. With the female characters so underdeveloped, this leaves Smith to carry the episode alone. However, the end result is only routine. The guest intruders fail to provoke any excitement, the humans and monsters being ponderously bland, with dialogue to match. The episode only livens up when Smith gets devious, and the scenes with Penny turned to gold by the remorseful Smith's stolen Midas touch are quite effectively spooky.

With the exception of a brief scene in "The Space Trader," Angela Cartwright's Penny had been little more than an extra piece of scenery in the background since "The Magic Mirror." Consequently, June Lockhart (last given something to do in "The Challenge"), Marta Kristen (in her first substantial scenes since "War of the Robots"), and Angela Cartwright have a reasonable amount of screentime available to them for a change. Lockhart, in particular, is always good when standing up to Smith, as she would again when left in charge in "The Golden Man," a second season classic; when Smith abandons Penny and pulls his "sell his life dearly to protect the children" routine after fleeing the scene yet again, she snaps "Well, you missed a golden opportunity!" Although it promotes the foolish myth of the criminal as romantic rascal (Larry Ward's Ohan is a sort of combination of Jimmy Hapgood and Raffles, but this rather stiff actor has no chance of pulling it off), this is a funny and entertaining episode from start to finish, and another soon-unlearned moment of growth for the stubbornly unteachable Doctor Smith, as two-faced and treacherous as ever, here playing out the Midas legend beautifully as he turns all around him to platinum. Gone forever now is the evil Smith of the early episodes, so much so that even when the women suspect he's up to something, no-one can be bothered to find out what. Indeed, in the early sequences with Ohan, a now high-minded Smith appears to have completely forgotten that he too is a criminal, and no-one thinks to remind him, either …

Larry Ward, a competent but nondescript actor usually seen in westerns, appears as the Mars shot captain in "One Way to the Moon" for *The Time Tunnel*, and as a troubled father in the *Land of the Giants* episode "Shell Game." He's also the recipient of Smith's new light-colored jersey, after the canny Harris changed back to dark again with alacrity. Werner Klemperer, best known as Colonel Klink in the '60s sit-com *Hogan's Heroes*, and a somewhat tougher prison warden here than he was on that show, but far less entertaining, also appeared in the *Voyage to the Bottom of the Sea* episode "The Blizzard Makers" and *The Man from UNCLE* episode "The Project Strigas Affair."

The name of Klemperer's alien always gives half-watching adult audiences a start and their offspring a wicked giggle in Britain, as although the spelling is completely different, when spoken it sounds like a vulgar English slangword! Most unfortunate, and although some writers have been known to do this deliberately (the late Stanley Ralph Ross famously sabotaged an episode of *Batman*), it is almost certainly an innocent coincidence here. Irwin Allen was not known for having much of a sense of humor for that sort of thing, or indeed self-indulgent in-jokes of any kind, and heads would have rolled had this ever had come to light at the time. Unfortunately, this unin-

tended *Carry On*-style name detracts from the genuine comedy being performed by Harris, who is wonderful in this, one of his favorite episodes. Production no.: 8526.

The Lost Civilization

wr. William Welch, dir. Don Richardson
   Will becomes Prince Charming for an extra-terrestrial Sleeping Beauty when he encounters the young princess of a warlike alien race.
   With Kym Karath (princess), Royal Dano (Major Domo)

Professor Robinson, Major West, and Will and the Robot are the only regulars to appear in this imaginative adventure, which drops the four of them into an underground civilization strongly reminiscent of 1940s movie serials like *Flash Gordon*, *The Secret Empire*, and *Undersea Kingdom*. The princess, portrayed by Kym Karath with some charm, and her first minister (the Ming-like Royal Dano in one of his very few science-fiction roles) reside with an army of sleeping androids (a mirror trick effect with the Robinson freezing tubes from the pilot) waiting to conquer the universe. To be fair to Dano, if he's recreating Ming and his ilk, his make-up and costume give him little say in the matter. A classic bottle show from William Welch, the adventure takes place on the re-dressed set of *Voyage to the Bottom of the Sea*. It's rather jarring to see the story played out in what is obviously a large chunk of the submarine *Seaview*.

Kym Karath was one of the children cast in *The Sound of Music* with Angela Cartwright, although she doesn't appear alongside her in this episode. There was no onscreen reunion as the cast had been split to put two episodes in the can simultaneously, and while all the male cast but for Jonathan Harris were on the *Voyage to the Bottom of the Sea* set filming this story, Cartwright was on the *Lost in Space* set filming "All That Glitters." Indeed, this episode is unique in the series for not involving Smith in the plot in any way, and it's a back-handed compliment to the cast and writer that he isn't missed. Surprisingly, the episode is strong enough to survive the absence of Doctor Smith, and certainly allows Williams and Mumy to shine, but the derivative nature of the story demonstrates just how wise Tony Wilson was to add Smith to the mix, and how bereft of inspiration the show would soon have become without Smith to make trouble—all the hazards encountered along the way (earthquakes, meteor showers, cave-ins, underground civilizations) have already been seen in the Smith-less pilot film. The story is a blatant retread of the *Sleeping Beauty* fairytale. When the planet explodes just three episodes later at the start of the second season, no mention is made of the underground civilization, the sleeping princess, or indeed any of the resident aliens encountered in the first season.... Production no.: 8527.

A Change of Space

wr. Peter Packer, dir. Sobey Martin

Will and Smith take separate flights in an alien spacecraft and enter another dimension, but while Will emerges as a child prodigy, Smith returns wracked by old age.

If ever there was a first season episode most like a second season offering, it is this one. The Robinsons are spectacularly dense in this story, failing to put two and two together even when discussing Will's absence and the mysterious departure of the spaceship simultaneously! However, stylistically, it shines with the production quality of the first season, particularly in the opening scenes and Will's space flight, in which Billy Mumy is superb. He does a fair job with some difficult dialogue, too. However, all pales next to Jonathan Harris' spectacular *Rip Van Winkle* tour-de-force as a hobbling, scheming, irascible, bitter, and fearful old coot. It's Smith, but it's not Smith. Harris has a wild time simpering and whining (a wheelchair has now been found inside the *Jupiter Two*), and Mark Goddard can barely keep a straight face.

The Robot is a curious mix of his early and later personas in this story. He's still being switched on and off and asked specific questions, but is also seen being timid and laughing at Smith. Again he has peculiar abilities he shouldn't have, translating the alien language effortlessly even though the alien is new to everybody ... new to everybody but viewers of Allen's other series, that is. The alien, when he arrives to reclaim his property "Wish Upon a Star"-style, is aquatic in appearance simply because he's swum over from the *Voyage to the Bottom of the Sea* episode "The Menfish," just filmed. He's photographed nicely though for his debut on dry land, with stunt man Frank Graham in the suit. Production no.: 8528.

Follow the Leader

wr. Barney Slater, dir. Don Richardson

While temporarily sealed in a cave, John Robinson is possessed by an alien force, and imprisons all of the Robinson party but Will.

A dry run for the third season's "Anti-Matter Man," and it's rather good. A rare perfect mix of drama and comedy. The first season episodes were seen very much through the eyes of the children watching it, and this was never truer than with this episode, which is powerful stuff for young audiences. The climactic scene, with the frightened Will on the edge of the cliff and bravely resigned to his fate, is uniquely strong and almost unbearably sad. The shockingly blunt, almost banal dialogue ("I know why you brought me here"/"Do you?"/"You're going to push me off, aren't you?"/"Yes, Will Robinson") is the perfect definition of less is more, not normally an Irwin Allen approach to drama. As the second and third seasons loomed, there would never be anything remotely this dramatic in the show again, and while one wouldn't wish the joys of those lighter years into oblivion, it is undeniable that the show would have been remembered differently and more respectfully had it ended here.

Voicing the alien entity is Gregory Morton, seen onscreen as the astronomer in "The End of the World," an episode of *The Time Tunnel*. He would later provide the voice of the judge for the Galactic Tribunal in the second season episode "The Prisoners of Space." Trivia hounds can listen for music from *The Day the Earth Stood Still,* or watch for the sacrificial altar from *Time Tunnel's* "Walls of Jericho" episode. Production no.: 8529.

SECOND SEASON (1966–1967)

Blast Off into Space

wr. Peter Packer, dir. Nathan Juran
    The Robinsons are forced to take off into space again when an eccentric space prospector starts an explosive chain reaction on their planet.
    With Strother Martin (Nerim)

Smith meets his match when a devious prospector, damaging the planet's stability with his mining explosions, exchanges a life-giving potion for a valuable component from the *Jupiter Two*. The Robinsons are forced to take off into space again when the eccentric prospector, costumed, cast, and played exactly as if he's stepped out of the Old West (complete with mule), starts an explosive chain reaction on their planet.

After a rather shaky start in every sense of the word, this second season opener, the first in color, develops into a patchy but enjoyable yarn, with veteran western star and B-villain Strother Martin on fine form as Nerim (it's an anagram of miner), the scheming prospector sweeping worthless diamonds out of the way with a stick-broom because he's mining for Cosmonium, "the quintessence of the living force that puts breath into everything that grows." The story flags in places, but the scenes in which Smith spills the magic elixir of life on a statue he's made, creating a greedy, violent creature hammering on the Chariot door for more, and the exciting take-off from the doomed planet with their valuable naviga-tion device lost (this is the episode in which the *Jupiter Two* model caught fire during effects work), offer more than adequate compensation. Much of the episode consists of (well-written and amusing) banter between Smith and the other members of the Robinson party. The one jarring element is the harsh and unpleasant new background music from Leith Stevens, which was happily not employed too often in subsequent stories. Stevens wrote some wonderful music for *Voyage to the Bottom of the Sea,* but his music for *Lost in Space* was horrible. There's a tedious card game sequence between Smith and Nerim which doesn't really work, and surprisingly little of the Robot after his funny pre-credits scene with Smith, Will, and Judy. All in all, it's a very weak start to the second season. Luckily, the series' major competitor, *Batman,* had also started the second season with poor choices.

This episode is the first of four which string together to form one complete lengthy adventure in which the Robinsons are back in space for the first time since the *Jupiter Two* crash-landed in the first season. During the course of this mini-series of sorts, the planet they spent the first season on is destroyed, and they narrowly miss a chance to return to Earth again before crash-landing on the world where they would spend the second season.

Best known for his appearances in numerous westerns, many of them classics (associate producer William Faralla, formerly employed on TV westerns, would be associated with Martin again; when he left *Lost in Space,* he went straight to work on *The Wild Bunch*), Strother Martin has little TV SF work to his credit, but appears in the 1950s film *The Magnetic Monster* and as a drunken vagrant in "Moonshot," an excellent episode of *The Invaders*. Production no.: 9501.

Wild Adventure

wr. William Read Woodfield, Allan Balter, dir. Don Richardson
    Smith, in the dog-house again, keeps spotting a

hypnotic space-mermaid outside the ship, a green girl who disappears every time the others on board are called to look, but who wants to feed off their valuable fuel.

With Vitina Marcus (Lorelei)

Some padding, which overdoes the scenes in which Smith is in a hypnotic state induced by the Lorelei, slows this episode down, and the single ship-bound locale doesn't help much either. Nevertheless, the episode holds the attention, despite the rather obvious attempt to recreate the tense moment of the first season's spacewalk (all now rather passé, and very 1950s, even then). The fiery sun that threatens the *Jupiter Two* at the episode's climax was also used in *The Time Tunnel* episode "The End of the World" at around this time to represent Halley's Comet. The first two episodes of the four part story that starts the second season are not particularly good, but the third and fourth show the series on top form. Fortunately for *Lost in Space*, the *Batman* series had made the crucial misjudgment of starting the second season with new, inferior adversaries rather than old favorites, and by the time this error had been corrected, Allen had the series back on top form and was now competing on a level playing field—in color. Although this story centers around Smith, the rest of the players feature equally.

Vitina Marcus would reappear as the space-siren, renamed Athena after the actress' young daughter, in "The Girl from the Green Dimension" later on in the season. As well as appearing twice in *Lost in Space*, she also made two appearances apiece in *Voyage to the Bottom of the Sea* and *The Time Tunnel*.

Woodfield and Balter wrote numerous scripts for *Voyage to the Bottom of the Sea*, and although this episode bears some similarity to the *Voyage* story "The Mermaid," that episode was not one of the many they wrote. They also contributed to *The Time Tunnel*, writing the research-heavy "Revenge of the Gods." Later, they became writers and story editors on the spy series *Mission: Impossible*, and its short-lived 1980s clone *Masquerade*. This was one of two contributions to *Lost in Space*, the other being the very different "Attack of the Monster Plants"; it plays very much like a take-the-money-and-run job. Woodfield said he didn't care for the characters, which is an odd get-out as *Voyage to the Bottom of the Sea* and *Mission: Impossible* weren't exactly known for their characterization. Production no.: 9502.

The Ghost Planet
wr. Peter Packer, dir. Nathan Juran
Smith is tricked into delivering the Jupiter Two *to a hostile planet populated by evil robots.*

Lost in space again, the *Jupiter Two* picks up radio messages from a planet which seductively claims to be Earth. Smith immediately steers the ship toward it, which turns out to be a world populated entirely by robots with designs on the Robinsons' machinery.

Quintessential *Lost in Space*, showing the series at its best and Doctor Smith at his wonderful worst. If ever proof was needed that the Smith character is not so much evil or stupid but just completely mad, it's this one—he's quite demented in the face of all evidence in opposition to his delusions; Smith's insistence that he's on Earth is rather stupid, even for him, but it's fun when he realizes he isn't. His first encounter with the robots is great stuff as his pomposity and greed turns to outright fear, and then back again when he discovers the robot treasure trove. The Robot's apparent betrayal and the exciting escape back to the ship are a highlight (although exactly how did the Robot get up the rungs of that ladder?).

The sets, although plainly constructed of numerous familiar props from other and later episodes are splendid and—with the series and American television itself having just introduced color—the pictures are vivid and attractive. Bit players Michael Fox (an actor and voice coach) and Sue England provide the voices for the inhabitants of the robot world. Sue England also provides the voice of the evil robot in the episode "Deadliest of the Species," and indeed that machine is built from several of the parts on display here! Production no.: 9503.

The Forbidden World
wr. Barney Slater, dir. Don Richardson
   Smith's carelessness turns him into a human bomb.
   With Wally Cox (Tiabo), Janos Prohaska (bird creature)

The fourth episode of what is very much a complete story, this excellent episode is a continuation of "The Ghost Planet," the story description of which couldn't possibly do justice to the amusement in store as Jonathan Harris turns in one of his funniest performances as the demented Doctor Smith with some choice dialogue, much of it undoubtedly improvised, alternately whining and whingeing, pompous, posturing, and preposterous. Aboard the *Jupiter Two*, before and after landing ("Stranded on another bleak and alien planet..." he sneers contemptuously, "oh lovely, absolutely lovely"), Smith goes through his library of catchphrases ("Spare me the barbs, Major," "Oh, the pain...") and alliterative put-downs ("you mechanical misery," "you ferrous Frankenstein"). Highlights of the episode include Smith's solo exploration of the planet after having been sent out to retrieve the Robot, and the sequences when he realizes he has been turned into a human bomb that could explode any minute. Particularly funny is the clear and obvious pleasure of the Robot at this turn of events! A hilarious sequence where the Robot decides to detonate Smith for the good of the others is milked until it moos for mercy.

Wally Cox was familiar in U.S. TV of the period in nerd roles before the term was invented. He starred as meek, mild-

mannered types in the series *Mr. Peepers* and *The Adventures of Hiram Holiday* and numerous anthology series and variety shows. He was in a memorable episode of *The Lucy Show*, although only as the set-up, and portrayed Mr. Biddle the birdwatcher in a series of stories for *The Beverly Hillbillies*, but fantasy fans will remember him best as the enthusiastic and bookish researcher in the superb TV movie *The Night Stalker*.

Janos Prohaska had made a profession out of playing unusual monster roles, and unlike most TV monsters, portrayed by stunt-men who just put on the suit that was handed to them, Prohaska very often made his own suits and hired himself out to SF series. He had previously appeared on *Lost in Space* during the first season as the giant Bloop in "The Oasis." The comical and non-threatening giant bird outfit seen here later turned up on two episodes of supernatural sit-com *Bewitched*, "Allergic to Macedonian Dodo Birds" in 1967 and "Sam's Witchcraft Blows a Fuse" in 1972. Prohaska was a guy who would go the extra few yards to make a suit convincing, whether it was staggering around on stilts as the Thetan in *The Outer Limits'* "The Architects of Fear," or scuttling around on the floor as the Horta (named after one of the behind-the-scenes guys) in *Star Trek's* "Devil in the Dark," although this particular comedy outfit was one of his lesser creations. Production no.: 9504.

Space Circus
wr. Bob and Wanda Duncan, dir. Harry Harris
   Will is persuaded by Smith to join a traveling space circus, in the hope that they will take them to Earth.
   With James Westerfield (Dr. Marvello), Melinda Fee (Fenestra)

This was the first script for the series by Bob and Wanda Duncan, who provided the show with some of its silliest moments. While the first season had featured its fair share of silliness (Peter Packer's hillbilly family in "The Space Croppers" come to mind),

"Space Circus" took the Robinsons irrevocably down the path they would travel for the bulk of the second season and parts of the third. From hereon, a straight adventure show with moments of silliness became a silly show with rare moments of seriousness. Now, Smith suddenly finds a straw boater and a cane aboard the spaceship for his admittedly funny song and dance routine with the Robot, and the die is cast.

There is more to be said for the lighter, comedic episodes of *Lost in Space* than some will allow, and they were certainly popular with younger viewers. "Space Circus" was a fun episode, and many of these stories provided opportunities for a variety of character actors to indulge themselves in great roles far removed from the banalities of most of the television they were offered. However, few would argue that the series itself was at its best when providing exciting sci-fi adventure and the thrills and spills promised by the first season. Many second season episodes at least offered both, but "Space Circus" is essentially a feel-good comedy, and offers no sense of menace, despite the slightly sleazy aspect of the circus troupe.

James Westerfield also appeared in *The Twilight Zone* ("Mr. Dingle the Strong") and *The Time Tunnel* ("The End of the World," filmed virtually next to this story). Melinda Fee would later co-star in the mid-'70s sci-fi adventure show *The Invisible Man*. She also appeared in the infamous *Bionic Woman* episode "Fembots in Las Vegas." Dawson Palmer is in the monster suit which will later feature as "The Abominable Snowman" in a gloriously silly episode of *Voyage to the Bottom of the Sea*. Production no.: 9505.

The Prisoners of Space

wr. Barney Slater, dir. Nathan Juran

An emissary from the Galactic Tribunal of Justice arrives on the planet and turns the Jupiter Two *campsite into a prison compound, charging the Robinsons with breaking the laws of outer space and informing them that they will be summoned to appear in court to justify their actions. Curiously, Smith is omitted from the list of the accused ... an error soon grimly rectified.*

A wonderful episode by one of the best writers. An archetypal edition of the series, and another second season classic, with Smith and the Robot in fine form, and some sadistic hectoring from Major West, who revels in Smith's predicament and gets some great digs in at the whining schemer's expense. Bearing in mind that the preferred and acclaimed opening episodes of the first season are not really representative of the direction the series ultimately took and the show the public came to know and expect, this episode—like "The Ghost Planet" and "The Forbidden World"—make for a perfect introduction for newcomers to the series, as well as acknowledging and rationalizing the severe change in emphasis and approach for regular viewers, who might have been wondering where the evil Doctor Smith had gone, and if he'd been forgotten. It's also useful when more timorous broadcasters start their run of the series with the color episodes, as it explains exactly how the Robinsons became lost in space as the trial progresses. Highlights are numerous, and include the glimpses of pilot footage on the Tribunal's memory machine (note the Robot's slower voice, and the separate legs that show him walking rather than gliding), the courtroom sequences laden with a gallery of monsters from various past episodes of *Lost in Space* and *Voyage to the Bottom of the Sea*, Smith's escape attempt from the fortress erected around the *Jupiter Two*, his midnight offer to betray the rest of the party for a return to Earth, and an amusing bit of business in which a worried Smith paces with the Robot, which is imitating his every move. In fact, there's not a dull moment in this story, which is perfectly constructed and perpetually entertaining. The first alien to appear on the scene—a giant furry black lump previously seen in "The Magic Mirror," with a huge protruding single eye on a stalk—is a hoot, and the other creatures are an intriguing motley crew.

Robert Kinoshita, art director for both *Lost in Space* and the classic 1956 feature *Forbidden Planet*, uses the same laboriously simple but effective trick photography technique to seal the Robinsons in their camp as Morbius used in that film to seal off his home from outside forces. Unfortunately, the effect is hurried here, and you can see the prop men's footprints dancing around in the sand as they remove or replace each piece of fencing individually between takes! Production no.: 9506.

The Android Machine

wr. Bob and Wanda Duncan, dir. Don Richardson

Smith orders himself a female android from an intergalactic department store ... but is unable to pay for his purchase.

With Dee Hartford (Verda), Fritz Feld (Zumdish), Tiger Joe Marsh (security guard)

Most of the excessively silly episodes came from the pen of writers Bob and Wanda Duncan, who started work on the series with "Space Circus" and then went on to produce a string of stories featuring either Verda, or Zumdish, or both, the two recurring characters introduced in this episode, their second of just five episodes for the show. Their stories were good comedy, and well-acted by old hams like Harris and Feld, but they played a major—although certainly not solitary—part in taking the series irretrievably down the path of spoofy camp juvenilia. Later, the Duncans would write for *The Time Tunnel* and *Land of the Giants*, although in a more sober vein.

This episode is one of the funniest and most entertaining of the second season, with Smith and the Robot's relationship highlighted, and the comedy sequences between them and Verda genuinely amusing. There's a wonderful classroom scene as the Robot embarrasses Smith, and Verda takes over the Robot's class ("She took my pointer!" whines a sulky Robot), strong action scenes, amusing set pieces, a typical

look-behind-you! monster moment outside the inevitable cave, and Harris is center-stage and loving it. Dee Hartford would return as Verda in "Revolt of the Androids," and would make a third appearance as a different character, Nancy Pi Squared in the episode "Space Beauty." She also appeared in "The Invisibles" in *The Outer Limits* as the wife of a military man possessed by aliens, as Miss Iceland in a *Batman* episode featuring Mr. Freeze, and a wicked scientist in the *Land of the Giants* episode "Target Earth."

The comic actor Fritz Feld made three appearances in *Lost in Space* as Zumdish, returning in "The Toymaker" and "Two Weeks in Space." He specialized in stuffy, posturing authority figures, and appeared in an episode of *Bewitched* with Jonathan Harris ("Samantha on the Keyboard") where they virtually recreate their Smith and Zumdish roles. He also appears in "The Napoleon's Tomb Affair" for *The Man from UNCLE*, "The Joker's Flying Saucer" for *Batman*, and "Comeback" for *Land of the Giants*. Tiger Joe Marsh, a former wrestler (he takes on "Herman the Great" in *The Munsters*), also returns in "The Toymaker," and appears as a torturer in *The Time Tunnel*, in "The Walls of Jericho."

The opening shot of a guilty Smith waking from his sleep is not included in the trailer in the previous episode, which starts with the Robot taking class. Verda appears (as does Smith, at the end) from the ordering machine inside one of the freezing tubes from the *Jupiter Two*. The base of the department store spaceship has been seen in many episodes and the psychedelic wheels on the ordering machine have been purloined from the set of *Our Man Flint*. Production no.: 9507.

The Deadly Games of Gamma Six

wr. Barney Slater, dir. Harry Harris

The cowardly Smith happily agrees to battle an alien midget in the boxing ring for a ticket home, un-

aware that the alien has hidden powers. With Mike Kellin (Myko), Harry Monty (Geo)

An episode very much in the tradition of late first season, with equal time for the Robinson party (although Smith and Will dominate, of course). There's a decent role for Guy Williams, allowing him to indulge in his two specialties, tough guy athletic combatant and sensitive, understanding dad, and we see a thoroughly devious Smith, whose scheming and accusations of cowardice to get Robinson to participate in the contest regardless of any potential danger smacks of his first season villainy. Further parallels with the first season include some thoroughly nasty aliens (rather than the usual second season eccentrics), and extensive use of first season background music—although why Smith's bout in the ring is accompanied by library western music is anybody's guess! There's also a good scene involving Smith imprisoned in a cage by the Robinsons (where did they get it?) and guarded by the Robot, whom Smith lures into a trap and effects an escape with typical Smith guile. For once though, we see where Smith gets his seemingly limitless supply of props ... Mrs. Robinson! She's seen at one point sewing his Tiger Smith dressing gown for the ring. One very peculiar inclusion is a little more fanciful though—the alien is seen refereeing the fight with a standard hang-down microphone from the ceiling. The catch? The bout is taking place outside!

Mike Kellin made a career out of portraying sneering bad guys, and had previously worked for Allen as a foreign dictator in "The Mist of Silence," a grim early episode of *Voyage to the Bottom of the Sea*. Dwarf actor Harry Monty, one of the *Wizard of Oz* Munchkins, was Billy Mumy's stand-in on the show, and frequently doubled as alien creatures, appearing in "The Dream Monster" and "The Questing Beast" to name but two. Gromack was portrayed by Ronald Weber, a regular Irwin Allen monster man, and the giant was stunt player Chuck Roberson. In a minor role as the alien leader was busy bit player Peter Brocco. The Russian Roulette-style gambling device is seen again as set decoration in "The Phantom Family." Production no.: 9508.

The Thief of Outer Space

wr. Jackson Gillis, dir. Don Richardson

Will and Penny are captured by a brash space sultan and his massive slave, who are hunting a runaway princess.

With Malachi Throne (the Thief), Ted Cassidy (the Slave)

Another good one for Smith and Robot fans. Typical second season fare, an enjoyable comedy. Malachi Throne played a number of wild-eyed exuberant baddies in all Irwin Allen's series, including Blackbeard in *Voyage to the Bottom of the Sea* and Machiavelli, "The Death Merchant," in *The Time Tunnel*. He appeared three times in *Voyage to the Bottom of the Sea*, in the first season episodes "The Magnus Beam" and "The Enemies," and "The Return of Blackbeard" in the fourth season. His other *Time Tunnel* was as Hera Singh in "The Night of the Long Knives." He appears in "Cold Hands, Warm Heart" for *The Outer Limits*, and was also Commodore Mendez in the *Star Trek* episode "The Menagerie," and the man behind False-Face in *Batman*. In *Land of the Giants*, he appeared in "The Secret City of Limbo." In the '70s he appeared in "The Bionic Woman" episode of *The Six Million Dollar Man*. A regular on *It Takes a Thief* in the '60s, he was still working in the '90s, in the series *Law and Order* as a judge, in *Melrose Place* as a troubled father, and as Pardek in the "Unification" story for *Star Trek: The Next Generation*, but today works mostly as a voiceover for commercials.

Although he longed for more ordinary roles, the towering Ted Cassidy was best known as Lurch the butler in *The Addams Family* and was doomed to play similar monstrous roles in other series, his most significant being a magnificent performance of fire and ice as the terrifying android Ruk in the *Star Trek* episode "What Are Little Girls Made Of?" He had a wonderfully sepulchral, tomb-like voice that he could put on, which served him well in the animated cartoon voiceover business. The thankless role of the Princess was played by Maxine Gates. Production no.: 9509.

The Curse of Cousin Smith

wr. Barney Slater, dir. Justus Addiss

Smith's equally wicked and untrustworthy cousin turns up to give the Robinson family double trouble.

With Henry Jones (Jeremiah)

This episode, barmy by even *Lost in Space's* deliriously daffy standards, offers two Smiths for the price of one, even though Jonathan Harris himself is unusually absent for the first half of the episode. Just as it looks as though the actor is off on extended leave (he may have had a few days off, or more likely, episodes were being filmed simultaneously), Harris returns on top form for a splendid comic piece with character actor Henry Jones and an intergalactic gambling machine (voiced, appropriately enough, by Sgt. Bilko's former henchman, Allan Melvin, the taller of Bilko's two stooges on *The Phil Silvers Show*) that more than compensates for the padding and stalling tactics of the first half. The episode is played, advisedly so, as pure comedy, and the story is quite foolish, with Jones playing Smith's Southern gentleman cousin Jeremiah, who literally drops in for a visit (this is almost the least of a number of absurd coincidences during the second season). For an episode with so much time to kill early on, the story omits to show us Jeremiah's eventual departure from the planet (where to, Earth?), explain how he found them in the first place, or even provide a satisfying resolution. Exactly what use Smith's inheritance would be while he is marooned in outer space is neither explained or explored. It may be that Slater's loose style of writing,

which often involved leaving spaces in the script for Harris to ad-lib to his heart's content, simply caused the director—Justus Addiss, relatively new to *Lost in Space*—to simply run out of time, necessitating a quick wrap-up ... but Slater often had trouble ending his stories, which although packed with incident, often just fizzle out at the end. Addiss, a regular *Voyage to the Bottom of the Sea* director doing his second and last *Lost in Space*, films the Robot in close-up from above his voice box, unlike those more familiar with the series. His previous *Lost in Space* was the first season's "Attack of the Monster Plants."

Henry Jones, another busy character actor prolific in '60s TV, appeared three times in *Voyage to the Bottom of the Sea* (twice as time-traveling eccentric Mr. Pem) and several episodes of *The Six Million Dollar Man*. As a series regular, he appeared in the '70s sit-com *Phyllis*. So silly is this story, that one can't help wondering whether this substitute Smith was a ploy to keep Jonathan Harris in line, a subtle warning for some real or imagined insubordination, and a common tactic at the time (it had been done on *Maverick*, *Cheyenne*, and *Bonanza* to name just three), particularly given his absence at the start—but Cousin Jeremiah is no substitute for the real article! Production no.: 9510.

West of Mars

wr. Michael Fessier, dir. Nathan Juran

Smith is forced to assume the identity of a looka-like western-style desperado and spirited away to a Wild West toytown.

With Allan Melvin (the Enforcer), Mickey Manners (townsperson), Eddie Quillan (bartender), Ken Mayer (gunslinger)

Inexplicably, unless you put it down to Michael Fessier's careless, shoddy writing, Smith is instantly able to explain the premise of this episode to Will, which is that a "super-swift" is an intergalactic gunslinger. Okay, but who told Smith? If that had been the only flaw in "West of Mars," then the episode might still have conceivably been a novel idea well-realized, but this idiocy was chicken-feed compared to the major misjudgments to follow.

Only weeks after being a dead ringer for a character in "The Thief of Outer Space" (which, while being as equally infantile as this episode, was at least fun to watch), Smith now has the misfortune to be a dead ringer for fugitive murderer Zeno, and is whisked away by a space marshal (Allan Melvin again, in person this time) to a surreal world, part western township, part toyland fantasy (the local cowboys ride stuffed nursery animals on wheels!). The fact that Fox had superb facilities for filming a genuine western episode of *Lost in Space* (as *The Time Tunnel* demonstrated on many occasions), and that it would have been great to see the cast in a western scenario (Mark Goddard previously co-starred in the series *Johnny Ringo*) only increases the disappointment of this 24 carat stinker, which is nowhere near as entertaining as its *Star Trek* counterpart "Spectre of the Gun." The episode could still have been partially redeemed in the credibility department by making the entire fiasco a dream, or explaining that Zeno was able to assume any form, but audiences weren't even given that much consolation.

"West of Mars" is the "Spock's Brain" of *Lost in Space*, one of the most embarrassing and stupid episodes, and an absolute debacle from start to finish. Although Jonathan Harris said in interviews that it was one of his favorite episodes, he hams it up horribly as the doppelganger outlaw Zeno, giving a truly dreadful and totally misjudged performance. The Robinsons are made to look absurdly slow-witted in this episode, as the differences between the two lookalikes are not only glaringly obvious, but have been causing consternation throughout. Guest player Allan Melvin was marvelous when mugging behind Phil Silvers' Sgt. Bilko, but his embarrassing over-acting

comes close to rivaling Harris' Zeno—and why is he named Claudius?? Melvin had also provided the voice of the gambling machine in "The Curse of Cousin Smith" in the previous episode, and regularly did vocals for cartoons.

On the plus side, the sequences in which Harris must play both Smith and Zeno were brilliantly realized and edited (although viewers with freeze-frame facilities can glimpse the profile of Harris' stand-in during Smith's first encounter with Zeno, if they're quick enough—or indeed, if they care enough—something the makers of '60s TV didn't have to worry about back then!); Nathan Juran, director of numerous limited budget special effects movies of the 1950s, was often Allen's first choice for optically complicated episodes of Allen's series. Michael Fessier—one of a team of writers who contributed to Dead End Kids movies and specialized, would you believe, in writing musical westerns—wrote no other *Lost in Space* episodes. Production no.: 9512.

A Visit to Hades

wr. Carey Wilber, dir. Don Richardson

Exiled alien Morbus allows the demented Smith to believe that he has traveled to the domain of Satan in order to dupe him into doing his bidding, and then sets out to seduce Judy.

With Gerald Mohr (Morbus)

At first, Smith dominates this story, and seeing him believe he is about to get his comeuppance at last is one of the delights of this episode, but as the story progresses, Marta Kristen enjoys a rare opportunity in the spotlight, using it only to show us how badly she can act when actually called upon to emote rather than just stand around looking gorgeous. It's hard to believe this is the same actress who was so good as her evil doppelganger in "Attack of the Monster Plants." The first twenty minutes of this episode (complete with clumsy disclaimer insert filmed on different film stock, presumably to appease the network censors and/or the Bible belt) rapidly begins to threaten to descend into another farrago on the same scale as "West of Mars," even to the extent of having an adult Smith appear in would-be comical flashbacks as disobedient child, delinquent teenager, and cake-stealing stowaway on the *Jupiter Two*. Was this really the extent of Smith's sins in space? Compare these idiocies with the superior "The Prisoners of Space" only a few episodes earlier, which reconciled the changing Smith persona with that of episodes like "The Derelict" effortlessly.

However, while the episode never fully recovers from these absurdities, the story does redeem itself as it progresses, and comes alive for the second half, if only to offer a number of tackily amusing shock sequences with cut-price creatures. Although the script is weak and clumsy, the sets and action offer enough compensation to keep the episode from deteriorating into another "West of Mars." Outstanding scenes include an attack on the Robot by Morbus, an assault on Smith with several deftly placed bolts of power, a classic bug-eyed monster of 1950s vintage, and an amusing fight sequence of special effects simplicity as Major West tackles Morbus. Goddard had good reason to want to slug Mohr in the episode's climactic fist-fight—when Mohr guest-starred on Goddard's earlier series, the western *Johnny Ringo*, in which Goddard co-starred as deputy Cully, he bumped off Cully's sweetheart!

Mohr, who also voiced Mr. Fantastic on Hanna-Barbera's enjoyable 1960s cartoon series of *The Fantastic Four*, and turns up in the *Voyage to the Bottom of the Sea* episode "The Lost Bomb," also appeared in such schlock feature films as *The Angry Red Planet*, *The Monster and the Girl*, *Son of Ali Baba*, and *Invasion: USA*. Production no.: 9513.

The Wreck of the Robot

wr. Barney Slater, dir. Nathan Juran
    Aliens steal the Robot, and then take him apart for study.

    With Jim Mills (Saticon)

After the increasingly poor quality of such foolishness as "The Curse of Cousin Smith," "West of Mars," and "A Visit to Hades," it was beginning to look as though the series was finished and the promise of the opening second season episodes would be unfulfilled. Happily, the following few episodes showed a marked return to form, and "The Wreck of the Robot" was a much-needed breath of fresh air. The Saticons are wonderful adversaries (they would return in "The Galaxy Gift"), with their swaying bodies, shadowy forms, and ludicrous bowler hats, and there was no eccentric guest star with an Earth-like premise to steal the show—just good old-fashioned hostile alien invaders. Like the later "Trip Through the Robot" and "Deadliest of the Species," "Wreck of the Robot" benefits from being centered around our mechanical friend, and the Smith and Robot double act are on top form. Smith gets to behave like a complete skunk, and then gets his comeuppance ... just what we like to see!

Even though Smith, Will, and the Robot rightly dominate the proceedings, most of the cast get a spot in the limelight, and there's a nice scene between Will and his father when it looks like the Robot might not be coming back. Guy Williams did a great wise old dad routine, particularly during the first season, and here he excels; it's good to see him with something to do. There's also a funny bit where June Lockhart does an affectionate send-up of the Robot. If one was looking for an archetypal example of the second season at its best, this would be it, and "Wreck of the Robot" is a worthy demonstration that all was not lost when the series went to color; many critics of the series fall all too easily into the erroneous assumption that *Lost in Space* was serious sci-fi in monochrome and fell apart when it went to color. In fact, many second season episodes could sit quite happily in the first season, while the first season had more than its fair share of comedic stories.

The truth is, that *Lost in Space*—with its cowboy, pirate, séances and hillbillies etc., all first season—changed pretty much the minute it went into all-original episodes after the pilot film was used up, and the best episodes of the first and second season were undoubtedly those featuring weird, hostile space aliens. What would be fair to say is that the series had a rather cheap, second-hand look to it when the color episodes began, and lost some of the visual class of the first season.

All the best elements of the second season are in "Wreck of the Robot," but none of the worst. There are only a couple of dubious scenes—Smith on an exercise bike? I don't think so! And the talking chess piece is a silly bit, and quite unnecessary. Otherwise, this is a classic episode. Props-spotters will have a fine old time looking around the Saticon hideaway—just about every piece of equipment seen during the second season can be seen littering the Saticon cave, including the robot from "The Ghost Planet," the wheel from "The Android Machine," the endlessly employed light towers from the *Voyage to the Bottom of the Sea* pilot and later UFO episode "The Sky Is Falling," and that ever-present archway most prominent in "The Dream Monster" and "The Colonists," but apparently available either rightside up or upside down from all intergalactic department stores! Production no.: 9514.

The Dream Monster

wr. Peter Packer, dir. Don Richardson

A scientist enlists Smith's assistance to drain the Robinsons of their emotions and place them in his android creations.

With John Abbott (Sesmar), Dawson Palmer (Raddion), Harry Monty, Frank Delfino (little cyborg helpers)

Sesmar, played engagingly as an eccentric mad scientist by gentle-looking bearded character actor John Abbott, is yet another odd character who has been residing on the same planet as the Robinsons for months

undiscovered. The family had been on this one planet since "The Forbidden World" (the atmosphere seems to have cleaned up nicely since Smith's first foray into the unknown) and there were still plenty more caves full of creatures to be discovered yet!

After the absurd excesses of other episodes filmed at around this time, "The Dream Monster" was like a breath of fresh air with Harris on top form as Smith (as he so often was during the second season), who finds himself reluctantly paired off with Major West for a riveting and fast-paced finale. For once, the episode lived up to the threatening teaser of the previous week (and watch for the wonderful double-take by the chimp when Raddion first emerges from behind the rock in the pre-credits teaser!). Also elevating the episode are the presence of the Chariot (seen less and less as the series goes on), excellent performances, sets and costumes, and liberal use of the spooky electronic music from *The Day the Earth Stood Still* that graced so many Allen productions. An example of the second season at its best, but it speaks volumes about the mindset of the networks at this time that the silliest second season episodes were juggled into prime position during important ratings months November and February, while two of the best, this one and the following, were buried in the Christmas weeks of December. Although *Batman's* ratings (and those of *Lost in Space*) were starting to slip, the television executives of all three networks were still married to the camp is king doctrine.

Elderly character actor John Abbott (who apparently did not enjoy or appreciate Jonathan Harris' acting choices) also played freedom fighter Gorak in "Underground" for *Land of the Giants*, and Ayrleborn in the *Star Trek* episode "Errand of Mercy." He also appeared in *Bewitched, The Munsters,* and an excellent episode of *The Man from UNCLE,* "The Birds and Bees Affair." His films include *Curse of the Werewolf.* Dawson Palmer was the series' regular monster man; former

Wizard of Oz Munchkin Harry Monty also frequently doubled as Billy Mumy's stand-in (it's common practice for actors of restricted growth to double for kids), while Frank Delfino also appeared as a midget disguised as a little boy in the *Voyage to the Bottom of the Sea* episode "Time Bomb," and as the alien in "Don't Open Till Doomsday" for *The Outer Limits*. Production no.: 9511.

The Golden Man

wr. Barney Slater, dir. Don Richardson

Smith and the women find themselves in the center of a squabble between two warmaking aliens, one handsome and benevolent, the other ugly and ill-tempered.

With Dennis Patrick (Keema), Ronald Gans (frog alien)

Doctor Smith (Jonathan Harris) discovers the true nature of "The Golden Man."

"The Golden Man" is a heavy handed morality play which blows the basic moral of the story—that friendly people bearing gifts are not always what they seem, and ugly, bad-tempered folk are not necessarily bad. This message is completely lost as when the handsome alien is revealed to be evil, he transforms into a hideous creature, while the frog instantly changes into a handsome prince, thus completely defeating the whole point of the story. True, it works on the level of showing the ugliness or goodness beneath surface appearances, but as a demonstration of the sage advice not to judge by appearances it falls a little short! The episode is further hampered by some uncharacteristically crummy production values. The frog creature is particularly childish, the other alien quite visually striking, but equally stiff and unrealistic. The low point of the episode though, if not the entire series, is a minefield represented by half-buried beach balls. Not all the dramatic music in the Fox library can make this scene look suspenseful; Marta Kristen must have thought she was back on *Beach Blanket Bingo*. And when the frog transforms into a good-looking prince, the guy who plays the role manages to give a bad performance just by standing there and saying nothing! Fortunately, the episode is tracked with some of the very best pieces of background music from the Allen series.

But for all its minor shortcomings, the episode is a major joy for the performances of Lockhart,

Patrick, Harris, and May. Will, Don, and Professor Robinson are completely out of the picture until the final scene, and it's good to see June Lockhart finally given something to do. She stands up to Smith quite well! Dennis Patrick, often a smooth villain in '70s and '80s series (he was a regular opponent of J.R. in *Dallas*) is fine as the oily Keema, and Harris is as great as ever. The sequence where he fawningly delivers the ship's entire supply of weapons to the beaming baddie, only to see the grateful alien transform into a grotesque potato-headed horror is classic, a change first signified by a friendly plant-like paw on Smith's shoulder, the oldest vaudeville gag in the book. The alien head—phony but fun, with a lovely lopsided long mouth and one eye sliding down its droopy, vegetable-like countenance—made frequent appearances in the Allen shows after this episode, with both this and the frog head being worn by John Carradine in "The Galaxy Gift," and both later doubling as alien gogglers at a space-menagerie in "A Day at the Zoo." The Frog Man's spaceship doubled as a time machine in two *Time Tunnel* episodes, while Keema's head was last seen sitting benignly on a shelf in an episode of *Land of the Giants!*

Dennis Patrick's credits include the low-budget SF film *The Time Travelers*. Ronald Gans, portraying the frog-creature, can be seen in (almost) human form in the third season story "Deadliest of the Species." He was a used car salesman who did voiceovers for Roger Corman trailers! Production no.: 9515.

The Girl from the Green Dimension

wr. Peter Packer, dir. Nathan Juran

Smith encounters his green-skinned seducer again, and interferes with an alien romance. With Vitina Marcus (Athena), Harry Raybould (Ursuk)

Smith and the Robot were naturally funny together, and Mark Goddard and many of the guest stars also demonstrated a talent for comedy, but—like *Star Trek* and *The Twilight Zone*—when *Lost in Space* went out of its way to try to be funny, the results were often more embarrassing than amusing, and so it was with this particular entry. The humor in the series needed to develop naturally from the story, and not be the reason for the episode itself. There are some funny moments, all of them concerning Smith and the Robot, but mostly the events are heavy-handed and over-the-top.

Vitina Marcus first appeared as the space-siren, now renamed Athena after actress Vitina Marcus' daughter, in "Wild Adventure," the second episode of this second season. She was clearly a favorite of Allen's, and was used by him more than any other TV producer, appearing more than once in three of his four series. Harry Raybould, cast as the green-skinned viking type who is enamored with Athena, and whose credits include a role in *The Amazing Colossal Man*, has a thankless task, but is not really muscular enough for the role—although it has to be admitted that a growl from anyone would send Smith scurrying for safety. Particularly puzzling is Smith's sudden assumption that Athena has the power to see into the future and bestow similar abilities to him. Nowhere is this notion suggested in the script earlier, and it can only be put down to either careless writing or such a scene being edited out of the show at some point for timing.

But there is little in the episode that does add up. A funeral sequence, in which Smith thinks he's seeing a flash-forward to his demise, while being the comedic highlight of a weak episode, makes no sense whatsoever—no-one gives a eulogy for a broken piece of equipment, which is the get-out; the poor old Robot has been treated with less respect—and the telescope is a huge device which seems to have come from nowhere, and is never seen again (other than as a prop representing other alien furniture in later episodes). The Robinsons' spaceship is a bit like the TARDIS in *Doctor Who*, given the amount of stuff that appears to be stashed away in there. Production no.: 9516.

The Questing Beast

wr. Carey Wilber, dir. Don Richardson

Will and Smith encounter Sagramonte of Antares, an aging knight in armor who is pursuing a coquettish female dragon across the galaxy.

With Hans Conried (Sagramonte)

Oh dear. It's one of the weakest episodes of the entire series. Before we lay into it, fists flying, a few quibbles. The official credits list Sue England as providing the voice for Gundemar, the dragon. England provided many voice-overs for Allen, notably female robots in "The Ghost Planet" and "Deadliest of the Species," but despite the credits, the voice used here sounds absolutely nothing like England's rich, sultry tones and the dragon has surely been redubbed. The voice on the finished product is plainly that of Sheila Mathews, seen a few episodes later in "The Space Vikings." Allen was not averse to doing this in post-production, having twice completely revoiced characters in *Voyage to the Bottom of the Sea*, both times to the episode's detriment ("The Fossil Men" and "Time Lock"). Still, no amount of re-looping could have saved this fire-breathing turkey...

If it wasn't for "West of Mars," this would easily qualify as the most embarrassing episode the series ever coughed up, resembling as it does little more than an amateurish children's stage play. Hans Conried was a comedy actor, broad, hammy, and unfunny. He starred in Arch Oboler's silly sci-fi broadside against TV, *The Twonky*, and was surprisingly good giving a rare subdued performance in the excellent creature feature *The Monster That Challenged the World*. Otherwise, he did mostly sit-coms (including regular turns on Angela Cartwright's *Make Room for Daddy*) and voicework (the Arthurian Disney film *The Sword in the Stone* among them). His dreary, indulgent and patronizing performance here is quite depressing, although it's hard to work out what else he could have done with the role. The dragon is a ludicrously false creation, little better than a pantomime horse, and the cast are forced to play for non-existent laughs. The dragon suit, here worn by stunt-man Jeff County, later turns up in *Batman* as a "neosaurus" ("How to Hatch a Dinosaur"), in which it turns out to be a costume rather than a real creature, thus heightening even more the artificiality of the suit. Perversely, it is this farrago of an episode that features one of the rare attempts in the series to inject some pathos into the relationship between Smith and Will, and there is a wonderful scene amidst this mess between the two of them in the *Jupiter Two*, as Smith confesses his human failings to a dispirited and betrayed Will and laments the fact that the boy will never have any real respect for him because of his weaknesses. Ordinarily, of course, Smith covers all his failings with self-deceiving posturing and pompous bluster, so this rare moment of honesty is a wonderful moment.

Somewhere in "The Questing Beast" is the touching message that while heroes aren't always the chivalrous mythological supermen that society demands of its legends, they can still be decent people doing the right thing in a burst of fearful courage and conscience once in a while, as the blustering Sagramonte finally demonstrates. In many ways, Wilber is returning to the theme of his first season story "The Sky Pirate," which also dealt with the unrealistic expectations young Will had for child-like adults such as Smith and Tucker, but in a far more subtle and poignant manner. Like Sagramonte, Smith and Tucker couldn't hope to meet Will Robinson's high standards even halfway, but their flawed humanity made their few bursts of decency all the more heroic. But it's ironic indeed that this dismal travesty of an episode should have been the one to feature such an important and moving scene between Will and Smith, a key moment in the series, a rare few minutes of character study for the series in a heavy-handed yarn otherwise flitting between scenes of Harris and guest star Conried clownishly indulging themselves with some humor-free slapstick and poor Angela Cartwright's futile attempts to play her scenes with the dragon with a straight face. Everyone gets into the spirit of the thing, but ultimately it's a spirit that would have been better exorcised. Production no.: 9517.

The Toymaker

wr. Bob and Wanda Duncan, dir. Robert Douglas

Smith has another run-in with the intergalactic department store, but this time ends up on sale ... as a clown!

With Walter Burke (the Toymaker), Fritz Feld (Zumdish)

One of the better episodes featuring an eccentric alien rather than a hostile one, enhanced by good sets, excellent use of the library music, a good performance by guest star Walter Burke (also "The Terrible Leprechaun" for *Voyage to the Bottom of the Sea*), and a fair-sized role for Guy Williams. It's unfortunate that this fairytale comedy should have followed "The Questing Beast," because although similar in tone, it works where the other one doesn't. Colorful and fun, this Christmas-based episode has a touch of Santa Claus' workshop about it, as Will and Smith encounter Walter Burke's Gepetto-like figure creating old fashioned toys for Zumdish and his intergalactic department store, last seen in "The Android Machine." Oddly, despite the theme, this episode didn't air until the end of January ... although having left the running order relatively intact during the first season (but for some minor switches around the sweeps months), nothing the network was doing with the sequence of episodes made much sense at this point.

Fritz Feld makes his second appearance as Zumdish, having previously appeared in

"The Android Machine." Credits can be found under that title, along with those of Tiger Joe Marsh, who plays his aide and bodyguard. Dawson Palmer is once more in the monster suit, with Larry Dean as the toy soldier. Dean was a mime who specialized in performing as a mechanical man. Despite this rather limited resume, he turns up in this guise or similar in episodes of *Bewitched*, *The Lucy Show* (twice, "Lucy and the Ceramic Cat" and "Lucy the Robot"), *Voyage to the Bottom of the Sea* ("The X Factor"), and *Land of the Giants* ("A Small War"). Zumdish returns in "Two Weeks in Space." Production no.: 9518.

Mutiny in Space

wr. Peter Packer, dir. Don Richardson

Banished from the Robinson camp for the latest in a long line of transgressions, Smith stomps off in a petulant sulk and stumbles upon an alien ship, which he deludes himself into thinking is an abandoned vehicle than he can repair and return to Earth ... until the owner of the ship, a blustering sea admiral type, reappears and shanghais Smith, Will and the Robot for his next voyage.

With Ronald Long (Admiral Zahrk)

A shameless parody of cinema's *Mutiny on the Bounty*, this is a lively and amusing yarn, with Smith particularly funny while ostracized from the *Jupiter Two* and bluffing to return to Earth alone in the derelict spaceship he has discovered. Like a child that never thinks beyond the immediate moment, it never occurs to Smith that the vessel might have an owner somewhere, and sure enough—like the owner of the magic helmet in "Wish Upon a Star" (which this episode's beginnings resemble)—he turns up in due course. The scenes with Will, Smith and the Robot all at sea are great stuff, and Ronald Long, a character actor sliced from the same joint of ham as Harris and many of the show's other guest performers, piles on the baloney as the cut-price Captain Bligh. The highlight of the episode is the Robot, who is very funny all the way through. If the series had to make campy, spoof episodes, then this was the way to make them.

However, the episode is dominated by Harris and Long to its detriment. Few of the series' would-be comical guest actors did not overstay their welcome, and Long's Admiral Zahrk is one-note and very loud; it all gets a bit much toward the end. It's typical second season fare, colorful and silly, and the fourth of six fairytale-style escapades in a row. Long's numerous telefantasy roles (at least eighteen) include Friar Tuck in "The Revenge of Robin Hood" for *The Time Tunnel*, a swingin' London fashion designer in *Batman*, and Santa Claus, the Beanstalk giant, and Henry VIII for *Bewitched*, a series for which he appeared in no less than five episodes. He also turns up in twice in *The Man from UNCLE*, *I Dream of Jeannie*, and *Get Smart*, and the first *Wonder Woman* pilot. Production no.: 9519.

The Space Vikings

wr. Margaret Brookman Hill, dir. Ezra Stone
Smith chances upon the hammer and gloves of the Norse God Thor during a cosmic storm, and finds himself transported to Valhalla to do battle with the gods.

With Sheila Mathews (Brynhilde), Bern Hoffman (Thor)

High camp comedy with Smith and the Robot on a jaunt to a curiously domesticated Valhalla, and Mathews (later to be Mrs. Irwin Allen) in fine operatic form as Brynhilde. Harris is by now completely out of control and Bern Hoffman plays Thor as a live-action Hagar the Horrible! Harris, in no way intimidated by the presence of the boss' wife, who arrives howling Wagnerian operatics on a winged horse, plays Loki to Hoffman's blustering Thor, completely demoralizing him just as the Frost Giants show up. This might just as well be The Adventures of Zachary Smith for all anyone else has to do, but Will and the Robot are around. This is the first of eight lighthearted comedic episodes directed by Ezra

Stone, who had just finished working regularly on *The Munsters*, another effects-heavy camp-fest, although at this point in the series, the directors were simply aiming the camera at Harris and going to lunch. To call it over the top is redundant—this is simply the campest TV episode of any '60s show, making the average edition of *Batman* look like *Mannix* in comparison.

Despite the events of so many earlier episodes, including the previous "Mutiny in Space," Will's experiences are once again dismissed as his wild imagination by his parents, who really should be ready to believe anything by now. The simulator the Robot pulls out of nowhere to make handy duplicates of objects is a curious unexplained and improbable device that Brookman Hill appears to have swiped from the drunken cook scene in *Forbidden Planet*; perhaps she got her robots mixed up.

The elves that appear in the enjoyable Niffleheim sequence are uncredited, but are almost certainly Harry Monty and Frank Delfino, from earlier episodes; it was, and still is, common practice to use dwarf actors as stand-ins for child actors, and Monty was Bill Mumy's double. The dragon from "A Visit to Hades" puts in a blink-and-you-miss-it appearance. Fun, but you've got to be in the right mood for it. Production no.: 9520.

Rocket to Earth

wr. Barney Slater, dir. Don Richardson
A mysterious wizard materializes on the planet, but only Doctor Smith can see him.

With Al Lewis (Zalto)

Par for the course during the second season, which tended to favor colorful eccentric human visitors to hostile alien creatures. This is the sixth episode in a row to feature storybook characters rather than a sci-fi concept as the theme. We had now had the knight, the toymaker and Zumdish, the Admiral, and the viking in quick succession, and there was a distinct shortage of otherworldly menaces as the series struggled to outcamp *Batman* on the opposing ABC network. Zalto's cave is stocked with the usual paraphernalia from the props department, including the large white bear also on show in the *Batman* Mr. Freeze episodes this season, and Zalto's spaceship is the *Seaview* diving bell with a paint job, sitting on the standard base of colored lights first seen in the first season's "The Sky Pirate" and seen frequently thereafter. The plot follows the usual second season pattern, opening with Smith, the Robot and the kids doing something preposterous, followed by a story dominated by Smith, Will and the Robot until the two men rush in at the end and mop up. Unusually, Maureen accompanies them on this rare occasion. It's not made clear how the space capsule actually gets back to the planet it started from after being fired on by Earth, although at this stage in the series it was almost pointless asking. At least there is plenty of humor to be had between Smith and the Robot, and when Smith thinks he's cracking up. Bob May performs double duties as the voice and operator of Zalto's ventriloquist's dummy.

New York actor Al Lewis was best known as the vampiric magician Grampa in *The Munsters*, and once again a lame adversary is balanced by Harris and May on top form. Curiously, former *Munsters* director Ezra Stone did not draw this assignment. One of the advantages of being obliged to pull episodes off the shelf for research that wouldn't normally be the first or second choice for pleasure is that one forgets just how often Harris saved a mediocre story with his antics—sample line from Smith to Don West: "I'm only mentally unbalanced, not completely barmy!" Production no.: 9522.

The Cave of the Wizards

wr. Peter Packer, dir. Don Richardson

A concussed Smith is transformed by alien machines into a cold, unfeeling wizard, and the Robot his golden slave, and the Robinsons are convinced that they have seen the last of the Smith and Robot they knew.

This episode makes so little sense that it sometimes seems as though the scenes are being shown cut or out of sequence! Written by Peter Packer, and not, as you might be forgiven for thinking, a pack of drunken monkeys, the episode provokes the nagging impression of having been apparently cobbled together primarily to find a use for numerous existing props and costumes from other programs, most notably *Voyage to the Bottom of the Sea*, from which series a number of familiar creatures enliven the action. Whether Packer was instructed so, or whether Allen and the props people simply plundered the storeroom rather than the piggy-bank will remain a mystery, but the use of the *Jupiter Two* standing set suggests an endeavor along the lines of William Welch's budget-conscious runabouts that he produced for *Voyage to the Bottom of the Sea* and *Land of the Giants*. Allen fans will spot *Voyage to the Bottom of the Sea's* "Fossil Men," the brain from "The Ghost Planet," and numerous familiar Egyptian bits and pieces from *Cleopatra* on view, and even one of the *Jupiter Two* models sitting in front of the computer eye. Of course it's possible that Jonathan Harris' frequent ad-libbing and rewriting created such inconsistencies as Smith declaring his intention to stay for the farewell meal and then being seen at the alien cave, but even so, there are many other incongruities. Whatever the story behind this particular yarn, it all works rather better than it ought to do, and became one of Jonathan Harris' favorite episodes because of the make-up opportunity(!). However, where an abandoned *Jupiter Two* came from, and why it even existed is never explained, and neither is anything else.

Smith, Will and the Robot dominate, and the Robot is particularly funny as the gold-plated servant of the alien-influenced Smith, who is gradually slipping away from Will during an increasingly elaborate make-up job that is transforming him into a whey-faced, pointed-eared stranger. This is one of a number of second season stories that explored, strengthened and defined the relationship between Smith and Will—schemer and innocent—and the usually playful Harris is almost convincing as he fights to break the spell of the alien machines in a dramatic and emotional finale. Despite the numerous great gaping holes in logic and continuity, the episode is consistently entertaining and amusing. There is no comedy guest star in this story, and this, plus Harris' performance as the alien, and the pulp sci-fi elements unseen since "The Golden Man," make what is actually a rather weak and substandard entry, more welcome than it should be. Spooky music from this episode is later used in "The Phantom Family," but more interesting, given the presence of composer John Williams, is the Royal Anthem played for Smith, which bears a striking resemblance to the theme of a certain banal sci-fi blockbuster of the late 1970s which also featured funny robots and the music of John Williams. Production no.: 9525.

Treasure of the Lost Planet

wr. Carey Wilber, dir. Harry Harris

Smith is haunted by a disembodied mechanical head and pursued by alien pirates in search of rare treasure.

With Albert Salmi (Tucker), Craig Duncan (Deek), Jim Boles (Smeek)*

A routine second season yarn enlivened by the Robot and some colorful aliens. In the midst of another run of oddball eccentrics as opposed to genuine menaces, and having endured the knight, the toymaker, the Admiral, the viking and the magician in quick succession, this probably wasn't the best time to bring back Albert Salmi as Tucker the pirate.

Salmi had previously appeared as wastrel Alonzo P. Tucker in "The Sky Pirate" during the first season. "The Sky Pirate" had

been a rather special and magical episode—this was a flatly-directed follow-up that illustrates quite how far in quality the production values of the writing and direction had fallen since those early episodes, unintentionally illustrating how the humanity in *Lost in Space* had been replaced by comedy. Whereas the first season was rooted in a certain reality it had found for itself, the second season had been fairytale pantomime and farce. Both seasons were enjoyable for different reasons, but there was no denying the integrity of the first and the foolishness of the second. Production no.: 9521.

Revolt of the Androids

wr. Bob and Wanda Duncan, dir. Don Richardson

Verda the android returns, pursued by a deadly killing machine.

With Dee Hartford (Verda), Don Matheson (first IDAK), Dawson Palmer (second IDAK/cave monster)

A colorful yarn in which a silver-skinned super-android bearing a strong resemblance to a certain comic-book hero arrives on the Robinsons' planet in pursuit of Verda, the android from the celestial department store. There's some good comedy with Smith, strong action scenes, amusing set pieces (at one point Smith is blissfully oblivious to the second Idak android preparing to pulp his silly head with a boulder), and a wacky space-machine in the form of a giant vacuum cleaner, sent to sweep up broken androids! After the knight, the toymaker, the Admiral, the viking, the magician, and now the pirate, the sci-fi elements were more than welcome, and as one of the superior comedies, not too bad at all.

The ruby-eating monster from the opening scenes (also on view in the next week teaser attached to the previous episode, "Treasure of the Lost Planet") will

---

*Israelen (probably Dawson Palmer), the fourth pirate, is the furry fellow seen in "The Keeper," "The Magic Mirror," "All That Glitters" and later "The Prisoners of Space."

be familiar to followers of *Voyage to the Bottom of the Sea* as "The Abominable Snowman." It previously appeared in "Space Circus" and turns up again for "Hunter's Moon." There is a rare chance to see Dawson Palmer, the series' most frequently employed monster man, in near-human form, taking a double role here as the cave monster and the second IDAK android. He also appears in human form in "The Space Croppers" and the *Land of the Giants* episode "The Golden Cage." This was the second *Lost in Space* appearance for both Dee Hartford and Don Matheson. Production no.: 9524.

The Colonists

wr. Peter Packer, dir. Ezra Stone
    An Amazonian warrior enslaves the male members of the Robinson party.
    With Francine York (Niolani)

A little more inspiration in the script and direction of this episode could have raised this story above the average, but instead some of the budgetary rough edges show through in places. Still, the entire cast feature in the proceedings, with the men put to work as slaves and the women treated like princesses, and there are some very funny sequences and no dull moments as Smith wheedles his way into the Amazon queen's good books as a fawning artist to avoid doing any real chores. While Smith's antics as a sculptor dominate, the opening scenes with the malfunctioning radio transmitters bring some rare second season drama into the proceedings. There was drama off-camera too, when guest player York missed her mark during a special effects scene to blow up the bridge and was grazed by a chunk of junk.

The gold bridge Smith is working on can be seen as a prop in numerous episodes of *Lost in Space* and other Allen series, including *Voyage to the Bottom of the Sea* ("Deadly Invasion") and *The Time Tunnel* ("The Kidnappers"), usually painted red. It appears to have been originally made for the spy spoof *Our Man Flint*. Francine York is excellent as the Amazon queen, although Niolani comes over as more of a 1950s-style spoilt starlet-type than a fierce warrior. In reality a good-natured queen of cult crap, York beat *Alien's* Ripley into space by over a decade as a pioneering female astronaut in the Sam Katzman quickie *Space Monster* (1965); never one to turn down a job, she has appeared in five Jerry Lewis films (but also with Brando and Elvis), and worked not just with Irwin Allen (she appeared in Allen's unsold pilot *The Time Travelers* and a *Land of the Giants* episode, "Doomsday"), but with Arthur Pierce, Larry Buchanan, Ted V. Mikels and Fred Olen Ray. She played the Bookworm's moll Lydia Limpet in *Batman*, the goddess Venus in *Bewitched*, and Lois Lane's mother in the 1990s *Superman* series *Lois and Clark*. Other TV includes *My Favorite Martian*, *The Wild Wild West*, *I Dream of Jeannie*, *Mission: Impossible*, *Future Cop*, and *Jason of Star Command*. Add on the daytime soaps, and she's been working continuously for four decades. Production no.: 9526.

Trip Through the Robot

wr. Barney Slater, dir. Don Richardson
    With the Robinsons unable to recharge him after Smith drains the Jupiter Two of its power supply, the Robot dejectedly wanders off into a forbidden area of the planet, where he becomes giant-sized ... Will and Smith must crawl inside their mechanical ally and return him to normal.

One of the better second season entries, despite being a blatant rehash of the first season's "The Oasis," in which it was Smith who became a giant; the Robot provided the catalyst for a few of the more tolerable second season adventures. One very nice touch has a repentant Smith making the futile gesture of briefly pushing on the Robot's mechanical heart to restart it when he sees how distressed Will is. The Robot's innards are constructed out of just about every spare piece of nuts and bolts in the prop department, including the usual familiar cogs and wheels and banks of computers. A mobile laser is adorned with the familiar circle of cylinders split by metal sides that made up the base of the bomb devices in *Voyage to the Bottom of the Sea's* "The Peacemaker" and *Time Tunnel's* "Raiders from Outer Space." The climax, with the guys trapped inside as the Robot shrinks, is well done for the time and quite exciting, although the special effects of the day could only replicate the shrinking effect by having the Robot's mechanics get closer rather than smaller.

This episode's trailer includes footage from "The Phantom Family" not present in the actual show; the following episode begins with different footage of Smith scuttling out of the *Jupiter Two* to join Don at the force field energizer and then starts from there.... Production no.: 9527.

The Phantom Family

wr. Peter Packer, dir. Ezra Stone

An alien replaces Don, Smith, and the girls with experimental android duplicates.

With Alan Hewitt (Lemnoc)

Director Ezra Stone has told how his actor friend Alan Hewitt was not too thrilled when he saw what he had been roped into—the alien head, familiar to *Time Tunnel* fans who saw two of them, painted blue, in the episode "Town of Terror," was hot and uncomfortable. The red clothing also appears in the *Lost in Space* episode "A Visit to Hades" and the *Voyage to the Bottom of the Sea* episode "Attack." Like their blue-hued compatriots in "Town of Terror," these particular aliens don't appear to be able to tell the difference between androids and humanoids; the script refers to humanoids when it means androids, while the *Time Tunnel* episode refers to androids when it means humanoids! The story focuses on Will, who—with the Robot—is forced to retrain the alien's inept copies to behave like their

human counterparts to secure the freedom of the originals, frozen in suspended animation by the alien in the same now over-used freezing tubes used in the *Jupiter Two*. A major drawback of the episode is that Don and Smith are automatons throughout most of the show, and while this is hardly a problem for certain cast members, it leaves the show minus its usual spark as Don, Smith, and the Robot are unable to bounce off each other (although even comatose and robotic, Harris steals the limelight). "The Phantom Family" is a highly appropriate title, as both Guy Williams and June Lockhart are absent from this episode until the final few scenes. Mumy, the alien, and the effects just about hold the interest, but it's all a long way from the far superior first season duplicates story, "Attack of the Monster Plants."

Some of the creepy music in the episode was previously heard in "Cave of the Wizards." Harris is clearly reading his lines when he has to list the ship's control panel functions—fair enough. When John and Don are leaving Lemnoc's cave, Mark Goddard bumps his head on Lemnoc's gun; lazily, the sequence was not edited out or re-filmed!

The previous episode "Trip Through the Robot" includes film from "The Phantom Family" not present in the actual episode showing Don, Smith, the girls and the Robot cowering on the floor of the ship from Lemnoc's artillery assault; this episode starts with Smith and Don checking out the force field energizer, preceded by a few seconds of different footage. Production no.: 9528.

The Mechanical Men

wr. Barney Slater, dir. Seymour Robbie

Tiny miniature copies of the Robot abduct Smith and exchange his personality around with the Robot, who then becomes their wicked leader.

A very silly one! There's no logic in the characterizations, and the writing is careless. To compound matters, the robotic dialogue has been recorded separately from the actors, and in several places it doesn't quite match. Given the total inability of either Jonathan Harris or Bob May to stick to the script, someone should have seen that one coming!

The miniature robots appear to be dozens of the hobby kit creations of the period; setting up each shot must have been murderously time-consuming. The most comparable reference point would be to liken the episode to those *Superman* comics of the 1960s in which anything, no matter how absurd, could happen within the limited frame of the characters' coincidence-cluttered environment. If the entire universe revolved around Earth in most science-fiction TV series, then during the middle year of *Lost in Space*, the entire universe seemed to revolve around not just Earth, but the Robinson party, most notably "The Curse of Cousin Smith," "West of Mars," "The Thief from Outer Space," and so on. Once again, the writers look back to the first season for inspiration, here the old cliché of Smith being turfed out of the camp and scheming away in the rocks and bushes as in "Attack of the Monster Plants" (again). However, this is one of those in which all concerned just throw up their hands in despair and get on with it ... Marta Kristen has told how she had particular problems getting her few lines out without laughing. The one good thing that can be said about this episode, which is at least amusing, is that we did not have to suffer yet another eccentric pantomime adversary (which may be why the *Batman*-obsessed network held it back until the end of the season). This did not last long, as we were about to meet ... Production no.: 9523.

The Astral Traveler

wr. Carey Wilber, dir. Don Richardson

Will and Smith are transported back to 19th century Scotland, where they encounter a ghost with a grudge against Smith's ancestor.

With Sean McClory (Hamish)

Given the look-behind-you style of jeopardy in *Lost in Space*, it was perhaps only natural that one of the writers would eventually drop Doctor Smith into the classic 1930s/40s haunted house set-up. Set in a spooky Scottish castle, the story makes little sense, and follows the now over-tired formula of letting Jonathan Harris loose with a loud over-the-top guest star. All your favorite clichés are here, and yet again the entire universe revolves around the Robinson party. He gets around, does Smith. This episode utilizes spooky sound effects from "The Forbidden World" and the island set from *Voyage*, and Angus the monster is "The Creature" from third season *Voyage to the Bottom of the Sea*. Professor Robinson is absent from this episode but for a voiceover. *Time Tunnel* fans can have fun spotting the props from various excursions into the past scattered around the castle. And having a warp in the space-time continuum represented by a 1930s-style revolving door covered in lights is original, at least.... Production no.: 9529.

The Galaxy Gift

wr. Barney Slater, dir. Ezra Stone

Hostile aliens recreate a copy of Chinatown in San Francisco to fool Smith into thinking he has returned to Earth and trick Penny into betraying a trust.

With John Carradine (Archon), Jim Mills (Saticon)

This entertaining episode ends the second season with some fine sequences, including the bogus Chinatown—a borrowed convenient standing set or I'm a Bloop's uncle—and some humorous moments with a giant fly (Harry Monty in the suit). The aliens are the same creatures that menaced the Robinsons in "Wreck of the Robot," and although they were not named in that story, and no reference is made to the earlier episode here, we must assume that they are also the Saticons. Archon is played by veteran horror film actor John Carradine, who made over 200 films during his career, many of them Grade Z horror. During the '60s and early '70s he made over a dozen TV appearances, including episodes of *The Green Hornet*, *The Munsters*, *The Girl from UNCLE*, and *The Man from UNCLE*, and later returned to work for Allen playing an unemployed horror actor (something he never was) in "Comeback," an episode of *Land of the Giants*. Jonathan Harris had worked with Carradine before, on the stage, and did not get on with him; he felt he had been snubbed by an off-handed Carradine when welcoming him to the set.

The two alien forms first assumed by Archon in a totally insane and typically second season intro (the kids and Smith are performing a pantomime for no-one in particular, complete with sets and costumes) are the two monster heads used for the warring aliens in "The Golden Man." The Robot is seen in drag in this episode, and later turns up in feminine guise in "Space Beauty"—a title not, thankfully, referring to the Robot! Production no.: 9530.

THIRD SEASON (1967–1968)

The Condemned of Space

wr. Peter Packer, dir. Nathan Juran

The Robinsons stumble onto a malfunctioning prison ship run by computers where the convicts are frozen alive.

With Marcel Hillaire (Phanzig)

This episode marked the start of the third season, and Allen pulled out all the stops to revitalize the show and give it a new lease of life with a complete overhaul. In this he succeeded, with the *Jupiter Two* taking off into space again and encountering a huge space station prison ship guarded by Robby the Robot of *Forbidden Planet* fame (now wearing fetching yellow stripes!). The direction could have been better (numerous jolt sequences were thrown away), and the use of music was below par, but it was good to see the Robinsons in space again, and to see a

different look in the sets (although we were soon to return to the standard sound stages and planet sets of the earlier seasons). Toward the middle of the second season, *Lost in Space* had begun to get a rather shabby, second-hand look about it; unfortunately, this would also happen again with the third season.

Another unhappy event—the cancellation of *The Time Tunnel*—benefited *Lost in Space*, as the show acquired much of the studio space and props from that series. With *Batman* in its third and final season and clearly in ratings trouble, camp was now declared officially dead and action and adventure was the order of the day. However, the Smith and Robot double-act that had sustained the show throughout the more ludicrous, campier moments of the second season suffered from Allen's half-hearted attempts to give less interesting characters equal screen time alongside Will, Smith and the Robot. Smith was consequently much more subdued in certain episodes, and although still flouncing around ad-libbing left, right and center, one has a sense of him being reined in, particularly during group scenes with the full cast, and the strain of the rest of the cast's growing dissatisfaction with the direction of the show is clearly evident in this season. The third season would be distinguished from the second by bringing in more action; Guy Williams in particular felt that the show had become a foolish joke during the second season, and from his perspective, one can hardly disagree. An established TV star from his lead role in Disney's heroic adventure series *Zorro*, he had signed on as the leader of a pioneering family in a space adventure series and through no fault of his own, rapidly found himself reduced to a supporting player on his own show, which had now transformed into a light comedy. Williams was not so much an actor in the theatrical sense as an athletic former male model who looked good, had some physical prowess, and knew how to stand and deliver lines with conviction and confidence. As such, he was perfect TV hero material, a point he had proven in *Zorro* and as a leading man in the superb heroic fantasies *Captain Sindbad* and *Damon and Pythias*. He was not happy, and despite attempts to placate him with more lines and action, he would frequently absent himself from the show toward the end of the run. For the series' young audience, it was fun to watch and as popular as ever, but the series had fallen a long, long way from the original intentions and standards of the stylish first season. In this episode Smith is not on form, his actions and dialogue even more ludicrous than usual—although if the third season took Smith away from Harris, no-one could take the Harris out of Smith; every episode had at least one laugh-out-loud gem from Smith, and at least one ad-lib from the Robot! In this episode, it's a thoroughly guilty Smith, having unleashed the usual cavalcade of life-endangering calamities, lamenting glumly "Poor Robot! I almost feel responsible!"

He's referring to the highlight of this particular episode, a gripping sequence when the Robot is put out into space by the bungling Smith. All the cast have new costumes for the new season, but the greatest change has been in Penny, as Angela Cartwright has become a young woman during the season's hiatus. Cartwright is wearing her hair attractively long, but only for this episode; Allen didn't like it. The series has lost its little girl, and unfortunately the character is now somewhat redundant for 1968 U.S. TV. The biggest problem any show casting kids has is that if it stays on the air long enough, the children grow up, and out of their roles. If the series hadn't ended with this season, it would have had some serious format problems to face by season five.

Marcel Hillaire would later play the Junkman in the final episode of the series, "Junkyard of Space," and was a prisoner on "Devil's Island" in *The Time Tunnel*. He appears in "The Virtue Affair" for *The Man from UNCLE*, which also features Ronald Long from "Mutiny in Space" as the villain of the week! Mark Goddard finds himself strapped to the familiar torture device from "The Cyborg" in *Voyage to the Bottom of the Sea* and "Raiders from Outer Space" in *The Time Tunnel*. This particular prop was used extensively in the Allen series—it's a life-size cut-out of a human figure decorated with flashing lights—and can also be seen in the second season's "The Dream Monster" in Sesmar's laboratory, and in "The Phantom Family" in Lemnoc's! Production no.: 1501.

Visit to a Hostile Planet

wr. Peter Packer, dir. Sobey Martin

The Jupiter Two *returns to Earth through a time-warp, where they inadvertently start a saucer-scare in a hick town in 1947.*

With Robert Foulk (Cragmire), Robert Pine (Craig), Pitt Herbert (Grover), Norman Leavitt (Charlie), Clair Wilcox (Stacy)

This episode swiftly became a fan favorite, mostly for being shot out of doors, showing the Robinsons back on Earth, and offering rare scenes of the full-size *Jupiter Two* on its legs (when the ship landed properly, as opposed to crash landing, it was usually with legs and steps). The full scale *Jupiter Two* was specially disassembled and reconstructed outside the studio for this episode, which starts well but veers dangerously close to second season silliness when Smith rallies the local hicks, all straight out of *Green Acres*. Still, Packer appears to have noted that UFOs have an infuriating habit of crashing in Bugtussle or Hooterville rather than downtown Manhattan ... There's a precognitive touch of Roswell here—and it's July, 1947! Smith, of course, sees a promising future for himself as a wise old despot because he knows the future, but tellingly rushes back to the others at the end when the Robinsons reluctantly realize this isn't home. Despite some heavy handed comedy moments, the dramatic sequences overrule them (Robot and *Jupiter Two* fire-power scenes contrast well with quieter, more mysterious moments) and the supporting cast save the day—the hayseeds are played by familiar and competent character actors, and Craig, who encounters Judy, and little Stacy, who befriends Will, are particularly good. This is the fifth episode put into production, and also the first to give the female cast some significant screentime since the season opener. Marta Kristen is particularly good, given some half-decent lines and realistic jeopardy to work with for once. The backlot used to portray Manitou Junction—when Will and the disguised Robot attempt their escape—can also be seen in "Town of Terror," an episode of *The Time Tunnel.* The lumberyard where the *Jupiter Two* lands is the Fox parking lot. Trivia spotters will note that the Robot somehow instantly repairs himself when shot by a bullet that seriously dents his frame!

Robert Foulk returned to portray Captain Kraspo in the dreary "Princess of Space." Pitt Herbert appeared in the "Billy the Kid" episode of *The Time Tunnel.* Recognized quite rightly as a strong high concept episode, the network moved this as near to the front of the run as possible. Production no.: 1505.

Kidnapped in Space

wr. Robert Hamner, dir. Don Richardson

When Smith boasts of his non-existent abilities as a surgeon, he and the Robot are forced to perform brain surgery on the computerized leader of an alien race!

With Grant Sullivan, Carol Williams (aliens), Joey Russo (young Smith).

An intentionally comedic episode, with Smith and the Robot absurdly coerced by time-controlling androids into performing brain surgery on their computerized leader. Smith's double-take when he discovers he has to operate on a machine is priceless, and Bob May's ad-libbing is on top form in this one too. Although Allen started the third

season visibly attempting to give the other cast members more screen time, the network clearly had other ideas, and this is plainly a Smith and Robot dominated comedy moved forward to the third in the run.

This was the first episode of the series to be aired from Robert Hamner, a regular contributor to *Voyage to the Bottom of the Sea,* and later story editor on the *Wonder Woman* TV series, although his first episode prepared appears to have been "Deadliest of the Species," which airs later. Hamner clearly relished the opportunity to get away from the comparatively poker-faced environment of the *Seaview,* where Allen demanded the show be played straight, and he produced a string of light-hearted Smith-and-Robot yarns, following this with the equally loopy "The Space Destructors," the ludicrous "Two Weeks in Space," and the moderately amusing "Fugitives in Space." With the exception of the latter, no matter how much comedy Hamner put into them, he could always be counted on to slip in the requisite action content too. One wishes he had come on board the show earlier. He also has the distinction of having penned the fan favorite "Anti-Matter Man," which was something of a stylistic departure for both himself and co-writer Barney Slater (represented on the credits by the pseudonym K.C. Alison). He captures the purpose and essence of Smith brilliantly and immediately.

The Space Pod—an enormous shuttle-craft that suddenly appeared on the *Jupiter Two* out of nowhere—makes its first appearance in this episode, although it actually premieres in "Hunter's Moon," as does Penny's new short hair-style, also putting in an early appearance as this sixth episode is moved forward to third (in fact, Angela Cartwright gathered her long hair up under a wig rather than cut it, but at least she doesn't have guest player Carol Williams' hair-style to deal with!). Grant Sullivan appeared in the *Land of the Giants* episode "The Creed"; child actor Joey Russo's other credits include

The Man from UNCLE and the Elvis Presley film *Harum Scarum*.

Most of the props from this episode are extremely familiar from both this series and *The Time Tunnel*. When *The Time Tunnel* ceased production, many of the props turned up on the third season of *Lost in Space*, and many of the bits and pieces seen here will be familiar to fans of both series. The aliens are more flamboyant versions of the silver-skinned guys seen in *Time Tunnel's* "Visitors from Beyond the Stars" and "Chase Through Time." There are some familiar sound effects, too. The machine leader's heartbeat is the same as that of the Robot in "Trip Through the Robot." When Smith is transformed into a child, the sound-effect is the same as that used when the time-travelers are transported through time in *The Time Tunnel*. Needless to say, all this gives the episode a slightly over-familiar, second-hand look to it, especially sitting as it does among the more expensive-looking earlier third season episodes. Production no.: 1506.

Hunter's Moon

wr. Jack Turley, dir. Don Richardson

John Robinson finds himself the unwilling substitute for a hunter's prey when he kills an attacking monster.

With Vincent Beck (Megazor).

Guy Williams, increasingly dissatisfied with the direction *Lost in Space* had taken in the second year, was promised more to do in the third season, with specific episodes to be built around him and other cast members. Although Smith has his fair share of screen time, this second episode prepared showcases Williams and Mumy in one of television's oldest story premises, the human prey pursued by a deranged hunter (according to writer Turley, one of story editor Anthony Wilson's favorites!). However, despite sections of the hunt being filmed outdoors, the constant switching from studio to outside location shooting and back again serves

only to heighten the artificiality of both, and the episode has a tatty, cheesy look to it, not helped by the uninspired appearance of Megazor (whose head-piece doesn't match his skin color), poor directing choices, an abundance of over-familiar hardware, and a familiar gallery of monsters in Megazor's cages previously seen on *Voyage to the Bottom of the Sea*, including the Scorpian (their spelling) from "Doomsday Island," the seaweed monster from "The Creature" (also seen in "The Astral Traveler"), the furry white monster from "The Abominable Snowman" (also seen in "Space Circus" and "Revolt of the Androids"), and a rock creature from "The Fossil Men," the latter of which has a hilarious bit of old-fashioned comedy shtick with Smith. The Scorpian suit would make two more appearances in the third season, and the rock men had already appeared in the second season's "Cave of the Wizards." The big furry guy with the horns from "Treasure of the Lost Planet" is also visible. As familiar as they all are (and why shouldn't the same life forms keep turning up?), it would have been good to see more of them, even if only as background. The finished result never looks quite as good as the storyboards (published in a 1980s fan publication) had hoped. Ironically, guest star Vincent Beck, who had appeared twice in *The Time Tunnel*, as a Viking marauder in "Merlin the Magician" and a towering android in "Town of Terror," was a giant of a man who could look and sound quite imposing when filmed right. No such luck here, buried under a thoroughly ineffectual outfit, and filmed in a flat and pedestrian manner by a director known for his contempt of the material. Beck also had the honor of appearing in the legendary turkey *Santa Claus Conquers the Martians* and a number of episodes of *The Monkees*.

When John Robinson is missing on the alien planet, the *Jupiter Two* follows him down, courtesy of Smith, who pushes all the wrong buttons in an impulsive fit of pique.

Knowing that color television was imminent (but oblivious to the syndication prospects for TV), Allen had special effects footage and location work filmed in long-shot with doubles filmed in color when he made the pilot, and this footage was indeed later used in subsequent color episodes, notably the *Jupiter Two* crash-landing; June Lockhart joked in interviews that they used to call Mark Goddard "Crash" West, because this was Allen's only footage of the ship landing—consequently no arrival on a planet's surface ever went smoothly! In actuality, however, the crash itself takes place offscreen (actual attempts to show the ship crash-landing were considered too phony, as outtakes on the series' DVD release demonstrate), and the long-shot footage of the *Jupiter Two* coming in for a landing (by Howard Lydecker) could easily have been used for a smooth arrival (and indeed was occasionally run backwards for a hasty departure). Closer to the truth is probably that Irwin Allen never landed a ship quietly when he could crash-land it!

However, there is also some new modelwork footage filmed for the third season (the Lydeckers' last for Allen) which gets a good airing before the series ends. This episode actually introduces the Space Pod shuttlecraft, which appeared from nowhere in the third season without any explanation or origin story. It emerges from underneath the *Jupiter Two*, despite being housed off the upper deck, and everybody behaves as if it has always been there (thanks to the network shuffling the episodes around, audiences actually encounter it first in "Kidnapped in Space," where a similar situation of full awareness prevails). Writers were simply told that this hardware was now available for inclusion, and duly wrote it in. Jack Turley wrote for numerous 1960s series, including *Land of the Giants* and *The Man from UNCLE*, and was writing for the series under duress for old friend story editor Anthony Wilson. Production no.: 1502.

The Space Primevals

wr. Peter Packer, dir. Nathan Juran

Smith and Major West become reluctant comrades when they are captured by primitives ruled by a computer.

With Arthur Batanides (Rangah).

A fun episode concentrating on the rocky relationship between Smith and Don, as they travel in the Chariot to plug a temperamental fissure and encounter a tribe of literate primitives (rather sweet little fellows in their ankle-high cave slippers, bopping about as if their feet are on hot coals, which, due to the proximity of the usual Irwin Allen volcano, they should be) ... and, while it makes for great entertainment, the idea of West entrusting the party's most dangerous and unreliable member to travel with him and transport an explosive device is beyond belief.

In fact, the whole episode is beyond belief. The tribe are in the thrall of Protinius, their governing computer, which has granted the caveman curious magical abilities, including teleportation of objects and people ("Back so soon, Smith?" gloats West as Smith tries to scuttle off and abandon him). The story is absolutely nonsensical, and the writer's research consists entirely of saying that things are "kind of prehistoric!" ... most absurdly, the Chariot supposedly achieves this transformation simply by acquiring a few vines draped over it. Needless to say, the *Lost World* lizard puts in a cameo appearance, and once again the Robot displays impossible and unusual powers that he shouldn't have. The computer in a cave bit had been done before in *The Twilight Zone*, and made no more sense then. Only Nathan Juran, who had dealt with concepts far more ridiculous during his schlock B-movie career, could have dared direct it.

Although the Robinsons are back in space for the third season, the space travelers are already on the planet when the story begins, a common occurrence in the third season giving the series more flexibility but a slightly disjointed look. Some episodes begin with the ship traveling through space, others with the ship crash-landed (always without feet), and none of them with an explanation; viewing the episodes in order of production creates no greater sense of continuity. The ship never lands on its legs when setting down in a desert-like locale, yet always does when descending on flat civilized surfaces. This is actually the third episode of the season (Major West debuts his new short, close-cut hair style he would keep for the remainder of the run), and there's more location filming, matching the studio sets a little better than the previously filmed "Hunter's Moon," and more new (later to be familiar) model footage of the Space Pod. The female cast members appear only briefly. Despite the ludicrous storyline, there is enough crammed in to keep the episode entertaining—color footage of the welcome return of the Chariot, the Robot on top form, exciting rescue scenes with Will and Professor Robinson (enhanced by the location filming), and amusing scenes between Smith and Don, who—believing their hours are numbered—begin to patch up their differences while damning each other with faint praise. The outdoors scenes and deployment of the series' hardware give the episode a classy appearance reminiscent of the first season (the opening travel scenes and John's search for the Chariot in the Space Pod are particularly good), but we would soon be back in the studio for the remainder of the run.

Arthur Batanides was the Mongol leader Batu in "Attack of the Barbarians," an episode of *The Time Tunnel*, one of his best and most enjoyable roles—quite the opposite of what he's given here. A fine actor ready to have a go at any role, Batanides has been rewarded in the SF TV arena with some of the most mundane episodes of shows such as *The Twilight Zone*, *The Outer Limits*, *The Green Hornet* and *Land of the Giants* ("Terror-go-Round"). Production no.: 1503.

The Space Destructors

wr. Robert Hamner, dir. Don Richardson

Will and Smith stumble onto an alien device that makes cyborgs, but Smith becomes drunk with power, and—under the influence of the machine—creates an army of Smith lookalikes.

A typical episode with all the usual ingredients—a scheme for Smith, a fight for John, a cave full of secrets and monsters (the same cave entrance used in all the third season episodes!). What have now become the *Lost in Space* clichés are all in evidence here, including John Robinson's token defending-the-family bit, Smith's let's-keep-a-secret routine, Will's sneaking out of the ship against orders, and so on. Robert Hamner had done his homework well.

Here, Jonathan Harris is on top form in what is essentially a remake of the first season episodes "Wish Upon a Star" and "His Majesty Smith," as Smith luxuriates in riches and culinary delights served up by his cyborg slaves before he inevitably comes unstuck. As with Hamner's previous "Kidnapped in Space," all semblance of logic goes straight out of the window to allow the Smith/Robot/Cyborg routines full comic leeway. The need for numerous cyborgs in Smith's image caused Jonathan Harris some hardship—he was claustrophobic, and hated spending hours under the paste to create the masks, the work of the award-winning make-up man John Chambers, who created David McCallum's marvelous future-man make-up for the classic "Sixth Finger" episode of *The Outer Limits*, Robert Culp's non-stereotypical Chinese disguise for his dual role in the *I Spy* episode "The Warlord," and the famous *Planet of the Apes* masks (an early incarnation of which can be viewed in the later *Lost in Space* story "Fugitives in Space"). Chambers was dismissive of "The Space Destructors," and regarded the finished job with supreme indifference, but a delightful still of Harris and Chambers posing with two of the heads (Chambers and the heads looming over Harris' shoulder while he theatrically and determinedly studies the script of that episode) shows that there were few bad feelings at the time. Harris was highly complimentary of Chambers' work, and the way in which he guided him through the personal trauma of the mask-making process, and kept one of the Smith masks on display in the hallway of his house until it finally fell apart.

Despite Chambers' efforts and Harris' bravery, the massed forces of the Smith cyborgs look somewhat phony, although Billy Mumy wears a more elaborate version for the spooky final scenes. The effect is as good as it can be by 1960s standards (such a concept would be effortlessly executed by computer today), and Will looks quite grotesque in a Hallowe'en kind of way as the miniature Smith. Never one to miss a trick in the recycling department, the plain cyborgs look very much like the ones used in the memorable *Voyage to the Bottom of the Sea* episode "The Cyborg" a year earlier, and there seems to be no reason, other than a whim of Smith's, why they should be dressed in various period costumes from Earth history other than to make use of the extensive 20th Century Fox wardrobes plundered for *The Time Tunnel!* Sharp-eyed viewers will spot the Time Tunnel's image area making up part of the device, along with the transformation tube from *Voyage to the Bottom of the Sea* episode "The X-Factor."

Another dream-like yarn best not examined too closely, "The Space Destructors" has lots of fireworks, fancy dress and fighting, and the cyborg construction process is a riot. One of the cyborgs is played by Tommy Farrell—the son of gangster movie actress Glenda Farrell (he appeared alongside her in the Elvis film *Kissin' Cousins*)—who has some nice moments as a fey cyborg slave conjured up by the arrogant Smith, and both he and Harris are clearly in their element camping it up shamelessly. Farrell kept busy on comedy series in the '60s, including episodes of *The Munsters, The Ad-*

dams Family, The Beverly Hillbillies, Captain Nice, and *Get Smart,* and appeared several times alongside Lucille Ball. He also appeared in "The Pop Art Affair" for *The Man from UNCLE.* Providing another of his sinister alien voices is Bart La Rue, also the voice of the Guardian in *Star Trek's* "City on the Edge of Forever." Production no.: 1508.

The Haunted Lighthouse

wr. Jackson Gillis, dir. Sobey Martin

The Jupiter Two—with a young alien boy and fellow castaway on board—find an ancient space lighthouse and a promise of enough fuel to reach Earth.

With Lou Wagner (J-5), Woodrow Parfrey (Silas Fogey), Kenya Coburn (Zaybo).

Even the splendid Woodrow Parfrey, who portrayed sleazy slimeballs in numerous episodes of *The Man from UNCLE* and was particularly wicked in "Fatal Cargo" for *Voyage to the Bottom of the Sea,* couldn't save this slop, in which he and fellow guest actor Wagner are obliged to play Disney-style loveable goofs. His character clearly modeled on the equally awkward and oddball Mirror Boy from Gillis' first season fairytale "The Magic Mirror," Wagner is one of those actors doomed to character roles thanks to his small stature and impish appearance; his films include *Planet of the Apes* and he played a Ferengi in "Chains of Command" for *Star Trek: The Next Generation.* Although essentially Penny's episode, there is enough of the entire cast to keep things interesting, and the lavish and spacious sets are a major plus. Production no.: 1509.

Flight into the Future

wr. Peter Packer, dir. Sobey Martin

On a world of illusions, the Robinsons get a nightmarish glimpse of their future ... (it didn't include a horrible feature film, though).

With Lew Gallo (Commander Fletcher), Don Eitner (Sergeant Smith).

With a story involving a Rip Van Winkle scenario and the descendants of the Robinson party, this episode isn't nearly so much fun as it ought to be—*The Flintstones* did it better, with "Groom Gloom"! The idea of Smith meeting a disgraced descendant from the future is a good one, but the writers don't seem to know where to go with it. Only the scenes with the Robot and his statue stand out, as the Robot discovers a proud monument to a "cybernetic hero." Gallo and Eitner are wearing the spacesuits from *Destination: Moon* and *Time Tunnel's* "One Way to the Moon," while Marta Kristen has some interesting scenes as her descendant in a groovy retro '50s atom age ensemble straight out of the pulp magazines. Production no.: 1507.

Collision of the Planets

wr. Peter Packer, dir. Don Richardson

The Robinsons have a run-in with some loutish aggressive bikers hired to destroy their planet, while Smith acquires Samson-like strength.

With Daniel Travanti (Ilan), Linda Gaye Scott (biker girl).

A group of lazy and lethargic space-bikers arrive on the Robinsons' latest stop-off point with orders to blow it up, but the angry and apathetic louts won't wait for the *Jupiter Two* to be made ready for lift-off.

Linda Gaye Scott appeared as the memorable Vama in "Invasion from Outer Space," an episode of *The Green Hornet* almost as ludicrous as this one. She had also recently played the female lead in a *Man from UNCLE*, "The Very Important Zombie Affair," and the Riddler's moll in a *Batman*. Daniel Travanti also appeared in *The Man from UNCLE* at around this time, and served time on the guest star circuit as a young man before being cast as Captain Frank Furillo in the quintessential cop show *Hill Street Blues*. Other fantasy roles include the splendid 1989 time travel feature *Millennium* and a recurring role in the 1990s cable series *Poltergeist—The Legacy*. His *Hill Street* co-star Michael Conrad appears under heavy make-up in the later episode "Fugitives in Space." The bikers are played by Joey Tata and Steve Marganian.

This is a truly awful episode, much worse than the famous forthcoming Carrot Man debacle. None of the cast look as though they want to be there except for Linda Gaye Scott, who appears to be having a great time going with the flow and is even caught laughing as one scene fades out. Ten years on from the juvenile delinquency panic of the '50s, television still can't deal with genuinely menacing bikers, so the louts are played as childish goofs. As if this isn't bad enough, Smith acquires green hair and Samson-like strength, and must also play to the infants. One of the few episodes in which Jonathan Harris just isn't funny, and Daniel J. Travanti, billed (as he was then) as Dan Travanty, and who gives a dreadful performance, looks as though he just wants the ground to swallow him up ... He seems reconciled to it today however, as he recently provided an autograph for a 2005 set of trading cards! Production no.: 1510.

The Space Creature

wr. William Welch, dir. Sobey Martin

An alien force that feeds on fear intimidates Will by abducting the Robinsons one by one while the Jupiter Two is in flight.

A suspenseful episode with an over-familiar premise—everyone on board is slowly disappearing. It's over-familiar because it's a time-honored cost-saving ploy of course, by Irwin Allen's master spendthrift William Welch, but having the creature represented by a guy under a bedsheet was one saving too many. Slinging a sheet over a stuntman in the manner of an old haunted house comedy must have made the cheapest monster ever. However, the biggest problem the story has is that a hasty rewrite for the better has also, less advisedly, changed horses midstream as to the origin of the menace.

Although *Forbidden Planet's* concept and execution of an invisible monster had already been filched for the first season story "Ghost in Space," this episode swipes the creature from the id explanation given to it, and makes a mess of the concept. Far superior is the episode's initial idea of a childish, infantile alien intellect at work, a common supposedly surprise twist in pulp SF that resurfaced at around the same time in *Star Trek's* "The Squire of Gothos," but the climax has been messed about with to rightly add a tense jeopardy scene between Will and the creature in the ship's storage areas and power core (it's good to see some thought given to this, but the *Jupiter Two* now has even *more* space inside than the exterior allows for). Having a genuinely malevolent menace undoubtedly helps, as does the goosed-up climax, but it's a shame it was revised in haste. Perhaps Irwin Allen's own id took a subconscious dislike to the overgrown child and his toys concept! The alien voice belongs to Ronald Gans.

Given that this is an obvious inexpensive bottle show of the sort Welch turned out frequently for *Voyage to the Bottom of the Sea*, it's surprisingly watchable. Unlike *Voyage*, which used interchangeable crewmen or guest stars for these sorts of stories, the regular *Lost in Space* characters are sufficiently familiar and well-defined to be concerned about and sustain the suspense in this sort of story. Production no.: 1511.

Deadliest of the Species

wr. Robert Hamner, dir. Sobey Martin

The Robot finds love and companionship ... with an evil robot fleeing the law.

With Sue England (female Robot voice), Ronald Gans (alien leader), Lyle Waggoner, Ralph Lee (androids).

Smith and the Robot are marvelous in this splendid episode that offers plenty of fireworks and lots of the Robot, who has a love affair with a malevolent female machine. As the fourth episode produced for the third season, Guy Williams and sidekick Mark Goddard dominate the action for the first half of the episode, with Jonathan Harris in the background and sticking to the script.

June Lockhart is curiously absent for the first half with no explanation. Harris, absent for the first ten minutes, is finally let out to play in the third act, and Smith's reaction to the Robot's "tawdry affair" is hilarious, with a wonderful scene where Smith spitefully gloats over the Robot's misfortune and makes the "ferrous Frankenstein" burst into tears before the female robot turns the tables and sees him off with a series of well-placed explosions. There's also more cornball comedy with the radarscope seen in the previous episode, "Hunter's Moon." The story's author, Robert Hamner, told how he built the entire episode around the Robot's closing comments that in the end "she was just another pretty face"—not that funny, but the pleasure he took from it resulted in a wonderful episode. As was often the case with incidents in companion show *Batman*, the sequence where the Robot "energizes" the grateful female robot is a perfect example of the sort of saucy thing that could be slipped past the censors which a different style of show would never have got away with. This is the later incarnation of the series at its best, with a perfect balance of action, humor and visuals. Although held over for a while, the November airdate suggests it may have been considered a strong one to keep by for sweeps week. The attack on the *Jupiter Two* by silver-skinned androids wearing headpieces similar to those in *Time Tunnel's* "The Kidnappers" is particularly exciting, with the family trapped in the ship, and Will trapped outside. Although an entire planet is blown up in "The Time Merchant," and a couple of pirates buy the farm in "Treasure of the Lost Planet," this is the only episode in which supposedly innocent aliens are destroyed onscreen, although visually they don't seem too hurt, cartoonishly spinning offstage. In the original storyline, the aliens were not destroyed, and returned to take custody of the defeated machine. Equally absurdly, the evil female Robot is pointlessly resurrected for a silly tag gag in the final scene.

Lyle Waggoner, the second choice to play *Batman* had Adam West declined the role, played Colonel Steve Trevor in the *Wonder Woman* TV series. The tiny role he plays here was one of his first TV appearances before finding more gainful employment in TV variety shows. His films include the *Time Tunnel* rip-off *Journey to the Center of Time*. Sue England also provided female voices for other Irwin Allen productions, including *Voyage to the Bottom of the Sea's* "The Human Computer" and the *Lost in Space* gem "The Ghost Planet." Ronald Gans voiced the Frog-like alien in "The Golden Man" and the Id monster in "The Space Creature" as well as securing a brief on-screen role here. Production no.: 1504.

A Day at the Zoo

wr. Jackson Gillis, dir. Irving Moore

The Robinson party encounter a fraudulent alien showman who claims to control time and space and captures them for his traveling sideshow.

With Leonard Stone (Farnum), Gary Tigerman (Oggo).

A dreary, derivative and plodding episode, with only the circus scenes and the Robot's boxing match with a knight in armor to recommend it. Vastly inferior to the first season's "The Keeper" and *Twilight Zone's* "People Are Alike All Over," and even the second season's "Space Circus," all of which this resembles in a negative, threadbare way, this is a cheap and tacky effort with too much talk and not enough action. When the Robinson party are put on display (Guy Williams doesn't appear in this episode at all, and June Lockhart appears only in the closing tag) they are observed through frosted glass by a variety of familiar alien visages. The monster mask from "The Golden Man" makes its third appearance (see also the intro of "The Galaxy Gift"), and also recognizable are heads from *Voyage to the Bottom of the Sea* episodes "Deadly Amphibians" and "The Menfish." The only completely visible aliens are a family of three

large-domed individuals representing a family unit, two of which are dressed in the alien costumes from *Time Tunnel's* "Raiders from Outer Space." One particularly poor and misjudged sequence of many has Will menaced by a purple papier-mâché carnival dinosaur head, which—when Major West blasts it—suddenly transforms itself into Allen's favorite *Lost World* footage, and a completely different creature! All this idiocy for one irrelevant shot, creating a continuity lapse that a two-year-old could spot.

The hazy images of blurred monster faces peering in at the exhibits could have been quite effective with a little bit of the magic and effort employed on shows like *The Outer Limits*, or even the first season of this series, but inept director Irving Moore, in one of two dismal outings on the Allen series (the Farnum follow-up episode "Space Beauty" is the other) has no such inspiration, and just films a bunch of extras milling about on the other side of opaque glass. Nice one, Irv. Where's Sutton Roley when you need him? Production no.: 1514.

Two Weeks in Space

wr. Robert Hamner, dir. Don Richardson

The Robinsons have their third encounter with the manager of the intergalactic department store, but now he's under the illusion he's operating a tour agency. Smith colludes with him to turn the Jupiter Two into a holiday hotel, but their first customers are dangerous convicts on the run!

With Fritz Feld (Zumdish), Edy Williams (Non), Richard Krisher (MXR), Eric Matthews (QZW), Carol Roebke (Tat).

As is apparent from the above synopsis, both the series and Jonathan Harris had now gone completely nuts. It would be a pointless exercise to criticize the foolishness of the story, as the episode is played entirely for laughs, with a token rescue of the womenfolk from a volcanic cavern by the guys at the climax (interestingly, Robinson disintegrates the two male aliens with his ray gun, willfully killing them, whereas the usual get-out would have been to have the aliens tumble into the handy lava pit themselves; it's a measure of how seriously the episode was being taken that no-one cared). Despite this being Hamner's purest comedy episode, he still manages to inject an element of menace into the proceedings (the coming attractions trailer plays on this, rather than the comedy), and the aliens are rather fun. Harris, of course, had played a hotel manager on *The Bill Dana Show* prior to *Lost in Space*, where he perfected many of his Doctor Smith characteristics, but there are no similarities with that role here, even if it possibly inspired Hamner. The result is well over the top, but tough not to like, with some classic lines from Smith ("Saucy baggage!"/"Also, elevator operator!") and some amusing exchanges between Smith and the Robot ("You mean it's not worth a king's ransom?"/"Not even a Doctor Smith's ransom!"). Even so, the idea that the aliens need a landing beam, or that the Robinsons can prevent them from landing is absurd. Jonathan Harris appears to have a double for his transformation scenes, which are very poorly dubbed, and despite Smith coming across as gay as the time he plans for his happy campers, this is the fifth episode in which he pursues, or is pursued by, a female!

The alien roles were played by bit players, including Eric Matthews, who had played an astronaut in the *Voyage to the Bottom of the Sea* episode "Journey into Fear," and ambitious up and coming starlet Edy Williams, who managed to turn up in most major 1960s TV series at one time or another, including *The Beverly Hillbillies*, *Batman*, and *The Man from UNCLE*, and made her name in the Fox feature *Beyond the Valley of the Dolls*. She is excellent in this, probably her most substantial TV role. She later married mainstream porn director Russ Meyer and she and her own two special effects later became a notorious familiar exhibit at the Cannes film market. Production no.: 1515.

Castles in Space
wr. Peter Packer, dir. Sobey Martin

Will and Smith encounter a bounty-hunting bandito and the ice princess he is pursuing ... and the Robot gets smashed out of his bubble on cheap drink!

With Alberto Monte (Chavo), Corinna Tsopei (Reyka).

One of Packer's rare forays into the parodic fantasy area of the show, with Don, Judy, Smith, Will, and the Robot encountering a silver-skinned bandito. Smith and the Robot dominate this episode with some amusing comedy routines and dialogue, the highlight being, of course, the sequence in which Chavo gets the Robot drunk. In *Forbidden Planet* it was the chef who got tipsy, by ordering Robby the Robot to reproduce liquor, but in *Lost in Space*, it was the Robot that got bombed! Other scenes of broad comedy follow, with Smith and the Robot staging a bungled rescue of cartoon-like dimensions, using a female dummy to lure the stereotypical bandito into a trap. Mark Goddard is on to hand to provide some traditional Major West slow burns and take care of the action sequences, and Judy has more to do than usual. Penny on the other hand is completely absent but for the closing scene at the Chariot, while Guy Williams and June Lockhart also appear only in this wrap-up scene and an insert during a radio conversation with Don. The *Jupiter Two* is not seen at all! This episode also features a nice little musical interlude when an entirely sober Will and Judy sing some folk rock. The rest of the music is unusually credited to frequent *Star Trek* composer Gerald Fried, a wise choice who specialized in incorporating the more recognizable sounds of world music into background scores for *The Man from UNCLE*, and does so here to give the episode a Mexican flavor. Interestingly, you can hear quite clearly some of the sort of background music used frequently in *Star Trek* during the scenes in which Chavo confronts Major West and threatens to harm Will.

Alberto Monte previously appeared in *The Time Tunnel* as Sgt. Garcia in "The Alamo." Like many Mexican actors of his generation, he was trapped in these stereotypical roles. Production no.: 1513.

Anti-Matter Man

wr. Robert Hamner, Barney Slater, dir. Sutton Roley

John Robinson is cast into a dark and threatening surrealistic dimension where he encounters evil versions of himself, Don, and the Robot.

Everyone loves a new idea, but sometimes an old idea done well can be just as enjoyable—formula doesn't have to be the f-word of science-fiction. The evil double is one of the oldest gems in the TV treasure chest, and it almost always works. The stories are fun, so the viewers like it. It saves money on guest stars, so the producers like it. It's foolproof as a publicity gimmick, so the networks like it. And it gives the actors an opportunity to stretch from their established characters and be center stage, so you can be sure that they like it. Jonathan Harris quoted one of the worst *Lost in Space* episodes ever made, "West of Mars," as one of his favorites for this very reason; David Hedison names his bodysnatching episode, the mediocre "Return of the Phantom," as his favorite *Voyage to the Bottom of the Sea*.

Although this episode was widely regarded as a return to first season quality after the total insanity of the past few episodes (there was even the return of a first season director, the inimitable Sutton Roley), there are the usual third season inconsistencies and oddities. We are never told what Will and particularly Smith are doing sitting round a campfire at night ... or where the book Will is reading came from, or why the pages mysteriously turn just as the evil John and Don are plotting their escape from the Shadow World. However, despite the usual lapses in logic that come with the territory where *Lost in Space* is concerned (the Robot casually remarking that the Anti-John casts

no shadow, Don's reluctance to believe the battered Robot about John, despite the overwhelming evidence that had swayed him only a few scenes earlier, John's symbolic but pointlessly disappearing chains at the end), "Anti-Matter Man" is rightly regarded as one of the all-time great episodes of *Lost in Space*, certainly of the color episodes and very variable third season. Had there been a fourth season, as was at one time likely, a return visit to the Shadow World was almost certainly on the cards.

After three 100 percent humorous entries in a row, this thriller showcasing Guy Williams and Mark Goddard was more than welcome, especially with Sutton Roley at the helm. His showing off in "Anti-Matter Man" includes a Roley trademark, the actors walking toward the camera until they envelop it, here done with Will and Don standing either side of the Robot until his control panel dominates. Other close-ups of the Robot are so tight you can see the brushstrokes of the silver paint! Elsewhere, a hand-held camera (quite a rarity in *Lost in Space*) is used for Will's dream and the dramatic fight scenes with Drun (Mark Goddard's evil double) and the inevitable rubber monster, which Roley makes the best of, keeping it and the camera moving.

In CGI-free 1967, special effects were done with models, sets, and camera tricks or not at all, and the images created for "Anti-Matter Man" were cheap but effective. Apart from the trees casting shadows on a supposedly distant mountain range every time lightning flashes, and one of the shadows in the Shadow World belonging to a technician manually pushing a rock, it all works beautifully. Roley works wonders with studio sets, a fluid, constantly moving camera, forced perspective, polythene, glitter, colored lights, shadow, and trick lenses. Arrival in the limbo between dimensions is done particularly well, with a simple sheet of glass in front of the lens. The spare long-distance Robot suit works double time this episode, taking a beating from the Anti-Matter Man, and then getting a paint job for the Anti-Matter Robot interlude.

The anti-matter world, and the bridge into it (mist-covered and surrounded by stars and an endless drop), is beautifully realized and both male leads revel in this rare opportunity to play parts of substance. Williams is so good as a villain that one can only regret his subsequent retirement from acting, as he could so easily and effectively joined the ranks of '60s heroes who went on to meaty villain roles in the '70s and '80s action shows. Roley's continuously swirling camera, ducking and diving to conceal the rough edges, contributes to several genuinely exciting scenes, including a shockingly brutal attack on the beloved Robot, Will's abduction, and the escape of the real John Robinson from the cave. Fans of *Voyage to the Bottom of the Sea* will recognize the Scorpian monster suit from "Doomsday Island."

Ironically, "Anti-Matter Man," one of the most dramatic and exciting episodes of the third season, was written under the pseudonym of K.C. Alison by two of the series' most capable comedic writers, Robert Hamner and Barney Slater. It's something of an irony—and a mystery—that one of the best of all the *Lost in Space* episodes should be graced with an alias. One wonders what could possibly have been the problem that encouraged them to remove their names. Slater, a favorite writer of Harris' for his habit of leaving dialogue spaces for Jonathan Harris to ad-lib, something clearly going on in this episode's closing tag scene, wrote almost exclusively for *Lost in Space*, authoring nine superb episodes for the first season, ten excellent second season stories, but only two third season stories besides "Anti-Matter Man." He was the best Smith and Robot writer on the show, and his only other work for Allen was a single *Time Tunnel*, the memorable "Pirates of Dead Man's Island." Robert Hamner also wrote a single *Time Tunnel*, "Attack of the Barbarians," and although

previously associated with *Voyage to the Bottom of the Sea*, had come aboard *Lost in Space* for the third season and swiftly shown himself to be an invaluable asset, again notably with Smith and the Robot. It was ironic indeed that two of the best Smith and Robot writers should provide the show with one of the best episodes to place them, although present, on the sidelines. Production no.: 1512.

Target Earth

wr. Peter Packer, dir. Nathan Juran
Only Will and Smith escape when shapeless aliens assume the forms of the Robinson family and head for Earth in the Jupiter Two.
With James Gosa, Brent Davis (aliens).

Splendid pulp sci-fi episode, with the Robinsons replaced by shape-changing globs who are all alike and want to sample life as individuals. Inevitably, once differentiated, they start fighting between themselves. This was the second episode in a row to feature an evil John Robinson and Don West, this time accompanied by doubles of the entire crew. The sets and creatures are excellent, although it would have been nice if the base of the monster costumes had touched the floor, or if director Nathan Juran had thought to obscure the fact that they didn't! However, Juran manages one excellent single take, using Smith's stand-in to crouch beside Will as they hide from the aliens, and then panning across without a cut to show Harris portraying the imitation Smith asleep in a chair. Smith and Will replace their duplicates, but end up with the fake Smith tied up and hidden on board the *Jupiter Two* as it attempts to leave with the alien crew. There is one glaring error when Will confronts the Robot, who has been reprogrammed to serve the aliens; Will struggles and loses, when all he had to do was remove the Robot's power pack, as Smith has done in countless other episodes—the error is magnified later when someone else does just that. Sadly, this is the last episode of *Lost in*

Space to feature any traditional hostile alien menaces as central to the plot; the remaining episodes in the series revolve around wacky extraterrestrial eccentrics. An excellent episode though, and the *Jupiter Two* does actually return to Earth, albeit briefly; tinted footage of the meteor shower from the pilot appears yet again, as does the missile sequence from "Forbidden World." Later, Juran—who had already helmed "West of Mars" with two Smiths—would helm a superb *Land of the Giants* episode, "The Clones," which also featured multiple doubles of cast members. Production no.: 1516.

Princess of Space

wr. Jackson Gillis, dir. Don Richardson

A space buccaneer is convinced that Penny is really his planet's long-lost Princess Alpha, and that once reunited with her Royal Scepter she will be able to quell the robot rebellion on his home planet.

With Robert Foulk (Kraspo), Arte Johnson (Fedor), Sheila Mathews (Aunt Gamma).

Angela Cartwright looks beautiful dressed up in two princess outfits, but there's not much else to this heavy handed yarn designed to put the character of Penny in the spotlight. As was typical of the third season, Guy Williams and Mark Goddard are sleepwalking through their performances; Williams and Lockhart put in only fleeting token appearances, and everyone but Cartwright and Mathews (Mrs. Irwin Allen) look utterly bored, as indeed they should—the story is little more than a catalogue of fairytale clichés, with Jackson Gillis, who established himself as Penny's writer with the first season gem "The Magic Mirror," forever rewriting that story every time Penny is given an episode in which she has more to do than stand around. The '60s gave pre-pubescent girls only one role in those days (Penny is supposed to be thirteen here), and that was to dream of fairytale princesses and fall in love with cheeky scamps or handsome princes. And even

though this is Penny's episode, it's still Will who gets to have most of the adventure, while Penny dresses up.

Robert Foulk, usually cast in folksy, hick roles, previously appeared in just that capacity in "Visit to a Hostile Planet." Arte Johnson, soon to be known for the cult show *Laugh-In* in the late '60s, later appeared in Allen's early '80s fiasco *Alice in Wonderland*, along with Allen's wife, by then calling herself Sheila Allen. This was Mathews third visit to the *Lost in Space* set; she appeared in the first season classic "Return from Outer Space," and featured in "The Space Vikings." Production no.: 1519.

The Time Merchant

wr. Bob and Wanda Duncan, dir. Ezra Stone

Smith swindles a being who can control time and makes his way back to Earth before the Jupiter Two *takes off into space, leaving John and Will to pick up the tab ... but then Professor Robinson makes a terrible discovery and the lives of the entire party depend on the Robot making sure that Smith boards the ill-fated spacecraft a second time.*

With John Crawford (Chronos), Byron Morrow (General Squires), Hoke Howell (Sergeant).

Don and the girls are completely absent from this episode, and it is a compliment to the fast pace of an intriguing storyline that they are never missed, although Don and Maureen appear in a flashback scene that appears to have been either specially prepared for this episode to include them, or excised from an earlier story at the eleventh hour. Footage from the pilot and—for no immediately discernible reason—"Wild Adventure" is employed, and Chronos' stooge is the orange fellow from "Anti-Matter Man." The sets for this episode match that memorable classic, with Chronos' world a dark and Dali-esque place where limp clock faces lie draped over trees and bushes. There are some clumsy attempts at comedy during Smith's brief foray at Alpha Control, but these are carried off quite well and don't linger or intrude on the action. For once, the humor sets just the right tone, is liberally employed but doesn't outstay its welcome, and provides an interesting contrast with the pilot episode that it joins full circle. Smith and the Robot are very funny (it's nice to see the series acknowledge that the Robot changed and developed a personality), the casting is good, the climax exciting (we get to see the Robot swing a few punches, and Smith perform a rare heroic act), and John Crawford, a fine player usually cast in more reality-based roles, seems to be enjoying his chance to play what is essentially pantomime. This was the only third season script by the Duncans, although a couple of other ideas—an *Alice in Wonderland* spoof and a Great Race concept—never got past the starting post. "The Time Merchant" is one of the best third season stories, and although the remainder have their moments, this is also, almost symbolically, the last *Lost in Space* episode of any significant quality, although the Robinsons still had six more episodes to film. A shame this could not have been held over to close with, but at the time, cancellation was by no means confirmed.

Contrary to some reference sources, none of the guest players previously appeared in the pilot, and vice versa. Production no.: 1518.

The Promised Planet

wr. Peter Packer, dir. Ezra Stone
> Smith and Penny succumb to the hypnotic persuasions of hostile ageless aliens who inhabit a psychedelic world where the generation gap is a canyon.

With Gil Rogers (Bartholomew), Keith Taylor (Edgar).

"Oh dear, I'm afraid this is all a bit too groovy for me!" laments Doctor Smith at one point in the proceedings, and most viewers are probably inclined to agree. This was a rather lame attempt to portray the arrival of '60s psychedelia in American culture, and watching predominantly middle-aged Hollywood scriptwriters desperately trying, and hopelessly failing to portray the counter-culture of the period in various television productions of the time was almost as sadly hilarious as the sight of the swingin' Smith. Virtually every long-running series on the air in the late '60s had what might loosely be termed a hippie episode trying to come to terms with what the media had coined the generation gap, but very few got away with this episode's extraordinarily unsubtle drug references ... feature films of the period were censored for less! As ever though, Hollywood's attempts to be hip in the '60s were comically incompetent; only the ugly punk phenomenon suffered such equally laughable misrepresentation on television a decade later.

That said, it's a fascinating period piece, and the youngsters' revelation as *Twilight Zone*-ish antennae blue aliens is great fun. The scenes where the Robinsons leave the planet, convinced they never had children, are quite powerful.

Keith Taylor had previously appeared in the first season's "Return from Outer Space." Production no.: 1520.

Fugitives in Space

wr. Robert Hamner, dir. Ezra Stone
> Smith and West find themselves unjustly confined to a prison planet to do hard time.

With Michael Conrad (Creech), Tol Avery (Warden).

Michael Conrad, later to be known for his memorable role as Sgt. Phil Esterhaus in the critically acclaimed police drama *Hill Street Blues*, is the familiar face hiding behind an ape-like monster mask in this routine, moderately entertaining but unspectacular episode. The episode is primarily interesting for being a trial run for the *Planet of the Apes* make-up then in development at Fox. Although reportedly not too thrilled with his role, and consequently (said director Ezra Stone) difficult and surly on the set, Conrad is clearly working hard under the heat of the mask, using his voice and eyes as best he can to give life to the convict Creech, and no doubt it was helpful to have a role into which he could channel his anger. It's a tough and demeaning task portraying Creech, as the episode is played entirely for laughs. The sets are sparse, but don't need to be elaborate; however, they don't help the episode either, which has a somewhat restricted and threadbare look. Everything is second-hand. The prison officers' bikes are those seen in the earlier episode "Collision of the Planets," ironically featuring another future *Hill Street Blues* player, Daniel J. Travanti; the prison uniforms are the "Devil's Island" costumes from the previous season's *Time Tunnel* episode; the robot head of the judge was a significant prop in "Treasure of the Lost Planet." The skull caps worn by the prison staff are particularly gormless.

Tol Avery, who had appeared in *Batman* and also turns up in "Shell Game" for *Land of the Giants*, has little to work with as the prison warden of Destructon, but does his best with what he has; the two guards, one of them uncredited, the other busy bit player Charles Horvath, are stiff and wooden. Although the episode holds the attention, not nearly enough is made of the potentially winning situation of having West and Smith incarcerated together, and the scenes between Smith and West carry none of the humor evident in the earlier "Dream Monster" or "Space Primevals" episodes. Actually, Smith and West are not fugitives at all for the majority of this episode, but prisoners—however, "Prisoners of Space" had already been used, and this title exploited the recognition factor of top-rated show *The Fugitive*. Penny, Judy, and the Robinson parents are absent; only four of the regular cast appear—Don, Smith, Will, and the Robot. Harris dominates competently, while everyone else looks bored. It was clearly a difficult episode to film, the wafer-thin ideas needing inspiration rather than dissension. What works is carried off between Smith and the Robot, particularly the visiting scene with

the cake; not the classic it should have been, though. Production no.: 1522.

Space Beauty

wr. Jackson Gillis, dir. Irving Moore

The Robinson party encounters the opportunist showman Farnum B. again, who this time wants to exhibit Judy in a beauty contest to appease the faceless dictator of an alien world.

With Leonard Stone (Farnum), Dee Hartford (Nancy Pi Squared).

Leonard Stone previously appeared as Farnum in "A Day at the Zoo," and gives a colorful, way-over-the-top return performance here in this threadbare but moderately entertaining time-waster. One could be forgiven for thinking that the two episodes were filmed back to back, as so many of the sets and costumes repeat themselves. The sets are depressingly sparse. Aside from the regular *Jupiter Two* and planet sets, we are offered only a bare darkened stage, one area cordoned off by a large expanse of the gold-colored curtain material that 20th Century Fox seems to have been buying in bulk throughout the '60s, decorated a little desperately from the props department's stock of period bits and pieces from historical epics. The other costumes are similarly familiar; the alien beauty contestants are luckless young women adorned with the heads of familiar monster costumes from previous episodes of *Lost in Space* and *Voyage to the Bottom of the Sea*, while the aliens from the cobalt planet are clad in suits of armor from the ever-handy stock room. The awful dragon suit from "The Questing Beast" also appears in a mercifully brief scene.

This is yet another episode that is carried by the humor generated by Smith and the Robot, and the opening scene, with the cobalt planet aliens haunting the *Jupiter Two*, are well done, even if the creeping around the cast's quarters routine is now beginning to look as overfamiliar as some of the props. Between them, Stone and Harris' broad pantomime performances carry the day in what is a particularly cheap-looking production, highlighted only by the director's clever use of red light on the face of Farnum whenever the selling of his soul is mentioned. Only two other scenes are particularly strong—a section when Farnum is transformed into a dangling puppet by his mysterious boss to remind him of his fiery fate if he fails to deliver Judy Robinson, and the climactic scenes outside the *Jupiter Two*, particularly the cheap but effective effects of the dictator's furnace-like visage and the snowfall.

Dee Hartford was previously the silver-skinned android Verda in two second season episodes and is fairly redundant here. Once again, John and Maureen Robinson are absent, and are not even mentioned, while Major West has a minor role in the proceedings at the end. A jaw-dropping moment of cartoon-like comedy aiming for cheap laughs has the Robot appearing in drag! (It's the pantomime costuming from the dreadful opening scenes in the second season's "The Galaxy Gift"). But the biggest laugh, as usual, comes from what is probably one of Harris' own typical ad-libs in a throwaway bit; presented with champagne by the obsequious Farnum, Smith sips it once ungratefully and disdainfully pronounces it "Domestic!" Production no.: 1523.

The Flaming Planet

wr. Barney Slater, dir. Don Richardson

The Robot comes close to being drafted into senseless warfare when Smith and West discover a dying alien culture devoted solely to battle.

With Abraham Sofaer (the Sobram).

Guy Williams returns to the series for an episode guest-starring prolific character actor Abraham Sofaer, with whom he previously acted in the superb feature film *Captain Sindbad* (Sofaer had played the wizard). Sofaer was the Thasian minder of "Charlie X" in *Star Trek* and had also appeared in *The Time Tunnel* in "Revenge of the Gods" and "The Walls of Jericho." His other fantasy

film credits include the *Time Tunnel* rip-off *Journey to the Center of Time*. The female cast members barely appear, with Maureen back for only one scene. Both Don and Professor Robinson figure prominently in the tale, which once again is dominated by Smith and the Robot, tormenting each other on top form. The episode only stalls when it makes a couple of awkward attempts at banter to give the others in the cast some token screentime alongside Smith and the Robot, most notably a soppy but happily brief interlude with Penny and Judy.

The Sobram is an impressive alien, and one of the Allen series' best; in fact, he looks a lot more impressive than some of those who passed through on *Star Trek*—and as beloved as those ol' silver-suited, silver-faced aliens are in many other Allen shows, it was nice to see an alien being dressed and colored differently for a change. Most of the props and effects had been seen before, however. The radiation belt that the *Jupiter Two* passes through came from "The Ghost Planet," as did the scenes of the missile attack, which appear frequently in the third season. The giant plant is a rather tacky and unconvincing prop, while the human-sized versions of the creature were recycled from a *Voyage to the Bottom of the Sea* episode, "The Plant Man." Nothing appears to be flaming, although there is an inexplicably exploding plant pot on board the *Jupiter Two*. Production no.: 1517.

The Great Vegetable Rebellion

wr. Peter Packer, dir. Don Richardson

The Robot's birthday celebrations end in disarray when Doctor Smith sends him to a planet where vegetation is the dominant life-form.

With Stanley Adams (Tybo), James Milhollin (Willoughby).

Although this infamous stinker is hardly one of the better episodes, it isn't quite as bad as legend has it either, even if the initial shock of being confronted by Stanley Adams in a carrot-suit can be a mite jarring! The episode has secured mythical status over the years as it is one that has stuck in the memories of many of the cast, who have a number of amusing anecdotes related to the filming of it. While there are no doubt nobler causes to champion in television than defending "The Great Vegetable Rebellion," it has to be said that the episode is livelier and much more fun than the *real* third season stinkers like "The Promised Planet," "The Haunted Lighthouse," "A Day at the Zoo," or "Collision of the Planets," all of which—to name but four—are far more stupid in idea, script, and execution. Neither does it commit the cardinal sin of being boring, a charge that may be leveled at "West of Mars" or "The Questing Beast." In fact, the episode is quite funny and well directed, and Adams' silly carrot suit looks rather good in a pantomime sort of way, as does Smith's transformation into a stick of celery; however this is yet another late third season entry that indicates the show was fast running out of steam. Confronted by the formidable sight of Jonathan Harris cornering him over the absurdity of the script, the hapless Peter Packer defended himself by admitting he hadn't "another goddamned idea in my head." If Packer was burnt out, then so was the series.

Taken as a comedy—and it's true that Mark Goddard can't keep a straight face—"The Great Vegetable Rebellion" is indeed a good laugh, particularly during the opening scenes celebrating the Robot's birthday. The plants that wail and moan when the Robinsons scythe through them are also a nice touch! On a 1985 TV reunion on the *America* show, Goddard joked "I'd studied acting very seriously for a long while, and now I'm doing a scene talking to a carrot...! And I figured I really should have stayed at the Actors' Studio longer, because we worked with trees and things like that...!" However, the worst idea in the episode was not the talking carrot man, but a speaking llama, an idea that Jonathan Harris swiftly

knocked on the head by refusing to work with the creature. Fiercely and wisely suspicious of any animal actor with regards to safety, and not one to be upstaged by anything, Harris had refused point blank to perform. The original idea had been Allen's, who—like the rest of Hollywood—thought Fox's 1967 *Doctor Dolittle* disaster (a musical about an eccentric veterinarian who talks to animals) was going to be a smash hit. Promotional stills and the end credit for the unlamented Willoughby (turned into a purple-haired human for the episode) still survive as testimony to a catastrophic near-miss.

It seems the rest of the cast of the show were also more mutinous than usual during the filming of this episode—Billy Mumy made some rather scathing comments about director Richardson to a fan publication—but given that this was undeniably written as a humorous episode, it does seem a little unfair that the already marginalized Guy Williams and June Lockhart were suspended from the next two episodes for insubordination! These were "Space Beauty" and "Fugitives in Space." This seems particularly arbitrary as it was Jonathan Harris who refused to work with the llama, and Mark Goddard who openly mocked the episode. No doubt the Robot's birthday party helped create a lighter than usual atmosphere on the set too.

Many of the props are quite familiar, notably the machine the carrot creature takes his moisture from, which was the score-keeping device in "Hunter's Moon." There's no action to speak of, but the episode stays interesting; all the cast share the spotlight equally, with Judy taking more airtime than usual. Stanley Adams was the Tribble salesman Cyrano Jones in *Star Trek's* "The Trouble with Tribbles," and also co-wrote dated doom yarn "The Mark of Gideon" for that series. Fellow broad character actor James Milhollin (the now humanoid Willoughby) was the store manager in "The After Hours" in *The Twilight Zone*, and appears in episodes of *Batman* and *The Man from UNCLE*. Production no.: 1521.

Junkyard of Space

wr. Barney Slater, dir. Ezra Stone

Smith finally finds his conscience in this final episode ... but not before selling the Robot and the spaceship to an intergalactic scrap merchant!

With Marcel Hillaire (the Junkman).

Very similar to the first season's "The Space Trader," this was to be the last episode of the series, and everything looks darkest for the Robinsons—Smith has been selling off the Robot's parts to the junkman (Marcel Hillaire was Phanzig the space convict in the very first episode of the third season, "The Condemned of Space"), the food is ruined, and then the junkman steals the *Jupiter Two* itself while the Robot appears to be going to a fiery doom! But this is also the episode that takes Smith's character full circle—after trying to kill the family in the earliest episodes, and then trying to return to Earth without them throughout the series, Smith (on board the *Jupiter Two* with the junkman and very possibly heading for home) demands that the junkman return to the planet and the Robinsons. Unintentionally, it was a nice way for the series to go out. Production no.: 1524.

Episodes in Order of Production

FIRST SEASON (29 EPISODES)

8501 The Reluctant Stowaway
8502 The Derelict
8503 Island in the Sky
8504 There Are Giants in the Earth
8505 The Hungry Sea
8506 Welcome Stranger
8507 My Friend, Mr. Nobody
8508 Invaders from the Fifth Dimension
8509 The Oasis
8510 The Sky is Falling
8511 The Raft
8512 Wish Upon a Star
8513 One of Our Dogs Is Missing
8514 Attack of the Monster Plants
8515 Return from Outer Space
8516 The Keeper (part one)
8517 The Keeper (part two)
8518 The Sky Pirate
8519 Ghost in Space
8520 The Magic Mirror
8521 The War of the Robots
8522 The Challenge
8523 The Space Trader
8524 His Majesty, Smith
8525 The Space Croppers
8526 All That Glitters
8527 The Lost Civilization
8528 A Change of Space
8529 Follow the Leader

SECOND SEASON (30 EPISODES)

9501 Blast Off into Space
9502 Wild Adventure
9503 The Ghost Planet
9504 Forbidden World
9505 Space Circus
9506 The Prisoners of Space
9507 The Android Machine
9508 The Deadly Games of Gamma Six
9509 The Thief of Outer Space
9510 The Curse of Cousin Smith
9511 The Dream Monster
9512 West of Mars
9513 A Visit to Hades
9514 The Wreck of the Robot
9515 The Golden Man
9516 The Girl from the Green Dimension
9517 The Questing Beast
9518 The Toymaker
9519 Mutiny in Space
9520 The Space Vikings
9521 Treasure of the Lost Planet
9522 Rocket to Earth
9523 The Mechanical Men
9524 Revolt of the Androids
9525 The Cave of the Wizards
9526 The Colonists
9527 Trip Through the Robot
9528 The Phantom Family
9529 The Astral Traveler
9530 The Galaxy Gift

THIRD SEASON (24 EPISODES)

1501 The Condemned of Space
1502 Hunter's Moon
1503 The Space Primevals
1504 Deadliest of the Species
1505 Visit to a Hostile Planet
1506 Kidnapped in Space
1507 Flight into the Future
1508 The Space Destructors
1509 The Haunted Lighthouse
1510 Collision of the Planets
1511 The Space Creature

1512 The Anti-Matter Man
1513 Castles in Space
1514 A Day at the Zoo
1515 Two Weeks in Space
1516 Target Earth
1517 The Flaming Planet
1518 The Time Merchant
1519 Princess of Space
1520 The Promised Planet
1521 The Great Vegetable Rebellion
1522 Fugitives in Space
1523 Space Beauty
1524 The Junkyard of Space

Episodes in Order of Broadcast

FIRST SEASON (29 EPISODES)

8501 The Reluctant Stowaway
8502 The Derelict
8503 Island in the Sky
8504 There Are Giants in the Earth
8505 The Hungry Sea
8506 Welcome Stranger
8507 My Friend, Mr. Nobody
8508 Invaders from the Fifth Dimension
8509 The Oasis
8510 The Sky Is Falling
8512 Wish Upon a Star
8511 The Raft
8513 One of Our Dogs Is Missing
8514 Attack of the Monster Plants
8515 Return from Outer Space
8516 The Keeper (part one)
8517 The Keeper (part two)
8518 The Sky Pirate
8519 Ghost in Space
8521 The War of the Robots
8520 The Magic Mirror
8522 The Challenge
8523 The Space Trader
8524 His Majesty, Smith
8525 The Space Croppers
8526 All That Glitters
8527 The Lost Civilization
8528 A Change of Space
8529 Follow the Leader

SECOND SEASON (30 EPISODES)

9501 Blast Off into Space
9502 Wild Adventure
9503 The Ghost Planet
9504 Forbidden World

9505 Space Circus
9506 The Prisoners of Space
9507 The Android Machine
9508 The Deadly Games of Gamma Six
9509 The Thief of Outer Space
9510 The Curse of Cousin Smith
9512 West of Mars
9513 A Visit to Hades
9514 The Wreck of the Robot
9511 The Dream Monster
9515 The Golden Man
9516 The Girl from the Green Dimension
9517 The Questing Beast
9518 The Toymaker
9519 Mutiny in Space
9520 The Space Vikings
9522 Rocket to Earth
9525 The Cave of the Wizards
9521 Treasure of the Lost Planet
9524 Revolt of the Androids
9526 The Colonists
9527 Trip Through the Robot
9528 The Phantom Family
9523 The Mechanical Men
9529 The Astral Traveler
9530 The Galaxy Gift

THIRD SEASON (24 EPISODES)

1501 The Condemned of Space
1505 Visit to a Hostile Planet
1506 Kidnapped in Space
1502 Hunter's Moon
1503 The Space Primevals
1508 The Space Destructors
1509 The Haunted Lighthouse
1507 Flight into the Future
1510 Collision of the Planets

1511 The Space Creature
1504 Deadliest of the Species
1514 A Day at the Zoo
1515 Two Weeks in Space
1513 Castles in Space
1512 The Anti-Matter Man
1516 Target Earth
1519 Princess of Space

1518 The Time Merchant
1520 The Promised Planet
1522 Fugitives in Space
1523 Space Beauty
1517 The Flaming Planet
1521 The Great Vegetable Rebellion
1524 The Junkyard of Space

Production Credits

Created and produced by Irwin Allen. Assistant to producer: Paul Zastupnevich. Story editor: Anthony Wilson. Art direction (pilot): William Creber. Art direction: Robert Kinoshita, Frank Barnette. Also: Carl Macauley, Rodger E. Maus, Art Loel. Art direction supervisor: Jack Martin Smith. Set decoration: Walter M. Scott, Norman Rockett, Sven Wickman, James Hassinger. Costume design and wardrobe: Paul Zastupnevich. Director of photography: Gene Polito, Frank Carson. Also: Charles Clarke, Winton Hoch. Special effects: Lyle B. Abbott, Howard Lydecker. Music: John Williams. Also: Herman Stein, Leith Stevens, Alexander Courage, Gerald Fried, Robert Drasnin, Cyril Mockridge, Fred Steiner, Joseph Mullendore. Music editor: Joseph Ruby, George Probert. Music editor (first episode): Morrie McNaughton. Music supervision: Leonard Engel, Lionel Newman. Theme music: John Williams. Sound effects editor: Don Hall Jr., Frank White, Robert Cornett. Supervising sound effects editor: Don Hall Jr. Production coordinator: Les Warner, William Faralla. Production supervisor: Jack Sonntag. Production assistant: Hal Herman. Production manager: Gaston Glass. Unit production manager: Hal Herman, Norman Henry, Ted Butcher, James M. Walters Jr. Assistant directors: Gil Mandelik, William Faralla, James M. Walters Jr. Also: Steve Bernhardt, Dave Silver, Don Gold, Joseph Lenzi, Pepe Lenzi, Norman August, Les Warner. Film editors: Roland Gross, James Baiotto, Frederic Baratta, Jack Gleason. Also: Clay Bartels, Tony Di Marco, Axel Hubert. Make-up: Ben Nye. Hair styling: Margaret Donovan. Post production supervisor: George Swink. Post production coordinator: Robert Mintz. Associate producer: Jerry Briskin (first season), William Faralla (second and third seasons). In charge of production: William Self, Guy Della Cioppa. Van Bernard Productions, Space Productions, and Jodi Productions for 20th Century Fox.

3 The Time Tunnel

September 1966–April 1967

If ever there was a show most deserving the over-used accolade of cult TV, it has to be *The Time Tunnel*. A one-season wonder of thirty episodes, it was renewed for a second season after a debut against three other popular fantasy shows of the period only to be canceled by new management. The television industry has been trying to make amends for its early demise ever since. Irwin Allen's extraordinary concept of two men "lost in the infinite corridors of time" remains, alongside *The Fugitive*, *Star Trek*, *The Invaders*, and *The Mary Tyler Moore Show*, one of the most constantly revisited and resurrected premises in television.

However, time travel TV series were thin on the ground when *The Time Tunnel* was conceived. Anthology series such as *The Twilight Zone* and *The Outer Limits* had dabbled with the theme, usually to produce personal stories about the futility of trying to change destiny, while the large majority of time travel feature films had been about adventures in the future (*The Time Machine*, *World Without End*, *Beyond the Time Barrier*, *The Time Travelers*). Invariably, these involved satisfied or struggling civilizations on the surface, and less satisfied, miserable mutant-types living underground (a plot that still turns up regularly in films and TV today). Those that featured encounters with famous figures from the past had usually been done as comedies (*When Knights Were Bold*, *Time Flies*, *Roman Scandals*, *Where Do We Go from*

Here?, and so on). On television, a 1950s series called *You Are There* had presented viewers with semi-educational reports from great moments in history, while TV hero *Captain Z-Ro* was an early prototype for *Quantum Leap's* Sam Beckett (affectionately parodied in the *Quantum Leap* episode "Future Boy," and knowingly acknowledged in the show's final episode). Britain's beloved *Doctor Who*, although then at the peak of mass market popularity, had not yet crossed the sea, other than in feature film form, where its extraordinary originality had been reduced to the cliché of the elderly, scatterbrained, eccentric professor.

The Time Tunnel concerned the high-spirited adventures of Doug Phillips and Tony Newman (Robert Colbert and James Darren), a couple of two-fisted, multi-skilled scientists who were plunged into episodic adventures in the past and/or future after trying to prove that their time travel experiments were worth every penny of the nearly eight billion tax dollars already spent on it. They proved that their time tunnel worked, but with one catch—once in, they couldn't get out.... All their harassed fellow scientists back at the Time Tunnel control center could do was switch them around in time from one sticky mess to another every time they got into too much trouble—which was every week, as they had an infallible ability for finding it. If they turned up in the wild west, it was just in time to meet George Armstrong

Custer or Billy the Kid; if they took a trip to Greece, it was inside a wooden horse; if they vacationed in Hawaii, it was a couple of hours before the bombing of Pearl Harbor; drop Doug in France, and he'd be brainwashed by Nazis days before D-Day or spirited away to have his head chopped off in the French Revolution; a nice cruise ship turned out to be the *Titanic*, a friendly sanctuary from a battlefield, the Alamo; put them on a desert island, and it would be Devil's Island, Krakatoa, or swarming with pirates. And the first thing they did on arrival anywhere was get into a fight.

The story begins with officialdom hold-ing the pursestrings to a pet project. A senator arrives from Washington at the secret desert locale of a project revealingly titled Operation Tic-Toc to pull the plug on the Tunnel project unless Phillips and Newman can prove some significant breakthrough in their experiments to travel through time. In a desperate attempt to prove the worth of their project, impetuous Tony Newman takes a midnight flit to the past, only to tumble onto the deck of the ill-fated so-called unsinkable ocean liner the *Titanic*, which hit an iceberg and did indeed sink with a huge loss of life. Newman's proved his point—the Tunnel works—but now, because

The series' regular cast pose in the mouth of the Time Tunnel. Standing left to right: James Darren and Robert Colbert. Seated left to right, Whit Bissell, Lee Meriwether, and John Zaremba.

the Tunnel has yet to be perfected, they can't bring him back, and the captain of the ship (Michael Rennie, of *The Day the Earth Stood Still* and the classic *Lost in Space* two-parter "The Keeper") has locked him below as a scaremongering stowaway ... just where the iceberg will hit, of course. Doug Phillips follows Tony into the Tunnel, belatedly convincing the doomed captain of his ship's fate, but now both men are lost in time. Each week they tumble into a new adventure, plummeting in slow motion into key moments of world history.

James Darren was cast as the young impetuous Tony Newman and Robert Colbert (pronounced Col-bear) was supposed to be the slightly older, more sedate and thoughtful Doug Phillips. Darren had been a star of teen exploitation movies (*Because They're Young, The Young Racers, Rumble on the Docks, Gidget, For Those Who Think Young*, etc.) before he came to the attention of Irwin Allen after guest-starring in an episode of *Voyage to the Bottom of the Sea* ("The Mechanical Man") with his former *Gidget* movies co-star Arthur O'Connell; Colbert's career began as a contract player for Warners, with a recurring role in *Maverick* and numerous guest appearances in Warner's western and detective shows. Colbert's character was an amalgam of the two quintessential leads in 1950s sci-fi, the brilliant scientist and the stoic, tough, can-do hero, while Darren was a slim, athletic former teen heart-throb. However, not only were the actors' lines interchangeable (it's Colbert who usually loses his cool), but Darren occasionally gave some of his lines to the sometimes short-changed Colbert quite willingly! The aspect of the characters that gave them depth was their friendship—each regularly risked his own life to help the other. They were authentic no-nonsense American heroes. Back at the Time Tunnel control center, General Heywood Kirk (Whit Bissell) was in charge, controlling the project for the U.S. government, working alongside scientists Ray Swain (John Zaremba) and Ann McGregor (Lee Meriwether). Swain was the pragmatic pessimist, erring on the side of caution, McGregor the emotional optimist.

Both Whit Bissell and John Zaremba were veterans of '50s SF; Whit Bissell had spent his early career playing weasels and villains thanks to his slight stature, but as he grew older and more dignified in appearance he drifted into playing authority figures—mayors, bankers, doctors, and scientists. He had played so many army generals (see "Nightmare" for *The Outer Limits*, "The Peacemaker" for *Voyage to the Bottom of the Sea*) that one suspects he came equipped with his own uniform; his General Kirk character was played as a humanitarian faced with making impossible decisions on the spot, but not afraid to make them and stick to them with conviction (very much a blueprint for the similar character in the *Time Tunnel*-ish 1990s series *Stargate–SG-1*). Bissell was a regular fixture in 1950s fantasy films, and can be seen in *The Atomic Kid, The Lost Continent, Target Earth, Creature from the Black Lagoon, I Was a Teenage Werewolf, I Was a Teenage Frankenstein, Invasion of the Body Snatchers, Monster on the Campus, The Time Machine,* and in the 1970s, *Soylent Green.* TV roles included a time-travel episode of *I Dream of Jeannie* set in the Old West. John Zaremba appeared in *Earth vs. the Flying Saucers, Twenty Million Miles to Earth, The Cosmic Man,* and during the 1960s, chalked up appearances in episodes of *The Twilight Zone, Batman, Get Smart, Voyage to the Bottom of the Sea, Mission: Impossible,* and *The Invaders.*

Lee Meriwether was a former Miss America who also played Catwoman in the 1966 *Batman* film. When *The Time Tunnel* was in production, her then-husband, Frank Aletter, was starring in the lame time travel comedy, *It's About Time.* Her films include *The 4-D Man,* and her other TV roles have included episodes of *The Man from UNCLE, Batman, Star Trek, Mission: Impossible,* and

Land of the Giants. Wesley Lau, who appeared periodically in *The Time Tunnel* as head of security Sgt. Jiggs, also made two appearances in *The Twilight Zone*, three *Mission: Impossible* episodes and *Land of the Giants.* A handful of episodes featured the youthful, green and eager Jerry (Sam Groom, later star of the short-lived *Otherworld* in the 1980s), panicky and volatile to offset the more restrained, laid-back maturity of the others. His patience was rewarded with a co-starring role sharing the lead (with Tom Hallick) in Allen's 1976 pilot *The Time Travelers.*

One of the best quotes about Irwin Allen can be found in the book *Fantastic Television,* in which authors Gary Gerani and Paul Schulman write that "Irwin Allen's career has combined two great gifts: the inventor's, for using imaginative special effects, and the farmer's, for using everything twice"! Nowhere was this policy more in evidence than on *The Time Tunnel.* As with all Irwin Allen series, production values were high for the time, with the series given a further cost-effective boost through the liberal use of 20th Century Fox's large library of stock footage from their numerous big screen epics. This made the task of the costume department twice as challenging, as they had to match up all the costumes with the clothing being worn in the library film. Happily, much of it was still in the costume department. Clearly, thousands of extras and epic battles were beyond the budgetary capabilities of a TV series, although *The Time Tunnel* enjoyed the usual high production values of all of Allen's series, and it is visually the most impressive looking of all Allen's shows. Library footage from Fox or other available sources was almost always integrated into the series seamlessly, and aided the series more than it hindered it (the only exceptions were "One Way to the Moon" and "Attack of the Barbarians," which didn't match up very well), and the employment of feature film clips ensured that viewers weren't cheated out of epic scenes by the financial realities of a TV budget. "Revenge of the Gods," set in ancient Greece and portraying the fall of Troy, and "Night of the Long Knives," concerning British Empire India and the Khyber Pass, in particular, look fantastic.

The visual effects on Allen's series were superb, and easily the best special effects on television at the time. They were the work of the talented and ingenious Lyle B. Abbott, who won three Emmy awards (two for *Voyage to the Bottom of the Sea,* one for *The Time Tunnel*) for his efforts. The control base set, where the Tunnel is located, is a fabulous and impressive creation, augmented by a striking matte painting in the first two episodes. The scenes where Doug Phillips and General Kirk show the visiting senator around the complex are feature film standard, and the futuristic sets for such episodes as the wonderful "Chase Through Time" and "The Kidnappers" were not matched for twenty years, until the series *V, Otherworld,* and *Star Trek: The Next Generation* showed up. Even the venerable *Star Trek,* in production at the same time as *The Time Tunnel,* looks positively shabby in comparison when the crew leave the *Enterprise.* The time travel effect itself was excellent, cleverly achieved—colored lights filmed with a wide-angle lens and blue-matted actors suspended on wires while the camera twirled around them for the time traveling effect. Although other time travelers who journeyed through the Tunnel usually just appeared from nowhere the same way they—and Doug and Tony—would suddenly depart, the two leads always arrived in a new time period by tumbling out of the sky. Different directors had different ways of achieving this—if filming outdoors, the boys might roll down a hill or across the ground. In the studio, they might glide down and jump from a wire in slow motion, or simply jump down from a box and roll, again in slow motion. Interestingly, their arrival was only witnessed once in the entire series, in "Crack of Doom," by superstitious primitive natives.

The Tunnel itself, housed in a typical Allen control center, all busy extras and flashing consoles, with a false perspective for the seemingly never-ending circular passageway, was a massive imposing cylinder that dwarfed the actors and really did look as though it might feasibly perform the awesome task of bridging the centuries. Smoke and sparks would surround the actors as they entered or emerged from the flickering Tunnel, after which an image of the traveler and the location might be viewed on the irritable and unreliable ghost-image of the Tunnel's view-screen. This shifting, infuriatingly unreliable picture added to the suspense in the control room scenes. Every time the two unfortunate adventurers strayed, the tense scientists would have to locate and lock on to them before effecting a transfer from danger; if they didn't know where they were, they'd have to work out their exact position in time and space before they could work out the co-ordinates to move them. The whole set-up was not unlike trying to get good results from an old television set that was past its best years, with an aerial that constantly needed adjusting—not an unfamiliar scenario for the audience in the 1960s. As fast as the scientists found their errant targets and whisked them away to a new time-period, the lads would drop in on another perilous situation where they were not welcome or did not want to be. Cynics and smart-alecks like to point out that time travelers never turn up in dreary, quiet locations where nothing momentous is about to happen, but it wouldn't be much of an adventure show if they did. The episode "Chase Through Time" suggests that there are quiet moments for both the time travelers and the frantic scientists ... they just don't last very long!

The father of time travel fantasy was H.G. Wells, with his 1895 novel *The Time Machine*, but thematically, the premise of *The Time Tunnel* owed no more to Wells than the numerous *Invisible Man* TV series did.

The prime source for Allen's inspiration would appear to be the 1964 novel *The Time Tunnel* by SF veteran Murray Leinster, which bears a resemblance in title only. In the original novel, the Tunnel is a Parisian alleyway leading to the Napoleonic era, and serving as a portal to the past for the covert activities of antiques dealers with connections nobody would believe. It was a nice idea—no portentous world-conquering or rewriting of history intended, no averting disasters or meeting historical icons, only greedy, unimaginative men trying to eke out a modest living with furtively smuggled antiquities. Inevitably though, someone does meddle with the past, resulting in the appearance of that old but irresistible SF cliché, the possible death of an ancestor. Allen made his version of *The Time Tunnel* not the time-warped stone passage of the book, but a top secret government research complex where the military are experimenting with a massive gateway to past centuries they have constructed deep underground in the Nevada desert; the opening scenes of the pilot, with the awed government official being shown around the complex (much as Allen liked to proudly show visitors round his sets) resembled the opening of his feature film *Voyage to the Bottom of the Sea*, already at this point an up and running TV series alongside fellow hit show *Lost in Space*. A further novel by Leinster, also titled *The Time Tunnel*, and featuring the characters from the television series, appeared in 1967; the series, although set in 1968, was aired in 1966, with pre-production going back as early as 1964. Although this second novel bears clear similarities to the pilot, there are some minor differences, with the tragedy the time-travelers are trying to avert being the somewhat more difficult to film Johnstown flooding of 1889, and the Indian attack of Adobe Walls attended by legendary western marshal Bat Masterson (who survived). The only significant differences are that Doug and Tony are in constant contact with the

Tunnel, and each wears a harness device to supposedly return them. It's possible that this novel was part of a deal worked out between Leinster and Allen for use of the title (Leinster later went on to write two of the novelizations for Allen's *Land of the Giants* series), or that it was a first draft for the pilot or premise (certainly, dropping a harness idea was wise). Others have indicated similarities with Ib Melchior's 1964 *The Time Travelers*, in which scientists step through a window into a ruined future Earth (not exactly a fresh idea itself), but even if this film nudged Allen's thoughts, he certainly put much more creativity into the end result. More interesting is that low-budget schlock-meister David Hewitt, who worked on *The Time Travelers*, later directed *Journey to the Centre of Time*, a 1968 Z-movie cheapie that was a blatant swipe of both *The Time Travelers* and *Time Tunnel's* "Chase Through Time" episode.

Wherever the initial idea came from, *The Time Tunnel* as we know it was conceived by Irwin Allen and written by Shimon Wincelberg, who had also been entrusted with the *Lost in Space* pilot and the first color episode of *Voyage to the Bottom of the Sea*. Wincelberg's script, although beginning the same way as the novel, placed the two time-tumbling scientists on board the doomed *Titanic* in 1912, and was then revised by Harold Jack Bloom (later creator of *Project UFO*), who made a few significant but minor changes, notably the removal of the clichéd and coincidental presence of Doug's parents on the *Titanic* passenger list.

The series was rich in bizarre imagery. There was Doug Phillips stepping into the Tunnel to attempt to retrieve his young colleague from the deck of the doomed *Titanic*, dressed in the costume of the period and armed with a newspaper detailing the disaster; Tony Newman meeting himself as a young boy before the attack on Pearl Harbor, and later weeping over the dead body of his missing father; the scientists inadvertently

bringing Halley's Comet back through the tunnel; a menacing silver alien striding in from the very far future and blithely abducting scientist Ann McGregor; a military policeman gunning down Trojan warriors with a machine gun and returning to the 20th century as a wizened old man; a stunned and disoriented 16th century pirate staggering out of the Tunnel and running riot in the control center with the luckless Ann McGregor as his hostage; alien beings removing all the oxygen from a small town, and draining the air from the Time Tunnel complex at the same time; the time travelers being mistaken for the visiting strangers of Biblical origin within the walls of Jericho; a poltergeist—the ghost of Roman Emperor Nero, no less—running amok in the control center; a military man joining his ancestor in the War of Independence to clear his name. And, like the later *Quantum Leap*, at least two episodes ("The Death Trap," "The Walls of Jericho") suggest the Hand of God, Fate, Destiny, or whatever at work.

Every single one of *The Time Tunnel's* thirty episodes was different in style and tone, but basically they can be divided into four categories—straight dramas with superb guest performances, straightforward action/adventure (what Allen called "running and jumping shows"), Hollywood-style historical romps, and glorious B-movie pulp SF. Into the first category of credible drama fall what might arguably be considered the best episodes—"Rendezvous with Yesterday," the pilot with Michael Rennie; "The End of the World"; "The Day the Sky Fell In," the Pearl Harbor story widely regarded as the series' finest hour; "The Last Patrol," with a superb dual performance by Carroll O'Connor; "Massacre," with Joe Maross magnificent as a psychotic and vainglorious Custer; the moving "The Alamo"; and "The Night of the Long Knives," boasting a wonderful cast and the best script William Welch ever wrote for Allen.

Into the straightforward action/adventure category would fall "The Crack of

Doom" (Krakatoa, swarming with hostile savages); the lurid melodrama "Devil's Island"; "Kill Two by Two," set in the WWII Pacific; "The Death Trap" (the inevitable Abe Lincoln episode, boosted by Ford Rainey's performance as Lincoln); the hokey Biblical adventure "The Walls of Jericho"; "Idol of Death"; "Billy the Kid," a wonderful western with Robert Walker Jr. a perfect Billy, and sterling supporting performances from John Crawford and Harry Lauter; and "The Death Merchant," with Niccolo Machiavelli loose at Gettysburg, a mad idea upgraded by the moving supporting performances of John Crawford and Kevin Hagen.

In the Hollywood-style historical romp category would fall "Revenge of the Gods" (the fall of Troy); "Reign of Terror," set in the French Revolution; "Invasion," a barmy WWII adventure set on the eve of D-Day; the wonderful "Revenge of Robin Hood," a knockabout Errol Flynn-style camp fest; "The Ghost of Nero," a deranged supernatural yarn slicing ham furiously; the legendary "Pirates of Dead Man's Island" with Victor Jory; "Attack of the Barbarians," featuring the series' only love story; and the loopy "Merlin the Magician," with Christopher Cary superb as Merlin.

In the pulp sci-fi category we have, in chronological order and getting progressively sillier, "One Way to the Moon," a '50s-style astronaut adventure; "Secret Weapon," a bizarre bottle show involving an Iron Curtain Time Tunnel in the '50s and a fraught over-the-top performance by Nehemiah Persoff; "Visitors from Beyond the Stars" (aliens in the Old West); "Chase Through Time" with a young Robert Duvall and a host of Allen's trademark dinosaurs and bodypainted aliens; "The Kidnappers" (alien abductions); the magnificently mad "Raiders from Outer Space" (cabbage-head bug-eyed aliens in Gordon's Sudan); and the Z-movie bodysnatching yarn "Town of Terror."

What we are left with is a one season

wonder that, because a second season never happened, remains a balanced mix of styles and surprises. *The Time Tunnel* wore many hats during its thirty episodes, and although the wacky ones come near the end, the final score is a fairly equal number of straight adventures with a respect for historical accuracy and serious dramatic development, traditional Hollywood costume romps with a cavalier disrespect for factual content or credibility, wild west myth-making, and *outre* pulp sci-fi with silver-skinned aliens and bug-eyed invaders. And, of course, a couple of episodes that fitted more than one category, or none of them. Where else could you see the ghost of Nero, Machiavelli at Gettysburg, monsters at Khartoum, or aliens in the wild west? As pure escapist entertainment, it takes some beating.

It is simplistic, but accurate, to say that the series got more bizarre and off-the-wall as it went on. The potential delights in store had the series gone on to a second season must remain one of the great torments of the B-movie aficionado. Allen gave script assignments to most of his regular writers from *Lost in Space* and *Voyage to the Bottom of the Sea* and they went straight to the stock footage library and then to the history books. Although some have carped about, or mocked the dependency on, expensively produced but cheaply acquired existing film, some of the series' very best episodes—"The Day the Sky Fell In," "Revenge of the Gods," "Revenge of Robin Hood," "Night of the Long Knives," "Merlin the Magician"—were specifically written around available footage. However, the eventual introduction of alien beings into *The Time Tunnel* midway through the run was a typical and not entirely unexpected ploy of Allen's that worked wonders for the series, as the inevitability of certain historic events ran the risk of making the series predictable.

While others still have complained about the arrival of aliens, monsters, and assorted creatures of fantasy into the storylines

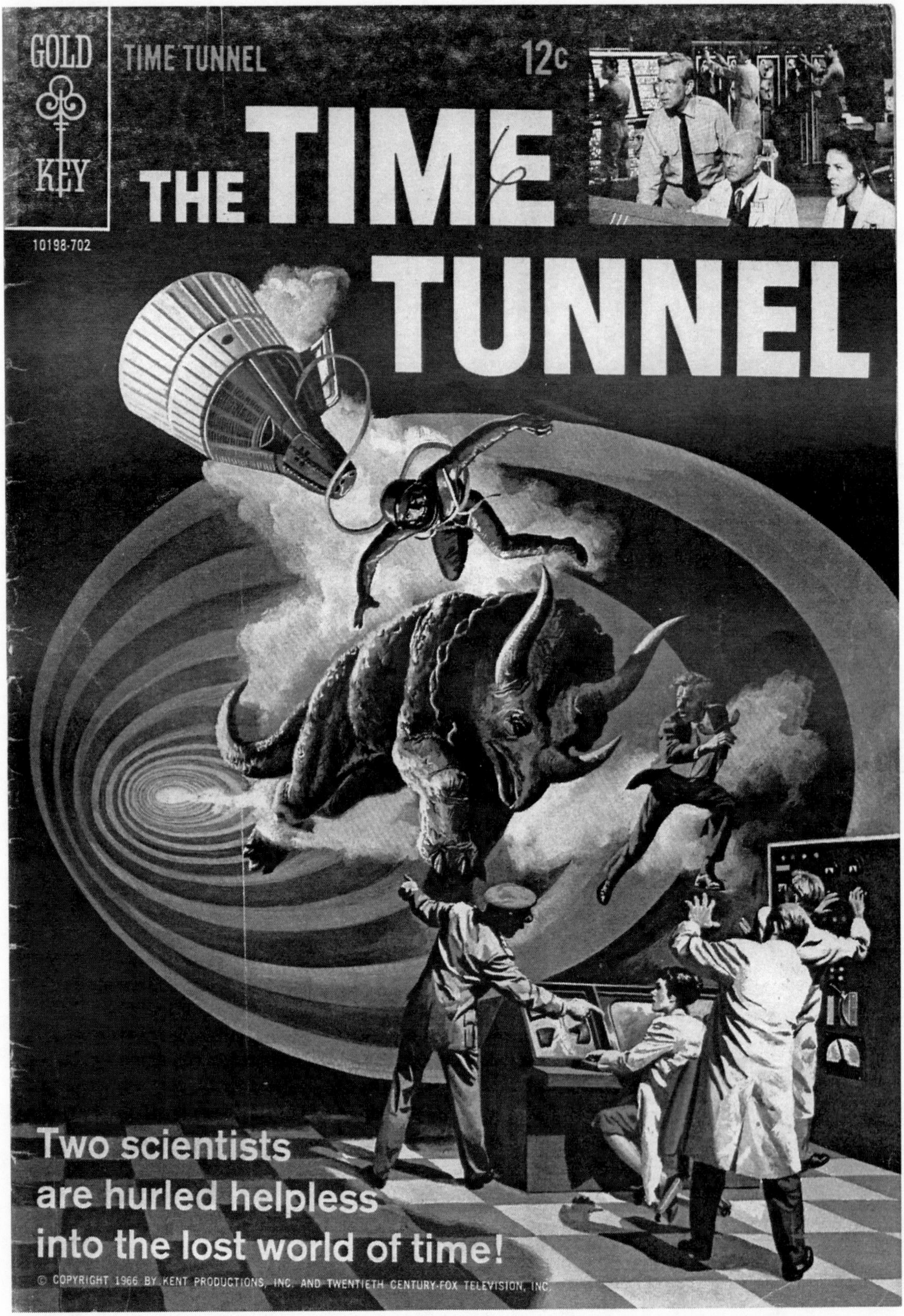
GOLD KEY
TIME TUNNEL
12c
10198-702
THE TIME TUNNEL
Two scientists
are hurled helpless
into the lost world of time!
© COPYRIGHT 1966 BY KENT PRODUCTIONS, INC. AND TWENTIETH CENTURY-FOX TELEVISION, INC.

of *Voyage to the Bottom of the Sea* and *The Time Tunnel*, the fact is that bizarre alien menaces were Allen's specialty, and the weirder the stories got, the higher the ratings of *Lost in Space* and *Voyage to the Bottom of the Sea* soared. Whatever the cloistered world of serious-minded sci-fi buffs might have felt, the general audience clearly considered Allen a welcome source of alien-fueled adventure and bug-eyed monsters. However, it is fair to say that as the first season of *Time Tunnel* neared its close, the series was in danger of becoming top heavy with extra-terrestrials, as the beings from space invaded nearly every episode.

The first episode to feature invaders from space was the aptly-named "Visitors from Beyond the Stars," written by *Lost in Space* stalwarts Bob and Wanda Duncan, in which the scientists materialize in a futuristic setting, only to discover that they are in fact above the Earth in a spaceship. Their second shock comes when they find out that the year is 1885, and the invaders have set their sights on a small town in Arizona. Back in 1968, the Time Tunnel scientists discover that the small western community is destined to become a mysterious ghost town that year. The last three episodes made were all pulp SF yarns, with the final story, "Town of Terror," having holes in the plot wider than the Tunnel itself, but while some episodes are obviously better than others, and "Invasion" and "Idol of Death" were the series' borderline turkeys, there were no real stinkers in the entire run. Every episode worked on its own level, even though the delights of "The Day the Sky Fell In" are quite different to those of "Town of Terror."

One constantly repeated legend is that the series utilized props from *Lost in Space*; while all the 20th Century Fox productions used the same props department, and a couple of items on display in *The Time Tunnel* did indeed come from that direction, it's probably more accurate to say that many of the *Time Tunnel* props turned up on *Lost in Space* during that series' third season after *Time Tunnel's* cancellation. See, for example, the *Lost in Space* episode "Kidnapped in Space," which is clearly being filmed on the just vacated *Time Tunnel* stage—the metal doors, the familiar banks of control panels, and even the sound effects of Doug and Tony disappearing into the Time Vortex are employed! All the props on the 20th Century Fox lot were interchangeable and used by all, including many of the locations; this is one of the reasons the wild west episodes of *The Time Tunnel* looked as good as any regular western show. Sharp-eyed viewers will note, for example, that the "Town of Terror" is also Manitou Junction in the popular "Visit to a Hostile Planet" episode of *Lost in Space*.

Another misapprehension provoked by a faulty reference source is that Doug and Tony returned to the deck of the *Titanic* in the final episode of *The Time Tunnel* to either be caught in a time-loop or have a second adventure there to open the second season. In fact, the sequence that started the fuss was a coming attractions trailer for the show's summer reruns in 1967. Happily for completists, it often appears in syndicated prints today (although not all episodes have the traditional cliffhanger opening to the next adventure; some appear to have been excised from some prints).

The Time Tunnel first aired in the U.S. on September 9th, 1966—one day after the first broadcast of *Star Trek*! The second season of *Lost in Space*, and the third season of *Voyage to the Bottom of the Sea* began the following week. As is often the case, the order in which the episodes were produced (or at least, assigned production numbers) varied from the order in which the network aired them, although in the case of *The Time Tunnel*, these variations were relatively

Opposite: An example of the Time Tunnel comics.

minor. The only significant difference is that episode ten, "Pirates of Dead Man's Island," was held over until much later in the series, and this is discussed under that title. Today, because most of the episodes still thankfully have their coming next week trailers attached, showing the opening scenes of the next adventure, broadcasters run the series in the sequence ABC originally aired them.

It has become accepted wisdom that the series was a ratings failure, an assumption repeated in numerous books and articles, but it wasn't. Although it only lasted one season, and ratings did decline, *The Time Tunnel* was tentatively renewed until new management came in at ABC and canceled all the borderline shows to demonstrate a new broom mentality. The series was all set for a second season when it was replaced by the infamous but now forgotten *Legend of Custer*, another 20th Century Fox show which employed a number of Irwin Allen's contributors but was quickly canceled. *Legend of Custer* picked the wrong time to try to produce an often unintentionally hilarious whitewashed picture of this notorious historical figure and paradoxically, *The Time Tunnel* had produced a far superior and factually sound portrait of Custer in the episode "Massacre." While this bone was thrown to Fox, the *Green Hornet/Time Tunnel* slot was filled by a series of children's films introduced by characters from *The Wizard of Oz*. Needless to say, *Time Tunnel's* former adversaries *Tarzan* and *The Wild Wild West* flourished...

Following *The Time Tunnel*, James Darren appeared in a twenty minute promo film for a proposed Irwin Allen series that never happened, *The Man from the 25th Century*, in which he played Andro, an alien abductee sent to Earth to prepare for an invasion, but who rebels against his masters and joins a secret government organization to oppose them. *Time Tunnel* guest players John Napier, John Crawford, and Ford Rainey also ap-

peared in this test footage that used vast chunks of stock shots from Time Tunnel headquarters. When this failed to sell, he played a brief cameo role as the oddly-named Doctor Talty in another busted Allen pilot, *City Beneath the Sea* (which also co-starred his old pal Robert Colbert), before returning to his singing career as a Vegas-style crooner for the rest of the '70s. He returned to TV, looking not much older, in the embarrassing William Shatner cop show *T.J. Hooker*, eventually turning to directing. Next came a spell hanging out with the Cannell/Lupo/Bellisario boys club, as he directed episodes of Cannell's *A-Team*, *Hunter*, and *Stingray*, Lupo's *Werewolf*, *Hardball*, and *Something is Out There*, among others, and—now silver-haired—appeared in episodes of Cannell's *Renegade* and Lupo's *Raven*. Darren was not the only beach movie boy in the group—fellow former teen hunk John Ashley co-produced many of the Cannell and Lupo shows. Darren's singing talents were put to use in the 1990s for a brief return to the SF arena, as hologram nightclub entertainer Vic Fontaine in a recurring role in the final season of *Star Trek: Deep Space Nine*. This gig reactivated his singing career. He was also reunited with former *T.J. Hooker* co-star Heather Locklear for a run of episodes in the final season of *Melrose Place*.

Like many TV heroes in the '60s, Robert Colbert went on to play a series of mostly villainous guest-starring roles following the demise of *The Time Tunnel*, starting with Irwin Allen's *Land of the Giants*, in which he played a devious and ruthless politician in the episode "Sabotage," and a heroic supporting role (as "Captain Dum-Dum" he said) in the unsold Allen pilot *City Beneath the Sea*. Following *The Time Tunnel* he has appeared in such series as *Quincy*, *Petrocelli*, *Mike Hammer*, *Crazy Like a Fox*, *50/50*, *Foley Square*, *Hunter*, *Murder She Wrote*, *Knight Rider*, *In the Heat of the Night* and *Wings*, as well as an ongoing role in '70s soap *The Young and the Restless*. Today, he's happily retired, although his staid, square-jawed persona in *The Time Tunnel* belies a wicked sense of humor, and he has made himself available for cameos in the hilarious B-movie spoof sequences of *Amazon Women on the Moon*, and as the pony-tailed supervisor of time-traveling tourists in the excellent made-for-cable time travel fantasy *Timescape*. He can also be seen—hiding behind a bushy white beard—in a minor role in "Guess Who's Coming to Breakfast?," an early episode of *Frasier*. Hiding out on the golf courses of America, "I never know who's gonna be coming at me, or what they'll remember me from!" laughs Colbert.

After her season on *The Time Tunnel*, Lee Meriwether returned to the guest-star circuit, narrowly missing out on a chance to appear regularly in *Mission: Impossible* after several guest turns in the show. It was a major disappointment to her. She appeared in episodes of *The FBI*, *Star Trek*, *Mannix*, *Hawk*, and as a worried parent of trapped children in "Rescue" for *Land of the Giants*, and then spent eight years in a dull but lucrative regular role in the awful *Barnaby Jones*, a ludicrous but long-running 1970s series about a geriatric detective! In the 1980s she was cast in the dire syndicated series *The Munsters Today* as Lily. Whit Bissell also went

Lee Meriwether and Robert Colbert pose with some familiar Irwin Allen hardware on the set of *The Time Tunnel*. Note that the sand-timer logo has still to be added to the floor.

straight back to work, doing "Dark Outpost" for *The Invaders* and "The Trouble with Tribbles" for *Star Trek* almost immediately he finished work on *The Time Tunnel*. The rest of his family was also enjoying success. His father-in-law, Alan Napier, had been gainfully employed as Alfred the butler in *Batman* and his grandson Brian Forster was a member of *The Partridge Family*. Meanwhile, Bissell was doing episodes of *The Man from UNCLE*, *Land of the Giants*, and Allen's *City Beneath the Sea* pilot. He also appeared in other series, including two episodes of *The Incredible Hulk*. John Zaremba returned to bit-parts, including a recurring role as the Jock Ewing character's doctor on *Dallas*. Whit Bissell and John Zaremba have since passed on.

In direct contrast to the easy launches *Voyage to the Bottom of the Sea* and *Lost in Space* enjoyed (*Batman* did not compete with *Lost in Space* until four months after the sci-fi show was established), *The Time Tunnel*, scheduled to follow *The Green Hornet* on Friday nights, had numerous obstacles to overcome. With the half-hour *Green Hornet* starting at the same time as hour shows *The Wild Wild West* on CBS and *Tarzan* on NBC, the dice were loaded against it from the start, and *The Time Tunnel*, starting on the half-hour, found itself competing not only with the back end of these two successful shows, but also the popular *Hogan's Heroes* on CBS and the first half of *The Man from UNCLE* on NBC. Consequently, *The Time Tunnel* had four different top rated shows to take on, one—*The Wild Wild West*—already established in a regular slot, another—*Man from UNCLE*—a cult favorite, and the third—*Tarzan*—a new series boasting a familiar and favorite character ... all of them of interest to the same target audience. And yet despite all this, *The Time Tunnel* had been penciled in for a second season.

The last episode of *The Time Tunnel* aired in April 1967, but its impact was immediate. Although only thirty episodes were produced, *The Time Tunnel* remains, like *The Twilight Zone* and *Star Trek* before it, one of the most successful so-called failures in syndication, possibly the most profitable and influential single season series ever ... and most significantly, in terms of proof of durability and popularity, the format continues to resurface regularly, employed endlessly by newer, wannabe hit series. Since *The Time Tunnel* ceased production, very few time travel adventures have failed to be influenced by it. Time travel stories proliferated in *Star Trek* (the final shape of the time portal in "City on the Edge of Forever" certainly bears a remarkable resemblance), *Lost in Space*, and *Voyage to the Bottom of the Sea*, where previously there had been none. Even *Mission: Impossible* and *The Wild Wild West* explored the theme. The short-lived secret agent series *Search*, with Burgess Meredith monitoring his spies *Time Tunnel*-style appeared in 1972 (following a pilot called *Probe*), and Allen reworked the concept himself with a little less inspiration in the entertaining pilot *The Time Travelers* in the late '70s, when a pilot film for a series based on *The Time Machine* also showed up (with Whit Bissell in the cast, also a player in the 1960 feature version). *Time Express* was a very short-lived series resembling the time travel forays into *The Twilight Zone*, while the modestly intriguing but credibility-challenged *Voyagers* brazenly reworked the *Time Tunnel* concept even more preposterously than the original (it's good fun, but no substitute—imagine *Time Tunnel* as a Disney film and you've got it...).

Donald Bellisario's *Quantum Leap* concerned a time travel project in Arizona that had gone horribly wrong and catapulted one of its creators irretrievably into a series of random escapades in time! While Bellisario does not list *The Time Tunnel* among his influences for *Quantum Leap*, and announced an intention to avoid similar stories while putting his own familiar stamp on the premise, themes in the second season opener

"Honeymoon Express" and the episodes "Killin' Time" and "The Leap Between the States" will ring bells for *Time Tunnel* fans. A series based on the film *Bill and Ted's Excellent Adventure(s)* did not catch on, while there is a strong case for arguing that *Sliders* and *Stargate–SG-1* both owe *Time Tunnel*—as well as *Star Trek*—a debt of gratitude. *Seven Days*, a two season run combining elements of *The Time Tunnel* (experimental time travel project rushed into use) and *Quantum Leap* (severe limits on time span traveled), struggled in a companion slot with *Star Trek: Voyager*. The difference here was that the hero *successfully* averted horrific disasters by traveling back the seven days of the title. However, since the beginning of the 1990s, it has become a certainty that every science-fiction or fantasy series enjoying a reasonable run will quickly turn up a time-travel episode or two, particularly into the recent past; forays into the '60s and '70s have become very popular, with *seaQuest DSV*, *Honey I Shrunk the Kids*, *Star Trek: Deep Space Nine*, *Star Trek: Voyager*, *Stargate–SG-1*, the new *Outer Limits*, and *Charmed* all turning out adventures in the latter half of the 20th century. Another favorite plot has been the *12:01/Groundhog Day*-style time-loop of the repeating day, which has manifested itself in episodes of *Xena*, *The X-Files*, *Buffy*, *Charmed*, and *Stargate–SG-1* to name just a few. In the early 2000s, although nothing came of it, two networks competed for the right to commission a new, updated version of *The Time Tunnel* itself—not bad for Irwin Allen's "only failure." With the budget-crunching possibilities now offered by computer trickery, we may yet one day see a return to the time travel adventure that takes place on the battlefields in ancient history.

The Cast

REGULAR CAST: Robert Colbert (Dr. Douglas Phillips), James Darren (Dr. Anthony Newman), Whit Bissell (General Heywood Kirk), Lee Meriwether (Dr. Ann McGregor), John Zaremba (Dr. Raymond Swain)

RECURRING CAST: Sam Groom (Jerry), Wesley Lau (Sgt. Jiggs)

The Episodes

SINGLE SEASON (1966–1967)

Rendezvous with Yesterday

wr. Shimon Wincelberg, Harold Jack Bloom, dir. Irwin Allen

When the Pentagon sends an official to investigate the economic viability of a billion dollar time travel project deep beneath the Arizona desert, impetuous scientist Tony Newman runs into the maw of the Time Tunnel before the device is ready for human testing, and tumbles onto the deck of the Titanic *hours before it's due to sink. Unable to retrieve him, his colleague goes to the rescue, but the two of them become "lost in the infinite corridors of time."*

With Gary Merrill (General LeRoy Clark), Michael Rennie (Captain Smith), Susan Hampshire (Althea Hall), Don Knight (Mr. Grainger), Gerald Michenaud (Marcel), John Winston (crewman), Brett Parker (technician)

LOCATION: The *Titanic*, April 13th, 14th, 1912.

Shimon Wincelberg wrote the original pilot script for Irwin Allen's *Lost in Space* that ultimately became the basis of four of the first five episodes of that series. He also wrote the *Star Trek* episodes "Dagger of the Mind" and "The Galileo Seven" (co-written with Oliver Crawford) and the first color episode of Allen's *Voyage to the Bottom of the Sea*, "Jonah and the Whale." He was a natural to be entrusted with the pilot script for *The Time Tunnel*, and came up with most of the background detail for the series and the *Titanic* as the setting of the first adventure, but the ABC network wanted changes. Afraid of losing the sale, Allen and Fox brought in a second writer to revise Wincelberg's script. Wincelberg wasn't pleased, but understood the politics of the situation. New writer Harold Jack Bloom made Tony rather than Doug the first of the scientists into the Tunnel, and wisely removed a hackneyed sub-plot about Doug's father and grandmother being on the ship, a corny coincidence and familiar contrivance from many a time-travel yarn even then. Bloom would later write regularly for Jack Webb's 1970s series *Project UFO*, including the pilot.

The pilot film for *The Time Tunnel*, like all of Allen's pilots, is quite spectacular. From the opening teaser, in which the investigating official's car sinks below the parched sand of the Arizona desert, to his guided tour of the extraordinary Time Tunnel complex, the series promises to be a real mindblast—and that promise does not go unfulfilled. Oddly enough, given Allen's inclination to reuse stock footage until it practically falls apart, many great visual effects were not seen again after this episode, including the entrance to the complex and the elevator journey. A beautiful establishing shot of the actors matted into an image of the entire floor of the complex where the Tunnel is housed was to be seen after this episode on only two more occasions ("One Way to the Moon" and "Night of the Long Knives"). *The Time Tunnel* comic book (two issues, by Western Publishing under their Gold Key imprint in 1966) refers to the Time Tunnel experiment by the rather transparent and silly codename of Operation: Tic-Toc. The pre-credits scene of this episode, in which Phillips requests permission to enter the base with Clark, is the first and only occasion in which this code-name is used in the series, when Doug refers to Tic-Toc base.

The Tunnel set itself is a fabulous piece

of work, banks of computers with a main desk for the controllers, and huge towers behind them. On the floor, a large yellow and black sands-of-time emblem, also seen on the staff badges ... and dominating everything, the massive imposing gaping maw of the Tunnel itself. Now *that's* a time machine! Elsewhere, a shot we do see many times in the series—the Tunnel's enormous power core, glowing towers linked on each floor by metal bridges and a gigantic globe that looks as though its destruction might take the whole world with it. This false perspective shot bears a striking resemblance to the Krel machinery in the 1956 feature *Forbidden Planet*, a film which also inspired *Lost in Space* and *Star Trek*, but it isn't the actual footage from the film. These shots were also used in Allen's test reel for the unsold series *The Man from the 25th Century*, which was to star James Darren. A trouble-in-the-Time-Tunnel shot of hordes of security men running across the bridges over the power core was employed frequently throughout the series, and was also used in this test film.

The *Titanic* was built, sold and launched as being an "unsinkable" ship, and no company's advertising ever dared tempt fate so carelessly again. More than 1,500 died and some were saved when this mighty passenger vessel hit an iceberg several days into its journey and slowly sank in icy waters in one of the most famous and terrible maritime disasters in history. Allen was searching for a well-known moment of dramatic power in history, and in the misery and bravery of that night in 1912, he found a story familiar enough for 1960s TV viewers to be aware of, but distant enough to be considered the stuff of drama. The pilot's structure, flitting back and forth from the *Titanic* to the Time Tunnel control room, is solid and the literate and intelligent dialogue is involving and flows comfortably. "Rendezvous with Yesterday" has itself stood the test of time impressively well. Scenes with a young child from the lower decks intruding on the opulence of the dining rooms to steal foodstuffs are amusing without being overly cute, and Michael Rennie is superb as the Captain. The only weak spot in the entire program is the silly business of Althea Hall's medical condition, a cornball contrivance more suited to a soap opera, and the sudden attack she suffers in the hallway is comically bad. However, this subplot is so minor as to be unobtrusive to the point where one wonders why it was even included. There is quite enough drama in the sinking of the ship, after all.

One scene jars. As the Captain realizes that the ship is sinking, he asks with dignity whether the time travelers are aware if he will die. Rather than enigmatically but tellingly replying "yes, we are," or simply not answering, Doug clumsily tells him he will! Other than this, the dialogue is excellent, capturing the period well. The scenes of the ship going down are quite elaborate for 1960s TV, and grimly effective (the pilot rivaled that of *Batman* as the most expensive of the time). Colbert's scenes with the kid are played with class rather than saccharine sentiment, and Darren's moments with Susan Hampshire as Althea are good, despite the hokey medical condition sub-plot. Her intended self-sacrifice however, is a very authentic reflection of the stiff upper lip attitude of the time, as historical anecdotes from the sinking of both the *Titanic* and the *Lusitania*, another seafaring tragedy of the period, are testimony to.

The undeniable drama of this terrible event has made it the subject of several films and TV productions, including a tasteless and historically dubious romantic indulgence in a 1990s big budget special effects production. All of them play up the fateful destiny and life and death scenarios rather luridly, but *Time Tunnel's* pilot, while certainly exploiting the drama of the situation, successfully gets across the horror of the disaster with respectful sympathy and without becoming ghoulish. Particularly impressive

is Doug's fleeting, touching glance at the surly engine room workers when he first materializes on board the *Titanic* to search for Tony. This brief, silent moment of grim sympathy achieves more than a page of handwringing dialogue would have and is a tribute to the acting prowess of the under-appreciated and under-used Colbert, who despite being on record as having enjoyed his life and acting career, and admiring both Allen and the *Time Tunnel* concept, claimed in an interview that "after (radio drama) *The Caine Mutiny Court Martial*, I never had nine words in a row worth a damn." Lack of strong dialogue never prevented him giving a strong performance. His mature determination contrasts with Darren's boyish urgent desperation effectively, and in this episode, as well as companion early adventures "The End of the World" and "The Day the Sky Fell In," one has a reassuring sense that their dialogue is not as interchangeable as it would become later in the series. In the best episodes, Tony's impetuous enthusiasm is kept in check by the big brotherly caution of Doug's undeclared leadership.

Since this episode was produced, the *Titanic* has proven a popular venue for other time travel adventures. The *Voyagers* series produced an episode on the ill-fated vessel, "Voyagers of the Titanic," while the 1981 feature film *Time Bandits* used the tragedy for black comedy in an only partly successful attempt to prove the old maxim that time plus tragedy equals comedy. It has to be said, however, that Allen was no stranger to milking humanity's baser instincts, as his disaster movies, *The Poseidon Adventure* and *The Towering Inferno* demonstrated in the early '70s.

Several scenes were excised from the pilot for reasons of length, but as we all know, Irwin Allen never wastes anything. The short sequence in "The End of the World," in which Tony briefly returns to the desert exterior of the Tunnel complex some years before he was known there originally belonged to the pilot, as did several scenes in prehistoric times utilizing Allen's famous *Lost World* lizards (about which, more later). These were later incorporated into the episode "Chase Through Time." Light-hearted moments during the filming of the pilot (Darren on the Tunnel set, Allen and Wesley Lau filming the 1956 desert scenes, Colbert and Darren clowning on the pre-historic jungle set, and Colbert and Darren filming the time-freeze scene over the *Titanic* railings and landing on a mattress below) can all be seen in the superb documentary *The Fantasy Worlds of Irwin Allen.*

Playing the Captain of the *Titanic* was Michael Rennie, who starred in the SF clas-sic *The Day the Earth Stood Still*, as well as Allen's film of *The Lost World* (as Lord Rox-ton) and the *Lost in Space* two-parter "The Keeper." He also turns up in a *Batman* episode of the period (as the Sandman) and *The Man from UNCLE* ("The THRUSH Roulette Affair"), but his other two '60s highlights, besides the Allen shows, were two superb stories for *The Invaders*, the mem-orable "The Innocents" and the two-part "Summit Meeting" (he could easily have been the same evil deceiver in both, but *The Invaders* was not known for its continuity!). In actuality, Michael Rennie looks nothing like the captain of the *Titanic*, as photos of the gentleman have survived. He does, how-ever, lend enormous weight and stature to the portrayal.

Susan Hampshire was a British actress who always played twee, demure precious young flowers of the sort she portrays here. There was, inevitably, not much for her in America, and she soon returned home, where she found her calling playing twee, demure types in BBC period romances. She ultimately made her name in two BBC pro-ductions, *The Forsyte Saga* in 1968 and the less successful *The Pallisers* in 1975, a rather transparent attempt to duplicate its success. Earlier, she had inherited the Julie Christie role in *The Andromeda Breakthrough* in 1962,

the sequel to *A for Andromeda*, an early '60s sci-fi effort from the BBC. The worldwide success of *The Forsyte Saga* however, left her trapped in the past as surely as Doug and Tony were.

British-born Don Knight also appeared in the pilot film for the 1977 SF series *Fan-tastic Journey* (which also had time travel el-ements) and the *Voyage to the Bottom of the Sea* episode "The Heat Monster," in which he struggled unsuccessfully to effect a Swedish accent. Mostly though, producers go to him when they have a British part to cast. In an interview with *Starlog* magazine in 1993, Knight revealed that actor Dennis Hopper—who had appeared as Napoleon in Allen's feature *The Story of Mankind*—had been cast in a minor role, but although vis-ible in background scenes, had been edited out of the final print. Sure enough, there he is in the scene on deck when Tony first lands on the *Titanic* and meets Susan Hampshire's character, and once you know he's there, you can see where his part was cut quite clearly.

The big, bear-like Gary Merrill, who lumbered comfortably through numerous war films, cop dramas and westerns, was very busy in sci-fi around the time he appeared in the *Time Tunnel* pilot, appearing in the cheapo underwater monster movie *Destina-tion: Inner Space,* and standing in for an ailing Richard Basehart in the *Voyage to the Bottom of the Sea* episode "The Menfish," which co-incidentally had a similar premise. He also ap-peared in episodes of *The Twilight Zone* ("Still Valley"), *The Outer Limits* ("The Human Fac-tor"), and the early '70s pilot *Earth II.*

This is the first of Wesley Lau's appear-ances as Sgt. Jiggs, the stereotypical mousta-chioed head of security at the Time Tunnel. His most famous scene is to come in "Re-venge of the Gods," when he travels through time himself, but he also appears in "One Way to the Moon," "The End of the World," and "Chase Through Time," five episodes altogether. Less distinctive without the moustache, he appeared in *Land of the Giants*, in a bit part as a cop in the episode "The Creed," and *The Twilight Zone* ("Twenty-Two" and "The Fugitive").

John Winston, who appears as a crewman guarding the quarters where Tony is imprisoned (and again as a soldier in "The Last Patrol"), was a more futuristic mariner in several episodes of *Star Trek*. He played Lt. Kyle, and was usually seen operating the transporter, including in two time travel episodes, "The City on the Edge of Forever" and "Tomorrow is Yesterday." He also appeared in *Star Trek II—The Wrath of Khan*. Gerald Michenaud shows up again in "Terror-go-Round," a drab episode of *Land of the Giants*. Brett Parker had also appeared in the opening episode of Allen's *Lost in Space*, as the unfortunate security guard disposed of by Doctor Smith. Curiously, although he gets an on-screen credit here for simply counting backwards, several other players, including the fellow who has an entire scene with Colbert while pursuing the boy on board the *Titanic*, do not! At the close of this episode, as the Mars flight lifts off, we hear the unmistakable metallic tones of Dick Tufeld, the voice of the *Lost in Space* Robot and *The Time Tunnel's* narrator. Production number: 6034.

One Way to the Moon

wr. William Welch, dir. Harry Harris

Doug and Tony are snatched from the deck of the sinking Titanic only to tumble aboard a 1978 flight to Mars just as the ship is about to take off! The four astronauts are alarmed to discover the time travelers adding to their weight and endangering the flight, and immediately suspect them of sabotage ... but the real threat to their safety is the presence of a number of enemy agents both on board the space flight, and inside the Time Tunnel complex itself.

With Larry Ward (Kane), Warren Stevens (Harlow), James Callahan (Beard), Ross Elliott (Dr. Brandon), Ben Cooper (Nazarro), Barry Kelley (Admiral Killian), Dick Tufeld (voice of mission control)

LOCATION: Mars Flight, and the Earth's moon, 1978.

"One Way to the Moon," which takes the time travelers on the first of just four trips into the then-future (the others are "Chase Through Time," "The Kidnappers," and "Town of Terror") also demonstrates the first of many time paradoxes during the series. The traitor Beard, watching in 1968, now knows that Doug and Tony will be aboard the moonshot, just as Washington can now warn the astronauts to expect the time travelers; the astronauts would therefore have been prepared for the inevitable arrival of Doug and Tony—and known the identity of the real saboteur ... Indeed, Beard would never have been on board in 1978, because although the Time Tunnel had lost visual contact and did not witness Beard's murderous acts, Doug and Tony could—and surely would—have informed them after the event. We can therefore only assume that Doug and Tony have effectively changed the future witnessed by them and the people at the Tunnel.

This episode also establishes the convention of having Doug and Tony revert to their original clothing before they depart a time-period, as their spacesuits miraculously disappear (where to?—they're not left behind) before they're whisked away. It would have been fun to see Doug and Tony arrive at each new location in the dress of the previous adventure, as the two time travelers in the later series *Voyagers* humorously did, but apart from complicating the scripts, this was an impossibility as no-one knew in which order the network would choose to run the episodes (in fact, "The End of the World" was the second episode produced). "One Way to the Moon" also features one of the clumsiest uses of stock footage (usually this was seamless) as the rocket that leaves the launch pad in the opening scenes (and in the previous episode's trailer) is quite clearly nothing like the one which ultimately lands on the moon (this footage is plainly swiped from George Pal's SF classic *Destination: Moon*). The plot of the episode bears some similarities to that of the *Lost in Space* pilot; we have the mission nearly being aborted because of additional weight, a saboteur for a foreign government on board, a risky space-walk, loss of contact with Mission Control, and of course the inevitable standard 1950s/'60s meteor shower! As the initial episodes of *Lost in Space* had already demonstrated, Allen's image of the Space Race was, understandably for the period, still firmly rooted in the tradition of the 1950s Hollywood space travel clichés that had been done to death the previous decade in such films as *Destination: Moon*, *Conquest of Space*, and their many, many imitators. However, whatever the episode's failings in terms of authenticity (and humankind was still three years away from the famous moon landing when this episode was made), it is a tense and dramatic episode, despite the familiarity of the plot's high points, and there are no slow moments.

James Callahan has kept busy in TV guest shots and supporting roles for over thirty years, with SF TV appearances ranging from *The Twilight Zone* and *My Favorite Martian*, to *Knight Rider* and *Amazing Stories*. His best sci-fi appearances outside his *Time Tunnel* however are probably his two *Invaders* episodes, "Nightmare" and "Labyrinth." He's particularly good in "Nightmare," as the baffled, aggressive, but well-meaning suitor of a frail young woman being persecuted by alien plotters.

Following his supporting role in the SF film classic *Forbidden Planet*, Warren Stevens made numerous appearances in SF TV series of the '60s. A close friend and former roommate of actor Richard Basehart, he made three appearances in Basehart's Irwin Allen series *Voyage to the Bottom of the Sea*, appeared twice in *Land of the Giants*, and as a hostile alien in "By Any Other Name," an Irwin Allen-ish *Star Trek*. Other roles in the '60s included *The Twilight Zone*, *The Outer Limits*, *The Man from UNCLE*, and Michael Rennie's time-travel cheapie *Cyborg 2087*.

Larry Ward was the escaped convict in "All That Glitters" for *Lost in Space*. He also appeared in episodes of *The Outer Limits*, *The Invaders*, *Land of the Giants* ("Shell Game"), and *Wonder Woman*. He was better known for—and better suited to—westerns. Barry Kelley played officious characters in numerous sit-coms including episodes of *The Munsters* and *The Addams Family*. Ben Cooper appeared in the *Twilight Zone* episode "Still Valley." Ross Elliott turned up again in *The Time Tunnel*, in the episode "Visitors from Beyond the Stars," and his numerous credits in the sci-fi arena can be found there. Production number: 9603.

The End of the World

wr. Peter Germano, William Welch, dir. Sobey Martin

> *Doug and Tony drop into a small mining town where a numb and fearful community are awaiting the end of the world. The catch—it's 1910.*

With Paul Fix (Henderson), James Westerfield (Sheriff), Gregory Morton (Professor Ainsley), Paul Carr (Blaine)

LOCATION: A small mining community somewhere in America, May 1910.

"The End of the World" offered a unique twist to one of the series' formula plots—the warning of imminent doom. This time, the situation was reversed; the time-travelers had to convince the townsfolk that there was *no* danger, while the locals believed that the appearance of Halley's Comet was the end of all life on Earth. If the boys can't make them realize the truth of the phenomenon, a group of miners trapped in a cave-in will be left to a grim fate underground. Interestingly, a silent film titled *The Comet* was made in 1910, which did portray scenes of panic and devastation as a passing meteor burns up the Earth in the 25th century. Humankind rebuilds, only to suffer one last catastrophe of the comet's making when the Earth's water disappears, leaving only a single man and woman surviving. Since then, of course, we have had *Meteor*, *Deep Impact*, *Armageddon*, and the unintentionally hilarious TV movie *Asteroid*. The series *Sliders* (in "Last Days") also makes use of this end of the world scenario, while the idea of the comet's magnetic pull affecting the Tunnel resurfaces as a black hole in the considerably more scientifically convincing episode of *Stargate—SG-1*, "A Matter of Time."

Some great imagery keeps this exemplary episode humming—the Tunnel scientists watching the scenes of mass panic around the world, the torchlight vigil on the mountain as the townspeople wait blankly for the end, the cataclysm back at the Time Tunnel control center, where futile attempts to rescue the time travelers result in the comet being drawn into the maw of the Time Tunnel by its magnetic pull, with Sam Groom's tremulous Jerry screaming for assistance as he's sucked into the Time Tunnel—after ominously building up the tension with his fears of the comet's powers in earlier scenes. An added plus at the close of the episode is a surprise short sequence crowded out of the pilot, in which Tony returns to the 1950s at a time when the Time Tunnel project had only just commenced. Disorientated that Doug has not yet met him, and doesn't know who he is, Tony is plucked back into the time stream just as a guard is about to shoot at him.

The script by William Welch—from a story by Peter Germano—is unusually good. Welch is not known for great dialogue, and Germano's only other contribution to the Allen canon was the ludicrous but enjoyable "Doomsday Island" for *Voyage to the Bottom of the Sea*, but this story is suspiciously intelligent and thoughtful, particularly in the scenes between Doug and Ainsley in 1910 and as the Time Tunnel scientists pause to debate the merit of their experiments and the potential for disastrous consequences. What the General and his people don't know is that the presence of the Time Tunnel's connection with 1910 actually saved the world from the collision with Halley's Comet, creating the black hole that diverted the comet from its trajectory. Such depth is unusual in an Allen show, and it's a rare treat here. Based on the evidence of Germano's "Doomsday Island," the later beautifully scripted Welch *Time Tunnel* episode "Night of the Long Knives," and the story only credit for Germano, it seems fair to credit Welch with the episode's virtues.

Sam Groom, later to star in Allen's time travel pilot *The Time Travelers*, appears for the first time in the series as technician Jerry (although we glimpse him briefly in a link between this episode and the previous one not repeated in this episode), a role later dropped from the series. His other episodes were "The Day the Sky Fell In," "Secret Weapon," "Crack of Doom" and "Night of the Long Knives," so he did at least have the distinction of appearing in some of the best. Other roles in SF TV include episodes of *The Bionic Woman* and *The Incredible Hulk*. After taking the lead in the early '70s syndicated series *Doctor Simon Locke* (later revamped as *Police Surgeon*) in Canada, he finally secured a leading role in a promising SF series in the *Lost in Space* tradition titled *Otherworld* in 1985. Following the unfair and cavalier treatment of *Otherworld* by CBS, Groom became disillusioned with Hollywood and returned to the New York theater. He still appears in TV productions filmed in New York, and appeared in a couple of episodes of quality legal drama *Law and Order* during the '90s.

Both Paul Fix and Paul Carr appeared in the first *Star Trek* episode, "Where No Man Has Gone Before." Paul Fix's career in sci-fi goes right back to the 1940s film *Doctor Cyclops*, which helped inspire *Land of the Giants*. He appeared in episodes of *Adventures of Superman*, *The Twilight Zone*, *The Wild Wild West*, *The Six Million Dollar Man*, and *Battlestar Galactica*. For Irwin Allen, Fix shows up in the *Voyage to the Bottom of the Sea* episode "The Terrible Toys" and went on to play a giant doctor in *Land of the Giants* ("The Creed" and "Deadly Lodestone"), while Carr appeared again in *The Time Tunnel* as Paris in "Revenge of the Gods" and as a giant photographer in "Framed" for *Land of the Giants*. He also chalked up a number of appearances in *Voyage to the Bottom of the Sea*. Carr has appeared in virtually every major fantasy TV series of the '60s and some of the '70s, and he's been lucky enough to be in some superior episodes, including that first Shatner *Star Trek*, a superb *Invaders*, two good *Time Tunnels*, the first weekly *Six Million Dollar Man*, and the first *Bionic Woman* story...

James Westerfield appeared in *The Twilight Zone* in the playful "Mr. Dingle the Strong" and later played a scurrilous showman in "Space Circus," a colorful portrayal for *Lost in Space*. Gregory Morton does a nice turn in "The King of Diamonds Affair" for *The Man from UNCLE*, and also turns up in the cast of the earlier and unrelated "The King of Knaves Affair" for the same series. He was also the alien voice in the classic *Lost in Space* episode "Follow the Leader." Elderly bit players Nelson Leigh and Bob Adler are listed in the publicity information for this episode, but not the end credits on screen; their roles as preacher and old man appear to have ended up on the cutting room floor. Nelson Leigh starred in the time travel feature film *World Without End* and the serials *Brick Bradford* and *Superman*; Adler later makes it to the screen in *Time Tunnel's* "Devil's Island." Production number: 9602.

The Day the Sky Fell In

wr. Ellis St. Joseph, dir. William Hale

The time travelers drop into the Japanese Consulate at Pearl Harbor the day before the Japanese attack, where—fleeing their interrogators—Tony encounters himself as a child and discovers the wartime fate of his father.

With Linden Chiles (Commander Newman), Susan Flannery (Louise Neill), Lew Gallo (Lt. Anderson), Bob Okazaki (Tasaka), Jerry Fujikawa (Okuna), Shuji Nozawa (Sumida), Caroline Kido (Yoku), Sheldon Golomb (young Tony), Frankie Kabott (Billy Neill), Robert Rior-

dan (Admiral Brandt), Pat Culliton (radio operator)

LOCATION: Pearl Harbor, Hawaii, December 6th, 7th, 1941.

"The Day the Sky Fell In," referred to erroneously in some promotional materials (and consequently in some sources) as "The Day the Sky Fell Down," is widely regarded as *The Time Tunnel's* finest hour. Its author, Ellis St. Joseph, has been responsible for other memorable TV science fiction episodes including the legendary "The Sixth Finger" for *The Outer Limits*, and "The Weird World," one of the best remembered and highly regarded episodes of *Land of the Giants*. St. Joseph also contributed other scripts to *The Outer Limits* (the first draft of "The Mutant") and *Land of the Giants* ("Underground"), and the Sandman/Catwoman team-up for *Batman*. Director William Hale would return to open "The Crack of Doom," set "The Death Trap," and exact "The Revenge of Robin Hood."

"The Day the Sky Fell In" is an exciting and intelligent episode, with many excellent scenes of pathos and irony, particularly—despite its Saturday morning serial connotations—when the time travelers are put under the influence of truth serum, and reveal the outcome of the war to their furious disbelieving captors. A tense moment at the Time Tunnel control center has the technicians bringing a live bomb from the attack back to their headquarters (this is the first of four explosive devices to terrorize the Tunnel—others appeared in "The Death Trap," "Chase Through Time," and "Raiders from Outer Space"). This is an exceptionally well-written episode (as well as splendid characterization and poignancy, there's a subtle inference that Tony's father and Louise Neill may be more than just friends, or would like to be), but one of the nicest aspects of the episode is the quiet, understated portrayal of Doug and Tony's friendship. Although the dramatics of the episode belong to James Darren and Linden Chiles

Doug and Tony (Robert Colbert, left, and James Darren) survey the carnage at Pearl Harbor in "The Day the Sky Fell In."

as future son and long-lost father, Robert Colbert manages to steal the show just standing in the background with a huge soppy grin on his face when the young Tony enters. Note also the look of genuine glee and happiness on his face for Tony as he realizes the importance of the moment. There's not a moment's hesitation of selfishness, disinterest or jealousy in his reaction to Tony's excitement, just immediate agreement to help Tony find out about his father.

Linden Chiles, cast as Tony's father, also appeared twice in *The Invaders* (once as David Vincent's brother), in the episodes "Wall of Crystal" and "Task Force." A lean, smooth-talking Ivy League type, he appeared in most '60s fantasy series at some point, including *The Twilight Zone*, *The Munsters*, *My Favorite Martian*, *The Man from UNCLE*, *The Green Hornet*, and Allen's *Land of the Giants* ("The Flight Plan"). Later roles included episodes of *The Six Million Dollar Man*, *The Bionic Woman*, *Logan's Run*, *Buck Rogers in the 25th Century*, *The Incredible Hulk*, *Knight Rider*, *V*, and *Lois and Clark*. Silver-haired since the '80s, he was reunited with James Darren when Darren directed an episode of *Werewolf* ("A World of Difference").

Lew Gallo returns to *The Time Tunnel* in the thankless role of futuristic alien Vokar in "Chase Through Time." Susan Flannery was in "Hail to the Chief," "The Traitor" and "Time Bomb" for *Voyage to the Bottom of the Sea*, and was briefly considered as a regular cast member for that series. She later appeared regularly on the daytime soap *Days of Our Lives*. Pat Culliton and Robert Riordan also served on board the *Seaview*, Culliton playing numerous bit parts and Riordan appearing as the ill-fated government man with James Darren in the teaser for "The Mechanical Man," the *Voyage* guest shot that got Darren his regular role in *The Time Tunnel*; Culliton, a regular bit-player on the Irwin Allen series, also shows up in *Time Tunnel's* "Revenge of the Gods," "Visitors

from Beyond the Stars," "Billy the Kid" and "Idol of Death."

Jerry Fujikawa also appears in *The Twilight Zone*, *The Man from UNCLE*, and *The Wild Wild West*. Bob Okazaki chalks up appearances in *Bewitched* and *The Man from UNCLE*. Shuji Nozawa also turns up in *The Man from UNCLE*, in "The Green Opal Affair," in a memorable fight scene with Robert Vaughn. No other SF TV credits could be found for Caroline Kido or Frankie Kabbott. Child actor Sheldon Golomb also appeared in "The Double-O-Nothing Affair" for *The Girl from UNCLE* and "A Piece of the Action" for *Star Trek*. Production number: 9606.

The Last Patrol

wr. Bob and Wanda Duncan, dir. Sobey Martin

Doug and Tony are taken for spies by a ruthless British General when they drop into the run-up to a decisive battle during the American War of Independence. Back in the present, the Pentagon has contacted the officer's descendant, who sees an ideal opportunity to discover why the battle went so calamitously wrong for his ancestor.

With Carroll O'Connor (General/Colonel Southall), Michael Pate (Captain Hotchkiss), John Napier (Captain Jenkins), David Watson (Lt. Rynerson), John Winston (British sentry)

LOCATION: New Orleans, January 6th, 1815.

This was the first script for the series by Bob and Wanda Duncan, who also contributed extensively to *Lost in Space*. The episode was filmed on the set of another Fox series, *Daniel Boone*.

Carroll O'Connor, who previously appeared alongside Michael Pate in "Long Live the King," a first season episode of *Voyage to the Bottom of the Sea*, gives a masterful performance here as both the British General and his descendant, providing this poignant tale with much of its class and credibility. He struts, he postures, he preens, he schemes, yet never once does he step over the line into caricatured villainy. This is not an actor reciting lines, it is a fully thought-out and considered performance of those lines;

everything is scripted, yet we see Southall reacting and thinking on the spot. Watch also his entrance as the 20th century Southall, and his seemingly ad-libbed awe at the Time Tunnel complex. Note that for his time travel sequence—missing from some prints—O'Connor was not suspended by wires as James Darren and Robert Colbert were, but simply stands before the effects footage of the time vortex. It doesn't really work, and this was the only occasion we saw anyone else who traveled through the Time Tunnel actually moving through time and space as Doug and Tony did each week.

While O'Connor will forever be remembered as the lead in his two long-running series, *All in the Family* in the 1970s and *In the Heat of the Night* in the 1990s, it is one-offs like this, and his sly gangster in the film *Point Blank*, which stand out as the gems in his career. Frankly, he was wasted all those years in *All in the Family*, and it is unfortunate that most of the public knows him only as Archie Bunker. O'Connor was not always well-served in his guest shots—his performance was impaired pointlessly by a wheelchair and dark glasses in "The Green Opal Affair," an early *Man from UNCLE* episode when it was still slavishly imitating Bond. He made the most of a lightweight *Outer Limits* ("Controlled Experiment"), and his *Voyage to the Bottom of the Sea* was unremarkable, but in *Time Tunnel* he shines. Consider for a moment that he was very nearly Doctor Smith in *Lost in Space*.

Michael Pate was also Captain of the guards in "The Walls of Jericho"; a wonderful heavy, he appeared to less effect in three episodes of *Voyage to the Bottom of the Sea* (in "Long Live the King" and "The Traitor" he played his usual pragmatic thug, in "Flaming Ice" a splendid alien). David Watson later gives a fine performance as the young Rudyard Kipling in "The Night of the Long Knives." John Napier was the escaped convict who ran off with the *Spindrift* into a pit of quicksand in the well-remembered *Land*

of the Giants episode "Manhunt." He was also lined up as a regular had Darren's proposed *Man from the 25th Century* test footage gone to series. John Winston, a regular bit-player on *Star Trek* as transporter chief Lt. Kyle, was also in the pilot episode of *The Time Tunnel*.

Despite the handicap of studio-bound exteriors, the strong script, the time travelers' usual camaraderie and loyalty, and O'Connor's wonderful turn as the two Southalls makes this one of the series' strongest offerings. Production number: 9607.

The Crack of Doom

wr. William Welch, dir. William Hale

> *Doug and Tony tumble onto the Pacific island of Krakatoa only hours before the famous volcano erupts.*

With Torin Thatcher (Dr. Holland), Ellen MacRae/Burstyn (Eve Holland), Victor Lundin (Karnosu), George Matsui (native)

LOCATION: Island of Krakatoa, August 27th, 1883.

Another powerful central performance, this time by Torin Thatcher, graces this studio-bound escapade filmed on the *Voyage to the Bottom of the Sea* island set. Thatcher's other SF TV roles have included "The Space Trader" in the talky first season *Lost in Space* episode, the treacherous Scotsman MacDougall in "Secret of the Loch" for the first season of *Voyage to the Bottom of the Sea*, the cowardly official in "Return of the Archons" for *Star Trek*, and the hapless scientist in "Nightmare" for *Land of the Giants*. However, he will always be best remembered for his wonderful turns as villainous wizards, in *The Seventh Voyage of Sinbad* and the underrated *Jack the Giant Killer*.

This episode is strongly reminiscent of the structure of the *Titanic*, Halley's Comet and Pearl Harbor episodes, and followed the pattern for the *"I know it sounds crazy, but you must believe me"* school of episodes prominent at the start of the series. It rapidly became apparent that the averting disaster strain of scripting would soon become formulaic, especially as history could not be changed, and contrary to what some have implied, *The Time Tunnel* fortunately never fell into that repetitive trap, with the writers later using the time travel concept in a variety of different ways. Of thirty episodes, only five have the time travelers trying to convince potential victims of a forthcoming historical tragedy—the sinking of the *Titanic*, the bombing of Pearl Harbor, the explosion of Krakatoa, Custer's Last Stand at Little Big Horn, and the Alamo. And only seven more involve specific, recorded major historical events (rather than periods or people)—Troy, Dreyfus on Devil's Island, the execution of Marie Antoinette, D-Day, the fall of Jericho, Gettysburg, and Khartoum.

Irwin Allen loved scenes of disaster unfolding on TV screens for the benefit of concerned observers as a severe stern warning was given in authoritarian tones about the lurid events that would or could occur if the peril of the week was not avoided (an early blueprint can be found in "Eleven Days to Zero," the pilot for *Voyage to the Bottom of the Sea*). These doom-laden predictions were invariably accompanied by stock footage of swaying palm trees in hurricane-force winds, crashing waves, tumbling buildings, abandoned cars, and panicking civilians. Allen wasn't going to be cheated out of his montage of mayhem just because Doug and Tony were whisked away before the explosion, and the disaster footage is awkwardly shoehorned into a silly scene in which the Time Tunnel moves its fix forward a day to absurdly confirm facts the scientists already know. An equally pointless interlude occurs when Kirk pumps Ray for useless facts and figures of the "did you know...?" schoolbook variety simply so that Welch can show off his research. It also doesn't ring true that an entire tribe of natives who have lived on Krakatoa for decades have been cowed by one crotchety old man and his daughter who arrived on the island less than two weeks

earlier. Holland's patronizing, dismissive and intolerant attitude toward the savages is entirely accurate for the British Empire period, but one wonders what gives him the upper hand when he has no military status, or troops. It is little short of a miracle that they haven't both been tipped into the lava pool days earlier.

Ellen McRae later changed her name to Ellen Burstyn. Her rather stiff and clipped period costume drama performance perhaps suits her role here, as the women of the period were obliged to play a specific preordained role in society, here the prim and proper doting daughter. Very young and inexperienced at this point in her career, she lacks conviction when required to be more fiery and argumentative. She later made her name in the 1970s, with films such as *Alice Doesn't Live Here Any More* and *The Exorcist*. Victor Lundin was wise to ask for a stunt double during his fight with James Darren; the stunt man's nose was broken! Lundin's other Irwin Allen assignments were "The Menfish" and "The Lobster Man" for *Voyage to the Bottom of the Sea*, two wonderful monster mash episodes. He portrayed a Klingon in the *Star Trek* episode "Errand of Mercy," and is probably best known as Friday in the silly *Robinson Crusoe on Mars*. Production number: 9608.

Revenge of the Gods

wr. William Read Woodfield, Allan Balter, dir. Sobey Martin

Doug and Tony tumble into ancient Greece, where they are taken for gods by Ulysses, who is on the verge of invading Troy with his legendary wooden horse.

With John Doucette (Ulysses), Paul Carr (Paris), Joseph Ruskin (Sardis), Dee Hartford (Helen), Abraham Sofaer (Epeios), Tony Brand (Trojan Captain), Kevin Hagen (Greek Captain), Pat Culliton (warrior)

LOCATION: Border of Greece and Turkey, 1200 B.C.

William Read Woodfield and Allan Balter wrote numerous thinly-veiled Red-bashing stories for *Voyage to the Bottom of the*

Sea before becoming story editors, and later producers, on the similarly inclined *Mission: Impossible*, but there were no Commies at Troy, and they had clearly done their homework on the story, as the dialogue demonstrates at every opportunity! Woodfield was fascinated by tricks and illusions (he had produced the oddball film *The Hypnotic Eye* and planned much wilder schemes that hadn't come off), and the wooden horse of Troy was, after all, one of the greatest sleights of hand in history. Visually, much of the episode consists of great chunks of spectacular stock footage from the otherwise stodgy *Helen of Troy* (1955) and *The 300 Spartans* (1962), and these dominate the action, leaving Woodfield and Balter's mythology lesson to simply shore up the numerous battle scenes and the entrance of the horse itself. This episode probably uses more stock footage than any other episode, but they are impressive scenes that a TV budget could never have hoped to afford, and expertly integrated into the adventure. Thus the episode is an extremely cheap one, but very lavish by TV standards.

Woodfield and Balter were an odd couple, an ill-matched pair thrown together while working on Allen's *Voyage to the Bottom of the Sea*. Balter was a short, quiet, unassuming bespectacled little fellow and former publicist who had worked on *The Outer Limits*, co-writing "The One Hundred Days of the Dragon" and contributing to "The Mutant" alongside Robert Mintz, who had since become a production executive at Fox on the Allen shows. Woodfield was a loud, blustering bear of a man, a former commercial and stills photographer who had taken nude pictures of Marilyn Monroe and been buddies with the so-called Rat Pack friends of Sinatra and JFK. Balter was an associate producer on early episodes of *Voyage to the Bottom of the Sea*, and Woodfield, who had written episodes of *Death Valley Days* and *Sea Hunt* in a classic case of "I can do better than that" after years standing around on movie

sets taking stills, wrote five first season episodes of *Voyage* alone before Balter and Woodfield teamed up to write eight more episodes for the second season. Both the leads of *Voyage to the Bottom of the Sea* regarded them as the series' finest writers. During this time, they wrote two episodes of *Lost in Space* and their one *Time Tunnel* before leaving the Allen operation after a blazing row over one of their *Voyage* scripts ("The Death Ship") being (temporarily) rewritten. They then wrote a fair number of *Mission: Impossible* episodes (Woodfield loved the show's gambling, illusions, and cons) before departing that studio after *another* furious altercation with *that* series' producer, whom they had fought with since day one ("I'd have killed him," Woodfield told Patrick White for his *Complete Mission: Impossible Dossier*, "I would have killed him without a moment's hesitation"). They wrote a dismally slow and outdated 1972 pilot for a proposed series titled *Earth II* (no relation to the later 1990s series that reworked early *Lost in Space*) before resurfacing in the early 1980s as story editors on a laughable and lowbrow so-bad-it's-good one season rip-off of *Mission: Impossible* by the notorious Glen Larson, titled *Masquerade*. This unintentionally hilarious parody of their greatest achievement opened with the now middle-aged Rod Taylor (of *Time Machine* fame) inviting the viewers to "Come spy with me!," as a montage of twenty-year-old spy clichés rolled on and he recruited dumb schmucks from the sticks to bring their special skills to global espionage capers. What made *Masquerade* funny was that crucially, and unlike *Mission: Impossible*, produced in more naive times, the convoluted ploys weren't remotely necessary—a bullet, bomb or fast car could have completed the job far more efficiently and effectively, as could even, in a couple of instances, a little old-fashioned diplomacy.

However, *The Time Tunnel* was one show that could rival the ill-fated *Masquerade* for lunacy. Watch out for the outrageous scene when Security Officer Jiggs slips back through time to help out Tony by machine-gunning a few Trojan soldiers ... only to re-emerge in the present day a wizened old man. So elated are the scientists to see him return safely a second time, that in another mad moment, they also inadvertently let one of the combatants back too, who wields a mean sword. The sequence—and unconsidered implications—of this single military po-liceman floating out of the sky and spraying bullets into sword-flailing warriors on the plains of Greece is quite extraordinary.

This episode is littered with performers who frequently worked with Allen. Dee Hartford was related to Allen's old pal Grou-cho Marx (Marx was one of many who put money into Lost in Space). She appeared sev-eral times in Lost in Space, as well as Land of the Giants, but she wasn't only in Irwin Allen productions. Other work in the '60s in-cluded The Twilight Zone, The Outer Limits, The Girl from UNCLE, and Batman.

Joseph Ruskin, a familiar TV face of the '60s, appeared as a genie in The Twilight Zone ("The Man in the Bottle") and as an alien being in Star Trek's legendary camp clas-sic "The Gamesters of Triskellion." He was in both seasons of Land of the Giants, a car-nival owner in "Terror-go-Round" for the first year, and a hawkish general in "Secret City of Limbo" during the second. The per-fect example of an actor condemned to vil-lainy because of his looks (he was once ar-rested by an eventually embarrassed cop who "knew his face from somewhere"), he's on top form as the villainous Sardis.

The gentle-voiced elderly character actor Abraham Sofaer has been frequently seen in 1950s fantasy films and 1960s SF TV, often in minor but significant and memo-rable parts. His weak, watery eyes cast him often in victim roles, but he could light 'em up and play fearsome when he wanted to. He had a recurring role in I Dream of Jean-nie, and appeared twice in Time Tunnel (re-turning for "The Walls of Jericho"). Other

roles included The Twilight Zone, Boris Karloff's Thriller, The Outer Limits, The Man from UNCLE, Star Trek, The Girl from UNCLE, Lost in Space, and Kolchak: the Night Stalker. Most memorably he was the wizard in Captain Sindbad.

Paul Carr, who has a more substantial role in this episode after a minor role in "The End of the World" as the leader of the trapped miners, appeared as an ill-fated crew member in "Where No Man Has Gone Be-fore," the first episode of Star Trek, and as a murderous photographer in "Framed" for Land of the Giants. He made a number of ap-pearances in Voyage to the Bottom of the Sea, and other roles include a classic Invaders ("The Innocent"), The Green Hornet, Get Smart, Circle of Fear, The Six Million Dollar Man, Logan's Run, The Amazing Spider-Man, Time Express, The Incredible Hulk, Buck Rogers in the 25th Century, and Airwolf.

John Doucette appeared three times in the 1950s Adventures of Superman series, and twice in Get Smart (the hilarious "The King Lives" and its sequel "To Sire with Love"). Other roles included guest shots in The Wild Wild West, Kolchak: the Night Stalker, and the unsold late '70s pilot The Time Machine. Kevin Hagen, later to play Inspector Kobick in Allen's Land of the Giants, makes the first of no less than four appearances in The Time Tunnel, (matching the number of appear-ances by John Crawford, with whom he ap-peared twice). Here, in a brief walk-on, he's a Greek warrior.

There are several funny behind-the-scenes stories relating to this episode ... In a Starlog interview, Paul Carr recalled his time as Paris "...in the most outlandish cos-tume you've ever seen ... I walked into the commissary wearing these flowing robes with all this make-up and a head full of curls—I mean, you could have scraped the make-up off with a shovel—and I ran into an old friend who was producing a picture at Fox. He looked up at me very casually and said 'Hi, Paul. Workin'?'!" In Epilog, a strange but useful fanzine of the early '90s, bit player Pat Culliton recalled the scene in which James Darren has a sword fight with Joseph Ruskin. In the script, Colbert's Doug offers to take on Sardis, but Darren's Tony replies that as the sword was thrown to him, he'll take the challenge. In the first take, Ruskin's sword apparently fell between the two of them, and Colbert and Darren jokingly bickered about who the sword was thrown to until the exasperated director shouted "cut"! Well—maybe you had to be there.... Production number: 9604.

Massacre

wr. Carey Wilber, dir. Murray Golden

Doug and Tony have the misfortune to attend Custer's last stand, while the Tunnel complex inadvertently snatches up one of the winning team.

With Joe Maross (General George Armstrong Custer), Lawrence Montaigne (Yellow Elk), Christopher Dark (Crazy Horse), George Mitchell (Sitting Bull), Perry Lopez (Dr. Whitebird), Paul Comi (Captain Benteen), Jim Halferty (Tim McGinnis), John Pickard (Major Reno), Bruce Mars (Tom Custer)

LOCATION: Little Big Horn and surrounding areas, the Indian Wars, June 24th, 25th, 1876.

20th Century Fox were no strangers to the western genre, having produced many conventional western films and series, and their large supply of sets, stock footage, locations and actors well versed with the traditions of the genre ensured that the western episodes of *The Time Tunnel* ("Massacre," "The Alamo," "Visitors from Beyond the Stars," and "Billy the Kid") looked as polished and professional as any regular western adventure from their studios. Indeed, any casual channel-zapper could quite easily have mistaken the shows for standard westerns, and received quite a shock when the aliens or *Time Tunnel* control center suddenly appeared! There are no science-fiction trappings in this episode, other than the Tunnel itself, which in this episode inadvertently snatches up a Native American brave

who thinks he's visited that great hunting ground in the sky!

Numerous versions of both Custer's life and the events at Little Big Horn have been filmed over the years, many of them just as fanciful as some of the events in this episode! With Custer as a central figure played by the leading man, many of those films were obliged to make apologies for Custer, or in some cases saw nothing to apologize for. By the 1960s, historians and counter culture alike were doing a little digging, and many were not impressed by some of the bones they dug up. As *The Time Tunnel* already had its two leading men as the heroes, it was not obliged to fudge about Custer or cast an image-conscious actor. Consequently, Joe Maross not only gives, like Carroll O'Connor in the earlier "The Last Patrol," one of the best performances of his career, but Custer is presented with some degree of honesty. Maross even looks like we might imagine Custer to have been (although history, as ever, has the last laugh, as photos of Custer show him to be a scrawny, worried-looking, ridiculous figure, highly unphotogenic for Hollywood purposes!). Without descending into preachy rhetoric like so many of the later guilt-ridden, handwringing anti-westerns that were just waiting round the corner in 1966, "Massacre" presents a balanced and historically fair account of the period, and Maross captures just the right mix of Custer's integrity, vanity, and stupidity, giving a subdued and powerful reading of Carey Wilber's script while making the emotional most of his few moments center-stage. He's easily the best Custer to date, even allowing for Richard Mulligan's fine effort four years later in the big screen feature *Little Big Man*, and—as in all the *Time Tunnel* westerns—the stock footage is integrated flawlessly (although 1960s TV restrictions ensure that it's a very clean and bloodless battlefield at the end).

Author Carey Wilber was quite a character, and something of an enigma as far as his writing was concerned. His career in SF TV started with work as a scriptwriter for *Captain Video* in the 1950s, and he was a frequent contributor to *Lost in Space* in the 1960s. *Star Trek* snobs will be dismayed to learn that several Irwin Allen writers contributed to *Star Trek's* first season, and Wilber's contribution was the excellent "Space Seed," which lead indirectly to the second *Star Trek* feature, *Star Trek II: The Wrath of Khan.* Wilber once claimed that he never watched his own episodes of a series, because he always knew what was going to happen! But, he said, he made an exception for *Lost in Space!*

Wilber's *Time Tunnels* are a mixed bunch from start to finish, mixing serious attempts at historical accuracy and genuine drama with pulp sci-fi and Hollywood-style period romps. While "Massacre" employed and enjoyed all the clichés of the western genre, particularly in the scenes at the Sioux camp, where the dialogue is a treat, it was a commendable effort toward authenticity and dramatic tension. If his second effort, "Chase Through Time," shared at least the dramatic tension and required no efforts toward historical accuracy, it beggars belief that the man who turned out "Massacre" could then hand in a farrago like "Town of Terror" for the same series. To produce "The Deadly Toys" for a series like *Wonder Woman,* his last found fantasy credit, is simply to understand the nature and requirements of the series; to deliver "Town of Terror" after submitting "Massacre" and "Chase Through Time" suggests it was written in the delirium of a fever! To praise "Massacre," one can point to "Space Seed." To explain "Town of Terror," one can single out *Lost in Space* turkey "The Questing Beast." But how can one explain Carey Wilber?

There is a glum postscript to this episode. Although "Massacre" takes the more modern accepted view that Custer was a pompous vainglorious fool, the following year Fox produced a short-lived series which pre-

sented him as a heroic figure. A bitter irony was that *The Time Tunnel* was tentatively renewed for a second season before a change in the ABC hierarchy caused a last minute reshuffle of the schedule that left *The Time Tunnel* out, and the new series, *The Legend of Custer,* commissioned from Fox in its place. Many of the *Time Tunnel* writers were moved to *Custer,* including Shimon Wincelberg, Bob and Wanda Duncan, and—ironically—the writer of this episode, Carey Wilber. With America slowly but surely wising up to the assumptions of western myth during the '60s, and reassessing their historical figures, the timing could not have been worse, and *The Legend of Custer* died midseason. Despite an excellent cast and production values, the series was as self-deceiving, and failed as badly, as the man himself—the public were just not buying Custer as a hero any more, and the network's own misjudgment had cost *The Time Tunnel* its place in the 1967–'68 schedule.

The performances in this episode are uniformly excellent, and as mentioned above, include a fine portrayal of George Armstrong Custer by Joe Maross, veteran of two good *Twilight Zone* stories, "Third from the Sun" and "The Little People," and the town sheriff in the memorable "Valley of the Shadow" for *The Invaders.* Paul Comi's other SF TV roles include three episodes of *The Twilight Zone,* two *Voyage to the Bottom of the Sea* ("Submarine Sunk Here" and "Deadly Creature Below"), *Star Trek* ("Balance of Terror"), and *The Invaders* ("Storm" and "The Life Seekers"). John Pickard mostly worked in more traditional westerns, but also appeared in *Land of the Giants* ("The Flight Plan"). Christopher Dark appeared in the SF time travel film *World Without End.* Other TV roles include *The Green Hornet, Mr. Terrific,* and *Land of the Giants* ("The Deadly Dart").

Lawrence Montaigne was a Romulan in *Star Trek's* "Balance of Terror," and a Vulcan in "Amok Time." He would show up again in *The Time Tunnel* in "Idol of Death." Other credits include *The Outer Limits, The Man from UNCLE, The Invaders, Batman,* and *Voyage to the Bottom of the Sea* ("Man-Beast"). Perry Lopez also appeared again in *The Time Tunnel* in "Night of the Long Knives," and in "Savage Jungle" for *Voyage to the Bottom of the Sea.* Other credits include *Star Trek, The Wild Wild West, The Man from UNCLE,* and *Airwolf.* Youthful Bruce Mars, a fair-haired football jock type, also appeared in "Killers of the Deep" and "The Abominable Snowman" for *Voyage to the Bottom of the Sea* and "Shore Leave" and "Assignment: Earth" for *Star Trek.* Young Jim Halferty also appeared in the excellent *Invaders* episode, "Nightmare."

What can you say about a guy who can play a Scotsman in *Voyage to the Bottom of the Sea* ("Secret of the Loch"), Chief Sitting Bull in *Time Tunnel,* and a murderous hick farmer in *Land of the Giants* ("Six Hours to Live")? Only that the elderly George Mitchell was another of those invaluable all-purpose character actors so scarce today. You've never heard of him, you wouldn't recognize him, and yet his numerous acting jobs included four *Twilight Zones* and two *Boris Karloff's Thriller.*

This was to be director Murray Golden's only contribution to *The Time Tunnel.* The previous season he had worked on the pulpy *Honey West* series and stayed with the bizarre to direct episodes of *Batman, The Green Hornet, The Invaders,* and *Star Trek,* the latter of which found him regular work on companion Desilu series *Mission: Impossible.* Production number: 9609.

Devil's Island

wr. Bob and Wanda Duncan, dir. Jerry Hopper
Doug and Tony arrive on the legendary penal colony Devil's Island just in time to inadvertently take the place of two fleeing convicts.

With Marcel Hillaire (Henri Boudaire), Oscar Beregi (Commandant), Theo Marcuse (Lescoux), Steven Geray (Perrault), Alaine Patrice (Claude), Ted Roter (Captain Dreyfus), Bob Adler (weakened prisoner)

LOCATION: 15th March, 1895, French Guyana.

Writers Bob and Wanda Duncan contributed most of the sillier episodes of Allen's *Lost in Space,* but contributed nine much better episodes to the thirty that made up *The Time Tunnel,* although this episode was a very poor follow-up to their excellent "The Last Patrol." The Duncans were never strong on logic, and the major flaw here lies in Doug and Tony's behavior once they have been captured and imprisoned. They *know* that all they have to do is sit tight in one spot until the Time Tunnel scientists get a fix and shift them, but instead of staying put, they start running around, lashing out, and generally causing trouble for themselves and everybody else around them, going through considerable hardship in the process. Most stupid of all, they attempt to escape with the prisoners ... but where are they escaping to, and why? The same irritating carelessness manifests itself in other contributions by the Duncans, notably "Kill Two by Two," which has the same flaw, and the enjoyable "The Death Merchant." Most frustrating of all is that all these flaws could have been excised with a few flicks of the pen; in almost every case, a couple of lines of dialogue could have justified the otherwise absurd actions that occur. For example, at the Time Tunnel base, the starving convict Henri Boudaire—plucked from Devil's Island by the Tunnel in error—is provided with a trolley of food, but is then returned to the past without eating from it!

Marcel Hillaire, although invariably cast as comedy Frenchmen (this is one of his few straight dramatic roles), was in actuality an Austrian actor who fled to America to escape the Nazis. He appears in many, many Hollywood productions of the 1960s portraying the archetypal French official and has a starring role in the *I Spy* episode "Chrysanthemum" as a bungling spy (would-be comedy episodes of normally serious shows are almost always awful, and this one is no exception; a little of Hillaire's performance goes a long way). Hillaire is less overbearing and more welcome when he plays bit parts or supporting roles. His other credits include *The Twilight Zone*, *The Man from UNCLE*, *The Girl from UNCLE* (all twice), and *Get Smart*. He was a prisoner once more for Allen the following year, when found frozen in suspended animation for his crimes on a floating penitentiary in space in the third season *Lost in Space* story "The Condemned of Space." He returned to *Lost in Space* that season for the final episode in the series, as the Junkman in "Junkyard of Space."

The episode is further hampered by being one of the more obviously stagebound stories, and there is no stock footage; the desert island set in this episode is familiar from *Voyage to the Bottom of the Sea*, and had already been seen in "The Crack of Doom." It is later employed in "Pirates of Dead Man's Island," while the prison uniforms were later utilized in the amusing *Lost in Space* episode "Fugitives in Space." They were initially—and accurately—red and white, but wisely dyed a more photogenic grey at the last minute.

The episode's saving grace is the presence of two of 1960s TV's best and busiest bad guys. Oscar Beregi appeared briefly in "No Way Out" for *Voyage to the Bottom of the Sea*, and notched up three appearances in *The Twilight Zone*. Big, bad, and Germanic, he was inevitably cast as a villain, and "Devil's Island" was neither his first or his last evil commandant role. Other roles included two episodes of *The Man from UNCLE*, three *The Wild Wild West*, several *Get Smart* and episodes of *The Girl from UNCLE* and *Batman*.

From bit parts in the anthology shows and the *Voyage to the Bottom of the Sea* pilot (from which he was virtually excised), Theo Marcuse moved up to larger roles later on (most memorably the wizard Korob in the Hallowe'en *Star Trek*, "Catspaw"). His small,

shifty eyes invariably cast him as a villain (his part in "Devil's Island" was typical fare for him), but a rare sympathetic role had him as a tortured scientist in "The Leeches," one of the grimmest—and best—of *The Invaders*.

This was the only episode of *Time Tunnel* directed by Jerry Hopper, best known for numerous westerns and tenures on *Burke's Law* (1963–'65) and *The Addams Family* (1964–'66). It's directorially undistinguished, and he was put to far better use helming some of the dafter episodes of *Voyage to the Bottom of the Sea*. The Dreyfus affair remains a sore subject for discussion to the French government even today; needless to say for 1960s television, only a vague injustice that the viewers are asked to take on faith is hinted at, and the anti-Semitism that put Dreyfus on the island in the first place was not addressed. Production number: 9611

Reign of Terror

wr. William Welch, dir. Sobey Martin

> *Tony joins forces with monarchists when Doug is captured as an aristocrat during the French Revolution, while a curious time paradox causes them to miss a chance to return home, and General Kirk to meet one of his ancestors.*

With David Opatoshu (Blanchard), Monique Lemaire (Marie Antoinette), Louis Mercier (Simon), Patrick Michenaud (Dauphin), Joey Tata (Napoleon Bonaparte)

LOCATION: Autumn, 1793, Paris, France.

During the course of *The Time Tunnel*, the two lost scientists returned to base on only two occasions—once in "The Crack of Doom," when Tony was brought back by a power surge, only to find his colleagues in 1968 frozen in a time warp, and again by magic in "Merlin the Magician," when both scientists were frozen themselves and unaware they'd even returned. Both episodes were written by the prolific William Welch, Allen's busy right-hand man. The scientists in the 1968 base themselves were never reunited with their time-traveling colleagues (except on one occasion when Ann time-traveled to the far future in Welch's "The Kidnappers"), although they did bring back seven other individuals, plus two bombs and one ghost! Of these seven (in "Revenge of the Gods," "Massacre," "Devil's Island," "Reign of Terror," "The Death Trap," "The Alamo," and "Pirates of Dead Man's Island"), only one was transported to the Time Tunnel base deliberately, and that was Querque, in this episode.

In "Reign of Terror," the Time Tunnel scientists learn the folly of sending even individual items back through time, when an antique ring General Kirk inherited from his family is intended to be used as an irradiated focal point with which to zero in on Doug and Tony, but instead turns out to be employed as evidence against Marie Antoinette to justify her execution. In a cruel twist of fate, Doug and Tony betray themselves to an official of the French Authorities who looks exactly like Kirk—it's his ancestor (played by Whit Bissell in a dual role), and the ring has traveled in a complete loop, passed through the ages to Kirk from his ancestors, but given to his ancestors by Kirk via the Time Tunnel.

It's an interesting episode with good sets, lighting, costumes, and cast (but watch out for the rubber lamp-post in the street fight). There's also one of the closest calls ever for the two time-travelers, who invariably departed time periods in a hurry (thus explaining why the Tunnel scientists never had time to get a proper fix to bring them back to base; critics of the series were fond of pointing out that the scientists seemed to be able to bring back anybody and everybody except their own two men, but as Ray Swain pointed out in the pilot, "it's only a matter of time"!)—here, they avoid a hail of bullets by a split-second.

One minor aspect of the story seems to be not thought out. As Kirk originally has possession of his ring in order to be able to send it back through time to Doug and Tony, it's a mystery as to why it's deemed

necessary to show the ring disappearing from his ancestor's finger at the close of the episode. If Kirk's ancestor *doesn't* retain the ring that has been sent back to him, how will he be able to pass it on to his descendants, and how will Kirk have it in 1968? The only (needlessly convoluted) explanation is that Kirk was given the ring by another branch of his family, and the ring returns to Kirk at story's end. On the other hand, if Querque got the ring from Kirk, and then passed it through *his* descendants to Kirk, where did the ring initially come from? The true explanation is probably just simple carelessness. However, the revelation that the chief of the French authorities is a lookalike for Kirk is cleverly concealed from first time audiences, and the sequence in which Kirk and Querque meet is similarly skillfully handled through the available trick photography techniques of the time. It's all done rather well. There are no rough edges on the technical side, even if the credibility of the coincidences in this yarn seems as bendy as the street lamp.

Whit Bissell does a fair job of portraying his ancestor; everyone speaks that comical language of Hollywood, Frenchman's English, but this is surely more practical than the unthinkable for TV, an entire episode in subtitles—consequently, one can only assume that Doug and Tony can speak fluent French (not to mention Latin, Greek, etc.) among their many talents! More bothersome than such unavoidable dramatic license are the scenes back at the Tunnel where the 20th century Kirk tries to deal with the behavior of his ancestor, which are handled clumsily, as though Kirk is somehow personally responsible for the repugnant and reprehensible actions of his ancestor. Ann's childish amusement in particular at Kirk's discomfort seems absurdly out of place. Also out of place, although standard for the series' own time period, is the squeamishness of Ann in some scenes; Meriwether was often obliged to play the helpless female card during the series' run, a now unfashionable trademark of the times that dates the show as surely and as slightly as Kirk's occasional cigarette. It is good to see the guest cast loaded with names of French origin though. Monique Lemaire had previously appeared in a *Voyage to the Bottom of the Sea* episode ("The Magnus Beam"), and at around the same time as her *Time Tunnel* appeared in *Batman* ("The Thirteenth Hat"/ "Batman Stands Pat"). Patrick Michenaud was the older brother of Gerald Michenaud, the little French lad on board the *Titanic* in the pilot. Patrick also secured a minor footnote in SF TV history as the young boy who briefly grabs hold of the *Spindrift* spacecraft in flight in "The Crash," the pilot episode of *Land of the Giants.*

Of the other players, David Opatoshu has numerous SF TV credits to his name, and had previously worked for Allen on *Voyage to the Bottom of the Sea* ("The Price of Doom"). Tiger Joe Marsh is credited as the executioner, but in the finished program we do not see anything but a brief shadow. It's possible that a filmed scene was cut before completion, either by the studio or by the network. More on Tiger Joe in the section on "The Walls of Jericho," where his performance survives. Joey Tata, a busy bit player at Fox in the 1960s most gainfully employed on the sets of *Batman* and *Voyage to the Bottom of the Sea*, appears briefly here as the young Napoleon and returns as a member of the French Resistance in "Invasion." He also appeared in episodes of *The Outer Limits*, and as a biker in "Collision of the Planets" for *Lost in Space*. During the 1990s, he had a recurring role as the owner of a soda bar on the teen show *Beverly Hills 90210*. Production number: 9612.

Secret Weapon

wr. Theodore Apstein, dir. Sobey Martin

The Time Tunnel scientists stumble onto the existence of a Russian time tunnel experiment in 1956, and manage to send Doug and Tony to the location ... only to have them consigned to a fate as guinea-pigs in a time travel experiment that is doomed to be fatal.

With Nehemiah Persoff (Dr. Biraki), Michael Ansara (Colonel Hruda), Gregory Gay (Alexis), Russ Conway (General Parker), Kevin Hagen (McDonnell)

LOCATION: Somewhere in Eastern Europe, June 16th, 1956.

"Secret Weapon" is one of the most unusual and enjoyable episodes in the series, cleverly utilizing the standing set of the Time Tunnel, which does double duty as the Iron Curtain Tunnel. There's a popular theory in scientific circles nicknamed the steam engine principle, which suggests that progress is inevitable and inexorable, that certain inventions are due to be discovered at certain times; that if Stevenson, for example, had not discovered the steam engine when he did, someone else would have stumbled onto the idea at around the same time. The notion of a Communist-controlled Time Tunnel, devised at the height of the Cold War, is an irresistibly exciting and provocative concept, and fits in neatly with the unwritten rules that *The Time Tunnel* set itself regarding Doug and Tony's participation in history (that history was immutable and they were already part of it). This inspired conceit, along with the usual madly deranged performance from Nehemiah Persoff, who could always be counted on to go wild-eyed over-the-top, makes the episode supremely enjoyable. At one point, Persoff's Biraki, as the head scientist of the Communist time travel project, asks Doug and Tony "Tell me—have your scientists come anywhere near to sending a man through time?," completely oblivious to the fact that he is talking to humankind's premiere time-travelers; the only regret of the story is that he never gets to discover that his two guinea-pigs were already traveling in time—to him! Witnesses of his glorious stunned, outsmarted, and defeated routine at the close of his assorted *Mission: Impossible* appearances will know exactly what I mean.

Contrasting Persoff's manic hamming are two laid-back gloating performances by Michael Ansara and Gregory Gay as two typical Cold War bad guys in the best tradition of Hollywood espionage thrillers. While Persoff chews the scenery (no doubt the Time Tunnel control center still carries his teethmarks), these two stand smirking as only truly evil Cold Warriors can...

By cleverly removing much of the dressing on the standing Tunnel set to make it look more basic and then relighting it, "Secret Weapon" was conveniently and effortlessly provided with a new set from the series' main standing set. Writer Theodore Apstein, in his only contribution to any of the Allen series, had ingeniously provided Allen with a relatively cheap episode on request, and *The Time Tunnel* with one of its most extraordinary and clever yarns, while director Sobey Martin wisely shoots the otherwise familiar set from a different angle. Given Allen's appreciation for a buck saved rather than a buck spent, it is curious that this was Apstein's only contribution to the Allen canon, but his initial story idea, concerning a meeting with Christopher Columbus in 1492, had apparently been rejected on the grounds of cost and in an interview with *Starlog* magazine, he expressed disappointment with the cost cuts made on the finished "Secret Weapon."

In fact, whatever might have been in Apstein's imagination, "Secret Weapon" looks good. The pre-credits sequence is particularly interesting, with the Time Tunnel control scientists experimenting with sending messages to the time travelers inside glowing red bricks which melt on arrival. These are a fabulous idea that provide a lively opening, although one wonders what would have happened if anyone had actually seen these noisy little packages arriving in the street. Another pleasure of the episode is that the time travelers have not been dropped into any particularly notable period of history, but just materialized at random; it stretched credibility somewhat for Doug and Tony to always show up on the eve of some momentous historical event, even if it was a necessity of the format. The only other time this happened in the series was at the beginning of "Chase Through Time," although one assumes the boys enjoyed other uneventful stopovers between the assorted catastrophes and bloodbaths they were catapulted into. What is not made clear is whether Doug and Tony were deposited in June of 1956 in Eastern Europe deliberately for the mission, which the Tunnel is not supposed to be capable of, or whether it is just a happy but unlikely coincidence that the Pentagon just happens to hear about as Biraki is knocking on their door. The series' format suggests chance.

Biraki's time capsule is later re-used in another above-average story, "Chase Through Time" (it also doubles as a frog-alien's transport in the *Lost in Space* episode "The Golden Man"). The European street (also used in "Reign of Terror," among others) will be familiar to viewers of *The Green Hornet*, the Fox series which preceded *Time Tunnel* in the ABC network's schedule—the street is seen in stock footage of the Hornet's car, the Black Beauty, speeding along after emerging from its secret hideaway, and these scenes can be seen in a number of *Green Hornet* episodes including "The Ray Is for Killing" and "Programmed for Death" to name but two.

Of the cast, Michael Ansara—shaven-headed for a theatrical engagement in *The King and I* (as he was in the *Voyage to the Bottom of the Sea* episode "Killers of the Deep," filmed within months of this episode)—is marvelous as the menacing and ruthless Hruda. Frequently appearing in SF TV, he would return to the series as a silver-skinned alien in "The Kidnappers."

Nehemiah Persoff was also rarely absent from the screen for long during the 1960s, usually cast as a loveable vulnerable immigrant or screaming villain. He's okay here, but seems uncertain at times whether he's a Russian or a Nazi! Nevertheless, it's an energetic and exhausting performance to watch. He played a convict in "Deadly Creature Below," an episode of *Voyage to the Bottom of the Sea* for the same director, and plays a character remarkably similar to Biraki (even lit the same way) in the fourth season *Man from UNCLE* episode "The Master's Touch Affair." He was also particularly memorable as the evil U-boat commander who gets his just deserts in the *Twilight Zone* episode "Judgement Day," after sinking a non-combatant passenger ship in a story presumably based on the sinking of the *Lusitania*. He was gainfully employed during the spy mania of the '60s, and spent the '70s confronting various TV super-heroes. Other credits include *The Wild Wild West*, *Land of the Giants* ("Land of the Lost"), *The Invisible Man*, *The Six Million Dollar Man*, *Wonder Woman*, *Logan's Run*, *The Bionic Woman*, *Battlestar Galactica*, and *Star Trek: The Next Generation*.

Russ Conway (no relation to the '60s crooner) came from Allen's stock supply of middle-aged figures of high-rank officialdom. His films included *Abbott and Costello Meet the Invisible Man*, *Abbott and Costello Go to Mars*, *War of the Worlds*, *Flight to Mars*, and *Our Man Flint*. On TV, he turned up in *The Munsters*, *The Green Hornet*, and *The Invaders*. Kevin Hagen, in his second of four *Time Tunnel* roles, hasn't much to do, but was always welcome in an Allen production for the integrity he brought to even the smallest role (however, nitpickers will note that a bit of business he devises with a cigarette inadvertently produces a minor continuity error in one scene). Gregory Gay's main claim to fame in the fantasy arena is as the evil Mota in the 1951 serial *Flying Disc Man from Mars*. He was also the recurring villain the Ruler in the 1955 *Commando Cody* TV episodes. His film credits include the '50s B-movie *The Creature with the Atom Brain*.

Although "Secret Weapon" aired in November 1966, it was actually made much earlier (and near the *Voyage* episode), as evidenced by the inclusion of clips from the story in promo films for *The Time Tunnel* in the first episode. Possibly, as a strong episode, it was held over for sweeps week, which would have been sometime around its November airdate. If so, this may have been a tactical error, as without any specific historical time period to appeal, it is very much an episode for hardcore fans of time travel and *Time Tunnel*. Production number: 9605.

The Death Trap

wr. Leonard Stadd, dir. William Hale

Doug and Tony stumble onto a fanatical plot to kill Abraham Lincoln four years before the time travelers know he will die.

With Scott Marlowe (Jeremiah), Tom Skerritt (Matthew), Ford Rainey (Abraham Lincoln), R.G. Armstrong (Pinkerton), Christopher Harris (David), Richard Geary (Carver)

LOCATION: February 22nd, 1861, Baltimore, USA.

An intriguing adventure, the most interesting aspect being the way the Time Tunnel assumes almost mystical significance here, with the implication that the time travelers are part of some pre-ordained destiny, or Grand Plan. Doug and Tony are not intruding on history, or interfering with it; as in the later "The Walls of Jericho" and others, they are *part* of it. The Tunnel scientists even get a useful glimpse of Lincoln's true demise before the picture shifts back to Doug and Tony.

Honest Abe Lincoln has long been a favorite figure for film-makers given his stature and distinctive appearance, chalking up time travel story credits in *The Twilight Zone* ("Back There"), *Doctor Who* ("The Chase"), *Voyagers* ("The Day the Rebs Took Lincoln"), and syndicated sit-com *Out of This World* ("Honest Evie" and "The Secret of Evie's Success"). But Lincoln's most bizarre posthumous appearance—even above his appearance in the 1989 time travel teen movie

Bill and Ted's Excellent Adventure—must surely have been in the absurd but enjoyable *Star Trek* episode "The Savage Curtain," in which an image of the famed U.S. President appears in space before the startled crew of the starship *Enterprise*, sitting sagely in repose as his statue does in Washington.

To avoid making the plotters of "The Death Trap"—two misguided brothers—racists who oppose Lincoln's promise to end slavery, or Secessionists who want to split the Union of the States, Stadd makes them over-zealous abolitionists in the John Brown tradition who feel that Lincoln will not deliver. Plot-wise, the highlights of the episode are Doug's meeting and conversation with Lincoln about the future (a strong performance by Ford Rainey) and the Tunnel's inadvertent snatching of young David, who is unwittingly holding an explosive device big enough to seriously damage the Tunnel, but understandably too terrified to believe the frantic pleas of the scientists to hand it over. The scene showing the Ford Theatre in 1865, as President Lincoln is assassinated, seems gratuitous and pointless and looks suspiciously like available stock footage (it's a different Lincoln, not Rainey); there's no reason for the Tunnel to suddenly acquire a mind of its own and leap forward, and for the ignorant few unaware of Lincoln's fate, it would have been enough to refer to it.

This is the first of three *Time Tunnel* episodes by Leonard Stadd, who also submitted two of the most *outre* later episodes, "The Revenge of Robin Hood" and "The Ghost of Nero." Next to those two little gems, this one is quite sober. It's also the episode that gave birth to Irwin Allen's much-quoted remark about *The Time Tunnel* being "a running and jumping show." Initially, there had been much more of a poignant discourse with Lincoln about the future, which both Stadd and director William Hale had wanted left in. Some of this remains, and is good stuff, but without seeing the original script it's difficult to

know who was right when Allen said to move on with the action. Either way, Stadd's three scripts worked well, and he had a good grasp of what *The Time Tunnel* was about, and was adept at exploiting the concept to the maximum with imagination and ingenuity without copying other writers' formulae. Stadd also contributed some equally creative and unusual *Man from UNCLE* episodes, including "The Discotheque Affair," "The Maze Affair," and "The Deep Six Affair." On both *The Time Tunnel* and *The Man from UNCLE*, Stadd could always be counted on to come up with an angle the series' other writers hadn't touched on.

Scott Marlowe appeared twice in *The Outer Limits*, in two classic episodes, "It Crawled Out of the Woodwork" and "The Form of Things Unknown" and *The Wild Wild West* ("The Night of the Howling Light"). Other credits include *Circle of Fear*, *Wonder Woman*, *Automan*, *Beauty and the Beast*, and *Freddy's Nightmares*. Tom Skerritt is today best known to sci-fi buffs as the ill-fated Captain of the *Nostromo* in *Alien*. SF TV fans are more likely to remember him in the superior *Kolchak: the Night Stalker* episode "The Devil's Platform" than for his brief appearance in an early episode of *Voyage to the Bottom of the Sea*, "The Enemies"; to everyone else, he's best known for a recurring role in *Cheers* and as the lead in the 1990s series *Picket Fences*. R.G. Armstrong's SF TV credits include *The Twilight Zone*, *The Invaders*, *Darkroom*, *Quantum Leap*, and a recurring role in *Friday the 13th—the series*. Richard Geary has appeared in *The Twilight Zone*, *The Girl from UNCLE*, *Star Trek*, and *Kolchak: the Night Stalker*. No further SF TV credits could be found for young Christopher Harris.

Ford Rainey, who portrays Lincoln, also appeared in *Voyage to the Bottom of the Sea* during its first season as the U.S. President, in the episodes "Hot Line" and "Doomsday." He played the U.S. President once more in the pilot for *Lost in Space* and makes a grand Lincoln—almost too grand, as we know Lincoln was thinner and not gifted with the resonant voice we imagine. As with Joe Maross as Custer in "Massacre," Rainey is more like Lincoln than Lincoln was! Meaning, of course, he lives up to our expectations rather than the boring reality. Rainey often found himself typecast as authoritative figures—he was the traitorous General Blaine in "Summit Meeting," a two-part story for *The Invaders* and cast as General Atwood in the promo reel for the aborted Allen series *The Man from the 25th Century*, starring *Time Tunnel's* James Darren.

Director William Hale's career is actually a curious mix of sci-fi and cops, with a brief run on the western series *Lancer* to confuse. This was his third of four *Time Tunnel* assignments, the others being "The Day the Sky Fell In," "The Crack of Doom," and "The Revenge of Robin Hood." His odd mix of dissimilar *Time Tunnels* boast some wonderful performances (but then so do many other episodes), while his *Invaders*, nothing special in comparison with other episodes of that series, resulted in further non-SF work for cop show king of the '70s Quinn Martin. Despite a wealth of work for Fox in the '60s and QM in the '70s, Hale did not devote himself exclusively to any one studio or *genre*. He was either adventurous or apathetic—the occasional flash of brilliance suggests the former.

The set for the brothers' home is used again, slightly shuffled around, for the rancher's home in "Visitors from Beyond the Stars." Trivia buffs may also be interested to know that Doug and Tony had a go at averting the assassination of Lincoln in the first issue of Western Publishing's two *Time Tunnel* comic books under the Gold Key imprint. Production number: 9613.

The Alamo

wr. Bob and Wanda Duncan, dir. Sobey Martin
   Doug and Tony inadvertently cause dissent within the ranks of the troops at the Alamo, when they try and warn the doomed Texan fort of the impending attack of the Mexican army.

With Rhodes Reason (Colonel William Travis), John Lupton (Captain Reynerson), Jim Davis (Colonel Jim Bowie), Rodolfo Hoyos (Captain Rodriguez), Edward Colmans (Dr. Armandez), Alberto Monte (Sergeant Garcia), Elizabeth Rogers (Mrs. Reynerson)
   LOCATION: Mexico, March 5th/6th, 1836.

A thoroughly enjoyable episode, belonging mostly to Robert Colbert, whose earnest smoothtalking to save as many necks as possible, and despondency and dismay as he realizes where he and Doug have materialized in the pre-credits sequence, contribute highlights to the episode. Darren's adventures outside the mission-turned-fort are less gripping, but make an intriguing diversion, while Travis' visit to the 20th century to foresee a fate not too well obscured in the first place is given power and resonance by Rhodes Reason's well-considered performance.

The Duncans' intelligent script does its best to stick to the fuzzy and contradictory facts of this futile and pathetic brave stand that, like so many famous military fiascos, has since become embellished and glorified by legend; ten years after this episode was filmed, the history of this event was still being researched and rewritten, and scholars and other more partisan individuals are still arguing over the minutiae today. The only major departure from confirmed fact is that the battle of the Alamo (Spanish for Cottonwood, a type of tree) took place in the darkness, in the early hours of the morning before dawn—here, the battle takes place in daylight. What is known is that 189 men died defending the former mission, the "back door" into Mexico, and that 600 Mexican troops under Santa Anna died taking it. One month later, Texans took an equally bloody and dismaying revenge, and Santa Anna surrendered.

The events of the Alamo have been immortalized in film before, most memorably in 1960, in John Wayne's intelligent and reverential *The Alamo*, a personal project of his. Other SF TV treatments include the 1985 time travel story "Alamo Jobe" in *Amazing Stories* and the 1987 *Once a Hero* episode "Remember the Cottonwood." The Duncans do not indulge in the legendary line-drawing of Travis immortalized in the John Wayne movie when the defenders know that reinforcements are unlikely to arrive ... but they find it difficult to have Jim Bowie die helpless in his sickbed without recreating the famous scene from the painting immortalizing and romanticizing his demise at the Alamo. Crockett, however, does not appear—the Duncans have written him out of the final battle, suggesting, as does history, that he died a couple of days earlier.

Rhodes Reason, who also appeared in the memorable "Bread and Circuses" episode of *Star Trek*, would return to play what amounted to a cameo as the Biblical character Joshua in "The Walls of Jericho." Although he looks nothing like the real Travis, who was a small, thin man with a moustache, he is excellent in a role that has attained near-mythical status. Again, this is not so much how Travis was, as how he should have been. Rhodes Reason was the older brother of Rex Reason, leading man of *This Island Earth* and *The Creature Walks Among Us*, and if it wasn't for a 1989 interview in *Starlog* confirming this, you could be forgiven for thinking they were the same actor with a name change, so similar are they in voice and appearance. Apparently, both young lads were pushed onto the stage by their mother, although neither took it too seriously, perhaps to their credit and indeed their sanity. Rhodes had the less prominent career, his other sole SF credit outside *The Time Tunnel* and *Star Trek* being *King Kong vs. Godzilla!* In the early '70s he made several thankless appearances in the *Here's Lucy* series as various hunky suitors for the ageing queen of comedy, Lucille Ball. Although Lucy was a superb comedienne and justly

deserves her stature as a TV icon (the author defers to no-one in his admiration for her '50s and '60s work), these were not her best years, and she was famously in denial about her age. Reason, better suited to drama than comedy anyway, looked wooden, miscast, and uncomfortable in these empty roles.

John Lupton also has a trashy fantasy film to his credit, the infamous *Jesse James Meets Frankenstein's Daughter*, made the same year as this. His TV work includes "The Lost Bomb" for *Voyage to the Bottom of the Sea* and "Moonshot" for *The Invaders*. Jim Davis, a credible Bowie, but actually looking nothing like the original, later went on to TV fame as Jock Ewing in *Dallas*. This was to be his sole SF TV credit, other than a *Project UFO* episode ("The Joshua Flats Incident"), although he also appeared in *Jesse James Meets Frankenstein's Daughter*, as well as the B-movies *The Monster from the Green Hell* and *The Day Time Ended*. Rodolfo Hoyos appears again in "Idol of Death." His credits include *The Twilight Zone*, *The Invaders*, *The Wild Wild West*, *The Man from UNCLE*, and *The Six Million Dollar Man*. Edward Colmans had previously appeared in *The Outer Limits* ("Tourist Attraction") and *Voyage to the Bottom of the Sea* ("The Mist of Silence"). Alberto Monte was the bandito in the enjoyable *Lost in Space* episode "Castles in Space." Elizabeth Rogers appeared in *Star Trek*, *Land of the Giants* ("Sabotage," alongside *Time Tunnel*'s Robert Colbert), and *Bewitched*. Production number: 9614.

The Night of the Long Knives

wr. William Welch, dir. Paul Stanley

Doug and Tony turn up in May, 1886 just in time for the battle at the Khyber Pass. Back at the Time Tunnel control center, the Tunnel has gone dead, leading the scientists to the inescapable conclusion that the same fate has befallen their time travelers.

With David Watson (Rudyard Kipling), Malachi Throne (Hera Singh), Peter Brocco (Kashi), Perry Lopez (Major Kabir), Brendan Dillon (Colonel Fettrech), George Keymas (Ali), Dayton Lummis (Gladstone), Ben Wright (Minister)

LOCATION: The border between India and Afghanistan, mid–May, 1886.

A wordy and literate script is finely performed by an excellent cast of familiar faces with conviction, as a number of players usually given much less to work with—Watson, Brocco, Dillon, Lopez, Keymas, Lummis, and Wright—make the most of their opportunity from a script that far surpasses the standard quality of Welch's work, so much of which was rushed, often written to order to accommodate standing sets, stock footage or existing props. This is easily Welch's most substantial and intelligent script for *The Time Tunnel*, or indeed any of Allen's series. So often he would resort to time-honored Hollywood cliché ("One Way to the Moon," "Reign of Terror"), or write for the sake of prop availability rather than story. Although he is obliged to get Kipling, Doug, and Tony into costume to match the superbly integrated stock footage, all this logically suits the storyline, rather than obviously dictating it (as with his "Merlin the Magician"). So often slumming it, here he delivers the goods, giving an honest and unbiased portrait of both sides' interests. Gladstone (correctly) foresees the fall of the British Empire, which would gasp its last some seventy years later at Suez after a slow, bitter decline, while Singh's perception of life under British rule—"You call us savages! You treat us like children! But we are intelligent men!"—is both valid and validated by his brutal behavior. Central to this episode, as with so many *Time Tunnel* stories, is the firm friendship between Doug and Tony. Doug's relationship with the elderly blind man also gives the episode power and resonance beyond the series' more typical historical romps. This story takes itself seriously.

The episode is further gifted with some superb location work that matches the stock footage perfectly, and excellent direction from Paul Stanley, who takes the time and trouble to employ a variety of different camera angles (notably in the pre-credits sequence) where half as many would have satisfied others, and manages to film the Time Tunnel complex from a number of fresh perspectives as well; we even get a quick flash of the rare establishing shot of the complex from the pilot at one point! This story is also the last stand for Sam Groom's panicky Jerry, who finally steps over the line...! We don't learn whether the Tunnel scientists work out what Jerry did, but he's never seen again after this episode! It would be fun to assume he was shown the door for his indiscretion, but the boring truth is that Groom's character was simply dropped from the series. This is also the only escapade that the Tunnel staff completely miss out on, seeing almost nothing of the adventure on the viewscreen.

The cast is uniformly excellent. David Watson as Kipling is earnest and adventurous, and Brendan Dillon perfect as the devious and scheming British commander, while Malachi Throne gives his standard bravura performance of brutish malevolence and flashing eyes that regular viewers of Allen's series have come to expect from him. The background music is welcomely familiar—the red, yellow and blue striped interior of Singh's tent a little less so, having also housed warriors in "Revenge of the Gods," "The Walls of Jericho" and—later—"Attack of the Barbarians" throughout the series' run! Some of the decor within is also noticeably familiar—and watch for Colbert throwing his cardboard shield down in the tent; it flies behind him like a frisbee.

Malachi Throne appeared in many science-fiction and fantasy shows of the 1960's, including all of the Irwin Allen productions. He would appear again in *The Time Tunnel*, as Machiavelli in "The Death Merchant." British actor David Watson had previously appeared in "The Last Patrol" in a much smaller role, and was Cornelius in *Beneath the Planet of the Apes* when Roddy McDowall proved unavailable. He also appeared in *The Girl from UNCLE*, *The Bionic Woman*, and *Project UFO*.

Brendan Dillon was also in an excellent *Man from UNCLE* episode, "The King of Diamonds Affair." His only other work for Allen was the role of Captain Jacob Wren, the leader of "The Fossil Men" for *Voyage to the Bottom of the Sea*. Although this was a hugely enjoyable episode, it was a shameful waste of his abilities, as not only was he hidden under a ton of rubber monster suit, his voice has been stupidly redubbed—the American anchorman tones that now grace the rock man sound like every alien invader that ever threatened the Earth circa 1950–'60, instead of the tortured British seaman that Dillon must surely have delivered. He did not fare much better in the cheapo early '70s SF series *Jason of Star Command*, in which he portrayed a pantomime pirate in "Marooned in Time." He deserved so much better than this, as his portrayal of the pragmatic Fettrech shows.

Elderly, grey-haired Peter Brocco later appeared in "Idol of Death" in a similar role and enjoyed a career that stretched back to the Rocketman serial *Radar Men from the Moon*, in which he played the earthbound extraterrestrial stooge of the bad guy. Although typecast, Brocco was fortunate enough to be typecast in several different ways, being considered for a number of different recurring types in bit roles. His frail, sad look frequently cast him as the helpless victim, but he was also an alien in *Twilight Zone* and *Lost in Space*, and often played scientists. He was particularly good as the ill-fated Doc Link in "I, Robot" for the original *Outer Limits*, with the small but key role of portraying a sympathetic victim. Films include *Invaders from Mars*, *Tobor the Great*, *The Three Stooges in Orbit*, and *In Like Flint*, and his numerous SF TV bit parts include roles in *Adventures of Superman*, *The Twilight Zone*, *Boris Karloff's Thriller*, *Voyage to the Bottom of the Sea* ("City Beneath the Sea"), *My Favorite Martian*, *The Man from UNCLE*, *Bewitched*, *I Dream of Jeannie*, *Lost in Space* ("The Deadly Games of Gamma Six"), *The Invaders* ("The Leeches"), and *Star Trek* ("Errand of Mercy").

Perry Lopez was previously on the other side of the Time Tunnel as Dr. Whitebird in "Massacre." Here, he hides behind a beard and turban. He also appears as the alien/crewman in "Savage Jungle," a ludicrous fourth season episode of *Voyage to the Bottom of the Sea*, and as an Enterprise officer in *Star Trek*'s "Shore Leave." Hard-faced heavy and stunt man George Keymas appears twice in *Voyage to the Bottom of the Sea* (in "The Buccaneer" and "The Lost Bomb"). He was Paul Mantee's stand-in and stunt double on *Robinson Crusoe on Mars*.

Dayton Lummis, sharing a single scene with Ben Wright here, had appeared alongside him previously in "The Last Battle," a first season episode for *Voyage to the Bottom of the Sea*. He plays the king in Nathan Juran's splendid *Jack the Giant Killer* (1961), and was in "The Cheaters" and "Cousin Tundifer," two highly regarded episodes of *Boris Karloff's Thriller*. Ben Wright played numerous bit parts and voiceovers in several episodes of *The Outer Limits*, *The Twilight Zone*, *The Man from UNCLE*, *The Wild Wild West*, and *The Invaders* ("Summit Meeting") and appears in the opening scenes of Allen's feature *The Lost World* as a British reporter.

By chance or design—probably chance—Paul Stanley has his name on three superior TV SF productions ("The Guests" for *The Outer Limits*, "My Friend, Mr. Nobody" for *Lost in Space*, and "The Night of the Long Knives" for *The Time Tunnel*). However, he directed three episodes of *The Outer Limits*, and the other two were among the worst in the series—the awful "Second Chance" and "Counterweight." It is impossible to assess Stanley's work comparatively, as not only does he flit from show to show before establishing himself, but the quality of the series he has worked on range from prestigious highly regarded shows like *The Outer Limits*, *The Untouchables*, *The Naked City*, *The Defenders*, and *Mission: Impossible* to regular everyday TV entertainments like *The Wild Wild West* ("The Night of the Spanish Curse"), numerous traditional western series, most of the major '70s cop shows, and even *The Six Million Dollar Man* ("The Ultimate Impostor"). Even in the fantasy arena his credits range from spooky *Ghost Story* ("The Dead We Leave Behind," "Legions of Demons") to the then hi-tech *Search* ("Flight to Nowhere"). He's also the only *Time Tunnel* director to have worked on the similar *Voyagers* series. Stanley seems to be not so much a man with a vision as a man with a mortgage, but given the ball he can run with it, and while so much of his stuff is routine, he's never made a mess of a good show, and—as "Night of the Long Knives" demonstrates—when offered a good script, he rises to the occasion. Production number: 9615.

Invasion

wr. Bob and Wanda Duncan, dir. Sobey Martin

Tony finds himself with the French Resistance during the Second World War just before D-Day, while Doug is a captive of the Germans, who have brainwashed him into believing that he's a German officer.

With Lyle Bettger (Major Hoffman), John Wengraf (Dr. Kleinemann), Michael St. Clair (Duchamps), Robert Carricart (Mirabeau), Joe E. Tata (Verlaine), Francis DeSales (Dr. Shumate)

LOCATION: Cherbourg Peninsula, June 4th, 1944.

From the sublime to the ridiculous. Each type of *Time Tunnel* episode delivered exactly what was expected of it, with hindsight at least, and the diversity and unpredictability of the show from one episode to the next probably accounts for both its success and its failure. Without the episode guides clutched by the fans with their inside knowledge of what to expect, the casual audience was constantly surprised, sometimes impressed, sometimes dismayed. In particular, the history buffs drawn to the show by such reasonably intelligent forays into the past as "The Day the Sky Fell In," "The Last Patrol," "Massacre," "Night of the Long Knives," and so on would overlook the duller ones but were certainly appalled by the show's gradual drift into the world of pulp sci-fi and extraterrestrials (personally, I love that stuff, but that's me). However no greater discrepancy between the variable quality of individual episodes could be found than that between the intelligent, exciting and literate spectacle of "Night of the Long Knives" and the inane, cheap and flat Poverty Row-style tedium of "Invasion," which features no flying saucers, silver-suited aliens or bug-eyed monsters, but refers to WWII and D-Day. "Invasion" is an extremely stupid episode, viss all der Chermans talkink like ziss, and all ze membairs of ze Fronsch Resistonse talking in Clouseau-speak. Particularly amusing is the way Colbert, while brainwashed, automatically starts talking in this silly Hollywood German! Even if we excuse the comical bogus dialects, having Doug adopt this speech pattern just highlights the artificiality of such generic short-cuts. Is he now supposed to be speaking German—or is it Germerican?

Lyle Bettger appeared in the *Voyage to the Bottom of the Sea* episode "The Creature." John Wengraf was a veteran of low-budget sci-fi (*Gog, Return of Dracula, Twelve to the Moon*). He, Michael St. Clair, and Robert Carricart all appeared in various episodes of *The Man from UNCLE* and other spy shows of the period. A regular cast member of adventure series *THE Cat* that season, Carricart was reunited over twenty years later with series star James Darren when he appeared in "Friendly Haven," an episode of *Werewolf* Darren was directing. Francis DeSales appeared in episodes of *The Outer Limits*, *The Twilight Zone*, and *The Wild Wild West*.

"Invasion" was supposed to be the directorial debut of Jerry Briskin, a script-consultant related to Allen. Instead, it ended up being directed by Sobey Martin, the most prolific *Time Tunnel* director, for reasons unknown. There are many amusing stories about the elderly Martin's lackluster and perfunctory attitude to his work, but the episodes he directed include some of the most dynamic and imaginative entries, and if he did allegedly direct some of his *Lost in Space* assignments quite literally in his sleep, then he did a more professional and lively job than many TV people who stay awake. Sadly, not much could be done for this stiff, the dullest episode in the series.

There are no disasters at the Time Tunnel control center in this episode, which is a sorry omission, because the episode needs the boost badly—the plot is the lowest Grade Z 1940s-style hokum, flat direction, threadbare sets an' all. It would have been fun to see the Time Tunnel control scientists bring back the brainwashed Doug, which at one point it seemed they were going to do. The shock of returning to 1968, and then back to 1945, could have broken the brainwashing spell far more effectively than the silly antidote get-out at the end. We also get a reprise of the truth serum scene from "The Day the Sky Fell In"; at least there it was submerged in a superior episode. Here, it just highlights how corny "Invasion" is. This is one of the most banal and disappointing episodes in the series, the only brief *frisson* coming from the brainwashed Doug inadvertently identifying the traitor in the French Resistance. This is the episode's one strong scene, and is quite murderously shocking.

One of the oddities of the nature of *The Time Tunnel* as an action/adventure show above all else was that Doug and Tony would frequently take life when propelled into battle scenarios; in "Revenge of the Gods" and "The Death Merchant," to name but two, the scientists have no qualms about participating on the battlefields, even though they shouldn't really be there. Not for them the moral questions of whether it's their fight, or whether they might be creating a time paradox by snuffing out various individuals. This excitement of taking part

in the historical adventure of the battles was, of course, integral to the show's format and intentions. Fortunately, the series frequently transcended Allen's narrow definition of it, but even so, *The Time Tunnel* was not a thoughtful science-fiction series in the manner of *The Twilight Zone* or *Star Trek*, and in essence is no different from the Hollywood fantasies it plundered footage from. This is particularly evident during this yarn, in which Tony blithely blasts away at the Nazi soldiers while on a mission with the French Resistance. Any ambiguity or philosophical depth inherent in the traitor's participation in the deaths of this Nazi cannon-fodder is purely unintentional. Production number: 9616.

The Revenge of Robin Hood
wr. Leonard Stadd, dir. William Hale

Doug and Tony turn up in Sherwood Forest, England, where they join Robin Hood and his band of Merry Men in their efforts to coerce King John into signing the Magna Carta.

With Donald Harron (Robin Hood), John Alderson (Little John), John Crawford (King John), Ronald Long (Friar Tuck), James Lanphier (Dubois), Erin O'Brien Moore (Baroness Elmont), John Orchard (Engelard)

LOCATION: June, 1215, Sherwood Forest, Merrie Englande.

With their usual lousy timing, Doug materializes in the throne room of King John just as Robin Hood, the Earl of Huntingdon, is battling for his life, while Tony tumbles into the castle dungeon.... By the end of the yarn, King John is captured by Robin, and Doug and Tony accompany him to Runnymede, where they witness the historic signing of the Magna Carta before disappearing once more into the Time Vortex!

There is absolutely no record whatsoever of the legendary Robin Hood having been present at the signing of the Magna Carta! While the stories of his exploits and records of his existence have been found dating anytime between the 12th and 14th centuries, it is generally assumed that Robin was most likely the Earl of Huntingdon, born sometime in the mid–1100s. This would make Robin eligible for medieval Medicare by the time the Magna Carta was signed in 1215 ... but of course, much of history is hearsay or myth to begin with, and the further back in time, the more questionable the facts. The Robin Hood legend, unencumbered by any requirement to adhere to known historical fact due to the notable absence of same, dominates Hollywood's historically hysterical stakes, with recreations ranging from Errol Flynn's campy, clean and colorful tree-swinger in the archetypical Hollywood role model *The Adventures of Robin Hood* (far from the first, even in 1938) to numerous TV and movie versions in subsequent decades, all more reflective of the period they were produced in than the 12th century. *The Time Tunnel's* contribution to the mythology also tips a feathered hat to Errol Flynn and all his imitators. It's a gloriously entertaining romp through Hollywood's Sherwood Forest which offers a bright, blond and bouncy Robin in various shades of green, a boisterous Little John, a shifty-eyed King John, his goateed sidekick, a treacherous Baroness, and a roly-poly Friar Tuck who bounces into battle sending combatants flying simply by bumping them with his girth!

The Time Tunnel's Robin Hood was Donald Harron, a chameleon-like supporting player who no doubt impressed Irwin by having an engagement at Stratford-on-Avon on his resume. He was memorable as loud Australian UNCLE agent Kitt Kittridge in *The Spy with My Face*, later "The Four Steps Affair" for *The Man from UNCLE*. In a reversal of the usual practice of making *UNCLE* features from two-parters, "The Four Steps Affair" was actually written around the extra set pieces filmed to beef up "The Double Affair" to movie length. As a result of this, Kittridge dies in *The Spy with My Face*, but lives on in "Four Steps"! Other roles included "The Inheritors," a two-part *Outer*

Limits, "Doomsday," an early *Voyage to the Bottom of the Sea*, and "The Pit" for *The Invaders*, all nondescript roles after the boisterous Robin and Kitt.

Rotund Ronald Long had a fine time in 1960s TV. As well as playing Friar Tuck here, he portrayed Henry VIII, the giant at the top of the beanstalk and even Santa Claus in various episodes of *Bewitched*, parodied Captain Bligh in *Lost in Space* ("Mutiny in Space"), and played many other wacky roles during this period in such colorful '60s escapades as *Batman*, *The Man from UNCLE*, *Get Smart*, and *I Dream of Jeannie*.

Writer Stadd and director Hale had worked together on Stadd's previous script for the series, Lincoln episode "The Death Trap." This episode was to be a rush job, but no-one had told John Crawford, cast as King John, who was making a meal out of his Magna Carta scene at the end. When he paused for effect, a voice shouted "cut" and Crawford protested he was still acting, and carried on. When the scene was finished, he found out the voice he had argued with was that of Irwin Allen! Happily, it didn't seem to have an effect on his employment record with the studio. Crawford would chalk up no less than four appearances in *The Time Tunnel*, following this episode with parts in "Billy the Kid," "The Death Merchant," and "Raiders from Outer Space."

If ever there was a patron saint of supporting players, it would be the chameleon-like Crawford, whose ordinary but instantly recognizable features have allowed him to play alongside virtually every significant SF TV icon. Outside of the SF arena, he has appeared with virtually every other American icon of 20th Century pop culture, from *The Waltons* and the *Mission: Impossible* agents to *The A-Team* and Dirty Harry—yet he remains almost totally anonymous. As a close friend of casting director Larry Stewart, a former acting colleague from his days in the serials, Crawford appeared in all the Irwin Allen series at one point, memorably as Chronos in "The Time Merchant" for *Lost in Space,* and as Alpha in a re-hash of "The Kidnappers" for *Voyage to the Bottom of the Sea* called "Time Lock"; ironically, both have time-travel themes, although Chronos was his favorite role and Alpha his least favorite after being forced to re-dub his performance. He also appeared in a loopy *Land of the Giants* called "Graveyard of Fools," and as a Federation official in *Star Trek* ("The Galileo Seven"). Crawford was in virtually every significant fantasy drama of the '60s, '70s, and early '80s, including *The Twilight Zone, My Favorite Martian, Batman, The Wild Wild West, The Invisible Man, The Bionic Woman, The Incredible Hulk, The Amazing Spider-Man,* and *Knight Rider.* He had a recurring role in the short-lived 1980s series *The Powers of Matthew Star* and also appeared in the serials *Blackhawk* and *Zombies of the Stratosphere* and the TV *Adventures of Superman.* Films include *Captain Sindbad* with Guy Williams. Superior roles outside SF include the films *Night Moves* (1975), in which he plays a pathetic slob seduced by jailbait, and *The Enforcer* (1976), as the mealymouthed Mayor rescued by Dirty Harry at great cost and to little visible advantage to the city. Interestingly, one of his own favorite roles was as the sheriff on *The Waltons!*

James Lanphier also appeared in the 1950s creature feature *The Deadly Mantis,* and episodes of *The Wild Wild West, The Green Hornet, Get Smart,* and *Batman.* Most memorably, he was the caterer who strangled the drunken waiter in the 1967 comedy classic *The Party.* The SF TV of John Alderson, a Britisher working in the U.S., includes *Voyage to the Bottom of the Sea* ("City Beneath the Sea"), *The Man from UNCLE* ("The Gazebo in the Maze Affair"), Britain's *Doctor Who, The Wild Wild West,* and *Automan.* John Orchard, usually cast as a clichéd working class Londoner type, also appeared in "The Gazebo in the Maze Affair" for *The Man from UNCLE* as well as *The Girl from UNCLE* and *Get Smart.* Erin O'Brien

Moore's films include *Destination: Moon* and *In Like Flint.* Production number: 9617.

Kill Two by Two

wr. Bob and Wanda Duncan, dir. Herschel Daugherty

Three days before the battle of Iwo Jima, Doug and Tony are trapped on a small Pacific island with a suicidal, murderous and embittered Japanese flyer.

With Mako (Lt. Nakamura), Kam Tong (Sergeant Itsugi), Phillip Ahn (Dr. Nakamura), Brent Davis (Marine Sergeant), Vince Howard (Time Tunnel medic)

LOCATION: Miname Iwo, a small Pacific island near Tokyo, February 17th, 1945.

This one gets better with repeated viewings, but it's still probably the only episode of the entire series besides "Invasion" which verges on the tedious ... a little of Lt. Nakamura goes a long way. And although the writers make some attempt to explain it away, it is irritating that Doug and Tony participate in the psychotic flyer's little games, when—as Ray points out—all they have to do is hide out until the Tunnel gets a fix on their location and retrieves them; saying "Go ahead and shoot" to a psychopath isn't really stalling for time!

Once again, a few flicks of a pen could patch the holes in the Duncans' script, as in their "Devil's Island" episode, the time travelers antagonize their captors instead of sitting still. There is at least a lame attempt to justify Doug's irrational and dangerous behavior by putting it down to blind machismo, but it doesn't really wash. Doug is too smart for that. There also seems little reason for Doug and Tony to get so worked up about getting a radio message warning out about the island, when they know full well the outcome of the battle and the war itself; again, Doug's argument doesn't really stand up. Indeed, they might even change the result for the worse.

Director Herschel Daugherty worked only twice for Irwin Allen, both times on *The Time Tunnel* (his other episode was "Town of Terror"). He took two assignments for the *UNCLE* franchise, "The Tigers are Coming Affair" for *The Man from UNCLE*, and "The Prisoner of Zalamar Affair" for *The Girl from UNCLE*, but seemed to draw the short straw where SF TV was concerned. He worked twice on *Star Trek*, but drew the Corman-esque "Operation: Annihilate" (which is essentially *It Conquered the World* without the happy little squat monster) and the bizarre "The Savage Curtain," the Abraham Lincoln episode far dafter than anything *The Time Tunnel* could have come up with. Hardly that legendary series' finest moments.

All three Japanese actors in this episode were familiar Hollywood faces with numerous credits. Mako Iwamtsu, who chose to be billed simply as Mako, became most famous for his martial arts movies of the '70s, and among his many TV roles was "The Preying Mantis," a superior episode of *The Green Hornet*, the half-hour Fox show scheduled directly before *The Time Tunnel* during its run and co-starring future martial arts icon Bruce Lee. Other TV included episodes of *Wonder Woman*, *Voyagers*, and *Greatest American Hero*. As the years passed and age took its course, he moved into mysterious mentor-style roles, including *The Incredible Hulk* ("Another Path," and the sequel "The Disciple," backdoor pilots) and Jackie Chan's U.S. debut, *The Big Brawl*. Mako is still busy today, and still turning up in cult TV—he was the publisher in the "Author, Author" episode of *Frasier*, in which the Crane brothers try to write a book together, and narrates the closing narration for Cartoon Network's superb *Dexter's Laboratory* cartoons. Other films include *Conan the Barbarian*, *Conan the Destroyer*, *Robocop 3*, and *Highlander: the Final Dimension*.

Philip Ahn's career goes all the way back to the 1939 *Buck Rogers* serial, in which he was billed as Philson Ahn. Since then, his numerous credits have included *The Man from UNCLE*, *The Wild Wild West*, *The Girl from UNCLE* and *Wonder Woman*. He is best known for his co-starring role in the TV series *Kung Fu*. Ahn is fine as the expert called in to assist the Control Centre—it's probably one of his best roles. Kam Tong also appeared in *The Man from UNCLE* (twice). Brent Davis played a *Seaview* crewman in "Deadly Invasion" for *Voyage to the Bottom of the Sea*, and was underneath the monster make-up in "Target Earth" for *Lost in Space*. Vince Howard appeared in *Star Trek* ("The Man Trap"), *The Invaders* ("The Spores"), *The Wild Wild West*, *I Dream of Jeannie*, *Bewitched*, *Kolchak: the Night Stalker*, and *Airwolf*. Production number: 9619.

Visitors from Beyond the Stars

wr. Bob and Wanda Duncan, dir. Sobey Martin
Callous, unemotional aliens orbit the Earth in the year 1885 to plunder the planet for food, intending to leave behind them a dead world.

With Jan Merlin (Centauri), Ross Elliott (Sheriff), Fred Beir (Taureg), Gary Haynes (Deputy), Tris Coffin (Jess Crawford), Byron Foulger (Williams), John Hoyt (alien leader), Pat Culliton (Johnson)
LOCATION: Mullins, Arizona, 1885.

The introduction of alien beings into *The Time Tunnel* was a typical and not unexpected ploy that divided the opinions of the writers but worked wonders for the scope of the series. There was only so much historical epic stock footage available, and the inevitable outcome of certain historic occasions ran the risk of becoming tiresome; there were only so many times the writers could get away with the "you must believe us!" warning of doom routine that had so far been employed for the sinking of the *Titanic*, the eruption of Krakatoa, the bombing of Pearl Harbor, Custer's last stand, and the Alamo (although it should be remembered that these stories were not only scattered among others of a different nature but also some of the best episodes).

This was the Tunnel's first encounter with aliens from other worlds, and the authors were Bob and Wanda Duncan, regular contributors to Allen's *Lost in Space*. Consequently, unlike later episodes in which extraterrestrials were a routine hazard, much time was taken to justify the presence of aliens and UFOs within the *Time Tunnel* premise in the control center scenes, with Kirk ordering Ann to pull the files on UFO sightings. Unfortunately, as the first season neared its close, the series was in danger of becoming top-heavy with extraterrestrials, and the aliens from space became a little too plentiful—indeed, there would be two alien invasions in 1885, one in the U.S. (this story), and another in India ("Raiders from Outer Space," also by the Duncans)! Oddly, "Visitors" is the episode that might more accurately be titled "Raiders from Outer Space"—the episode that *does* bear this title is not specifically about raiding!

A nineteenth century sheriff (Ross Elliott) encounters a typical Irwin Allen silver-skinned extraterrestial (Jan Merlin) in "Visitors from Beyond the Stars."

The footage of the alien spaceship is the much-used shot from "The Sky Pirate," a *Lost in Space* episode, and it is used again in the final *Time Tunnel* episode, "Town of Terror," while the aliens brainwash Doug and some of the Mullins townsfolk in the same *Invaders from Mars*-style as the amoeba-creature that took over the *Seaview* crew in the *Voyage to the Bottom of the Sea* episode "Monster from Outer Space"—little tell-tale spots behind the ear! Stock footage of stampeding cattle (frozen in time by the aliens at one point) and Apache Indians wiping out a troop of cavalry (no doubt from Fox's extensive library of traditional western films) contrast intrigu-ingly with the silver-clad silver-skinned aliens and their sci-fi shenanigans in the town that the Time Tunnel researchers discover is destined to become a ghost town that year, and the control base, for the first and last time, regards the appearance of extraterrestrials as surprising. The same footage of cattle stampeding through town was used in a *Batman* story, "Come Back, Shame"/"It's the Way You Play the Game," that same year. The opening scenes on board the spaceship include much material cut out from the previous episode's trailer.

The indoor Crawford ranch set is actually the same as used for the modest home of Jeremiah and Matthew in "The Death Trap," with only a few minor changes—there's a different picture on the wall in the neighboring room, and a different one by the door, a clock has replaced some tins, and the stove is in a slightly different position (although the coffee pot—and even the rag to lift it!—is exactly the same)! The chairs in the saloon can also be found scattered around the Pinkerton detectives' cobwebbed base in the same episode. On the walls of the alien spaceship are the ever-present rods found in "Chase Through Time," one of which is used as the infamous Homing Pole in "Revenge of Robin Hood."

Each episode featured the opening ritual of Doug and Tony having to guess where they were, and a nice touch in this story is their obvious assumption that they're in the far future; then, once aware that they're in a spaceship over the Earth, Tony draws the obvious but erroneous conclusion that "somebody's air force will be swarming all over us in a minute." It's quite a revelation when we discover that they're in the year 1885! It was also a refreshing change to see Doug and Tony casually introduce themselves as time travelers, something they hadn't been able to do with credibility since "One Way to the Moon"—in fact, it's quite jarring when they blurt it out to the aliens at the start of this story!

The writers were divided about the shift toward alien invaders. Harold Jack Bloom had advised against adventures into the future after turning in the revised pilot script, and Ellis St. Joseph was equally apprehensive, although pragmatic about the reasons. Leonard Stadd was for it, feeling the constant trips back to known history would become repetitive. Surprisingly, given that they wrote a few, the Duncans were against the appearance of extraterrestrials too. "The series' basic premise had to be taken with more than a grain of salt" they explained to *Starlog* magazine, "but aliens from outer space were more than the show could han-

dle!" James Darren, whose favorite episodes were "The Day the Sky Fell In," "The Death Trap," and "Billy the Kid," agreed. "To me, the most interesting thing about going forward in time is to see what the future will bring. To go there and meet a couple of guys with silver faces who speak mumbo-jumbo doesn't mean anything." "I wouldn't have changed the format, but felt that going into the future was a mistake," said Lee Meriwether.

Of the performers, Jan Merlin makes a brave stab at the thankless task of portraying the cold, robotic alien leader. A regular on the early '50s series *Tom Corbett–Space Cadet* as the junior wisecracking trainee, in later years he got to play on the bad guys' side. He appeared three times in *Voyage to the Bottom of the Sea*, as an assassin in the first season story "No Way Out," a wicked assistant in the second season's "The X-Factor," and a Nazi officer in the third season's "Death from the Past." He also appeared in an early *Man from UNCLE* ("The King of Knaves Affair"). More recently, he appeared in the Roger Corman time travel film *Time Trackers*, a delightful obscurity. In a 1995 *Starlog* interview, he told how he had recently seen Robert Colbert in a restaurant and "crept up behind him and said I was going to take him to my planet as soon as I got the silver paint off. He fell over in his chair!"

Fred Beir, as his extraterrestrial colleague, is less well cast, but has nothing to do anyway. Underneath the silver paint is an actor who gave terrific performances as a terrified astronaut in "Death Ship" for *The Twilight Zone*, and a demon in "Fire Fall" for *Kolchak: the Night Stalker*. Beir has shown on numerous occasions that when given something to work with in the script, he could really deliver, but when given nothing, he gave nothing. He also appeared in episodes of *The Outer Limits* and *The Six Million Dollar Man*.

SF veteran John Hoyt (real name John

Hoysradt) did double duty for *The Time Tunnel*, appearing here as the alien leader who materializes in the Time Tunnel complex to discover the fate of his predecessors in the previous century, and returning in the following episode to play an expert in psychic phenomena in "Ghost of Nero." A former teacher, he played many strict, cold, authoritarian roles, in both sit-coms and drama. He was previously an alien in "The Bellero Shield," a classic episode of *The Outer Limits*, appearing in human form in that series in two other good episodes, "Don't Open Till Doomsday" and "I, Robot." His numerous other roles in the genre include the memorable "Will the Real Martian Please Stand Up?" episode of *The Twilight Zone*, "The Cage," the first, unsold pilot for *Star Trek* (in which he played the ship's doctor), and the films *The Lost Continent*, *When Worlds Collide*, *Attack of the Puppet People*, *X—the Man with X-Ray Eyes*, *The Time Travelers*, and the '70s sci-fi sex spoof *Flesh Gordon*. He has also appeared in episodes of *Voyage to the Bottom of the Sea* ("Hail to the Chief"), *The Munsters*, *Get Smart*, *The Man from UNCLE*, *The Monkees* ("I Was a Teenage Monster"), *The Wild Wild West*, *Planet of the Apes*, *Kolchak: the Night Stalker*, *The Six Million Dollar Man*, and *Battlestar Galactica*. Byron Foulger, cast as the craven town coward and saloonkeeper, appears alongside Hoyt in the *Monkees* spoof "I Was a Teenage Monster," as well as *Superman and the Mole Men*, *The Magnetic Monster*, and the classic time travel episode of *The Twilight Zone*, "Walking Distance." His career goes all the way back to 1934 and *Flash Gordon Conquers the Universe*. As the terrified town traitor, he plays a vintage western cliché to the hilt with lilting, fearful voice and wide eyes. As was the case with so many character actors, *The Time Tunnel* gave him one of his best and most distinctive roles.

Ross Elliott (a veteran of numerous straight westerns—he was the sheriff for many years in *The Virginian*) was previously the crazed traitor in "One Way to the Moon," and gives an excellent credible performance here as the local lawman well out of his depth. He had previously worked alongside James Darren in the 1964 teen movie *The Lively Set*, and has small film roles in *The Beast from 20,000 Fathoms*, *Tarantula*, *Monster on the Campus*, and *The Indestructible Man*. Other TV roles include a walk-on in "Superman on Earth" (the very first episode of the 1950s *Superman* series), two *Twilight Zone*, a *Voyage to the Bottom of the Sea* ("Death Ship"), three of *The Invaders*, and episodes of *The Wild Wild West*, *The Six Million Dollar Man*, *The Bionic Woman*, and *Wonder Woman*. Gary Haynes, his deputy, later appeared as the hapless teenager Pete, again facing an extraterrestrial menace in "Town of Terror," the final *Time Tunnel* episode.

Tris Coffin was a veteran of the Saturday morning serials (he was Rocketman in *King of the Rocket Men*, and also appeared in *Spy Smasher*, *Perils of Nyoka*, *Bruce Gentry*, and *Radar Patrol vs. Spy King*, among others) and several episodes of the 1950s *Superman* series. He appears only briefly as the rancher, yet is dignified and brave enough that we mourn his passing during his and Doug's brief resistance. Pat Culliton, cast as an unfortunate cowboy who gets blown away by the aliens in a show of power, was a prolific bit player in Irwin Allen productions, and appeared many times in different minor roles for *Voyage to the Bottom of the Sea*, *The Time Tunnel*, and *Land of the Giants*. On one occasion he worked on three Allen shows—two *Time Tunnel* and a *Voyage*—during three consecutive days. He had a recurring role in the '80s series *Starman*.

Robert Colbert gets an early taste of playing the villain (he played silver-haired bad guys in numerous series when his leading man days were over), and it's interesting to note that this is the second time in the series (after the D-Day story "Invasion," also by the Duncans) that poor Doug is brainwashed! The direction, by Sobey Martin, is flawless, with several menacing close-ups of the aliens (full face close-ups being Martin's giveaway trademark), but sadly, as usual, the same can't be said for the Duncans' fun, fast-paced, inventive but inevitably slap-dash script. The aliens should realize that their extermination of the Earth will fail, as Doug and Tony have already announced that they've come from Earth's future, and the awe-struck Time Tunnel staff automatically assume that the alien craft on the Time Tunnel image-area is a UFO, even though the dialogue confirms that they have neither seen inside the ship, or achieved a time-fix. As this is their first encounter with alien beings (they would be taken for granted in the episodes to follow), a more logical assumption would be to presume they are looking at an Earth ship from the far future. Production number: 9618.

The Ghost of Nero

wr. Leonard Stadd, dir. Sobey Martin

The Time Tunnel comes under attack from a poltergeist when Doug and Tony discover the tomb of the Emperor Nero while stranded in Italy during World War One.

With Eduardo Cianelli (Count Galba), Gunnar Hellstrom (Neistadt), Richard Jaeckel (Mueller), John Hoyt (Dr. Steinholtz), Nino Candido (Benito Mussolini)

LOCATION: the Villa Galba, on the edge of the Alps, northern Italy, October 23rd, 1915.

Director Sobey Martin seems to have neither helped nor hindered the production of his episodes to any great extent with regard to performances, and it is Eduardo Cianelli who brings this one to life as the elderly aristocrat Count Galba, on whose family the ghost of Nero pursues his revenge for their part in overthrowing him (this is historically accurate, incidentally; the Galbas are not a fictional creation). Cianelli, a short, sharp-faced, elderly Italian, was a frequent movie villain and starred in the title role of *The Mysterious Doctor Satan*, a wonderful early (1940) sci-fi serial with a masked hero and a tin robot from *Undersea Kingdom.*

He also appeared in the films *The Mummy's Hand* and *The Monster from the Green Hell* and three *UNCLE* escapades. Once again, *The Time Tunnel* gives an under-used performer one of his best opportunities.

Richard Jaeckel, a veteran of many war films, is pretty bad as a German officer, and Gunnar Hellstrom fades into the wallpaper as the commanding German officer. Tired of playing a succession of Nazis, Hellstrom later turned to directing, including two episodes of *The Wild Wild West*. Jaeckel's other SF TV credits include *The Outer Limits*, *The Wild Wild West*, *The Gemini Man*, and *Fantastic Journey*. Nino Candido was the props master on *Timescape*, the excellent 1992 time-travel fantasy that featured Robert Colbert in a supporting role as the boss of a tour guide leading the rich and bored of the future on ghoulish sightseeing tours of terrible disasters. As an in-joke, Candido's name appears on a list of casualties. John Hoyt, who appeared in the previous episode as an aggrieved extra-terrestrial, the leader of the alien looters, returns *sans* silver skin as the scatty Doctor Steinholtz, the authority in the paranormal called in by the Time Tunnel staff. Often, but not exclusively seen as stern, rigid, unemotional characters (like his silver-skinned alien), he's clearly having fun in a different kind of role than he usually plays. The music editor makes good use of Bernard Herrman's spooky theramin music from *The Day the Earth Stood Still*, and the entire episode is good fun, an unusual and original entry. The scenes in which the ghost comes back through the Tunnel are splendid, and the delightful twist ending caused the normally sedate and profoundly unimpressed film buff and program purchaser for British TV Leslie Halliwell to sarcastically single the episode out with undisguised admiration as "a lulu" in his 1979 *Teleguide* reference work. If you watch carefully during the scenes where the poltergeist hurls the library books around, you will see one of the wooden blocks being used to manually push the books off the shelf come into view.

This was the third and final contribution to the series from writer Leonard Stadd, after "The Death Trap" (Abe Lincoln) and "The Revenge of Robin Hood." He fell out with Allen over an unproduced script set in an over-populated future-world. A shame—it would have been good to see more, just to find out what he would have come up with next. Production number: 9620.

The Walls of Jericho

wr. Ellis St. Joseph, dir. Nathan Juran

When Doug and Tony tumble into the tent of Joshua as he prepares to attack the walled city of Jericho, the Time Tunnel staff relish the opportunity to witness an event of truly Biblical proportions.

With Myrna Fahey (Rahab), Linda Gaye (Ahza), Arnold Moss (Malek), Abraham Sofaer (Rahab's father), Michael Pate (Captain), Rhodes Reason (Joshua), Tiger Joe Marsh (torturer), Cynthia Lane (Shala)

LOCATION: the city of Jericho, Biblical times

Whoops—the walls of Jericho almost come tumbling down too soon in the scene where Tony fights with the torturer to rescue Doug. Of all the episodes of *The Time Tunnel*, this is the only one which really doesn't work in the way intended. What by its nature should have been one of the most daring, extraordinary, and thought-provoking episodes in the series is in fact reduced by the constraints of TV to one of the slower, duller adventures. An episode which should have set the mind thinking, instead sends it wandering. The supporting cast is competent but undistinctive, although Colbert and Darren's performances are as lively and as solid as ever, and just about hold this installment together. Writer Ellis St. Joseph, who was thrilled with the way his other *Time Tunnel*, the magnificent "The Day the Sky Fell In," came out, blamed himself for being too ambitious and forgetting the budget, but he also disliked the performances (except for Abraham Sofaer) and the costumes. It's fair comment. Arnold Moss and Michael Pate

do what they can with what they're given, but both Myrna Fahey, who portrays Rahab, the privileged survivor of Jericho's destruction, the original tart with a heart, and Linda Gaye, the treacherous Ahza, play their roles with the same flat melodramatics found in sword-and-sandal epics of the '40s and '50s.

Ironically, the fact that this is a Bible story allows for far darker and grimmer events occurring than would otherwise have been allowed in yarns based around other historical periods, which were remarkably clean and healthy by comparison; note the casual (offscreen) slaughter of the torturer for allowing Doug's escape, the reference to the cruel blinding of Rahab's father, the gruesome end of Malek, and the then-unheard of references to virgins and harlots, all acceptable to the twisted logic of the censor because it's a Bible story.

Although it was a rare achievement to get the character of a prostitute on TV in the '60s, let alone an early evening show, the source material undoubtedly swayed the censors from attempting to rewrite the Bible. Nevertheless, the script skirts delicately around Rahab's occupation. Consequently, this coyness, coupled with dialogue that turns Doug, Tony, and General Kirk into religious zealots, results in a dreary episode with much bogus wonderment and all the religious posturing of a Hollywood Bible epic; as Joshua is on the side of Christianity, neither the writer or the episode question the rights and wrongs of the Israelite army, which is essentially imposing its will on a society that has been deemed evil because it has chosen to go another way. Rahab—who has actually betrayed her city by aiding Joshua's spies—is portrayed not as the person who sold out her fellow citizens, but as the only citizen who deserves to survive what was essentially little more than yet another all-too-common historical massacre in the name of religion. Interestingly, the very next episode, "Idol of Death," takes the side of the heathen natives against the Spanish Conquistadors, whose leader Cortes was doing much the same thing, in the same brutal way, as Joshua. In "The Walls of Jericho," the non-believing despot Malek's brutality, barbarism and prejudice is much the same as that of fanatics of every shade; the concept of a totally evil city is, of course, ridiculous to anyone but a fanatic. All we see of Jericho are mad priests worshipping demonic idols, brutal soldiers, treacherous thieves, torturers, and sniveling citizens waiting to die their deserved death for backing the wrong side—including, presumably, the young girl Doug and Tony fight to save at the start of their adventure.

The destruction of the city is done as best as possible, and one bizarre image that sticks in the mind is the sight of General Kirk back at the control center, brandishing a Bible instead of the usual computer file, as they excitedly follow events. One scene that does make the episode worth catching is Malek's speech to Doug while he's being tortured in the cells, tormenting Doug by ridiculing his faith as he asks why God let his friend escape while leaving him to a sticky end.

As with its 1980s counterpart, *Quantum Leap*, it had long been apparent in *The Time Tunnel*, that, although not actually stated, Doug and Tony's adventures in time were part of some fateful destiny, a cosmic plan that dropped them in the right place at the right time to be part of history. Unlike *Quantum Leap's* producer, whose previous TV series *Airwolf* was loaded with religious symbolism and who portrayed quite literal interpretations of Heaven in episodes of his series *Magnum P.I.* and *JAG*, Allen is more ambiguous about such notions as fate or destiny. In fact, it's doubtful he gave the matter much though at all, his series not exactly being known—thankfully—for their philosophical or preachy tendencies. Bible stories were just another Hollywood genre to him. If *Quantum Leap* went out of its way to specifically portray its hero as a sort of time-traveling angel, *Time Tunnel's* take was determined only by the dramatic requirements of the story, nothing more, and nothing less. While *The Time Tunnel's* time travelers couldn't change events, it was clear that they had always been participants; in the course of the series they had, or would, save a woman and child on board the *Titanic*, prevent the sabotage of a 1978 space-flight ten years into their future, speed up the rescue of trapped miners in 1910, save a young trooper from Little Big Horn and a soldier's wife at the Alamo, and so on. In "The Walls of Jericho," not only are Doug and Tony destined to become the two spies in the city mentioned in the Bible, but divine intervention appears to be preventing the Time Tunnel from interfering with the course of events, just as Ott will do in "The Kidnappers" and Merlin in "Merlin the Magician." Author St. Joseph claimed to leave the interpretation of miracles up to the viewer. Was the cyclone sent by God? Or was it just a natural phenomenon? However, the author's position is fairly apparent, with much preaching by the regular cast and two specific examples of divine intervention when Ann, the disbeliever of the bunch, tries to retrieve Doug and Tony before Biblical prophecy has come to pass. This episode makes it perfectly clear within the format of the show that not only are Doug and Tony a part of history, but so is the Time Tunnel itself; their present situation is as pre-ordained as the sinking of the *Titanic* or the events at Custer's last stand. Conceptually, this is dangerous ground to establish, albeit unintentionally.

This particular story got an equally hokey, almost science-fictional treatment in the extraordinary and little-seen 1970s Biblical series *Greatest Heroes of the Bible*. In this, the two strangers are incandescent angels!

Rhodes Reason, who is striking as Joshua, but seen again only briefly after the initial teaser scene (filmed in a by now all-too-familiar pink and yellow striped tent—

see "Revenge of the Gods," "Night of the Long Knives" and "Attack of the Barbarians"!), had previously been in "The Alamo," where he portrayed Colonel Travis. As Malek, Arnold Moss (Noubar Telemakian in "The Deadly Toys Affair" for *The Man from UNCLE,* Anton Karidian in "Conscience of the King" for *Star Trek*) is an adequate villain. Michael Pate, excellent as the British captain in "The Last Patrol," returns to practice his unique brand of callous bullying villainy as another cruel Captain.

Abraham Sofaer had previously appeared in *The Time Tunnel* in "Revenge of the Gods." Myrna Fahey's best known credit is for Roger Corman's *Fall of the House of Usher.* She also encountered *Superman* ("All That Glitters") and *Batman* ("True or False-Face"/"Holy Rat Race"). Linda Gaye, the sister of actress Debra Paget, started her career in low-budget teen exploitation fare such as *Rock Around the Clock* and *Shake, Rattle, and Rock* in the 1950s. By the mid–'60s, she was working mostly in TV, and appeared in episodes of *The Wild Wild West, Get Smart,* and *I Dream of Jeannie.* She should not be confused with another '60s actress, Linda Gaye Scott. Tiger Joe the torturer, left on the cutting room floor as the executioner in "Reign of Terror," was a former pro-wrestler who also played a heavy in *Lost in Space.* No other SF TV credits could be found for young Cynthia Lane.

Nathan Juran was frequently handed the tougher episodes of Allen's series to shoot, but this one seems difficult only in terms of subject matter. It is notably stagebound, with no location shooting of any kind. Juran was essentially a technician, working better with special effects than actors, some say. But whatever one might think of such films as *The Deadly Mantis, Attack of the Fifty Foot Woman,* or *The Brain from Planet Arous,* they are fondly remembered and enjoyable. *Twenty Million Miles to Earth* and *First Men in the Moon* are excellent, and while Juran might not have been able to save

a stiff, he certainly never stood in the way of a good performance if it was there to be had. If the actors were ignored or hampered by Juran's attention to the complex special effects challenges, it did not show in the finished work. Production number: 9621.

Idol of Death

wr. Bob and Wanda Duncan, dir. Sobey Martin

Arriving in a Mexican jungle in the sixteenth century, Doug and Tony are taken prisoner by the notorious Ferdinand Cortes ... However, the historical expert the Tunnel staff have enlisted to help them retrieve Doug and Tony only has eyes for an ancient artifact.

With Teno Pollick (young Chief), Lawrence Montaigne (Alvarado), Anthony Caruso (Cortes), Rodolfo Hoyos (Castillano), Peter Brocco (elderly retainer), Abel Fernandez (bowman)

LOCATION: 1st October, 1519, Vera Cruz, Mexico.

"Idol of Death" was withdrawn from circulation for some years due to undisclosed but now apparently resolved legal problems. Fortunately, it is a run-of-the-mill story with little to distinguish it other than the cast, many of whom appear in other episodes. While it's not a bad episode, there's nothing great about it either.

The official synopsis of the storyline does clear up one absurdity in the episode, which is that the corrupt Castillano inexplicably throws the Mask back into the Tunnel after he has forced the Time Tunnel personnel to retrieve it; in the story description, it is supposed to have been Kirk who does this, which makes much more sense. This synopsis also refers to the young chief as Quexcotl, but perhaps unsurprisingly, nobody calls him by this name in the episode!

Anthony Caruso, often the bad guy, starred in the B-movie *The Most Dangerous Man Alive,* and also appeared in episodes of *Adventures of Superman, The Wild Wild West, The Girl from UNCLE, Star Trek,* and *The Incredible Hulk.*

Virtually all the other players in this

episode had previously appeared in earlier *Time Tunnel* stories. Having been brought through the Tunnel as Sioux brave Yellow Elk in "Massacre," Lawrence Montaigne here stays where he belongs, as Alvarado, while Hoyos was in "The Alamo" and Brocco in "Night of the Long Knives." Patrick Culliton, a regular bit-player on the Irwin Allen series, also shows up in "The Day the Sky Fell In," "Revenge of the Gods," "Visitors from Beyond the Stars," and "Billy the Kid." Further information on all these actors can be found in the details of those episodes. Abel Fernandez, formerly one of *The Untouchables*, also appeared in the *Batman* episode "Penguin's Clean Sweep." No further SF TV credits could be found for young Teno Pollick. The two elderly victims of Cortes are not credited. Production number: 9622.

Billy the Kid

wr. William Welch, dir. Nathan Juran

The Time Tunnel personnel are amazed to see Doug Phillips shoot Billy the Kid three months before he was supposed to die at the hand of Pat Garrett.

With Robert Walker Jr. (Billy the Kid), Allen Case (Pat Garrett), John Crawford (John Poe), Harry Lauter (Wilson), Pitt Herbert (McKinney), Phil Chambers (Hayes), Pat Culliton (lynch mob leader)

LOCATION: Lincoln, Arizona, April, 1881.

This was Nathan Juran's second of four *Time Tunnel* assignments, the first having been "The Walls of Jericho"; "The Death Merchant" and "Raiders from Outer Space" would follow. Interestingly, while "The Walls of Jericho" spent much of its time hammering home the idea that Doug and Tony are part of an inescapable destiny that can't be altered, much of the tension in the first fifteen minutes of "Billy the Kid" is derived from the uneasy suspicion and mystifying possibility that the time travelers have changed history, as Doug is forced to draw a gun on infamous outlaw William Bonney, aka Billy the Kid.

As ever, historical fact is both less melo-dramatic and yet more interesting than presented here. The "Billy the Kid" episode of *The Time Tunnel* is a long way from historically accurate, even in the confusion of fact and legend that makes up the story of William Bonney, and in fact goes out of the way to be vague. However, the episode is faithful to the known facts in spirit, playing with what is known—the writers have made the effort to set the story in Lincoln County, Arizona, where the Kid's legend began and ended during the events of what came to be called the Lincoln County War; the deputies of Pat Garrett are correctly named, the dates are as close as can be determined, and Ann even makes a reference to the fact that the Kid was born in New York; Billy is shown to be popular with his men, even loved; and it was commonly acknowledged that no jail could hold him, stories of his effortless jail-breaks being an accepted part of history. If Robert Walker's otherwise definitive portrait of a snake-like killer is unfairly missing Billy's sense of outrage and injustice at his lot, it is perhaps worth noting that the Billy the Kid, Alamo and Custer episodes of this science-fiction series are far more accurate than many of the conventional westerns of the period.

This is yet another one of those episodes where the viewers find themselves wondering why Doug and Tony don't just head for the hills and hide behind a rock until the Time Tunnel scientists can locate them and transfer them in their own good time—but then there wouldn't be an adventure, would there? Doug does briefly point out at one stage that they don't want to move around too much while the Tunnel tries to locate them. Still, having spent the first quarter of the program puzzling over how they've managed to change history when they know that Pat Garrett will kill Billy the Kid in July of that year, it does seem rather odd that they then feel obliged to go back into Lincoln and alert the sheriff's office that they've captured Billy. One of the best scenes in this episode comes after the break at the end of act one, when Doug is overjoyed at seeing that Billy wasn't killed by his bullet—even though his own life is now in danger again. It's a telling moment that illustrates Doug's inherent goodness, just as Billy's puzzlement over Tony's concern for the shot deputy in the opening teaser shows up Billy's callous inhumanity. During the scenes at the deserted ranch as Doug and Tony casually discuss their situation and even, at one point, find the humor in it, there is a lovely moment of wry self-awareness as the time traveling duo speak to each other in TV western dude-speak, as if to acknowledge and mock the absurdity of their situation. Too much of this would have ruined the series and turned its already tenuous grip on reality into outright smartass parody. But almost every episode delineated and reaffirmed their friendship and camaraderie in some way, and brief, warm moments of light humor like this were rare.

The beauty of the wild west episodes of *The Time Tunnel* was that the Fox studios were particularly adept at making westerns, and well-equipped for sets, props, and performers; consequently, these episodes always looked top-notch and authentic, at least in TV terms. Billy the Kid also turns up in a *Voyagers* episode, "Bully and Billy," and in the time travel teen comedy film *Bill and Ted's Excellent Adventure*, but this is by far the best of Billy's temporal exploits. Robert Walker Jr. is perfectly cast as Billy, and made two other notable appearances in '60s sci-fi, as "Charlie X" in *Star Trek*, and as a frightened, selfish alien in "Panic" for *The Invaders*. The rest of the cast is uniformly excellent, particularly Allen Case as Pat Garrett and the chameleon-like John Crawford as the loutish, swaggering deputy John Poe. It's incredible to think that the same actor had only a few episodes earlier made such a splendid King John in "The Revenge of Robin Hood." He has told how he had a lot of trouble persuading Irwin Allen that he

could convincingly portray a cowboy after appearing as King John! Fortunately, he had a handy film still of himself looking surly and unshaven! The episode is greatly enhanced by the thoughtful performances of Case, Crawford, and the very underrated Harry Lauter, all of whom bring more to the stage than there is on the page. Both Lauter and Crawford are particularly good in their portrayal of eager, hero-worshipping subordinates.

Crawford would make two more appearances in *The Time Tunnel*, matching Kevin Hagen (with whom he appeared twice) at four, playing military men in "The Death Merchant" and "Raiders from Outer Space," both again for Juran. Lauter was a veteran of the Saturday matinee serials (he actually took the leading role, his only lead ever, in the last serial Republic ever made, *King of the Carnival* in 1955). He was one of those anonymous jobbing actors endlessly employed in bit parts who brought skill and realism to every role he tackled, and yet never received his due in recognition. Like John Crawford, Kevin Hagen, George Mitchell, and other chameleons, audiences saw him bring life to many roles without ever knowing his name. For example, he is the military man in charge of the troops that confront Klaatu in the classic *The Day the Earth Stood Still*. His fawning moronic sidekick to Billy in this episode is a treat, and he shows up again in the upcoming *Time Tunnel* episode, "Pirates of Dead Man's Island" (although it was filmed much earlier).

Allen Case later appeared in the pilot for *The Man from Atlantis*. Pitt Herbert, often cast in country roles, is one of the townsfolk in the time-travel *Lost in Space* episode "Visit to a Hostile Planet." Other roles include *Boris Karloff's Thriller, The Twilight Zone, The Munsters, Get Smart, The Wild Wild West, Batman,* and *Kolchak: the Night Stalker.* Phil Chambers appeared in the 1950s creature feature *The Mole People.* Other credits include *The Twilight Zone, The Wild Wild West,* and the classic "Valley of the Shadow" for *The Invaders*. Production number: 9623.

Pirates of Dead Man's Island

wr. Barney Slater, dir. Sobey Martin

While attempting to free Doug and Tony from the clutches of a band of sadistic Barbary Coast brigands, the scientists inadvertently bring the brutal leader back to the Time Tunnel complex, where he takes Ann hostage and runs amok.

With Victor Jory (Captain Beal), Pepito Galindo (Armando), Regis Toomey (Dr. Berkhart), Charles Bateman (Captain Stephan Decatur), James Anderson (Mr. Hampton), Harry Lauter (Mr. Johnson), Alex Montoya (Spanish Captain)

LOCATION: April 10th, 1805, the Barbary Coast.

A powerful central performance from Victor Jory and the exciting and memorable scenes of a Barbary Coast pirate running amok in the Time Tunnel complex are the high points of this adventure otherwise filmed mostly on the Fox island set seen in many Irwin Allen series episodes. It's a rare treat to see one of the Tunnel's frequent inadvertent visitors actually get out of the control center and into the complex itself, and the scenes in which Ann is captured and the scientists must lure the crazed pirate back into the Tunnel are tense and well played. Jory's reaction when, as the ill-fated Captain Beal, he looks over the barrier on the walkway to see the huge power core beneath him is priceless. After all this, the rest of the story, detailing Doug and Tony's exploits on the island ducking the pirates, can only pale in comparison, but it's a solid adventure with some impressive and beautiful stock footage of the galleons in battle with rich and evocative colors. The same stock had been employed in "Dead Men's Doubloons," a pirate-themed episode of *Voyage to the Bottom of the Sea* the previous year and, suggests the excellent documentary *The Fantasy Worlds of Irwin Allen*, Allen's legendary 1957 turkey *The Story of Mankind*.

Most of the episodes of *The Time Tunnel* were aired in the order they were filmed, with only a few earlier episodes being shuffled around for maximum effect, but "Pirates of Dead Man's Island" is an exception. The tenth episode filmed, it was held over until an airdate that would appear to suggest sweeps week, a period in November and February when the TV networks traditionally air their strongest fare to get maximum ratings that determine their ad rates. As a consequence, it would seem this episode was clearly judged by all concerned to be one of the strongest in the series, even though it became episode 23. Certainly, it is one of the episodes most often remembered and referred to.

Alongside Carroll O'Connor's superb turn as Colonel Southall in "The Last Patrol," and Joe Maross' definitive Custer in "Massacre," Victor Jory as Captain Beal qualifies as one of the series' best guest performances in a long list of contenders. It is certainly the most energetic. Although he was in his sixties, Jory was a strong, powerful man, and Lee Meriwether has told many times how she ended up exhausted and badly bruised after her scenes on the North Bridge. Within months, or more likely weeks of appearing as Beal, Jory appeared as a gangster in "The Frog Is a Deadly Weapon," a weirdly titled episode of *The Green Hornet* (the super-hero crime series preceding *The Time Tunnel* in the schedule), and a deposed dictator in "Return to Glory" for quality adventure series *I Spy*. The following season he opened the fourth and final year of *Voyage to the Bottom of the Sea*, as the fanatical alchemist in "Fires of Death." Cast throughout his career as a vicious villain, other fantasy credits include the infamous *Cat Women of the Moon*, in which he gets to play the hero, and the fascinating cheapie *The Man Who Turned to Stone*, while his most prestigious screen roles were in *A Midsummer Night's Dream* (as Oberon), *The Adventures of Tom Sawyer* (as Injun Joe) and *Gone with the Wind*. In the

'70s he appeared as a mysterious Native American in "Bad Medicine," for *Kolchak: the Night Stalker.*

Regis Toomey, a regular on the Gene Barry Aaron Spelling series *Burke's Law* with Gary Conway of *Land of the Giants,* was also the bogus politician who enjoyed a lengthy ride in the Flying Sub in "The Left-Handed Man" for *Voyage to the Bottom of the Sea* the previous season, thus enjoying the distinction of appearing in two excellent Allen episodes. The sub-plot with Toomey's Doctor Berkhart is fun, but silly, with the doctor staying behind to change the course of history quite drastically by saving 17th century sailors with his little black bag full of penicillin (a word which the baffled Decatur pronounces perfectly). Although it's been established that the events in the Tunnel are part of history, rather than an addition to it, it does seem a rather bizarre development! The somewhat doomed look on Toomey's face when he gets his wish agreed to is almost unintentionally funny.

The variety of time periods and costumes exploited on *The Time Tunnel* allowed Allen to be even more faithful to his regular performers than usual, and as we have already seen, many actors and bit players appeared several times in different roles. By a quirk of scheduling, Harry Lauter appeared in the previous episode, "Billy the Kid" as the villainous Wilson, and then exchanged his cowboy duds to play Decatur's right-hand man Johnson, although as mentioned, "Pirates" was actually filmed much earlier. Lauter's career began in the serials, and he was one of those invaluable actors who always gave a perfect performance in nondescript roles. He had roles in the serials *Flying Disc Man from Mars* and *Canadian Mounties vs. Atomic Invaders,* and the films *The Creature with the Atom Brain, It Came from Beneath the Sea, Earth vs. the Flying Saucers,* and *The Werewolf.* TV work included *My Favorite Martian, The Wild Wild West, The Green Hornet, Voyage to the Bottom of the Sea*

("Deadly Waters"), *The Invaders* ("The Innocent"), and *Land of the Giants* ("The Creed").

For Charles Bateman, who also guested almost invisibly in episodes of *The Munsters, The Green Hornet* and *The Invaders* at around this time, *The Time Tunnel* would yet again provide one of a jobbing actor's better roles. James Anderson appeared in the films *Five* and *I Married a Monster from Outer Space.* He previously worked for Irwin Allen on the *Voyage to the Bottom of the Sea* episode "And Five of Us Are Left." The same year young Pepito Galindo played Armando, he also appeared in a fondly remembered (and much imitated) episode of *I Spy,* "Bet Me a Dollar."

Barney Slater was a regular writer for *Lost in Space,* where he had a hand in almost all the very best episodes, particularly during the first season. Sadly, this was to be his only *Time Tunnel.* Unusually for *Time Tunnel* (although quite common for *Lost in Space*), the trailer sequence for the following story, "Chase Through Time," is edited slightly differently than it appears in the actual episode, mostly for time. Production number: 9610

Chase Through Time

wr. Carey Wilber, dir. Sobey Martin

In pursuit of a saboteur who has placed a bomb in the Time Tunnel complex and fled into the Tunnel, Doug and Tony discover him working on a time travel device for a bizarre insect-like colony one million years into the future, where he's been hiding out for ten years. Attempting to retrieve all three time travelers, the Time Tunnel scientists transfer a room full of people from this future world into prehistoric times.

With Robert Duvall (Raoul Nimon), Vitina Marcus (Zee), Lew Gallo (Vokar), Joe Ryan (the Magister)

LOCATION: Grand Canyon, Arizona, 1547, then One million AD, One million BC.

Robert Duvall, later a successful movie star who was most active in the '70s, made several of his early appearances in 1960s science-fiction series, appearing twice in *The Outer Limits* (in "The Chameleon" and the two-parter "The Inheritors"), and in *The*

Twilight Zone ("Miniature") and *Voyage to the Bottom of the Sea* ("The Invaders"). In "The Chameleon," he plays a hard-bitten, world-weary hired gun for the government, in "The Inheritors" a strait-laced by-the-book FBI man. In "Miniature," he's what the cruel-hearted might call a loser, or a nobody, a shy man who develops an obsession with a doll house. In his *Voyage to the Bottom of the Sea* episode, a superior first season black-and-white adventure, he is a sleeping alien menace, ill-advisedly revived by the *Seaview* explorers. There were other, more conventional TV guest shots, but by the 1970s he was working exclusively in the cinema, notable appearances including *The Outfit*, *M*A*S*H*, *The Godfather*, *The Killer Elite* and *Apocalypse Now* (he also appears in the 1970s SF features *THX-1138* and the *Invasion of the Body Snatchers* remake). While he never gives the same performance twice, he has often portrayed haunted psychotics and loners, and traces of all the aforementioned TV roles and feature film roles can be found in the traitorous, murderous spy Raoul Nimon. Here, in his only color SF TV appearance (other than the borderline "Night of the Falcon" for *The Wild Wild West*), he gives a fierce and energetic performance, particularly good in the opening scenes in the Time Tunnel complex, and in the futuristic beehive, although he appears to be struggling with his lines on a couple of later occasions. However, few other guest players could have duplicated Duvall's inspired mix of anxiety, confidence, and inadequacy for Nimon. Catch the look on his face when he stands before Doug and Tony next to the Magister, defiant, terrified, untouchable, pathetic.

The sets, direction, and photography on this episode are flawless (although one backcloth is rumpled); the episode looks fabulous, including the scenes in the prehistoric jungle (although sharp-eyed viewers will catch a glimpse of David Hedison putting in an unintentional cameo in the well-worn dinosaur fight footage from *The Lost World*). The jungle sequence prior to the reappearance of unintentional time travelers Vokar and Zee actually belongs to the pilot film, in which Doug and Tony were to be briefly thrown back to prehistoric times, but which was excised for time. Never one to waste an inch of footage, Allen inserts it here. Sobey Martin, renowned for directing episodes mechanically and almost literally in his sleep, stages the action well and positions the camera with care. To be fair, he was always efficient, and sometimes impressive.

The erratic Carey Wilber, who also wrote for *Captain Video*, *Lost in Space*, and *Star Trek*, turned in two other *Time Tunnel* episodes ranging from the sublime ("Massacre") to the ridiculous ("Town of Terror"). It's quite extraordinary to imagine that any two examples of Wilber's work were written by the same person ... but they were. More on Wilber's credits in the section on "Massacre." Possibly Wilber secured this assignment having shown his ability to integrate the pilot footage of *Lost in Space* into a new script ("There Were Giants in the Earth"). Possibly, Allen requested a script utilizing the prehistoric footage and set largely on the series' standing set ... but if it is a so-called bottle show, the futuristic sets—bearing a very strong resemblance to the Krel designs of 1956 feature film *Forbidden Planet*, as do the images of the Time Tunnel power core, lifted from the pilot—seem a little too high quality for the episode to have been very cost-effective, despite the employment of some familiar existing props.

The time-travel capsule Nimon is building for the people of the future is the same one used in "Secret Weapon" by the East European scientists (also the spaceship of the frog-alien in "The Golden Man" for *Lost in Space* that season). As one might expect from the chase premise, the Time Tunnel control center plays a slightly larger and more prominent part in the proceedings than usual. (Note that ultimately the Time Tunnel staff only locate the trigger to Nimon's bomb—it's never mentioned, but can we trust they eventually found the bomb itself?)

The opening scenes of this episode have some curious but unimportant differences from the trailer in the previous episode. As this episode begins, we see Doug and Tony landing near the Grand Canyon as Doctor Stiles, the episode's equivalent of the ill-fated nightwatchman, watches on the Time Tunnel viewscreen, whereas before we accompanied Doug and Tony ... and the red alert alarm in the trailer is not only shorter, but the voice is that of a different actor, Dick Tufeld, the series' regular narrator and voice of the *Lost in Space* Robot. Here, the warning sequence is somewhat longer, and the voice belongs to someone else. There's also now an insert of Stiles slumping forward and knocking a lever with his hand when Nimon shoots him, which is the cause of Doug and Tony's distress.

A number of nice touches include the revelation that when Doug and Tony arrive in the far future civilization where the spy has been hiding out, he's already been there a decade. A larger budget might have allowed the aliens to be a bit more bee-like to accommodate Wilber's obvious attempts at a beehive motif (Nimon comes to a gruesome end in a prehistoric beehive in an uncharacteristically grim and poignant final scene), but Allen's standard silver-skinned aliens always look good; the Magister is a particularly impressive creation, and we see too little of him. The sequence in which all the protagonists blink out into the time vortex by rote is quite jolting. Regular viewers are suddenly aware that, like the flight of Captain Beal into the complex in "Pirates of Dead Man's Island," they are seeing something new and special and unexpected. Particularly chilling is the sudden, blunt ending, in which Duvall huddles despondently in the corner of a giant beehive, resigned to

his fate as the ominous hum of the bees draws uncomfortably closer. It's a rare moment of quiet horror as opposed to the more usual loud spectacle of an Irwin Allen production!

Cast as Zee was Vitina Marcus, an Allen regular, appearing twice as the space Lorelei Athena in *Lost in Space* ("Wild Adventure" and "The Girl from the Green Dimension") and again in *The Time Tunnel* as the princess Sarit in "Attack of the Barbarians." She was the native girl in Allen's feature film adaptation of *The Lost World*, and so chalked up her first of two appearances in *Voyage to the Bottom of the Sea* when she appeared in Allen's brazen re-use of his own footage in "Turn Back the Clock," recreating her role in new scenes with her former co-star—and *Voyage* series star—David Hedison. The second was in "Return of the Phantom." She played another native girl—a female Tarzan, in fact—in "The My Friend the Gorilla Affair" for *The Man from UNCLE*. Die-hard *UNCLE* fans despise this episode for its camp frivolity, but it's a hoot, and Marcus is beautiful.

Lew Gallo has worked in many aspects of stage and screen work, and it was while working as a dialogue coach on the 1963 war film *PT-109*—detailing the wartime exploits of JFK—that he was personally suggested for a role in the film ... by Kennedy himself. Interestingly, he previously appeared in the 1960 film *Ocean's Eleven*, alongside several members of the infamous Kennedy Rat Pack. He appears briefly in the Pearl Harbor episode of *Time Tunnel*, "The Day the Sky Fell In," but while "Chase Through Time" offers him a considerably larger role, it is hardly his greatest moment. Painted silver, he wrestles with some truly thankless dialogue. After numerous film roles and over 150 small TV roles, including undistinguished appearances in three episodes of *The Twilight Zone*, a *Lost in Space* ("Flight into the Future"), and two *Voyage to the Bottom of the Sea* ("The Death Ship" and "Deadly Waters") he turned to producing, for *Love, American Style* in the '70s and *Mike Hammer* in the '80s. He would still occasionally act, and turned up as a ghostly angel in *It's Garry Shandling's Show*, a cable sit-com which also employed regular Allen announcer Dick Tufeld. Joe Ryan also appears as an alien in the *Lost in Space* episode "Invaders from the Fifth Dimension." Production number: 9624.

The Death Merchant

wr. Bob and Wanda Duncan, dir. Nathan Juran

The Tunnel control center inadvertently transfers the 13th century warmonger and schemer Machiavelli to the time of the American Civil War, where Doug and Tony must prevent him from influencing the outcome of the battle of Gettysburg.

With Malachi Throne (Machiavelli), John Crawford (Major), Kevin Hagen (Sgt. Maddox), Kevin O'Neal (Corporal)

LOCATION: Gettysburg, U.S.A., summer of 1863

A bizarre and entertaining episode with plenty of action, inspiration and excitement peppered with a smattering of oddball flaws. Visually, the episode looks great, vastly improved for being shot out of doors rather than on a studio set. Darker in tone than most episodes, the horror and futility of war, particularly one between two sides from the same country, is well-drawn with a series of grim, sudden and senseless deaths. Tellingly, only the evil Machiavelli survives, even though he is ultimately cheated of the bloodthirsty spectacle he has been awaiting with undisguised relish.

Malachi Throne, in his second *Time Tunnel* appearance (the other was "Night of the Long Knives"), gives perhaps the best and most three-dimensional of his many performances in 1960s SF TV, and his theatrical, glee at the blood and carnage around him contrasts well with the more realistically played battle-weary performances of the two opposing officers in the conflict, who have seen enough young men die to last them a lifetime. The dark side of war is ably demonstrated by some grim shots of young men's bodies draped over trees and fences, a young corporal's horror when a man next to him gets his face blown off, and the corporal's own death when the Major shoots him at the river. The remorseless daisy chain of unnecessary, sudden, pointless death as each protagonist unquestioningly and unhesitatingly takes the life of the next, along with a total absence of melodrama, speechifying or heroism, makes this one of the darkest and most authentic portrayals of warfare produced for television. When the Major dies, there is a brief but moving scene when Doug assures him that the Union will win, and relates how the battle of Gettysburg will end; the Major doesn't have time to question how he knows all this before he dies from a sword wound inflicted by the manic Machiavelli, absurdly colorful and incongruous in the grimy, muddy surroundings the Tunnel has dropped him into. It's a relentlessly downbeat episode. The scene in which Machiavelli puts paid to the Confederate Sergeant (another flawless performance from the talented Kevin Hagen) is chilling and horrific, as he blithely shoots the soldier in cold blood after the other man's bullets have flown harmlessly through him. Having established in the mind of Maddox that he is an indestructible ghost, the brutal warmonger calmly takes aim and fires.

Typically for a Bob and Wanda Duncan episode, the invulnerability of Machiavelli in the Civil War time period is one of a number of careless flaws in the script, for if the infamous schemer can't be killed because he's past his own death, then this fortunate circumstance should surely apply to Doug and Tony on their many journeys into the far future. As it clearly doesn't—and shouldn't—this renders Machiavelli's power nonsensical. This is such a glaring inconsistency that it is particularly difficult to get past. Another careless slip is Kirk's assumption back in 1968 that it is the Time Tunnel that has conveyed Machiavelli to the Civil War time period, and Ray's declaration that they have the "only" time mechanism; they have already seen at least two other time travel devices in previous episodes ("Secret Weapon" and "Chase Through Time"), and there were more time travelers to follow. When playing with time and space, the possible means for Machiavelli to have traveled through time are literally infinite. Furthermore, the implication that Machiavelli arrived on the coat-tails of Doug's identical signal goes against the obvious evidence that Machiavelli clearly arrived well before them to have set his scheme in motion. Also, it's odd that it's Doug's pattern that resembles Machiavelli's, given that the power surge presumed responsible is used to save Tony. It would have been a much cleaner plot device the other way round; in fact, very little logic seems to have been employed in devising an explanation for Machiavelli's presence. On a lighter note, it's amusing to see that when Crawford and Colbert cross the river early in the story, Colbert emerges bone-dry while Crawford is soaked. Watch the previous scene closely where they enter the water, and you'll see Colbert's stand-in take over.

All three of the main performers in this episode had appeared previously in *The Time Tunnel* and worked extensively for Irwin Allen. As was becoming the rule in this series, Nicollo Machiavelli was presented more as we would presume him to look, than as he really did. In actual fact, Machiavelli was a plotter rather than a doer, a writer and schemer rather than an active protagonist, and a thin, sly-looking fellow; Malachi Throne looks nothing like him.

John Crawford, a great King John in "The Revenge of Robin Hood," and loutish lawman John Poe in "Billy the Kid," would make his fourth and final appearance in *The Time Tunnel* in "Raiders from Outer Space," bowing out in fine form as the terribly British Captain Henderson. Not only was each performance different, but Crawford also adapted his performance to the tone of the piece. For example, here he gives a moving, serious performance, whereas in "Raiders" he is clearly—and appropriately—having fun with the role.

Kevin Hagen also appeared in all Irwin Allen's sci-fi series for Fox at some point, including four different roles in *The Time Tunnel*. He became a recurring character in *Land of the Giants*, making a meal of an otherwise colorless role as the crafty and pragmatic Inspector Kobick, an adversary who appeared in fourteen episodes. In the 1970s, he enjoyed another recurring role, as the town doctor in *Little House on the Prairie*. Kevin O'Neal is the younger brother of actor Ryan O'Neal, who was then finding TV fame at Fox in his breakthrough role in the prime-time soap *Peyton Place*. The younger O'Neal also appears in the *Twilight Zone* episode "The Changing of the Guard." Production number: 9625.

Attack of the Barbarians

wr. Robert Hamner, dir. Sobey Martin
Doug and Tony fight alongside Marco Polo against the Mongols in the 13th century, but Tony falls in love with a princess and considers staying.

With John Saxon (Marco Polo), Arthur Batanides (Batu), Vitina Marcus (Sarit), Paul Mantee (Ambahai)
LOCATION: Somewhere in Eastern China or Mongolia, 1287.

Irwin Allen was not a great one for character studies, and certainly not romantic stories, describing *The Time Tunnel* as a "running and jumping" show—which it certainly was. This dictate, narrow-minded and limiting though it was (and no doubt a source of frustration to some writers and actors) actually helped make his four SF series the lively and fast-paced adventures they were, and prevented them getting mired in the Captain Kirk romance-of-the-week syndrome. Consequently, when *The Time Tunnel* (or any Allen show) did pause for a character study or romance, the event was special and memorable. There are only two serious romantic storylines in the entire Irwin Allen canon—this one, and Mark Wilson's infatuation with the castaway Marna in "The Golden Cage" for *Land of the Giants*. Only rarely, for example, did we ever get any insight into the inner self of cartoon cut-out Dr. Smith in *Lost in Space* (only brief moments in "The Raft," "Trip Through the Robot," "The Questing Beast" and "The Time Merchant" come to mind), and those scenes are memorable for it. Only two or three times, in the entire 110 episode run of *Voyage to the Bottom of the Sea*, did we see David Hedison's Captain Crane romancing a woman. Too often, fake, contrived conflict and shallow, simplistic waffle are passed off as characterization on contemporary sci-fi shows, generating false and phony melodramatic pit-stops that slow down the action or the plot rather than developing or explaining events. Soap opera dialogue does not give characters depth; such insights come from the performances if they come at all. When Ann shows her feelings for Doug in "The Kidnappers" and General Kirk shows his tiredness and weary resolve in "Pirates of Dead Man's Island," these moments become special and unique rather than contrived because they are one-offs, not recurring one-dimensional characteristics. We saw the fate of Tony's father and a glimpse of his childhood in "The Day the Sky Fell In," but otherwise we knew little about the two time-travelers other than that Doug had joined the Time Tunnel project first—yet their unspoken camaraderie comes across in every single episode through their actions, not endless verbiage about how much they respect each other. We know these men without having a third party recite all their virtues in the script.

"Attack of the Barbarians," for all its cheesy production values (which will be discussed in a moment), is a special episode, not only because it gives us *Time Tunnel's* only love story but because it's one of those episodes—like "The Day the Sky Fell In," "The Last Patrol," and "Massacre"—that revolves around the usually understated closeness between Doug and Tony, rather than

simply leaving it implied by events. (There are critics, as we know, who like to read undertones or implications of closet homosexuality into any strong male friendship in film, but this tired old song says more about the lonely person singing it than the production in question! Such people can't be argued with, because any scenes showing the characters romancing or womanizing are dismissed as covering up or over-compensating!) Although they were too busy "running and jumping" to be allowed to show it, Doug and Tony had been to hell and back on their travels—they'd seen countless wars, battlefields, and disasters, living through traumatic events that were not only an endless procession of horror, grandeur, and tragedy, but of enormous magnitude in history and myth. Throughout all this, they had stayed steadfastly loyal to each other, and dependent on each other, the only constants in a kaleidoscopic miasma of past, present and future, and this episode is valuable to the series for showing the devotion and dedication the two time-travelers had for each other ... making history while experiencing history. Very few time travel films have attempted to deal with the psychological effects of time traveling—only *Slaughterhouse Five* and *Twelve Monkeys* come to mind in cinema, while on TV we have *Twilight Zone's* "Walking Distance" and a rare gem from the otherwise insipid 1990s version of *The Outer Limits*, "A Stitch in Time." Tony's love for Sarit, whether it was due to a young man's natural lust, deprivation, or infatuation, was entirely understandable and justifiable, as is his desire in this episode to stop "running and jumping" and settle down.

On a more mundane and less profound level of criticism and observation, this episode was also shot outdoors on location, as was the episode that preceded it ... but unlike "The Death Merchant," which benefited greatly from the privilege, the opening scenes of "Attack of the Barbarians" look hopelessly unconvincing, giving every impression of having been shot in a park (complete with tire-tracks and freshly mown grass!). The opening conflict between the time-travelers and the Mongols resembles a theme park pageant, and the stock footage, which is usually integrated seamlessly, looks horribly phony and out of place. When one stray warrior comes galloping toward the time travelers after we've just seen hordes of them in the film clips, it's laughable. Fortunately, this is not the case with the rest of the episode (or, indeed, the rest of the series), which once past the lame opening is as gripping and intriguing as ever, with a spectacular battle scene at the close integrated with the conflict between Doug and Tony. However, the famous pink, yellow, and blue striped tent interior is rapidly overstaying its welcome at this point!

Like Barney Slater, the *Lost in Space* writer who submitted the memorable "Pirates of Dead Man's Island," Robert Hamner—a regular contributor to *Voyage to the Bottom of the Sea* and *Lost in Space*—wrote only this one episode of *The Time Tunnel*.

Veteran TV and film actor John Saxon was James Darren's roommate for a while during the early '60s. He did more film work than TV, albeit almost exclusively in unspeakable schlock, and—as a martial arts enthusiast—is best known for his role in the Bruce Lee classic *Enter the Dragon*. His sci-fi CV is a cavalcade of Z-grade junk, as is most of his other work in straight-to-video drivel. These include Roger Corman's *Queen of Blood*, Gene Roddenberry's unsold pilot *Planet Earth*, and a recurring role in three of the *Nightmare on Elm Street* film series. This was his only assignment for Irwin Allen.

Although an excellent actor able to invest his parts with some humanity, Arthur Batanides has not been lucky in the SF field, where he has endured foolish roles as a caveman in *Lost in Space* ("The Space Primevals") and a bogus alien in an unintentionally hilarious SF episode of *The Green Hornet* ("Invasion from Outer Space"), encountered a leprechaun in *Wonder Woman* ("Pot o'Gold"), and featured in one of the few undisputed lemons of the original *Outer Limits* ("Specimen: Unknown"). He was better served here as the Mongol leader Batu, a role he enjoyed. "I played Genghis Khan's grandson, and I loved the make-up," he told Mark Phillips, interviewing him for *Starlog*. "It took over two hours to put it on and they had a whole stretch cloth over my head to bald me. It was a great role to play. I loved the concept of *The Time Tunnel*. It had great potential. Frankly, I've had great reservations about some of these science-fiction things."

Fair comment, under the circumstances. His films include *The Unearthly* and *The Leech Woman*, and despite a small role in the pilot for *The Man from UNCLE* and a reasonable *Star Trek* ("That Which Survives," alongside *Time Tunnel's* Lee Meriwether, a role he enjoyed as for once he wasn't the heavy), most of his SF TV work—*The Twilight Zone*, *Get Smart*, *The Wild Wild West*, *Land of the Giants* ("Terror-go-Round"), *Galactica '80*, and *Knight Rider*—when not embarrassing, has been undistinguished.

Paul Mantee is best known for one of his earliest acting jobs, *Robinson Crusoe on Mars*. TV includes episodes of *Batman*, *The Invaders*, *Voyage to the Bottom of the Sea*, *The Gemini Man*, *The Six Million Dollar Man*, *Fantastic Journey*, *Logan's Run*, and *Buck Rogers in the 25th Century*.

All credit to Vitina Marcus, who despite her over-exposure in Irwin Allen productions, managed to look different in all of them. She is excellent as the princess Sarit, yet had just played Zee in "Chase Through Time." Her sultry beauty was subjected to all manner of challenges throughout the '60s, particularly by the Irwin Allen studios. They painted her green, they painted her gold, menaced her with giant spiders, ghosts, and dinosaurs, but still she looked gorgeous. Production number: 9626.

Merlin the Magician

wr. William Welch, dir. Harry Harris

Merlin the Magician materializes in the Time Tunnel complex and causes havoc while ensuring that Doug and Tony assist him in his machinations to get the young Arthur Pendragon on the throne of England.

With Christopher Cary (Merlin), Jim Mc-Mullan (Arthur), Lisa Jak (Guinevere), Vincent Beck (Wogan)

LOCATION: Cornwall, England, 544 A.D.

Both this episode and the following story begin with the premise of someone from another time period visiting the Tunnel, instead of the other way round. Here, the legendary Merlin abducts Doug and Tony to the time of King Arthur, while in the next story, Ann is spirited away to the year 8433 by an intruder who turns up at the Time Tunnel complex in much the same way as the aliens at the close of "Visitors from Beyond the Stars." Indeed, the last three episodes of *The Time Tunnel* all feature futuristic aliens, which would seem to indicate the future direction of the series had it made a second season.

Here, a very silly but thoroughly entertaining episode is saved by Christopher Cary's performance as Merlin, and the usual antics back at the complex provide an interesting diversion from the escapades with the Vikings. The abundant battle footage (although even more was available) came from the 1954 movie of *Prince Valiant* (based on a popular and long-running newspaper comic strip), so explaining the silly lopsided wig Jim McMullan is forced to wear as the young Arthur, and why Merlin is obliged to transform the knights into Vikings. Director Harry Harris, an Irwin Allen regular working on only his second and last *Time Tunnel* (his other was the third filmed, but second aired, "One Way to the Moon"), endeavors to film the Tunnel set from more creative angles, and one scene is very odd, with the General discovering Ann and Ray standing inside the Tunnel numb with shock after they've witnessed Doug cut down by a sword. A prolific director for Irwin Allen, he directed half-a-dozen episodes of *Lost in Space*, but mostly occupied himself with *Voyage to the Bottom of the Sea* and *Land of the Giants*, directing nearly half of the latter series. Given his interesting use of the *Time Tunnel* standing set in both this and "One Way to the Moon," one wishes he had done just a couple more *Time Tunnels*, if only to see what else he came up with; in many episodes, control scientists Whit Bissell, Lee Meriwether and John Zaremba rarely left their marks, but both times Harris has them moving round the set. A former director of TV westerns, he returned to the genre almost immediately when the Irwin Allen factory wound down, although as the westerns themselves declined, he seemed to be scraping around for a new niche, eventually spending most of the 1970s directing the soapy feelgood drama *The Waltons*.

Whatever the truth behind the mixture of fact and fantasy that has become the legend of King Arthur, this episode takes the usual, and I must say preferable, path of films and television of portraying Merlin as a purely supernatural being. This Merlin is a wizard, pure and simple. He freezes things, he floats gracefully through the air (actor Christopher Cary was a former ballet dancer in his native England), he moves people in time with a wave of his hand, he sees the future because he has been there, he turns time backwards with a flick of his wrist. This is not an alchemist, an alien (like the Pied Piper in the *Land of the Giants* episode "Pay the Piper"), or a sleight-of-hand conjurer, this is a supernatural being. Quite why such a powerful entity should need the assistance of two lowly mortals to achieve his aims, even allowing for the occasional brief moment to rest his powers, is a question neither properly asked or sufficiently answered, but then in a yarn such as this it doesn't need to be. This, like the earlier "Revenge of Robin Hood" episode, is a historical romp in a Hollywood version of history, and happily, the cast and audience are left in no doubt of it. It's plain, joyous fun.

The episodes set in the Middle Ages were always the ones on shakiest ground—it's difficult to take big burly guys with horns on their helmets seriously in any circumstances—but while this story isn't as enjoyably loony as the colorful "Revenge of Robin Hood," it's not as cheesy as the Marco Polo yarn that preceded it either. As said, Merlin's transformation of the knights into Vikings was necessitated to fit the battle footage from *Prince Valiant* (along with most of the props and costumes by the looks of it), while the castle sets look remarkably similar to those fortresses in the Troy, Marco Polo, and Robin Hood stories. Music from the *Prince Valiant* film is liberally sprinkled throughout the entire series, and in fact, the stomping opening theme from *Prince Valiant* graces not this episode, but "The Revenge of Robin Hood."

As with Robin Hood, Billy the Kid, and Custer, *The Time Tunnel*'s Merlin is by far one of the best of numerous interpretations of Merlin in film and television. Being magical, the famous wizard has done his fair share of time-traveling in other productions, although in nothing very memorable or notable. Christopher Cary, one of the better actors on television, was a regular on the 1960s war series *Garrison's Gorillas*. This blond-haired, hard-faced young man also appeared in *The Man from UNCLE*, *The Girl from UNCLE*, *The Wild Wild West*, *Batman*, *Land of the Giants* ("Chamber of Fear"), the unsold Gene Roddenberry pilot *Planet Earth*, *Wonder Woman*, and *Voyagers*. Only months after the broadcast of "Merlin the Magician," he would again be involved in the legend of King Arthur, this time playing Mordred in the 1967 film of the musical *Camelot*.

Tall, deep-voiced, and menacing, Vincent Beck never quite got the parts he deserved. In fact, many of them were downright embarrassing. After the much-mocked

Santa Claus Conquers the Martians, his role here as the Viking warlord in "Merlin the Magician" resulted in a recall to don one of the monster suits for the series' final episode, "Town of Terror." He then played blue-faced alien hunter Megazor in "Hunter's Moon" for third season *Lost in Space*, where he was let down by a cheesy outfit and uninspired direction. Other TV included *The Man from UNCLE*, *The Girl from UNCLE*, *Get Smart*, *The Wild Wild West*, and *The Invisible Man*. Jim McMullan continued on the guest star circuit throughout the 1970s, turning up in episodes of *The Six Million Dollar Man* and *The Bionic Woman*, and went on to star in his own short-lived sci-fi show during the 1979–'80 season, when he took the lead in what turned out to be only five episodes of the intriguing but disappointing *Beyond Westworld* (blink and you missed it in March, 1980). No further SF TV credits for Lisa Jak have been located. Production number: 9628.

The Kidnappers

wr. William Welch, dir. Sobey Martin

Ann is kidnapped from the Time Tunnel complex by an alien scientist as bait to lure Earth's premiere time-travelers to attempt a rescue mission that is to end with their capture for his private collection of stolen historical figures.

With Michael Ansara (alien scientist), Del Monroe (OTT)

LOCATION: A star near Canopis, many light years away from Earth, 8433.

"The Kidnappers" is textbook Irwin Allen B-movie pulp sci-fi adventure, but with Grade A sets and visuals to shame every other SF show of the period. William Welch wrote or co-wrote 52 episodes of Allen's TV series (a sixth of Allen's entire output), including seven *Time Tunnels*. Given the unusually high quality of his contributions to *The Time Tunnel*, "The Kidnappers"—although good by the standards of a typical Welch script—is both the last and the least of his *Time Tunnel* offerings, the action based rather transparently around a succession of children's party games! They play tag, they play hide and seek, they play statues, they play hunt the thimble! However, Welch's obvious interest in history shines through—everyone's had a go at the fate of Hitler, who turns up here on ice yet again, but he didn't have to name OTT's earlier captives as Cicero and Sir Thomas More! Also appearing is one Bob May, glimpsed briefly in a blink-and-you-miss-him shot as the frozen Adolf Hitler; May was usually incarcerated, quite happily it has been said, inside the *Lost in Space* Robot, and equally happily doesn't bear the slightest resemblance to who he's supposed to be here!

After appearing in the feature film of *Voyage to the Bottom of the Sea* with his then-wife Barbara Eden for producer Irwin Allen, Michael Ansara, tailor-made for Hollywood villainy, was used frequently in Allen's TV productions, and appeared in virtually every significant fantasy TV show of the '60s. He also inevitably worked frequently on Eden's long-running *I Dream of Jeannie* series. Of all the actors to cross from the swinging '60's SF to the grim and grey gloomy sci-fi of the '90s, Ansara is one of a select few performers whose career has spanned almost every phase of film fantasy, having appeared on just about every significant TV SF show ever made. Del Monroe, Kowalski on Allen's *Voyage to the Bottom of the Sea*, probably wisely turned down the role of Inspector Kobick on *Land of the Giants* (which went, fortuitously, to the talented Kevin Hagen), and moved on to a career playing bit parts as heavies when the submarine adventure series closed production. Among the heroes he ill-advisedly tried to menace were *The Amazing Spider-Man* in "The Kirkwood Haunting," and *The Incredible Hulk* in "East Winds."

As had by now become the norm with both Welch scripts and *The Time Tunnel's* more fanciful yarns, the plot is full of holes as wide as the Time Tunnel itself. Welch was quite capable of turning out scripts of good quality, as proven by "Night of the Long Knives" and "Billy the Kid" among others, but more often he dashed them off quickly to order as Irwin Allen's rewrite man or pinch-hitter; he knew Allen's stock footage library and props department better than the people in charge of it, and many of his episodes are recognizable as Welch scripts not by their style or characteristics, but by their deployment of available materials. "The Kidnappers" is all too clearly one of his cynical rush jobs. There are numerous unsubstantiated statements, including such howlers as Kirk's immediate assumption that OTT must be a time-traveler, when he looks no different from any other Irwin Allen extra-terrestrial, Tony's instant assumption that the future-men are hostile, and some absurd behavior on the parts of all concerned. Why does Kirk announce dramatically that he's going to switch Doug and Tony—why not just do it, before he can be stopped? Why does Doug just blithely reveal to the future-men that he, Tony, and Ann hid their drugged food instead of eating it? And most obviously of all, why do the scientists back at the Time Tunnel assume that switching the guys to another time-period will solve their problems? They *know* that they're dealing with opponents who have mastered time travel, and can instantly return Doug and Tony from wherever the Tunnel sends them.

The ending, for this reason, is ambiguous. Doug and Tony destroy the time machine of the kidnappers, but there is no indication that they have lost the knowledge or facilities to simply build another. Are OTT and his master killed in their final confrontation with Doug and Tony, or only stunned? If stunned, then they can continue abducting Doug and Tony *ad infinitum*. We must therefore presume that they are killed; the episode ends very suddenly, in the manner of many of Welch's scripts for *Voyage to the Bottom of the Sea*, when the alien menace concerned, having kept everyone running around for 49 minutes, would be conveniently blown up right at the end of the show. And what became of the historical figures that were abducted?

Poor Welch. He wrote under the impression, as all TV workhorses believed in the '60s, that his efforts would fly from the minds and memories of viewers as soon as they had aired, two runs and into the mists of time. If only he had known that TV buffs and sci-fi fans would be nitpicking his words to threads for decades afterwards alongside multiple reruns of the source, while people within the industry would be using Allen's shows as templates for future SF TV, studying them for wisdom regarding what to do—and what not to do—when making potential long-running hit series of their own.

The episode also features some classic dumb dialogue, including two personal favorites. As mentioned, OTT is a standard silver-skinned Irwin Allen alien. For absolutely no discernible reason, General Kirk announces authoritatively, "You know, he *looked* like he might be a time traveler!" Later comes my number one candidate from an Irwin Allen show, when Ray Swain demands "Check all channels, from one hundred through to infinity!" Which, of course, will take forever ... literally, forever! In Britain, the initials OTT are shorthand for Over The Top, meaning too extreme to be taken seriously. That certainly is appropriate for this episode, which is enormous fun and hugely enjoyable for all the wrong reasons.

Despite all this, the episode is fast-paced and imaginative, with never a dull moment. The sets are excellent, a kaleidoscope of colors and lights, and the performances are fine (if you don't look *too* closely at OTT, who bears a striking resemblance to crewman Kowalski from *Voyage to the Bottom of the Sea!*). Only Lee Meriwether's sign-of-the-times helpless female routine grates on modern sensibilities in places, although the scenes in which she is reunited with, and then parted from, Doug and Tony are sub-

tly moving, a rare moment of brief emotion amid the usual rough and tumble.

There are also some nice ideas hidden within Welch's unusually original scenario—the roofless rooms open to the skies, the aliens becoming motionless at night, OTT's necklace weapon, the spotlight that Doug and Tony must follow on arrival, and the central concept of Michael Ansara's impressive alien scientist kidnapping and collecting people from Earth's past (a theme that resurfaces in Welch's "Time Lock," a fourth season episode of *Voyage to the Bottom of the Sea* the following year, as well as Britain's *Doctor Who,* in "The War Games" and *Star Trek: The Next Generation's* "The Most Toys," to name but three). The sets are superb—only the alien ray-guns brandished in one scene look tacky, and the few daft plot inconsistencies are easily overlooked in deference to a cracking good, crisply efficient adventure story that is eminently watchable and entertaining. Production number: 9627.

Raiders from Outer Space

wr. Bob and Wanda Duncan, dir. Nathan Juran
Materializing in North Africa, just before the battle of Khartoum, Doug and Tony discover a nest of extraterrestrial aliens preparing to use Earth as a battleground for their own wars.

With John Crawford (Captain Henderson), Kevin Hagen (alien leader)
LOCATION: November 2nd, 1883, Sudan, North Africa.

Where to start? With the wonderful 1950s-style alien invaders, with their thin legs, green scales, bug eyes and bat ears, all in glorious color? With the spectacle of the tumultuous battle footage from an expensive historical epic? With the humming, whirring six-foot explosive device made up of familiar bits and pieces from the *Lost in Space* and *Voyage to the Bottom of the Sea* props room? With the faceless zombie slaves guarding the alien base in the rocks? With the hilarious performance of John Crawford as the stereotypical British Empire soldier, whose response to stumbling onto an ant-nest of extraterrestrials is not "oh my ghod" but a curious "Hel-leau?" Or with the wonderfully subtle character actor Kevin Hagen, valiantly trying to look menacing and retain his dignity with a giant plastic cabbage on his head? This, folks, is *The Time Tunnel* at its best, and its worst. You've never seen anything quite like it, and you'll never see anything like it again.

Regular viewers of Irwin Allen series will have much to look for in this lively adventure, one of the most fast and furious and thoroughly enjoyable in the series. The background music, which includes much of Allen's regular stock music for weird alien episodes of his shows, noticeably includes as well some background music from *Lost in Space* early on, and even some spots of the *Prince Valiant* score at one point. Most amusingly, the alien headquarters appears to be made up of several parts of the *Seaview* missile room from *Voyage to the Bottom of the Sea*, Admiral Nelson's transparent world map (mostly seen in that series' first season) and that familiar human form cut-out as seen in "The Dream Monster" and "The Condemned of Space," to name but two *Lost in Space* stories utilizing it, and the *Voyage to the Bottom of the Sea* episode "The Cyborg." More interestingly, the scenes inserting Colbert, Darren, and Crawford into the film footage defending the fort are filmed on the dock of the Nelson Institute harboring the *Seaview* from *Voyage to the Bottom of the Sea*. Had the camera panned slightly to the left of the action, we would have seen a very incongruous body of water in the middle of dry and dusty 1880s India!

Director Nathan Juran (sometimes known as Jerry Juran or Nathan Hertz) directed enjoyable episodes of *Voyage to the Bottom of the Sea* ("The Machines Strike Back," "The Shape of Doom," and "Deadly Invasion"), two classic first season *Lost in Space* ("Return from Outer Space" and "The Magic Mirror," alongside the less exciting

"The Space Trader"), six assorted second season *Lost in Space* episodes of varying quality ("Blast Off into Space," "The Ghost Planet," "The Prisoners of Space," "The Girl from the Green Dimension," "West of Mars," and "The Wreck of the Robot"), and three excellent third season stories ("The Condemned of Space," "The Space Primevals," and "Target Earth"). For *The Time Tunnel*, he directed "The Walls of Jericho," "Billy the Kid," "The Death Merchant," and "Raiders from Outer Space." Following *The Time Tunnel*, he moved on to *Land of the Giants*, where he seems to have fallen on his feet, laying claim to the much-remembered first season story "Ghost Town," and the second season's "The Deadly Pawn," "Land of the Lost," "The Clones," and "Nightmare," the latter three of which feature some of the series' more unusual effects sequences. For this task, the Austrian-born former art director was more than qualified, having previously worked in the cinema, where his body of work included such special effects-laden sci-fi extravaganzas as *The Deadly Mantis*, *Attack of the Fifty Foot Woman*, *The Brain from Planet Arous*, *Twenty Million Miles to Earth*, *The Seventh Voyage of Sinbad*, *Jack the Giant Killer*, and *First Men in the Moon*. Many of these were films with special effects wizard Ray Harryhausen, who had animated Allen's stop motion dinosaurs for *The Animal World*. *Sinbad* and *Jack* are fairytale adventures; *Twenty Million Miles to Earth* and *First Men in the Moon* are second league sci-fi classics. Juran was also very adept at handling material utilizing footage from other films; his numerous earlier B-pictures included *Siege of the Saxons*, which filches action scenes from other films, and *East of Sudan*, which uses stock from *The Four Feathers*. Both the latter were probably sourced for this episode's action scenes, some of which are foolishly and obviously compressed, elongating the bodies and drawing attention to their outside source. The feature film *Khartoum*, released at around the same time as this episode was produced, was *not* a source of stock footage or sets.

For both John Crawford and Kevin Hagen, this was their fourth appearance in the series, and their second together in the same episode (previously, they both fought on opposite sides in "The Death Merchant"). Three of Crawford's and two of Hagen's *Time Tunnels* were also Nathan Juran's. Hagen, who gave his best performance in an Irwin Allen show in Juran's "The Shape of Doom" for *Voyage to the Bottom of the Sea,* can put his talents to any role, and he carries off this impossible assignment perfectly, and with as much gravitas as he can muster with a big green plastic brain and bat-ears balanced on his head. Bizarrely, Hagen's role is referred to as Planet Leader in the credits and promotional materials, but if he is the "planet leader," who sent him to Earth to prove himself? Furthermore, why is he being demoted to Prince? In fact, why are they even using a terrestrial term like Prince in the first place? British-born John Crawford is clearly having great fun as Colonel Henderson, yet another fine opportunity to exercise his craft in this actor's dream of a series (unless of course, you draw the short straw and get the cabbage head). The Major's aide and the other aliens and alien stooges are sadly not credited. Production number: 9629.

Town of Terror

wr. Carey Wilber, dir. Herschel Daugherty

The time travelers tumble into a deserted New England town in the year 1978, where invading alien beings have set up a beach-head to destroy all life on Earth.

With Gary Haynes (Pete), Heather Young (Joan), Mabel Albertson (Sarah), Vincent Beck, Kelly Thorsden (aliens)

LOCATION: September 10th, Cliffport, Maine, New England, 1978.

In a plot-line reminiscent of the then-current series *The Invaders,* the aliens (inexplicably referred to as androids) are masquerading as humans in a plot to steal the Earth's oxygen and transfer it to their own planet. Exactly why they need oxygen if they are androids, and what became of their own supply is never explained! But then this is pure 1950s-style B-movie bilge, and great fun if watched purely in that context—but expect nothing so sophisticated as *Invasion of the Body Snatchers* and its ilk from this arrant nonsense, which makes no sense at all.

The basic flaw from the point of view of the series' concept is the closeness of the time period (bearing in mind that 1978 was ten years in the future here). The problem with both this episode and the earlier "One Way to the Moon" is that the Time Tunnel control center, armed with the knowledge of what to expect in the future, would be able to alert the authorities and thus prevent the events they have witnessed from ever taking place, thus creating a time paradox. It's also peculiar that Doug and Tony never once regard 1978 as being as good as home—and are whisked away as usual at story's end, and into the infinite corridors of eternal syndication and cable TV. After all, 1978 is only a decade away from their starting point in 1968—why, after the aliens have been routed, don't Doug and Tony simply make their way back to the Time Tunnel complex for a pleasant month or two looking over the newspapers of the last ten years?

Such hopes for pause for thought amid the monster mayhem rapidly fade amid the avalanche of minor throwaway gaffes in plot logic, the major ones concerning such questions as why Doug and Tony instantly assume that the aliens they see are androids (a fact not verified by the aliens themselves until much later in the proceedings) and how they know that these creatures can't stand up in the stormy weather that brews up. These are powerful, unearthly creatures encountered for the first time—how do they *know* these things? As in "Visitors from Beyond the Stars" and "The Kidnappers," these things are so because the scriptwriter says they are, not because the characters discover them to *be* so during the course of the story.

What became of the alien device hidden in the Time Tunnel complex? Like Nimon's bomb in the same author's "Chase Through Time," we never hear of it again, or see it discovered or removed—it has served its function as a plot device, and is forgotten. What became of the townspeople who disappeared when the aliens inhabiting their bodies vanished?

But of course it's futile to pick holes in an episode in which nobody knew, cared, or bothered to consider such questions. Production values are high for the time, and the alien heads—although blatantly phony—are colorful and serve their purpose, and as usual in *The Time Tunnel*, there are several nice creative touches, including a number of wacky scenes with the aliens. Mabel Albertson's transformation into a hideous, towering monster is a hoot, and the alien visit to the Time Tunnel complex and the two surviving townspeople's reactions when asked to believe that on top of their sudden extraterrestrial problems, they have just encountered two time travelers are other highlights. There's also the inevitable calamity back at the Time Tunnel control center to look forward to when the oxygen starts to disappear in 1968, sucked away by the aliens' device through the Tunnel's connection to '78. In the sequence where Doug and Tony attempt to break out of captivity by smashing a bench through a window, Robert Colbert sustained a slight injury to his forehead, necessitating a few quickly administered stitches at a nearby hospital.

Writer Carey Wilber's other two *Time Tunnel* episodes were the excellent "Massacre," concerning Custer's last stand, and the fascinating Robert Duvall starrer "Chase Through Time," and despite the uncharacteristic plot inconsistencies in his work here, he was one of the more inspired contributors among the Irwin Allen canon. He rarely repeated his ideas, and there are enough of

them here to keep the 49 minutes fast and furious. Plainly and simply, it's pulp SF, and is best enjoyed at that level.

Playing two teenagers who find that they are the only townspeople not to be taken over by the alien invaders were Gary Haynes and Heather Young. Gary Haynes previously played the Deputy in "Visitors from Beyond the Stars," while Heather Young was to be cast as stewardess Betty Hamilton in Allen's next series, *Land of the Giants*. As Patti Petersen—her real name—she makes a brief appearance in the first Mad Hatter story for *Batman*. Also returning from "Visitors from Beyond the Stars" was stock footage of an alien spacecraft, previously used in Wilber's *Lost in Space* episode "The Sky Pirate."

Mabel Albertson was Darrin's mother in *Bewitched* during the '60s, Dick Van Dyke's mother in his splendid but forgotten 1970s series, the so-called *New Dick Van Dyke Show*, and a regular fixture in many other sitcoms of the period dating back to the 1950s. This was her only SF work, and in one brief scene, with the actress presumably unavailable, she is replaced by a very obvious stand-in. As this appearance is pointless and literally for one second of screen time, you can only wonder why director Herschel Daugherty, in his second of only two Irwin Allen assignments (the other was "Kill Two by Two"), even bothered to film it.

In the alien suits were two gentlemen with perfect credentials for a production like "Town of Terror"! Vincent Beck was Megazor in the "Hunter's Moon" episode of *Lost in Space*, and could also count the notorious *Santa Claus Conquers the Martians* among his film credits. He had previously appeared in "Merlin the Magician" as the viking Wogan. Kelly Thorsden was in the cast of *Invasion of the Saucermen*, a super little trashy teen movie of the '50s. These two courageous performers stagger around the Fox backlot blindly trying to see out of their antennae headpieces, no doubt grateful every time Daugherty stops the camera. Wiggle wiggle wiggle go their evil fingers whenever they're about to take someone over with a prod to the forehead. Love those wiggly fingers. One of the monster heads used in this episode did double duty on *Lost in Space* at around the same time, painted red to adorn the alien in "The Phantom Family"; you can actually see the red paint beneath the purple in some shots...

And that was how this extraordinary series ended, from the highs of "The Day the Sky Fell In," "The Last Patrol" and "Massacre" to the lows of "Town of Terror." Not with a bang, but a wiggle. But what a ride.... Production number: 9630.

Episodes in Order of Production

SINGLE SEASON (30 EPISODES)

6034 Rendezvous with Yesterday
9602 The End of the World
9603 One Way to the Moon
9604 Revenge of the Gods
9605 Secret Weapon
9606 The Day the Sky Fell In
9607 The Last Patrol
9608 The Crack of Doom
9609 Massacre
9610 Pirates of Dead Man's Island
9611 Devil's Island
9612 Reign of Terror
9613 The Death Trap
9614 The Alamo
9615 The Night of the Long Knives
9616 Invasion
9617 The Revenge of Robin Hood
9618 Visitors from Beyond the Stars
9619 Kill Two By Two
9620 The Ghost of Nero
9621 The Walls of Jericho
9622 Idol of Death
9623 Billy the Kid
9624 Chase Through Time
9625 The Death Merchant
9626 Attack of the Barbarians
9627 The Kidnappers
9628 Merlin the Magician
9629 Raiders from Outer Space
9630 Town of Terror

Episodes in Order of Broadcast

SINGLE SEASON (30 EPISODES)

6034 Rendezvous with Yesterday
9603 One Way to the Moon
9602 The End of the World
9606 The Day the Sky Fell In
9607 The Last Patrol
9608 The Crack of Doom
9604 Revenge of the Gods
9609 Massacre
9611 Devil's Island
9612 Reign of Terror
9605 Secret Weapon
9613 The Death Trap
9614 The Alamo
9615 The Night of the Long Knives
9616 Invasion
9617 The Revenge of Robin Hood
9619 Kill Two By Two
9618 Visitors from Beyond the Stars
9620 The Ghost of Nero
9621 The Walls of Jericho
9622 Idol of Death
9623 Billy the Kid
9610 Pirates of Dead Man's Island
9624 Chase Through Time
9625 The Death Merchant
9626 Attack of the Barbarians
9628 Merlin the Magician
9627 The Kidnappers
9629 Raiders from Outer Space
9630 Town of Terror

Production Credits

Created and produced by Irwin Allen. Assistant to producer: Paul Zastupnevich. Story editor: William Welch (pilot). Story editor: Arthur Weiss (series). Art direction: William J. Creber, Rodger E. Maus. Art direction supervisor: Jack Martin Smith. Set decoration: Walter M. Scott, Norman Rockett. Costume design and wardrobe: Paul Zastupnevich. Director of photography: Winton Hoch, A.S.C Special effects: Lyle B. Abbott, A.S.C. Music: John Williams (pilot). Music: Lyn Murray, Paul Sawtell, Robert Drasnin, Leith Stevens, Joseph Mullendore, George Duning. Music editor: Joseph Ruby (pilot). Music editor: Sam Levin (series). Music supervision: Leonard Engel, Lionel Newman. Theme music: John Williams. Sound effects editor: Robert Cornett. Supervising sound effects editor: Don Hall Jr. Production coordinator: Les Warner. Production supervisor: Jack Sonntag. Production assistant: Hal Herman. Unit production manager: Eric Stacey (pilot). Unit production manager: Bob Anderson (series). Assistant directors: Ted Butcher, Fred Simpson, Steve Bernhardt. Film editors: James Baiotto, Dick Wormell, Axel Hubert. Make-up: Ben Nye. Hair styling: Margaret Donovan. Post production supervisor: George Swink. Post production coordinator: Robert Mintz. Associate producer: Jerry Briskin. In charge of production: William Self. Kent Productions for 20th Century Fox.

4 *Land of the Giants*

September 1968–March 1970

Looking for his next hit series, Allen did what every TV producer does—knowing that the last thing the play-safe networks want is something really new, he looked back at his past work for the nearly new. He found it in the first season of his biggest hit, *Lost in Space*, the format and two episodes of which ("There Were Giants in the Earth" and "The Oasis") showed him which way to go.

The fourth of Allen's popular and impressive science-fantasy adventure series of the 1960s was an extraordinary and expensive story relating the fate of the crew and passengers of a small "sub-orbital" flight from Los Angeles to London (in the far future of 1983) which is mysteriously diverted by a green-glowing magnetic force to a strange world where everything is gigantic in size—the grass is six feet high, the trees are as tall as skyscrapers, insects are the size of dogs, and the human inhabitants are 70 foot tall lumbering sadists, simpletons, or mad scientists. His new group of castaways (just two inches high) are hunted by the authorities for the benefits of their science and technology, which is fifty years in advance of the giants (the castaways are not the first Earth people to have traveled through the space warp to the giant world).

Allen's series were always well cast, and *Land of the Giants* was no exception. Starring were Gary Conway and Don Marshall as Steve Burton and Dan Erickson, the pi-

lots of the *Spindrift*, Don Matheson as temperamental and hard-headed businessman and engineer Mark Wilson, Deanna Lund as spoilt, wealthy heiress Valerie Scott, and Kurt Kasznar as sly but panicky Alexander Fitzhugh, a soft-hearted (and soft-headed) embezzler and con-man. Stefan Arngrim was the dim but good-hearted orphan Barry Lockridge, Heather Young was motherly stewardess Betty Hamilton, and Kevin Hagen was Inspector Kobick, the man assigned to locating and capturing "the little people." The giants' world—or at least the part of it reached by our unfortunate but intrepid adventurers—looks something like early 1930s America, but is a totalitarian state run by a government known as the Supreme Council and policed by the S.I.D. (Special Investigations Department), from which the timorous citizenry cower; it's a fusion of USA and USSR. Early stories detailed the castaways' attempts to survive in their new hostile environment, avoid capture by the giant people and repair their spaceship to return home, although later stories sometimes revolved around the problems of giant people they had become involved with and decided to help out. There's a reward out for their capture, too—the evil state police force, lead by Hagen's sly and intimidating Kobick, has put it about that the so-called little people are deadly dangerous aliens.... Kobick is a ruthless and treacherous man whom even his fellow giants can't

The "little people" contemplate their future outside the poorly camouflaged space shuttle the *Spindrift* in the *Land of the Giants*.

trust, and pursues the castaways throughout various (but by no means all) adventures, spreading propagandist scare stories to the gullible populace and offering a hefty reward for the capture of the "dangerous aliens" ... a move sending all manner of unsavory characters tramping through the overgrown forest with nets, boxes and jars. Fortunately, the giants are slow in physical speed as well as mental agility, which is doubly fortunate for the castaways as—unlike the Robinsons of *Lost in Space*, who seemed to have everything they could possibly require stashed aboard for their pre-planned voyage, plus quite a bit more—the *Spindrift* had been a passenger flight, and day-to-day survival played a much more prominent part in the

land of the giants. Indeed, many episodes started from that premise, with the group making various finds, turning trash into gold, or getting into peril while foraging for food, chemicals, or other materials to fix the ship for a return flight home.

The three male leads were of the brave, all-American square-jawed tough guy breed favored by Allen in all his other series, and as such they were required to do little more than run around and be athletic and heroic, tasks they performed admirably. Gary Conway, Don Marshall and Don Matheson spent much of their time waving lighted branches at snarling back-projected rodents or poking them with giant needles and sticks. When they weren't doing that they'd be shinnying up to tabletops on knotted ropes with grappling hooks made out of giant safety pins, dodging giant eyes by scurrying mouse-like between book displays and tins of food on table tops, or scuttling across dimly-lit floors and around skirting boards to crawl underneath conveniently raised doors (they discovered early on that giants don't see too well in the dark). The travelers were also kept smartly clothed too, presumably by the women in the party; the show being a product of its time, the two female members of the group were frequently being ordered back to the ship for safety, and traditionally feminine chores and attributes were unquestioningly assigned in that direction. While Heather Young's stewardess Betty was the epitome of the domestic housewife, Deanna Lund's spoilt rich girl Valerie defied her new role and was refreshingly feisty and disobedient; even when she was obeying snappy orders from the men, her eyes were projecting the message that she would do whatever she felt like doing. She was particularly well-written in the pilot.

Despite this one sign of the times, the series has—like Allen's other series—aged remarkably well. While slower paced than its predecessors, it is eminently watchable and entertaining, with more frequent attempts at character delineation and pathos than those before it. Particularly well-played was Don Matheson's fiery, short-tempered and aggressive businessman Mark Wilson, who didn't take orders easily, and frequently played practical devil's advocate to the bossy moral center of Gary Conway's Captain Burton. Another source of tension was the double-act of the boy and the scoundrel that had worked so well before in *Lost in Space*. This, Allen and collaborator Anthony Wilson reasoned, would also provide the prerequisite conflict that the belated addition of Doctor Smith had brought to *Lost in Space* (which Wilson also story edited). Like the other Allen series, *Land of the Giants* took itself far more seriously than *Lost in Space* in compar-

ison, and the amusing excesses of Jonathan Harris' antics as Smith would have been badly out of place in this series. However, the Smith-and-Will ploy had worked too well not to be employed again. Wilson went directly to "The Reluctant Stowaway" (the first episode of *Lost in Space*), even to the extent of rerunning the scam-that-doesn't-matter-anymore sequence where Smith tries to flim-flam the boy only to have subsequent sudden shocking developments make his efforts redundant; in *Space*, the attack of the Robot negates Smith's yarn about Will's phony illness, while in *Giants* Fitzhugh's nonsense about top secret documents is exposed by the encounter with the giant cat. We also see Fitzhugh writing off other members of the group as hopelessly lost in a thoroughly Smith-like manner.

While Barry and Fitzhugh were clearly intended to fill the same function as Will and Smith in *Lost in Space*, they did not dominate the series, even though the writers inevitably drifted toward the more colorful character of Alexander Fitzhugh to at least launch the adventures. Fitzhugh was obviously devised as a Doctor Smith-style catalyst, and the writers naturally played on this, but because Kasznar created and protected his own character the interpretation tended to differ from week to week, writer to writer. Sometimes he was a coward, sometimes a schemer, sometimes a playful con-man, sometimes a cold-hearted villain, sometimes a loveable bumbler, each writer picking on a different aspect of the Smith persona. Treated with disdain by the others as a liar and a liability, the cowardly and self-interested Fitzhugh began as a bad guy, but softened up and rallied round as the series progressed. However, his characterization also tended to jump around a bit from one episode to the next because of the network's irritating decision to radically alter the running order of the series.

Gary Conway's career began in '50s B-movies like *The Saga of the Viking Women and* the Sea Serpent, I Was a Teenage Frankenstein, How to Make a Monster, and Young Guns of Texas; before taking the lead in Land of the Giants he co-starred with Gene Barry in the 1960s detective series Burke's Law. His real name is Gareth Carmody. Before securing the lead in Land of the Giants he made the unsold pilot Attack and tested for the leads in The Alaskans and The Long Hot Summer. Following Land of the Giants he made the unsold pilot The Judge and Jake Wyler, guest-starred in Columbo, Ghost Story, and Police

Story, and appeared in various low-budget films, eventually moving into producing. Conway has been trying to resurrect Land of the Giants as a feature film for some years now.

Don Marshall had made guest appearances in over a dozen different TV series of the period, including a memorable Star Trek ("The Galileo Seven"). After Giants, he would be seen in The Bionic Woman and The Incredible Hulk. Don Matheson had already appeared in Allen's Lost in Space (twice) and Voyage to the Bottom of the Sea, and went on to appear in Allen's disastrous TV production of Alice in Wonderland.

Before Land of the Giants, Heather Young (real name Patricia Kay Peterson) had appeared in episodes of The Felony Squad, Batman, Judd for the Defense and The Time Tunnel. Following Giants, she retired from the business to raise a family. Deanna Lund's career is an almost parodic litany of '60s starlet credits—the Riddler's moll on an episode of Batman, a "slutty girlfriend" (her words) in the thriller Johnny Tiger, two uncredited bit parts in Elvis films (Paradise, Hawaiian Style and Spinout), a screen debut as a dolly bird in Doctor Goldfoot and the Bikini Machine ("I really didn't want to stand around in a gold bikini for six weeks"), and a part as a lesbian stripper in the Sinatra film Tony Rome. There were also roles in the sci-fi thriller Dimension

Kurt Kasznar hollers in the grip of the ubiquitous giant hand that represented all grasping giants as another seeks the reward for "little people."

Five with *Star Trek's* Jeffrey Hunter, infamous turkey *The Oscar*, and other gems with titles like *Sting of Death* (her first film), *The Swinger*, *The American Wife*, and *Out of Sight*. Following *Land of the Giants* she appeared in episodes of sci-fi spy show *Search*, *Love American Style*, *The Waltons*, and *The Incredible Hulk*. She also worked on the daytime soaps *General Hospital* and *One Life to Live* and the breakfast show *Good Morning New York*. More recently, she found a new career in low-budget movies, appearing in *Witch Story*, *Transylvania Twist*, *Naked Force*, *Red Wind*, and *Hammer*.

Stefan Arngrim's screen debut was in the film *The Way West*; TV roles followed. As a teenager, he appears in the schlock horror film *Fear No Evil* and has a small role in 1992 sci-fi feature *Strange Days*. As with most child actors, work has been harder to find as an adult, but he has kept busy; he's played small roles in *The X-Files*, *Highlander*, *Poltergeist—the Legacy*, *Viper*, and *Seven Days*. Kurt Kasznar died in 1979; he also appeared in *Search*, and the pilot film for *MacMillan and Wife* (quite a treat for Irwin Allen fans, "Once Upon a Dead Man" also features a wonderful turn by Jonathan Harris). His numerous TV roles include the fantasy series *The Man from UNCLE*, *The Girl from UNCLE*, and *Wonder Woman* and prior to *Land of the Giants* he had appeared in over thirty films.

However, although the series was graced with a likeable cast (who very rarely met or acted alongside their guest stars, most of whom were cast as giants and filmed separately), and the set pieces with giant animals and insects were excellent, the quality of individual episodes of *Land of the Giants* depended very much on the ideas and the guest stars (who included Ron Howard, Bruce Dern, Robert Colbert, Broderick Crawford, Stuart Margolin, Richard Anderson, Sam Elliott, John Carradine, Jonathan Harris, Lee Meriwether, and Yvonne Craig).

The special effects people, who had their work cut out for them, were Fox's award-winning in-house team of Lyle B. Abbott, Art Cruickshank, and Emil Kosa Jr. As ever, Allen got it right from the start, and little had to be amended or changed, although the foggy and noisy giants' world, with its swirling mists and eerie sounds, quickly emulated the new worlds of *Lost in Space* by clearing up and quietening down with indecent haste in subsequent episodes. The bright orange spaceship remained grounded for most of the series (although very poorly concealed!), and insects and other passing creatures of the ground were noticeably absent. In later episodes, for the sake of dramatic license, the giants became more human-like and conversational, a change which occurred more quickly on air than in production when ABC shuffled the running order. Equally inevitably, less complicated shots were employed in later episodes, with some natural and practical re-use of props (but hardly ever stock footage, except for the occasional establishing shot; however, Allen's inevitable dino-lizards did show up!). Although we never saw the giants visibly pick up the tiny Earthlings after the pilot (they would be conveniently obscured from view when in the hands of the actors playing the giants), for the second season little clockwork toys were developed, showing wriggling feet struggling in the giant's hands. The actors did most of their own stunts, and all the giant props had to be physically built.

While the pilot was far and away the best of all the episodes, the next in production, "The Weird World," with Glenn Corbett playing another marooned astronaut, comes an easy second. The episodes offered some memorable and imaginative images— the little people cowering in an egg-carton, or sticky-taped to a giant's work bench; a giant screeching bird setting its beady eye on them; a gopher hole ominously beginning to shake and crumble as the owner ploughs toward them; a fatal spider's web spread inside an air vent. According to Fox's literature, the pilot was originally to have ended with the *Spindrift* castaways discovering Kagan's tape recorder from "The Weird World," so revealing that others had come to the land of the giants before them, but this scene was apparently excised when the network decided to shuffle the running order.

Although there had already been a short-lived 1950s series titled *World of Giants* (about a deliberately shrinking crimefighter, a theme that would resurface in pop culture periodically—comic book *The Atom*, puppet show *The Secret Service*, mid–'80s series *Misfits of Science*, straight-to-video film *Dollman*), and other precedents obviously included *tom thumb, Gulliver's Travels, The Devil Doll, The Incredible Shrinking Man, Attack of the Puppet People*, and *Fantastic Voyage, Land of the Giants* was most clearly inspired by the 1940s B-movie *Doctor Cyclops* (the episode "On a Clear Night You Can See the Earth is a blatant remake of the movie, even to the uncharacteristic intent of the space travelers to kill the threatening giant scientist). In *Doctor Cyclops*, a pompous elderly biologist and a prim young female doctor coerce a fellow scientist into accompanying them on an expedition to Brazil where—with their guide and another local—they become human guinea-pigs for a mad scientist with a shrinking ray. With the remarkable frankness that only a B-picture of the period could bring to the screen, the party decide to kill their tormentor, and interestingly, it is the sole woman in the group who takes charge and has all the good ideas—quite a novelty for the 1940s! Despite pedestrian, uninspired direction and giveaway tell-tale dialogue that leaves the development of few scenes open to speculation, it was filmed in eerie blues and greens and the sets and trick photography were flawless. The early episodes of *Land of the Giants* were in much the same vein, and visually very similar, although after the first few excellent episodes ("The Crash," "The Weird World," "The Trap" and "The Bounty Hunter" were the first filmed) the

mists cleared to reveal a more conventional forest area, and the sun came out over the area of woodlands where the *Spindrift*, the castaways' spaceship, was marooned.

With the camp craze now over, and color TV no longer a novelty, Allen opted for realistic color and to play the series straight, at least during the first year; a lighter tone crept into some of the episodes in the second season, which is distinguished from the first by a photo montage and different theme instead of the first season's animated credits. Gone were the colorful, garish sets and toyland props and costumes of *Lost in Space*, with regular Allen costumer Paul Zastupnevich producing a set of more subdued, realistic outfits. The colors, sets and props were mostly naturalistic, the costumes blending in without appearing drab, and the characters were treated far more realistically than the sugar-coated Robinsons. They were even allowed to quarrel frequently, but, as with all Allen series, the action never slowed down long enough for any in-depth characterization. As the series developed it became necessary to give the giants more to say and do in order to create and develop stories, but unfortunately, the writers made the mistake midway through the first season of shifting the emphasis away from the interests of the Earth party to the dilemmas of the giant guest stars into whose lives the little people appear. Examples of this trend include "Shell Game," "Rescue," "Return of Inidu" and the sentimental but chilling "Night of Thrombeldinbar," in which devious con-man Fitzhugh is mistaken by two unhappy and mistreated orphans for a sort of mythical Santa's elf. It would spoil the story to reveal the surprise twist here, but as a one-off, the story made a pleasing diversion from the usual good giants/bad giants conflicts, and still manages some imaginative moments of horror and menace through the kids' innocent beliefs in magic and myth.

One strong episode that concentrated

on the regular cast was "Target Earth," in which the crew and passengers quarrel and split up over a proposed alliance with giant scientists that might get them home. But one of the series' best remembered yarns is "Ghost Town," the fourteenth episode filmed but the second aired, in which a sadistic and spiteful little girl menaces the group in a mock-up model Earth town built by her eccentric grandfather, and which— despite a mystifying lack of living souls— briefly leads them to hope against hope that they may have somehow stumbled back to Earth. There's a marvelous sequence in which Fitzhugh is trying to use a fake phone box which is suddenly plucked off the ground and suspended in the air by a giant hand. In "Genius at Work" the tables are turned when a child prodigy (the teenage Ron Howard) whips up a formula that can make the Earth people giant-sized—a development which causes the put-upon Fitzhugh to become vindictive and careless as he struts around the giant world bumping smaller men aside into the gutter!

Other first season highlights included "Framed," in which the Earth people corner a murderer; "Flight Plan," with a treacherous miniaturized giant; "Manhunt," in which a convict trapped in quicksand takes the spaceship with him; "The Golden Cage," with Mark seduced by a young girl used as bait by giants; and "Sabotage," with *Time Tunnel's* Robert Colbert as the bad guy. Weaker episodes included the circus-based "Terror-go-Round," "The Lost Ones" with a group of marooned louts, the zoo-based "Seven Little Indians," "Return of Inidu," which flounders after a great start, and "Shell Game," which utilizes the giant seashell prop from the *Doctor Dolittle* film.

No tribute to *Land of the Giants* would be complete without a huge tip of the (giant) hat to composer John Williams, who also scored the early episodes of *Lost in Space* and the *Time Tunnel* pilot, and is today best known for the equally rousing themes for *Jaws, Star Wars, Superman, Jurassic Park,* and many, many others. As was the case with *Lost in Space,* Williams' music was tracked through the rest of the series, and *Land of the Giants* benefited enormously from it. Many of Williams' pieces for the pilot became almost signature music for the show, secondary themes, and as interesting as the later contributions of Joseph Mullendore and others were, it was the blasts of Williams' warning trumpets and blaring crescendos that audiences associate with the series today.

A clever employment of camera angles—below for the giants, up high for the little people—and John Williams' superb trumpeting backing score accentuated the impression of an oversized world and added to the illusion. Of course, when the series was being planned, the actors knew nothing of what the finished effects would look like on screen, or how huge a part the talents of L.B. Abbott, John Williams, Tony Wilson and others would contribute. Talking up to corners of the studio, running and screaming from objects that weren't there, and feeling even sillier when they were (Gary Conway and Don Matheson can clearly be seen laughing in the pilot's drainpipe sequence), the cast members—cowering in giant egg cartons, strapped to table tops with giant swathes of stickytape—were undoubtedly relieved and impressed when they saw the finished film. Far from looking ridiculous, they were part of one of the most elaborate and extravagant special effects displays in the history of television.

Unfortunately, the show took a crippling blow it never quite recovered from when story editor Tony Wilson left the show shortly after it started and took the characterization with him ... What characterization there was in *Land of the Giants* was down to the efforts of Wilson, the man who gave *Lost in Space* Doctor Smith and the Robot and helped bring *The Invaders* and *Planet of the Apes* to television. Having been the story editor

10230-901
JANUARY

LAND OF THE GIANTS

COUNTDOWN TO ESCAPE!

on *Lost in Space* for all three seasons, he helped set up *Land of the Giants* as well, giving the most strongly defined characters yet to an Irwin Allen production (something which completely evaporated when he left), and left them with around twenty embryonic storylines before he departed to work his magic on a western series, the now forgotten *Bonanza*-clone *Lancer*. Those episodes with his name on the credits are distinguished by a strength of characterization that was noticeably absent from later episodes. Conway's Captain Steve Burton, like *Star Trek's* Captain Kirk, was blessed with the self-assurance that comes with being the leading man of a TV series with the scriptwriters on his side, although Matheson's quarrelsome Mark Wilson, despite having the scripts loaded against him in the role of Burton's antagonist, was sometimes more likeable and pragmatic. Deanna Lund was excellent as the impulsive and impetuous sexpot Valerie Scott, a wealthy young woman not used to being told no, while Don Marshall's co-pilot Dan Erickson and Heather Young's motherly stewardess Betty Hamilton were pretty much stoic ciphers; Marshall was rarely used to the best of his abilities (ably displayed in the classic *Star Trek* episode "The Galileo Seven"), while Young was hindered by pregnancy through much of the second season. Equally uncharismatic as cute lil' orphan Barry Lockridge was Stefan Arngrim, a young lad whose bland role and sudden growth spurt between the two seasons relegated him to little more than scenery in the later episodes. Adding the most color to the cast was Austrian-born character actor Kurt Kasznar as the devious Alexander Fitzhugh.

Kasznar was superb as the greasy, sweaty and fearful ne'er-do-well "Commander" Fitzhugh, but young Arngrim, although apparently excellent with his lines and everybody else's, was a poor substitute for Billy Mumy. Fortunately, the cast did not sink into the same discontent and apathy that plagued the Smith-led *Lost in Space*, as Fitzhugh was not the only malcontent in the party. Whereas the Robinsons had been a tight-knit family, the crew and passengers of the *Spindrift* were a disparate bunch, and both Mark Wilson and Valerie Scott, the other two passengers, considered themselves free spirits and frequently argued with the sanctimonious Captain Burton and went their own way. Unlike the Robinson castaways there was no protocol as to who was in charge, even though Burton assumed responsibility and co-pilot Erickson and stewardess Hamilton remained loyal. Sadly, the conflict between the party was never quite so fully exploited as the excellent opening episodes by Wilson suggested it would be, although the aforementioned "Target Earth," in which the passengers split with the crew and Barry after arguing over an attempt to get home that may or may not have been a trap, was a rare non-Wilson exception.

For the second season, Allen shifted the emphasis of the stories back to the regular cast, rather than making the guest stars the focus of the story. Exceptions included "Six Hours to Live," in which the Earth people try to clear a convicted man of murder and expose the true culprits, a nasty old man and his shrewish wife, "Giants and All That Jazz," in which Dan introduces a giant trumpet player to jazz, and the light comedy "Comeback," guest starring John Carradine as a washed-up horror film actor. Other light-hearted escapades included "The Inside Rail," with Fitzhugh endangering everybody trying to play the horses; "Our Man O'Reilly," a daft yarn that seems to have forgotten the giant world isn't Earth; the bizarre "Pay the Piper," with Jonathan Harris of *Lost in Space* as the Pied Piper, an extraterrestrial traveler it turns out, who offers to rid the giants of the little people for the

Opposite: An example of the *Land of the Giants* comic books from the 1960s.

benefit of a self-aggrandizing politician; "A Small War," with the Earth people menaced by a little boy's toy soldiers; and "The Marionettes," in which Betty and Fitzhugh pose as circus puppets. In the second season's unusual change of pace "Home Sweet Home," Steve and Fitzhugh actually return to Earth, but in the 19th century. However, the best second season episodes were probably the darker ones—"The Mechanical Man," with a dangerously lethal android; "The Unsuspected," in which Steve accidentally ingests hallucinogens that turn him treacherously paranoid; "A Place Called Earth," featuring murderous time-traveling telepaths; "Nightmare," in which the Earth people find being invisible is a two-edged sword; "Panic"; "The Deadly Dart"; and "Doomsday." *Land of the Giants* probably had a more limited life-span than Allen's other series, and by the end of the first season, ideas were wearing thin. There were only so many times the audience could get excited by a barking dog, mewling cat, or pecking bird, and after 51 episodes the well was running dry. As had been the procedure with *Time Tunnel* and *Voyage to the Bottom of the Sea*, Allen added further fantastic concepts to a show already boasting an outrageous premise—the castaways now encountered killer robots, madmen, time travelers, underground civilizations, bizarre hallucinations, a teleporter device, and—in "The Clones," a memorable episode—were duplicated by a giant scientist who creates

doubles of them all. With the limited novelty of the giant world now wearing off, it was these more unbelievable yarns that were the most entertaining. The final few episodes filmed show desperation setting in, as the series had clearly run its course. However, it was the cost factor that finally sank the show. Cancellation due to the high cost of production may have ultimately been a mercy killing that left fans with two good seasons (only about a dozen duds in the run, with just a couple of outright stinkers) rather than a slow death *Star Trek*-style. It was the most expensive TV series in production when it was made, and it still looks great.

Most of the Allen series were aired relatively sequentially by the networks concerned with a minimal amount of reorganization. However, as the ABC network decided to air the episodes in a completely different running order from that in which they were made, consistency, continuity, and character development in *Land of the Giants* is all over the place when later broadcasters have followed the network sequence rather than the production order (as they often do). Consequently, the *Land of the Giants* episodes will be discussed sequentially, in the order episodes were given a production number, rather than in the wildly haphazard network running order, for reasons concerning the development of the series which will become apparent as we proceed.

The Cast

REGULAR CAST: Gary Conway (Captain Steve Burton), Don Matheson (businessman Mark Wilson), Kurt Kasznar (embezzler Alexander Fitzhugh), Deanna Lund (heiress Valerie Scott), Don Marshall (co-pilot Dan Erickson), Heather Young (stewardess Betty Hamilton), Stefan Arngrim (orphan Barry Lockridge)

The Episodes

FIRST SEASON (1968–1969)

The Crash

wr. Anthony Wilson, Irwin Allen, dir. Irwin Allen

June 12th, 1983: A sub-orbital flight from Los Angeles to London encounters a strange magnetic force that sucks them into another dimension.

With Don Watters (entymologist), Anne Dore (lab assistant), Patrick Michenaud (giant boy)

"The Crash" may be one of the best hours of television ever produced, a non-stop roller-coaster ride of what was then— and still is—an extraordinary accomplishment of special effects magic. Without wishing to denigrate the other episodes, it's easily the best in the series.

Obviously, much of this has to do with the fact that it's the pilot. "The Crash" not only sets the scene, but has to sell the show to the audience (the network had already okayed the series, but the quality of the finished result dictates the amount of promotional and executive support the series gets, not to mention how many viewers come back the next week). Consequently, Allen pulls out all the stops, with endless effects scenes and exciting confrontations with perils of all description—if only subsequent episodes had featured such continuous action. No appearance of a giant creature occurs without being preceded by a scene of ominous predatory growling noises, and only a brief sequence with some giant spiders fails to deliver credible special effects. Elsewhere, scenes with a giant cat and later, a giant dog, are dazzling—even today. The sets are superb, particularly a completely convincing lab tabletop, and a giant junkyard. Absolutely no visual or planning aid from computer technology was available at the time; everything had to be meticulously planned, built and pho-

tographed the hard way (there was one short-cut—a scene featuring Mark Wilson in the *Spindrift* was filmed on a portion of the *Jupiter Two* from *Lost in Space*). The whole episode has an almost dreamlike quality, particularly in the lab sequence, as in the early episodes, the giants are silent, almost somnambulistic, until the need for stories forced them to become more talkier, bigger versions of ordinary people.

"The Crash" overcomes some pretty bad acting in the opening scenes (particularly from Kurt Kasznar, later one of the series' prime assets) to develop into quite a striking little mini-film. Nitpicking further, it's difficult to resist remarking that the safety authorities ought perhaps to be informed that the *Spindrift*'s seats aren't fastened to the floor! It would also be interesting to know how Fitzhugh intends to spirit a suitcase so blatantly full of banknotes through customs, although a bribed official is plausible. But then, if Fitzhugh had something more discreet, his bag couldn't burst open so spectacularly when the giant cat attacks!

Little is known of Don Watters and Anne Dore, who portrayed the two giant scientists in the pilot (even though the still of Watters clutching Deanna Lund in his fist has become one of the most famous images associated with the series; one of the very rare occasions a giant was shown visibly holding one of the Earth people until the second season introduced tiny wind-up dolls to the effects options). Anne Dore did have a bit part in the *Lost in Space* episode "Return from Outer Space," and Watters, looking very different, plays a wordless heavy in the early '70s action film *Truck Turner*. Patrick Michenaud is the older of two brothers working as child actors in the '60s. He appears as the dauphin in the French Revolution episode of *The Time Tunnel*, "Reign

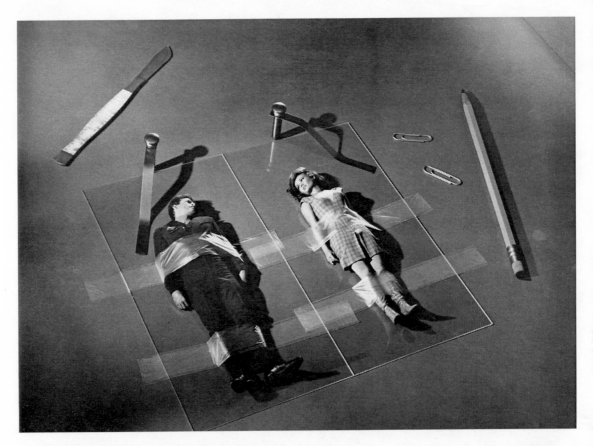

Gary Conway and Deanna Lund in an iconic image from the *Land of the Giants* pilot.

of Terror," while his younger brother Gerald can be seen aboard the *Titanic* in the pilot episode of *Time Tunnel* and as a gypsy boy in the later *Land of the Giants* episode "Terror-go-Round." Both lads can be seen together in the *Mission: Impossible* episode "Shock," as two kids snooping around the set of one of the team's operations. Production no.: 2401.

The Weird World

wr. Anthony Wilson, Ellis St. Joseph, dir. Harry Harris

The Earth people meet a lonely sole survivor from a previous flight.

With Glenn Corbett (Major Kagan), Don Gazzaniga (night watchman)

This story establishes that the giants' technology is approximately fifty years behind Earth's, and that the giants have difficulty seeing in the dark. While "The

Crash" was easily the best of all the episodes, the next in production, "The Weird World," with Glenn Corbett of *Star Trek's* "Metamorphosis" playing Kagan, another marooned astronaut, comes an easy second. The pilot was originally to have ended with the discovery of Kagan's tape recorder from "The Weird World," so revealing that others had come to the land of the giants before them, but this scene was lost when the network decided to shuffle the running order. Although its loss is a shame, it does remove one of those happy but unlikely movie coincidences, as the Earth people were destined to meet Kagan himself in the following episode. In fact, although the second episode produced, it became the eleventh broadcast, even though Fitzhugh has not yet mellowed, tries to betray everyone, and is still lugging his suitcase full of money around with him wherever he goes. Fitzhugh began the series as a selfish coward but gradually became a loveable rogue, a character development somewhat obscured by the ABC network's episode juggling. No other Allen series was shuffled around in so cavalier a fashion, and it is in order to properly examine the development of the series that we look at the episodes in order of production rather than order of broadcast.

If *Star Trek's* original Cochran had been the embodiment of Robinson Crusoe, with an ethereal and female Friday, then Corbett's Major Kagan certainly looked the part. Well-remembered for his role as the original Zephram Cochran in the aforementioned *Star Trek* episode (a completely different interpretation was presented by another actor in the '90s feature film *Star Trek: First Contact*), he also appeared in *The Man from UNCLE* ("The Hong Kong Shilling Affair") and starred in the unsold parallel world-/man-on-the-run pilot *The Stranger.* He also appears to have worked in some capacity on un-used footage for Allen's proposed *City Beneath the Sea* series.

Writer Anthony Wilson went on to contribute a number of story ideas to the series which were then scripted by other writers. As the episodes with the strongest plots and character development are those with Wilson's name on them, it would seem as though he got the series off to a good start. The job of transposing *Robinson Crusoe* to the *Land of the Giants* format went to the talented Ellis St. Joseph, who also wrote such SF TV classics as "The Sixth Finger" for *The Outer Limits* and "The Day the Sky Fell In" for *The Time Tunnel.* He was thrilled with Corbett's portrayal of Kagan, telling *Starlog* interviewer Mark Phillips that "The Weird World" "was done beautifully. It turned out just as I had envisioned it." The sequences with the giant crow and giant gopher, and the climactic scenes as Kagan confronts the menace in the drainpipe so horrible he'd blanked it from his mind, are among the

best in the series. Later, St. Joseph would write "Underground" for the series, and would have happily written more, but for a higher paid film offer that materialized.

"The Weird World" was the first of no less than 24 episodes that Harry Harris would direct of *Land of the Giants.* Together, he and Sobey Martin directed the entire series with the exception of Allen's pilot and "Ghost Town" in the first season (which was directed by Nathan Juran), and five second season episodes (four of which were also by Juran). A former director of westerns, with numerous episodes of *Gunsmoke* and *Rawhide* to his credit, Harris contributed extensively and almost exclusively to all the Allen series during the '60s, directing seven *Lost in Space* episodes, two *Time Tunnel,* and eleven *Voyage to the Bottom of the Sea,* dividing his time on *Land of the Giants* with another western, *The High Chapparal.* Despite working on some of the most challenging episodes of the other Allen series, most of his *Land of the Giants* episodes following this classic were among the most mundane and straightforward, with the really unusual assignments going elsewhere. Following *Land of the Giants,* Harris went on to direct for *The Waltons,* his only other SF credit being a *Man from Atlantis* episode, "Hawk of Mu." Production no.: 2402.

The Trap

wr. Anthony Wilson, Jack Turley, dir. Sobey Martin

While trying to salvage materials for the ship from a giant alarm clock, two of the Spindrift party are hunted down and captured by giant scientists with a sound-sensitive device.

With Stewart Bradley (scientist), Morgan Jones (assistant)

One of the earliest episodes made, and the first episode in which the giants and the Earth people communicate; note that the giants use a microphone to receive the voices of the little people, a device not bothered with in future episodes for obvious practical reasons. The episode gets off to a bad start credibility-wise when Steve and Dan creep around in the undergrowth trying to retrieve a discarded silver foil chocolate bar wrapper right under the noses of the giants, when all they have to do is wait for the two men to move on. This sequence, with the mantis, and the one with Valerie and Fitzhugh with the animal trap were added to the episode at the last minute; some nice dialogue in the opening campsite scene and a sequence with Betty and Valerie finding a mud puddle had to be cut from the script to accommodate these jeopardy sequences. Originally, the episode had opened at the campsite in a scene now trimmed down to a few lines about Fitzhugh never missing a meal; a shame, because moments of characterization were lost. On the plus side, there is an excellently realized scene when a falling giant sprawls and knocks Fitzhugh unconscious, and a wagon the castaways have built out of a giant sardine can and bottle tops looks good. This is the episode in which Fitzhugh finally relents and pitches in to be one of the gang; there is a redemptive moment when the passengers and crew watch Barry present him with a homemade hero medal. Unfortunately, by the time it aired, as the eighth episode instead of the third, this metamorphosis was redundant.

"The Trap" was the first of Sobey Martin's 21 episodes of Land of the Giants, alternating with Harry Harris but for seven episodes. A former MGM film editor, Martin had worked on a number of undistinguished and long forgotten 1950s TV series (including Big Town, Public Defender, Paris Precinct, Crusader, The Millionaire, and U.S. Marshal) before joining the Irwin Allen operation for the '60s, where he directed thirteen of some of the most unusual episodes of Voyage to the Bottom of the Sea, twelve Lost in Space (of which at least half are classics), and thirteen Time Tunnel.

Jack Turley, not a great admirer of the Allen series, but a friend of Anthony Wil-son, also wrote "Hunter's Moon" for Lost in Space and the later Land of the Giants episode "The Golden Cage." Stewart Bradley plays a giant police sergeant in the second season episode "Six Hours to Live." Bit player Morgan Jones' extensive credits include the films Forbidden Planet, Not of This Earth, and The Giant Claw, and episodes of The Twilight Zone, The Invaders, Star Trek, Bewitched, and The Six Million Dollar Man. The two muggers and their victim are not credited; at the time Allen's series were made, onscreen credits were arbitrary, at the discretion of the production. Production no.: 2403.

The Bounty Hunter

wr. Anthony Wilson, Dan Ullman, dir. Harry Harris

The Earth people discover there's a price on their heads ... and Steve and Mark fall out when a bounty hunter brings a gun into the forest that Mark wants to steal for protection.

With Paul Sorensen (the bounty hunter), Kimberly Beck (his daughter)

Filmed back to back with "The Trap," and using exactly the same campsite set (this duplication is less obvious when the series is shown in U.S. network running order, because they aired quite a way apart), this is a nice episode that neatly sets the boundaries for the space travelers' future encounters with the giants. They have realized that these aren't monsters, but giant human beings, while the giant man is moved to compassion by his young daughter. In only one other episode will the little people deliberately try to take a life—and succeed—and that is the uncharacteristic "On a Clear Night You Can See the Earth," featuring the demise of a menacing mad scientist who can see in the dark with special glasses. "The Bounty Hunter" is the episode that establishes that the giants are aware of the little people and want to hunt them down and capture them. Again, the revelation is rendered meaningless when the series is shown in the network running order, which places this episode fifteenth. Both "The Trap" and "The Bounty Hunter" further hammer home the plot point that the giants can't see too well in the dark.

Once again, the episode has been overseen by Anthony Wilson and is heavy on character development; Valerie and Fitzhugh are remarkably three-dimensional for an Allen production. Also established is that, like Professor Robinson and Major West in the earliest episodes of *Lost in Space*, calm, cautious Steve and hot-headed, short-fused Mark are frequently in disagreement about the course of action that should be taken (Steve always turns out to be right of course, because Gary Conway is the star of the show, which does tend to make Burton a little insufferable at times!). Dan Ullman was a former western writer and a regular contributor to 1960s TV SF, writing the excellent "Cold Hands, Warm Heart" for the second season of *The Outer Limits* and the superb "The Leeches" and "The Saucer" for *The Invaders*. He returned to write "Six Hours to Live" and "Doomsday" for the second season. Production no.: 2404.

The Golden Cage

wr. Anthony Wilson, Jack Turley, dir. Sobey Martin

Mark and Steve fall out over a trap baited by the giants with a beautiful Earth girl who has grown to womanhood in captivity.

With Celeste Yarnall (Marna), Douglas Banks, Dawson Palmer, Page Slattery (the scientists)

The nature of television in the 1960s, combined with the status of this series as an early Sunday evening entertainment, prevented Allen's writers from ever exploring sexual tensions among the castaways even if Allen had allowed it. The consensus among those who knew him was that he was not remotely interested in characterization (or what passes for it in TV sci-fi), or anything else that would slow down the action. With regard to his other three series, this was al-

most certainly the right decision. Nevertheless, of all Allen's series, *Land of the Giants* had the most strongly defined cast, and the opportunity was there for the sort of in-depth character exploration that his other series did not allow for. While the situations in *The Time Tunnel* and *Voyage to the Bottom of the Sea* were too fast moving to offer the chance for human drama that the situation of the *Spindrift*'s crew and passengers did, and while such scenes in *Lost in Space* would have been a hindrance that slowed down the action and the humor, *Land of the Giants* cried out for a depth of character development (in terms of conflict rather than wishy-washy feelings or romance) that was sadly rarely attempted. Once again, what characterization there was, was clearly the work of story editor Anthony Wilson, who set the scene for the series with the opening episodes by farming out completed stories to hired hands for finished teleplays. When the assignments went directly to the scriptwriters as notions to be developed, the characterization quite noticeably suffered, with (upon Wilson's departure) a number of the writers putting the dramatic emphasis on the giant characters. This story though is difficult to fault, rich in intriguing imagery, particularly the teaser in which the Earth party discover the girl in the bottle. It was as close as the series got—or wanted to get—to exploring the sexual feelings of the castaways. In real life, at least two of the cast seemed to have no such qualms—Don Matheson and Deanna Lund later married, and they have both said that had the series gone to a third year, a wedding for their characters was on the cards! Although they later amicably divorced, actress Melissa Matheson is their daughter.

Celeste Yarnall, a model turned actress who is today a successful businesswoman, appears as Yeoman Landon in *Star Trek's* "The Apple." Of the supporting cast in this story, Dawson Palmer was the regular monster man on *Lost in Space*; Douglas Bank had a memorable bit-part as a scientist in the opening scene of the *Voyage to the Bottom of the Sea* episode "Werewolf." He returns to *Land of the Giants* to play a bit part in "Sabotage." Production no.: 2405.

The Lost Ones

wr. Bob and Esther Mitchell, dir. Harry Harris
The Earth people encounter a group of marooned juvenile delinquents.

With Zalman King (Nick), Tommy Webb (Dolf), Jack Chaplain (Joey), Lee Jay Lambert (Hopper), Dave Dunlop (trapper)

More castaways from an earlier flight, this time a party of unlikable street kids. This was the first story by husband and wife team Bob and Esther Mitchell, who wrote twelve episodes of *Land of the Giants* altogether, "The Lost Ones" being followed by "The Creed," "Double-Cross," "Sabotage," "The Night of Thrombeldinbar," "Rescue," "Shell Game," "Return of Inidu," "Genius at Work," "The Unsuspected," "The Clones," and "The Secret City of Limbo." Particularly memorable were "The Night of Thrombeldinbar," "Genius at Work," "The Unsuspected," and "The Clones." A thirteenth script, featuring the fascinating concept of the little people saving the giant world from giant-sized space invaders, was never produced after the series was suddenly canceled, and they later wrote two episodes of *Buck Rogers in the 25th Century*, "Journey to Oasis" and "The Crystals."

Zalman King, who went on to take the lead in the series *The Young Lawyers*, is today best known for producing a string of rather tame and decidedly unerotic sex films and the equally dreary *Red Shoe Diaries*. The episode is primarily notable for the anecdote about New York method actor King breaking Gary Conway's nose in a fight scene not once, but twice—a yarn far more interesting than anything on the screen here. "The Lost Ones," however, falls prey to the old rule of thumb that an episode featuring boorish and obnoxious people can result in a boorish and obnoxious hour for the audience. Like the castaways, we can't wait to get rid of this sorry bunch. Had the hooligan routine been played to the hilt to create a genuine sense of menace, we may have had a suspenseful episode in which the thoughtful and pragmatic *Spindrift* passengers are placed in peril by the careless and brainless thugs. Instead, we get a bunch of overage Dead End Kids. Production no.: 2406.

Manhunt

wr. Robert Lees, Stanley Silverman, dir. Sobey Martin
The Earth people attempt to save the life of a giant escaped convict who has found and taken the Spindrift and become lodged in quicksand ... with some of their party trapped inside the ship.

With John Napier (fugitive)

This is one of the most consistently tense and exciting episodes, with a constant sense of jeopardy and a unique situation. All the cast members enjoy equal screen time, and the *Spindrift* interiors are seen more than usual. Amazingly, perhaps, it is the only episode in the series besides "Shell Game" in which anyone stumbles onto the bright orange spaceship in the forest. Although the cliché of quicksand was one of Irwin Allen's favorite perils, turning up at least once in all Allen's series, it is employed effectively here, generating a genuine sense of terror and suspense. Unfortunately, the matte work when Steve first reveals his presence to the sinking convict is not up to the series' usual standard, the miniature mannequins used to briefly represent Valerie and Betty look like the store-bought dolls they are (Valerie is having a very frizzy bad hair day and Betty has a completely different hairstyle!), and Dan is a little too panicky, but these are minor quibbles. A larger one rests on the castaways' decision to slip the convict his gun to enable him to escape from the police; unaware of his crimes before they helped each other, how did they know he wouldn't use it, leaving them with a death or two on their collective conscience? The episode also addresses a problem that many later episodes would conveniently (if necessarily) gloss over, which is that the giants can easily outpace the little people, and frequently obviously do—yet the castaways always seem to be only a few minutes from any given location. Here, the members of the party left outside the stolen ship have serious problems keeping up with their companions abducted with the *Spindrift*.

Scriptwriters Robert Lees and Stanley Silverman had previously written "Ace in the Hole" for *The Green Hornet*. Robert Lees had written for comedy duos Abbott And Costello, Olsen and Johnson, and Dean Martin and Jerry Lewis, but having been blacklisted during the McCarthy era in the 1950s, was obliged to write under the pseudonym of Jay Selby. Stanley Silverman was the head writer on popular adventure series *Sea Hunt* and *Flipper*. This was their only script for the series; they didn't get on with associate producer Jerry Briskin. Guest player John Napier had previously appeared in "The Last Patrol" for *The Time Tunnel*. He does well here with a virtually wordless and difficult part. The two police officers and the homeowner are uncredited. Production no.: 2407.

Framed

wr. Mann Rubin, dir. Harry Harris

The little people witness the murder of a model by a photographer, and set out to prove the innocence of a hobo who has been set up to take the fall.

With Paul Carr (photographer), Doodles Weaver (vagrant), Linda Peck (model), Dennis Cross, Baynes Barron (police officers)

In this episode, the eighth to be produced but the third to be aired, the audience learned prematurely that the government is aware of the existence of the little people, and has posted a reward for their capture (a continuing theme in the series), although the search has yet to become the

problem of the S.I.D. (Special Investigations Department) of later episodes. An insert has been filmed with two police officers to establish this fact. In the correct running order, we would have already learnt these details in the first few episodes.

Writer Mann Rubin's career started with the sci-fi series *Tales of Tomorrow* in 1951, but he has since become more connected with message shows, often railing against bigotry or fascism (he wrote the TV movie about racial tensions that developed *Kojak*). The inspiration for his one and only contribution to *Land of the Giants* was a little less lofty; on his way to the story meeting he passed a cinema showing Michelangelo Antonioni's then-revolutionary art film *Blow Up*, which concerns a photographer who believes he has witnessed a murder on freshly developed negatives! Here, of course, and more mundanely, the photographer was the murderer, the little people the witnesses after the incriminating film.

The whole episode is built around the premise that the little people badly need the murderous photographer's camera lens for their ship repairs, but a glaring flaw in the final scenes has them leaving the valuable lens behind as they make their escape after the police take away the photographer. Although it has been established that the photographer's house is difficult to get into, the building is now empty, so it hardly follows that after all the risks taken, the entire team can't stay behind in the now-deserted house and secure the lens in their own sweet time. Apart from this niggling irritation—which rather spoils the whole episode—it's a tense and interesting yarn with a number of clever and convincing trick shots and a beautiful recurring piece of melodic background music from Leith Stevens that was sadly rarely used again, although it does turn up in "Ghost Town." To be fair, Rubin's script had the lens sacrificed to get the picture to the police, but the finished episode has the picture more effectively fluttering out from hiding into the policeman's line of vision. Now the line is that the lens is left behind because it's too heavy, but there seems no reason why the castaways couldn't have kept it without disturbing the format—by itself, it was not a ticket home.

The scenes in the forest, and those in the photographer's house are carried off superbly, and there's never a dull moment, including Steve and Fitzhugh trapped in a gopher hole by the murderer, Steve and Valerie inside the camera, and Dan's close call in the street, where the cigarette pack he's been hiding in gets stamped on as soon as he's left it. Another last minute addition to the episode, this was one of the very few sequences in the series which effectively and realistically demonstrated the constant, ceaseless peril the Earth people were exposed to every second they were running around outside the spaceship. "Framed" was highly regarded by director Harry Harris and, curiously, was the series' highest rated episode.

Despite the heavy cast list, only Paul Carr as the solitary lensman has any substantial screen time, and much is without dialogue. Carr was an Allen regular, and although well cast, this is one of his less substantial roles. Production no.: 2408.

The Creed

wr. Richard McDonagh, Bob and Esther Mitchell, dir. Sobey Martin
When Barry is taken ill, the Earth people are forced to seek out a sympathetic medic.

With Paul Fix (Doctor Brulle), Henry Corden (janitor), Harry Lauter, Wesley Lau, Grant Sullivan (police officers), Garry Tigerman (delivery boy)

This was the second of twelve contributions to *Land of the Giants* by husband and wife writing team Bob and Esther Mitchell, and the story is credited to Richard McDonagh, who took over as the story editor for *Land of the Giants* after Anthony Wilson left; he had previously held the same position on the war series *Combat*. The character of Doctor Brulle would return to the series in the episode "Deadly Lodestone," but McDonagh was cruel to him—a benevolent, helpful and sympathetic character who loses everything by helping the castaways, he is one of the few good-hearted giants to come off the worse for his encounters with them.

Veteran supporting actor Paul Fix mostly worked in westerns, but he appeared in *Voyage to the Bottom of the Sea* in "The Terrible Toys," and in "The End of the World" for *The Time Tunnel*. He was also the second of the *Enterprise* medics in *Star Trek*, appearing in the episode "Where No Man Has Gone Before." Henry Corden's main claim to fame was taking over the voice of Fred Flintstone following the passing of Alan Reed.

The bit players are an interesting bunch. Wesley Lau was Sgt. Jiggs, head of security in *The Time Tunnel*, and best remembered for his trip back to Troy in "Revenge of the Gods." Grant Sullivan played an alien in the *Lost in Space* episode "Kidnapped in Space"; Garry Tigerman played a prehistoric boy in the *Lost in Space* episode "A Day at the Zoo." The third cop is Harry Lauter, a veteran of the Saturday morning serials who appeared twice in *The Time Tunnel*, and his extensive credits are referred to there. One of the best anonymous bit players in the industry, his films include *White Heat* and *The Day the Earth Stood Still*. Not all the actors playing police officers appear to have been credited.

This episode establishes, perhaps not deliberately, that the giant world—or at least the country the castaways are marooned in—not only uses the English language, but also the same Latin-based medical terms. German, however, is an unknown language! It is implied early on that Betty is the person best qualified to perform the operation, but she demurs to Steve. There seems to be no reason why she shouldn't so do the surgery, other than the convention that the star of the show must always be the hero. Production no.: 2409.

The Flight Plan

wr. Peter Packer, dir. Harry Harris

A giant scientist has the power to shrink himself and tries to gain the Earth people's trust to steal their advanced scientific knowledge.

With Linden Chiles (Joe), William Bramley, Myron Healy (plotters), John Pickard (guard)

A flight plan is the intended route a pilot leaves behind him in case of difficulty, so that rescue teams, if required, can save valuable hours in search time by retracing the plane's journey. In this case, the title refers to the scheme three treacherous giants have hatched to get their hands on the *Spindrift*, although we never learn exactly who they are and where they came about their extraordinary drug to shrink one of their number down to little people size. One of the more amusing anomalies of the series was that although Earth's science was supposedly further advanced than that of the giants, the castaways were forever stumbling onto giant scientists who had come up with incredible inventions!

Although hardly a household name, Linden Chiles holds a special place in SF TV history for playing Tony Newman's father in the classic *Time Tunnel* episode "The Day the Sky Fell In" and David Vincent's brother in "Wall of Crystal" for *The Invaders*. A likeable actor, he usually played solid, stand-up types. Although cast as the bad guy here, he eventually returns to form when he realizes his loyalty to his new-found friends is greater than to his luckless colleagues (even though he appears to have been the driving force behind the scheme). William Bramley's menacing voice had been well employed providing alien voices on *Lost in Space*, notably "My Friend, Mr. Nobody." He returned to *Land of the Giants* for "Giants and All That Jazz" in the second season, and previously appeared in the *Star Trek* episode "Bread and Circuses." Myron Healey was a

veteran of western B-movies and co-starred in the Republic serial *Panther Girl of the Congo.* He often took roles in the *Adventures of Superman* series of the 1950s, and later appeared in episodes of *Kolchak: the Night Stalker, Amazing Spider-Man,* and *Knight Rider.* John Pickard, another western regular, was in the "Massacre" episode of *Time Tunnel* concerning Custer. Other SF TV roles include *The Twilight Zone,* four episodes of *The Wild Wild West,* and *The Immortal.*

A regular writer on *Lost in Space* throughout its three year run, this was Peter Packer's only contribution to *Land of the Giants.* Although hardly the most original idea ("The Flight Plan" would shrink a giant, "Genius at Work" would enlarge the little people), it's an okay yarn, and surprising that Packer, having done so many *Lost in Space,* provided only one script for *Land of the Giants.* It's an enjoyable episode, marred only by some poor matte work when Joe and the Earth people confront the bad guys at the story's end. Conversely, a scene where a giant sits down on a step, unaware the little people are scurrying around his feet, works beautifully and is one of the best special effects sequences in the series. Although the music is credited to Paul Sawtell, the episode uses John Williams' music from the pilot extensively. Production no.: 2410.

Underground

wr. Anthony Wilson, Ellis St. Joseph, dir. Sobey Martin

The little people are coerced into assisting an elderly giant involved with an underground movement dedicated to overthrowing the dictatorship.

With John Abbott (Gorak), Paul Trinka, James Gosa (guards), Jerry Catron (sentry), Lance Le Gault (police officer), Ivan Markota (fugitive)

In actuality, Irwin Allen had made eight episodes of *Land of the Giants* before he gave any of the planet's inhabitants the opportunity to talk fluently and extensively, but audiences in 1968 were dropped into the new format dramatically by the network's decision to shuffle the running order around. With scenes added to the eighth episode, "Framed," to enable it to air third, and this eleventh episode airing fourth, episodes in which the giants were noticeably more silent aired later, giving the series a decidedly erratic format. Here, the totalitarian nature of the giant world is finally and firmly established, but when the series is shown in the ABC network running order viewers are brought up to speed much quicker. Although the episode is adequate, Ellis St. Joseph could and did do much better, as "The Weird World" demonstrates, along with his *Time Tunnel*, *Batman*, and *Outer Limits* credits. It's a rather slow episode that only just holds the interest, mostly thanks to the spaceship deception scene and the sequence with Fitzhugh inside the package.

John Abbott was Sesmar, the android maker in "The Dream Monster," one of the best second season *Lost in Space* episodes, and Ayrleborn in "Errand of Mercy," one of the best of the original *Star Trek*s. His extensive fantasy credits are detailed in the *Lost in Space* section.

Again, the bit players are interesting. Paul Trinka was crewman Patterson in *Voyage to the Bottom of the Sea*; he also appears in the episode "Genius at Work." His only other notable credit was in the Russ Meyer sleaze-fest *Faster, Pussycat! Kill! Kill!* Jerry Catron also appeared in a number of bit-parts in *Voyage to the Bottom of the Sea*, as well as "The Last Flight," an episode of *The Twilight Zone*, and "Operation: Annihilate" and "The Doomsday Machine" for *Star Trek*. James Gosa was under the monster suit in the *Lost in Space* episode "Target Earth." Ivan Markota appears again in the *Land of the Giants* episode also titled "Target Earth." Lance Le Gault would later play recurring roles as Colonel Decker in *The A-Team*, and Alamo Joe in *Werewolf*; a former friend, stand-in, bit player, stunt person, musician, and choreographer for Elvis Presley throughout the

1960s, he appeared regularly in action/adventure series of the '80s, including Donald Bellisario's *Airwolf* and *Quantum Leap*. Heather Young has a one-off ghastly perm in this episode which is clearly a wig, leading to speculation that this may have been the episode in which she famously devastated the production staff by returning from lunch with a brand-new hairstyle—mid-episode! Production no.: 2411.

Double-Cross

wr. Bob and Esther Mitchell, dir. Harry Harris
An amnesiac Fitzhugh becomes involved with jewel thieves.

With Willard Sage (Hook), Lane Bradford (Lobo), Joseph Ryan (police officer), Howard Culver (curator), Ted Jordan (museum guard)

The costumes that the thieves wear in the opening scene are *Lost in Space* monster suits, the Cyclops from "There Were Giants in the Earth" and others, and an alien head from "Two Weeks in Space." Sadly, that's the extent of the excitement in this talky episode, which involves a long-winded effort to break into a museum. And although it affords Kurt Kasznar the chance to have some fun, giving a regular character amnesia was a bit of an old chestnut even back in 1968. The best scenes involve Barry in the giant keyhole, and the hiding place for the ruby is inspired. Much of the music comes from the pilot. Also re-used is the trellis set from "Framed."

Willard Sage plays one of the aliens in the dismal *Star Trek* episode "The Empath" and also appears in "The Experiment" for *The Invaders*. He returns to *Land of the Giants* as the ill-fated Inspector Swann in "The Deadly Dart." Lane Bradford appeared in the *Lost in Space* episode "West of Mars." Billed under the name of Joe Ryan, Joseph Ryan appeared as aliens for *Lost in Space* in "Invaders from the Fifth Dimension" and *The Time Tunnel* in "Chase Through Time." Howard Culver often did voiceover work on Allen's series, and others. Ted Jordan returned in "Target Earth." Production no.: 2412.

On a Clear Night You Can See the Earth

wr. Anthony Wilson, Sheldon Stark, dir. Sobey Martin

An embittered and paranoid scientist develops a pair of glasses that enables the giants to see in the dark, and the little people find themselves threatened by torture and a giant dog.

With Michael Ansara (Murtrah)

An interesting episode in that the little people willfully murder a sadistic scientist to ensure their own safety ... just as the persecuted little people in the film *Doctor Cyclops* do. One of the sources of inspiration for *Land of the Giants*—although by no means the only one—was undoubtedly this 1940 film, to which this episode bears a slight resemblance (in *Doctor Cyclops*, the little people—reduced in size by the mad scientist of the title—escape the doctor because he can't see without his bottle-thick glasses). This is a very odd episode of *Land of the Giants*, as it lifts the notion that the little people must kill in a kill-or-be-killed situation from *Doctor Cyclops* and transposes it to this story, where it really doesn't fit. Consequently, part of the episode is taken up with some very clumsy efforts to justify this decision rather than simply write the script a different way, and as a result of this, "On a Clear Night..." blatantly contradicts the spirit of the earlier episode "The Bounty Hunter" and the style of the rest of the series. One other aspect of the episode is slightly jarring to contemporary audiences; at one point, the girls show up at the scene and Dan snaps rudely and harshly at them to "get back where they belong—at the ship!" This book's author is not one to bandy the word sexist around in a kneejerk manner, but this is very much out of character for Dan, and unacceptable behavior even then.

As the paranoid and sadistic Murtrah, Michael Ansara, acting completely alone

and with little to do except laugh wickedly a lot, gives what is probably his poorest performance ever in anything. He had done many episodes of various SF TV series, including five other Irwin Allen episodes and the *Voyage to the Bottom of the Sea* film, and he is not to blame for having nothing to work with here.

Former comic book writer Sheldon Stark was also the author of "Turn Back the Clock," the infamous *Voyage to the Bottom of the Sea* episode that utilized great chunks of Allen's feature film of *The Lost World*. Stark's other writing credits include "Crime Wave" for *The Green Hornet,* "The Monks of St. Thomas Affair" for *The Man from UNCLE,* and "Fine Finny Fiends/Batman Makes the Scene" for *Batman*. Despite the story credit for Anthony Wilson, not much of his characterization is in evidence here. Act Two of this episode opens with some music from *Lost in Space*. Production no.: 2413.

Ghost Town

wr. Anthony Wilson, Gilbert Ralston, William Welch, dir. Nathan Juran

A spiteful little girl terrorizes the Earth people in a built-to-scale toy town constructed by her grandfather.

With Percy Helton (Akman), Amber Flower (grand-daughter), Raymond Guth (vagrant)

Chosen as the second episode to air by the ABC network in its original run, this one actually works much better as the later episode it really is (fourteenth), not just because Fitzhugh's relationship with Barry is further along, but for the tease that the little people might have got back to Earth ... This discovery of an apparent Earth town has much more impact mid-season than as the second episode, for the viewers as well as the space travelers, because we have come to understand and identify with their dilemma over the past weeks and the profound emotional significance of such a discovery. It also makes an interesting change of environment from the usual pathways through oversize plants.

"Ghost Town" was written from a story idea by Anthony Wilson, and ultimately revised by Allen's Mr. Fix-It man William Welch (a prolific contributor to all four of Allen's sci-fi series), but the interesting name involved here is that of Gilbert Ralston. Ralston, whose other fantasy TV credits include the first aired episode of *The Wild Wild West* ("The Night of the Inferno") and two superior episodes of *I Spy* ("Dragon's Teeth" and "The Time of the Knife"), had just written "Who Mourns for Adonais?" for *Star Trek*, and unintentionally or otherwise, the episode bears a number of similarities with that story, which of course may be attributable to his writing process. Both stories involve an all-powerful benevolent jailer (Akman/Apollo) who plans to lord it over helpless and unwilling subjects as a well-intentioned dictator, and patronizes his captives as though they were needy children. Both groups of captives are imprisoned on his home turf, both groups scheme to trick their way to freedom, and in both cases the first plan fails and the second one works. At one point, *Star Trek's* Apollo even becomes giant-sized. Both stories involve the nullification of a force field and the removal of that artificial power before escape is achieved. In "Ghost Town" the captor is an eccentric old man, aided and abetted by his granddaughter. In "Who Mourns for Adonais?," the god-like adversary Apollo plays both captor and spiteful child. In the early '70s, Ralston would script two minor-league horror films, *Willard* and its sequel *Ben*, in which a misfit, and then a young boy, lord it over a private kingdom of pet rats! Clearly a theme is present!

Ralston was very happy with his *Star Trek*, but dissatisfied with the way "Ghost Town" turned out. For *Land of the Giants* fans and TV buffs in general however, it has many pleasures. First of all, the performances of the guest players (even Raymond Guth's ill-fated and quite nasty vagrant) are fine. Percy Helton, who was born in 1894, and passed away a couple of years after this episode aired, was another in a long line of Irwin Allen's eccentric old loons. He had previously appeared in such films as *Miracle on 34th Street* and *20,000 Leagues Under the Sea*, as well as two *Twilight Zones* ("Mute" and "Mr. Garrity and the Graves"), and encountered *Superman, Honey West, The Green Hornet, The Girl from UNCLE*, and *Batman*. He was in the rock and roll movies *Shake, Rattle and Rock* and *Jailhouse Rock* and memorably brutalized in the Mike Hammer film *Kiss Me Deadly*. Amber Flower as the resentful little girl who terrorizes the castaways every time her father is absent is not so much a realistic portrayal of childhood as she is a special effect, but bearing in mind that so many child actors can completely ruin a show, she represents her function in the proceedings effectively. Had the story been more about the child's jealousy and less about running around the town, casting might have been more difficult, particularly back in 1968 when child actors had little range and subtlety.

Best of all though, the episode offers an original and unusual premise, a story that involves the castaways rather than the problems of the giant guest stars (a trend in the latter half of the first season), a number of superbly executed set pieces, and—uniquely—a guided tour of the backlot's town and city streets seen in so many television productions of the period. The reason Akman's town looks like Anytown, USA is because that's exactly what it was built to represent. Midburry's Main Street also stands in for *Batman's* Gotham City when dressed up with cars, people, and other city trimmings (*Batman* and *Green Hornet* fans will recognize many locations, particularly the green storefront window next to the Bar And Grill saloon), but when dressed down it becomes small town America. Around the corner you're in picket fence suburbia. Because the story calls for the town to be deserted, the effect is fascinating, like visiting Disneyland Paris in January.

The episode is creatively shot by Nathan Juran, a veteran of composite shots and special effects work who directed such giant creature movies as *The Deadly Mantis, Twenty Million Miles to Earth, Attack of the Fifty Foot Woman, The Seventh Voyage of Sinbad,* and *Jack the Giant Killer,* as well as the delightful *First Men in the Moon.* All of Juran's episodes of *Land of the Giants* are interesting, particularly "The Clones" and "Nightmare," which makes it more of a shame that virtually the entire series was directed by competent and super-efficient, but boringly straightforward craftsmen such as Harry Harris and Sobey Martin. They were professional and knew what they were doing, but there was no innovation or experimentation involved. Juran always seems to have been called in when a challenge was presented. The miniatures are expertly matched with the regular sized backlot, notably the phone box, stew pot, and truck, and the backlot blends in perfectly with the giant gazebo where the old man controls the town. In many later episodes props would occasionally be out of proportion (hand-held radios would suddenly be half the size of the little people when held by the giants, for example), but here the props and mattes are matched perfectly. Particularly impressive is the scene in which Steve tries to persuade Akman to let them go—Akman is leaning casually on a perfectly matched rooftop and then lifts the life-size toy truck from the street.

There are minor anomalies in the completed story. Akman tells how he constructed the Earth town from picture books, but of course the giant world is exactly the same! Possibly this is due to stories being prepared before the writers were clear on the format (finished scripts were being commissioned and submitted at least a year before the series' first airdate), although this line should have been excised. And why does the force field kill a giant, but only knock out Barry? Fitzhugh survives it twice. And how is it Akman can run a lethal force

field anyway? Finally, Percy Helton's name is misspelled in the closing credits. But this is nitpicking, and "Ghost Town" remains one of the best—and best remembered—episodes of *Land of the Giants.* Production no.: 2414.

Brainwash

wr. William Welch, dir. Harry Harris

Two giants lure the Earth people into a trap by using abandoned Earth equipment.

With Warren Stevens (Captain Ashim), Leonard Stone (Doctor Kraal), Len Lesser (prisoner), Robert Dowdell (police officer)

Although this story involves the security forces, it takes place—like the later and similar "Sabotage"—before the production staff had come up with the S.I.D.; Ashim is simply a conniving, ladder-climbing bureaucrat. Both he and Kraal meet well-deserved ends, with the story establishing both as callous, corrupt murderers. Stevens and Stone together effectively represent the crushing banality of evil.

As was often to be the case as the series progressed, Betty and Barry appear only fleetingly, and Deanna Lund has only a couple of lines as well. Fitzhugh is in comical coward mode. As was also often the case with this series, one is overcome with the urge to shout at the characters onscreen as they make obvious errors to further the plot. Most significantly, we know that Fitzhugh should not be left alone with the transmitting equipment, and when Steve leaves him while saying not to touch, we realize it's a foregone conclusion that he will. Also, given the proven lethal nature of Kraal's foam, both the giants and the Earth people are extraordinarily blasé about it. Kraal orders Fitzhugh to wipe himself down, but his clothes are clearly soaked with the stuff—and Kraal puts the handkerchief back in his pocket! Surely something so lethal only needs to seep through the clothing into the skin? Similarly, when Steve is sprayed, Mark should have warned him to remove his jumpsuit. Another of the series' recurring flaws has the giants creeping up on the Earth people twice in the woods. It's quite ridiculous to believe that these lumbering creatures can't be heard, seen, or sensed until it's too late. Equally silly is Steve's behavior at the end when he insists on pulling the destruct switch so swiftly. Mark was quite right to ask for an extra couple of minutes to reach Earth, and the time they spent fighting could have provided those valuable moments. As with the David Vincent character in *The Invaders*, when writers start allowing the heroes to start making stupid mistakes, the audience begins to lose sympathy with their predicament. When this happens, the series is lost.

Technically, the episode is good, with Ashim's desk set particularly well realized. The dialogue is a bit over the top when Steve and Fitzhugh first find the cavern; the scriptwriter has them marveling over the magnificence of what the props department finally delivers as the usual Irwin Allen hand-me-down computer banks. Snatches of John Williams' pilot film music, and even a few bars from *Lost in Space*, can be heard at opportune moments. Kraal's foam dispenser was previously seen as a vital component in the *Time Tunnel* episode "The Kidnappers." Most significantly in the trivia department, Betty and Valerie debut new outfits in this episode.

Warren Stevens was an Irwin Allen regular, having chalked up three appearances in *Voyage to the Bottom of the Sea* and one *Time Tunnel*. Later, he would appear in the second season episode "A Place Called Home." Leonard Stone was Farnum B. in the *Lost in Space* episodes "A Day at the Zoo" and "Space Beauty," and played the title role in "The Hitch-Hiker," a sinister episode of *The Twilight Zone*. He returns in a different role in the second season episode "The Unsuspected." Robert Dowdell was Lt. Chip Morton in *Voyage to the Bottom of the Sea*; other SF TV roles include bit parts in *V* and *Max Headroom*. Len Lesser was frequently cast as

thugs and scuzzos; during the 1990s he was often seen in *Seinfeld* as the ghastly Uncle Leo. Production no.: 2415.

Terror-Go-Round

wr. Charles Bennett, dir. Sobey Martin

The Earth people are captured by a seedy traveling circus.

With Joseph Ruskin (Carlos), Arthur Batanides (Luigi), Gerald Michenaud (Pepi), Arch Whiting (police officer)

Scriptwriter Charles Bennett's contemptuous attitude toward Allen and his programs has been documented in the *Voyage to the Bottom of the Sea* section, and there is nothing in his single contribution for *Land of the Giants* to suggest he had amended his views for this series. It holds the interest, but little else—most of the action appears to have taken place offscreen. Both Joseph Ruskin and Arthur Batanides remember the episode for the bad behavior of the circus bear, which ran amok on set. At the time this episode was filmed, there were fewer regulations regarding the treatment of animals, and both Ruskin and Batanides felt the bear was mistreated. Nevertheless, general audiences tend to recall this episode not for the bear, but its climax involving escape from the circus by balloon. Several photographs from this sequence were used in the *Land of the Giants* gum cards from A&BC in 1969, and as the angles indicate that they are not frames from the filmed episode, it can be assumed they were taken by an on-set stills photographer. The music for the balloon flight comes from the beginning of the pilot.

Joseph Ruskin returned in the second season to play in "The Secret City of Limbo." His other TV SF roles are numerous, and include *The Twilight Zone*, *The Outer Limits*, *Voyage to the Bottom of the Sea*, *The Time Tunnel*, *Get Smart*, *Star Trek*, *The Wild Wild West*, *The Man from UNCLE*, *Planet of the Apes*, *The Six Million Dollar Man*, *The Bionic Woman*, *Project UFO*, the unsold pilots

Doctor Scorpion (1978) and *Captain America* (1979), *Airwolf*, *Max Headroom*, and three episodes of *Star Trek: Deep Space Nine*. Most recently, he's been seen in episodes of *Enterprise* and *Alias*. Arthur Batanides appears in "That Which Survives," in a dreaded red jersey for *Star Trek*, and as the leader of a group of primitives controlled by computer in "The Space Primevals" for *Lost in Space*. Other roles include the Mongol leader Batu in "Attack of the Barbarians," an episode of *The Time Tunnel*, "Specimen: Unknown" for *The Outer Limits* and a bogus alien in the trashy Z-feature-like "Invasion from Outer Space" for *The Green Hornet*.

Gerald Michenaud played much the same sort of role as he does here in "Rendezvous with Yesterday," the first episode of *The Time Tunnel* ... wearing what is surely the same beret! Arch Whiting was Sparks in *Voyage to the Bottom of the Sea*, and also appears in the closing scenes of the "Ma Parker" episode of *Batman* and "The Alternative Factor," one of the very worst *Star Trek* episodes. As with his colleague Paul Trinka in "Underground," make-up has stuck a phony-looking moustache on him to avoid viewer recognition. Allen was loyal to his actors in this way; there was no need for him to use players from his earlier series in bit parts that any jobbing actor could play, but it was one of the most frequently seen characteristics of both the man and his series to find work for people he liked. Production no.: 2416.

Sabotage

wr. Bob and Esther Mitchell, dir. Harry Harris
The Earth people are implicated in an act of sabotage engineered by a power-hungry security chief to discredit a politician sympathetic to their plight and further his own attempts to create fear and hostility toward the tiny "invaders."

With Robert Colbert (Bolgar), John Marley (Zarkin), Parley Baer (Senator Obek), Elizabeth Rogers (secretary), Douglas Bank (police officer), Keith Taylor (newsboy)

Robert Colbert was Doug Phillips, one of the two time traveling scientists in Irwin Allen's *Time Tunnel*, and would later co-star for Allen in his unsold pilot *City Beneath the Sea*. He would have been familiar with the street in which he vacuums up two of the little people as he met Alexis on it in *Time Tunnel's* "Secret Weapon" and was taken to the guillotine on it in "Reign of Terror"! Here, he plays a sleazy bad guy working from the same police building seen in "Framed" (the S.I.D. have yet to be introduced to the series). Colbert's character of Security Chief Bolgar appears to be an early incarnation of the later recurring character Inspector Kobick; the little people already know him when he shows up, and Bolgar knows the number and gender of the entire *Spindrift* party, right down to the boy and the dog. The episode ends with the friendly, humane, and sympathetic Senator Obek in possession of an incriminating tape clearing the little people of the act of sabotage and revealing Bolgar and Zarkin as the conspirators. Foolishly, Obek has barged in on Bolgar and Zarkin without the police back-up, who, he announces, are close behind him. In the Mitchells' original script, the story continues with Zarkin pulling a gun in panic and shooting Obek dead. Realizing they've gone too far, Bolgar then kills Zarkin and gives the tape to the police to exonerate himself. He's been forced to clear the Earth people of sabotage and make Zarkin the fall guy for both Obek's murder and the attempt to frame the castaways. The episode would then have ended with the three male leads realizing that in Bolgar, they have made a formidable new enemy, but for whatever reason, the Colbert/Bolgar character was dropped, and the story ends with Obek alive and Bolgar and Zarkin under arrest. Otherwise, the script is filmed virtually as written.

Elizabeth Rogers was Lt. Palmer in the *Star Trek* episode "The Doomsday Machine" and "The Way to Eden," and turned up in "The Alamo" for *The Time Tunnel*. Her character as Obek's secretary is the weak link in the script—it is preposterous that having been told the time of an explosive act of sabotage she would not alert either Obek or the authorities. A way round this would have been for the Mitchells to implicate her in the plot.

Character actors John Marley and Parley Baer are well known, but not for SF roles—Marley usually gets cast as mobsters, Baer as a country hick. However, Marley has appeared in episodes of *The Twilight Zone*, *The Outer Limits*, *Kolchak: the Night Stalker*, and *The Incredible Hulk*, and Baer also appeared in *The Outer Limits*, *My Favorite Martian*, *I Dream of Jeannie*, and several episodes of *The Addams Family* and *Bewitched*. In later years he appeared in episodes of *Project UFO*, *The Incredible Hulk*, *Quantum Leap*, and *The Flash*. Douglas Bank previously appeared as a scientist in both "The Golden Cage" and the *Voyage to the Bottom of the Sea* episode "Werewolf." Keith Taylor usually found himself cast as loutish slobs, and appears as such in *Star Trek's* "Miri" and twice in *Lost in Space*, in "Return from Outer Space" and "The Promised Planet." Production no.: 2417.

Genius at Work

wr. Bob and Esther Mitchell, dir. Sobey Martin
   Fitzhugh becomes giant sized thanks to a young prodigy's scientific formula, but soon gets himself into trouble.

With Kevin Hagen (Inspector Kobick), Ronny Howard (Jodar), Jacques Aubuchon (Zurpin), Paul Trinka, Pat Culliton (police officers), Vic Perrin (man in street), Rusty Jones (young boy)

"Genius at Work" stars child actor Ronny Howard of *The Andy Griffith Show* (later Ron Howard, teenage star of *American Graffiti* and sit-com *Happy Days*) as a child prodigy who devises a formula to enlarge the little people to regular size on his world. Perhaps not coincidentally somewhere along the line, he had earlier appeared in the very similar feature *Village of the Giants*, a Bert Gordon production. Although he made a

variety of low-budget B-features, Gordon specialized in sci-fi cheapies featuring giant menaces, and had already filmed the likes of *The Amazing Colossal Man* and its follow-up *War of the Colossal Beast*, the *Giants*-like *Attack of the Puppet People*, and such giant bug epics as *Earth vs. the Spider*, using many of the same techniques as the special effects technicians of *Land of the Giants*. "Genius at Work" swiftly moves along in its own direction to become a very different production, but it's difficult to imagine that *Village of the Giants* didn't provide some sort of initial inspiration for the Mitchells somewhere along the way, especially as both this episode and their first filmed script, "The Lost Ones," feature aspects of that movie—Ronny Howard and growth serum in one, juvenile delinquents in the other. Like "The Flight Plan," "Genius at Work" does not show the actors growing or shrinking (given the special effects capabilities of the time, this was probably wise), but it does thankfully avoid implying that the characters' clothes grow and shrink with them. In fact, Fitzhugh's stolen giant clothing is the catalyst for the story, which is solid and entertaining, even if the giant-sized Steve, posing as a lawyer, is exposed by Kobick with one of the oldest tricks in the book (the same vintage ruse traps *The Prisoner* in "The Schizoid Man").

Kevin Hagen made numerous appearances in Irwin Allen productions, appearing once in *Lost in Space*, twice in *Voyage to the Bottom of the Sea*, and no less than four times in *The Time Tunnel*. This was his first appearance as the recurring character Inspector Kobick. Interestingly, it falls to the Mitchells to introduce the S.I.D. and the replacement for Security Chief Bolgar and his Department of Security—or did their first draft initially feature Bolgar? Whatever the case, Kobick is a more interesting and credible adversary, as he is simply a callous bureaucrat on a mission, whereas Bolgar was palpably evil. Kobick is not comic-book evil—he's just mean, a product of a totalitarian environment.

Bit player Jacques Aubuchon had played various roles in episodes of *The Twilight Zone, Voyage to the Bottom of the Sea, The Man from UNCLE, The Green Hornet, Bewitched,* and *Project UFO. Voyage to the Bottom of the Sea's* Paul Trinka makes his second of two appearances in *Land of the Giants* (he previously played a cop in "Underground"), once again behind a moustache. Pat Culliton was a regular bit player in *Voyage* and *Time Tunnel.* Vic Perrin, a familiar face in SF TV (turning up in *Twilight's Zone's* "People Are Alike All Over" and *Star Trek's* "Mirror, Mirror" among many), provided the sinister narration for the original *Outer Limits* series. Production no.: 2418.

Deadly Lodestone

wr. William Stuart, dir. Harry Harris

Dan realizes he must send himself into exile when the giants start using a tracking device sensitive to a surgical pin in his leg that keeps betraying them.

With Kevin Hagen (Inspector Kobick), Paul Fix (Doctor Brulle), Robert Emhardt (Mr. Secretary), Bill Fletcher (Sergeant Karf), Sheila Mathews (Nurse Helg), Gene Dynarski (warden)

This was the second appearance of Kevin Hagen's recurring character Inspector Kobick. It's another story just about kept interesting by a few tense moments, including an encounter with a spider and a suspenseful phone call made from Kobick's own office.

Paul Fix returns as the virtuous Doctor Brulle, now imprisoned for aiding the Earth people in the earlier episode "The Creed." It's a shame nobody thought to write an episode in which the Earth people engineer his escape. Screen slimeball Robert Emhardt puts in a brief appearance as a member of the imposing Supreme Council. He was often to be found in sinister roles, notably in *The Invaders* (the superb "Nightmare") and *The Man from UNCLE* ("The Apple-a-Day Affair"). Sheila Mathews was Mrs. Irwin Allen, and would return in the second season in a different role, in "Wild Journey."

Gene Dynarski appeared twice in both *Star Trek* and *Voyage to the Bottom of the Sea.* William Stuart wrote two further scripts for the series, "The Mechanical Man" and "The Deadly Dart." Production no.: 2419.

The Night of Thrombeldinbar

wr. Bob and Esther Mitchell, dir. Sobey Martin

Fitzhugh happily poses as a mythical elf for two deprived orphans, unaware of the lethal consequences of the myth.

With Alfred Ryder (Mr. Parteg), Teddy Quinn (Garna), Michael A. Freeman (Tobek), Jay Novello (Okun), Miriam Schiller (housewife)

A traditional, heartwarming tale in the classic tradition, although Mr. Fitzhugh nearly gets warmed in a quite different way. Concerning a fairytale of the giant world, the episode has the dark ambience of a Grimm's tale, with adult players Parteg and Okun resembling storybook scares themselves. Fitzhugh is mistaken for a gift-giving elf of giant mythology by two little orphan boys, and gleefully goes along with the gag to light up their lives ... unaware that he's likely to light up as well—literally. The *Twilight Zone*-ish twist is worthy of Rod Serling himself, utterly believable and inspired. It's darkest before the dawn—again, literally—but it all gets warm and fuzzy toward the end.

Alfred Ryder appeared three times in Allen's *Voyage to the Bottom of the Sea,* twice as the ghostly Captain Krueger in "The Phantom Strikes" and "The Return of the Phantom," and again as an obsessed scientist in "The Heat Monster." He was Professor Crater in "The Man Trap," an excellent early *Star Trek,* and also appeared twice in *The Invaders,* on both occasions playing one of the aliens. Jay Novello had played a similarly shifty role in Allen's film of *The Lost World.* Other credits include the 1944 *Captain America* serial, *Atlantis, the Lost Continent,* and episodes of *The Outer Limits* and *I Spy.* Bit player Miriam Schiller appears briefly again in "A Small War" and as Miss

Teutonium in the *Lost in Space* episode "Space Beauty." Production no.: 2420.

Seven Little Indians

wr. Bob and Wanda Duncan, dir. Harry Harris

The Earth people flit around the animal cages of a giant zoo while trying to retrieve Barry's dog, who just became an exhibit to lure the castaways into a trap.

With Kevin Hagen (Inspector Kobick), Chris Alcaide (Sergeant Arnak), Cliff Osmond (Grotius), Garry Walberg, Rico Catani, Erik Nelson (S.I.D. men)

This was the third appearance of the recurring character Inspector Kobick. Hagen makes what could easily have been a nothing part work quite well, and proves conclusively here that he is much more three-dimensional than his predecessor, the cartoonishly wicked Bolgar. Kobick, in this episode, sees himself involved in a battle of wits with worthy adversaries, and Hagen plays him like a cold-hearted, puritanical old-fashioned schoolteacher engaged in a war of nerves.

Cliff Osmond is also quite good as the slimy, obsequious Grotius, playing both sides against each other for all he can get. Garry Walberg, playing a sadistic guard, played a corrupt cop in *The Green Hornet* and also appeared in episodes of *Star Trek* and *The Invaders*. Erik Nelson appeared in several episodes as an S.I.D. man—as well as "Seven Little Indians," also "The Chase," "The Mechanical Man," "Collector's Item," and "Wild Journey."

Bob and Wanda Duncan wrote extensively for Allen's *Lost in Space* and *Time Tunnel*, but less successfully for *Land of the Giants*. "Seven Little Indians" is set in a zoo and exists only to show off the not very special effects with the animals, which consist solely of various cast members running backwards and forwards across matte shots of the animals in their cages. Things pick up near the end during the little people's escape. The Duncans' second and last script, "Panic," was marginally better. Production no.: 2421.

Target Earth

wr. Arthur Weiss, dir. Sobey Martin

The passengers split with the Spindrift crew in an argument over whether to attempt a risky trip home through a scientist's invention.

With Arthur Franz (Franzen), Dee Hartford (Altha), Kevin Hagen (Inspector Kobick), Peter Mamakos (Logar), Ted Jordan (S.I.D. man), Denver Mattson, Ivan Markota (police officers)

This was the first and best episode written by *Voyage to the Bottom of the Sea* contributor Arthur Weiss, who also wrote the episodes "The Chase," "Chamber of Fear," and "The Deadly Pawn." However, what is never considered either by Weiss or his characters, large or small, is exactly how the giants are going to invade a world as small as Earth, even if they do travel there. The notion conjures up absurdly comical and preposterous images of a Tex Avery cartoon like "King-Size Canary," or giant human invaders stamping around *Godzilla*-like through a screaming city. The opening scenes employ music rejected by Allen for the pilot, who then commissioned a whole new score from John Williams, the one ultimately used.

Arthur Franz often portrayed the archetypal pipe-sucking scientist of the 1950s, appearing in such roles in *Abbott and Costello Meet the Invisible Man*, *Flight to Mars*, *Invaders from Mars*, *The Flame Barrier*, *Monster on the Campus*, *The Atomic Submarine*, and the *Voyage to the Bottom of the Sea* episode "The Condemned." He was also the co-star in the 1950s *World of Giants* spy series. Other TV roles included *The Invaders* and *The Six Million Dollar Man*.

Dee Hartford was Verda in "The Android Machine" and "Revolt of the Androids" in *Lost in Space*, and would make a third appearance as a different character, Nancy Pi Squared, in the episode "Space Beauty." She also appeared in "The Invisibles" in *The Outer Limits* as the wife of a military man possessed by aliens and in *Batman* as Miss Iceland. Peter Mamakos has credits

Stefan Arngrim, Kurt Kasznar, Deanna Lund, Don Matheson and Gary Conway pose
with some of the series' oversized props in this promotional shot.

for *Adventures of Superman, Voyage to the Bottom of the Sea, Batman, The Girl from UNCLE, Get Smart,* and *Night Gallery.* Ted Jordan was previously a guard in "Double Cross," and an astronaut in "The Silent Saboteurs" for *Voyage to the Bottom of the Sea.* Ivan Markota previously appeared as the fugitive in "Underground." Production no.: 2422.

Rescue

wr. Bob and Esther Mitchell, dir. Harry Harris
The Earth people try to rescue two giant children from a deep hole while avoiding the attentions of Inspector Kobick and the SID.

With Kevin Hagen (Inspector Kobick), Tom Reese (Sergeant Gedo), Michael J. Quinn (Lieutenant Emar), Lee Meriwether (mother), Don Collier (father), Buddy Foster (Tedar), Blair Ashley (Leeda), Roy Rowan (newscaster)

This was Kevin Hagen's fifth appearance as Inspector Kobick, and as evidenced by this very basic storyline, the series was now in a rut. Episodes repeatedly revolved around Kobick and the castaways trying to outmaneuver each other and uniformed heavies tramping through the forest in pursuit. To the series' credit, the writers kept coming up with new ways to attack and pursue the Earth people, but nevertheless everyone just seems to be going through the motions. "Rescue" is a straightforward save-the-kids-from-the-well drama, a competent time-waster but little more than that, and hindered by some rather flat acting and directing. Unimaginative dialogue and a pedestrian plot is not helped by the lazy and hackneyed device of having events and information related through a TV newscaster.

Lee Meriwether was a regular on Irwin Allen's series *The Time Tunnel.* A former Miss America, she also played the Catwoman in the 1966 *Batman* feature film and an alien killer in "That Which Survives" for *Star Trek,* but here she has little to do but look worried as the distressed mother, looking like and playing the role in the same manner as her *Time Tunnel* role. Child actress Blair Ashley

grew up to become Blair Tefkin, one of the cast of 1980s sci-fi series *V.* Production no.: 2423.

Return of Inidu

wr. Bob and Esther Mitchell, dir. Sobey Martin
The Earth people stumble into a haunted house while sheltering from a storm, and encounter an elderly illusionist.

With Jack Albertson (Inidu), Peter Haskell (Enog), Tony Benson (Grot), Jerry Davis (Torg), Steven Marlo (police officer)

An episode with a difference. The first twenty minutes are fine as the castaways stumble through an oncoming storm into a haunted house and encounter ghostly noises, green lights, the ghost itself (comically, a man with a sheet over him), and two spook-baiting louts, but once the occupant is revealed as a friendly old magician, the episode turns into a merry bore as the space travelers receive magical lollipops and turn into giggling fans of the loveable old rogue. Although a simple illusionist unjustly jailed, the magician has absurdly supernatural powers second only to the magical stars of *Bewitched* or *I Dream of Jeannie,* teleporting the little people from place to place for example, and telling a story of unjust imprisonment even more unlikely than his powers. Now he's hiding out and naturally they must help clear his name, at which point the episode slows down to a crawl. The real problem with "Return of Inidu" though (a deceptive title for researchers as this is his first and last appearance) is that Inidu's tricks are quite impossible for a simple stage magician to perform, and are even accompanied by the traditional *Lost in Space*-style electronic pop more rightly associated with aliens. If Inidu can do all this, he hardly needed the little people to help him...

Heather Young and Stefan Arngrim are absent from this episode. Veteran character actor Jack Albertson returns in a different role in the second season's "Panic." Steven Marlo appeared in the *Star Trek* episode "A

Piece of the Action." He turns up again in "The Mechanical Man," "The Deadly Pawn," and "Panic." Production no.: 2424.

Shell Game

wr. Bob and Esther Mitchell, dir. Harry Harris

The Spindrift *spaceship is discovered and taken by an impoverished fisherman's son, and the Earth people offer to build a hearing aid to restore the boy's hearing in return for their valuable craft.*

With Larry Ward (Talf), Jan Shepard (Osla), Garry Dubin (Dal), Tol Avery (Mister Derg)

A very ordinary feelgood yarn that takes place on the seafront location seen in *Time Tunnel's* "Town of Terror" and various *Batman* adventures. All the Mitchells' episodes suffer from dreary, deadly dull dialogue, and this one is no exception. Their stories move along in the expected direction to the inevitable conclusion with few surprises. This is the second and last time the *Spindrift* is discovered and moved, and as in "Manhunt" and the pilot, viewers get a good look at the spaceship's design. The giant seashell interior was a set built for Fox's then-recent *Doctor Dolittle* film, an expensive flop. Larry Ward was the escaped prisoner in "All That Glitters" for *Lost in Space* and the commander of the Mars shot in "One Way to the Moon" for *The Time Tunnel*. Jan Shepard is probably best known for her two Elvis Presley films, *King Creole* and *Paradise, Hawaiian Style*. Tol Avery was the Warden in "Fugitives of Space" for *Lost in Space*. Once again, a routine episode plods along, the giant menace this week being an irritable lobster! There is, however, an exciting scene in the forest when Mark and Dan are menaced by rather more lively wildlife. Production no.: 2425.

The Chase

wr. William Welch, Arthur Weiss, dir. Sobey Martin

S.I.D. Inspector Kobick forces the Earth people to help him crack a counterfeit money operation.

With Kevin Hagen (Inspector Kobick), Robert F. Lyons (Nalor), Timothy Scott (Trilling), Patrick Sullivan Burke (Golan), Erik Nelson (S.I.D. man), Norman Burton (Sergeant)

Kobick is back for the last episode of the first season, another contrived storyline borrowed from the Big Book Of Plots. This was Kevin Hagen's sixth appearance as Kobick and there is a sense that the series is relying too much on this character to provide the show with storylines. Naturally, Kobick has no intention of letting the castaways go when the job is done. The show is looking tired—even an encounter with a giant rat in the drainage system is muted and anti-climactic. And why do the counterfeiters have a drain in the middle of their living space?

Stefan Arngrim's Barry is absent from this episode. Arthur Weiss also wrote the episodes "Target Earth," "Chamber of Fear," and "The Deadly Pawn." Production no.: 2426.

SECOND SEASON (1969–'70)

The Inside Rail

wr. Richard Shapiro, dir. Harry Harris

Fitzhugh's passion for a flutter on the horses—even giant-sized ones—endangers his companions.

With Ben Blue (Moley), Arch Johnson (Chief Rivers), Joe Turkel (police sergeant), Vic Tayback (gangster), John Harmon (groom)

The first episode of the second season out of the starting gate (but third aired) was this frivolous racetrack yarn, and it wasn't too much of a stretch to imagine Fitzhugh playing the ponies. The scene where he enthusiastically runs out onto the track and the horses run over him is brilliantly done. However, Fitzhugh behaves like a complete idiot in this episode, his greed overpowering his fear, and the ghost of Doctor Smith looms large. The episode is okay, but *Land of the Giants* works better as dramatic adventure rather than comedic adventure, and the problem with comedy episodes is that the rest of the cast have to go along with the gag.

Writer Richard Shapiro later went on to create 20th Century Fox's '80s super-soap *Dynasty* and follow-up prime-time soaps *Emerald Point* and *The Colbys* with his wife Esther Shapiro. He joined *Land of the Giants* from the second season, and this, his first script for the series, was his favorite of the four he wrote. All were whimsical, light stories laced with humor—"The Inside Rail," "Giants and All That Jazz," "Comeback," and "Pay the Piper."

However, the first thing one notices about this episode is how much Stefan Arngrim has grown during the summer hiatus. He would grow even taller during the months to come, making him somewhat redundant, having outgrown his usefulness as the cute little orphan cherub of the early episodes. As if in recognition of this, the writers found it increasingly difficult to include him, as Barry's childish naiveté was now beginning to make him look a bit of a doofus now that he was too old to be the token kid. Another regular who would take a back seat this season was Heather Young, who returned to work pregnant, and spent most of the second season either standing on the sidelines or, for a while, absent without explanation.

Ben Blue was an old time vaudevillian and it showed in his performance. Both Vic Tayback and John Harmon appear in the light-hearted *Star Trek* gangland episode "A Piece of the Action" (as does frequent *Land of the Giants* bit player Steven Marlo). Tayback could play straight if asked (he appears in the opening scene of *Bullitt*, for example), but he was usually cast as a comedy gangster, a role he plays again here. Harmon was also the unfortunate hobo who disintegrates himself in the *Star Trek* episode "City on the Edge of Forever." Arch Johnson also usually played bluff blowhards in light-hearted fare (he was the army sergeant in the Elvis Presley film *G.I. Blues*, a typical role). TV roles include episodes of *The Twilight Zone*, *The Munsters*, *The Invaders*, quite a few *Bewitched*,

The Bionic Woman, *The Invisible Man*, and *Wonder Woman*.

With an exciting new title sequence and theme (again by John Williams), and the re-emphasis for the most part on the travails of the castaways rather than the lives of the giants, the series returned refreshed, but with more of the same. However, the writers were clearly receiving little guidance in the continuity of the series, with some writers on the show, such as Richard Shapiro, Dan Ullman, Jerry Thomas, William Stuart, Jackson Gillis, and even Allen's right-hand man William Welch using Earth-style names for the giants, and others, including Arthur Weiss, Sidney Marshall, Oliver Crawford, Shirl Hendrix, and Bob and Wanda Duncan, sticking to the original concept of weird, alien-sounding names. The blame for this ridiculous and lazy state of affairs can only be laid at the feet of the show's story editor, Richard McDonagh, who had no excuse for such carelessness as he had been with the show since the early days of the first season. It was his responsibility, but one has to wonder why the actors didn't question it, or Allen himself notice.

This episode also introduces a third set of new outfits for everybody but Steve, Dan, and Fitzhugh, and the series' new mechanical dolls, used to show the little people's legs kicking when they are picked up by the giants. In the first season, after the pilot, actors picking up little people simply cup their hands most of the time. Now they have a prop to handle. The dolls—and the new theme—are a good example of how Irwin Allen always tried to come to a new season with something fresh. Not many TV producers—if any—bothered to commission new themes to revitalize their shows just for the hell of it. Production no.: 4701.

Chamber of Fear

wr. Arthur Weiss, dir. Sobey Martin

Steve and Dan are menaced by a giant dog while trying to rescue Fitzhugh, and Valerie and Mark ex-

perience mechanical dangers in a wax museum, when the Earth people become involved in the plans of two jewel thieves.

With Cliff Osmond (Jolo), Christopher Cary (Deenar), Joan Freeman (Mara), Dan Kennedy (police officer), Robert Tiedemann (monk)

Inevitably, when actors spend two years on a series, there are stories to tell. Don Matheson and Deanna Lund are now both able to laugh about their misfortunes on the mechanical mannequin set in this episode, and even perhaps embellish it; simply put, Matheson found himself caught in the mechanism and trapped on a rotating wheel that kept banging his head on a pipe every time it turned. Lund was unable to free him, and everyone on set thought they were giving a marvelous performance. This scene is actually the most exciting part of the episode, and Lund is very good in it—there's a genuine sense of desperation, even though Matheson's difficulties have not made the final cut (you do see the poor man bump his head once).

Cliff Osmond previously appeared in the first season episode "Seven Little Indians" as the unctuous zoo caretaker. Here, he plays a completely different kind of role, a vicious bully, with fellow guest star Christopher Cary in the meek stooge role. Cary, best known for his role in the '60s war series *Garrison's Gorillas*, was Merlin in *The Time Tunnel* and appeared in Gene Roddenberry's pilot film *Planet Earth*. Joan Freeman also appeared in "Behold Eck" for *The Outer Limits* and "The Bat-Cave Affair" for *The Man from UNCLE*. She is best known for the Elvis Presley film *Roustabout* (*Land of the Giants* was fast becoming a retirement home for former Presley film girls!). Here, she's cast as yet another of the giant world's shrill, East European-style dowdy harridans. Heather Young and Deanna Lund certainly never had any worries about being upstaged by the female guest stars!

Arthur Weiss also wrote the episodes

"Target Earth," "The Chase," and "The Deadly Pawn." He cleverly splits the seven leads and has two storylines going at once (three, if you include Young and Arngrim's few scenes at the end). Given the number of cast members, it's surprising this never occurred to some of the other regular writers, particularly the Duncans or the Mitchells, whose stories could have used a goose. Production no.: 4702.

The Mechanical Man

wr. William Stuart, dir. Harry Harris
The Earth people stumble onto a scientist who has created a homicidal robot.

With Broderick Crawford (Professor Gorn), Stuart Margolin (Zoral), James Daris (mechanical man), William Chapman (Secretary Mek), Richard Carlyle (police officer), Steven Marlo (S.I.D. official), Erik Nelson (S.I.D. man)

This episode, which opened the second season, might better have gone by the more dynamic title the robot's creator gave his invention—the Hydraulic Man. The intention, however, is clearly to do the Karloff *Frankenstein*. A sequence in which the robot tenderly rescues Barry's dog Chipper from quicksand, while emulating Karloff's quizzical look, and the scenes later in which the robot is chained in a seat at the lab clearly indicate the intention of both writer and director to nudge the collective memory of the audience. Unfortunately, through no fault of his own, James Daris looks more like Peter Boyle in *Young Frankenstein* than Karloff's monster or any of his heirs.

During the hiatus between seasons, the little people appear to have acquired some rather fancy new technology, including a stylish cutting torch and a telescopic vertically extendable spy device for looking through windows. As with the *Lost in Space* Space Pod, it has all appeared out of nowhere, but in theory could have been built by Mark. This episode also introduced the mechanical kicking dolls first used in "The Inside Rail" to the viewing audience;

indeed Broderick Crawford poses rather unconvincingly with one for a publicity still. These tricks were better seen from a distance. Heather Young is absent from this episode, as is the *Spindrift* set but for the tag, but it was admittedly a strong one to start the second season.

Broderick Crawford was best known for the 1950s series *Highway Patrol*, and is very good as the brusque, blunt, pragmatic and cold-hearted scientist. Stuart Margolin would go on to play Angel Martin in *The Rockford Files*, one of a number of working associations with James Garner. Given the *Frankenstein* connotations in the script, one feels that Margolin was cast in the Ygor role, but happily the production does not go in this hackneyed direction. James Daris appears in the *Star Trek* turkey "Spock's Brain." Richard Carlyle had a minor role in the *Star Trek* episode "The Squire of Gothos." Steven Marlo was the police officer in "Return of Inidu" and shows up again in "The Deadly Pawn" and "Panic." The backlot street in which the robot first runs amok is the shorefront one from "Shell Game," looking very different in darkness.

William Stuart contributed "Deadly Lodestone" to the first season. His third and final script for the series would be "The Deadly Dart," which pointlessly revives the Zoral character, portrayed by a different actor. Production no.: 4703.

Collector's Item

wr. Sidney Marshall, Bob and Wanda Duncan, dir. Sobey Martin
Valerie becomes a pawn in a murder plot when she is held captive in a music box by a crazy collector.

With Guy Stockwell (Gorak), Robert H. Harris (Tojar), Susan Howard (Gorak's wife), George Sperdakos (goldsmith), Erik Nelson (S.I.D. man)

The second season was notable for featuring giant characters with more depth than before, but although this is true of this episode, the characters are clichéd and the

storyline silly. Guy Stockwell (the brother of *Quantum Leap's* Dean Stockwell) and Robert H. Harris (usually cast as timid mouse-like types, here playing a grasping, Scrooge-like, hateful old man) are fine in their roles, but the episode plods. Apart from an exciting but brief scene where Steve hangs from the back of a speeding car by a rope, little else happens that hasn't been seen before (the prerequisite jackbooted S.I.D. man and slavering dog for example). Susan Howard, later to appear regularly in the 1980s primetime soap *Dallas*, is this episode's dowdy, doormat wife—giant women in *Land of the Giants* always seemed to be relentless, sharp-tongued nags or plain, browbeaten mice—and Howard's isn't even granted the privilege of a name! Once again, Heather Young and Stefan Arngrim have only minor roles in the proceedings. Production no.: 4704.

Giants and All That Jazz

wr. Richard Shapiro, dir. Harry Harris
Dan introduces the pleasures of jazz music to the giant world.

With Sugar Ray Robinson (Biff), Mike Mazurki (Loach), William Bramley (Hanley), Diana Chesney (Nell)

The giant world's only black man (apparently) is former boxer Sugar Ray Robinson as jazz club owner Biff Bower, and the derelict building seen at the end of the street at the beginning of "Collector's Item" is the seedy joint in question. The only problem is that no one has invented jazz yet, and worse still, two Hollywood heavies are making Biff's life a misery. Barry just happens to be learning the trumpet, and Dan just happens to be an expert player. What follows is a reworking of that hoary old time travel movie chestnut where a form of popular music is introduced to the world prematurely (it would turn up yet again in the *Back to the Future* movie and the *Quantum Leap* TV series to name but two). When professional crone Diana Chesney turns up with a snake wrapped around her eccentric neck, it isn't too hard to guess where this episode's jeopardy is coming from. This tedious feelgood yarn is another whimsy from Richard Shapiro, the second of four scripts for *Land of the Giants*; the others, equally light and whimsical, were "The Inside Rail," "Comeback," and "Pay The Piper."

As was often the case, the props representing the property of the little people are much too big when held in the giants' hands. They are half the size of the Earth people. However, the episode has more pressing problems. Having managed to tap a giant's phone and posed effectively as an S.I.D. official, Steve could have said anything to get the none-too-bright giant to release Barry and Valerie. Instead, he simply secures an hour's grace to embark on an elaborate and ridiculously convoluted scheme to free them. All he had to do was get the giant out of his apartment or tell him to leave them somewhere. A less glaring flaw in this story is that, once again, all the giants have ordinary, Earth-like names. William Bramley previously appeared in "The Flight Plan." Production no.: 4705.

Six Hours to Live

wr. Dan Ullman, dir. Sobey Martin

After hearing two giants gloating nervously over the impending execution of a convicted killer, the Earth people go to the aid of a wrongly convicted murderer sentenced to die.

With Richard Anderson (Joe Simmons), Sam Elliott (Martin Reed), George Mitchell (Harry Cass), Anne Seymour (Martha Cass), Bill Quinn (warden), Larry Pennell (guard), Michael Quinn (gateman), Stewart Bradley (sergeant)

It's not hard to work out why the network decided to move this episode up to second in the season. As hackneyed as the premise is, it has a strong story, strong cast, and high stakes. As the two greedy, fearful, thoroughly wicked farmers, George Mitchell and Anne Seymour are excellent. Sam Elliott as the innocent man is sympathetic, and Richard Anderson convincing as the reporter. The scene where Elliott discovers the

little people hiding in his last supper is almost unintentionally comical, but he plays it well. It's a wonderfully realistic human touch that the stupid Cass couple are caught because the wife won't run out without her best china ... and "leave it for someone to steal!" Even with their stolen money, Mr. and Mrs. Cass—a cowed drunk and a nagging witch—are in purgatory already.

After some of the bland stereotypes of the first season, someone seems to have decided to make the giants more realistic this second season, and it's a welcome move. When Reed returns to the farmhouse playing on their guilty fear of retribution, writer Dan Ullman treads the line perfectly between humor and drama, particularly when the devious old woman realizes Reed is mortal. It would have been nice to see the castaways using some poltergeist-style stalling tactics until the police arrived, but the ending still works, thanks to smiling Stewart Bradley's playsafe policeman, a man who occasionally relishes his work.

A veteran writer of low budget westerns, Dan Ullman co-wrote the fondly remembered *Outer Limits* episode "Cold Hands, Warm Heart," and two excellent *Invaders*, "The Leeches" and "The Saucer." Previously, he scripted the early episode "The Bounty Hunter." Sensibly, and like Arthur Weiss in "Chamber of Fear," Ullman splits the seven leads and has two storylines going at once.

Richard Anderson later became a busy actor in the 1970s, playing Oscar Goldman, the boss of both *The Six Million Dollar Man* and *The Bionic Woman*. He was also the immortal Doctor Richard Malcolm in *The Night Strangler*, the second *Kolchak* TV film, and appeared in the '50s SF classic *Forbidden Planet*. The chameleon-like George Mitchell had previously appeared in *Voyage to the Bottom of the Sea* and *Time Tunnel*. Larry Pennell was recurring character Homer J. Noodleman, alias movie hunk Dash Riprock on *The Beverly Hillbillies*. Michael J. Quinn was in charge of the rescue operation in "Rescue" and plays a third role in "Our Man O'Reilly." Stewart Bradley was a scientist in the early episode "The Trap."

Understandably, sets and props were starting to get some re-use by this point. The farmhouse wall interior is the one from "Return of Inidu," the prison cell was seen in "Genius at Work," and the camera from "Framed" also makes a return appearance. The lamp stand was also a regular design fixture in giant households. Stefan Arngrim is absent from this episode, and Heather Young is seen only briefly. Production no.: 4706.

The Unsuspected

wr. Bob and Esther Mitchell, dir. Harry Harris
The Earth people are terrorized by a series of mysterious disappearances among their number.

With Kevin Hagen (Inspector Kobick), Leonard Stone (Sergeant Eson)

It's the old dark house chestnut transposed to the planet of the giants, as cast members disappear, one by one … *Lost in Space* had done a similar storyline as "The Space Creature," and *Voyage* had played the notion to death. Unfortunately, although Steve—transformed into a paranoid by mushroom spores, and bundling the castaways into an abandoned building's air vent one by one—refers to the comment Mark innocently made that triggered off his delusion, the line had been left out of the relevant pre-credits scene. Several small dialogue exchanges have been snipped, and the cast often only approximate the Mitchells' dull dialogue, but this is a key plot point. Fortunately, the episode still works without it.

This seventh episode, moved forward to fifth aired, sees the return of Inspector Kobick to the series, although it seems the decision to bring him in was a last minute one—the script refers to a character called Dobbs. Several other episodes this season bring in Kobick rather than a different intended adversary, testimony to the fine work

of Kevin Hagen, who now allows himself a little quiff in his hair, which last season was greased down flat to give him a more puritanical appearance. The only other guest player in this episode is Leonard Stone, who previously appeared in the first season episode "Brainwash" in a similar but different role.

After all the whimsy and complicated yarns of the previous few weeks, it's a pleasure to enjoy a fast-paced, genuine thriller involving the main players. Although Steve is swiftly revealed as the abductor, this increases the tension as the remaining castaways race against time to stop Steve betraying the others to Kobick. It's a second season highlight, and one of Gary Conway's favorites. Production no.: 4707.

A Place Called Earth

wr. William Welch, dir. Harmon Jones
Time-traveling criminals from Earth's future arrive on the giants' world to use it as a beach-head for their plans to conquer the Earth.

With Warren Stevens (Olds), Jerry Douglas (Fielder), Jerry Quarry (Bron), Scott Thomas (messenger), Rex Holman (Mezron), Gene Le Bell (Mezron's brother), John Mooney (pharmacist)

This is a typical William Welch yarn of the type he contributed frequently to *Voyage to the Bottom of the Sea* and *The Time Tunnel*, full of silver-clad alien beings and strange alien devices. As usual, there is no plot as such, only an initial premise that allows the players to run around energetically for the duration of the episode until the time is up, at which time a convenient resolution is whipped up to wrap things up as quickly as possible. As such, it's a pleasant diversion, and as there were only a handful of futuristic alien stories in *Land of the Giants* (although no doubt there would have been more had the series gone to a third season) they are tolerable in the general scheme of things without harming credibility too much. As loathed as they are by some, aliens and monsters may have been the way to go, had *Land of the Giants* faced a third season.

However, it has to be said that at this late date the Irwin Allen version of the universe was starting to look a little threadbare and passé. The futuristic Earth is a typical Allen set of a darkened room laden with familiar flickering computer banks and dominated by a huge illuminated ball on a pedestal (the *Time Tunnel* power core by the looks of it) giving the orders! All the suits, props and sets (regular size and giant) are existing stock from previous episodes of *Land of the Giants* and other Allen series (the time travelers initially pose as naval men simply because *Voyage to the Bottom of the Sea* uniforms are available; one suspects the guests were cast by shirt size and leg measurements). This was obviously one of Welch's budget cheapies to order, even to the extent of footage of the *Lost in Space* Space Pod doubling for the time-travelers' transportation which even the most casual viewer must have recognized. Welch was a master of constructing stories out of existing materials when budgets got tight, and this—along with a sequel of sorts, "Home Sweet Home"—is undoubtedly one of them. It's also enjoyably different from the standard *Land of the Giants* fare.

Warren Stevens was an Irwin Allen regular, and had already appeared in the first season episode "Brainwash." Rex Holman played Abraham Lincoln in "The Passersby" for *The Twilight Zone*, one of the pasty-faced aliens in the classic "Demon with a Glass Hand" for *The Outer Limits*, and one of the Earp boys in "Spectre of the Gun" for *Star Trek*. Other TV fantasy roles have included *Boris Karloff's Thriller*, and *The Man from UNCLE*. Production no.: 4708.

The Deadly Pawn

wr. Arthur Weiss, dir. Nathan Juran

The Earth people are used as living chess pieces by a deranged and self-indulgent millionaire.

With Alex Dreir (Kronig), John Zaremba (Doctor Lalor), Charlie Briggs (guard), Steven Marlo (technician)

This was Arthur Weiss' final foray into the *Land of the Giants*, one of the silliest of the series, a contrived gimmick show with the castaways compelled to play chess on a lethal giant board. Giant chess boards had already appeared in *The Prisoner* and *The Man from UNCLE* to name but two, and the novelty wears off very quickly, with only the absurdity remaining. Previously, Weiss wrote the equally off-kilter episodes "Target Earth," "The Chase," and "Chamber of Fear." Alex Dreir does what he can with a ridiculous role, while John Zaremba simply looks uncomfortable. Bit player Steven Marlo makes his third appearance in the series, hidden behind glasses and moustache. The most exciting moment in the episode appears to have occurred offscreen, as Stefan Arngrim related many years later how Irwin Allen's toupee fell victim to a wind machine. Heather Young, now heavily pregnant, is seen briefly back at the ship, herself hidden behind some control panels. She will be absent from the series for the next six episodes. Production no.: 4709.

Land of the Lost

wr. William Welch, dir. Sobey Martin, Nathan Juran

The Earth travelers float off in a balloon and land in the hostile territory of a tyrannical ruler.

With Nehemiah Persoff (Titus), Clint Ritchie (Andros), Bob Braun (balloon seller), Peter Canon (slave), Brian Nash (young boy)

Despite the planet Earth being covered with different cultures and different environments, science-fiction and fantasy often present us with entire planets that are presumed to be the same all over. When *Star Trek*, for example, presented audiences with Roman cultures, Nazi societies, and even a planet run by mobsters, the implication was not that this was one portion of the world in question, but the whole world. This episode of *Land of the Giants* suggests, quite adventurously and sensibly, that the totalitarian dictatorship where the *Spindrift* has crash-landed does not cover the whole world, an interesting and unusual, but quite obvious assumption. Unfortunately, the land the castaways inadvertently travel to is not much better than the one they left, a despotic, isolated society run by a brutal tyrant! After witnessing miles of lights indicating a huge sprawling metropolis, we also don't see much of it—one room and a power source next door. Budget restrictions, obviously—but the idea has not been thought through.

Nehemiah Persoff had previously appeared in fairly good episodes of *The Twilight Zone*, *Voyage to the Bottom of the Sea*, *Time Tunnel*, and *The Man from UNCLE*, but his character of Titus is by far the weakest of his sci-fi roles, one-dimensional to say the least, and there is little rationale to anything he says or does, something even the script acknowledges. As for direction, this is the only Allen episode to feature two named directors, although it is not apparent who replaced who or why. The result is not a great episode, but certainly a different episode ... and the initial balloon ride is an exciting highlight. But as a story, there's nothing there. Heather Young begins a six episode absence from this episode. Production no.: 4710.

Every Dog Needs a Boy

wr. Jerry Thomas, dir. Harry Harris
   Barry's dog requires the attention of a sympathetic veterinarian after tangling with a giant-sized four-legged opponent.
   With Michael Anderson Jr. (Ben), Tom Nardini (Carl), Oliver MacGowan (Doctor Howard), Robert Shayne (Mr. Clinton)

Jerry Thomas had been a regular writer for *The Green Hornet*, another Fox series, and worked as story editor on that show. While the *Hornet* series, a more sober crimefighter series from the *Batman* stable, was quite lively low-budget escapism, this—his sole

contribution to *Land of the Giants*, and indeed the entire Allen output—is as dull as dishwater. The giant characters are uninteresting and the castaways take absurd risks, starting by leaving Barry alone after telling him that they can't risk everybody's safety for the sake of rescuing the dog. Naturally, as soon as they turn their backs, he's off...

Oliver MacGowan was the caretaker in the *Star Trek* episode "Shore Leave." Robert Shayne's appearance here is bookended by two recurring roles with D.C. Comics superheroes—as Inspector Henderson in *Adventures of Superman* in the 1950s and as Reggie the news vendor in *The Flash* in the 1990s. Michael Anderson Jr. appears in the underrated mini-series of *The Martian Chronicles*. Tom Nardini later became a regular in the dreary *Cowboy in Africa* series. Heather Young's character is still absent. The title is a play on the old adage that "every boy needs a dog." Production no.: 4711.

The Clones

wr. Oliver Crawford, Bob and Esther Mitchell, dir. Nathan Juran
   A scientist creates flawed and dangerous duplicates of the Earth people.
   With William Schallert (Doctor Arno), Sandra Giles (Doctor Gault)

Although the technology of cloning is still in its infancy, this Irwin Allen version of the process (performed with the aid of two suspended animation tubes from *Lost in Space*), while no doubt scientifically dubious, offers sobering food for thought. The banal motivation of the scientists, concerned mostly with their funding and social standing with their peers, and the casual callousness with which they work on the captive castaways, presents a chilling and credible fantasy scenario that is not only memorable as an exciting and adventurous yarn, but insightful as a terrible warning. This is not to say that scientific experimentation should be stalled or feared—only that there are very real and human consequences to be considered when human beings play with life. The horror that permeates the episode comes from two dreadful side effects of the experimentation—firstly, that the subjects do not know whether they are their own original selves or not, and are all equally certain that they are, and secondly, that the duplicates gradually become aggressive and paranoid and are doomed to deteriorate physically and mentally, before returning to oblivion.

With several versions of the leads to account for onscreen, this was an absurdly difficult episode to film, and in 1969 it had to be done the hard way, with split screens and stand-ins. As *Land of the Giants* was already an optical-heavy special effects show, not only was all the usual trickery required, but in many scenes there were two sets of half the cast to co-ordinate! (This being 1960s TV, the cloning process duplicates identical clothing as well). Happily, veteran director Nathan Juran, a special effects maestro with a well-paced, waste-free ability to tell a story effectively was to hand, and he was already familiar with both the Irwin Allen *modus operandi* and the show itself. Although virtually the entire series was directed by Allen stalwarts Harry Harris and Sobey Martin, five others would be directed by Juran, a master of difficult shoots. For the first season he had directed "Ghost Town."

All the effects scenes with the cloned duplicates are filmed with good old-fashioned trick photography, with stand-ins keeping their backs toward the camera ... but the scene in the air vents, when doubles of four of the six regulars (Heather Young, pregnant during much of the second season, is still absent, again without explanation) are blown through the air ducts alongside their originals, are uniquely weird and professionally show-offy in an unobtrusive way. The sight of the series regulars doubled up is totally bizarre, and this action sequence is cleverly cut in such a way that by the time the viewer has figured out which is the stand-in, the scene has changed to another shot. The illusion is brilliantly upheld.

The writing also is exemplary. The story is Oliver Crawford's, given the once-over by *Giants* regulars Bob and Esther Mitchell. Crawford's other fantasy credits include *The Outer Limits*, *The Wild Wild West* and *Voyage to the Bottom of the Sea*, and he was not averse to doing rewrites and collaborative work himself—he collaborated with Shimon Wincelberg on the classic *Star Trek* episode "The Galileo Seven" and rewrote David Gerrold's "The Cloud Minders" for the same series. Structurally, Crawford's story is clever and scary, although exactly what the Mitchells brought to the table in the rewrite is uncertain. With two, and in some cases, three of the series regulars running around, the story is cleverly constructed to confuse the audience as much as the characters. The scenes at the campsite with the tortured clone of Dan, whoever wrote them, are rich in a rare poignancy and pathos not usually associated with the mechanical A to B scriptwriting of *Land of the Giants*. Don Marshall, who also appeared in "The Galileo Seven," grabs this unusual opportunity to give a strong and three-dimensional performance.

William Schallert is best remembered in the U.S. for a series of cozy dad roles, but can claim two classic TV SF episodes for his resume, the overrated "Little Girl Lost" for *The Twilight Zone*, and "The Trouble with Tribbles" for *Star Trek*. He was also in one of the earliest sci-fi films of the '50s era, 1949's *The Man from Planet X*. Former B-girl Sandra Giles later appeared as a circus dancer in "The Marionettes." Production no.: 4712.

Comeback
wr. Richard Shapiro, dir. Harry Harris
The Earth people become involved with a washed-up horror film actor and a sleazy film producer.
With John Carradine (Egor), Jesse White (Manfred), Fritz Feld (Quigg), James Jeter (gateman), Olan Soule (cameraman), Janos Prohaska (gorilla)

Veteran horror film actor John Carradine plays veteran but washed-up horror film actor Egor Krull, who stumbles onto four of the little people, potential co-stars in a cheap movie project that will now feature them as extraordinary living special effects à la *Attack of the Puppet People*—or indeed, *Land of the Giants*. Unfortunately, the cleverness of this conceit ends there, and the finished episode is not so different from the sort of fare it is sending up. Perhaps the best moment is the scene in which the castaways have to improvise some movie dialogue themselves, and this is hilarious, but with the rest of the episode free of genuine comedy material, the guest cast—broad character actors Jesse White and Fritz Feld, more often seen in, and better suited to, comedy— are obliged to play their stereotypical roles (cigar-chewing vulgarian producer, beret-clad foreign director) with a degree of dramatic seriousness the story doesn't warrant. Surprisingly, Alexander Courage is credited with the clichéd background music, which heavy-handedly tries to compensate for the laugh-free script.

John Carradine made over 200 films during his career, many of them well-documented, most of them Grade Z horror. He also made numerous TV appearances during the 1960s, in episodes of *The Twilight Zone*, *The Munsters*, *Lost in Space*, *The Green Hornet*, *The Man from UNCLE*, *The Girl from UNCLE*, and the TV movie *The Night Strangler*, the second *Kolchak* story. The comic actor Fritz Feld made three appearances in *Lost in Space* as the eccentric Zumdish, in "The Android Machine," "The Toymaker" and "Two Weeks in Space." Janos Prohaska, here wearing the gorilla suit, had made a profession out of playing unusual monster roles, and unlike most TV gorillas, portrayed by stunt-men who played for vaudevillian laughs, Prohaska took the opposite route of trying to appear as convincing as possible. He appears in his monkey suit for *The Outer Limits* ("The Sixth Finger"), *Lost*

in Space ("The Oasis"), and *Bewitched* ("Darrin Goes Ape"), and while flat direction let him down when he put on his white gorilla suit for *Star Trek's* "Friday's Child," his tour-de-force is the *Voyage to the Bottom of the Sea* episode "Fatal Cargo" in the same outfit. He's back again a few episodes later for "The Marionettes."

Following the success of the whimsical but also dark and threatening "Night of Thrombeldinbar" in the first season, some second season episodes—particularly those by Richard Shapiro and William Welch— had started to play the Fitzhugh character purely for comedy (forgetting the dark side that the Mitchells always included in their scripts, which for all their failings were possessed by a sense of perpetual uneasy menace). While this was preferable to seeing Fitzhugh as an Aunt Sally figure for Captain Burton to bully and shove around, it was (as is so often the case with humor in TV SF) often overplayed at the expense of a story's and character's credibility. In this episode, as in Shapiro's "Inside Rail," Fitzhugh behaves like such a buffoon that he is totally out of character. As with the later interpretation of Doctor Smith in *Lost in Space*, one wonders if the stressfulness of his situation hasn't driven him slightly mad. Production no.: 4713.

Nightmare (aka The Delta Effect)

wr. William Welch, dir. Nathan Juran

A malfunctioning scientific device turns the Earth people both invisible and delusional as they experience a variety of trippy hallucinations.

With Kevin Hagen (Inspector Kobick), Torin Thatcher (Doctor Berger), Yale Summers (Andre)

Another William Welch cost-cutting time-filler. As the episode opens, the castaways have met another friendly and sympathetic giant scientist (similar to Jody and Franzen in "Genius at Work" and "Target Earth" respectively) who is helping them build a device to take their spaceship home to Earth. Instead, the device malfunctions, and a form of radiation causes the Delta Effect (the original title of the episode) to create a succession of bizarre delusions as people appear and disappear in a blaze of photographic effects. "It doesn't make sense" says Dan, shortly before he disappears into thin air, not just invisible, but in a strange limbo-land—and he's right. Similar nonsensical time-wasters were written for *Voyage to the Bottom of the Sea* when real stories were in short supply. The visual effects are quite interesting, a surreal neon nightmare, making this one of the better of such stories, marred only by the unnecessary inclusion of over-familiar images from the Time Tunnel base during the hallucination scenes with Steve and Mark fighting.

Character actor Torin Thatcher was a favorite of director Nathan Juran, who had used him in "The Space Trader" for *Lost in Space.* Here, he plays the blustering colleague of the friendly scientist. This was Kevin Hagen's eighth appearance as the recurring character Inspector Kobick, although in the credits he is billed simply as S.I.D. Inspector. Juran used Hagen several times in Allen shows, and would have had no hesitation in calling him in for a role that should have been his anyway. Kobick is being used more sparingly in this second season, and the dream sequences give him the chance to do a little more acting than usual. Production no.: 4714.

Home Sweet Home (aka Return)

wr. William Welch, dir. Harry Harris

Steve and Fitzhugh take a trip back to Earth in an abandoned alien spaceship ... but find themselves in the 19th century.

With William Bassett (Ranger Jack), John Milford (Ranger Wilson), Mort Mills (police constable), June Dayton (Mrs. Perkins), William Benedict (Mr. Peabody), Bob Adler (Mr. Sloacum), Pete Kellett (guard)

Anyone coming fresh to the show with this episode is going to be very confused, as it strays far from the path of a typical *Land of the Giants* episode. Indeed, very little time is spent on the giants' world, and those scenes appear to be an attempt to shoehorn in the expected lilliputian action scenes promised by the title. Despite this, "Home Sweet Home," originally titled simply "Return," is a refreshing change and an enjoyable yarn, continuing indirectly from the earlier episode "A Place Called Earth" by opening with the discovery of Olds and Fielder's abandoned time machine (in actuality, the Space Pod from the third season of *Lost in Space*). Captain Burton and Fitzhugh are then spirited away not only back to Earth, but into the past, where—at one point—the superstitious locals of the 19th century township the vehicle has appeared in, are frozen in time. The set is not one of the usual standing sets on the lot employed in the Allen series, leading one to suspect it has been constructed for something else and that Welch has built a story around its availability. The highlight of the episode, an old time-travel movie chestnut, has the locals building a bonfire around the Space Pod, with Steve and Fitzhugh in it, to dispose of supernatural demons they don't understand.

John Milford had appeared in *Voyage to the Bottom of the Sea* and *The Invaders.* Bob Adler had experienced "Devil's Island" in *The Time Tunnel.* Peter Kellett was William Shatner's stand-in in *Star Trek* and the evil Kirk's henchman in the *Star Trek* episode "Mirror, Mirror." Production no.: 4715.

Our Man O'Reilly

wr. Jackson Gillis, dir. Sobey Martin

The Earth people become involved with an oafish but harmless fellow who mistakes them for leprechauns.

With Alan Hale (O'Reilly), Alan Bergmann (Krenko), Billy Halop (bartender), Eddie Marr (Brynie), Lindsay Workman (Cunningham), Michael J. Quinn (night watchman), Dusty Cadis (store guard)

Jackson Gillis wrote for a variety of series, dividing his time between murder mysteries for *Columbo* and *Perry Mason* and adventure series ranging from *Adventures of Superman* and *Lost in Space* to *Knight Rider* and *The Equalizer*. However, no one seems to have bothered to tell him that the giant world is another planet and not an oversized Earth, and so we are greeted with the spectacle of his central character, a stereotypical drunken Irishman, raving about the "leprechauns" he's seen. *Land of the Giants* always was schizophrenic regarding the names of the giant-sized characters—sometimes they had silly pulp mag SF names, other times Earth-like WASP names—but this tedious episode, by any name, is a colossal bore, as are television's loveable drunks. The production is also getting lazy—the giant shoebox from "Comeback" makes a reappearance in this episode without any alterations to redress it. Previously when props were re-used, efforts were made to look them look slightly different to all but the most dedicated viewer.

Alan Hale is best known for his starring roles in two other earlier series, *Casey Jones* and *Gilligan's Island*, and boisterous bit parts in historical adventures. A little of his jolly Irishman, already bordering on offensive stereotype, goes a long way—funny drunks are rarely particularly funny unless they advance the plot, and certainly don't carry entire storylines. Alan Bergmann was one of the aliens in the *Star Trek* episode "The Empath." He also appeared in episodes of *The Six Million Dollar Man*, *The Bionic Woman*, and *Wonder Woman*. Of the bit players, *Bilko* fans will spot Papperelli behind the bar in the form of Billy Halop, Lindsay Workman appeared in *The Twilight Zone's* "Valley of the Shadow," and Dusty Cadis appeared in the "Abominable Snowman" episode of *Voyage to the Bottom of the Sea*. Michael J. Quinn previously appeared in "Rescue" and "Six Hours to Live." Bit player Eddie Marr had appeared in *20,000*

Leagues Under the Sea, I Was a Teenage Werewolf, and *How to Make a Monster*. TV roles included parts in *The Twilight Zone* and *The Addams Family*. Heather Young returns to the series after an absence of six episodes. Production no.: 4716.

Panic (aka No Escape)

wr. Bob and Wanda Duncan, dir. Sobey Martin

The Earth people must evade a ruthless and ambitious official while trying to return to Earth in a friendly scientist's teleportation device.

With Jack Albertson (Kirmus), Peter Mark Richman (Marad), Diane McBain (Mrs. Evers), Edward G. Robinson Jr., Patrick Culliton, Steven Marlo (S.I.D. men)

With the story involving much running around, electronic popping about, and ending with a handy explosion, it would be fair to assume this is another William Welch filler, but in fact it's the third and last script for the series (after "Seven Little Indians" in the zoo, and a teleplay for Sidney Marshall's "Collector's Item") by Bob and Wanda Duncan. The Duncans had written extensively for *Lost in Space* and *The Time Tunnel*, however, and were well versed on how to fill up an hour slot Irwin Allen-style. Guest star Jack Albertson, distinguished from his earlier turn as magician Inidu in "Return of Inidu" by a beard and moustache, is once again mysteriously moving the little people around in space, but this time with the aid of a teleportation device he has invented. For a planet that is scientifically backward in comparison with Earth, there were certainly a lot of stories concerning super-science ... although perhaps it says something about totalitarian societies that many of the inventions were being kept away from the government and most of those that weren't failed to work properly. Tyrannical societies are invariably more scientifically backward than free ones, as Woody Allen's hilarious 1973 film *Sleeper* pointed out so memorably; in a more liberal environment, perhaps the scientists would have been working with the government, and the giant world would have been further along.

Although Stefan Arngrim's Barry is absent, the rest of the cast enjoy an equal amount of screentime—it's particularly refreshing to see, as in the second season's "Doomsday" and "The Marionettes," Heather Young's Betty with plenty to do, although by rights the poor woman surely shouldn't have survived the fall to the floor in the gun barrel. One thing the Duncans did always acknowledge more than the series' other writers was what would be the large amount of animal life in proximity to the castaways, something many episodes failed to bother with. All the Duncans' episodes feature brief encounters with various pets and wildlife, although the giant world does appear to be significantly bug-free.

Oddly, the guest cast are divided between those who have alien names and the supporting characters who have Earth-style names (including the S.I.D. men). The three guest stars are all well-cast, but if Albertson has a substantial center stage role, Mark Richman (seen to advantage in episodes of *Voyage to the Bottom of the Sea*, *The Invaders*, and *The Man from UNCLE*) has little option but to phone his part in, restricted by the mattes and dull, small sets. Diane McBain's treacherous housekeeper (she was frequently cast in witchy roles and is another former Elvis babe) is significant primarily for her being the only giant in the entire series to actually move quickly while trying to catch the little people. Production no.: 4717.

Pay the Piper

wr. Richard Shapiro, dir. Harry Harris

The Earth people discover that the legend of the Pied Piper was inspired by a space-traveling troublemaker who has turned up on the giant world to offer to rid it of an infestation of tiny Earth people.

With Jonathan Harris (the Piper), Peter Leeds (the Senator), Michael James Wixted (Timmy)

This was the fourth and final story

from writer Richard Shapiro, who joined *Land of the Giants* from the second season, contributing "The Inside Rail," "Giants and All That Jazz," "Comeback," and this story, "Pay the Piper." All four were light and frothy escapades—one is set at a racetrack, one has the giant world discovering jazz, another features a variety of ham actors in a send-up of the movie business—but this one takes the cake. A fascinating premise suggests that the Pied Piper of legend was actually a visiting alien space traveler, and when he turns up on the giant world, a shifty politician (is there any other kind?) hires him to scare off the little people and make him a hero. Shapiro's scripts were graced with a selection of notable character actors to make them even more frothy and non-threatening, and his Pied Piper is portrayed by the camp Jonathan Harris, Doctor Smith from *Lost in Space*. Following the demise of that series, Harris had returned to the guest star circuit, and although notorious for famously departing from the scripts on *Lost in Space*, here he is word perfect with lines that seem written for him in mind. Production no.: 4718.

The Secret City of Limbo

wr. Bob and Esther Mitchell, dir. Sobey Martin

The Earth people discover a strange underground civilization where a power struggle is in process between a benevolent dictator and a warmonger.

With Malachi Throne (Taru), Joseph Ruskin (General Aza), Whit Bissell (Doctor Krane), Peter Jason (Mylo)

If the "Land of the Lost" had been noticeably compact, this problem was rectified by the large and spacious set employed for the series' second and last lost civilization, this time located underground. However, why there would be a teleportation grid the right size for Earth people hidden in a hole in the ground is never considered! Initially, the writers had envisaged a society of pale-skinned, big-eyed mole people, but the budget and Allen's usual futuristic humanoid society won out. "The Secret City of Limbo," a meaningless title, is another thoroughly routine story by the Mitchells which unfolds exactly as the audience expects.

Both Malachi Throne and Joseph Ruskin had appeared several times in Irwin Allen productions, as had Whit Bissell, who was of course General Kirk in *The Time Tunnel*, making four of that series' five regulars guest stars in *Land of the Giants*. Joseph Ruskin had previously appeared in the first season episode "Terror-go-Round." This was the last of twelve scripts from Bob and Esther Mitchell. Production no.: 4719.

Doomsday

wr. Dan Ullman, dir. Harry Harris
The Earth people stumble onto a terrorist plot to set off a series of fatal explosions in the giant community.

With Kevin Hagen (Inspector Kobick), Francine York (Doctor North), Charles Dierkop (Kamber), Ed Peck (Warkin), Tom Drake (S.I.D. man)

A rather confused yarn which offers no obvious aim or motivation for the terrorist violence other than anarchy ... a bizarre rationale for a bogus female doctor living in opulent surroundings with a pet monkey! This scenario, alongside North's ruthless cold-hearted killings of her two stooges, suggests Ullman may have been aiming for some sort of cod-Bond scenario that got lost somewhere in the production process. However, the script, while far from Ullman's best, has been filmed faithfully, even down to the insipid final tag, showing the monkey outside the *Spindrift*, a cause for much merriment, rather than terror and concern for their safety and security. All the castaways think it's hilarious, and we're supposed to as well—which is absurd, as the creature can not only do serious damage to the spaceship and little people, but also lead anyone else back to the secret campsite. It's a serious dilemma worthy of an entire storyline rather than a cheap closing gag. But despite this *faux pas*, the rest is an acceptable entry. The end credits suggest that the S.I.D. inspector was named Turner, although in the script and the episode the character is our old adversary Inspector Kobick, played as usual by Kevin Hagen. Hagen is as solid as ever, and gives strength and credence to every scene he appears in, something the shaky plotting sorely needs, although the series does not seem particularly committed to the character—this is his ninth and last appearance, and events in the forthcoming "The Deadly Dart" (with Kobick absent on "special assignment") suggest he was to be replaced and/or that the series was trying to replace him.

Charles Dierkop appeared as "The Left Handed Man" in an excellent *Voyage to the Bottom of the Sea*, and as yet another crooked stooge in the Allen pilot *City Beneath the Sea*. He spent the mid-'70s as a hippie cop in the silly *Police Woman* series. Ed Peck's gravel voice adorned many tough guy bit parts in drama and sit-com; he was the head of security who faced down Kirk in the "Tomorrow Is Yesterday" episode of *Star Trek*.

Whereas many actors enjoyed some of their most unusual and flamboyant roles in the other Allen series, *Land of the Giants* often showcased their drabbest, dullest acting opportunities. Francine York can do little with her role here, and is even denied her final shot of impotent fury as offered in the script; she was more fun as Neolani the Amazon in the *Lost in Space* episode "The Colonists," where her other fantasy credits are detailed. Although Barry is absent yet again, the rest of the cast enjoy an equal amount of screentime. Production no.: 4720.

Wild Journey

wr. William Welch, dir. Harry Harris
When they encounter two aliens with a time travel device, Steve and Dan plot to return to the time of their departure from Earth to change their fate.

With Bruce Dern (Thorg), Yvonne Craig

(Berna), Sheila Mathews (Miss Collier), Louise Lorimer (Miss Smith), Erik Nelson (S.I.D. man), Win Liverman (security guard), Marshall Stewart (man in street)

"I was running around with a ray gun on the Fox lot," Bruce Dern told a reporter from *Films and Filming* in the 1970s, "when I got a call from Jack Nicholson...." The call was for him to co-star in the movie *Drive, He Said*, a film that was to make him a major star of the '70s, and the "ray gun" was in fact nothing less than a "Space-Time Manipulator." Dern's indifference and disdain towards this acting assignment was entirely justified, as this is a truly dreadful and embarrassing botch, an ineptly scripted catalogue of absurdities that is outlandish not in the way that Irwin Allen's TV series are enjoyably outlandish, but in the hopelessly incompetent script, which blows the potential of a wonderful idea. What should have been one of the best episodes of *Land of the Giants* turns out to be one of the dumbest.

As the episode opens, Steve and Dan are being pursued by an S.I.D. man when they notice that the object of his attention is not them, but another tiny fugitive who is revealed to be one of a pair of aliens, Thorg and Berna, a male and female with extraordinary powers to control time and space. The production process edits out or omits to film certain exchanges that would have explained at least some of the inconsistencies the episode produces. Without a break in the story, and with a previous scene omitted, Dern refers to the castaways mentioning Earth—which they haven't—and projects an image of the Earth on a rock. Having seen this image, having no reason to fear or distrust these two, and having been told by the aliens that they can manipulate time and space, Dan suggests "losing these two" and getting back to camp! What, no questions? No requests? Think hard, guys!

Later, having been shown L.A. airport and their spaceship, the *Spindrift*, in flight, Steve is told that the aliens won't let the ma-

chine out of their hands. Entirely reasonable of course, and Steve and Dan think so too ... but instead of doing the next obvious thing, and asking Thorg and Berna to return them to Earth, they just shrug their shoulders, and off they go...

The aliens, who have still not shown the slightest demonstration of hostility, then ask if they might visit the camp of the Earth people, but—despite the fact that these two seem friendly, despite the fact that they can obviously get them home, and despite the fact that they can surely find the campsite in about fourteen different ways—Steve refuses ... and despite their amazing powers, the aliens then follow them surreptitiously on foot! (A scene with Steve realizing the aliens will follow, and so leading them along a false trail is also omitted).

Saving the aliens from the clutches of the S.I.D. officer, who is now looking for his quarry in the forest, Steve and Dan—still without asking the obvious and attempting to strike up either a deal or a friendship—steal one of the Space-Time Manipulators with a view to getting back to Earth. Surely they realize that the aliens can simply find and retrieve them from any part of time and space with their remaining device? Instead, they decide that it's "now or never" for themselves to return to Earth on September 25th, 1983 (the pilot film clearly states the date of the flight being January 16th, but Welch has looked up the episode's airdate) and try to stop the flight from ever happening. But this is crazy—nobody died, and the castaways actually saved lives on the giant world and did good ... With history changed, the photographer gets away with murder, the kids in the mineshaft are killed, the wrongly accused murderer is executed, and so on. Why not simply return to Earth two years later, with all exciting memories and experiences intact? This thought occurs neither to writer, producers, or characters (Harry Harris, a competent enough director, never seems to question a script).

What does occur to the two aliens is that they will be "in trouble" if the past is changed and events don't happen exactly as they did. Steve and Dan return to 1983, and sure enough, there are Thorg and Berna waiting for them. Dan suggests Steve send the aliens back with the Space-Time Manipulator, even though the aliens have one themselves and can simply keep coming back! Steve can't reset it anyway, so they barge into the Flight Office and announce that they won't take the flight out. But where are the Steve and Dan of 1983 while all this is going on? Can't they take the flight out? Or have this Steve and Dan become the other Steve and Dan? Why, when as two pilots in charge of taking out a flight, Steve and Dan tell the Flight Officer to call a security officer to evict Thorg and Berna, does she refuse?

The Flight Officer, enquiring about Steve and Dan's refusal to fly, inadvertently feeds them with numerous easy options to get out of the flight to London (illness, bomb hoax, etc.), and there are doubtless other numerous delaying tactics that a child could think of, but instead, the two pilots drivel on lamely about "bad feelings" and other soft excuses that carry no weight. Why not feign illness? Why not expose the embezzler Fitzhugh? Why not invent, or cause, some spurious equipment malfunction? Now that they have revealed themselves as a thoroughly suspicious pair of characters, any sane Flight Officer would remove them from duty immediately anyway.

At this point, the Flight Officer attempts to organize two different pilots, while Thorg and Berna now reveal that they cannot return to their mission on the giant world until everything is as it was; the events of history must not be changed in any way. Despite this, Flight 612 is transferred to the *Spindrift* because the Flight Officer must cancel the seats of 41 passengers due to Steve and Dan's refusal to fly, while the four who will now take the *Spindrift* to London are—

of course—the series' regulars. Consequently, not only have Steve and Dan changed history, they've actually shaped the events that will take them on a one way trip to the land of the giants. To further confuse matters, Thorg and Berna are perfectly willing for the flight to take place with the substitute pilots—yet all this changes events in the past, leaving Steve and Dan on Earth ... something they earlier said they couldn't do.

The next revelation comes when the aliens start employing all sorts of bizarre powers that they could have used hours ago to achieve their aims, freezing time in the departure lounge, and shrinking Steve and Dan down to the miniature size they are in the giant's dimension—another new ability the aliens have pulled out of a hat (a pre-credits teaser sequence, with Thorg growing to giant-size on the giant world and making his pursuer the little person, was scrapped, while another sequence with him moving everyone around with the Space Time Manipulator was modified to such an extent it became a meaningless series of explosive charges). Thorg and Berna, we now realize, could have frozen them, shrunk them, returned them, and/or reversed time at any point during the adventure. Why was Thorg running from the S.I.D. officer earlier when he possesses the sort of powers he later demonstrates?

The episode continues in similar fashion throughout its entire duration, including more silliness in the departure lounge, as Steve and Dan first try to contact Mark while in the form of little people, and then full-sized try to persuade various members of the party to stay behind. Once again, the two of them ramble on incoherently about "crashes" and "being marooned," never once using more devious storytelling to scuttle the flight. Would you fly with these men at the controls?

Although the episode has one or two nice touches (it's fun to see the passengers before their flight, and Fitzhugh has an amusing scene with the dog Chipper that appears to have been added at the last minute to make up time for the scenes unfilmed), for once they can't compensate for the disastrous failings of the plot. Certainly there were duller episodes, but none offered such banal or excruciatingly insipid dialogue, and few had such a persistent parade of gaping flaws in the plot in terms of credibility or common sense. Time travel stories are always on shaky ground by their very nature, but never has one been so thoughtlessly conceived as this silly tale, which desperately needed rewriting before filming. Somewhere along the way the production came to the same conclusion, and an already weakly written yarn became mincemeat, and this is a shame, because the idea is excellent, and written with care would have made a wonderful inadvertent last episode, as it takes the show full circle, literally back to its beginnings in the final scenes.

Bruce Dern did much television work in the '60s before hitting the big time, including the legendary "The Zanti Misfits" for *The Outer Limits*. He later starred in the SF film *Silent Running*. Yvonne Craig, previously Batgirl in the third season of the *Batman* series, was a major figure in 1960s SF, chalking up appearances in *My Favorite Martian*, *Voyage to the Bottom of the Sea*, *Star Trek*, *The Man from UNCLE*, *The Six Million Dollar Man*, and the films *In Like Flint* and *Mars Needs Women*. Sheila Mathews (Mrs. Irwin Allen) previously appeared in "Deadly Lodestone." Stefan Arngrim was by now far too tall to participate in the flashback scenes and appears in this episode only in stock footage. Production no.: 4721.

The Deadly Dart
(aka The Retaliator)

wr. William Stuart, dir. Harry Harris
    Mark is framed for the murder of an S.I.D. inspector.

With John Dehner (Lt. Grayson), Madlyn Rhue (Bertha Fry), Christopher Dark (Sergeant Barker), Willard Sage (Inspector Swann), Kent Taylor (Doctor Jelko), Donald Barry (Zoral)

When regular characters are accused of murder, we know that a series is coming to the end of its natural life and script ideas are in short supply. At least *Land of the Giants* gets some credit for waiting until the last few episodes to introduce such desperation. The episode opens with the castaways privy to information the audience has been denied, with the script telling us that Inspector Kobick has been replaced by the sadistic and weird upcoming murder victim Inspector Swann, an adversary the little people have already had several encounters with when this story begins. However, the story does reference Stuart's earlier episode, "The Mechanical Man," an escapade we did witness, pointlessly bringing back the scientist Zoral from that story, played by a completely different actor. Stuart had already brought back Doctor Brulle from William Welch's "The Creed," and was the only writer on the series to attempt to create and follow some form of continuity, but it was clearly not a priority of anyone else on the show; if only he had been the story editor. The episode's best sequence involves an improbable and elaborate trap set by Swann before his death, utilizing the poles from the force field in "The Chase" and the teleporter, redressed and customized, from "Panic." The series is also starting to use blue-screen, or chromakey as it was then called, rather than back projection, and the decline in quality of some of the effects scenes is there for all to see when Dan examines Swann's fallen body.

Madlyn Rhue, cast as another of the series' string of malevolent women prevalent toward the end of the series, was Lt. McGivers in the *Star Trek* episode "Space Seed," and Willard Sage plays one the aliens in the dismal "The Empath." He previously appeared in *Land of the Giants* as Hook in "Double Cross" and also appears in "The Experiment" for *The Invaders*. Christopher

Dark was Crazy Horse in *Time Tunnel's* "Massacre."

Kent Taylor had played a minor role in the *Voyage to the Bottom of the Sea* episode "And Five of Us Are Left" after starring in some very minor league SF B-movies in the 1950s, including *Phantom from 10,000 Leagues* and the empty *The Day Mars Invaded Earth,* all title and no content. Donald Red Barry was a former western star (as Red Ryder) and stunt player in the serials who had also turned to bit parts by the 1960s, including episodes of *The Munsters, Batman,* and *The Wild Wild West.* In the 1970s, he turned up in *Kolchak: the Night Stalker, The Six Million Dollar Man, The Bionic Woman,* and *Project UFO* among others.

As mentioned under "Doomsday," while *Lost in Space* and *The Time Tunnel* often supplied 1960s character actors with some of their best and most memorable parts, *Land of the Giants* frequently showcased wonderful performers at their dullest. A veteran of three *Twilight Zones,* John Dehner was great fun as a mad scientist in "The Menfish" for *Voyage to the Bottom of the Sea* and a would-be world conqueror in *The Man from UNCLE,* but can make little of his dreary part here. He looks as bored as we are.

This would be William Stuart's third and final script for the series, following "Deadly Lodestone" and "The Mechanical Man." Production no.: 4722.

Graveyard of Fools

wr. Sidney Marshall, dir. Sobey Martin

Giant scientists force the Earth people to travel to a dangerous and uncharted area of the giant world.

With Albert Salmi (Melzac/Bryk), John Crawford (Tagor)

Toward the end of the series, *Land of the Giants* was increasingly reliant on bells and whistles episodes—that is to say, meaningless time-filling non-stories where the characters would simply pop and bleep around from one pointless jeopardy sequence to another while in pursuit of what

screenwriters call McGuffins, some sort of goal or device that would solve their manufactured problems ("A Place Called Earth," "Nightmare," "Home Sweet Home," "Panic," "Wild Journey," etc.). Like "Panic," this is a William Welch episode in every way but name, another of those episodes where the crew experience a variety of bizarre, nightmarish hallucinations that conveniently employ existing props and stock footage (Irwin Allen's *Lost World* footage is clumsily employed; the main interior set is made up of pieces from *Voyage to the Bottom of the Sea's Seaview*). While four of the cast endure this, Mark is kept captive in the same force field device used by the S.I.D. in "The Chase," and the second season's fancy breaking and entering equipment from "The Inside Rail" and "Six Hours to Live" is employed again. Again, the story revolves around another fantastic scientific device way beyond Earth science, let alone the backward technology of the giant world. More worryingly, some of the matte work on the special effects is still looking noticeably shoddy. The cast are superimposed clumsily in front of the insect and lizard footage, and when Dan announces he's going to follow Bryk ghost-like through the wall, the obvious bluescreen (the same telegraphed effect used with Deanna Lund in "The Secret City of Limbo") tells us that he'll be successful well before he tries it. Perhaps the best sequence features Fitzhugh being menaced by a malevolent giant-sized version of himself.

Taking the money and running were two of the finest character players in film and TV, Albert Salmi and John Crawford. Playing two different characters at least gives Salmi the best role here, but Marshall's dialogue for the giants is awful (and once again, the castaways appear to have information the audience has not seen them acquire—Steve has already heard of the "graveyard of fools" of the title, a sort of Bermuda Triangle which although supposedly mysterious to the giants, is already inhabited by

Melzac's malcontent twin brother! How did *he* get there?). Both Salmi and Crawford were wonderful actors, and deserved far better than they got here—and their bored, smirking performances suggest they knew it. Although bit player Marshall Stewart, who previously appeared in "Wild Journey," is credited as playing a janitor, no such character appears in the finished episode, suggesting a sequence cut for time. Production no.: 4723.

A Small War

wr. Shirl Hendryx, dir. Harry Harris

The Earth people are forced into participating in a young boy's war games with his toy soldiers and tanks.

With Sean Kelly (Alek Erdap), Charles Drake (Mr. Erdap), Larry Dean (toy soldier), Miriam Schiller (toy nurse)

"A Small War" was written from a five-line premise by long-gone story editor Anthony Wilson. It was a rush job done as a favor to story editor Richard McDonagh, and looks it. Nothing has been thought through. Endless repetitious scenes of toy soldiers marching through the forest slow an already tiresome story down to a crawl, and although the mimes playing the soldiers are good, it still doesn't obscure the fact that they are not toys. However, the biggest problem with the episode's credibility is that the boy is much too old not to realize that the little people aren't sophisticated toys; he would have to be at least three or four years younger to not understand he's dealing with living beings. For this reason alone, the first season's "Ghost Town" is a model example, to excuse the pun, of how to pull off this sort of storyline, while "A Small War" demonstrates how not to. To compound the fault, when the boy discovers that the little people can bleed, and his father tells him that if they can capture them, they'll be rich, the boy aids the little people in escaping from his father. As his father is portrayed as a decent man, there seems no logical reason for

the boy's betrayal (had the father been a violent bully, then his actions might have made sense). A sensible rewrite, perhaps pitting two five year old boys against each other, could have produced a classic episode, instead of the silly misfire we have here.

Charles Drake appears in the SF feature film *It Came from Outer Space* as the sheriff. His TV roles include a substantial role in "The Saucer" for *The Invaders*, and a minor role as boorish officialdom in "The Deadly Years" for *Star Trek*. Larry Dean was also a toy soldier in episodes of *Lost in Space* and *Voyage to the Bottom of the Sea*, among others. Miriam Schiller appeared briefly as a housewife in the earlier episode "Night of Thrombeldinbar," and as Miss Teutonium in "Space Beauty" for *Lost in Space*. Production no.: 4724.

The Marionettes

wr. William Welch, dir. Sobey Martin

When an elderly puppeteer in a traveling show injures his hand saving Valerie from a giant gorilla, the Earth people repay his kindness by posing as his marionettes until he recovers.

With Frank Ferguson (Goalby), Victoria Vetri (Lisa), Bob Hogan (Brady), Sandra Giles (dancer), Janos Prohaska (gorilla), Martin Liverman (trainer), Carl Carlsson (knife thrower), Al Lampkin (fire eater), Diane Krabbe (little girl)

The last episode to go into production (or at least to be assigned a production number), and the series finally got its chance to do *King Kong* again with Valerie and the giant gorilla from "Comeback." The first fifteen minutes, in pursuit of the gorilla, are quite good, but afterwards, when Fitzhugh and Betty pose as marionettes, it all gets a bit cute. But it's an unusual episode, giving Kurt Kasznar the chance to have some fun and Heather Young the opportunity to show off her dancing skills. The problem is that the show's audience doesn't tune in to see the cast indulging themselves.

Frank Ferguson's other roles include bits in *Adventures of Superman*, *The Twilight*

Zone, and *Voyage to the Bottom of the Sea*. Victoria Vetri had just changed her name from Angela Dorian (her real name), and was wonderful in "I'll Be a Mummy's Uncle" for *Batman*, as one of King Tut's inappropriate molls. Despite film roles in *Rosemary's Baby* and *When Dinosaurs Ruled the Earth*, nothing much happened career-wise afterwards. Bob Hogan later changed his stage name to Robert and appeared in several '70s and '80s cop shows. Fantasy TV roles include episodes of *Twilight Zone*, *Batman*, *I Dream of Jeannie*, *Six Million Dollar Man*, *The Incredible Hulk*, *Automan*, *Airwolf*, and *Knight Rider*. Sandra Giles previously appeared as Doctor Arno's lab assistant in "The Clones." Janos Prohaska previously did his gorilla bit for "Comeback." Production no.: 4725.

Episodes in Order of Production

FIRST SEASON (26 EPISODES)

2401 The Crash
2402 The Weird World
2403 The Trap
2404 The Bounty Hunter
2405 The Golden Cage
2406 The Lost Ones
2407 Manhunt
2408 Framed
2409 The Creed
2410 The Flight Plan
2411 Underground
2412 Double-Cross
2413 On a Clear Night You Can See the Earth
2414 Ghost Town
2415 Brainwash
2416 Terror-go-Round
2417 Sabotage
2418 Genius at Work
2419 Deadly Lodestone
2420 Night of Thrombeldinbar
2421 Seven Little Indians
2422 Target Earth
2423 Rescue
2424 Return of Inidu
2425 Shell Game
2426 The Chase

SECOND SEASON (25 EPISODES)

4701 The Inside Rail
4702 Chamber of Fear
4703 The Mechanical Man
4704 Collector's Item
4705 Giants and All That Jazz
4706 Six Hours to Live
4707 The Unsuspected
4708 A Place Called Earth
4709 The Deadly Pawn
4710 Land of the Lost
4711 Every Dog Needs a Boy
4712 The Clones
4713 Comeback
4714 Nightmare
4715 Home Sweet Home
4716 Our Man O'Reilly
4717 Panic
4718 Pay the Piper
4719 Secret City of Limbo
4720 Doomsday
4721 Wild Journey
4722 The Deadly Dart
4723 Graveyard of Fools
4724 A Small War
4725 The Marionettes

Episodes in Order of Broadcast

FIRST SEASON (26 EPISODES)

2401 The Crash
2414 Ghost Town
2408 Framed
2411 Underground
2416 Terror-Go-Round
2410 The Flight Plan
2407 Manhunt

2403 The Trap
2409 The Creed
2412 Double-Cross
2402 The Weird World
2405 The Golden Cage
2406 The Lost Ones
2415 Brainwash
2404 The Bounty Hunter
2413 On a Clear Night You Can See the Earth

2419 Deadly Lodestone
2420 Night of Thrombeldinbar
2421 Seven Little Indians
2422 Target Earth
2418 Genius at Work
2424 Return of Inidu
2423 Rescue
2417 Sabotage
2425 Shell Game
2426 The Chase

SECOND SEASON (25 EPISODES)

4703 The Mechanical Man
4706 Six Hours to Live
4701 The Inside Rail
4709 The Deadly Pawn
4707 The Unsuspected
4705 Giants and All That Jazz

4704 Collector's Item
4711 Every Dog Needs a Boy
4702 Chamber of Fear
4712 The Clones
4713 Comeback
4708 A Place Called Earth
4710 Land of the Lost
4715 Home Sweet Home
4716 Our Man O'Reilly
4714 Nightmare
4718 Pay the Piper
4719 Secret City of Limbo
4717 Panic
4722 The Deadly Dart
4720 Doomsday
4724 A Small War
4725 The Marionettes
4721 Wild Journey
4723 Graveyard of Fools

Production Credits

Created and produced by Irwin Allen; Assistant to producer: Paul Zastupnevich; Story editor: Tony Wilson (pre-production); Story editor: Richard McDonagh (series); Art direction: Rodger E. Maus, Stan Jolley, Stan Johnson; Art direction supervisor: Jack Martin Smith; Set decoration: Walter M. Scott, Norman Rockett, Raymond Paul; Also: James Cane, Robert Signorelli; Costume design and wardrobe: Paul Zastupnevich; Director of photography: Howard Schwartz, Frank Carson; Also: Charles Clarke, Richard Kelley; Special effects: Lyle B. Abbott, Art Cruickshank, Emil Kosa Jr.; Music: John Williams, Joseph Mullendore, Paul Sawtell, Leith Stevens; Also: Alexander Courage, Harry Geller, Irving Gertz, Richard La Salle, Robert Prince; Music editor: George Probert; Music supervision: Leonard Engel, Lionel Newman; Theme music: John Williams; Sound effects editor: Robert Cornett; Supervising sound effects editor: Don Hall Jr.; Production coordinator: Les Warner; Production supervisor: Jack Sonntag Production assistant: Hal Herman; Unit production manager: Ted Butcher; Assistant directors: Ray Taylor, Eli Dunn, David Whorf, Gil Kissel, E. Darrell Hallenbeck; Film editors: James Baiotto, Jack Gleason, George Watters, Dick Wormell; Make-up: Ben Nye; Hair styling: Margaret Donovan; Post production supervisor: George Swink; Post production coordinator: Robert Mintz; Associate producer: Jerry Briskin, Bruce Fowler Jr.; In charge of production: William Self; Kent Productions for 20th Century Fox.

Bibliography

Abbott, Jon. "100 Faces You Know...." *TV Zone* 100th Issue Special, 1998.

_____. "*Land of the Giants*: The Crash." *TV Zone*, no. 93.

_____. "*Land of the Giants*: Ghost Town." *TV Zone*, no. 105.

_____. "*Lost in Space*: Anti-Matter Man." *TV Zone*, no. 92.

_____. "*Lost in Space*: My Friend, Mr. Nobody." *TV Zone*, #111.

_____. "*The Time Tunnel*: Starburst Yearbook." 1989/'90.

_____. "*The Time Tunnel*: Pirates of Dead Man's Island." *TV Zone*, no. 90.

_____. "*The Time Tunnel*: Visitors from Beyond the Stars." *TV Zone*, no. 97.

_____. "*The Time Tunnel*: Chase Through Time." *TV Zone*, no. 112.

_____. *Voyage to the Bottom of the Sea. Starburst*, no. 84, August 1985.

_____. "*Voyage to the Bottom of the Sea*: Eleven Days to Zero." *TV Zone*, no. 95.

_____. "*Voyage to the Bottom of the Sea*: Fatal Cargo." *TV Zone*, no. 101.

_____. "*Voyage to the Bottom of the Sea*: Journey with Fear." *TV Zone*, no. 116.

Balter, Allan. Quoted in *TV Guide* letters page, October 1964.

Bassom, David. Interview with June Lockhart. *TV Zone*, no. 85.

Brooks, Tim, and Marsh, Earle. *The Complete Directory to Primetime Network and Cable TV Shows, 1946–Present*. New York: Ballantine Books, 1995.

Clark, Mike. Interview with Jonathan Harris. *Starlog*, July 1985.

_____. Interview with David Hedison. *Starlog*, July 1986.

_____. Interview with Marta Kristen. *Starlog*, October 1988.

_____. Interview with Guy Williams. *Starlog*, January 1987.

_____. Interviews with the writers of *Voyage to the Bottom of the Sea. Starlog*, August, September, October, 1992.

_____, and Cotter, Bill. Interview with Robert Kinoshita. *Starlog*, April 1982.

_____, and Cotter, Bill. Interview with Bob May. *Starlog*, April 1982.

_____, and Cotter, Bill. Interview with Bill Mumy. *Starlog*, July 1981.

_____, and Cotter, Bill. Voyage to the Bottom of the Sea episode guide. *Starlog*, April 1980.

_____, and Cotter, Bill. Article on Voyage to the Bottom of the Sea. *Starlog*, June 1980.

Cline, William C. *In the Nick of Time*: Motion Picture Sound Serials. Jefferson, NC: McFarland, 1997 {1984}.

Cook, Jonathan. Interview with David Hedison. *TV Zone*, Special no. 3, early 1990's.

Counts, Kyle. Interview with Robert Colbert. *Starlog*, June 1992.

_____. Interview with Gary Conway. *Starlog*, February 1990.

_____. Interview with James Darren. *Starlog*, July 1992.

_____. Interview with Deanna Lund. *Starlog*, August 1992.

_____. Interview with Lee Meriwether. *Starlog*, April 1990.

_____. Interview with Bill Mumy. *Starlog*, February 1991.

Cox, Stephen. *Dreaming of Jeannie*. New York: St. Martin's, 2000.

Crutchfield, James Andrew. *Legends of the Wild West*. Lincolnwood, IL: Publications International, 1995.

Dern, Marian. Interview with Richard Basehart, *TV Guide*, 1965.

Eisner, Joel. Interview with Robert Colbert, *SFTV*, February 1985.

_____. Interview with John Crawford, *Starlog*, February 1996.

_____. Interview with Lee Meriwether, SFTV, June 1985.

_____. Interview with Malachi Throne, *Starlog*, May 1993

_____. *The Official Batman Batbook*. Chicago: Contemporary , 1986.

Eramo, Steven. Interview with Marta Kristen. *TV Zone*, Special no. 35.

Evans, Jeff. "The Forsyte Saga/The Pallisers." *Guinness Television Encyclopedia*. London: Guinness, 1995.

Fidelman, Geoffrey Mark. *The Lucy Book*. New South Wales: Renaissance, 1999.

Florence, Bill, and Florence, Jennifer. Interview with Paul Carr. *Starlog*, June 1990.

Fulton, Roger. *The Encyclopedia of TV Science Fiction*. London: Boxtree, 2000.

Gerani, Gary, and Schulman, Paul. *Fantastic Television*. Survey: LSP/Harmony, 1999.

Goldberg, Lee. Interview with David Hedison. *Starlog*, August 1989.

Gross, Edward. Interview with Carey Wilber. *Starlog*, April 1987.

_____, and Altman, Mark. *Captain's Logs—The Complete Trek Voyages*. London: Boxtree, 1993.

Halliwell, Leslie. *Halliwell's Filmgoer's Companion*. London: Granada, 1980.

_____. *Halliwell's Teleguide*. London: Granada, 1979.

Hedison, David. Uncredited interview. *TV Guide*, July 1996.

Heitland, Jon. *The Man from UNCLE Book*. New York: St. Martin's, 1987.

Hirshorn, Louis. Interview with Bill Mumy. *TV Zone*, nos. 35, 36.

Hrushack, Ted Michael, and Meyers, Richard. Interview with Angela Cartwright. *Starlog*, April 1979.

Jankiewicz, Pat. Interview with Stanley Ralph Ross. *Filmfax*, no. 16, August, 1989.

Johnson, Richard. Feature article on SF TV. *Radio Times*, September 1994.

Julius, Marshall. Interview with Jonathan Harris. What's on in London, November 13, 1991.

Kinnard, Roy. *Science-Fiction Serials*. Jefferson, NC: McFarland, 1998.

Linaweaver, Brad. Interview with David Hedison. *Filmfax*, no. 68, August–September 1998.

Lisanti, Tom. Interview with Irene Tsu. *Filmfax*, no. 68, August–September 1998.

_____. Interview with Francine York. In *Fantasy Femmes of Sixties Cinema*. Jefferson, NC: McFarland, 2001.

Lockhart, June. Uncredited interview. *TV Guide*, August 13, 1994.

McGee, Mark Thomas. Roger Corman: The Best of the Cheap Acts. Jefferson, NC: McFarland, 1988.

_____. The Rock and Roll Movie Encyclopedia of the 1950s. Jefferson, NC: McFarland, 1990.

Messman, Richard. Interview with Pat Culliton. Epi-Log Journal, May 1992.

_____. Interview with Marta Kristen. Unidentified fanzine, 1979.

_____. *Lost in Space Anniversary Tribute Book*. 1987.

_____. *The Lost in Space Technical Manual*. Movie Publisher Services, 1988.

Monroe, Paul. *The Lost in Space Handbook*. Star Tech, 1989.

Passerelli, Alison. Interview with Terry Becker. *Filmfax*, no. 93–94, October–November, 2002.

_____. Interview with Del Monroe. *Filmfax*, no. 92, August–September, 2002.

_____. Interview with Arch Whiting. Irwin Allen News Network, 1999.

Peary, Danny. *Cult Movie Stars*. New York: Simon and Schuster, 1991.

Phillips, Mark. Interview (posthumously published) with John Anderson. 1992, *Starlog*, July 1995.

_____. Interview with Stefan Arngrim. *TV Zone*, Special no. 60, 2005.

_____. Interview with Arthur Batanides. *Starlog*, April 1993.

_____. Interview with Barbara Bouchet. *Starlog*.

_____. Interview with Paul Comi. *Starlog*, August 1990.

_____. Interview with Ray Didsbury. *Filmfax*, no. 81–82, October 2001.

_____. Interview with James Goldstone. *Starlog* Platinum, no. 3, 1994.

_____. Interview with Jonathan Harris. *TV Zone*, no. 158.

_____. Interview with Allan Hunt. *Starlog*, November 1993.

_____. Interview with Don Knight. *Starlog*, March 1993.

_____. Interviews with Land of the Giants scriptwriters. *Starlog*, October 1990.

_____. Interviews with Lost in Space scriptwriters. *Starlog*, October–November 1995.

_____. Interview with Victor Lundin. *Starlog*, March 1996.

_____. Interview with Don Matheson. *Starlog*, January 1991.

_____. Interview with Jan Merlin. *Starlog*, March 1995.

_____. Interview with Bob and Esther Mitchell. *Starlog*, January 1991.

_____. Interview with Sutton Roley. *Starlog*, September 1995.

_____. Interview with Joseph Ruskin. *Starlog*, March 1993.

_____. Interview with Liam Sullivan. *Starlog*, January 1991.

_____. Interviews with *Time Tunnel* writers. *Starlog*, September 1991.

_____. Interviews with *Time Tunnel* writers. *Starlog*, October 1991.

_____. Interview with Shimon Wincelberg. *Starlog*, October 1990.

Pilato, Herbie J. *The Bewitched Book*. New York: Bantam, 1992

Reeves, Richard, "PT 109." In *Past Imperfect: History According to the Movies*, ed. Mark Carnes. New York: Holt, 1995.

Schow, David, and Frentzen, Jeffrey. *The Outer Limits: The Official Companion*. Ace Trade, 1986.

Spelling, Ian. Interview with Jonathan Harris. *Starlog*, March 1998.

Swires, Steve. Interview with June Lockhart. *Starlog*, July 1983.

Trent, Sue, and Whittaker, Carole. Richard Basehart biography. *Seaview* Crew Fact Sheet, 1996.

_____, and _____. Robert Dowdell biography. *Seaview* Crew Fact Sheet, 1997.

_____, and _____. David Hedison biography. *Seaview* Crew Fact Sheet, 1996.

Uncredited, interview with June Lockhart. *TV Guide*, August 13th, 1994.

Vincent-Rudzki, Jan, and Briggs, Nicholas. Interview with Jonathan Harris. *TV Zone* Special no. 3.

Voger, Mark. Interview with Mark Goddard. *Filmfax* no. 33, June/July 1992.

_____. Interview with Jonathan Harris. *Filmfax* no. 32, April/May 1992.

Warren, Bill. *Keep Watching the Skies*, 12 vols. Jefferson, NC: McFarland, 1982 (vol. 1), 1986 (vol. 2).

Weaver, Tom, Interview with Michael Ansara, *Starlog*, April 1996.

_____. Interview with Charles Bennett. *Starlog*, August 1993.

_____. Interview with Mark Goddard. *Starlog*, May 1993.

_____. Interview with David Hedison. *Starlog*, October 2002.

_____. Interview with Nancy Kovack. *Starlog*, February 1990.

_____. Interview with June Lockhart. *Starlog*, January 1994.

_____. Interview with Bob May. *Starlog*, April 1994.

_____. Interview with Rex Reason. *Starlog*, March 1989.

_____. Interview with William Read Woodfield. Fangoria, mid–2000.

White, Patrick J. *The Complete Mission: Impossible Dossier*. New York: Avon.

Wicking, Chris, and Vahimagi, Tise. *The American Vein*. Directors and Directions in Television. New York: Dutton, 1979.

Williams, David. Interview with Jonathan Harris. Prime-Time, Summer 1986.

Zicree, Marc Scott. *The Twilight Zone Companion*. New York: Bantam, 1982.

Index

Numbers in **boldface** indicate a main entry in the text.
Numbers in *bold italics* indicate photographs.